SIXTH EDITION

An Introduction to Human Services

Policy and Practice

BETTY REID MANDELL
Bridgewater State College
Professor Emerita

BARBARA SCHRAM
Northeastern University
Professor Emerita

PEARSON

Boston   New York   San Francisco
Mexico City   Montreal   Toronto   London   Madrid   Munich   Paris
Hong Kong   Singapore   Tokyo   Cape Town   Sydney

Series Editor: Patricia Quinlin
Editorial Assistant: Sara Holliday
Marketing Manager: Kris Ellis-Levy
Editorial-Production Service: Omegatype Typography, Inc.
Composition Buyer: Linda Cox
Manufacturing Buyer: JoAnne Sweeney
Electronic Composition: Omegatype Typography, Inc.
Cover Administrator: Kristina Mose-Libon

For related titles and support materials, visit our online catalog at www.ablongman.com.

Between the time website information is gathered and then published, it is not unusual for some sites to have closed. Also, the transcription of URLs can result in typographical errors. The publisher would appreciate notification where these errors occur so that they may be corrected in subsequent editions.

Library of Congress Cataloging-in-Publication Data

Mandell, Betty Reid.
    An introduction to human services / Betty Reid Mandell, Barbara Schram. — 6th ed.
      p. cm.
    Includes bibliographical references and index.
    ISBN 0-205-44214-5 (paperbound)
     1. Social service.   2. Social case work.   I. Schram, Barbara.   II. Title.

HV40.S387 2006
361—dc22
                                                   2005045892

Printed in the United States of America

10 9 8 7 6 5 4 3 2 1   RRD-VA 09 08 07 06 05

To our clients, our students, and our children—
with gratitude for all they continue
to teach us.

Contents

SECTION TWO

Implementing Human Service Interventions

SECTION THREE

Thriving and Surviving in This Field

Preface

In the previous five editions of this text, we have used the analogy of taking a ride on a seesaw to describe how we learn and teach about the human service field. When we sit on the end of the seesaw closest to the ground, we can observe in vivid detail a troubled individual struggling with his or her particular life circumstance. Based on this observation, we can describe the options that might be available to that individual in a human service network. Then we might map out the steps that need to be taken to provide him or her with the most appropriate social services and emotional support.

But as we soar high above the ground on our seesaw, we see that individual in less detail. Now we can see how that single life situation complements or conflicts with others in the community. From our vantage point, we can also learn about the world events and cultural or sociopolitical forces that might influence an individual's fate. At this height, we focus less on one person's struggle and think instead about the ways in which a community or a whole society can tackle the vexing problems of violence, abuse, poverty, or lack of opportunity. Looking at individuals in the context of society also helps us sort out, among many conflicting schools of thought, how their problems came about and how their problems should be prevented or solved. As human service providers, we are always looking at both the intimate portrait and the big picture. Both are equally important. In this text, we place more emphasis on *social systems* than on *individual psychology* because we believe it is important for beginning students to understand the context of the field before they take specialized courses in psychology and intrapsychic development.

Our understanding of social problems and the social services they require is made far richer but much more ambiguous by this dual set of perspectives. It also prevents us from accepting simplistic, one-size-fits-all solutions to complex social problems.

The seesaw analogy also expresses our feelings about the vast changes we have all experienced since the first edition of our book. As we look back, we realize with surprise that in our first edition the word *AIDS* did not appear anywhere in the text. It is hard to believe that a disease that has spread so quickly and taken such a high toll was barely recognized as a major social problem when our book first went to the printer in 1983. After many years in which AIDS was a death sentence, things are finally improving in developed countries. Many PWAs (People with AIDS) are now living many years beyond the one to two years that used to be their predicted life expectancy. New medications, a societal increase in condom use, and the postponing of early sexual activity appear to be helping to contain this devastating medical and social problem. This help, however, has still not become widely available to people in poor countries. In fact, AIDS now claims the lives of increasingly large numbers of persons in Africa and Asia.

In the last edition, we noted with regret that the problem of affordable housing and homelessness had steadily risen to alarming proportions. Temporary shelters have become permanent institutions, and most of us have become used to seeing people sleeping on the streets of our large cities. Previous solutions to the housing crises, such as subsidized public housing, have virtually been abandoned, but no new ideas or the will to implement them have surfaced. We have worried that the entitlements and social services designed to help people through hard times seemed to be diminishing as the cries for tax relief were becoming louder and more insistent. Now it is clear that the restructuring of welfare in the United States has done nothing to solve this thorny problem.

Since our first edition, some awesome positive changes have occurred in the rest of the world. The tearing down of the Berlin Wall and the breaking up of the Soviet empire have lifted the ominous threat of nuclear destruction. We have noted with pleasure the dismantling of the racial-segregation system in South Africa and the rising interest in the positive rewards of diversity in our own country. We have applauded the increased spirit of volunteerism that has been spreading across the land and the continued healthy growth of the self-help movement.

In the preface to our last edition, we predicted that there would be a groundswell of interest in finally solving the problems of delivering adequate physical and mental health care for all of our citizens. We anticipated then that we would be writing about some new form of universal national health insurance. *But we have proved to be poor prophets.* Universal health care proposals have been completely wiped off Congress's agenda. Private, managed health care schemes, many for profit, have proliferated. Groups across the country are now struggling to retain even a part of the gains that had been made in health care for those over the age of 65, through Medicare, and through Medicaid, for low-income people.

Now, as we write the preface to our sixth edition, we cannot help but note the alarming rise in violence in the world in which we live and deliver human services. Although crime statistics have shown a remarkable decrease in many of our cities as we entered the new millennium, high school shootings and similar violent acts shattered many lives and occupied the worried attention of pundits and parents. The secure world of the middle-class schoolyard has been irretrievably altered.

After thinking there could not be many things worse for our country than disaffected young people turning on their classmates, we now face an even greater escalation of violence. Since the World Trade Center Towers were demolished, much has been altered in our lives. Along with the loss of life and property has gone a substantial amount of our sense of security and comfort. Many of the gains made in civil liberties, in communication technology, and in the embrace of a multicultural society may be whittled back as our government attempts to stop further terrorist acts and has embarked on two wars. We cannot even begin to estimate what losses this will bring to our clients. Obviously, with the defense buildup and downward spiral in the economy, there will be less and less money available to house the homeless, educate the disabled, and provide needed medical care for all.

Perhaps the most important message of this text in all its editions is that our work is always intimately connected with both the history and future of society. Every shift in the social fabric impacts hugely on the daily life of the people you are learning to serve. In our many years in the field there has never been a time when knowledgeable, skillful human service workers have been so needed. To act with and on behalf of clients and communities, you will need to understand the root causes that underpin social service interventions and social policy. As you enter this field, you will be called on to be a *generalist*—able to interview and counsel an elderly citizen so he can obtain the services that will sustain him in his home and then advocate for him when a faceless bureaucrat decides the services are no longer needed. When day-care facilities or job-training programs for teen parents lose their funding, you will need to know how to join with other groups to go to the courts and legislative chambers to design new programs or salvage old ones. But you will also have to learn how to present your arguments in a clear way, marshaling accurate evidence of need, proposing creative strategies, and documenting the potential for success of your programs.

To make this text more accessible to the beginning student, we organize the chapters into three sections. In the first we present the context of human service work, answering the major questions you are probably asking: *What is a human service agency, what do human service workers do, and what are the barriers that keep people from using human services?* Then we describe how human service work has changed through the years, discuss different intervention strategies, and explore the attitudes, values, skills, and knowledge that bind together all workers, regardless of their problem area or credentials. After that, we discuss the conflicts and dilemmas that are likely to occur as we try to incorporate the values of our field into our daily practice. Finally, we pose and then try to answer questions about the social welfare system. We discuss the major social welfare programs and how we can keep ourselves up to date so we can guide our clients through this ever-changing maze of rules and regulations.

After first exploring the foundations of human service work, in the second section we examine in detail the ways in which human service workers implement each of the interventions. This section begins with a chapter on working with diversity. Subsequent chapters describe the skills involved in interviewing, counseling and case management, working with groups, planning programs, and organizing for systems change.

In the final and shortest section, we present information that human service workers need to know about the legal issues that cut across all the interventions.

Fittingly, the final chapter offers words of wisdom about keeping your spark alive and avoiding burnout. This is an especially important chapter because in the next several years, all of us will be challenged to work harder and more creatively until the current wave of slash-and-burn budget cutting has abated.

Each chapter begins with an introduction that links it to the ones you have already read. This field is filled with "alphabet" agencies and jargon, so when new terms are introduced they are highlighted and defined within the text and again in the glossary at the back of the book. Finally, each chapter ends with a summary so you can review the information presented. These summaries can also be read before beginning the chapter, which can be helpful to the student who likes to study a road map in advance of a journey. Questions for discussion and web sites for further information on the topic just discussed close each chapter.

Interviews with human service workers and quotes from case records, newspaper clippings, and novels are included to keep the text lively and help readers feel greater empathy for problems that might be distant from their own life experiences.

We hope that the charts, checklists, and samples of interventions will continue to be useful as you venture out to a volunteer job or internship. All of the examples have been drawn from the authors' combined total of more than fifty years of work in social service agencies. Between us, we have had experience in a family service agency, a neighborhood poverty program, a program for youth at risk, a large recreation center, and a research bureau. We have taught for many years in college human service programs. Both on the campus and in community agencies we have led training groups and done research on adoption, special needs, and the social welfare system. Both of us have raised children and have struggled through our own developmental milestones, both giving help and receiving support from others.

We would like to thank the reviewers of the previous editions for their thoughtful and valuable feedback: Donna Blake, Genesee Community College; Patricia A. Dolan, Northern Kentucky University; Karole Kinsey Fuller, Kirkwood Community College; Sharon K. Hall, University of Houston Clear Lake; Sandra Haynes, Metropolitan State College of Denver; Carabelle McNeill, Touro College; Larry Sheffield, La Sierra University; and Cate Solomon, Lasell College, as well as David Birnbach, who reviewed the section on managed care.

We would also like to thank the reviewers of this edition: Susan E. Claxton, Floyd College, and Pamela Kiser, Elon University.

We have tried to infuse this book with some humor. Although human service work can be intensely draining, we think there is as much need in this field for a good laugh as there is for an empathetic tear or a flash of rage at injustice. We are passionate about our work and hope we communicate that.

CHAPTER 1

What Are Human Services? What Do Human Service Workers Do?

In this chapter, we begin to sketch a picture of the surprisingly large variety of human service agencies. We introduce you to the many workers—with different titles and varying responsibilities—who are employed by these social services. You will also meet Kathy Holbrook and her family, who have been struggling to deal with the upheaval precipitated by her father's alcohol abuse. We tell Kathy's story in three different ways to help you visualize the diverse aspects of the problem of addiction and the many services that might provide help.

The Holbrooks and their neighbors turn to human service agencies when their problems are too heavy to carry alone. But though they may desperately want to find help, many barriers of internal emotions and external pressures may stand in the way of their getting the services they need.

You may be surprised by the enormous diversity of the human services field. Until members of the community actually encounter a human service worker, most have little accurate knowledge of what our work involves. While this array of options in the human service network may be confusing, we will point out that this diversity is inevitable and desirable. Not only does it offer many choices for clients but it also can give each worker a chance to find a niche that meets his or her unique interests and attributes.

HUMAN SERVICE NETWORKS

What are human services? What do human service workers do? These are logical questions for a beginning student to ask and for an introductory text to answer. But the answers are not as straightforward as you might expect. A professor of human services described the challenge of answering these seemingly obvious questions.

> While I was in college, my friends and family kept asking me, in a challenging way, exactly *what* is a human services major? They wondered what a big guy like me was doing studying for that kind of a field. I'd try to give them a short, clear answer. They never seemed completely satisfied.
>
> That was irritating enough when I was in college, but even after I graduated with a BS in human services, my friends and relatives kept right on asking me what I was *really* going to do to earn my living. If I fell back on my stock answer, about how I was in the business of helping people to help themselves, I always sounded hopelessly muddled.
>
> How do you explain all the things you are *really* doing when it looks as if you are just "hanging out" on a street corner with a gang of teenagers? As a young outreach worker hired by my town, "hanging out" was a large part of my job description. Sometimes I'd be playing pool or shooting baskets with the kids in the local recreation center.

Later on in the day I might spend a few hours drinking coffee with a family around their kitchen table. I took kids on camping trips. I held their hands when they ended up in the hospital with an overdose of drugs or a broken leg from a gang fight or football game. I'd chew the fat with the clerks at juvenile court and visit with my kids going in or coming out of the courtroom.

I was a sounding board for the parents, the kids, the local merchants, and the police. Of course I can't point to an adult and say it's because of my work that he made it up and out of trouble. But I think that what I did made a difference in some of the kids' futures.

Twenty years later, one of my students complained to me that she had the same problem. How could she justify the usefulness of spending three hours sitting in front of a television set with five retarded adults? How could she explain what she was doing when she was eating a hamburger in a luncheonette or throwing a Frisbee around the park with her clients?

She'd get frustrated when one of her friends would say, "You get paid for doing *that*? You have to go to college to learn how to do *that*? Now, *my major*—engineering, business, computers, etc.—that's *real* work!"

Helping is such a natural part of our everyday lives that it is hard to think of it as a specialized activity for which people must be trained. Think back over the last few weeks. The chances are that someone—a coworker, friend, or relative—has asked you for help. Perhaps a friend was having trouble with a love relationship and needed to talk about it. If you listened with empathy and tried to understand her view of the problem, you were giving a human service.

An attentive listener and a strong shoulder to cry on might have been all your friend needed. However, if the same type of problem continues to occur, she might need more than a warm, accepting friend. She might need to talk with an experienced counselor who has helped other young adults juggle the conflicting needs of intimacy and independence.

Professional counselors work in private practice, at family service agencies, in hospital outpatient clinics, in mental health centers, in women's advocacy programs, or in the guidance offices of high schools or colleges.

All of us, at some time in our lives, will be on both sides of the helping process, giving or asking for support. Problems are part of living, and no one—regardless of education, income, or profession—is immune. The college president might have a disintegrating marriage, the business tycoon might give birth to a severely retarded child, and the famous sports star might contract AIDS. When the economy dips or a hurricane hits the coast, thousands of people from all walks of life lose their jobs, their homes, and their sense of security. If we live long enough, we will have to cope with the death and illness of many people we care about. And throughout the life span, we will face our own critical junctures, transitions, and changing capacities.

People can follow many different routes to find help within the human service network. The route chosen is likely to be influenced by:

- The nature of the problem
- Someone's hunch about the causes of the problem
- The resources available in the local community
- The cost and the person's ability to pay
- The climate of the times that creates fads about "the *right* thing to do when you have problem X, Y, or Z"
- The history of the circumstances confronting that person
- Luck or chance (e.g., an aunt mentions that she knows a counselor who has helped her or perhaps the topic is discussed in advice columns such as *Dear Abby* or *Ask Beth*)

Research indicates that most referrals are made by word of mouth. When people are in pain, they are likely to ask the advice of someone they trust. A member of the clergy, doctor, bartender, or hairdresser can often inspire the courage to walk into a social service agency. Human service workers spend a great amount of time, energy, and creativity getting their message out to the public.

Throughout the pages of this book and in your own work in the field, you will quickly discover that there is no simple path to finding help. Because people are complex, human service problems are multifaceted. So we have had to create a variety of social services. Programs that cluster around one particular problem area are called **human service networks** or **delivery systems.**

Human service networks (or **delivery systems**) The programs and entitlements that offer help in dealing with different but complementary parts of an overall problem.

The following paper, written by Kathy Holbrook, a first-year student at Westwood Community College, paints a vivid picture of the variety and complexity of one of these networks.

The assignment was called "The Helpee Paper." Kathy's instructor asked the students to think back to a time in their lives when they faced a painful personal crisis. They were asked to describe that situation and then evaluate the help they received from professionals, volunteers, family, or friends.

In the many years this paper has been assigned, the instructor has never had a student who was unable to remember a painful episode. Students have written about homesickness at camp or the death of a pet; problems with drugs, alcohol, and eating disorders; the divorce of parents; or conflicts around the choice of a college or career. Because the students select their topic, they decide how much personal material they want to reveal.

Some students choose to share their papers with the class. While listening to these stories, class members feel the intensity of the emotions that conflict engenders. They also learn about the complex barriers that surround the acts of asking for and receiving help. In addition, the students receive a true-to-life picture of the patchwork quilt of agencies and worker roles that make up each of the human service networks.

After reading about Kathy's attempts to tread her way through the human service network of alcohol abuse, you will read about two other paths Kathy *might* have followed if her problems had developed differently. As you read these three accounts, try to identify all the human service agencies and workers Kathy encountered.

My Experience Receiving Help

by Kathy Holbrook

When I read the assignment for this paper I had mixed feelings. On the one hand, it opens up a lot of wounds. On the other hand, I know that if I want to be a human service worker I have to learn from my own experiences. And every time I talk about the problems my family had with my dad's alcoholism, it can help someone else. That's the main lesson I learned from the Alcoholics Anonymous (AA) meetings I've attended. Well, I guess I've started this paper already.

I can't pinpoint when the problem began. As I look back, I realize the problem was always with us but I didn't have a name for it. I thought the way we lived was just the way things were in everyone's family.

We had a big house in Westwood. My father worked for years for the same stock brokerage firm. He could make or lose thousands of dollars a day of other people's money. It was high pressure all the time.

When I was little we didn't see much of Dad. He had to work very hard to keep up with the rest of the community. People where we live keep moving: a bigger house, a pool, a summer place on the lake, a boat, ivy-league colleges for their kids. Mom was the "typical" housewife. She did all the chauffeuring to Scouts and swim team and came to all our plays alone when Dad was in the city. The first ten years it seemed like we were mostly like everyone else. I knew Mom and Dad always kept liquor around because they did a lot of entertaining.

But in my first year of high school everything got worse. Sometimes I'd get up in the morning and Dad would be asleep on the sofa with his clothes on. Sometimes he wouldn't get up for breakfast. I'd hear Mom phoning his boss, saying he was sick or that he couldn't get the car started. I began to notice that she often didn't tell the truth about Dad.

Then he started coming home during the day. He'd drink until he'd pass out, sometimes right in the living room. I'd ask Mom if I could have friends over and she'd say I couldn't. After a while no one was invited to our house for dinner parties anymore. I felt as if we were living in a cave with a locked door across it. Mom even kept the window blinds down in the afternoon. I think she didn't want the neighbors to see Dad at home, especially when he hadn't shaved or changed his clothes.

I tried to talk to my brothers about it, but they would blow me off. My brother Dennis and Dad got into such a bad fight that Dennis moved into his girlfriend's room at college. Chuck, my oldest brother, has always been a bookworm. He'd just crawl into his room and read or listen to music all the time. Even at dinner we were never together anymore. If we were all there, Mom was nervous or Dad would get up and leave in the middle. She'd cook a big meal and he wouldn't come home or he'd say the food was no good and he'd yell. He never hit her, but he would slam his glass down so it would break or knock over his chair when he left the table.

I was still his special little girl, though. He'd always ask me to stay around the house and he'd give me dollar bills for being so good. Sometimes I'd take off his shoes when he was asleep on the sofa. A couple of times I got up at night and covered him when he was lying on the couch.

My mom started to go to church a lot. The priest came to our house to talk to my dad. Finally, I came home from school one day and Mom said we were leaving. We would stay at my aunt's house until Dad packed his things and left. Then we could come back. That's when she told me that he was an alcoholic. He was sick and it wasn't his fault, but he had to make himself well if we were going to be a family again.

We stayed at my aunt's house for two weeks. Mom finally went to court and got a **restraining**

order. The marshal made Dad leave the house, and he wasn't even supposed to visit us. The only time we got together was at the meetings with our psychologist, Dr. Hightower. I hated those sessions. My brother Dennis would shout insults and Dad looked like he was going to cry. Chuck wouldn't say anything.

Mom and I started going to **Al-Anon** meetings together. That's a support group like AA but it's for families and friends of people who drink too much. I had one teacher at school whom I really liked, so one day I broke down and told her about Dad. She took me by the hand to see the guidance counselor. He was the one who got me to go to my first **Alateen** group. I went a few times during activities block. I liked talking to him alone in his office, but I wasn't comfortable in the group. There were kids in it I didn't trust. I was sure they would spread it around about my family being such a mess.

Dad went away to a hospital for alcoholics. His company wanted him back so badly that they sent someone to our home from the personnel department to convince him to go into a program. They were willing to pay for his treatment through his health insurance. We had family meetings with him at the hospital. My mom would see the same social worker because she was pretty depressed by now. I think she took medication for her nerves.

He stayed there for three months. Then he went to the state rehabilitation office and got vocational counseling because he knew he couldn't go back to the tension of wheeling and dealing in the stock market. It was too stressful a place for him and most of the people in his company drank too much at business lunches and dinners.

After ten months Dad moved back home. He started a small landscape company. A retired man who used to run a business in town helped him get it all together and they became buddies. My mom works now as a nurse's aide.

Last January the whole family celebrated the seventh anniversary of Dad's sobriety. We went to his AA group. It was a terrific family reunion. Father Brian was there, too, because he had so much to do with helping my family get straightened out. The only dark spot is Dennis. He came to the party, but he is still very angry. He holds Dad responsible for all the bad times. Actually I think Dennis is drinking now, too. He is very bitter.

I'm not glad that I had to go through this mess, but some good things came out of it. Dad is a really laid-back guy now. He sort of takes things as they come. He and Mom are closer than ever.

Through this I got interested in the field of alcohol counseling. I have paid my dues. I'd like to work in schools teaching kids about alcohol and drug abuse. I've been a member of Students Against Drunk Driving (SADD) and have become very self-confident. I can speak before groups now and I don't feel like I have to please everyone anymore. I speak my mind.

Alternative Scenario 1

Finally I came home from school one day and Mom said we were leaving. We would stay at my aunt's house until Dad packed his things and left. Then we could come back. That's when she told me that he was an alcoholic. He was sick and it wasn't his fault, but he had to make himself well if we were going to be a family again.

Until then Dad had never lifted a hand to anyone in the family, but now he was so angry at Mom he tried to strangle her. He followed us to my Aunt Catherine's house and kept banging on the door. Mom kept calling the police, but he kept coming back. My aunt has two little kids and we were messing up her family. Even though my dad was in bad shape, he managed to get to the bank and withdraw all their money. My mom had to call my brother Dennis and ask him for enough cash to get us through the next couple of days. She got a restraining order from the court forbidding Dad to come near us.

Finally, Mom phoned Renewal House and they sent a van to pick us up. Chuck stayed on with my aunt. Renewal is a shelter for **battered women.** Would you believe we heard about it from my aunt's cleaning woman? She had a sister who was being beaten by her boyfriend and she lived there for a couple of months. They won't give out their address over the phone in case there is someone looking for you who might hunt you down and hurt you. They have to be secretive.

The whole thing was really humiliating and scary. I didn't like the neighborhood; there were a lot of empty lots and rundown houses. But when we walked in it was quite a surprise. The shelter was old but clean and very homey. They had travel posters on all the walls and lots of plants. The center director was our lifeline. She told Mom about everything she needed to do.

A volunteer drove me back and forth to school. Mom went to the Welfare Department and eventually she got us **AFDC (Aid to Families with Dependent Children)**.* It wasn't nearly as much money as we were used to, but it was enough to contribute for the room and board at Renewal House. She got a **Medicaid** card so I could go to the hospital for my allergy shots.

Mom started getting very short-tempered. I couldn't blame her, but it was awful for me. I didn't like living there and not being able to go to my friends' houses or to after-school clubs. All I did was go to school and come home. I went to a social worker at the Westwood Mental Health Clinic, but I didn't like him.

After two years my folks got divorced. I have seen very little of my father and it hurts that he doesn't call. He is remarried. Mom went back to school, so she was never around and I hated where we lived. Dennis and Chuck have just gone their own ways.

By the time I began my sophomore year I was very depressed by the whole situation. One night I thought about killing myself and how I would do it. I called the Samaritans, a **hot line** for people who are thinking about suicide. The woman on the phone talked to me for a few nights and then suggested I go to Alateen at the Mt. Auburn Hospital. I stuck with that group and made a lot of friends there.

Now I am a member of **ACOA, Adult Children of Alcoholics.** Groups have been really important for me. There are other people out there like me and we are tough survivors. I'm also active in SADD, Students Against Drunk Driving. I think when I finish my degree I'd like to become an organizer. The women from MADD, Mothers Against Drunk Driving, are really dynamite people. I'd like to try to change the laws that make alcohol so available.

I finally got my act together enough to finish high school and get into college. I see Ms. Applehorn at the counseling center here. She has a way of making me feel I am worth something. She reminds me how far I have come. I guess I got the help I needed, but my dad

never did. He went to AA and to a place called Emerge for men who use violence. But he hasn't changed much.

Alternative Scenario 2

Finally I came home from school one day and Mom said we were leaving. We would stay at my aunt's house until Dad packed his things and left. Then we could come back. That's when she told me that he was an alcoholic. He was sick and it wasn't his fault, but he had to make himself well if we were going to be a family again.

We stayed with my aunt and uncle for four or five months. I began to notice that Mom was changing. She had always had one or two drinks to keep my dad company, but I never saw her as a drinker. She started not getting up to give me and Chuck breakfast. Some days she didn't even get dressed. My uncle had a bad temper and I know he wasn't happy we had moved in. I spent a lot of time with my brother Dennis and his girlfriend, but they were both working and going to school. Chuck got an apartment with another guy and moved out.

I started not coming home so as to avoid the whole scene. I did a lot of stealing things from local stores. I always had a pocket full of change. I even tried drinking beer with the high school kids, but luckily it just made me fall asleep. I know that with both my parents being alcoholics, I could easily become addicted also. I won't even take a social drink now.

The youth patrol officer would pick me up, give me a lecture, and send me home. The only things that still mattered to me were Scouts and my brothers. My Scout leader was more like a mother than Mom was. She took me to a child-guidance clinic and the worker there tried to get my mom to come in and talk. When she wouldn't do it, they filed a complaint with the Department of Social Services. They accused her of neglecting me and took me out of my aunt's house. I was very angry, but the worker found me a foster home. I didn't have a choice, so I went. Ms. Braun is an older, single lady whose kids have grown up. She was what I needed, strict but very loving.

*The title and regulations of this income support program were changed by the Welfare Reform bill of 1996. This will be discussed in Chapter 6, The Social Welfare System.

Mom died two years later. She'd had a heart condition for a long time, and with all the trouble with Dad and her drinking she didn't give herself proper care. My two brothers weren't settled down enough to take care of me. My foster mother asked me if I wanted to be her daughter permanently.

The people in the Department of Social Services who supervise adoptions felt she was too old. They wanted to put me with a younger couple. Ms. Braun got a lawyer from legal services and she fought for me. The judge finally gave me to her. In some ways social services was right about her being too old. She doesn't always understand about this generation. At times I resent her. I was in a group for teenagers who have been adopted. It was good to talk it over with the leader and the other kids. I found out I had it really good. The leader signed me up to get a "big sister" from Catholic Charities. I could *really* talk to her. She

was attending Westwood Community College. Dolores is the one who convinced me I could go to college and maybe study for the same degree.

For a while I saw a psychiatrist and I was on anti-depressant medication. I don't feel I need to use it now that I am getting on with my life.

Ms. Braun and my Scout leader and my two brothers are my family. When I graduated from high school they all gave me a surprise party.

I sometimes think about what would have happened to me if I hadn't had Dolores, my Scout leader, and my foster mother. They were able to see that even when I was acting up, I really did not want to be in trouble. Even the youth patrol officer, he had the right combination of toughness and caring.

Though I'm in human services now, I want a job in a business firm. I want to dress up, buy a decent car, and get away from all of these problems.*

*To read an in-depth autobiographical portrait of the impact of alcohol abuse on family life, see Suzanne Somers's *Keeping Secrets,* 1988. For a new approach to treating alcoholism, see Jay and Jay (2000). For an excellent description of the tasks involved in treating adult children of alcholics, see Ruben (2001).

Helpers Have Varied Backgrounds and Job Titles

In the three scenarios described in the previous section, Kathy, a young woman who could have been sitting next to you in a college class, encountered twenty-five different helpers at various agencies. Although each had a different job title and performed somewhat different tasks, they all offered human services. How many of these did you identify?

1. Priest
2. Psychologist
3. Family therapist
4. High school guidance counselor
5. Teacher
6. Vocational counselor
7. Self-help group leaders (AA, Al-Anon, Alateen)
8. Personnel department counselor
9. Rehabilitation specialist

10. Drug counselor

11. Social worker (at drug clinic)

12. Shelter director

13. Shelter volunteers

14. Hot-line worker

15. Organizer for a social action group (e.g., SADD, MADD)

16. Welfare claims worker

17. Therapist (in college counseling center)

18. Scout leader

19. Youth patrol officer

20. Child-protective services worker

21. Foster parent

22. Adoption caseworker

23. Lawyer (at public legal services)

24. Psychiatrist

25. Volunteer Big Sister

Each of these twenty-five people brought to his or her work a different mixture of education, training, and life experience. For example, the teacher and guidance counselor performed their human service tasks as only one part of their overall jobs. They probably graduated from college with a bachelor's or master's degree in education. It is likely that they have some formal certification or license from their cities or states that permits them to call themselves "teacher" or "guidance counselor." Along with their formal training in education methods, they had some psychology and sociology courses as undergraduates. The guidance counselor probably took a few additional courses that involved working with people and their problems.

In Kathy's high school there might have been a school adjustment counselor, school social worker, or school psychologist. Any one of them might have started Kathy on the path of finding services. All of them have been certified by their school boards and have advanced degrees.

The family therapist, the counselors, the rehabilitation and vocational workers, and the shelter staff director are likely to have graduated from college with a two- or four-year degree. Some might have studied beyond college, earning specialized degrees in clinical psychology, counseling, social work, rehabilitation, health education, or perhaps one of the newer fields, such as family systems therapy, drug and alcohol counseling, or human sexuality.

Most states have boards or professional associations that certify psychologists, social workers, and psychiatrists, but there are no uniform standards. Each state is free to establish its own criteria. So the term *counselor* is like a generic-brand label. Each social agency can decide what combination of degrees and years of experience it will require for the counselors it hires. Sometimes these decisions are made clearly and rationally, according to the demands of the job. Often, however, these decisions are made with one eye on the budget. Selection of staff might also be governed by the biases of the board of trustees or director, who are convinced that only workers trained in one specific therapeutic model should be hired. Thus we cannot predict the scope or depth of a particular counselor's expertise simply by knowing his or her job title.

The term *social worker* is also used loosely. Some agencies apply it to almost every position of helping at their agency. Thus the claims worker, the care and protection worker, and the foster care and adoption workers from the Department of Social Services are all referred to as social workers. Officially, the term *social worker* should be applied only to a professional who has earned an undergraduate bachelor in social work degree (BSW) or a graduate master of social work degree (MSW).

Human service worker is also an umbrella term. It identifies workers—a youth patrol officer, an organizer of a SADD chapter, or a director of a shelter—who, regardless of qualifications, fill the role of helper.

Several of the workers Kathy encountered had little or no formal education in the helping professions. Hot-line workers, self-help leaders, and foster parents often have education and training totally unrelated to the helping professions. For some of these individuals, providing human services is their central career, but for most of them it is something they do on a part-time, interim, or volunteer basis.

In the past, these part-time or volunteer workers were not always viewed as an important part of the human services network. In recent years, however, that attitude has begun to change. Now these workers are being offered on-the-job training through workshops and seminars. Often they can earn academic credits that enable them to obtain college degrees and grow in knowledge, self-confidence, and public respect.

Helpers Have Different Agency Affiliations and Orientations

Human service workers are found in a wide variety of settings, ranging from a storefront center to the carpeted offices of the personnel department of the personnel department in a high-tech firm. Some human services, especially for the middle and upper classes, are provided in the homes or offices of private practitioners. But the majority of professional human service workers are financed by the public and are found in social service departments, community mental health centers, hospitals and health clinics, college counseling centers, and ministers' or rabbis' offices. Many private nonprofit groups, such as the Family Service Association, the Jewish Family Service, Catholic Charities, the Protestant Federation, and the Salvation Army, conduct large numbers of direct-care and social change programs. Although most human services are provided on an outpatient basis, some are given in **residential treatment centers** or **community residences**.

Residential treatment center A facility providing mental and physical services for a specific problem population which reqires that the person being treated stay within its walls for a specified period of time.

Community residences Small living units, houses, or apartments located in communities that serve people who have disabilities or other special situations that render them unable to live on their own. (Also known as halfway houses; group homes.)

Raising the public's awareness of the devastating impact of drug and alcohol addiction is a never-ending task to which many workers devote their careers.

Many valuable social services are offered by citizen groups, which conduct programs that advocate for the rights of tenants, immigrants, veterans, homeless families, or some other special population. Citizen groups often hire human service workers to educate and mobilize the public. They work toward changing behaviors such as substance abuse, violence, or destruction of the environment. Often they lobby public officials or the courts to change the way social programs are funded and laws are enforced.

Although there is no way to collect accurate statistics on the number of people in this country who conduct or attend self-help groups, it is possible that these groups are now the single largest source of human services. These groups, usually patterned on the model developed by **Alcoholics Anonymous (AA)**, tackle every conceivable emotional, social, and physical problem that affects some subgroup in the community (Kerrin & Rothblatt, 2004; Wuthnow, 1994; White & Madera, web version).

Most human service agencies are entirely or partially funded through grants from the local, state, or federal government. Many others are private nonprofit groups, often sponsored by religious denominations that raise money from fees, public appeals, and philanthropic foundations.

A smaller but fast-growing type of agency is the private, profit-making one. Some of these operate on the model pioneered by the fast-food restaurant chains.

Alcoholics Anonymous (AA) A self-help organization that uses a specific twelve-step program for recovery from the addiction to alcohol.

Entrepreneurs develop a model for a preschool child care center or for the treatment of head-injured people. If it is successful in one location, they open branches of the program in other towns. Perhaps they franchise the model, selling the agency name and method of operation to another entrepreneur. These agencies make their profit entirely from the fees paid by consumers and insurance companies or in performing under a contract with a public agency. Opinions are many and mixed about the emergence of "for profit" social services. This is a controversial topic that you will likely debate in your classes and internships. This movement is often called the "privatization of social services."

Most staff members earn a salary, but agency volunteers work just for the gratification they receive. And there are differences in the hours that workers are on duty. A family worker in a day care center has to work evening hours to telephone or meet with working parents; a counselor for a group of special-needs adults might live in a community residence, working a few days a week around the clock.

Some agencies expect their workers, volunteer or paid, to operate within a particular treatment model or theoretical orientation. Their approach to the clients may be built on the theories of Sigmund Freud, Erik Erikson, or B. F. Skinner. You will read the work of these pioneer scholars in introductory psychology or human development classes. Other theories, such as those of Carl Rogers, Jean Baker Miller, or William Glasser, you are likely to read about in counseling courses or hear spoken of in your field work (Hackney & Cormier, 1996; Okun, 1991; Seligman, 1996). The **twelve-step** and **co-dependency** models, on which many addiction support groups are based, are currently much in vogue.

In addition, some agencies adhere to a specific set of religious or ethical principles. A staff member in a social service department of a Catholic hospital, for example, would be expected to suggest to clients only those options that are acceptable to the overarching principles of that religion. These agencies are currently being referred to as "faith-based social services." The extent to which public monies should support their services has been hotly contested in Congress and the media (Kaminer, 1997, 2001).

There is no overall approach that everyone in the human service field agrees is the most effective. A classic research study by Carkhuff and Berenson (1968) indicates that the variations among counselors' styles are so great that it is impossible to compare their methods and outcomes. With no clear evidence that one theorist has found the best method for creating mental health or social change, most counselors evolve a method for creating out of bits and pieces of many theories. This eclectic approach is further refined through years of experience. And, finally, styles are filtered though the individual personalities of workers and the demands of the population they work with.

With the widespread movement to **managed health care** programs, for example, much of a counselor's action plan is dictated by how long the client's health care provider will pay for mental health services.

Differences in social welfare laws from state to state add more diversity to the field. As you read about the history of social welfare in the United States, you will learn about the tug of war that has been going on between the federal government

Twelve-step program A program of healing activities designed by the founders of Alcoholics Anonymous.

Co-dependency A mutually destructive relationship between a person who is addicted and his or her significant other that helps to continue, rather than break, the addiction.

Managed health care A prepaid system in which an individual must choose among the doctors included in a particular plan, such as a Health Maintenance Organization. It generally stresses preventive health care but is often used as a cost-cutting measure.

In recent years there has been a big push to get people out of what many deemed a "failed" welfare system. However, too often, the buck has simply been passed from the federal government to the state and local government with insufficient job opportunities and job training, leaving families without the money for food, shelter, and health care.

and the states in responding to social needs. Diversity and uniformity of social programs exist side by side. On the one hand, you could travel from California to Maine and find reasonably similar **Head Start** preschool programs in each state. On the other hand, if you visited foster care agencies in each state as you went from east to west you would find fifty different sets of rules and regulations. Head Start is a federal program, so the rules that govern it are made in Washington, D.C., and disseminated to each state. But foster care and adoption laws are made on the state level, so we find wide variations in these programs.

  These discrepancies underscore our assertion that human service workers cannot assume they know what social services exist, even in their hometown. In order to practice their profession, they must know how to construct a currently accurate profile of the services available in each specific community.

Head Start A federally funded preschool program that aims to increase the readiness for public school of children from low-income families. It was begun by the War on Poverty in the 1960s.

FINDING THE APPROPRIATE HUMAN SERVICES PROGRAM

The local town hall is usually the first place to begin the search for an appropriate social service agency. There you will find the local health, recreation, and education departments; juvenile and elder services; and the like. The workers in these departments can describe the social services they fund, monitor, or license. They might have listings of services in each area.

The next source we turn to in exploring the human service network is the directories of social services published by various private agencies. One type of directory is *comprehensive*; it lists a broad range of social problems and the agencies that deal with them. This sort of directory is generally compiled and distributed by the group that coordinates and raises funds for social services in a particular town. Such groups include the United Way, Community Chest, Community Council, Social Service Coalition, or Red Feather Agency.

In larger cities where the task is a major undertaking, the work of compiling resources might devolve on a private publishing firm. In Massachusetts, for example, a book entitled *The Human Services Referral Directory of Massachusetts* (2002) is larger than the phone books of many towns in our country. A well-thumbed copy of that directory is likely to adorn the desk of almost every human service worker in the state.*

The table of contents of a comprehensive directory affords a vivid display of the diversity of problems and agencies. The index of a human services directory might start off like this:

A	B	C
abortion	battered women	child care centers
abuse, physical	bereavement support	children's services
addiction	birth control	consumer protection
adoption	block associations	counseling
aging	bulimia	correctional institutions
AIDS		

The other types of directories are *problem specific*; they focus on one particular service area. Thus individual booklets might list services for the developmentally delayed, addiction support groups, or early-childhood centers. Some directories are published by national organizations, which have chapters across the country; others are just for local services. A booklet listing services for senior citizens, for example, is likely to include some of the resources shown in the box on page 15.

Some directories list only the *objective* information about an agency: location, activities, costs, and eligibility requirements. The *subjective* directories provide a more in-depth picture by describing agency services and then evaluating their quality of service. An excellent example of the more subjective type of directory was compiled by a group of students studying health care issues at the State University of New York at Stony Brook (Lefferts, 1982). In the process of this research, students learned an amazing amount about the quantity and quality of services in their town. An evaluative directory empowers both the consumer and human service worker, who can thereby make informed decisions when they choose an agency. Subjective directories are much harder to compile than the factual listings. Each agency must be visited, all

***The Human Services Referral Directory* is now also published in New York (2002) and by other publishers under slightly different titles in many other states.

American Association of Retired Persons
Congregate-living programs
Council on Aging
Day-activity programs
Elderhostel educational programs
Elderly legal services
Exercise programs
Homemaker/home health aides
Meals on wheels
Nursing homes
Recreation centers
Residences
Retired Seniors in Volunteer Programs (RSVP)
Shuttle-bus service
Social action or issue groups
Visiting nurses

its materials must be read, and data must be found that offer feedback on the care that clients have received. And they must then be updated on a regular schedule.

Some agencies maintain hot-line phone services. One can call them, for example, to get information on sexually transmitted diseases, learn about various forms of cancer, or find a service agency for stepfamilies.

Newspapers also contain information about new agencies that are opening or about the special projects and problems of agencies. The calendar page of the newspaper often lists workshops, seminars, and meetings of support groups. Often there are notices placed by social agencies seeking volunteers or donations. Computer bulletin boards and chat rooms on the Internet can also be rich sources of information on virtually every social problem and program.

The classified section of a local newspaper can provide clues to the social service networks in a town. Figure 1.1 shows a selection of want ads clipped from the local newspapers of several cities.

BARRIERS THAT PREVENT PEOPLE FROM GETTING HELP

Despite the problems caused by her father's alcohol addiction, Kathy was quite fortunate in some ways. Her town had a variety of social services, and she was able to find and use them. For many people, things do not work out as well. Perhaps they resist seeking help or have difficulty locating, choosing, paying for, or using it.

Many barriers are encountered on the pathway to seeking help. When they are insurmountable, small problems balloon into large, often tragic ones. Because barriers

CASE MANAGEMENT SUPERVISOR

Starting approximately August. BA degree with 6 years experience or MA degree with 3 years experience. Salary competitive. Submit resume to: P.O. Box 462, Little Rock, AR 72217

PART-TIME EXPERIENCED TRAINER

to supervise volunteers, organize & conduct workshops on alcohol & drugs, communication skills, building self-esteem. Send resumé to Box 911, Maryland, AR 72204

FULL & PART-TIME POSITIONS

open for single applicants. Work with emotionally disturbed teens in residential treatment setting. Experience preferred. Box 976

COORDINATOR

Colorado Community Improvement Program. Plan and implement Community Improvement Program including recruitment of entrants, technical assistance during program year, provide communities, neighborhoods, and organizations with information relating to community problems. Meet with city officials, chambers of commerce, civic leaders in public meetings. Related degree and experience preferred. Salary negotiable. Apply and send resumé to: C. Brill, ETO, Inc., 1470 S. Vermont St., Aurora, CO 80012

COORDINATOR/JOB PLACEMENT

Fulltime. Develops and coordinates vocational services for adult psychiatric population. B.A. + 1 year relevant exp. and 6 mo. exp. in industrial setting. Exp. may be substituted for part of education. Apply through July 10,

at Mental Health Center of Denver Co. Inc. 1333 Iris, Affirmative Action M/F, EOE.

CITIZEN ACTION

Progressive social change organization seeks individuals with political motivation for community outreach. Travel opportunities. 617-291-6090 before 1 p.m.

PSYCHIATRIC YOUTH WORKER

St. Agnes Home for Boys has immediate opening for experienced person to work closely with emotionally disturbed adolescent boys in our intensive treatment unit. Qualified applicant must be at least 21, have drivers license and car, have min. 2 years college with courses in the behavioral sciences, plus psychiatric work experience with disturbed children. Excellent benefits. Call TR9-2362 Monday through Friday between 10 a.m. & 3 p.m.

DIRECTOR

Mondale halfway house for alcoholics. Position requires BA or BS degree, related area preferred & 2 yrs experience in treatment of alcoholism. May be a recovered alcoholic with at least 2 yrs of sobriety. Contact Human Services Center, P.O. Box 14, Mendenhall, MS 39114. An equal opportunity employer.

RELIEF houseparents/child care worker, 12:30 p.m. to 8:30 a.m., 5 day work week, 2 yrs. college or 1 yr. exp., to work at Boys Ranch. Call Mr. Yate, 726-9012.

COMMUNITY CASE WORKER.

Duties include: recruiting Indian foster homes for public or private, assisting Indian families w/state courts concerning children.

Perform these services for the Indian People in Tucson. Call after 9:00 a.m., 712-9000.

ADOLESCENT CHEMICAL DEPENDENCY PROGRAM

Stoughton Medical Center, LaCrosse, Wis., is pleased to announce the start of a newly organized Adolescent Chemical Dependency Program. Program will consist of a 16 bed unit within an accredited medical center. We are seeking:

- Director—Full time, master degree level.
- Family Therapist—Full time, master degree level.
- Alcoholism Counselor II—2 full time positions, bachelor degree level.
- Counselor I—2 full time and 2 part time positions, knowledge of chemical dependency required.
- Recreation Therapist—full time, bachelor degree level. Excellent salary and fringe benefits. Send resume to :

Stoughton Medical Center Personnel Dept., 1 Timm Ave. LaCrosse, WI 54601

CARE Givers—for pre-school, N.W. Detroit, min. 2 yrs. of child development courses required, call 812-9602.

EXECUTIVE DIRECTOR

For newly formed Homemaker-Home Health Aid Agency. Private, non-profit voluntary agency. Experience in health related field. Education required: B.S. degree, experience in fields of social work and public health. Submit resumé including references to:

Circle-Homemaker-Health Care, Box 26, Granville, OH 43023

FIGURE 1.1 Classified advertisements for human service jobs that have appeared in newspapers from different parts of the country

Source: *Denver Post,* Denver, Colorado; *Kansas City Times,* Kansas City, Missouri; *New Orleans Times-Picayune/States Item,* New Orleans, Louisiana; *Arizona Daily Star,* Tucson, Arizona; *Minneapolis Tribune,* Minneapolis, Minnesota; *Detroit News,* Detroit, Michigan; *Columbus Dispatch,* Columbus, Ohio; *Arkansas Gazette,* Little Rock, Arkansas.

interfere with our ability to serve prospective clients, we need to develop skills to recognize them and then negate or surmount them.

Some barriers, such as feelings of indecision and ambivalence, are inevitable. How could Kathy's father be certain that he had crossed the line that separates a social drinker from an alcoholic? How could he be certain that he needed professional help? How could he be sure that the hospital or group he ultimately chose was the right one for him? These kinds of feelings we call **internal barriers** to receiving help.

Other, more tangible barriers can stand in the way. Often there are no beds available in a detoxification unit when the client is ready. Frequently there is not enough money to train or pay staff to learn about a new treatment modality. The red tape of bureaucrats in government and in the insurance industry often interferes with a well-thought-out service plan. We call these **external barriers.**

We cannot always remove or mitigate the impact of these internal and external barriers, but we must be aware of them. Both client and worker interact within the constraints these barriers impose and are challenged to work creatively around them, using all the intervention strategies we will be describing in a later chapter.

Following is a list of barriers to finding and using human services. The first six are primarily internal barriers that will need to be dealt with in the worker–client counseling relationship. The last five are more external to the client and are most appropriately dealt with by using the strategies of organizing and advocacy. But here, as with most categories, lines do blur.

Each of the first ten barriers is followed by some inner thoughts or questions that reflect them. The last one we will discuss in more detail.

Internal barriers
Emotions or attitudes within a person that make it difficult for him or her to seek help.

External barriers
Barriers in the environment that make it difficult for a person to receive help.

1. *The Difficulty of Evaluating the Seriousness of a Problem*
   - Does my child have a learning disability that needs special help, or is he or she just developing a little bit more slowly than the other kids in the class?
   - Is it normal to be so furious at my parents? Are other teenagers as depressed as I am?
   - Is this kid in my class just mischievous or is there some other more serious problem? Does he just have a high energy level or is he biologically hyperactive?

2. *The Tendency to Deny the Gravity of a Problem*
   - I'm just a social drinker who sometimes has a bit too much. I can stop anytime I decide to. Can I really?
   - Well, I know he hits me once in a while. But don't all marriages go through rough spots?
   - There is no discrimination in this company; we just can't seem to find any qualified women (or disabled or Latino) supervisors. No one can say I didn't try, can they?

3. *The Fear of Being Judged, Labeled, or Punished*
   - If I get tested for AIDS and it turns out I'm positive, will I lose my job and my medical insurance? Will my family stick with me?
   - If I ask for an evaluation of my child's learning problems, will she be labeled retarded or be stuck in a low track for the rest of her schooling?

- I know I don't have enough food in the house, but if I apply for food stamps, will my neighbors begin referring to me as the old lady who's a "welfare cheat"?

4. *The Suspicion or Distrust of Human Service Workers and Agencies*
   - I know they assure you that complaints of child abuse are anonymous, but how do I know they won't give out my name? Maybe my neighbor will come after me.
   - If I admit how mad I get at my child, will they try to take him away from me?
   - If I agree to a voluntary commitment to the hospital for an evaluation, will they decide I'm crazy and throw away the key?

5. *The Shame of Not Being Able to Solve One's Own Problems*
   - I don't see any other men bursting into tears when they get turned down for a job. Why can't I act like a "real" man?
   - I was always taught that you don't air your dirty linen in public; so, although I know the landlord is not giving me enough heat, won't I look like a crybaby if I complain to the rent board?
   - How can I ask for help paying my medical bills? My family has always taken care of its own.

6. *Fear of the Unknown*
   - If we start marital counseling and I say what I really think, will we end up in divorce court?
   - Maybe this school isn't as good as it should be, but if the parents start making decisions, won't it get worse? What do they know about education?
   - Living at home might be lonely for our son, who's developmentally delayed, but maybe when he's older we'll think about his moving into a community residence. How can we be sure he won't be hurt if he moves out into the world?

7. *The Difficulties of Choosing the Appropriate Program and Helper*
   - I've heard about three special programs for autistic children; how do I know which one is best?
   - Our committee has interviewed six candidates for the job of hot-line director, and they are all different. What kind of person (race, gender, age, degree) would make the best director?
   - My family has been going to this clinic for three years, and we don't seem to be getting along any better. Whom can I talk with to see if maybe we shouldn't try another approach?

8. *The Inadequacy of Services*
   - Will there be anyone in that program who understands my culture and speaks my language? Will any of the other staff be disabled the way I am? (Sue, Ivey, & Pederson, 1996)
   - We worry that the steep stairs will be hard to maneuver for many of the senior citizens, but what can we do? It is the only building we could afford.
   - No one wants to have this prison (halfway house for addicts, drop-in center for teenagers) in the neighborhood; should we locate it on the edge of town, even though it can't be reached by public transportation?

9. *The High Cost of Services*
   - We don't have enough money for our day camp, so we have to save the spaces for those most in need. But how do you decide whom to reject?
   - I know that your mom needs this nursing home, but Medicaid doesn't pay the full cost and we never get those payments on time anyway.
   - We could try to run a reform candidate for the school board who is in favor of racial integration, but can we pay the advertising costs to get enough publicity?

10. *Past History, Reputation, or Public Image of a Program*
    - First it was the antipoverty program, then Model Cities, now it's privatization. I've seen them all come and go. Our neighborhood never seems to get any better. Why should I participate in this new program?
    - With all the taxes I pay, why do the schools still turn out kids who can't read?
    - As a legislator, I'm convinced that this town does not need another shelter for the homeless. Do you think the social workers complain about problems so they can keep their jobs?

11. *Myths and Lack of Information about the Human Services*

Because the field is so broad and the barriers to finding and using help so pervasive, the public is understandably confused. This lack of clarity can lead to hostility. Much of what people *think* they know about the role of the human service worker is, in fact, either incomplete or just plain wrong.

Unlike many other professions—fire fighters, doctors, secretaries—the public rarely sees human service workers doing their jobs. We don't wear uniforms or have any observable symbols or tools of our trade. People usually visualize the human service professional primarily in the role of therapist, counselor, or welfare investigator, working one-on-one to solve individual problems or ferret out wrongdoing. Although these are important roles, they do not show the full dimensions of human service work.

Instead of working in a one-on-one counseling relationship with Kathy, for example, some human service workers tackled the problem of alcohol abuse by trying to change the social system that supports it.

- They made speeches about the need for funding alcohol education programs.

- They designed training programs for schools and private industry.

- They met with legislators to change the laws governing the advertising and sale of addictive substances.

- They conducted research to find out what kind of prevention programs work best.

- They published newsletters, books, and journal articles that disseminated the wisdom they have gleaned about alcohol intervention.

- They designed computer programs so that information about addiction could be easily retrieved.

These social change activities are just as important as the therapy or counseling interventions that the public identifies as our province. The media does little to help the public get a well-rounded picture of the varied work of the field. Television programs show the exploits of doctors, emergency medical technicians, lawyers, detectives, newspaper reporters, and an occasional schoolteacher, but rarely those of a human service worker.

Only one major network show—*Eastside, Westside*—has featured a human service worker as its "hero." Each episode showed him interacting with people who were struggling to overcome difficult situations. The program dealt with racial prejudice, prostitution, alcoholism, marital discord, labor strikes, and runaway children. Most of the dramas were real-life situations, filled with suspense, emotion, conflicting values, and expectations. Because the program tried to hold a mirror up to life, many of the problems could not be resolved in neatly packaged, hour-long segments. Sadly—but accurately—the black family depicted on the show was not welcomed with open arms by their neighbors in an all-white suburb; the divorcing couples and runaway kids were not always reunited, and alcoholics often drifted back to the bottle. Although the critics liked it, *Eastside, Westside* ran for only one season. The uniqueness of the program lay not only in its portrayal of the excitement and frustration of human service work but also in its depiction of the wide-ranging activities of the human service worker.

Worse than the paucity of information about the field are the myths and misinformation projected by the popular media using human service workers as the objects of ridicule: "Hello," says the client. "Hmmm, now what do you *really* mean by that?" asks the counselor.

Encouraging responsible behavior and reducing the self-defeating cycle of alcohol and drug abuse require creative approaches. This wrecked car raises frightening questions about the fate of its once carefree driver. Change in drinking patterns is painstakingly slow, yet we believe that change is always possible.

On the rare occasions that the theater or Hollywood movies depict us at all, they often portray us as narrow, rigid, inept snoopers. The social worker in Herb Gardner's often-performed comedy, *A Thousand Clowns* (1962), is a classic portrayal of this stereotype. In it, a children's protective worker (with hair pulled back, glasses halfway down her nose, flat shoes, and a man-tailored suit) is sent to investigate charges that a man is corrupting his young nephew. He is romping with him through New York's parks and neighborhoods instead of sending him to school, where the boy could be taught to take life seriously. The uncle and nephew are portrayed as witty, energetic, loving people, while the young female social worker and her stuffy male supervisor represent the boredom of society, full of rigid rules and unfeeling bureaucracy.

The definitive parody of human service workers was written by Stephen Sondheim for *West Side Story*. Set in an urban ghetto, this musical drama is an updated version of the tragedy of Romeo and Juliet. In this saga of poverty, prejudice, and conflicting emotions, a group of teenage gang members tell a police officer about their misadventures with the human service workers they have been sent to. Each "helper" disagrees with the others and comes to a ridiculous, simplistic conclusion about the teenagers' delinquency. A judge says they are misunderstood neurotics, so he sends them to a therapist. The therapist says that delinquency is a social disease, so he sends them to a social worker to get a "good honest job." The social worker says they're not antisocial, they're only "antiwork" and could use a year in jail. And so they are sent back to court, right where they started from!

A PARADOX

When we consider the barriers strewn along the path to getting help, we should think about them in their current context. When placed in perspective, these barriers reveal a frustrating paradox.

At no time in the history of the social services has there been such a wide array of program approaches for solving social problems as there is today, although many programs are struggling to stay solvent. Thirty years ago, Kathy's father would probably have been fired from his job when his alcohol addiction began interfering with his performance. Back then, few companies hired trained mental health counselors for their personnel departments, and most workers could not afford the luxury of an inpatient facility to "dry out" and regroup. But Kathy's dad overcame barriers with the help of a professional **employee assistance program** (EAP) counselor at his firm. His health insurance plan paid for his stay at the rehabilitation center. He was lucky!

And certainly, attitudes toward addicts have improved. Thirty years ago, if a police officer had encountered Kathy's dad sleeping off his binge in a public park, he probably would have arrested him, and a judge might have charged him with disorderly conduct, public drunkenness, and the like. But by the time Kathy wrote this paper, most police officers had learned to define alcohol addiction as an illness.

So the barriers of inaccessibility and stigma, for example, should be toppling down for families facing the kinds of problems Kathy described. Right? Wrong!

Employee assistance program (EAP) Supportive services dealing with mental health or financial or legal issues that are offered directly to employees by their company or agency. Their goal is to reduce worker turnover and raise productivity.

Strangely enough, this isn't happening. In actuality, in this new millennium, most health care plans, which at their inception were fairly generous with mental health benefits, are drastically cutting back on these treatments.

At the same time, in public forums in the mass media and in the halls of Congress, the following demands are being shouted with louder and louder voices:

- Give the public tax cuts instead of social services.

- Allow each of the fifty states to make its own decisions about whether to fund specific social services.

- Bring to a halt the days of massive public support for social services.

- Admit that social services hinder rather than help troubled individuals.

In later chapters, we will return to these themes to see how they play out as human service workers try to ameliorate social problems in an ever more complex world, in which priorities are moving away from dealing with social problems through governmental intervention.

CHOOSING OUR WORK ROLE

From one perspective, this wide range (some might call it a hodgepodge) of human service agencies can seem overwhelming. It is especially confusing to the student just starting a human service career. On the flip side of the coin, however, this incredible diversity offers each worker a chance to find the particular combination of worker roles, agencies, clients, populations, and problems that fits his or her unique talents.

As you read about Kathy's experiences, reflect on your own, and glance through directories and want ads, you will probably be attracted to some human service roles and repelled by others. These are natural reactions. While one person thrives working with youngsters with cerebral palsy, another might drown in feelings of frustration or hopelessness. That same worker who cannot cope with the physically disabled child might be able to coolly trade put-downs with the angriest streetwise teenager. One worker who can listen patiently and nonjudgmentally all day long to folks like Kathy's dad would be tongue-tied trying to convince the zoning board to let her agency purchase a building when the neighbors have organized to block the sale.

We need to tune in to our instinctive feelings of attraction or repulsion to different human service tasks and roles. But we also need to keep our options open. We often surprise ourselves by discovering that we can do work that we thought we could never tolerate. We can also find ourselves unstimulated by a work role that we always thought we wanted.

Currently many students are being trained to be human service generalists. The **generalist** is knowledgeable about a wide range of resources, strategies, and subgroups and can operate comfortably in many agency roles. He or she does not nec-

Generalist A worker who is knowledgeable about a wide range of resources and subgroups and who can use a variety of helping interventions.

essarily identify with one human service subspecialty but works with a small number of clients, helping them confront and solve the gamut of life's problems. The generalist is often a team member or assistant whose daily tasks grow out of a job assignment that complements the role of other helping professionals.

Some students take the reverse path, specializing in a specific role from the start of their careers. Trained to work as alcohol and drug abuse counselors or as mental health technicians, they develop depth rather than breadth. Later on they might need to expand their skills as priorities shift or as they move up the career ladder. Whichever direction students take at the start of their career, they will probably continue to do a significant amount of growing as they search for the academic degrees and experience that suit them best.

Whether returning to school for advanced training or switching jobs, workers need to make choices about (1) the specific problems or populations they want to deal with, (2) the type of agency setting they enjoy, and (3) the strategies of intervention they are best at. These choices will be determined by *personal attributes, lifestyles,* and *ideologies* and by the *accessibility of certain occupational roles.*

Our Attributes

Most of us have been taught since childhood that talking about our good points is bragging or showing off, but in the human services we must develop insight into precisely what we do best and least well. We need to estimate what our chances of growth or change will be in a specific job.

Although the same values and attitudes are basic to all types of human service work, there are differences in the kinds of people who can do intensive, one-to-one counseling and those who fare best in the rough-and-tumble atmosphere of community organization. Some of us are outgoing and articulate, others more introspective and quiet. Some are comfortable filling a niche in a traditional structure; others like to be in charge or work alone. Each time we try a new field experience, meet clients and workers at different agencies, or read about human service work, we should try to visualize ourselves as full-time workers in that role. We need to figure out how its demands fit our personality and how much we are willing to change.

Our Lifestyles

Even as we start our human service education, we should think about the elements in an environment that bring out the best in us. Some of us, for example, are night people, so working a 2:00 P.M. to 10:00 P.M. shift in a teen residence or running evening parents' groups would be possible. Others are nine-to-fivers. Perhaps they will choose to work in a school or on the day shift at a hospital or mental health clinic. All jobs require some mix of time, location, and structure. These are dictated by the sorts of populations the agency serves.

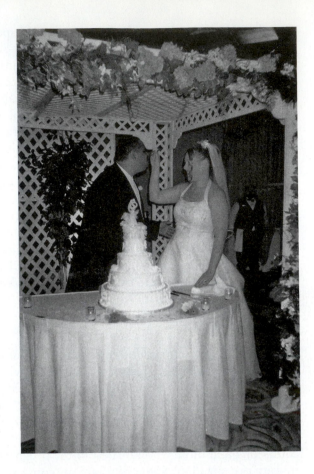

As our lives evolve through marriage, raising children, caring for elderly parents, facing an empty nest, or perhaps moving to a new area, our work life needs to accommodate to those changes.

Some people feel strongly about dressing in a certain fashion; however, that desire might not fit a particular setting or subgroup. Others insist on having privacy or a place of their own. Obviously, a live-in job in a residence might not suit them.

Although we need to compromise on certain issues, others are vital and legitimate personal needs. As our lives change, the kind of work that makes sense for us also changes. The choice of a specific role need not be lifelong. Optimally, it should support the other parts of our lives as family members and citizens. The broadness of the human service field offers a unique chance to shift gears as circumstances require.

Our Personal Ideologies

Each of us comes to human service work with a unique set of philosophies, drawn from our religion or a general ethical framework. These beliefs must be compatible with the work we do. If a person has strong religious convictions about war, contraception, suicide, special types of food, or days of rest, these must be taken into account in choosing a place to work. We must not be self-conscious about acknowledging the primacy of these issues in our lives. Usually, we can find jobs that allow their expression. Although our values will come under constant scrutiny in the course of learning about the field and though many values might change, they should never be suppressed. If we try to deny them, they may subtly affect our work.

Likewise, many of us have political beliefs about how society should be organized—our personal visions of utopia. We choose the human service work that seems to be moving the community in that direction. As long as our politics or visions do not engulf our work, they add dimension and intensity to it. Some jobs might make demands that we cannot in conscience fulfill. We need to acknowledge these problems openly. Needless to say, having our own beliefs never means that we insist our clients agree with us. If we have too many rigid beliefs, it may turn out that human services is not the right field for us.

Agencies in the Local Community

Throughout this book, we underscore the changing nature of human service work. For example, priorities are not the same in a rural setting as in an urban center. Priorities change as the population shifts in age or ethnicity; inventions affect people's lifestyles; and election results redirect the national agenda.

When the country is at war, having an economic recession, or embarking on a new crusade against mental illness, disability, or domestic violence, some agencies become obsolete and others expand. Funding patterns change dramatically in short periods. Sometimes the human services help to shape the political climate in the country; more often they are shaped by it.

You might, for example, read about shelters for young mothers who have AIDS. You might decide to work in one, only to discover that your state does not appropriate money for such shelters. This does not necessarily mean you won't ever work in one. Perhaps you will first have to join with others and use your organizational skills to create a public outcry for such programs. Once successful, you can retool, using less of your social change skills and more of your counseling skills.

To get a visceral feeling for the highs, lows, and realities of human service work, let's meet Stephanie Lake, a worker whom Kathy might have encountered on her college campus.

INTERVIEW

Stephanie Lake, Program Coordinator, Drug and Alcohol Education Project

My work on the Drug and Alcohol Education Project began while I was a human services student. I met the director of the project, Margie Crooks, when she came to my class as a guest speaker. She was new on campus and looking for students to help get the program off the ground.

My college is hard to get to know. We are a work-study school. The students are on campus for several months and then leave for their job placements for the same amount of time before they return again. We are smack in the middle of a poor-to-working-class urban area. About half the students commute. A lot of our students have limited incomes and have to work part time. They have the usual problems of college kids—separation from family, roommate problems for the dorm students, and the tensions of traffic, parking, and home problems for the commuters. Then there are problems of studying, career choice, and all the baggage around social relationships and sexual identity. As on most campuses, there can be social pressures to drink too much and to experiment with marijuana. A lot of the kids come out of high school with these habits, or they come to college and think it is a chance to bust loose.

Although we have a Department of Student Counseling and a half-time counselor who specializes in drugs and alcohol, the administration decided to put more energy into education about, and the prevention of, substance abuse. That way, they don't just sit around waiting for the problems to come to them.

They made a really good choice in hiring Margie, because although she is youngish, she has a great background. She worked for several regional drug prevention centers. I volunteered to help her recruit students for a peer-counseling program called *Peers Reaching Out,* or PRO. We started with nine students. The first thing we did was a survey of attitudes and behavior. We walked around the student lounge for days with our clipboards. Because they knew their answers were anonymous, kids really opened up to us. We found out a lot about the services they used and what they might want. We also recruited a few peer counselors that way.

The next thing we did was form a committee. This was made up of university staff from different programs and student leaders. They became a brain trust to come up with ideas about the rules that needed to be changed and make suggestions for programs. I became the secretary to the group and still am.

They suggested that we needed more awareness on campus of the problem and the new program. The president declared a DRUG-AHOL Awareness Week. Faculty members agreed to invite speakers into their classes, and the resident assistants organized discussions in the dorms. We set up a table in the quad and took turns sitting at it every day for a week. We gave out literature on different aspects of the problem, had a drug board that showed the paraphernalia and effects of drugs and alcohol. We also had drug wheels that you use to figure out how much alcohol it would take to make you legally drunk.

The idea I was proudest of was the display of a totally wrecked car donated by a junkyard. We had it towed right into the center of the quad. The students could see in gruesome detail what can happen when you drive drunk. They stopped and asked a lot of questions. We also had a video going constantly in the main lobby about the crash involving that car.

After I volunteered for two quarters, Marge was able to hire me as a work-study student. I was put in charge of DRUG-AHOL Awareness Week and each one has gotten better since then.

At first I was afraid to speak in front of student clubs, but I eventually got over that. I wrote articles for the student newspaper and was interviewed on the student radio station. I also used all my own contacts and was able to recruit a solid group of forty-five students. Some of them were in recovery themselves and some of them, like me, had alcohol abuse in the family. I organized the weekly training sessions, set up speakers, got videos, and stayed in touch with the peers between training sessions.

Margie taught me a lot about writing grants. I assisted her in gathering background information and in making presentations to foundations. One of them funded us for two years. As soon as I graduated, I was able to come on full time. Since then I have planned, organized, and implemented a twenty-four-hour DRUG-AHOL telephone hot line. This way, we can give out information and make referrals, and the students don't have to identify themselves if they don't want to.

I think I've also been especially pleased with the development of the campus task force. I've gone from being a student member to being one of the professional staff to whom people turn for suggestions. We had a major problem with our senior "bash." For years it's been a tradition for the seniors to bring champagne onto the quad the last day of classes and just get totally drunk. They would destroy the grass, break the bottles, and have a series of nasty accidents. We needed to stop it and yet, we recognized the seniors' need to celebrate. Our committee proposed that the university take over the celebration, providing the champagne, soft drinks, and plenty of food. That way, the seniors could have their party and we could help them drink in a responsible way. They grumbled the first year, but we pulled it off.

But this year the university decided we couldn't repeat it. The president felt we couldn't take the ethical or moral risk of providing liquor to students who would later drive home. So they gave them a beautiful, fancy, nonalcoholic party. Of course, the students went to the local bars right after it, but there is only so much you can do.

The other project I work on is a program called INSTEAD. From the student court, we get referrals of residents who have caused damage while drunk or who have been caught with liquor in the dorms. The university used to expel them from the dorms. Now we recognize they have a problem. They have to attend a six-session training course and do community service. I think this has helped a lot of them turn around. Some of the INSTEAD members go on to join AA. Some even stay with their volunteer work with neighborhood kids.

I have learned so much about administration and planning in this job. It is ending within the next month because the grant is over. This gives me a chance to explore going back to school for my advanced degree. I think maybe it's time to leave, but it's been great to grow with a program that has so much meaning for students and faculty.

SUMMARY

1. Three possible routes for a young woman looking for help with her father's alcohol abuse were described. By following these paths we encountered twenty-five different human service roles.

2. A picture of the human service programs in any one particular town can be discovered by calling the town hall or an umbrella funding agency, searching out directories of services, calling hot lines, and reading the local newspapers.

3. Although services might be available, clients frequently have difficulty finding and using them. Barriers generated by internal and external pressures clutter the paths. We looked at a variety of these barriers by listening in on the nagging doubts and questions that reflect them.

4. The public often accepts stereotypes about who we are and what we do. People often lack accurate information about the full range of human service work.

5. The complexity inherent in human service problems leads to a proliferation of agencies and professional roles. This diversity can offer much choice to those seeking appropriate services or roles. People choose their work roles in the field by considering their own:

   Personal attributes

   Lifestyle

   Philosophy or ideology

   Available programs

6. The description of the daily work of a program coordinator for a drug and alcohol abuse education and prevention project reveals many important roles in the human service network.

7. Although treading the maze of the human service system is complex and frustrating, it is never routine and is often exhilarating.

DISCUSSION QUESTIONS

1. Some people believe that alcohol or drug abuse is a crime best left to the criminal justice system. Others believe that addiction is a moral failing and thus should be cured by the family and the church. Others assert that it is a problem that should be dealt with by the medical establishment and the social service networks. What do you think of each of these positions?

2. What is the situation with drug and alcohol use and abuse on your campus? What approaches does the administration appear to be using if there seems to be a problem, and how effective do you think these approaches are?

3. If you were assigned to write a helpee paper the way Kathy was, would you be willing to write about a personal problem? Would you be willing to share your paper with your classmates after you wrote it (if you decided to fulfill the assignment)? To what extent do you think that asking students in a Human Service class to share personal information with the instructor or with other students is an appropriate learning device? To what extent does it feel an unjustified invasion of your privacy?

4. What human service workers have you personally met? Which ones do you know about in your community or on your campus? Which of their jobs seems like a set of tasks you might like to try out? Which would you prefer to avoid?

WEB RESOURCES FOR FURTHER STUDY

Research Navigator Guide
www.researchnavigator.com

To obtain a broad overview of the field and be guided through a multitude of human service related web sites, see *Research navigator guide: The helping professions* (Kjosness, Barr, & Rettman, 2004). Or, if you register with a code listed on the front page of the book, you can access its web site.

Hazelden Publishing and Educational Services
www.hazelden.org

Prevline: National Clearinghouse for Alcohol and Drug Information
www.health.org and www.samhsa.gov.

Web of Addictions
www.well.com/user/woa

These resources are especially helpful for more extensive reading materials and factual information on issues of addiction.

The National Mental Health Consumers Self-Help Clearinghouse
www.mhselfhelp.org

An excellent web site that connects individuals to self-help and advocacy resources in many areas of mental health from the vantage point of consumers.

CHAPTER 2

The Changing Nature of the Helping Process

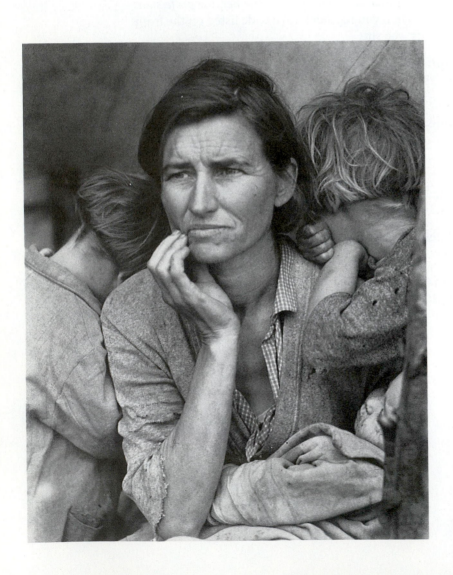

Now that we have looked at the many ways in which human services are organized and delivered to families like Kathy's and to students on an urban campus, we will take a step backward to see how the services of today have evolved over the years. Communities have always reached out to help their neighbors in a crisis, but social upheavals, new knowledge, inventions, and the pressures of the social environment shape the ways in which that help is given. Attitudes toward people in distress and the ways to help them have changed dramatically and erratically through history.

The methods used to offer help have followed a complex, unpredictable course, taking one step forward, two steps backward, often circling around to the place they started. Through case examples, we will show the changes that have occurred in the treatment of the poor, the disabled, the mentally ill, and those accused of crimes against property and people.

Finally, we will try to answer the question of why you need to understand where we have come from to chart a course for your work in the future. We hope you will see how we can revive valuable attitudes and behaviors that have been thoughtlessly cast aside in the rush to be modern. And you will note ways in which we must be careful to avoid repeating some of the worst mistakes our predecessors made in their efforts to cope with the age-old problems of human beings.

A woman who is active in a welfare rights group called EMPOWER in Rochester, New York, describes how the group helped her change from feeling worthless and powerless to feeling in control of her life.

> I felt worthless and ashamed receiving a welfare check. I didn't even go to the bank on welfare-check day. I didn't want people to see me with that manila envelope—the one welfare checks come in....
>
> The image that I would use for the way I felt about myself would be a social leper. I felt like I had a dreaded, contagious disease.... It took the beauty from my eyes, causing me to feel ugly; it took the hope from my heart, causing me to feel discouraged; it took the ideas from my mind, causing me to feel useless....
>
> These feelings started to change when I met the founder of EMPOWER.... Mr. Ingram treated us like respectable human beings.... My sense of worth was enhanced when church members treated me with courtesy and respect.... (Ingram, 1992, p. 95)
>
> As I began to feel good about myself, I began to entertain the notion that, as a person with worth, I was entitled to fair and legal treatment by the welfare establishment.... EMPOWER gives people the opportunity to take charge of their lives. Those who choose to do so then encourage others to do the same.... Together, using a collective

voice, welfare recipients are growing in their ability to address with dignity a system that has too long failed to recognize their individual worth and value. (Maxwell, 1988, p. 13)

Welfare rights groups such as EMPOWER that help AFDC/TANF recipients overcome welfare stigma stand firm as the ocean of anti-welfare sentiment threatens to engulf the country. Resentment against welfare recipients is not new, but its intensity has vastly increased since the early 1980s.

The poor have not always been treated with such suspicion and mistrust. In feudal times, people believed that their economic status was decreed by God, and the poor were not blamed for their condition. Each historical period creates the conditions that shape people's attitudes about helping people. In this chapter, we trace some of those historical changes.

SOCIETY SHAPES HELPING BEHAVIOR

Human beings are social animals who have always helped each other (and, of course, also hurt each other). The kind of relationships that a society expects from its citizens and the way it organizes its important institutions—the family, the system of governance and control—can either nurture or stunt people's impulses to give help to relatives, friends, and needy strangers.

Anthropologists have shown that behavior varies widely among cultures. It is shaped by the food supply, the kinship system, the system of production, and relationships with other societies. It is easier to be loving and helpful in some societies than in others. Yet, if a modern society is to stay intact, it must encourage some form of mutual help. This is what the anthropologist Claude Levi-Strauss (1974) called the **principle of reciprocity,** which he considered the basic glue that holds a society together. That principle points to people's mutual obligations toward each other, based on caring and a sense of justice.

Principle of reciprocity The principle that social relationships are based to some extent on an analysis of trade-offs that determines what each person must give to the relationship in order to get back certain benefits.

HELPING IN WESTERN CULTURE

Not only do different cultures vary in their helping behaviors, but our government, churches, and even private groups have always reacted differently to those in need of help. By exploring a small part of the history of a few institutions that are supposed to provide help, we see this evolution in concrete form. "But," you might ask, "why must I bother studying the past in order to do my job as a mental health aide (or probation officer) in the twenty-first century?" Each new view of the way people should be helped, or not helped, has left behind its skeletons. Buildings constructed during one era are still standing many years later; staff trained under outmoded theories continue to practice. Lingering myths and misconceptions about crime, mental illness, and poverty are almost impossible to stamp out, even in the face of overwhelming scientific evidence proving them wrong.

Social attitudes about behavior go through cycles. Sometimes they reverse themselves from one era to another. These immigrants to the United States, landing at Ellis Island early in the twentieth century, faced adversity, but their labor was welcomed. Now, many of their descendants vote to restrict the entry and social benefits of new waves of hopeful immigrants.

Change as a Cyclical Path

Change is not an upward, linear progression. Rather, changes in social attitudes and treatment methods tend to be cyclical. Yet, although the next spin in the cycle may look familiar, it doesn't come out exactly like the previous one. The philosopher Hegel called change a **dialectical** process. First there is the idea or action (a thesis), which inspires its opposite idea or action (antithesis). Out of the struggle of these two opposites comes a new synthesis. Then the process begins all over again. As you will see in the examples that follow, these cycles are strongly influenced by warring political ideologies, often seesawing between conservative ideas and more liberal ones.

We find ourselves periodically returning to the same debates about the legitimacy and effectiveness of such issues as:

- Capital punishment
- Mercy killing
- Birth control
- Women's rights
- Educational methods

Dialectical   Refers to the principle that an idea or event (thesis) generates its opposite (antithesis), leading to a reconciliation of opposites (synthesis) and a continuation of the dialectical process.

To understand the hodgepodge of rules, regulations, and social attitudes that surround our daily work in a hospital ward, a prison, or an old-age home, we need to know the possibilities, limits, and trade-offs of the many methods used in the past. Some of those may be, with variations, the methods of the future.

Tracing the overall history of helping in the United States as well as in Western Europe reveals a tortured path, starting from the times when people in need were viewed as the responsibility of their families alone and perhaps were also given a little help from the church or a benevolent feudal lord, owner, or other master. With the decline of feudalism and the rise of mercantilism and industrialism, the responsibility for those people who could not help themselves began to shift more and more to town governments. Official overseers of the poor gradually replaced the church and almsgivers as the primary sources of help outside the family. Eventually, this task of providing help became a profession for volunteers or trained professionals.

Some governments have been reluctant to take on the full responsibility. The United States, for example, has been called a "reluctant welfare state" in comparison with most other industrialized nations. Today we watch as our government dismantles services that it once offered citizens. When George H. W. Bush was president, he wanted volunteers to take the place of government services and called for "a thousand points of light." When his son, George W. Bush, became president in 2001, he continued his father's efforts to increase dependency on voluntary organizations in social services. His "faith-based" approach proposed giving religious organizations more money to deliver social services and more freedom from government restrictions. This strategy is reminiscent of the nineteenth century, with volunteers and private philanthropies. Some officials have even suggested that we return to the practices of feudal days, when the church gave whatever help was available. Churches protest that they are not equipped to handle the job, and the Catholic bishops have called for more government help for the poor and oppressed (National Conference of Catholic Bishops, 1997).

Except for a generous outpouring of giving to the victims of the attacks on the World Trade Center and the Pentagon, many charities nationwide have experienced sharp drops in contributions since September 11. Even before September 11, people were reacting to the economic pinch by cutting back on their giving.

Along with the shifts between private and public responsibility for helping has come a slowly changing set of social perspectives on people who need help. In feudal times, people were pretty much locked into their social status, and the rulers of society, buttressed by theologians such as St. Augustine, spread the word that the poor were poor because God willed it. If God willed it, the rulers argued, then it would be sacrilegious to change their status. The rich, however, could assure their own entrance into heaven by giving to the poor.

Sixteenth-century theologian John Calvin helped wed Protestant theology with the ideology needed for the rise of capitalism. He extolled the virtues of thrift, industry, sobriety, and responsibility as essential to the achievement of the reign of God on earth. The Puritan moralists of New England used his ideas to reinforce the work ethic needed for the newly emerging industrialism of the United States. The moral imperative to make money made it a stigma to be poor, and ensured that programs which give money to the poor would be linked to efforts to get them to work for wages. (Mothers have always worked as caretakers, but without wages.)

A powerful influence on the treatment of the poor during the late nineteenth century was the adaptation of the ideas of Charles Darwin on evolution to the realm of sociology. Although Darwin did not draw any sociological conclusions from his work, Herbert Spencer, an English philosopher and one of the first sociologists, used Darwin's work to coin the phrase *survival of the fittest.* According to Spencer's interpretation, the fittest people in society were those who were able to make money. Poor people were declared unfit and accorded the same treatment doled out to common criminals. This philosophy is called **Social Darwinism.** Even before Spencer, this attitude had currency:

> Christian charity…enjoins a personal interest in the lower orders; visiting them in their cottages, even though they may seem "little better than savages and barbarians, with whom any familiar intercourse would be degrading…if not dangerous," might nurture in the poor a sense of gratitude to their superiors. (Trimmer, 1801, p. 11)

Social Darwinism The application of Charles Darwin's theories of evolution to the human sphere by sociologist Herbert Spencer. The concept of "survival of the fittest" was used to justify accumulation of wealth and disregard of the needs of the poor.

Blaming the Victim versus Blaming the Social System

The beginnings of the industrial age ushered in the view that people with problems were morally depraved, almost as if they had a self-inflicted contagious disease. It was thought that they deserved punishment or removal from society. William Ryan calls that point of view **victim blaming** (Ryan, W., 1976). It is a point of view that has sunk roots deep into our society.

An equally radical but opposing point of view, and generally less popular, has been battling the blaming-the-victim ideology ever since the sixteenth century. It defines human problems as a result of interacting personal and social forces, often beyond the control of the individual. It looks at individuals as embedded in families and communities and in economic and political systems that exert a powerful pull on personality development, social status, and life chances.

Victim blaming Blaming a person for his or her own misfortune rather than considering the social forces that contributed to the problem.

This alternative point of view, which looks at social systems, asserts that life situations are an inevitable part of the human condition in an industrialized society. Everyone gets old and most old people retire from work; working parents need help with child care; everyone gets sick at some time; wage earners who support a family sometimes die or become disabled; women get pregnant and need prenatal care; everyone needs education in order to be a contributing member of society; many workers are injured; some babies are born with crippling diseases or develop one later in life. In an economic system that doesn't guarantee employment, some people lose their jobs. Life stresses take their toll on everyone, on some people more than others.

These opposing philosophies have resulted in very different approaches to giving help. The blaming-the-victim ideology always sees character defects in individuals. At best, it results in remedial programs to "cure" those defects. At its worst, it

Deserving versus undeserving The discriminatory classification of people into higher and lower categories, considering some people to be more worthy of receiving benefits and services than others.

Means-tested programs Programs that are only available to the poor, whose assets fall below a certain set eligibility level.

Residual philosophy of social welfare A philosophy that believes the problem that requires help is not a "normal" social need, but arises because of special circumstances brought about by individual deficiency.

Institutional philosophy of social welfare A philosophy that looks at people as being embedded in a social system and as having predictable developmental needs.

Universal programs Programs that provide income supports and social services to both the affluent and the poor.

Entitlements Benefits and services that people are legally entitled to, as compared to those that are given at the discretion of officials.

punishes people for what it construes as perverse or immoral conduct. Entire groups of people are blamed for their behavior—the poor, for example, are assumed to be poor because they lack initiative and the work ethic. The homeless are thought to have brought their condition on themselves by personality defects or lack of careful planning.

Means-Tested versus Universal Programs

Victim blamers feel superior to the victims. They assume that they could never be in the shape the victim is in. They separate people into "them" and "us." They are likely to give help sparingly, and to separate people into **deserving versus undeserving.** They prefer **means-tested programs** for the most desperate people and they investigate people's financial situations with a fine-toothed comb. They create demeaning and unattractive welfare programs so that people will be reluctant to accept the help.

The means-tested approach is often called the **residual philosophy of social welfare.** Proponents of means-tested programs are more likely to believe that the problem that requires help is not a "normal" social need, but arises because of special circumstances owing to individual deficiency. Help is often given on a temporary basis until the person is "rehabilitated"—educated, retrained, or otherwise made self-sufficient. Because recipients of these programs are assumed to have some deficiency, they are often regarded with suspicion, suspected of fraud, and subjected to various efforts to change their character. Applicants must prove that they have so little money and assets that they meet the criteria of poverty that the agency sets for eligibility. Temporary Assistance to Needy Families (TANF), the federal name for the program formerly called Aid to Families with Dependent Children (AFDC), is an example of a means-tested program.

Those who look at people as being embedded in a social system, and thus having predictable developmental needs, are more likely to regard social supports as a universal right. That philosophy of social welfare is called the **institutional,** or **developmental, philosophy of social welfare.** Programs subscribing to this philosophy are called **universal programs.** Their adherents know that problems are bound to occur, so they provide for people in need in a way that respects the dignity of the individual. The programs they create—unemployment insurance; workers' compensation; family and children's allowances; old-age, survivors', and disabled persons' pensions; Medicare—are given as **entitlements,** which do not distinguish between "deserving" and "undeserving." Universal income supports and social services include both the affluent and the poor. Wealthy people who receive such aid will pay some of the cost through **progressive taxes,** whereby the rich are taxed at a higher rate than the less affluent.

Some social welfare programs are more politically protected than others. Because the middle class feels entitled to programs such as Social Security, it uses its political clout to protect those programs. Congress is cautious about cutting back Social Security, but felt no need to put on the brakes in cutting back AFDC.

Universal programs are much more widely used in European countries than in the United States. For example, most industrialized countries except the United States have what they call a *family allowance*, which gives a certain amount of money to families for each child they have. Most industrialized countries, except for the United States, have a national health insurance system. France has universal day care for working mothers.

Liberals tend to prefer universal programs which they believe create more solidarity between social classes, show more respect to claimants, and are easier to defend politically. Conservatives tend to prefer means-tested programs (programs in which people must prove great need). The words used to describe people who get these benefits reflect attitudes toward the programs. *People who receive benefits under universal programs are called* claimants; *people who receive means-tested benefits are called* recipients. *Claimants are claiming their rights; recipients are receiving whatever someone chooses to give them.*

Progressive taxes
Taxes that tax the rich at a higher rate than those who are less affluent.

Programs to Provide Money

From the seventeenth to nineteenth centuries, local officials gave meager amounts of cash to the poor in their homes or put them in almshouses or workhouses. The fear of having to go to the poor house served to deter people from even admitting their hunger. Eventually welfare programs were taken over by states, and some were later run by the federal government.

In the 1930s, the turmoil and massive unemployment that resulted from the Great Depression gave rise to the first large-scale federal involvement in income supports. The Social Security Act in 1935 established two categories of programs—universal and means-tested. This implicitly separated beneficiaries into the "deserving" and the "undeserving" poor. People who receive the universal programs (Old-Age, Survivors', and Disability Insurance, popularly called Social Security) are automatically considered "deserving." People who receive the means-tested programs such as Temporary Assistance to Needy Families (TANF) are contemptuously viewed as "undeserving."

During the civil rights era of the 1960s (as in the period of labor union organizing in the 1930s), many people redefined poverty as the result of an unjust social system that blocked people's opportunity. Those who subscribed to this **opportunity theory** of poverty viewed the poor as men and women who shared the same qualities and aspirations as everyone else but were kept from realizing their potential by barriers of social class, ethnicity, sex, disability, age, or a combination of them all (Cloward & Ohlin, 1964; Ryan, W., 1976)

Opportunity theory   The theory that people are prevented from getting out of poverty because of the lack of social opportunities rather than because of individual defects.

The War on Poverty

The last major expansion in the welfare state was the federal government's War on Poverty, which began in 1964 with the passage of the Economic Opportunity Act.

Despite the name of the act, most programs of the War on Poverty did not follow the tenets of the opportunity theory. This theory (sometimes called *structuralism*) requires major structural changes in society, including the creation of more jobs and housing by the government and businesses. Secretary of Labor Willard Wirtz proposed a large-scale public jobs program that would have attacked poverty by transforming local labor markets (Glenn, 2001a, p. 102). However, neither President Johnson, the Congress, nor businesses were willing to do this, preferring instead to cut taxes, which they claimed would stimulate business to create jobs. "By default, the War on Poverty in the 1960's adopted the culture of poverty theory" (Ryan, W., 1976, p. 94) and aimed to change the social characteristics and potential of the poor rather than redistribute society's resources. One of the ways it did this was through educational programs—the Head Start program for early childhood education and the Job Corps for adolescents. It was also instrumental in securing the passage of the Elementary and Secondary Education Act of 1965.

The other major strategy of the War on Poverty—community action—had some prospect of changing social systems. It encouraged residents to participate actively in creating community change and challenging existing institutions. Bypassing structures of state and local government, the federal government sent money directly to citizen groups. This stressed the value of citizen participation, a belief that grew out of the settlement house tradition.

For a few years, the exciting folks in the community action programs challenged business as usual in school systems and in welfare offices. It upset local officials to see one level of government and party financing the harassment of another level of government and party. Eventually those same officials muted the program's militancy. Present-day community action programs are generally content to run Head Start day care centers and fuel subsidy, surplus-food, and weatherization programs to conserve heat in houses. Hardly a challenge to anyone!

The War on Poverty did, however, raise the consciousness of the nation to the plight of the poor. Although poverty was not abolished, it was greatly reduced during the 1960s, due to both an expanding economy and expanded social welfare benefits.

The Welfare Rights Movement

One of the most notable accomplishments of the community action program was the welfare rights movement. In 1966, Frances Fox Piven and Richard Cloward saw the movement as a strategy to end poverty (1966). They argued that the welfare rolls should be expanded to include everybody who was eligible (only half of all eligible people received AFDC), and this explosion in the rolls would create a political crisis for the Democratic party that would lead them to construct a more adequate system, such as a guaranteed annual income. Although the government did federalize the programs for the aged, disabled, and blind under the Supplemental Security Income program, by the time the National Welfare Rights Organization had ended in 1975, AFDC was still stigmatized and left recipients in poverty.

Nevertheless, the movement won important victories. The Legal Services Corporation, funded by the poverty program, provided poor people with lawyers to fight for their rights. Going all the way to the Supreme Court to strike down welfare residency requirements and "man in the house" rules that had created welfare "fraud squads," which were used to search for men in mothers' homes during unannounced raids, the corporation won the right to appeal unfavorable welfare decisions.

The poverty movement also got more money for many poor people and created a fundamental change in consciousness about their rights. Women on welfare declared that their job as mothers is *work* and deserves society's respect and recompense. Their demands foreshadowed the later feminist demands for wages for housework and caregiving. The most important demand of the National Welfare Rights Organization was for a guaranteed annual income to provide an income floor beneath which no one could sink.

At the same time, or perhaps in reaction to these more radical explanations of poverty, victim-blaming theories resurfaced in the 1960s and became stronger up to the present time. These theories have a stranglehold on the country and a powerful hold on people's thinking about the poor. Because they are helping to shape the destiny of the nation, it is important to trace their development.

Culture of Poverty versus Opportunity Theory

The backlash against the gains of the 1960s began with a movement of conservatives headed by Barry Goldwater, who ran for president in 1964. A concerted attack on welfare culminated in the Personal Responsibility Act of 1996. It was implicitly an attack on minorities and on women.

In the 1960s, some social planners and theorists revived long-dormant theories that place the onus for poverty on inferior heredity (it was called *bad blood* in our grandparents' time) (Eysenck, 1971; Herrnstein, 1971). They were especially eager to apply this theory to African Americans and other people of color.

Other social scientists asserted that the poor had a culture of poverty, a system of self-defeating beliefs passed on from parent to child. According to this theory, some groups of people stay mired in poverty because they lack basic psychological discipline. They cannot control their desires to own a VCR, buy a bottle of whiskey, or have unprotected sex long enough to save sufficient money, study hard, or plan for their futures (Banfield, 1974).

Anthropologist Oscar Lewis first coined the phrase *culture of poverty* as he studied poor people in Mexico and Puerto Rico (1961, 1966). He believed, however, that people could fight their way out of this culture by political activism. Conservative social scientists who lacked this faith in the empowering potential of political action believed that the culture of poverty was unchangeable. Sociologist Edward Banfield (1974) argued that none of the programs of the 1960s' War on Poverty had done any good. He believed that only authoritarian policies such as institutional care, separation of children from parents, or preventive detention based on the statistical probability of criminal behavior could even begin to eradicate it.

Because these policies would be politically unacceptable, he advised the government to do nothing, since its growing bureaucracy of programs had no effect on the problem. Daniel Patrick Moynihan echoed this when he served in the Nixon administration, advocating "benign neglect" of the poor (Lindlom & Cohen, 1979).

"Benign neglect" gained favor in the cynical and anxious 1980s and 1990s. In their study of what has gone wrong in the United States, Don Barlett and James Steele (1992) conclude that the "social contract" was canceled in the 1980s. *People had stopped believing that society had a responsibility to care for all its citizens.*

Victim-blaming theories captured the allegiance of many citizens in the 1980s. Earlier they had been grudgingly willing to allow some expansion in the welfare state, but in the eighties they worried about their own downward mobility and their children's future. So they "returned to an older psychology of scarcity" (Katz, 1989, p. 138). Rather than looking at the larger economic picture, especially the growing inequality of wealth, people often blamed welfare for *causing* their problems. Conservative critics capitalizing on those anxieties argued that welfare was not good for people or for business. Their prescription was to cut benefits, calling it "welfare reform." The criticism of welfare was lumped together with a call for a return to traditional puritanical or family values.

One of the critics of welfare, George Gilder, wrote a book called *Wealth and Poverty* (1981), described by one reviewer as "the Bible of the Reagan administration" (Silk, 1981, p. 44). Gilder's advice to the poor was to work harder than the classes above them, and to stay in monogamous families. According to him, men need to marry in order to channel their aggression, and the rise in female-headed families "unleashes the primitive impulses in men." Men in their natural states are "naked apes" in need of taming by women (Katz, 1989, p. 145). When the state provides for their children, men are "cuckolded by the compassionate state" (Gilder, 1981, p. 153). Gilder believed that inequality is good for society because it raises everyone's living standards, including those of the poor. The welfare system demoralizes the poor; it "erodes work and family and thus keeps poor people poor" (p. 82).

The Goldwater Old Right, which was focused on anticommunism, associated the War on Poverty with communism. In the 1970s, the New Right shifted its focus to social issues and developed the stereotype of the welfare queen, a stereotype that was skillfully used by President Reagan to political advantage (Williams, 1997). The welfare queen was presented

> as a socially deviant woman of color (unwed teen parent, non-wage worker, drug user, long-term recipient). With shrewd use of dissembling imagery, exaggeration, and stereotyping, the New Right played to fears of the welfare recipient as "other." (Williams, 1997, p. 1)

President Reagan's budget director, David Stockman, asserted that "there are no entitlements—period" (Katz M. B., 1989, p. 151). In his book *Losing Ground* (1984), Charles Murray argued that illegitimacy, crime, and family deterioration are caused by AFDC (TANF) payments and rules, and he recommended the elimination of virtually all social benefits except Social Security (Katz, 1989, p. 151). Ten years later in his book *The Bell Curve* (Murray & Herrnstein, 1994), Murray's racism was blatant. He argued that welfare should be abolished, not simply because of the economic incentive it creates, but because it encourages dysgenesis, the outbreeding of intelligent whites by genetically inferior African Americans, Hispanics, and poor European Americans (Williams, L., 1997, p. 14).

In response to the conservative alarm about welfare dependence, advocates for the poor countered that the problem was an undependable state. The Catholic bishops, in their pastoral letter on the U.S. economy, claimed that poverty violated a sense of community, deprived people of citizenship, and left them powerless. It "assaults not only one's pocketbook but also one's fundamental human dignity" (National Conference of Catholic Bishops, 1986, p. 93).

The bishops trumpeted their outrage like biblical prophets: "That so many people are poor in a nation as rich as ours," they wrote, "is a social and moral scandal that we cannot ignore" (p. 101). And in response to the call to "put those welfare mothers to work," the bishops took an increasingly unpopular stand in favor of giving mothers (or fathers) the right to stay home to care for their children and to be supported in this important work by welfare grants.

By the mid-1980s, the buzzword in poverty discourse was the *underclass*. No one could define it precisely, and it sometimes seemed to have grown out of a vague, undefined fear of inner-city violence and drug use, teenage sexuality, minority teenage mothers and jobless youth, and single-parent families.

The underclass became another name for the "undeserving poor," and much of the focus was on teenage mothers and jobless youth. Once more, policymakers paid less attention to the structural causes of poverty, such as inadequate education, lack of jobs, or low salaries, than they paid to behavior that was largely caused by lack of opportunity. Instead of providing training and employment for black and Hispanic males, the policy response was to put more of them in jail. Rates of incarceration in the United States soared above those in every other Western industrial democracy (Katz, M. B., 1989, p. 195).

As wages have declined, more married women have had to enter the workforce to help meet their families' needs. This has helped to fuel hostility toward TANF recipients who stay home to care for their families. Politicians have found that anti-welfare programs win them votes.

By the time Bill Clinton was elected president in 1992, welfare bashing seemed to have become a national sport, right along with baseball. Although welfare bashing has always been popular, the flood of anti-welfare sentiment reached tidal wave proportions by the 1990s. Both the Democrats and the Republicans railed against what they termed the "dependency" of welfare mothers and vowed to get them off the rolls and make them "self-sufficient." President Clinton promised to "end welfare as we know it." The Republican-controlled House of Representatives, led by Speaker of the House Newt Gingrich, promised in 1994 to roll back the gains in the welfare state that began with the New Deal of the 1930s, and it set forth a proposal called the Contract with America. Opponents dubbed it the Contract on America. It proposed to eliminate many federal social welfare programs, including AFDC, turning such programs over to the states with federal block grants, and ending federal oversight. In August 1996, Congress passed and President Clinton signed the Personal Responsibility and Work Opportunity Act, ending sixty years of federal entitlement to cash assistance for poor families.

In the 1980s, Charles Murray provided the ideological backing for the dismantling of the welfare state by the Republican-controlled Congress that had been elected in 1994. In a *Wall Street Journal* article, "The Coming White Underclass" (1994), Murray wrote that "illegitimacy is the single most important social problem of our time—more important than crime, drugs, poverty, illiteracy, welfare or homelessness because it drives everything else" (1994, p. 20).

Murray believes that when teenagers realize that there are no benefits that come to them when they become unmarried parents, they will stop having children. Not only would he deprive these individuals of an AFDC grant, but he would also deprive their children of child support from the father of the child. Children should receive support from the father only when the mother is married to him.

Of course Murray's idea that cutting off AFDC benefits will prevent pregnancy is absurd. Instead it will help to restigmatize having babies without getting married, which is what the right wing quite clearly says it wants to do. Title I of the Personal Responsibility Act, entitled "Reducing Illegitimacy," declared that "marriage is the foundation of a successful society" and went on to give a laundry list of so-called facts about illegitimacy that featured teenage mothers and linked criminality with absent black fathers. States have joined in this warfare against teen parents, passing laws restricting welfare and giving them rewards (dubbed "Bridefare" or "Wedfare" programs) if they marry any man, not necessarily the father of their child.

The Personal Responsibility Act was particularly tough on teen parents, requiring unmarried parents under the age of 18 to live with an adult and stay in school in order to receive benefits. About two-thirds of unmarried teen parents do live with their parents, but the ones who don't may be required to live in a group home or institution sponsored by the state.

This law has resulted in many teenagers being dropped from the welfare rolls. A follow-up study in Massachusetts, where a similar law has been in effect since November 1, 1995, found that out of the 668 mothers under the age of 18 who were on the welfare rolls on November 1, more than half—350 teenagers, plus their children—were dropped as a result of the new law. Under pressure, the Massachusetts Department of Social Services hired two private agencies to find missing families. The two private agencies couldn't find 124 of the 350 teenage families. Investigators say the missing girls may have left no forwarding address or telephone numbers. But they also suspect that some girls remain underground because they don't understand the law and fear, mistakenly, that the state will take their children (Mandell, 1997, p. 36).

On closer examination, Murray's "facts" are simply wrong. In 1994, only 6.3 percent of AFDC families were headed by teens, most of them 18 or 19 years old (U.S. Congress, 1996b). Between 1970 and 1993, the total number of births to teenagers dropped from 656,000 to 501,000 (U.S. Bureau of the Census, 1996b). The rate dropped consistently through the 1990s, falling 20 percent for the decade. By 2000, the teen pregnancy rate dropped to the lowest rate in sixty years (CNN.com. U.S. News, 2000). Although pregnancy rates are more than twice as high for African American and Hispanic girls than for white girls, the pregnancy rates are falling in all racial categories, and most dramatically among black teens (*Sojourner,* 2001).

A rise in pregnancy rates does not necessarily mean a rise in sexual promiscuity. Most sexually active adolescents are involved in stable, intense relationships with only one partner (U.S. Department of Commerce, 1995, p. 46). TV sitcoms and soap operas leave no doubt that society has become much more permissive about sex in the past three decades, and birth control has become much more available. Yet one cannot assume that a rise in sexual activity automatically translates into a rise in pregnancies. Research has shown that the most powerful factor in the decision to delay pregnancy until later in life is an adolescent's commitment to education and a future career apart from motherhood. Those who go on to higher education or fulfilling careers are not as likely to have babies as those who drop out of high school. Teens who have high educational expectations and school success are more likely to use contraception effectively. In discussing population control,

President Clinton acknowledged that the best approach to birth control in third-world countries is to educate the women, but he didn't apply that insight to teenagers in the United States. Instead, he blamed the AFDC program for encouraging teen pregnancy.

Sex education and easily available contraception lower the likelihood of getting pregnant, but in the United States, communities hold pitched battles over introducing sex education into the schools. It is the rare high school that makes condoms available. Even when a school does offer a sex education course, it may be introduced too late and be too superficial to really help prevent teen pregnancies.

AFDC/TANF does not encourage family breakup and out-of-wedlock births. Single-parent households are on the rise, but this is not due to AFDC/TANF. The increase in childbearing by unmarried women cuts across class, educational attainment, and age lines and is happening worldwide. Most of this increase is in births to adult unmarried women, not adolescents (U.S. Congress, 1996). One-third of births in the U.S. are out of wedlock, and 40 percent of the out-of-wedlock births are to couples who are living together but are not married (Turnbull, 2004). While the value of the AFDC benefit fell during the past twenty years, the number of mother-only households rose. The size of a welfare grant has no correlation with the number of pregnancies. Mississippi, which has the lowest AFDC (TANF) grant, has the highest rate of teenage pregnancies, whereas Vermont, with the highest AFDC (TANF) grant, has the lowest rate.

It is ludicrous to think that welfare causes poverty or teenage pregnancy. Suppose you studied accidents. Those who had to be carried away on a stretcher died more frequently than those who walked away from the accident. That doesn't mean that stretchers cause death. Welfare is like that stretcher. It does not cause poverty, although the meager welfare grants ensure that recipients will remain poor.

Welfare Reform and Racism

When Aid to Dependent Children was begun as part of the Social Security Act in 1935, the program was mainly for white widows, excluding most people of color. In the early years of the program, African American women were often excluded by rules imposed by the states such as "suitable home"* and "man-in-the-house"** rules, which were struck down by the Supreme Court in the 1960s. This was particularly true in the South. One southern field supervisor summed up the prevailing attitude toward African American women in the 1940s and 1950s:

> The number of Negro cases is few due to the unanimous feeling on the part of the staff and board that there are more work opportunities for Negro women and to their in-

---

*"Suitable home" rules excluded women from AFDC if officials decided that their home was not suitable in some way and were most often used against mothers who were not married.

**"Man-in-the-house" rules stated that women were forbidden to have a man in the house. Welfare workers often conducted midnight raids to try to find a man in the house.

tense desire not to interfere with local labor conditions. The attitude that "they have always gotten along," and that "all they'll do is have more children" is definite.... There is hesitancy on the part of lay boards to advance too rapidly over the thinking of their own communities, which see no reason why the employable Negro mother should not continue her usually sketchy seasonal labor or indefinite domestic service rather than receive a public assistance grant. (Bell, 1965, pp. 34–35)

In the 1960s, the civil rights and welfare rights movements resulted in the inclusion of many who had been excluded from the original AFDC program. Legal service lawyers challenged exclusionary rules and won many victories. As a result, the number of African American women in the program increased by about 15 percent between 1965 and 1971. "The evolution of a right-wing critique of welfare in the early 1960s coincided with this shift in the racial composition of the AFDC population" (Williams, 1997, p. 1). Public officials, aided by the media, made people believe that AFDC was largely a program for African Americans, even though, until very recently, the highest percentage of people on AFDC were European Americans.

However, as the welfare rolls continue to plunge, white recipients are leaving the system faster than black and Hispanic recipients. By 2001, African American families comprised 39 percent; 26 percent were Hispanic, 1.3 percent Native American, 2.1 Asian percent (U.S. Department of Health and Human Services, 2004). A study by the Census Bureau showed that minority welfare recipients were significantly more disadvantaged than their white counterparts. They face discrimination from prospective employers and landlords, and Hispanic recipients face the problem of learning English when there are not enough English as a Second Language (ESL) programs. The time limits imposed on the federal level, and in many states, will be especially hard on African American and Hispanic recipients.

The assumption that AFDC was primarily for African Americans led to racially based policies based on stereotypes. Conservative views about the proper place of women being in the home might still apply to American women of European descent, but African American women have always been expected to work outside the home, predominantly as domestic and agricultural workers. The 1967 amendments to the Social Security Act placed mandatory work requirements on AFDC recipients for the first time, and subsequent laws such as the Family Support Act of 1988 stiffened the requirements, culminating in the current draconian work requirements of the Personal Responsibility Act.

The restrictions placed on teen parents were also directed against minority teenagers, who are disproportionately represented in the teen parent population. Among many people, "teenage parents" has become a code word for minority women, and the attack on welfare has become an attack on them.

The War against Women

Welfare is one of the battlegrounds of a war on women. The National Organization for Women says that not only does the Personal Responsibility Act inflict suffering on poor women and their children, but it also heralds a broader effort to pressure all women into a repressive sexuality, limited reproductive choices, and conventional family arrangements. The radical Right understands the connection between a safety net and women's autonomy. By withdrawing federal assistance for women without male support (and also by attacking affirmative action, Title IX, and college financing), by branding welfare mothers with demeaning racial stereotypes, and by pauperizing them and questioning their fitness as mothers, the Right is forcing every woman to depend economically on a man within a traditional marriage whether or not she wants to and whether or not the man is dependable. The economic alternative is made so harsh that women may find themselves unable to provide for their families and may have to give up their children to foster care or adoption.

Conservatives are worried about the decline of two-parent families. The 2000 Census showed that the number of families headed by women who have children, which are typically poorer than two-parent families, grew nearly five times faster in the 1990s than the number of married couples with children. For the first time, nuclear families comprised less than 25 percent of all households in the United States (Schmitt, 2001a).

The Personal Responsibility Act provides for an "anti-illegitimacy" bonus that gives extra federal money to states that lower their nonmarital birth *and* abortion rates. States have enacted a variety of programs to get this bonus. In Virginia, for example, cities are conducting Marriage Before the Carriage contests, in which youths ages 12 to 21 can enter a drawing for a new car if they haven't fathered or conceived a child in the past year. Mississippi has established an abstinence unit of the state government, even though numerous studies have shown that abstinence education alone is unsuccessful in lowering birthrates. States have a financial incentive to promote abstinence to the exclusion of other family planning education through federal "abstinence only" money available under the federal welfare bill. More draconian measures have so far been voted down, as was Arizona's unsuccessful proposal to automatically make children of unmarried teen parents wards of the state and put the infants in the custody of the state's protective service system. A private group in California is offering $200 cash rewards to vulnerable low-income or drug- or alcohol-addicted women who agree to have a Norplant implant or undergo sterilization (Davis, 1998).

Everyone knows that if women are to enter the waged labor market, they will need child care. The right wing has always resisted public provision of day care on the grounds that a woman's "natural place" is in the home; George Gilder (1981) said that a woman finds dignity and security beneath the authority of her husband. A bill providing for universal day care was vetoed by President Nixon. One of his aides said that it would "Sovietize child care." On the other hand, conservatives are agreed that a single-mother welfare recipient should be in waged work. The double standard for middle-class mothers and welfare mothers was revealed when Congress—soon after it passed the Personal Responsibility Act—passed a law in 1998 giving tax deductions to middle-class women who choose to stay home to care for their children.

All these policies limit the choices of poor women and further deepen the rift between poor women who have no choices and affluent women who do. These reproductive issues affect only poor women now, but they are related to the drive to limit reproductive choice for *all* women. The conservative talk about putting poor children into orphanages is not really about orphanages but about women: about reinforcing the sexual double standard.

Yet all the talk about taking their children away and putting them in orphanages serves to terrorize welfare recipients still further. The Latin root of *proletariat* is "people who have no other wealth but their children." That took on a poignant meaning when Charles Murray proposed a policy of cutting off AFDC payments to teenage mothers and using the money saved to provide orphanages for their children. Shortly before Christmas of 1994, Speaker of the House Newt Gingrich championed a bill that would have let states use federal welfare money for orphanages. Critics invoked Charles Dickens and Scrooge; Gingrich countered with nostalgic images of *Boys Town* and Spencer Tracy. By the time President Clinton denounced the plan as "dead wrong," Mr. Gingrich was protesting that he had been misunderstood (Bernstein, 1996a).

Changes in the Economy

The state of the economy has a powerful influence on what kind of social welfare system a society provides. Since the 1970s, there have been vast changes in the U.S. economy, and in the global economy. A process of **deindustrialization** has taken place, in which manufacturing work has declined—especially in heavy industries such as auto, steel, and aircraft—and both high technology and service work have increased. Corporations have downsized, manufacturing jobs have been automated, and jobs have moved overseas. Transnational corporations are increasingly dominating national as well as international economies. Corporate leaders influence legislators to cut back on funds for social welfare because as they are eager for funds to expand their corporations and are eager to slash the safety net in order to lower wages. When there is no safety net, people are forced to take any job at any wage rather than starve. At the same time, a massive corporate restructuring creates growing impoverishment of both the working class and the middle class. As the middle class falls into the lower class, there is a widening gap between the rich and the poor, and the ranks of poor people swell.

deindustrialization
A shift in the economy from manufacturing jobs to service and high technology jobs.

> Belinda Schell worked at the Diamond Glass Company plant in Royersford, Pennsylvania, from 1984 to 1990, earning more than $10 an hour. In 1990, she and 500 coworkers lost their jobs because the plant closed. The Diamond Glass Company plant was one of the thousands of corporations in the United States that were involved in the corporate takeover craze of the 1980s. In those leveraged buyouts, managers and investors bought companies with money borrowed from the company's future earnings, and to pay off their debts, they laid off workers and often closed plants. (Barlett & Steele, 1992, p. 15)

In her new job as a nursing-home aide, Belinda earns considerably less than she earned at Diamond Glass. "It is an occupation that the federal government touts as a growth industry that will provide many jobs, mostly low paying, as the aged population continues to grow" (Barlett & Steele, 1992, p. 15).

Workers without a college education have been particularly hurt by the decline of manufacturing jobs. Also, since men have historically held the vast majority of manufacturing jobs, deindustrialization has caused their earnings to decline. Most men can no longer support an entire family on their paychecks. Working in an auto plant in Detroit used to pay good wages. Flipping hamburgers at McDonald's will not support a family.

Women have been moving into the labor force in increasing numbers, partly due to increased desires to have more economic independence and partly due to financial necessity, but on average they earn about one-fourth less than men (Albelda & Tilly, 1997, pp. 6–7). Close to half of all employed women work in clerical and service jobs, compared to one-sixth of men. The Bureau of Labor Statistics predicts growth in women's job opportunities—but low-paid jobs will provide the bulk of that growth. Many are pink-collar jobs that pay low wages and generally offer only part-time hours or part-year employment. The 800,000 nurses projected to join the workforce between 1992 and 2005 will be offset by the 600,000 waiters and waitresses and nursing aides (Albelda & Tilly, 1997, pp. 48–49).

Most of the well-paid jobs require higher education. This makes it hard for welfare mothers to earn a living wage because most of them do not have any college education and the Personal Responsibility Act supports no more than one year of vocational education. For women, education is particularly important in staving off poverty. Four years of college sharply reduce their chances of being poor (Albelda & Tilly, 1997, p. 26). But college-educated women still earn less than college-educated men; a woman with a bachelor's degree earns, on average, $3.90 less per hour than a man with a bachelor's degree (p. 46).

The booming economy of the 1990s, especially in the years 1997–2000, was the best economy in thirty-five years. Although the official unemployment rate was only 4 percent, incomes for the poorest citizens rose only slightly. Even middle-income people did only a bit better than they did in the 1980s.

The economy slowed down to a recession in 2001. By the fall of 2001, unemployment was 5.7 percent. The September 11 attacks on the World Trade Center and the Pentagon furthered a lack of confidence. Stocks in insurance companies, airlines, and the tourist industry especially spiraled downward. Massive layoffs increased the unemployment rate. Since the September 11 attacks and the nation's subsequent economic downturn, food pantries and homeless shelters nationwide have seen a spike in the number of people seeking help, more than they can handle.

Government officials declared the recession to be officially over by November 2001, but the economy continued to lose jobs. Three years after the recession began, 2.4 million U.S. jobs had disappeared. A larger share of layoffs have been permanent, rather than the temporary cyclical layoffs dominant in most previous recessions (Miller, 2004). By 2003 corporate profits were up and productivity had increased, but wages remained stagnant. "In the fourth quarter of 2003, profits as a share of the total economy reached their highest level in more than 50 years. The share of the pie going to wages and salaries hit a 50-year low" (Stein, 2004). Affluent families benefited most from the growing economy. They received significant gains from the rising value of their stocks and homes, and they were the major beneficiaries of President Bush's tax cuts. The median income of the middle-class, on the other hand, actually *dropped* by about one percent during 2002 (*Boston Phoenix,* 2004).

The official unemployment rate undercounts the unemployed. It does not count many people: "discouraged workers" who have given up looking for a job; part-time workers who would prefer to work full-time; people available for work, but not looking due to family, school, or health issues; and the enormous prison population. The United States incarcerates people at ten times the rate of European countries, keeping them off the streets and out of unemployment lines. If all those people were counted, we would find that the unemployment rate is 8 percent and the underemployment rate is 15 percent of the workforce (Albelda & Tilly, 1997, p. 50).

> Scott Gelinas spent the first eight years of his working life at the same manufacturer and planned to make a career there. His layoff in the summer of 2002 changed all that.
>
> In the two years since. Gellinas, 27, of Dracut (Massachusetts) has worked at two other companies and, before too long, he could well be working at a third. Of course, he says, he'd prefer more stability. But frequent job changes just happen to go with his current career: temporary worker.
>
> "Am I afraid of losing my job again? Yeah," said Gelinas, an electronics technician now working a three-to-six month assignment at a Concord medical device-maker. "Is there a chance I'll go from temp to temp? Probably." (Gavin, 2004)

Job insecurity increased as businesses lowered labor costs by turning full-time jobs into temporary and part-time work, without health and retirement benefits. Employment in temporary agencies has expanded twenty-fold since the early 1960s, to the point where Manpower, Inc., employs more people over the course of a year than any other private employer in the country (Tilly, 1998, p. 20). All jobs are becoming more contingent. "Businesses are disavowing implicit lifetime employment guarantees, and telling workers they are hired only on an 'as-needed basis'" (p. 21).

Globalization and technology are not only reshaping the U.S. economy but also widening income inequality among workers. "With traditional middle-class jobs vanishing along with factories, some economists worry that the nation's labor force is stratifying into a skilled, well-paid elite and a mass of lesser-skilled workers struggling to hold on to their standard of living" (Gavin, 2004).

The gap between the rich and the poor has widened dramatically. Between 1979 and 1997, the average after-tax income of the wealthiest 1 percent saw a 157 percent increase, growing from $263,700 to $677,900, according to the Congressional Budget Office. And during that same period, the average after-tax income of the lowest-earning one-fifth of U.S. citizens actually dropped from $10,900 to $10,800 (Overholser, 2001). Family incomes are diverging more widely than they have at any time since the 1920s, before the upheavals of the Depression, the New

Deal, and World War II (Reich, 2001). "In the 1960s, the ratio of chief executive pay to average worker pay was about 70 to 1. Today it's around 700 to 1" (Kuttner, 2004). In sharp contrast, one in four workers, 28 million, live at the federal poverty level, earning less than $9.04 an hour (*FRAC News Digest*, 2004).

The income gap tells only part of the story. There is an even wider gap in wealth (the total resources of a household minus its debts). The gap between the very rich and the poor is reminiscent of the Gilded Age in the 1890s. By 2001, income inequality had reached unprecedented levels:

- The wealthiest 1 percent of Americans controlled about 38 percent of America's wealth.

- The bottom 80 percent controlled only 17 percent of America's wealth.

- The top 1 percent of stock owners had 48 percent of stock holdings.

- The bottom 80 percent had only 4 percent of stock holdings (Jackson, 2001).

In the summer of 2001, Congress and the Bush administration enacted a tax cut of $1.35 trillion and sent tax rebate checks to millions of people. President Bush and his allies argued that the money they sent to citizens would boost a slowing economy by increasing consumer purchasing power. They also believed that the tax cut would take much of a projected budget surplus off the table, therefore reducing the size of the government and making it impossible for the Democrats to spend money on social programs. This tax cut left less money for child care, affordable health care, job training, and better schools. The tax cut benefited the rich more than the poor: The bottom 80 percent received less than one-third of the benefits; 40 percent of the benefits went to the richest 1 percent of taxpayers (Reich, 2001).

CYCLES OF HELPING

To illustrate the dialectical nature of human service issues, we shall discuss three issues on the front burner of public attention: welfare, mental illness, and juvenile justice.

Cycles in Welfare Reform

We are using the term *welfare* in the way that the public generally understands it—Aid to Families with Dependent Children (AFDC) or, as it is now called, on a federal level, Temporary Aid to Needy Families (TANF).* If we called all government financial transfer programs "welfare," then financial-aid grants to college students and veterans' benefits would come under that category. Although the amount paid to the AFDC program has been relatively small—less than 1 percent of federal government spending and about 3 percent of state spending—it garners a huge amount of public scorn. Much larger welfare grants go to the middle class and rich.

Fraud and abuse in Medicare billing cost taxpayers as much as $28.6 billion a year, about $7 billion more than the total federal spending for AFDC (United for a Fair Economy, 1997). Yet, women on welfare are frequently accused of welfare fraud. Most people do not know that most of the welfare cheating is done by vendors—doctors, dentists, pharmacists, and businesses that earn money from welfare. A study in Massachusetts showed that more than 93 percent of the money recovered from welfare fraud came from vendors. Two of the largest fraud cases in the nation were against for-profit hospitals for defrauding government health insurance programs. Three executives of the nation's biggest hospital chain, Columbia/HCA, were indicted in 1997 for conspiring to defraud government health insurance programs. The U.S. Attorney's office fined TAP Pharmaceutical Products

*States have given different names to TANF. In Massachusetts, for example, the program is called Transitional Assistance to Families with Dependent Children (TAFDC).

of Illinois $875 million in September 2001 for price manipulation, the largest settlement ever in health care fraud. Fraud in Medicare and Medicaid due to inflated drug prices and loopholes is costing taxpayers over $2 billion a year, according to a study by the General Accounting Office (Dembner, 2001).

People are beginning to express their resentment toward the unfairness of a system that gives large tax breaks and subsidies to the rich while increasing the tax burden of the poor and middle class and removing the safety net for the poor. Former Secretary of Labor Robert Reich has attacked "welfare for the rich." He suggested that over $200 billion in corporate welfare could be trimmed within five years. President Clinton discouraged Reich from taking the campaign further, for fear of alienating big Democratic party funders (Collins, 1995). Consider these facts:

- Taxpayers earning over $1 million paid taxes on 76 percent of their income in 1940, but only 31 percent in 1997. The tax bill passed by Congress in 1997 gave them an even bigger break. It gave the richest 1 percent of Americans more tax-cut savings than the bottom 80 percent. It actually increased taxes on the poorest 20 percent of Americans (United for a Fair Economy, 1997).

- Lockheed received $1 billion to cover plant shutdowns and relocations.

- Home mortgage interest is deductible up to $1 million per year. Reducing the limit to $250,000 would save the government $10 billion a year.

- In total, profit-making corporations grab $170 billion per year in federal funds (United for a Fair Economy, 1998).

Welfare provides a good example of the cycles of reform. Frances Fox Piven and Richard Cloward (1971), two of the leading proponents of the opportunity theory, believe that welfare expands and contracts in response to changes in the economy and the political climate. The leading architects of the welfare rights movement, they believe passionately in political activism as a way to empower the poor.

Piven and Cloward argue that government officials expand welfare (public assistance) in times of civil turmoil. When the turmoil dies down, they cut back on welfare and use it to enforce work norms. They document the following cycles of expansion and contraction in welfare:

- Beginning of large-scale federal relief programs during the Great Depression as a response to civil turmoil.

- Cutbacks during the 1940s and 1950s after the turmoil of the 1930s subsided. Welfare was often withheld from people in order to force them into low-paid agricultural and factory work.

- Expansion during the 1960s as a response to civil turmoil (and as an attempt to build a new urban base for the Democratic party).

- Cutbacks from the 1970s to the present, after the turmoil of the 1960s subsided. During this period, welfare has been withheld to force women into the low-wage labor market.

We are now witnessing the implementation of punitive workfare programs at the same time that relief and other programs for the poor are being cut back. The struggles of the poor and working class and their allies will ultimately affect the outcome.

THE DOWNWARD SLIDE

The upward climb of social welfare expenditures reversed in 1975. Expenditures then took a downward turn for the first time in three decades, beginning with the Ford and Carter administrations, moving down and even picking up roller-coaster speed during the 1980s. Congress and the Reagan administration conducted a massive assault on all entitlement programs for the poor and near-poor. Programs for the middle class suffered also.

Some states replaced the lost federal funds with state funds, but during the recession of the late 1980s and early 1990s, states raced to cut social welfare and implement punitive measures. Across the nation, state legislators and governors slashed benefits for low-income people more drastically than they had done since the 1980s. Fourteen of the thirty states with supplemental welfare programs, known as General Assistance, cut those budgets, affecting nearly half a million people.

At the same time that corporations were being restructured, social welfare programs were also being restructured. As wages went down, so did welfare payments—no coincidence. According to a principle known in welfare circles as the **principle of less eligibility,** welfare payments in the United States are almost always kept below the lowest wages in order to encourage people to take any low-wage job rather than go on welfare. Many people assumed that the welfare state would expand forever. But, as Abramovitz (1992) points out,

> As long as investment in social reproduction meshed with the needs of profitable production and political control, social welfare programs remained intact and grew. But in the mid-1970s, changing economic and political conditions rendered the postwar social policies less conducive to the needs of business and the state, which then began to turn them around. (p. 33)

Twenty-five years ago, the consumer advocate Ralph Nader warned that the Republicans were engaged in a campaign to undermine people's trust in government so they could dismantle it, because government sometimes prevented the worst depredations of capitalism. Now we see how farsighted Nader was. Once people can be stopped from thinking that the government owes them anything, the safety net of the welfare state, never very strong, can be shredded entirely. Then there is no buffer to protect people from having to take any low-wage job, or to protect women from having to stay in a bad marriage, or even to protect them from homelessness. It seems that we have returned full cycle to the nineteenth century in welfare reform.

Welfare is like society's lightning rod, attracting people's anxieties and ambivalence about dependence and self-reliance, about work, about race, about sex, about mothers living without husbands, about our responsibilities toward one another,

Principle of less eligibility The principle that the amount of welfare given to people should be less than the lowest wage so that people will not be tempted to take welfare rather than get a wage-earning job.

and about the nature of a just society. It has been more of a politically hot issue in the United States than in any other industrialized country. Some Europeans say that following the United States' welfare scene is like reading the musty historical pages of the development of European welfare.

Cycles of Treatment of Mental Illness

If you have ever gone to a nursing home, you have probably seen a person who was acting so strangely that you thought she or he might be mentally ill. Did you wonder why that person was in a nursing home? Why wasn't she or he in a hospital, a group home, or an apartment with supportive services? The answer to that question reveals one of the many twists and turns that treatment of the mentally ill has taken throughout history.

Again, we see the eerie similarity of present conditions to earlier times. In 1985, the president of the American Psychiatric Association, John A. Talbott, said

> In trying to reform the mental health system, we've gone from atrocious to awful. In colonial times, hordes of mentally ill people wandered from town to town. They lacked food, shelter, and care. That's exactly the situation today: we've come full circle. (Nickerson, 1985, p. 18)

One of the problems in discussing mental illness is that the very concept is like quicksand. Cancer or heart disease is diagnosed by laboratory tests. The diagnosis tells where the problem is located and what it looks like and offers clues on how to treat it. Not so with mental illness.

The imprecision of the diagnosis of schizophrenia, for example, is illustrated by a study done by thirteen psychology researchers. They presented themselves at the door of various mental hospitals, telling the admitting officers that they heard voices saying "empty," "hollow," and "thud." Otherwise, they told the truth about themselves. All of them were diagnosed as schizophrenic and admitted to the hospitals. After stays of varying lengths, some lasting as long as six months, each was discharged with a diagnosis of "schizophrenic on remission."

Interestingly, their fellow patients were inclined to think they didn't belong in the hospital, while the staff were convinced they did. One nurse, commenting on the note-taking activities of one of the researchers, wrote on his chart, "Patient engages in compulsive note-taking activity" (Rosenhan, 1973, p. 253).

Mark Vonnegut (son of novelist Kurt Vonnegut) was diagnosed as schizophrenic and hospitalized for mental illness. However, when he recovered and wrote a book about his experience, most members of the psychiatric profession concluded that he had been misdiagnosed and was in fact simply depressed. "Mark's first response to news of this rediagnosis was to say, 'What a wonderful diagnostic tool. We now know if a patient gets well, he or she definitely did not have schizophrenia'" (Vonnegut, 1991, p. 33).

Except for organic conditions such as brain tumors, mental illness can only be diagnosed by observing behavior. This has led some psychiatrists, such as Thomas

Szasz, to say that it is inappropriate to label behaviors as diseases when, as far as anyone knows, they have no organic cause. Rather, Szasz says, these are behaviors that are intolerable to the patients' family and friends and so are diagnosed as mental illness. Once labeled, the offending patient can then be removed from his family and put in a hospital (Szasz, 1961). Szasz does not deny that people who were labeled as mentally ill might be experiencing intense emotional anguish, but he argues that this is not a disease in the same sense as a physical disease, and he argues against forcing patients to accept treatment if they do not want it. This theory is, of course, very controversial. Many people who study the brain and treat mentally ill people believe that physiological malfunction can be demonstrated and treated.

There are a disproportionate number of people of color in mental hospitals. This is partly because of racial discrimination and partly because disproportionate numbers of them are poor. As Chesler (1972) points out, "Women of all classes and races constitute the majority of the psychiatrically involved population in America, Britain, Sweden, and Canada," (p. 333) "and most 'patients' over sixty-five, in asylums or in old-age homes, are, of course, women. Our society does not overly like old age or women" (p. xxii).

Political philosopher Michel Foucault (1987) points out that certain behaviors are regarded differently in different cultures and at different historical periods. For example, the holy man of the Zulus, the shaman, might be diagnosed as a hypochondriac or a hysteric by Europeans. In earlier times in some societies, the village idiot and the epileptic were thought to have special wisdom. Society, he says, locks up or excludes the mental patient because it does not want to recognize itself in the ill individual. "As it diagnoses the illness, it excludes the patient" (p. 63).

Foucault says that, up to about 1650, "madness was allowed free reign" (1987, p. 67). Society neither exalted it nor tried to control it; in fact, in France in the early seventeenth century, there were famous madmen who were a great source of entertainment for the public. But "about the middle of the seventeenth century, a sudden change took place; the world of madness was to become the world of exclusion" (1987, p. 67). Throughout Europe, institutions were built to house many different categories of people:

> the poor and disabled, the elderly poor, beggars, the work-shy, those with venereal diseases, libertines of all kinds, people whose families or the royal power wished to spare public punishment, spendthrift fathers, defrocked priests; in short, all those who, in relation to the order of reason, morality, and society, showed signs of "derangement." (Foucault, 1987, p. 67)

What all these groups had in common, Foucault says, was their *inability to work*. Whereas in the Middle Ages the cardinal sins were pride and greed, in the seventeenth century, sloth became the cardinal sin. Institutions imposed severe discipline, rules of silence, lockstep routines, strict spiritual guidance, and solitary reflection. Mentally ill people were stigmatized and made to feel guilty. That stigma is still powerful.

In about the middle of the eighteenth century, Europeans began to protest the widespread internment of people. The French Revolution of 1789 wanted to abolish internment as a symbol of ancient oppression, particularly for the poor. But this liberation did not apply to the mentally ill, who were considered dangerous. "Hence the need to contain them and the penal sanction inflicted on those who allow 'madmen and dangerous animals' to roam freely" (Foucault, 1987, p. 70). Thus, the mentally ill were left behind in the old houses of internment.

Internment of the mentally ill then became more medical (Foucault, 1987). Treatment freed the patients from some of the physical punishment but substituted "moral chains that transformed the asylum into a sort of perpetual court of law." Threats, punishment, deprivation of food, and humiliation were used to "both infantilize the madman and make him feel guilty" (p. 71).

In the nineteenth century, madness was thought to be contagious. Because it was thought unfair to criminals to expose them to the mentally ill, mentally ill people were separated into asylums. The doctor was not the servant of the patient but of the society. Foucault believes that the psychologization of madness that occurred in the nineteenth century was "part of the punitive system in which the madman, reduced to the status of a minor, was treated in every way as a child, and in which madness was

Unfortunately when our society embarks on a positive social reform the effort is often underfunded or incomplete, leading to new types of problems.

associated with guilt and wrongdoing.... None of this psychology would exist without the *moralizing sadism* in which nineteenth-century 'philanthropy' enclosed it, under the hypocritical appearances of 'liberation'" (1987, p. 73).

Foucault did not see the disciplines of psychology or any of the other behavioral sciences as liberating. Rather, he saw them as a means of disciplining people for the economic needs of modern industrial society. Clearly this is a radically controversial point of view. We present it here not because we agree with all of Foucault's views, but because it is being hotly debated in some academic circles and is forcing a reexamination of traditional views.

THE PROGRESSIVES AND THE REFORMERS

During the early twentieth century in the United States, social activists known as **Progressives** were shocked by the oppressiveness of the overcrowded prisons and mental hospitals that helped so few people. They did not, however, want to abolish them; rather, they thought that each inmate or patient would be cured if professionals could tailor a case-by-case treatment plan.

On the surface, the policy of treating prisoners or mental patients as individuals, collecting each one's life history, and making personalized treatment plans, seems kinder and more scientific than predetermined prescriptions that ignore these people's backgrounds. However, what often happened in practice was that the professionals who planned or delivered such individualized treatments—judges, doctors, therapists, and wardens—were given an extraordinary amount of authority that was often abused (Rothman, 1971).

Progressives
Members of the Progressive party in the early twentieth century who favored social reforms such as abolition of child labor, juvenile courts, and more individualized treatment of the mentally ill.

Modern reformers are closing the mental hospitals and returning the inmates to their communities, the very same places they were kept during colonial times. Indeed, treatment of the mentally ill has come full circle, but now the rationale behind it is different. The colonists of early America believed in the inevitability of problems; modern reformers believe that hospitals institutionalize people but do not heal them. The latter argue for the healing power of kin, community ties, and normal, everyday routines.

In the 1970s, the mental patients' and prisoners' rights movements joined in the fight for more humane, community-based treatment. Following is an interview with Judi Chamberlin, who has been part of this liberation movement.

INTERVIEW

Judi Chamberlin, Mental Patients' Liberation Front

Judi Chamberlin calls herself a "psychiatric survivor" of the mental health system. She not only survived but she also went on to write a book about her experiences with mental illness and psychiatric hospitals. She also started an alternative service for discharged mental

Mental Patients' Liberation Front (MPLF) An organization of people who are or have been patients in psychiatric hospitals and who oppose many established psychiatric practices. They have established support groups and alternative institutions.

patients and is one of the leaders of the **Mental Patients' Liberation Front (MPLF)**. In May 1992, she received a Distinguished Service Award from the President's Commission on Employment of People with Disabilities for "promoting the dignity, equality, independence, and employment of people with disabilities." When people tell Judi that she is not the "typical" ex-mental patient, she says, "My experiences aren't atypical. I'm typical. I went looking for help, and the state oppressed me."

Judi speaks at conferences all over the nation and the world. The best conferences, she says, have been those to which users of the mental health system are invited. A 1988 conference in England, for example, called "Common Concerns," was attended by an equal number of workers and users. In the United States, the National Institute of Mental Health sponsored a pioneering set of dialogues in Florida. Users and service providers explored issues together. Judi was surprised and pleased when the National Conference on Mental Health Statistics contacted her to ask for her involvement in the first conference involving users as well as researchers. She had not expected statisticians to be particularly interested in mental patients' liberation, but it is a hopeful sign that they want users of the services to help them figure out the questions to research. Researchers cannot study outcome measures unless they know what kind of outcomes the users want.

People don't usually seek out the opinions of mental patients, Judi said. They think, "If you're mentally ill, what do you know?" Whatever a person has to say is suspect. When students learn about the mental health system, they only hear the views of the professionals. They seldom empathize with the mentally ill or try to understand how it feels to be on the receiving end.

If they want to have an honest dialogue with the mentally ill and ex-patients, service providers have to be prepared to face their anger and mistrust. People who use services have been treated in paternalistic and controlling ways, and this understandably has made them angry.

The interviewer, Betty Reid Mandell, shared with Judi an experience she had as a social work graduate student in a Veterans Administration psychiatric clinic. Sometimes VA doctors would refer veterans to the clinic without telling them it was a psychiatric clinic. When the veterans saw the name over the door, they were furious, and it was hard for them to get beyond their anger and feelings of betrayal. Judi said that this is not unusual. Professionals assume that because patients are mentally ill, they can't understand. People are sometimes coerced into mental hospitals, the rationale for this being, "We know they need to be there, but they wouldn't understand."

This kind of attitude has caused a split between the Alliance for the Mentally Ill (AMI), a support group for relatives and friends of mentally ill people, and the Mental Patients' Liberation Front (MPLF). Parents in the AMI argue, "We love our sons and daughters and want them to get help. We may trick them if we have to, whether they say they want it or not." The patient may not want to take drugs, but relatives often think they should, and complain that patients don't take their medications. (Judi pointed out that recent research has shown that a high percentage of all drugs, not just psychotropic, are not taken according to the doctor's prescription.)

Judi has tried to promote dialogue between AMI and MPLF. Ex-patients and families have one thing in common—they didn't choose to be in the system. Professionals choose to be there. It is important to recognize that families have a valid perspective.

Some people accuse the MPLF of being totally opposed to drugs. Judi says it believes in choice. Patients need to have all the facts, which are often kept from them. The professionals sometimes feel that if they give patients information, they only scare them. Judi has tried drugs, but hasn't found one that helps her. For her, drugs don't work, but she wouldn't tell anyone else what to do.

Research on phenothiazines shows what happens when patients don't have all the information. Although it is now well known that phenothiazines cause tardive dyskinesia (involuntary tics), not until recently did it come to light that they also cause tardive dementia, a loss of brain function. Patients can deteriorate mentally by taking the drugs. Professionals had not realized this earlier because they assumed that mental patients were deteriorating because of their illness.

The average doctor knows very little about drugs, often only what the advertisers say. Journals are filled with drug ads, and at medical conferences drug salespeople are all over the place. The field is controlled by profitable pharmaceutical companies. For example, there are two identical drugs for a heart condition, one generic and one with a trade name. The trade drug is six times as expensive as the generic, and that is the one that doctors prescribe most. A tranquilizer called clozapine used to cost $9,000 a year but has come down in price because of so many complaints. It doesn't cause tardive dyskinesia, as do all of the phenothiazines, but it can kill users if not correctly monitored.

Almost everyone in the psychiatric field has gone into diagnosing and drugs. Most of the professionals doing talking therapy are psychologists and social workers. There is very little clinical psychological training for doctors anymore, except for long, arduous psychoanalytic training. The conventional psychiatric wisdom is that you can't talk with psychotics. Most psychiatrists, and the AMI, believe that mental illness is primarily biological and can be controlled or cured only with drugs. The Alliance quotes statistics by the World Health Organization, which indicate that schizophrenia affects 1 percent of the human population worldwide. The AMI denies that stress or trauma causes mental illness, yet Judi says there is a good deal of research that challenges this belief. Researchers have tracked unemployment and mental hospital admissions showing that mental illness rises with unemployment. Research about women in mental hospitals indicates that as many as 50 to 80 percent have been sexually abused.

Interestingly, the rate of recovery of mental patients is higher in third-world countries. Judi believes that is because they have stronger family and community ties. Also, traditional healers, who would be used more in third-world countries, sit with the patient, sometimes for days. In Africa, for example, a native healer spends several days observing the patient. That presence sets up a powerful therapeutic alliance. The healer does not think that it is important to ask questions but that it is important just to be there.

A few psychiatrists still believe in talk therapy and are cautious about using drugs. Judi thinks one of the best is Peter Breggin, who wrote an excellent book called *Toxic Psychiatry* (1991). Another important book is *Community Mental Health: Principles and Practice,* by Loren Mosher and Lorenzo Berti (1989), which proposes a blueprint for a comprehensive community mental health system. The authors maintain that before taking drugs, people should have a chance to get real community support. Once people start on drugs, they are likely to stay on them and have a hard time getting off. Mosher and Berti believe that a society can run mental health systems without hospitalizing anyone.

Drugs are used extensively all over the world. Most of the alternative mental health programs of the 1960s and 1970s have died, although a few proposals have been made for new ones. Although there has been a lot of talk about the innovative programs in Italy, where there are no long-term institutions, Italian practitioners still rely on drugs. Some community cooperatives have been set up there (not sheltered workshops, but co-ops actually owned and run by ex-patients).

In her book *On Our Own* (Chamberlin, 1988), Judi describes her encounters with the mental health system. Following are a few excerpts:

> I got married at twenty. Of course, that wasn't the origin of my troubles, it just seems that way. Lots of things brought me to that point. Like hating school. Bright New York Jewish girls are supposed to love school, bring home perfect report cards, and make their parents proud. By the time I got to high school, I was counting the days to freedom. Although I had the marks, and the hopeful urging of my parents, I knew I didn't want to go to college. Which led to a secretarial job, boredom, and marriage. I had freed myself from one trap only by entering another. It's all a familiar story today, but this was 1965. No women's liberation, or even the recognition of the need for it. (p. 22)
>
> When I got pregnant, I felt I was beginning a great adventure. Three months later, after a miscarriage, the adventure was over. Everyone waited for me to "snap out of it." I wanted to retreat to someplace inside myself for a while, but my parents, my husband, my obstetrician, expected me to be cheerfully getting on with my life. I couldn't find words for my need to withdraw. The more demands people made, the more frightened I became. Couldn't they see that I needed to be alone, to cry, to lie in bed and pull the covers over my head, to figure out what I wanted, what I needed? (p. 23)

Judi goes on to tell about seeing a psychiatrist, who gave her orange, blue, and white pills and advised her to go back to work. "And take my pills. There was something very important about taking my pills. If they were supposed to make me happy, they didn't. I felt drugged, lethargic—the very feelings the pills were supposed to cure" (p. 23).

Judi was in and out of various mental hospitals, but none helped her. Finally, she found the Vancouver Emotional Emergency Center, an alternative mental health center, and there "there was always someone to talk to." She describes her first day:

> The first afternoon David and Dave were on shift. I sat in the dining room and watched them make dinner. I didn't feel like doing very much or saying very much, but there was something comforting about watching them. There were eight for dinner—the residents, David, Dave, and a volunteer. We sat around the big dining room table. The food was delicious. Later David asked me if I wanted a massage. We went upstairs to one of the bedrooms, and I lay down on the floor. The massage was incredibly relaxing. I went downstairs to the living room and sat with a few other people. After a while I lay down on the couch again. When people started going off to bed, I asked David if I could stay on the couch. I wanted to be near other people, and the upstairs part of the house, where the bedrooms were, felt very isolated. He said that I could and brought me a blanket. (p. 57)

After a few weeks' stay, Judi went to the "screaming room" with a staff member. The staff member helped her work through her feelings of powerlessness to discover new energy and joy.

[I was] amazed by my energy. I had followed my pain and fear toward what I thought would be death, and instead I had found a source of life, my own sense of self, which had always been hidden from me. Out of struggle and pain, I had been reborn. (p. 62)

Judi says that human service workers enter the field with idealism but get caught up in an oppressive system. They need to seek out support in working to humanize their agencies, and they must encourage dialogue between workers and patients. Like patients, workers are oppressed by a hierarchical system. They have very little control over their work.

It is important to remember that patients need someone to be there for them. They need human contact. Alternative health systems are actually cheaper than the hierarchical ones because they do not have layers of highly paid professional staff. Psychiatric training often gets in the way of reaching people. Psychiatrists feel compelled to interpret. Rather than constantly interpreting speech and behavior, they should simply listen respectfully. The feeling of acceptance thereby imparted to the patient is critical in establishing the rapport between doctor and patient that is essential to healing.

Since this interview, Judi has been a consultant to the Psychiatric Rehabilitation Center at Boston University and a staff member of The National Empowerment Center in Lawrence, Massachusetts (see their web site at the end of this chapter). There has been a fierce debate about this center, resulting in the loss of their federal funding. A conservative scholar and author of a book excoriating liberal politics in mental health care, Sally Satel, said, "These are people who really don't represent the severely mentally ill.... They're not on the street, incoherent, frostbitten, sitting in their own excrement" (Barry, 2002). A Washington research psychiatrist who specializes in schizophrenia, E. Fuller Torrey, said, "I think the center has done damage by implying—by saying quite explicitly—that medications are not necessary, that if you just provide community support and housing that everyone can live like Daniel Fisher (a staff member of the center). I think it's false" (Barry, 2002). Daniel Fisher and Judi Chamberlin, on the other hand, believe that it is possible to completely recover from mental illness without medication.

RECENT DEVELOPMENTS IN TREATING MENTAL ILLNESS

Beginning in about 1955, the state mental hospitals began to undergo **deinstitutionalization**. Ultimately, most of the patients were "reinstitutionalized" into shelters for the homeless, nursing homes, and rest homes.

The almshouses of the eighteenth and nineteenth centuries seem to have returned. Now they are called shelters for the homeless. Although some cities build shelters for different categories of people (e.g., men, women, families), the shelters in some cities are similar to the almshouses in the way they lump together a great variety of people—poor families with children, runaway adolescents, veterans, the

Deinstitutionalization
A large-scale reform movement that took people out of institutions and hospitals and returned them to their community with special services to aid their reintegration.

aged, mentally ill, substance abusers. Many homeless people find shelters so frightening that they would rather sleep on the streets or in abandoned buildings.

Between 1955 and 1984, the population of state and county mental hospitals in the United States declined from 558,922 to 118,647 (Blau, 1992, p. 80). Some of the patients went home to their families, some went to halfway houses, foster care, or jail. Some were discharged to the streets or to shelters for the homeless. The rest went to nursing homes. Officially, patients who left the hospitals were supposed to be mainstreamed into the community, where they would receive supports. The Mental Retardation Facilities and Community Mental Health Centers Construction Act, signed into law by President Kennedy in 1963, was supposed to fund 2,000 mental health centers by 1980, but only 789 were eventually funded (Blau, 1992, p. 82). And even those did not serve the chronically mentally ill in the way that was originally intended. Mental health professionals found the chronically mentally ill less rewarding to work with than the acutely ill or the neurotic. "Hence, a mere ten years after passage of the act, chronic mental patients had too few places to go, and even in those places, they were not exactly welcome" (82).

Sixteen percent of the inmates of U.S. prisons and jails suffer from severe mental illness (Smith, A. C., 1999). Dorothea Dix, who campaigned in the late nineteenth century to get mentally ill people out of jails and into mental hospitals, would be sad to see her work undone in the late twentieth century (Steadman, McCarty, & Morrissey, 1989).

THE FAILURE OF DEINSTITUTIONALIZATION

Most psychiatrists assert that deinstitutionalization was made possible by the discovery of antipsychotic drugs, which allow patients to live a stable life outside the hospital. Although it is true that these medications have helped some people return to mainstream life, Blau points out that psychiatrists often relied too heavily on drugs in their eagerness to empty the hospitals. An overreliance on drugs can prolong social dependency and produce neurological damage (1992, p. 81).

Unintended consequences of reform Events that occur as a result of reform measures that were not planned or anticipated by the reformers.

The failure of deinstitutionalization to live up to its promise is an illustration of a principle that sociologists call the **unintended consequences of reform.** Sometimes a reform can become so perverted in the way it is carried out that its advocates, who held such high hopes for it, feel betrayed.

Mentally ill people are less likely to be considered unemployable when there is a labor shortage. In the United States during World War II, people who would later be labeled as unemployable were employed. "Virtually none of the disabled workers in the San Francisco Bay area was unemployed in 1942–1943" (McGowan & Porter, 1967). It is interesting to see how differently people are viewed when they are urgently needed. All adults were needed during World War II. That is when middle-class women worked outside the home in large numbers. After the war, they were told to go back home and raise their children.

THE PRIVATIZATION OF CARE

Medicaid stimulated the growth of private nursing homes and was paid for partly by the federal government. This encouraged states to shift much of the financial burden to the government by discharging patients to private nursing and boarding homes. Patients were federally subsidized by Social Security Disability Insurance (SSDI) and Supplemental Security Income (SSI). Yet money to develop community facilities was simply not allocated (Warner, 1989, p. 23).

As patients were discharged from large state hospitals, many general hospitals created psychiatric wings for people in crisis. The concept of short, crisis-oriented hospitalization replaced the old long-stay "back ward." In some states, psychiatric care is being almost completely privatized.

Patients' rights advocates won significant victories in the 1960s and 1970s, establishing the right to treatment in the least restrictive setting. In 1971, a precedent-setting Florida case, *O'Connor v. Donaldson*, determined that people could not be committed involuntarily to a mental hospital unless they were dangerous to themselves or others. Other states followed suit. However, we may now be witnessing a return to involuntary commitments. There is some public sentiment, sparked by a few well-publicized cases, that mentally ill people, and particularly those who are homeless, should be forced to go to hospitals for their own or the public's protection. Several states have revised their laws to allow involuntary commitment.

Cycles in Juvenile Justice

Closely following the adult prisons and insane asylums of the late nineteenth and early twentieth centuries came the establishment of reformatories or training schools for juvenile delinquents. This **child-saving movement,** as it is often called, was also spearheaded by the Progressives. Ironically, although the Progressives were appalled at the brutality of the asylums and prisons of the 1830s, they created new asylums of their own—this time for children who had gotten into trouble with the law or who had no parents able to care for them.

Criminal justice reforms during the Progressive era were aimed at professionalizing the police and other agencies of social control, diversifying their methods of operation, and extending the coercive functions of the state into new areas of working-class life. The Progressives were critical of the police and prisons, because they often "aggravated conflict through corruption, brutality and general incompetence," consequently undermining the "legitimacy of the capitalist system itself" (Platt, 1977, pp. xxvi–xxvii).

Sociologist Anthony Platt (1977) believes that both compulsory education and the institutions of the child-saving movement (reformatories, orphanages, foster care homes, juvenile courts) were devised by certain segments of the middle and upper classes as new forms of social control and occupational tracking. Industrialists wanted to preserve social stability, and the juvenile courts and reform schools

Child-saving movement A term used to describe the efforts of reformers in the late nineteenth and early twentieth centuries to rescue children from "unwholesome influences." The movement led to the development of children's institutions, foster care, and the juvenile court.

helped to do this. Furthermore, affluent women wanted careers, and social service was a respectable career for them. Of course, there are other scholars who would disagree with this interpretation, believing that the creation of juvenile courts and reformatories was motivated by primarily humanitarian concerns to protect society and rehabilitate youngsters. And there are many, including the present authors, who believe that both points of view have some validity.

The juvenile court system was based on the belief that children who break the law should not be punished as if they were adults. Children's cases were reviewed informally by judges. Lawyers generally did not handle juvenile cases, as juvenile court is not based on an adversary model. Court-based probation officers investigated the backgrounds of the youthful offenders and reported to the judges. No jury sat in judgment, and no lawyer and prosecutor debated.

Juvenile reformatories were supposed to protect youngsters humanely from the corrupting influences of adult criminals. Although this sounds rational, in actual practice it meant that a youth found guilty was assigned to a reformatory *without trial and with a minimum of legal protection.* Legal due process was assumed to be unnecessary because reformatories were intended to reform, not punish. The judge and probation officer were assumed to be enlightened, free of self-interest, incorruptible, and always working in the best interest of the youth. Reformatories were built in the country, far from the residents' homes. Inmates were "protected from idleness, indulgence, and luxuries through military drill, physical exercise, and constant supervision" (Platt, 1977, p. 54). They were required to work at industrial and agricultural jobs but were given no more than an elementary education so that they did not "rise beyond their station in life." The reformatories were supposed to teach "the value of sobriety, thrift, industry, prudence, 'realistic' ambition, and adjustment" (p. 55).

CHANGE IN THE SYSTEM

Fifteen-year-old Gerald Gault challenged the fairness of the entire juvenile court procedure. He declared that he had not been treated in a humane way. In 1964 he was sentenced to a state industrial school in Arizona for six years for making an obscene telephone call. This misdemeanor carried a maximum sentence of two months in jail and a fine of $5 to $50 for adults. Gault brought suit against the state of Arizona, and in 1967 the U.S. Supreme Court declared that the juvenile court had indeed ignored the legal due process that is required by the U.S. Constitution (*In Re Gault* 967). Speaking for the majority in the Gault case, Justice Fortas said:

> However euphemistic the title, a "receiving home" or an "industrial school" for juveniles is an institution of confinement in which the child is incarcerated.... Under our Constitution, the condition of being a boy does not justify a kangaroo court." (Platt, 1977, pp. 27–28)

This decision finally gave juveniles certain due-process rights. Now they have a right to know the charges against them, the right to have their own lawyer, and the right to confront and cross-examine their accusers and witnesses. They must be warned about self-incrimination and their right to remain silent. (Juveniles still do not have the right to a jury trial unless they are bound over to an adult court.)

So, once again reform had soured. The court the Progressives had hailed as a great reform in the nineteenth century was called a "kangaroo court" in the twentieth century!

Soon after the Gault decision, a reform-minded commissioner of the Massachusetts Department of Youth Services, Jerome Miller, shut down every state training school and reformatory in the state. He condemned them as unworkable and unreformable. Miller was brought in to reform the system after a series of scandals—including stories of beatings, isolation, and rape—had rocked the state's prison-like reform schools. His decision to shift state policy from warehousing juveniles in institutions to counseling and educating them in community-based group homes set off a debate that is still raging.

Critics charged Miller with being soft on crime and have continually called for more locked facilities, especially for repeat offenders. The 1991 "get tough on crime" climate prompted Massachusetts governor William Weld to file legislation calling for the prosecution of violent teenagers in adult criminal court, saying, "For too long, the response to violent crime in our cities has been to treat juvenile offenders like victims" (McNamara, 1991, p. 24). Weld was about to recommend the death penalty for juveniles who kill until Amnesty International suggested that Massachusetts would be altering its criminal code to conform to Iraq's.

Despite the calls for getting tough on juveniles,

> the system of small-scale detention centers devoted to treating and educating delinquent youth has not been discredited. On the contrary, it has been hailed by the National Council on Crime and Delinquency as a model.... Massachusetts ranks 46th of the 50 states in reported juvenile crime" (Ibid.). Yet Miller's story about the Massachusetts experiment (Miller, 1991) almost didn't reach the public. One book editor rejected the manuscript because it might be "too compassionate for the times." (McNamara, 1991, p. 24)

Governor Weld's call to get tough on juvenile crime was echoed throughout the nation. Many juveniles have been bound over to adult courts and put in adult prisons. Boot camps grew substantially in the 1980s and 1990s. Thousands of juveniles have been put in them, where they were often treated harshly. There are no national regulations for these boot camps, and states are lax in their supervision. At least thirty-one teenagers in eleven states died at these camps since 1980. A 14-year-old boy named Tony Haynes died in July 2001 at an Arizona desert boot camp. Investigators said they were told before he died that counselors physically abused him and forced him to eat dirt (Janofsky, 2001, p. A1). However, states are now scaling back the controversial programs or shutting them entirely. The boot camp that Massachusetts opened in 1992 was closed in 2002, with the recognition that boot camps fare no better in rehabilitating criminals than traditional lock-ups. Commenting on the rise of boot camps, the Northeastern University criminologist James Alan Fox said,

> From the beginning, there was very little evidence that this would work. But once a couple of boot camps opened, and they showed them on '60 Minutes' and '20/20,' filming these kids being screamed at…it was suddenly terrific. That's all Americans and political leaders really needed to invest in boot camps in a wholesale way. (Latour, 2002)

BEHAVIOR DEFINED AS A SOCIAL PROBLEM

When does a particular kind of personal or social behavior become defined as a "social problem"? Why did social-problems textbooks of the pre-1970s rarely mention such issues as sexism, wife abuse, incest, sexual harassment, rape, and discrimination against the disabled, whereas post-1970s textbooks prominently discuss these as social problems?

Behaviors become social problems when some people and organizations force those issues to the top of the public agenda. Wife abuse and rape were widespread before 1970, but they weren't defined as social problems until the feminist movement challenged traditional assumptions about women's place in society (Best, 1989).

More than most other countries in the world, the United States has clung to an individualistic philosophy, believing the Horatio Alger rags-to-riches myth that anyone can make it if he or she works hard enough. Sociologist C. Wright Mills (1959) distinguished between "private troubles" and "public issues." *Troubles* happen to individuals and to the relationships between individuals. Troubles are private and threaten private values. *Issues,* on the other hand, transcend one individual's inner life and are widespread within the community. Mills gives the following example:

> When, in a city of 100,000, only one man is unemployed, that is his personal trouble, and for its relief we properly look to the character of the man, his skills, and his immediate opportunities. But when in a nation of 50 million employees, 15 million men [sic] are unemployed, that is an issue, and we may not hope to find its solution within the range of opportunities open to any one individual. The very structure of opportunities has collapsed. Both the correct statement of the problem and the range of possible solutions require us to consider the economic and political institutions of the society, and not merely the personal situation and character of a scatter of individuals. (p. 9)

We know that as unemployment rises, so do alcoholism and drug use, homelessness, child abuse, divorce, domestic violence, crime and delinquency, mental illness, and so forth. The human service worker who treats each case as a personal trouble is doing a disservice to clients, society, and the profession. As novelist Kurt Vonnegut said, "Workers in the field of mental health at various times in different parts of the world must find themselves asked to make people happier in cultures and societies which have gone insane" (Vonnegut, 1991, p. 32). Troubles call for personal struggle; social issues demand wide-scale social change.

DEFINING PROBLEMS

The Drug Scare

The process of defining problems and treating those problems is often more political than scientific. Both the definitions and the treatments go through cycles that depend more on the political and economic climate than on objective analysis. For example, two sociologists, Craig Reinarman and Harry Levine (1989), studied the crack-cocaine "epidemic," concluding that *crack use was no greater than it had been in previous years*. Rather, it was being called an epidemic as a dramatic ploy to sell newspapers, increase TV program ratings, and get votes for politicians. The drug scare led an overwhelming majority of both houses of Congress to vote for new antidrug laws with long mandatory prison terms, the death sentence, and massive funding for drug enforcement. Reinarman and Levine point out that during drug scares, all kinds of social problems are blamed on drugs and certain groups are scapegoated, most often people of color and youth of all races.

In support of their argument, Reinarman and Levine examined nationwide surveys of drug use and showed that the percentage of 18- to 25-year-old young adults who had ever tried cocaine peaked in 1982, four years before the current epidemic was announced, and it has *declined* since then. The issue became prominent before the 1984 presidential election, and dropped sharply in both political speeches and media coverage after the election, only to return during the 1988 election year. As a *New York Times* story put it, the drug scares filled an issue vacuum, since "there were no domestic or foreign policy crises looming on which the two parties could easily differentiate themselves" (Reinerman & Levine, 1989, p. 129). In evaluating the "epidemic" of drugs as compared to other substances, the sociologists point out that

> for every *one* cocaine-related death in the U.S. in 1987 there were approximately *300* tobacco-related deaths and *100* alcohol-related deaths. Seen in this light, cocaine's impact is somewhat less dramatic than media and political accounts suggest. (p. 120)

The media has embedded in the public's mind the image of drugs running rampant in the ghettos. But studies have shown that a higher percentage of whites than blacks have used cocaine; whites are more able to conceal their drug deals and can hire lawyers when they are arrested. A study in 1999 showed that tobacco use was higher among white youths 12 and older (27 percent) than among black youths (22.5 percent) or Hispanic youths (22.6 percent), and that binge alcohol drinking was lower for blacks (16.5 percent) than for all other races (20–21 percent) (SAMHSA, 1999).

Despite these statistics, much stiffer prison sentences are given for the possession of a small amount of crack than for a larger amount of cocaine. Poor people are more likely to use crack, because it is cheaper, and people of color are disproportionately poor, so a disproportionate number of people of color are jailed for drug use ("All Things Considered," 1992).

Again, we see the blaming-the-victim ideology winning over the systems analysis approach. While they were defunding social programs, the Reagan administration blamed

> unemployment, poverty, urban decay, school crises, crime, and all their attendant forms of human troubles…on *individual* deviance, immorality, or weakness…. *People in trouble were reconceptualized as people who make trouble;* social control replaced social welfare as the organizing principle of state policy. (Reinarman & Levine, 1989, p. 127)

This has profound implications for the human services, because the programs that get government funds are the ones that have been defined by officials as important. Methods of treatment are shaped by official philosophy.

The largest proportion of antidrug money has been spent on law enforcement and jails rather than on drug treatment programs and supportive services for addicts. And, despite the seeming concern for "crack babies," there are fewer treatment resources for pregnant mothers than for any other population.

How the Media Demonize People

People get much of their information from the media, and when the media distort facts, people are more likely to have distorted views. We will examine how the media dealt with AIDS and with welfare to illustrate how the media can demonize a group of people.

AIDS

In his study of the way magazines dealt with AIDS, Edward Albert (1989) shows that national magazines were slow to pay attention to AIDS. When they first printed news about it in 1982, they focused on the homosexual lifestyle, sometimes in a sensationalized manner. This encouraged readers to conclude that AIDS was something that happened to "them," not "us," because "we" don't do those things. This raised the question of whether homosexuality, and AIDS, was a moral or a medical issue.

Since the public assumed that AIDS happened to "them," a socially devalued and powerless group, they did not insist that officials pay more attention to the disease. Newspaper coverage increased in 1983 when stories appeared about children being at risk but decreased when the Centers for Disease Control indicated that there was no change in the at-risk populations. Media coverage increased in 1985 with the disclosure that the actor Rock Hudson had AIDS and it was implied that he was gay.

In 1985, the press began to suggest that AIDS was a threat to heterosexuals. "Beginning around the time of the death of Rock Hudson, a climate of fear emerged, quite different from that created when the press first typified AIDS as a disease of deviance" (Albert, 1989, p. 47). The press began to claim that the disease was spreading throughout the population. This climate of fear led to bitter debates about how to respond to the threat. Some people called for mandatory widespread testing; some advocated quarantine of those with the illness. William F. Buckley Jr. even suggested in an April 25, 1986, editorial in the *National Review* that those with AIDS be given a tattoo so the rest of us could avoid them.

When the media finally presented AIDS as a disease that could affect anyone, it began to be seen as a disease of the normal rather than just of the *deviant*. Increasingly, celebrities, homosexuals and heterosexuals alike, admitted to having AIDS. Arthur Ashe, a champion tennis player, got AIDS from a blood transfusion, and basketball star Magic Johnson got HIV from heterosexual contact. In the 1990s, the media became more sympathetic, speaking out against the stigmatization of AIDS victims, which was created in part by their early inadequate coverage of AIDS (Albert, 1989, p. 50). By the year 2000, most U.S. adults were relatively well informed about the causes of AIDS ("HIV-Related Knowledge and Stigma," 2001).

The AIDS epidemic has increased people's homophobia about gays and lesbians. Although AIDS is caused by a virus, the fact that in the United States it first began and spread the fastest among male homosexuals propelled the belief that the disease was *caused* by being gay. Although 75 percent of people with the HIV virus across the world are heterosexuals, gay men have been hit the hardest in the United States. However, their contagion rate is leveling off, and the fastest growing categories of victims of AIDS are minority women and their children.

Much of the change in public perception and official response to AIDS was created by organized groups of AIDS activists working tirelessly to educate the public and to force officials to act.

While new drug therapies and prevention education have made it possible to control the AIDS epidemic in the developed world, AIDS has reached epidemic proportions in the developing world, particularly in Africa and in many Asian countries. The same process of denial that took place in the United States is taking place with regard to AIDS in the developing world. After three years of frustrated lobbying to get permission to study the burgeoning growth of AIDS worldwide, two intelligence officers for the U.S. Central Intelligence Agency finally got permission in 1990 to do the study. Their study, "The Global AIDS Disaster," projected 45 million infections by 2000—inexorably fatal, the great majority in Africa. "The number beggared comparison. There were not that many combatants killed in World War I, World War II, Korea and Vietnam combined" (Gellman, 2000, p. 1). The author of the report, Kenneth Brown, said that the official reaction to the report was indifference.

NOTHING FOR YEARS

Nothing for years,
life continues as if
something hideous wasn't
coiled within;
then the sudden purple lump,
death's calling card,
a warrant to strip-mine flesh.
At the end, each ounce
of muscle razed,
only wasted bones left,
yet the eyes grown
huge with knowing
they did
nothing for years.

—Chris Mandell

Although many leaders were aware of the coming catastrophe for a decade, "Individually and collectively, most of those with power decided not to act" (Gellman, p. 1). James Sherry, director of program development for the Joint United Nations Program on HIV/AIDS, speaks bitterly of the crisis, "I can't think of the coming of any event which was more heralded, to less effect," he said, "The bottom line is, the people who are dying from AIDS don't matter in this world" (Gellman, 2000, p. 1). Racism was a big factor in this denial. One of Mr. Brown's colleagues at the National Intelligence Council said, "Oh, it will be good, because Africa is overpopulated anyway" (Gellman, p. 1).

In 2003, the World Health Organization adopted a plan called "3 × 5," setting a target of getting three million poor people on antiretroviral drugs by the end of 2005. At the AIDS conference in Bankok in July 2004, WHO officials said their 3 × 5 program was "just short" of the July goal of 500,000 in treatment, but Laurie Garrett, a senior fellow for global health at the Council on Foreign Relations, criticized the lack of progress, saying, "We are 18 months away from WHO's self-appointed deadline, and the pool of new HIV infections grows at the rate of 8,000 a day (Garrett, 2004).

Welfare

Conservative policymakers have successfully dismantled the safety net for poor people, often using the media to turn the public and government officials against the poor, particularly welfare recipients. They created think tanks such as the Heritage Foundation, the Manhattan Institute, and the American Enterprise Institute that put out a stream of books and magazines, and flooded the press with news releases.*

Fairness and Accuracy in Reporting (FAIR), an organization that analyzes press coverage, conducted a three-month study of the media's coverage of welfare issues from December 1, 1994, to February 24, 1995 (Flanders, Jackson, & Shadoan, 1997). Most of the people interviewed by the media were males, most were politicians and government officials, and most gave the official line that spending on the poor ought to be restricted. State and local officials most often interviewed were Republican governors who ran punitive programs, such as Tommy Thompson of Wisconsin and John Engler of Michigan. Few of those reports included any dissenters from the get-tough approach.

Welfare recipients were seldom interviewed, and when they were, they were given limited roles, and at worst they were attacked. In one vivid example, multi-million dollar earner Diane Sawyer of ABC devoted a segment to grilling a group of teenage mothers receiving Aid to Families with Dependent Children (*Prime Time Live*, 2/16/95). Explaining that "to many people these girls are public enemy No. 1," Sawyer harangued them on behalf of "taxpayers" who were "mad as hell." "Answer their question," she demanded: "Why should they pay for your mistake?"

Sixteen-year-old Lisa Wright, one of *Prime Time*'s interviewees, tried to point out that when it comes to taxpayer dollars, AFDC is "such a small percentage now, you know, of the amount of money taxpayers send in. Most of the money is going for defense." But Sawyer was having none of it: She dragged the discussion right back to female "irresponsibility" (Flanders et al., 1997, pp. 30–31).

"Lascivious teenagers" were linked to "every threat to the fabric of this country" by Jonathan Alter (1994). *Newsweek* harped on the theme of shame for poor young women, comparing them to drunk drivers (p. 41). When they attacked teenagers on welfare, neither Diane Sawyer nor Jonathan Alter pointed out that 70 percent of so-called teen pregnancies are the result of sex with men over 20. A study by sociologist Mike Males suggests that 50,000 teen pregnancies a year are caused by rape, and two-thirds of teen mothers have histories of sexual abuse by a perpetrator averaging 27 years of age (Flanders et al., 1997, pp. 33–34).

The welfare recipients that the media selected to be interviewed often reinforced stereotypes. In a *U.S. News & World Report* cover story, "six of the seven pictures were of women of color, mostly African Americans. The only white woman pictured was described as clinically depressed, as if poverty only affects white people who are in some way handicapped" (Flanders et al., 1997, p. 34). Recipients shown in the media often had several children, even though families on welfare have an average of 1.9 children, slightly less than the national average.

---

*For a valuable analysis of the Right's assault on welfare, see Lucy Williams's booklet *Decades of Distortion* (1997).

Reminiscent of much reporting on the AIDS crisis, stories on welfare drew a stark distinction between poverty's innocent and guilty victims. The acceptably innocent were children, the guilty were their moms. Although poor children certainly need defenders, poor children come from poor families. In the media, however, "innocent children" were often ominously separated from their guilty moms (just as "AIDS babies" were often described as more or less self-conceived) (Flanders et al., 1997, p. 33).

Research and advocacy groups made up only 9 percent of media sources during the period that FAIR studied. After participating in two hours of a *Firing Line* debate on welfare, Frances Fox Piven commented to the *St. Petersburg Times* "I am struck by how little evidence matters in talk about welfare" (Flanders et al., 1997, p. 37).

Yet the stereotypes that conservatives had created returned to haunt them when they wanted to persuade businesses to hire welfare mothers. How could you ask a CEO to hire people whom you had previously described as lazy, undependable, and oversexed? A year after the Personal Responsibility Act had been passed, a *New York Times* article reported that "welfare recipients, last year's political pariahs, are shedding their outcast status" (DeParle, 1997).

The NBC affiliate in Montgomery, Alabama, WSFA, has a weekly feature portraying a welfare family in favorable terms. On St. Louis radio, an advertising campaign praises those with the "guts to get off welfare." In Charlotte, North Carolina, there are billboards—paid for by the county and posted by the Chamber of Commerce—urging employers to give recipients a chance.

The effort to erase the stigma of welfare is being coordinated by the Welfare to Work Partnership, which was established in 1997 with President Clinton's encouragement. It includes corporate executives and aims to persuade business leaders to hire welfare recipients. It is conducting an advertising campaign with the slogans, "Welfare mothers make responsible employees" and "Welfare to work is a program that creates independence" (DeParle, 1997). The welfare recipients that conservatives had demonized are now being rehabilitated by politicians and corporate executives, with the help of the media.

Preventive Health Care

If we all ate tofu, carrots, green vegetables, and brown rice, gave up smoking, dieted, and got plenty of exercise, would we all be healthy? Filled with advice from nutritionists and doctors, the Living and Health pages of newspapers give that message. They cite studies showing the beneficial effects of exercise and a healthy diet.

How can these healthy habits help the poor? *Poverty is bad for your health.* A British commission, named for its chairman, Dr. Black, studied the health of people in several countries, including Great Britain. It found that health policy directed to individual health (regarding smoking, diet, and exercise) improved the health of middle-income and rich people but not the poor. The poor are exposed to such deleterious conditions by their work, housing, and low income that individual behaviors often cannot overcome these disadvantages. The death rate of a blue-collar worker is 2.6 times higher than that of a doctor or lawyer. The Royal Commission called for a return to the **public-health approach,** which asserts that life span is more influenced by improvements in housing, living standards, and sanitation than by improvements in medical intervention, surgery, and acute care (Townsend, 1992).

During the 1970s in England, despite countrywide improvement in living standards, the gap in health between the rich and the poor widened. The Royal Commission, after studying scientific evidence, said that gap could only be closed by (1) providing better housing and adequate income to the poor, (2) increasing wages, and (3) increasing government payments to the aged, single parents, the disabled, and the unemployed.

Food programs, vaccination, and fluoridation are three examples of the success of preventive public-health measures. The WIC (Women, Infants, and Children) food program in the United States for low-income mothers and children has proved that providing healthy food to children and pregnant women has prevented health problems such as infant mortality, low birth weight, and low resistance to disease. Fluoridation of the water has prevented millions of cavities. Today, immunology is such an accepted practice in Western culture that it receives little public attention. Only when there is a breakdown in controls and specific disease rates rise does the general public become aware of the existence of the public-health prevention approach (Friedlander & Apte, 1980, pp. 368–369).

Public health is concerned with preventive health care, and that is a concern of human service workers. Where an illness is a large-scale problem—as is black lung disease among coal miners; brown lung disease among textile workers; hypertension among black people; cancer among asbestos workers and people living near hazardous wastes; and stroke, cancer, and heart disease among the general population—human service workers deal with the problem on three levels:

1. They work to prevent the causes of illness when they are known.
2. They work to develop appropriate and adequate services.
3. They work with the victims of these public-health problems in giving health-related services.

public-health approach A preventive approach to social problems as opposed to a remedial approach. It implements large-scale programs to meet people's basic health and nutritional needs in order to prevent illness.

THE HISTORY OF HUMAN SERVICE WORK

Human service is a broad umbrella category that includes many different kinds of work. Among the first human service workers were doctors and nurses, teachers, lawyers, and the clergy. During the nineteenth century, the people whom we generally call human service workers today began to define their work and organize themselves into professions. They have taken a variety of routes to define their work

MEDICATION   INCARCERATION

A judge must decide the fate of a person who is accused of committing a crime but who also might be mentally ill or stressed out by homelessness. Should special courts be set up to diagnose and mandate treatment? Can therapy or medication be useful when it is coerced?

as they responded to changing definitions of problems, technological innovations, and political and economic realities. Some of the professions under the human-service umbrella today are:

- Claims workers in government benefit programs—e.g., welfare, unemployment, Social Security, Medicaid, food stamps
- Cooperative extension workers (often called extension agents or county agents)
- Counselors (school, employment, rehabilitation, career planning and placement)
- Music therapists, art therapists, dance therapists
- Residential-care workers with children, the disabled, the aged, people with drug or alcohol problems, parolees, delinquents
- Psychologists
- Social workers and social service aides
- Speech pathologists and audiologists
- Therapy and rehabilitation workers (occupational, recreational, and physical therapists)

We shall briefly trace the history of the profession of social work as it evolved from nineteenth-century forms to the present and the history of the newer human service profession.

The COSs and the Settlement House Movement

The roots of social work were nurtured by two major wellsprings: the **Charity Organization Societies** (COSs), from which casework and counseling grew, and the settlement house movement, which pioneered group work, community and social change, and advocacy.

The COSs first began in England, expanding later to large cities in the United States. They tried to be orderly in their distribution of relief funds through what they termed *scientific charity*. Their "friendly visitors" sought to separate the "deserving" from the "undeserving" poor through a case-by-case investigation of their life situations. The COSs thought that poverty was perpetuated by indiscriminate relief giving, which made people lazy, or by defects in character. The present-day Family Service Societies grew out of these Charity Organization Societies, and most of the schools of social work in the United States were organized by people who worked in them. The kind of thinking that dominated the COSs certainly exerted an influence on the entire social work profession. The Columbia University School of Social Work (originally the New York School of Philanthropy), the first university school to award the degree in social work, opened in 1898 under the auspices of the New York Charity Organization Society.

Social work also derived from the **settlement house movement** of the late 19th century. Although the early settlement house workers did not call themselves social workers, social work graduate schools began in the 1940s to include group work and community organizing in their curricula.

The settlement house movement was exemplified by the work of Jane Addams at Hull House in Chicago. A young woman from a rich family who was profoundly shocked by the poverty and exploitation of immigrant families in the urban slums of Chicago, she established a community center to help immigrants solve their social, educational, recreational, and survival problems. Hull House attracted a dedicated core of privileged, yet concerned young staff, mostly volunteers, who "settled" (lived) in the house (thus the name "settlement house"). They helped the newly arrived families to care for their young children and conducted classes in English, citizenship, and the like. Addams imprinted on the field the values of respect for cultural differences and reaching out to clients where one finds them—on the stoops of their houses, at the corner bar, in the factory, and on assembly lines. She also promulgated the belief that society needs to work in a variety of ways to conquer social and personal problems. She loved the city and understood the power of groups to give support to their own members and to apply pressure for needed changes in the laws and customs of their communities. Four labor unions were organized at Hull House. Chambers (1980) records the history of the settlement

Charity Organization Societies (COSs) The earliest professional social work agencies, organized first in England and later in the United States; they claimed to deliver "scientific charity" through case-by-case work of "friendly visitors."

Settlement house movement The movement of the late nineteenth and early twentieth centuries that established agencies in city slums of England and the United States, where professionals gave group services and engaged in social action on behalf of the slum dwellers.

house movement. He describes how settlement leaders supported the organizing efforts of working women, walked picket lines to demonstrate labor solidarity, testified before civic groups about the needs and rights of working women, and helped raise strike funds.

The settlement workers wanted to bring together the privileged and the underprivileged to share some of the finer things of life. Music, drama, art, and dancing clubs and classes were opened to the immigrant neighbors. Workers, college students, and alumni could live for a time in the settlements, playing basketball, chatting on stoops, and participating in the life of poor neighborhoods.

Jane Addams drew a sharp distinction between her kind of work and the work of the "friendly visitors" of the COSs. She did not think they were "friendly" at all in the moralistic way they drew distinctions between the "deserving" and the "undeserving" poor. She wrote about the

> difference between the emotional kindness with which relief is given by one poor neighbor to another poor neighbor, and the guarded care with which relief is given by a charity visitor to a charity recipient. The neighborhood mind is at once confronted not only by the difference of method; but by an absolute clashing of two ethical standards. (Addams, 1902, pp. 19–20)

Mary Richmond, one of the leading lights of the COSs and author of the first major theoretical work on social casework in 1917, *Social Diagnosis* (1917/1971), reciprocated Jane Addams's contempt, accusing the settlements of doing harm by their misguided charity.

Like the organizers of the COSs, most of the settlement house workers came from a religious tradition and viewed their human service work as an expression of their beliefs. However, the settlement house workers had a somewhat different vision of the causes and the remedies of poverty. Although not usually radical in their political views (anarchists, communists, and socialists would not have claimed them as their own), they were more inclined than the organizers of the COSs to put some of the blame for poverty on greedy businessmen, landlords, and corrupt politicians.

Many of the settlement house workers were Progressives who struggled to expand the role of the state in social welfare. They sponsored reforms such as the juvenile court movement and the establishment of kindergartens. As we have seen, in their trust of the state they ignored the state's potential for violations of human rights. At their lowest, they sought to force the immigrants' rich kaleidoscope of lifestyles and values into a more docile, homogenized U.S. style. At their best, they had a vision of a more just society and believed that their reforms could create it. That thread of reform resurfaced in the New Deal of the 1930s, the New Frontier of the Kennedy era, and the Great Society of the Johnson era. Not until the liberation struggles of the late 1950s and 1960s was the view of the state as benign parent challenged, and the "rights revolution" begun.

Bertha Reynolds, an outspoken advocate of social change, summed up the difference between the settlements and the COSs. She commented that although the

COSs and settlements were interested in the same reforms, *the settlements organized neighborhoods to act for themselves, whereas the charities helped families in need.* A settlement worker told her:

> You caseworkers see people only when they are in trouble and at their worst. We live with them in good times or bad, and see them at their best. It makes our attitude different. We encourage them to take social action and help them to do it effectively. We abhor charity. (Reynolds, 1963, p. 30)

As the Progressive reform movement died, so too did much of the reform thrust of the settlement houses. Workers no longer live in the houses and often do not even live in the same neighborhood. Many settlement houses are now primarily social and recreational centers. The sounds of square dance music and then of rap and heavy metal replaced the angry arguments of union organizers exhorting crowds of garment workers to fight for their rights. Some settlement houses, however, continued to be involved in social action in their communities, particularly during the War on Poverty. Chicago settlement houses helped to shape Chicago's War on Poverty, brought about major changes in the city's police department, and reformed the child welfare system in Illinois (Seever, 1987).

Social Work Schools

Thus, from two groups attempting in their own fashion to aid the troubled and poor, emerged a profession with noble aims but built on a shaky alliance. When schools of social work developed their curricula, the COSs wielded the most influence. As social work developed its education during the next fifty years, the casework model of the COSs became the major skill in the field. Social workers counseled families, worked in child protection agencies, arranged foster care and adoption for children, helped the families of sick people plan for release and rehabilitation, and worked on mental health teams with psychiatrists and psychologists.

Jane Addams drew on sociological rather than psychological theory. She was well connected with the world-renowned sociology department of the University of Chicago. But at that time, clinical psychology had not yet been developed, and sociology "offered little in respect to managing face-to-face interaction with clients; and that is where psychiatry could be applied" (Specht, 1990, p. 348). The individualistic philosophy of the COSs laid the foundation for social work's almost wholesale acceptance of psychiatric theory, beginning in the 1920s. The most popular of these theories was the psychoanalytically oriented theories of Sigmund Freud.

Beginning in the 1950s, social workers were increasingly influenced by the humanistically oriented psychologies of Carl Rogers (1951), Abraham Maslow, and others, and some later incorporated what Specht (1990) calls popular and New Age psychologies—"transcendental meditation, rolfing, hypnosis, and the scores of other therapies now available" (p. 19).

Although there was no return to the theory of moral depravity that held sway in the nineteenth century, the adoption of psychology as the almost exclusive theory of social work education slowly moved professionals away from the neighborhood and group work of Jane Addams. The adoption of behaviorist theory by many schools of social work, beginning in the 1960s, did little to change the individualistic focus of the profession. The introduction of social systems theory in the 1970s (Pincus & Minahan, 1973) emphasized the interaction of the person with the environment; but although systems theory is widely discussed in social work schools, the overwhelming majority of social workers are trained to work one-on-one. Group work and community organizing expanded to meet the social ferment of the 1960s and early 1970s, but contracted when the ferment subsided.

Current Trends in Social Work

As social services are becoming increasingly privatized, so is social work. The fastest-growing sector of social work is private practice (Barker, 1995). As states passed licensing laws, workers became eligible to receive **third-party payment** for therapy through the clients' insurance.

Third-party payment Payments made by insurance companies or government programs for medical expenses incurred by individuals.

Social workers' reasons for preferring private practice over agency practice vary. Earning more money is certainly one of the major reasons, but many workers are dissatisfied with the bureaucracy and restrictions of agency practice and yearn to control their working conditions and choose the types of clients they will serve (Abramovitz, 1986). There is intense debate within the profession, and pitched battles among the National Association of Social Workers (NASW), the National Institute for Clinical Social Work Advancement, and the American Board of Examiners (Battle, 1990, p. 232). Those who oppose the trend believe that the rise in private practice amounts to turning our back on the poor, who cannot afford to pay $70 to $150 an hour for therapy and cannot get insurance coverage for it. Those who favor it argue that social workers are as qualified to do therapy as are psychologists and should have that choice.

As more social workers with an MSW degree go into private practice, the public social services are increasingly staffed by those without an MSW. College graduates with degrees in social work, psychology, sociology, or human services fill those jobs. They provide care for the elderly, neglected and abused children, the disabled, and the mentally ill, a large proportion of whom are poor and minorities.

Undergraduate social work programs were established in state colleges, mostly in sociology departments, during the Depression, to staff the new public welfare agencies created by the Social Security Act. The Bachelor of Social Work (BSW) credential was accepted by the Council on Social Work Education (CSWE) in 1966, but it was not until 1970 that NASW admitted BSW workers as members. The CSWE allows graduate schools to admit BSW members with advanced standing if they choose. Thus BSW graduates can often finish an MSW degree in one year rather than the two years that is usually required.

The Roots of the Human Service Field

The field of human services was born in the 1950s and since then has expanded in fits and starts. The term *human service,* as opposed to *welfare,* was given the official stamp of approval when the federal Department of Health, Education, and Welfare (HEW) changed its name to Health and Human Services (HHS) in 1980.

Having declared MSW social workers as nonessential and too expensive, the federal government set out to create a new profession of human service workers. Although saving money may have been one reason for this, there were also other factors at work. Some liberal federal bureaucrats saw social work as too traditional and rigid to deliver adequate services to the poor. The civil rights movement created pressure to open up service professions to minorities who had previously been excluded. Then too, there was money available for social services, and many professions wanted a piece of this action. Government expenditures on social welfare rose dramatically, nearly tripling between 1960 and 1970, and another infusion of funds came with the passage of Title XX legislation in 1975, which funded social services. College educators from a variety of disciplines—counseling, education, special education, psychology, social work, and others—scrambled for Title XX funds.

> In the 1960s, Dr. Harold McPheeters of the Southern Regional Education Board (SREB) applied for and received a grant from the National Institute of Mental Health (NIMH) for the development of mental-health programs at community colleges in the Southern region of the country. This was the beginning of the associate's-level human service degree in the United States. Therefore, some consider Dr. McPheeters to be the "founder" of the human services field. (Neukrug, 1994)

The National Organization for Human Service Education (NOHSE) was founded in 1975 at the 5th Annual Faculty Development Conference of the Southern Regional Education Board. In 1976, the National Institute of Mental Health (NIMH) gave funds to the Southern Regional Education Board to create national standards for training and reviewing human service programs (Brawley, 1980). Out of this project came the Council for Standards of Human Service Education (CSHSE), formed in February 1979. In 1982, the National Commission for Human Service Workers was incorporated to provide a national system for voluntary registration and certification of human service workers (National Commission for Human Service Workers, 1982, p. 1).

The new human service workers include: the indigenous neighborhood people ("new professionals") recruited during the War on Poverty by social agencies, schools, and hospitals; community college graduates with an associate degree and a major in human services or a related field; and graduates of four-year human service programs. The following influences helped the human service profession to grow:

1. *The civil rights and liberation struggles.* During the civil rights and liberation struggles of the 1960s, people of color, feminists, gays, and youth declared that

mainstream social work was irrelevant. It was too white, too middle class, and too patriarchal. They created their own alternative self-controlled agencies: the Black Panther breakfast program, feminist health collectives, parent co-op daycare centers, shelters for battered women, gay and lesbian counseling centers, shelters and drug counseling centers for alienated and runaway youth. Most of these were not staffed by professional social workers, although an occasional social worker sympathetic to the agency's ideology might work with it.

2. *The OEO War on Poverty.* In its War on Poverty, the Office of Economic Opportunity (OEO) challenged the COS mentality of established social work. The OEO set up new agencies to do battle with the social work gatekeepers to get more benefits and services for clients. Actually, since most workers in Departments of Welfare are not BSW or MSW social workers, OEO's war with welfare was not in a strict sense a war with the social work profession, but instead with a government bureaucracy. However, OEO officials tended to view the profession of social work as the enemy of change.

Many establishment agencies eagerly accepted OEO money, and some highly professionalized agencies, such as Family Service Societies, for the first time hired "indigenous workers" from the communities they served in order to forge links between the agency and the service users. Many professional child welfare social workers were challenged, for the first time in their careers, by poverty lawyers defending parents of foster children. Poverty lawyers entered areas that had hitherto been the domain of social workers.

New Careers for the Poor movement A movement that began in the 1960s to train workers who do not have extensive formal credentials for human service jobs.

3. *The New Careers for the Poor movement.* The **New Careers movement,** conceived of and best articulated by Arthur Pearl and Frank Riessman (1965), was begun as part of the War on Poverty to create human service careers for poor people. Finding that they were blocked in their quest for upward mobility by lack of credentials, one of the movement's leaders, Audrey Cohen, started the College of Human Services in New York City. She announced her intention to "change the whole pattern of credentialing as it now exists" (Houston & Cohen, 1972, p. 22).

Career ladder A specific path of jobs that relates accomplishment and tenure to upward mobility.

The **career ladder** concept, in which a worker with incomplete training could move up through on-the-job experience and training, was built into some antipoverty legislation. Many agencies and colleges drew upon antipoverty funds to set up training courses and programs.

4. *The growth of community colleges.* The burgeoning growth of community colleges in the late 1960s and the 1970s spurred the growth of human service programs, more than 500 by 1996 (di Giovanni, 1996). This gave the New Careers students another way to gain a credential and, aided by antipoverty money and grants, many associate's degree graduates found jobs in agencies and schools.

5. *Deinstitutionalization and contracting out.* Deinstitutionalization created a demand for workers in community residences, prerelease centers, mental health clin-

ics, and other community settings. This, along with the increase in contracting out of services to private agencies, created new agencies that were not part of the MSW or BSW tradition. Workers came from many disciplines. (For example, a Massachusetts Department of Youth Services treatment program for juvenile delinquents on Penikese Island was begun by marine biologists from the Woods Hole Oceanographic Institute.) Contracting out not only took some turf away from social work, but it also weakened public-service unions, bringing down the wage scale in both the public and the private sectors.

New Disciplines

Among the first professionals to retool for the human service field were elementary and high school teachers who were faced with layoffs because of declining student enrollment. A 1979 survey "revealed that more than 300 schools, colleges or departments of education had human services programs" (Vogel, 1979). One of the authors of this book, Barbara Schram, started a human service program in one of them. The American Association of Colleges for Teacher Education recommended relieving the current oversupply of teachers by diversifying to produce a new kind of teacher, a human service educator.

Although psychologists have always been in the human services, a branch of psychology called *professional psychology* is more oriented toward counseling than toward research. The first school of professional psychology, accredited by the American Psychological Association in 1974, seems especially oriented toward health services, the field that accounts for a large proportion of the growth in social welfare spending since the 1960s.

In sociology, a specialty called *clinical sociology* has developed, whose practitioners, particularly family sociologists, do therapy with individuals, groups, and families. Their counseling theories include a sociological perspective that examines the difference between private troubles and public issues.

Finally, in the field of child abuse and neglect, which for decades had been the almost exclusive province of social work, doctors and lawyers gained prominence. Advances in radiology in the 1960s made it easier to diagnose abuse, and the term *battered-child syndrome* was coined. Since then, many child abuse units have been located in hospitals rather than in social agencies. Lawyers also became involved in defining abuse and neglect and in representing the parents, the child, and the state in court cases.

Declassification and Deprofessionalization

Many states have moved to declassify civil service jobs, removing them from the exclusive province of social work and broadening the qualifications. The National Association of Social Workers (NASW) and the Council on Social Work Education

(CSWE) countered the move to declassify social work jobs by lobbying for state licensing legislation. State NASW chapters were urged to make licensing a high priority on their agenda. NASW also countered declassification moves by seeking to prove the worth of the BSW and MSW credentials to state civil service and merit system boards. Ironically, social workers, many of whom had never wanted to be in the public welfare agencies in the first place, were now fighting declassification efforts to keep them out.

Breaking Down Boundaries

Much of the human services literature, particularly the New Careers literature, displays the missionary zeal of a movement. To the extent that human service workers are struggling on the side of the poor and the dispossessed, as in the New Careers movement, we applaud their efforts. They enabled thousands of poor people, especially poor women, to get jobs they would never have had otherwise and provided a vital missing link between the poor and their communities. We also agree enthusiastically with the pleas of human service workers to break down the artificial boundaries between disciplines and open up the field to anyone who can enrich it. The New Careers people from the communities served by social agencies have a gut-level knowledge of their neighbors' lives that a social worker commuting from an affluent white suburb cannot hope to match.

Many people are made tense by the introduction of a staff member with different credentials. In highly stratified organizations such as hospitals, much effort can be wasted and tempers strained as the traditional helpers try to find ways to fit the newly arrived worker into the pecking order. Some new workers or students in field placements have walked into the middle of such power struggles, inheriting long-smoldering conflicts. Tensions are often greater where staff morale is low, communication is poor, and there is a lack of adequate orientation before a new role is inserted into an existing system. Thus, if a residential treatment center hires, for the first time, a human service worker, everyone involved in that system needs to do some serious thinking about the new person's job description. Often, if other workers are given a voice in shaping it, they are less resistant to change when the eager generalist appears on the scene. If newcomers are left to carve out their own job description or are given superimposed ones, toes are bound to be stepped on.

There are no easy ways to avoid turf battles in institutions, but forewarned is forearmed! Professions tend to solidify their boundaries, and most workers have understandable concern about their responsibilities and privileges. Good humor and a nonthreatening attitude, coupled with a sense of your potential contribution, can go a long way in dealing with boundary disputes.

Many of the conflicts within a profession and between professions center on social class, race, and gender differences. Sometimes the fight may seem to be about credentials, but it is *really* about white people, middle-class people, heterosexuals, or nonhandicapped workers wanting to preserve their exclusive status.

Whether we are called human service workers or social workers, we still give the best service possible. There is room for many flowers to bloom in the social service field, but each of those flowers must prove its competence and its dedication.

SUMMARY

1. People have always helped, as well as hurt, each other. The nature of a society shapes people's helping impulses. One anthropologist believes that the principle of reciprocity is the basic glue that holds a society together.

2. A review of the history of helping gives perspective on how changes in society shape the methods of helping. To understand the present, we need to know the past.

3. At the beginning of industrialization, people who needed help were regarded as morally depraved. That attitude shifted somewhat to the view that problems are often beyond the control of the individual.

4. Universal programs, such as Social Security, cover people of all social classes. Means-tested programs, such as Temporary Assistance to Needy Families, cover only the poor and are usually stigmatized.

5. Welfare gradually shifted from local, to state, and then to federal responsibility. In recent years, it has drifted back to the responsibility of state and local governments.

6. During the rise of Protestantism, especially Calvinism, the poor were regarded as people who had been denied the grace of God and were treated as criminals. They were placed in debtors' prisons and workhouses. This attitude pervaded American society until well into the twentieth century.

7. During the civil rights era of the 1960s, many people redefined poverty as a result of an unjust social system. This gave rise to an opportunity theory of poverty, as opposed to a victim-blaming theory.

8. Political ideologies often define personal and social problems. Such influence characterizes, for example, the following issues: the drug "epidemic"; the response to welfare; an individual versus a systems approach to health care; and the roles and privileges of men and women.

9. The forms of helping go in cycles. For example, welfare reform, the care of the mentally ill, and the treatment of delinquents have all run a cyclical course.

10. The Progressives attempted to individualize the treatment of prisoners and mental patients. However, given unchecked authority, professionals often violated clients' rights.

11. The contemporary response to mental illness is deinstitutionalization, which places clients in more normal settings in the community although there are not enough community facilities.

12. The Progressives instituted the child-saving movement, creating juvenile courts, foster care, compulsory education, and orphanages. These institutions are regarded by some as new forms of social control and occupational tracking of the poor.

13. Ostensibly, the juvenile court system was more humane for children, but its failure to provide the due process of adults courts resulted in many injustices. The Supreme Court's 1967 Gault decision gave juveniles some due-process rights.

14. The first professionals to do social welfare work with the poor were social workers. The two early strands of the profession were the Charity Organization Societies and the settlement house movement.

15. The human service field began in the 1950s and since then has grown with the impact of deinstitutionalization, the War on Poverty program, the New Careers movement, and the proliferation of community colleges.

DISCUSSION QUESTIONS

1. The minimum wage in 2004 was $5.15 an hour. Why do you think Congress and the President are unwilling to raise that wage to an amount that would support a family? What amount do you think the minimum wage should be?

2. The government of Finland gives each new mother a complete layette for the baby, or 150 Euros (about $185 in 2004). A parent who gets on a bus in Helsinki with a baby in a carriage or stroller does not have to pay the bus fare because people think the parent should not be distracted from caring for the baby. Single mothers not only suffer no stigma in Finland, they are considered to be doing valuable work for the country by raising children. There are no shelters for homeless families in Finland because people believe that families should be in apartments, not shelters. These attitudes are quite different from attitudes toward mothers in the U.S. who receive welfare. Why do you think there is such a difference?

3. Why do you think welfare has become a political issue in the U.S.?

4. J. P. Morgan recommended that the difference in pay between a chief corporate executive and the average worker in that corporation should be in a ratio of 20 to 1. Today in the U.S. it is 700 to 1. Why has there been no public outcry about this?

WEB RESOURCES FOR FURTHER STUDY

The National Empowerment Center
www.power2u.org

The mission of the National Empowerment Center, Inc., is to carry a message of recovery, empowerment, hope, and healing to people who have been diagnosed with mental illness. "We carry that message with authority because we are a consumer/survivors/expatient–run organization and each of us is living a personal journey of recovery and empowerment. We are convinced that recovery and empowerment are not the privilege of a few exceptional leaders, but rather are possible for each person who has been diagnosed with mental illness."

National Network of Abortion Funds (NNAF)
www.nnaf.org

Access and Equality Contingent
www.access.nnaf.org

An organization that raises funds to help low-income women get abortions when necessary. They lobby to increase access to choice, which includes the choice to have children and to have the resources to care for them. The Access and Equality Contingent seeks to broaden the feminist agenda to be more inclusive of issues that affect low-income women such as welfare and poverty. They lobby against the Family Cap provision and marriage promotion programs in welfare law and against the Hyde Amendment, which prohibits federal funding for abortion. They organized several welfare rights groups nationwide to attend the March for Women's Lives in Washington, D.C., on April 25, 2004.

National Organization for Women (NOW)
www.now.org

Official home page of the National Organization for Women. Offers information about the organization and its agenda, as well as feminism, women, abortion rights, violence against women, racial and ethnic diversity, and economic equity.

National Organization for Human Service Education (NOHSE)
www.nohse.com

Established in 1975, the National Organization for Human Service Education unites educators, students, practitioners, and clients in a conversation about preparation of effective human service workers. It is a membership organization. It encourages and supports the development of local, state, and national organizations of human services. It sponsors forums through conferences, institutes, publications, and symposia that foster creative approaches to human service education and delivery.

Physicians for a National Health Program (PNHP)
www.pnhp.org

The goal of Physicians for a National Health Program is a health program that covers all U.S. residents for all medically necessary care including preventive, acute, mental health, long-term care and prescription drugs in a publicly administered, publicly financed program. It would replace private insurance premiums and out-of-pocket payments with a progressive tax program to finance medical care. PNHP has 10,000 members, representing every medical specialty and every state, and many other health care professionals and concerned individuals. Through public education, research, and mobilization of their members, they have played a key role in focusing the health-care policy debate on the need for fundamental reform.

CHAPTER 3

Strategies of Intervention

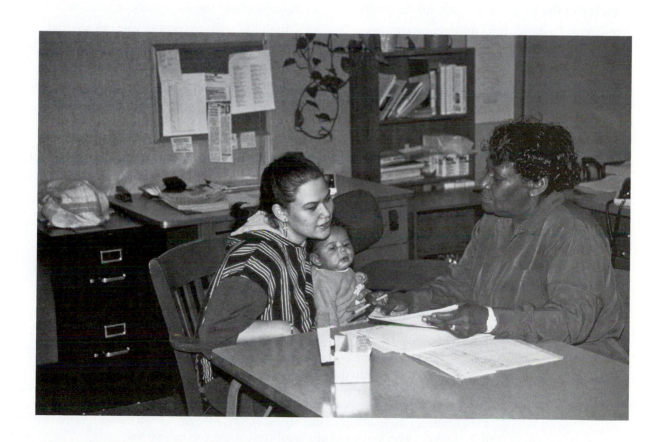

In Chapter 1, we glimpsed the incredible diversity of human service roles and agencies. Then we looked backward to see how help has been delivered in the past and to learn from this history. Now we are ready to describe the ways in which a human service worker takes a public mandate and turns it into action. These actions are called *strategies of intervention.*

Workers choose the interventions they think will be most effective based on their understanding of the roots, or reasons, for the problem. To understand these underlying reasons, we introduce the concept of *multicausality,* a concept that will appear many times in the following chapters. Its principles assert that there is never one simple reason for a complex social problem. Multiple causes lead to multiple strategies of intervention. Further, the uniqueness of each personality and life experience argues for diverse approaches.

After showing how we analyze the factors that lie behind a problem such as child abuse, we describe fourteen of the interventions that human service workers implement to cope with this problem. The interventions can be divided into those that aim at changing the *behavior or internal attitudes* of the troubled individual and those that aim at changing the *external pressures* exerted by the environments within which people live and work.

Then we describe the tasks that must be carried out to make each intervention successful. By reading about the daily work of the director of a disability resource center, you can see that whether she is counseling one mobility impaired student or researching the physical barriers that make navigating the campus difficult for all students in wheelchairs, her work follows a similar pattern. All interventions begin with the collecting of relevant data and end with the careful evaluation of what has been accomplished and the way in which the work was done.

A human services student intern in a human resource department of a high-tech corporation wrote this entry in her fieldwork journal.

> While I was covering the reception desk yesterday, a woman who works in the employee cafeteria came into the office. She is convinced that her boss is sexually harassing her. I described to her all the possible places she could go to get some action on her complaints. Then I told her my honest opinion of the trade-offs of each pathway. After a few sentences she interrupted me, saying, "Okay, enough, just tell me what is the best thing to do!" I gave her one of our usual yes-but-then-again answers.
>
> "Damn it!" she shouted, "How come you middle-class professionals never give a simple answer to a simple question?"

This student knew that with personnel problems, just as with all other human service problems, there are no easy, one-size-fits-all solutions. Action plans cannot be designed like the chemist combines elements—two parts of hydrogen mixed with one part of oxygen produces water. In our field, we never can predict exactly what the outcome of our words or acts will be. Because that reality is often forgotten, people become frustrated by the endless duplication, contradictions, and lack of clarity they find when dealing with human service problems.

Irritating as this situation may be, it is inevitable. Three basic forces create this endless diversity:

1. *Value conflicts in a pluralistic society*
2. *Historical changes*
3. *The concept of multicausality*

We will briefly introduce the first two factors, but in this chapter we will focus primarily on the impact of the concept of multicausality on the design and implementation of intervention strategies.

Value Conflicts: As you read the chapters on value conflicts and working with diversity, you will find that there is very little agreement in our society on issues as basic as the nature of human nature and the legitimate functions of government. The definitions of what constitutes proper parental discipline, the appropriate role of males and females, attitudes toward sexuality, consumerism, and even the legitimacy of social protest vary according to our race, religion, ethnic heritage, and the extent of our assimilation into U.S. society. Our socioeconomic class, sex, region of the country, ideology, age, and stage in life also exert an impact on our opinions and actions.

Historical Changes: The attitude of society toward social problems, and the helping process, undergoes constant shifts. New theories on the causes of and cures for social problems keep emerging. Programs established in one era reflect the state of theory at that time. But agencies rarely change as fast as the dominant views. People trained at one time, when certain theories held sway, continue to operate under those theories long after they have been discarded or revised by others. Sometimes, if people keep on working in their old-fashioned way, old theories are likely to come back into fashion, just like clothes stored in the attic.

THE CONCEPT OF MULTICAUSALITY

When a person sets out to solve a problem, the most logical first step is to try to find out what has caused it. Once the cause has been identified, a rational plan to solve the problem can then be designed. But as we try to neatly match solutions to problems, the following six principles of **multicausality** complicate the process.

Multicausality
The view that personal or social problems are caused by many interacting factors, often too complex to allow a precise assessment of causality.

1. *In dealing with social problems, we can never establish causality with any solid degree of certainty.* Even though we may have collected all the data we could about a

person, we still end up with a best guess, an informed hunch, or a hypothesis to explain the causes of his or her problem. For example, it is easy to make the assumption that if infants are picked up every time they cry, they will become spoiled. But it is equally possible that if infants are allowed to cry for long periods of time, they will become frustrated. As we watch a child who constantly seeks attention from a teacher, we cannot tell if the child's behavior is caused by *too much* or *too little* parental supervision at home. We also cannot tell if it is because of a genuine inability to understand the work and the child needs more instruction, or if it is because the work is too easy and the child is bored and ready to move on.

If we were to read all the books on the shelf of a library under the heading "Child-Raising Manuals," we would find many different views among the experts. Whether children should be spanked, breast-fed, sent to day care or kept at home, taught the alphabet early, and so forth are questions with many different answers (Breitbart & Schram, 1978). Dr. Benjamin Spock, author of the best-selling manual on raising a healthy child, did a major revision of his book (Spock, 1946, 1976). If you tried to follow his parenting advice in 1946, you would have raised your little boy or girl very differently than if you read his revised book thirty years later. Spock looked back at his first book and was shocked by his own sex-role stereotyping. In his later books, he confessed that his thinking had undergone a dramatic change (Spock & Morgan, 1989).

When we read about the lives of famous people, we find every possible kind of parenting. Some have excelled in life presumably because of supportive home environments, but others have excelled despite their negative home environments. Some of these people were orphans, some were the only child in the family, and some had many siblings. In landmark autobiographies, such as *Manchild in the Promised Land* (Brown, 1965), authors struggle to understand the impact of their early experiences on their adult personality and life choices, and rarely can they come up with answers. Jerome Kagan (1989), an eminent Harvard University child development specialist, has found that the more he studies, the less he is convinced that there are very many linkages between a person's early childhood characteristics and his or her personality as an adult.

2. *There is rarely one simple cause of a problem.* When we observe negative behavior, either in a social system or in an individual, we can be absolutely sure that more than one factor is responsible. Beware of popular wisdom and tabloid newspapers that will try to sell you simple reasons for a complex phenomenon. Headlines shout:

POLITICIAN DECLARES LACK OF DISCIPLINE
IN HOME IS MAJOR CAUSE OF RISE
IN JUVENILE DELINQUENCY

or

SCHOOL AUTHORITIES SAY INADEQUATE CRIMINAL
JUSTICE SYSTEM IS CAUSE OF CRIME INCREASE

or

SOCIAL REFORMERS DEMAND INCREASE IN JOBS
TO STEM YOUTH CRIME

or

LACK OF RECREATIONAL FACILITIES CITED AS
CAUSE OF JUVENILE DELINQUENCY

And as newspapers search for reasons that can be crammed into eye-catching head-lines, supermarket magazines offer articles entitled:

THE SECRET OF A HAPPY MARRIAGE

or

HOW YOUR BIRTH ORDER DETERMINES
YOUR PERSONALITY

Pop culture encourages people to blame their problems on a single event in their lives—the "one cataclysmic event" theory of social causation. In television dramas, the kindly therapist helps the distraught woman remember the horrible experience that led, twenty years later, to her mental breakdown; and, released from the prison of her repressed memory, she walks out of his office into the waiting arms of husband and children, made whole again. Veterans, refugees, and victims of violent assaults often do suffer post-traumatic stress disorder (PTSD) from the devastating things they have seen and felt. But neither the development of their problems nor the solutions to them are ever that simple.

3. *Human service problems are the result of many intertwined personal pressures and social forces.* The problem of delinquency among young men and women in-volves so many different developmental stresses, such as family, peer, and school pressures, that it would not be possible to overcome delinquency by changing only one aspect of a teenager's life.

If we look at another of the headlines, we will find there is no compelling re-search data proving that when fewer women worked outside the home, youth crime was substantially lower. Historically, poor and working-class women have al-ways had to work outside their homes to feed their families. And given both the current economy and the realities of many women's desire for jobs and careers, it is hardly practical to expect all mothers to stay at home, even if that would solve the problem.

It is also unlikely that just increasing the length of prison sentences would stop the crime epidemic. Who gets caught, the bail set, and the kind of punishment given are more often connected to the socioeconomic status and race of the alleged perpetrators than to guilt or innocence. And the debate on capital punishment

THE NEW SEXUAL REVOLUTION

Each major social change, for example, the sexual revolution, brings with it a host of both negative and positive consequences. This leads to the further proliferation of social programs to deal with them.

waxes and wanes, with no compelling evidence that it reduces the incidence of major crimes.

Although a severe lack of jobs, especially for young people, undoubtedly does encourage youngsters to resort to criminal behavior, jobs alone do not stop crime. Youth need to be trained adequately for rewarding jobs, and the ones offered must hold the promise of a future. In addition, if simply having a job assured honesty, we would not have the widespread white-collar fraud that has led to the downfall of many banks and stock companies.

Too much leisure time with nothing to do surely encourages some juvenile crime, especially vandalism, but recreation centers alone would not account for a large reduction in crime statistics. Video arcades, movie theaters, and even sports teams do not necessarily create mentally healthy people.

Rising delinquency rates probably do result from inadequacies in the family, the courts, the economy, the schools, and recreational facilities. Delinquency may be encouraged by lack of opportunity due to discrimination. It is also propelled by social attitudes that place an inordinate stress on consumerism. And it may also be encouraged by a general breakdown of social supports such as the church and extended family networks.

Finally, there is the individual enmeshed in all of these systems. Individuals bring with them their own strengths and weaknesses, some inborn and some learned, as well as their unique combination of luck and chance.

Another human service problem that is the result of many complex personal and social events is child abuse. Many people believe that child abuse is caused by poverty or that parents who were beaten as children will become abusive parents. But these two reasons account for only some unknown percentage of abuse. All victims of child abuse do not come from poor families, and many adults who were abused do not become abusers.

To understand the full dimension of any social problem, we must systematically analyze all of the contributory causes. To do this type of multicausality analysis, we drew a circle to represent the *whole problem* (see Figure 3.1). Then we divided it into several pie-shaped pieces. Each piece contributes to the whole problem.

As you study Figure 3.1, remember that many of the theories of causation are tentative. Some reasons have yet to be found, and we are not sure of the relative importance of each of the wedges to the total problem. Research in the field of child abuse reveals much contradictory data (Gary, 1991; Kadushin, 1980). After a few more years of study, we will probably omit one wedge or diminish its size. For example, we

When we work for social change, rarely do we expect to be the target of police action. But Cheri Honkala, a member of the Chippewa tribe, discovered what it felt like to be treated like a criminal when she joined a protest against the lack of affordable housing.

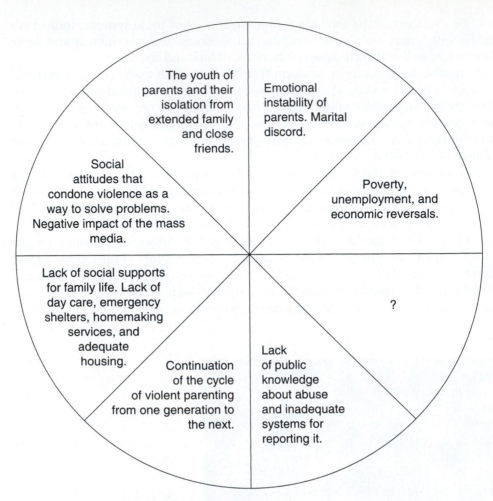

FIGURE 3.1   The possible causes of child abuse

used to think that poverty and harsh working-class-style discipline were the major contributors to abuse. Then, as our reporting systems improved, we became aware of many middle- and upper-class families who abused their children. These families might have avoided detection earlier because they used private doctors who were less likely than those in public hospitals to diagnose a bruise as a result of parental abuse or neglect. And in suburban schools, as opposed to inner-city schools, teachers rarely considered the possibility that a child's injury had been inflicted by his or her parents.

We have also realized that there are different forms of abuse and neglect. When sexual and emotional abuse are included in the definition, there is little doubt that this problem does not respect boundaries of socioeconomic class.

As you study the pie, you will notice that the several reasons for child abuse described are generated from different sources. The inner psychological pressures that drive adults to hurt children are intertwined with the exterior pressures exerted by social institutions and world events.

4. *Some causes of social problems are deeply rooted, and others are secondary causes or symptoms of a deeper problem.* After we look at the many causes that lie behind a human service problem, we must try to rank them in some order of priority. Then we focus our efforts for change on the causes that might have the most powerful impact. These are called the **root causes**—the reasons behind the reasons.

Usually the root causes are the most deeply buried and the most intractable. Visualize a large tree you want to remove from your garden. It is held in place by a series of roots, some close to the surface and others firmly embedded. The surface ones may be the easiest to remove, but they do the least to dislodge the whole tree.

Root causes The critical causes of a particular problem that seem to have contributed most significantly to its emergence.

We know, for example, that during periods of economic recession, there seems to be a rise in family violence. Yet we can do little to stop job layoffs in the automobile factories or recapture the market from foreign competitors. However, by recognizing the social costs of unemployment, we can work to establish more job-retraining programs. We can also lobby the federal government for extended unemployment benefits and organize support groups that help families deal with the upheaval in their lives without taking it out on their children and each other. And we can work for political candidates who share our values.

Exploring root causes, like everything else connected with causality, is a matter of action and reflection, trial and error. For example, a woman enters counseling convinced that her constant depression is a result of her husband's infidelity. Her husband complains that she is no longer willing to go out with him or entertain their friends as they used to. He feels rejected by her and has sought companionship in a series of brief affairs. After meeting with the couple together and separately, the counselor suggests that she visit yet one more physician. Although her family doctor had given her a clean bill of health, the specialist diagnoses her constant lack of energy as chronic fatigue syndrome. Unfortunately, there is no quick cure for this biological condition.

Perhaps the couple's situation will remain the same for a while, but the definition of the root causes of their problem is now very different. They might still need supportive therapy. He might still be unhappy with her inactivity, but he is likely to feel less rejected. Now, perhaps, he can be more understanding. If he is less angry, her mood is likely to improve. And if the basic commitment to each other is still strong, perhaps they can find new, more sedentary ways to enjoy being together.

5. *Although many people appear to have the same problem, they may have it for a different set of reasons.* If one were to visit a meeting of Alcoholics Anonymous (AA), it would be easy to assume that the participants were all there for the same major reasons. True, they all have problems with alcohol. But what constellation of

causes has led them to become alcoholics? There are many subgroups within this seemingly homogeneous assembly:

- Subgroup A includes people who were raised in an alcoholic family.

- Subgroup B includes people who are in a relationship with an alcoholic lover or spouse.

- Subgroup C includes people who have an undiagnosed and untreated biological condition such as **anxiety disorder** or **attention deficit hyperactivity disorder.**

- Subgroup D includes people who are in a profession that requires a great deal of social drinking.

- Subgroup E includes people who have recently experienced a major life trauma such as death, divorce, job loss, or diminished physical capacity.

Likewise, if one were to observe a group of eighteen third-grade students in a townwide tutoring program, it would be easy to assume that they all have the same problems. Even though they are all labeled learning disabled and their scores on a standardized reading test place them two years behind their peers, we may discover after getting to know them that:

- Three need eyeglasses and one needs a hearing aid.

- Two are very bright but have short attention spans.

- Three have a specific learning disorder, such as dyslexia.

- Five are attending a school that has large classes, inexperienced teachers, and a high staff turnover.

- Two have serious problems at home that divert their energy.

- One frequently comes to school hungry, cold, or physically ill.

- For two we can find no reasons at all (maybe they are just late bloomers).

Of course, each of the six causal factors just described are filtered through the screen of the child's unique personality and habitual way of coping. Just as there are no two identical faces in the world (except for identical twins), there are no two identical psychological profiles.

Figure 3.2 shows a multilayered maze that illustrates the many forces shaping our attitudes and actions. These forces begin to influence us from the moment our genetic makeup is determined by the combining of a sperm with an egg. The impact that sex, race, and physical abilities and disabilities will have on a specific child's future life will be mediated by his or her family, culture, neighborhood, and other significant events and groups.

Anxiety disorder
A biological condition in which feelings of extreme fear, tension, and dread often overwhelm the person, even when there is no apparent threat to their well-being.

Attention deficit hyperactivity disorder (ADHD)
A biological condition with early onset and often long duration that interferes with a person's capacity to focus and sustain interest, especially when the agenda is set by an outside authority, as in the school or work setting.

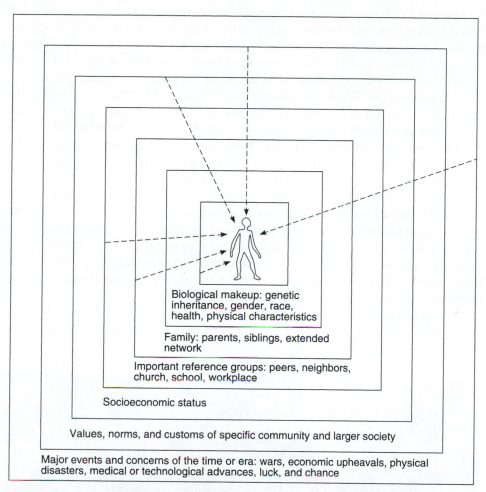

Biological makeup: genetic inheritance, gender, race, health, physical characteristics

Family: parents, siblings, extended network

Important reference groups: peers, neighbors, church, school, workplace

Socioeconomic status

Values, norms, and customs of specific community and larger society

Major events and concerns of the time or era: wars, economic upheavals, physical disasters, medical or technological advances, luck, and chance

FIGURE 3.2   Six sets of forces that shape our actions and attitudes

6. *Even when people encounter similar experiences, they do not necessarily react in similar ways.* In a very personal account of his internment in a Nazi concentration camp during World War II, the late psychologist Bruno Bettelheim (1950) wrote about being both victim and professional observer. He described the ways inmates adjusted to life under intolerable circumstances. Many died resisting the guards, others acquiesced almost humbly, some escaped, some collaborated, some took leadership roles for the first time in their lives. Differences among the prisoners seemed to be based on their life experiences before their internment and their personal characteristics, occupations, and skills, as well as on large doses of luck and chance.

It was impossible to predict in advance how concentration camp survivors would fare in the future. Some, like Bettelheim, gained strength from adversity and went on to have outstanding careers. Some became bitter, withdrawn, and distrustful. Still others became profoundly more appreciative of the basic pleasures of family and friends. Likewise, children who are too bright or creative for the class they are placed in do not all act alike. One simply grins and bears it, another withdraws into daydreams, another becomes the class clown, and another becomes the star pupil.

The concept of multicausality also helps to explain why siblings are often so different. Even though they grow up with the same set of parents, go to the same school, live in the same neighborhood, perhaps even have the same type of physical disability, we can never predict precisely how each one of them will think or act. Surprisingly, the reverse is also true. Scientists have identified cases in which identical twins, reared apart from birth, displayed remarkable similarities in adulthood. Although their environments were very dissimilar, their DNA—their genes—exerted a remarkable impact on their abilities and personalities.

Learning about the concept of multicausality helps us to understand why so many different strategies are needed to alleviate personal and social problems. It also helps us understand why so much experimentation accompanies any effort to intervene in a social problem. As our understanding of a problem deepens and the world changes, our strategies expand and change.

For example, those who believed that the availability of alcohol was the root cause of alcohol abuse lobbied long and hard to get it outlawed. They succeeded in

An excellent way to increase one's understanding of the world, both as a worker and as a citizen of the world, is to volunteer for a program such as Habitat for Humanity International. Volunteers work alongside local people to erect low-cost, quality housing.

passing the Eighteenth Amendment to the U.S. Constitution. The Prohibition Act banned the sale of alcoholic beverages all across the United States. Although it appeared to be a logical strategy of intervention, the act was a disaster. Criminals quickly took the place of the alcohol producers, and we had a situation that looked very much like the drug wars that are being fought in the streets of many U.S. towns today. The Prohibition Act was repealed in 1933 and liquor again became widely available. And, once again, it wreaks havoc on family life. Should we try to decriminalize drugs in the same way? What are the pros and cons of doing that? The debate rages on.

Some people are working to make alcohol less available by banning alcohol advertisements, raising the drinking age, and banishing alcohol from campus events. Can you think of five other strategies that might be used in the battle against alcohol abuse?

THE STRATEGIES OF INTERVENTION

Although workers use many strategies and assume different roles in various settings, their actions are neither random nor idiosyncratic. The Southern Regional Education Board (1969) surveyed a large number of human service workers in the field. They identified thirteen of the most consistently used worker roles or strategies of intervention. They have stayed the same from that time to the present even though many of the problem areas have changed. We added one more, and in Table 3.1 divided them into three categories: **direct-service strategies,** which deliver services directly to those in need; **systems-change strategies,** which create, maintain, or change the institutions and groups in which services are delivered; and a middle category of strategies that combines elements of direct-service work and elements of systems-change work. See also Ginsberg (1998) on careers in social work.

The boundary lines that separate one intervention from another and those that divide the direct-service from the systems-change strategies are fluid. A worker

Direct-service strategies Worker actions that deliver services directly to clients.

Systems-change strategies Acts aimed at helping clients by creating or improving the organizations that are supposed to deliver services to them.

TABLE 3.1   The Strategies of Intervention

Direct-Service	Both Direct-Service and Systems-Change	Systems-Change
Caregiving	Group facilitating	Planning
Case managing/counseling	Outreaching	Administering
Teaching/training/coaching	Mobilizing	Data collecting and managing
Behavior changing	Advocating	Evaluating/researching
	Consulting	
	Assisting a specialist	

Source: Categories derived from Southern Regional Education Board, 1969.

might shift from one intervention strategy to another over the course of a week or in the course of an hour. We warn the student that these worker strategies are not brand names like products on a supermarket shelf. Agencies may use them interchangeably or in ways that differ from the way we are defining them. But categories, although imprecise, are useful insofar as they help us visualize the two overarching goals of all human service interventions:

Disabilities Resource Center (DRC) An office that coordinates the academic support services that enable students with physical, mental, or educational disabilities to pursue their class work.

- Helping individuals change their lives

- Helping to improve the environments in which people function

The following interview with the coordinator of the **Disabilities Resource Center (DRC)** at a large university shows Ruth Bork using virtually every one of the direct-service and systems-change strategies. Once you have read the descriptions of the strategies that appear after the interview, go back and see if you can identify how she employs each of them in her daily work.

I N T E R V I E W

Ruth Bork, Administrator, Disabilities Resource Center

It is hard to believe that I've been in this job for over nineteen years. I was the first staff member hired, so I had the rare opportunity of starting an agency from the bare walls. My job has grown and changed so much. I work on a variety of levels, from the individual students all the way up to the president's office. Since the passage of the **Americans with Disabilities Act (ADA)**, my job has expanded even more.

Americans with Disabilities Act (ADA) A congressional mandate that guarantees many rights to people with physical and mental disabilities, especially in the fields of employment and architectural access.

My primary task is meeting the special needs for supportive services and accommodations of any student at the university who has a documented disability. This includes students who have significant visual or hearing impairments, problems with mobility, learning disabilities, or psychiatric conditions. Some of the students are permanently disabled from birth or through accident or illness. Some are temporarily disabled.

As my staff has grown, I've delegated more and more of my direct-service work. Now I do a great deal of supervision and administration. I keep one day each week to catch up on all my administrative paperwork but try to keep my contact with the students ongoing. I get much of my job satisfaction from meeting young people and watching them grow in self-esteem and confidence.

Counseling begins from the moment students are accepted. They need help in finding the package of resources that can get them through the class work and social life of a large university. For example, if a student has a mobility impairment, I review his or her program to make sure that the classes needed for his or her major are held in accessible buildings. If they aren't, I get the class moved. I also have to make sure that a student in a wheelchair can get from one part of the campus to another in the class break time. Nothing is worse for the student's morale than to have the class start without him or her or to keep everyone waiting.

Sometimes I advocate with a department chairperson for changes in the student's academic program because a learning disability makes mastering certain subject matter almost impossible. Perhaps a major is very prescribed, requiring certain courses in sequence, but the student can only handle a limited number of courses at one time. The university will have to make an exception. If there is fieldwork, we may have to arrange transportation; if there is a conference with an instructor, the student might need a sign language interpreter.

The DRC hires, trains, and schedules note takers, who sit in on classes and provide the student with a coherent set of notes. We have one staff member whose whole job it is to schedule sign language interpreters and note takers for students with a variety of limitations.

I'll arrange for books to be delivered if the student has a condition such as arthritis and has a hard time standing in a two-hour line at the bookstore. We make sure that the university library has the latest Braille writers and that the dorms are equipped with alarm systems and telephones for the visually and hearing impaired. Our students have a right to anything that gives them a level playing field with the able-bodied students. Equal opportunity means many different things.

Training and teaching the faculty and staff takes up a lot of my time. They need to be aware of the needs as well as the feelings of the different segments of the disabled population. I run workshops and conferences. I am available to consult with faculty on individual students in their classes.

The fastest-growing segment of the population we serve is the learning-disabled (LD) students. Their disabling condition is invisible. It requires a lot of consciousness raising to help professors realize that being late or incomplete on an assignment can be part of a biological disability. Many of the LD students take untimed tests in our office, where there are few distractions. Faculty members have to change their mindset from "lazy and unmotivated" to "student who needs organizational support services."

I encourage the students to tell the faculty what their abilities and disabilities are and what it is they need in order to get the most from school. Labels don't tell us much because every student, whatever his or her disability, has a different set of circumstances and personality.

I serve as the adviser to the DSO, the Disabled Students Organization. This is a social group, but more importantly, it is a voice for the students. One voice isn't very loud, but when several are raised all at once, the university pays attention. Sometimes the students win their demands and sometimes they have to compromise, but I still encourage them to make decisions and take action. Now the DSO is protesting because the administration plans to move our office. The new space is larger, but it will be in the subbasement. Some students see that as an insult. They have felt swept under the rug in their own communities, so they want a central location. I don't think they will win this battle, but I think it is worth voicing their opinions.

We also run support groups. These are led by the disabled students, counseling interns, and occasionally a faculty member. They help the students to realize that they aren't alone, and the more experienced students can pass on wisdom about the system. Instead of me deciding and telling others what needs to be changed, I can get varied opinions through the groups. They have been catalysts for improvements.

We've been working for many years to make the buildings on campus more accessible. Federal laws require that physical barriers be removed. For example, we now have chair lifts installed in the buildings, so wheelchair riders can go from one level to another. We also have published special maps of the campus so that a new student who uses a wheelchair can quickly learn how to get around. We take the barriers one at a time, and we work on a specific architectural modification. In the older buildings, that is very hard to do.

When I was a student here, the elevator in the main building had heavy doors that had to be opened by hand. This was impossible for a person in a wheelchair or for anyone with a back problem. That elevator has finally been replaced. Ramps have been built, and bathrooms have been modified in all the buildings. Elevators now have Braille numbers on the floor selector panels. Each of these improvements was carefully thought out and took months to accomplish.

I thought that the study of architectural modifications was completed in 1990, but additions to the ADA required us to reassess the campus for barriers. We reconvened a committee to do that. I also serve on several other committees representing the interests of our students. I am on the orientation committee, the student retention committee, and the group that advises the counseling center.

I don't have a disabling condition myself but several of the staff do. They help me to stay sensitive. I also try to keep up with my reading. I've just finished a book on counseling students with learning disabilities (Orentstein, 1999). It always amazes me how much more there is to learn. Our library is here for any students on campus who want to use it for their research.

I'd like to tell you what a typical day is like, but there is no such thing. A student may come in with a problem concerning a class or an internship. I may get a call from an administrator who wants information on the cost of a chair lift. Lately the university attorney has been struggling with some lawsuits that have been brought by staff members who have disabilities and don't feel they have been treated fairly. As people with psychiatric conditions move into the mainstream, there are more students and staff on campus who present challenges to faculty and administrators. I act as a consultant on those cases.

The problems I deal with range from A to Z—from administrative problems to zero sensitivity. For example, I might advocate on behalf of someone who's living in a building that needs to be made accessible and the landlord wants him or her out of there. So my work isn't contained just within the school. I deal with all the facets of our students' lives if they ask me to.

Networking and referral and resource collecting are important aspects of my work. If a student is having trouble with financial aid, the athletic department, or a roommate, that can be their most pressing concern. It needs to be addressed.

Resources for my students are everywhere. For example, I was working with a student who had a head injury from a car crash. She wanted to get involved with other young people like herself. I called around and found a Head Injury Foundation group in the suburbs. There wasn't one in this area, but she collected names of others who were interested. They met and I helped them start a group. I strive to empower people to help themselves and others.

I also have to keep sharpening my administrative skills as the job gets more complex. I have learned how to propose and keep a budget, do annual reports, write memos and action plans, do research, chair meetings, and speak up on behalf of the disabled-student population.

As the civil rights of people with disabilities expand, my office and my job also expand.

DIRECT-SERVICE STRATEGIES

Caregiving

When using a caregiving strategy, the bulk of a worker's time and effort are spent meeting the client's immediate needs. In jobs such as home health aide for the elderly, provider of **respite care** for the family of the physically handicapped child, or counselor in a residence or family planning clinic, the worker gives emotional support and physical care and helps in obtaining additional services. Ruth's office recruits part-time personal care attendants, workers who give direct care by helping a disabled student get ready in the morning, by note taking, or by reading to a student who is blind. They perform caregiving tasks in almost every one of the interventions. Many entry-level jobs in human service require that a large percentage of worker time be spent on caregiving tasks.

Respite care
Provision of a paid worker to relieve a person who is a primary caretaker so that the caretaker can pursue outside tasks or have some free time.

Case Managing/Counseling

Case-managing and counseling interventions aim at making sure that individuals locate and obtain the services for which they qualify. Vocational rehabilitation agencies, welfare departments, family agencies, hospitals, school systems, children's protective agencies, and large institutions such as city governments or universities employ workers who use these strategies.

Sometimes the worker is referred to as an *ombudsperson,* a Scandinavian word for a professional go-between, a red-tape cutter who carries a person's complaints to the highest authority. Workers who do counseling or case management are assigned a number of clients—a case load. They stay in touch with these people to make sure that services are reaching them. Because entitlements are often buried in many different laws, programs, or agencies, few people can find their way through the maze alone. Human service workers often organize hot lines and special resource centers so that connections can be made between the public and the programs they need.

Although human service workers provide emotional support and assist clients in finding and using services, generally they do not perform the type of insight counseling or therapy done by a more highly trained psychologist or clinical social worker.

Teaching/Training/Coaching and Behavior Changing

In recent years, more and more human service workers have been using teaching/training/coaching and behavior-changing interventions. They prepare clients of institutions or hospitals for an eventual move into a community residence and from there to living on their own. Through role-playing, guided field experiences, modeling, and reward systems, they teach survival skills to people who are physically or mentally disabled. These skills, which include finding and keeping a job, managing money, using public transportation, and enjoying recreational outlets, are called "the skills of daily living."

Such intervention strategies are also employed by public school staff workers as they try to mainstream (integrate) children with special needs into regular classrooms. A special-education worker may go into the home of a family to show parents techniques that will help their developmentally delayed preschooler do routine tasks and prepare for school. The use of an **early intervention program** is increasing in importance with every age group. The government agencies that fund programs have realized that money invested in solving problems early on saves a great deal of money down the line.

Early intervention program   Program that attempts to deal with a person's (often a child's) problem at the first sign of difficulty.

Human service workers often train peer leaders or mentors to help in the running of drug and alcohol awareness programs. Ruth uses these interventions when she orients new note takers and tutors or models techniques for faculty members to use when they have a student who is hearing impaired.

DIRECT-SERVICE AND SYSTEMS-CHANGE STRATEGIES

Group Facilitating

Traditionally, YMCAs and YWCAs, Scouts, 4-H clubs, Junior Achievement groups, settlement houses, and recreation centers have used group facilitating strategies. Group workers help members develop their leadership qualities, build confidence, and expand their skills and cultural awareness.

In recent years, the use of group techniques has grown beyond the recreational setting. The deinstitutionalization of the mentally ill and physically handicapped has led to the creation of many small, community-based programs. There are social clubs for ex-mental patients, prerelease centers for people completing jail sentences, and group homes for juvenile offenders. Day care programs for preschool children as well as for elderly and disabled adults also use group interventions.

Support groups bring together divorced parents, adult survivors of battering, persons caring for a person with AIDS, compulsive gamblers, overweight individuals, or older women entering the workforce for the first time. Human service workers may facilitate such a group. When an able peer leader emerges, they often withdraw, providing consultation as needed.

Many agencies use groups to orient new clients and volunteers. Some adoption and foster care agencies ask experienced parents to orient prospective ones, just as Ruth asks a junior or a senior to lead a support group for first-year students who share his or her disability.

Outreaching

Because she has learned that she can never simply sit in her office and wait for clients, Ruth has developed many creative outreach strategies. Through meetings, phone calls, and extensive networking, she spreads the message about the DRC's services to members of the university community. She invites them to visit the office and get to know her staff.

Mental and physical health agencies, recreation centers, and both private and government youth-serving agencies often employ outreach workers. They work with youth gang members to lessen inner-city violence. During the summer months, many suburban towns employ college students to monitor the town parks. They mingle with the neighborhood teenagers and try to head off the problems that often develop when teenagers with too much time and money hang out together. After they become accepted by the teens, they can plan recreational programs with them.

Outreach workers at day care centers and other early-childhood programs might visit churches and clinics to obtain referrals. They also spend their time sitting in living rooms and around kitchen tables answering questions about their program or sharing educational techniques. Departments of social service use outreach workers—sometimes called "home finders"—to locate and monitor appropriate foster homes for children, teens, and the elderly.

Prevention programs rely a great deal on outreach strategies. Some of you may have encountered a human service worker visiting your high school or Scout troop. Perhaps he or she showed a film and gave a talk to raise awareness about alcoholism, drug abuse, safe sex, or domestic violence. Perhaps the worker was there to recruit volunteers.

Mobilizing and Advocating

There has probably never been a day in the years she has worked at the DRC that Ruth has not heard at least one complaint from a student, a faculty member, or a staff member. Complaints are warning signs that something is not going as well as it should and needs to be improved. Working in a large university, she has often had to mobilize a great deal of clout to smooth out the rough spots. Perhaps a faculty member refused to let a student use a tape recorder even after the student explained why it was necessary. Ruth might have had to go up to the next level of authority, exerting pressure through the department chair, the dean of the college, or the academic provost.

Perhaps parents are futilely demanding that the city park department clean up a rubble-strewn lot so it can be used as a safe play space. They may turn to a human service worker to learn how to mobilize enough citizen pressure to get action.

On a more sophisticated level, perhaps a citizens' task force with a human service staff person is mobilizing public sentiment to exert pressure for the reorganization of an unresponsive school board or police department. Human service workers mobilize the power that brings about change at board meetings, at public forums, in the courts, and occasionally on picket lines.

Consulting and Assisting a Specialist

Human service workers using these interventions share their special knowledge and skills with clients, the public, and other professionals. Since July 1992, when the Americans with Disabilities Act was supposed to be fully implemented, Ruth has been serving on a task force that monitors how well the university is complying with it. If there are problems with an employee who is deaf, she calls on her staff member who specializes in hearing impairments. If there are issues she does not know enough about, the university seeks another consultant.

Professionals from other fields tap the special knowledge of human service workers by organizing interdisciplinary teams. In an adolescent psychiatric unit of a hospital, for example, each patient is assigned a team composed of a doctor, a nurse, and a human service worker. The human service worker generally interviews or visits the family and represents their needs when the team meets to evaluate each patient's progress.

When employed by a government licensing or monitoring board such as the Office of Elderly Affairs, human service workers visit nursing homes, for example, to make sure they are providing adequate care. If there are inadequacies, they share their expertise in programming, budgeting, or staff relations.

Some lawyers, doctors, and therapists employ human service workers to act as their eyes and ears with community groups or other mental health professionals. In this role, human service workers are likely to employ any one, or all, of the strategies discussed so far.

SYSTEMS-CHANGE STRATEGIES

Planning

Of course, planning is an integral part of all interventions. But some human service workers develop special expertise in this role. They spend most of their time researching, designing, organizing, monitoring, and evaluating a new or expanded program to fill a gap in the human service network. You are likely to find a planner hard at work in a library, at a computer terminal, or in the offices of foundations and government bureaucracies.

In small agencies such as community residences, all of the staff use planning interventions to organize fund-raisers, outings, social events, and volunteer orientations. Ruth started out using mostly counseling interventions, working one on one with each student. But now, as her staff has grown and her expertise has expanded, she has become so adept at planning that she could move into any setting and put together a program proposal to start a new service.

Administering

Although traditional human service agencies and government bureaucracies are most likely to be administered by an experienced staff person with an advanced degree in psychology, medicine, social work, or public administration, newer, small-scale institutions assign staff with human service degrees to administrative roles. Even a recent graduate may be given the job of directing a small program for mothers with AIDS or a shelter for women who have been battered. Although the center may only accommodate five or six women at a time, it requires the same range of skills needed to run a large hospital or school. Money must be raised and accounted for, the facility must be furnished and maintained, forms must be submitted, staff must be recruited and trained, and mailing lists and other clerical details must be completed.

Collecting and Managing Data

If a student at Ruth's university who has broken a leg on a ski trip cannot find out about the services available at the DRC, then the services are worth very little. The mushrooming of human service programs and entitlements on college campuses and in the larger community has led to new methods for finding, assessing, and utilizing resources. Compiling specialized resource booklets and designing web sites that are attractive and accessible are a vital human service skills. Keeping a computer updated with information on programs for eating disorders or narcotic addiction enables a counselor at the DRC to make a useful referral.

Laws are constantly changing. They are also written in legal language and are difficult to understand. Human service workers write pamphlets that translate complex legal jargon into standard English. With this information, a mother with a sick child and no money can find out how to apply for Medicaid or file an appeal if she is denied fuel assistance or food stamps.

Evaluating/Researching

Although human service workers are likely to turn to a variety of experts to find statistics and research data they too must be prepared to carry out a small-scale survey or a library search for up-to-date information on a particular disability or medication.

As community-based programs have become more decentralized, their funding sources have had to work harder to keep track of them. Human service workers need to learn to help design and implement evaluation plans. They collect statistics, interview clients, and write reports of program events. The funding or renewal of a program often depends on how well they have assessed client attitudes and needs and kept their services responsive to the population they serve.

At the end of each fiscal year, Ruth submits a budget request for the DRC for the upcoming year. She has been able to document the need for expanded budget and services through her systematic research. In addition, an outside evaluator visits the program each year, and Ruth assigns two staff members to help the evaluator assess student satisfaction with the services of the DRC.

ACTIVITIES AND TASKS USED TO IMPLEMENT EACH STRATEGY

The interview with Ruth Bork showed her using all of the strategies of intervention. What you could not see, however, is the way she goes about implementing them. Whether she is counseling a head-injured student, drafting a plan to remove an architectural barrier in a dormitory, or organizing an orientation meeting for faculty, she proceeds in an orderly way, using the same activities for each intervention.

Seven tasks must be performed in order to implement each strategy of intervention. A worker always begins by gathering data and ends by evaluating his or her work. Although we have listed these activities and tasks by number, we do not mean to imply that one must be completed before proceeding to the next. In actual practice, several may be done simultaneously. But the message we wish to impress on the reader is that our work is never random. *There is an underlying pattern of tasks needed to implement each strategy. If we skip one of the following tasks, we risk a failed intervention.*

1. Gathering data
2. Storing and sharing information
3. Negotiating contracts and assessing problems
4. Building a trusting relationship
5. Designing an action plan
6. Implementing the action plan
7. Monitoring and evaluating the work

Gathering Data

Ruth needs to paint the fullest picture possible of each student's problem situation. Yet it is much harder for her to collect relevant information than it would be if she were a biologist or physicist. Much of the data she collects and acts on is at best incomplete and variable. We cannot take a temperature or do a blood test to find accurate information. Sometimes a person's words may be cheerful but the tone of voice reveals pain. To more fully understand the emotions behind words and to grasp the complexity of each student's situation, Ruth uses many data-gathering techniques.

She collects data through interviews, reading, research, and attending conferences and workshops. Only after the data have been gathered can she begin to plan how to help each student.

INTERVIEWING

Interviewing underlies all of Ruth's work. The quality of information she gathers before making a plan depends on how skillfully she conducts an interview. The first part of the interviewing process is asking appropriate questions. Through role-playing in a class or a training situation, students develop skill in phrasing questions in a way that avoids steering the listener into a preconceived path or into a verbal trap. Ruth has learned when to ask open-ended questions that provoke maximum expression. She uses focused questions to elicit accurate information about dates, times, and places. She often asks for clarification.

When asking questions and listening to a client's or colleague's thoughts, she uses her active-listening skills. *Active listening* is distinguished from the more passive kind of *social listening* by its total concentration. She remembers precisely what has been said and reflects back ideas and feelings to make sure she understands.

Active observing is also part of interviewing. Ruth tries to grasp the full significance of what is being said by assessing the emotional tone of the words as well as by observing facial expressions, hand movements, posture, and gestures—in other words, body language.

READING, RESEARCHING, AND ATTENDING
CONFERENCES AND WORKSHOPS

Usually some historical records can be gathered before starting an intervention. The counselors at the DRC have access to each of their clients' test scores and high school grades as well as statements from guidance counselors and doctors. When a new worker is assigned to the Learning Disabled Students' Support Group, notes from past meetings that were compiled by previous group leaders can be useful. Human service workers read whatever background data they can find. But all information has limitations. Records are written by people who have brought their own biases to the recording or testing process.

Much data gathering goes on at case conferences or committee meetings. Sometimes workers do their data gathering at libraries. In the professional journals, they learn about a research or demonstration project on a particular problem. They go to workshops where clients, coworkers, or professionals from allied fields gather to share information.

An integral part of data gathering is focused visiting and observing. In some programs, this involves visiting the homes, classrooms, or workplaces of clients to gain some firsthand insights into their strengths and weaknesses as they interact with the system. Visiting another program can be a refreshing treat for workers who have been locked into the routine of their own agency.

Storing and Sharing Information

One of Ruth's crucial responsibilities is keeping records. Information is never randomly jotted down. Recording has a purpose, and the DRC workers practice the skills of focused note taking. Professional recordings or minutes separate a worker's personal evaluation or judgment from the observable or verifiable data.

Careful collecting and sharing of information is a direct expression of respect for clients and coworkers. It also protects workers from accusations of mismanagement. Ruth needs to document how money has been spent by her staff, and she must keep track of her clients' unmet needs.

Negotiating Contracts and Assessing Problems

Nothing defeats the helping process as much as a lack of direction. For each new intervention, Ruth negotiates a working contract, which articulates mutual expectations and the rules of the road with clients, faculty, and colleagues. A contract might be written or verbal, but it must be clear. And it often changes over time as reality shapes goals.

Building Relationships

Ruth begins building a relationship with a student (or faculty member or administrator) from the first moment of contact. She continues to nurture the relationship throughout the helping process. The primary tool all workers must have is their ability to communicate warmth, concern, empathy, and knowledge.

If Ruth cannot gain the trust of students or colleagues, she will be ineffective, no matter what else she is able to do. In each of the strategies, relationship building is critically important. The case manager/counselor must be able to energize and empower people just as much as the agency administrator or researcher.

Designing and Implementing Action Plans

Many social agencies, especially those that receive public funds, require that a formal action plan be written and accepted by client and worker before any services begin. These plans commit to paper the problems, the goals, and the specific ways they will be worked on within a set period of time. Formal written plans are used extensively with special-education services in public schools. By law the school staff, the human service workers, the client (if old enough or competent enough), and the family must all sign a statement that they have been part of the process of deliberation and agree to implement the Individual Education Plan, or IEP.

In programs that employ behavior modification approaches or in which basic survival skills are being taught, Individual Service Plans (ISPs) help both worker and client be clear about the small tasks that must be worked on from day to day. In Ruth's office, there is a written plan in each student's file. Both the student and the case manager sign the plan and review it periodically.

For a first-year student who has both receptive and expressive language problems, Ruth suggested the following items for her action plan:

1. For the first semester she will take a reduced load of two courses.

2. A note taker will accompany her to class.

3. Three times a week she will attend the DRC for skill building with a tutor and three other students.

4. She will continue seeing an occupational therapist twice a month to help her with eye–hand coordination.

5. She will attend two workshops on study skills offered by the counseling and testing center.

6. She will arrange to take some vocational preference tests at the counseling center to help her decide on a major.

7. She will check back in with Ruth three times during the quarter for fifteen-minute sessions to evaluate each of the preceding activities.

To make sure each part of the plan is implemented, Ruth will write a memo to the staff member who schedules tutors, write a letter to the department chair explaining the need for the reduced course load, and send a referral form for testing. During the fifteen-minute check-in sessions, she will offer an attentive ear and a *lot* of encouragement.

Monitoring and Evaluating Our Work

Because individuals, environments, and social interactions are in perpetual motion, human service workers become skilled at critically looking at and reshaping their contracts, relationships, action plans, and methods of implementation. A worker who is in tune with the dynamic state of the problem-solving process is always asking questions: How are we doing? What seems to be getting in the way of X, Y, and Z? Have I fully understood how the client feels about this?

In order to answer these questions, the worker needs to learn how to use a variety of evaluative feedback techniques. Obviously, the client is the primary source of feedback. Workers also use supervision or consultation from more experienced colleagues to check on how their work is progressing.

Sometimes workers administer small survey questionnaires. Case records, statistical data on meetings, referrals, visits, and other daily activities form the basis of evaluation reports or summaries. These reports can then compare one period of time with another, one client group with another, and one intervention strategy with another.

PUTTING TOGETHER THE INTERVENTIONS AND THE ACTIVITIES

Now that we have described the human service interventions and the activities that are used to implement them, the pattern underlying all of Ruth's work should become clear.

Figure 3.3 is a page from Ruth's calendar book listing the notations that she made about three appointments. On this particular day, she will be using a planning intervention for a meeting with the architects, using a group-facilitating intervention with new faculty members, and using a counseling intervention with a student in crisis.

Figure 3.4 shows the three interventions from the appointment book listed down the left-hand side of the chart. The seven activities Ruth will use to implement each intervention are listed across the top. As you can see, she has already begun each of these interventions by gathering data. Of course, what Ruth needs to find out and where she will go to get that information will be different for each intervention.

To collect data for her meeting with Larry Colvin, an architect, Ruth read two manuals on modifications of alarms for the hearing impaired and the blind and visited a college with a building similar to the one they will be discussing.

Before she speaks to the new faculty members about teaching students who are handicapped, she will review the results of a recent attitude survey. Each of the students served by the DRC was asked to describe specific faculty behaviors that encouraged their learning and those that hindered it. The faculty members need to hear these statements "from the horse's mouth."

Before she interviews Margaret, she will gather data by looking at the student's admissions file, speaking to the nurse at the health service, and interviewing the

---

Schedule for Tuesday, September 10th

10:00 A.M.:   Meet with the architect to review plans for new fire alarm system for disabled students in Croner Hall.

(A PLANNING INTERVENTION)

12:00–2:00 P.M.:   Lunch meeting—Lead a discussion on teaching students who have documented disabilities. Orientation of new faculty members.

(A GROUP-FACILITATING INTERVENTION)

3:00–4:00 P.M.:   Meet with Margaret Clinton; she has severe asthma and is thinking of dropping out.

(A COUNSELING INTERVENTION)

FIGURE 3.3   Sample calendar

ACTIVITIES NEEDED TO IMPLEMENT THE INTERVENTIONS							
		Gather Data	Store and Share Information	Negotiate Contract	Build Relationships	Design Action Plan	Implement Plan	Monitor and Evaluate
THE INTERVENTIONS	Drafting the plan for the dormitory	Read manuals and visit a college dorm						
	Organizing orientation meeting for faculty	Review results of survey of students' attitudes toward faculty behavior in class						
	Counseling a new student	Review admission file; speak to dorm counselor; interview student						

FIGURE 3.4   A model of the activities a worker engages in for each intervention employed
We have filled in the first column. On the left side of this chart, we list three interventions that a worker would likely carry out during the day. Across the top of the chart, we list each of the activities the worker would perform to carry out the interventions. We filled in the activities for gathering data; can you fill in the rest?

dorm counselor who knows her best. She will also tap into her many years of experience to assess the degree of crisis in Margaret's situation.

After she collects the necessary information, Ruth will store it in the form of notes, memos, or other written communication. She will need to file it carefully so it is at her fingertips when she needs it again. Then she will think about the contract she has negotiated with the architect, the faculty group, and the student. What can she do for them? What does each of them expect of her? And so it will continue through each of the activities, until she completes the intervention and evaluates how it has gone and how it might go better next time.

The next time you are assigned a new task in your fieldwork, before you panic, take a deep breath and visualize this chart. Begin to make a list of the background information you will need. The more systematically you proceed in collecting data, the more confident you will be when you negotiate contracts, build relationships, and design and implement your action plans.

The chapters in the second section of this book (Chapters 7–12) will describe the strategies and activities we have just introduced in this whirlwind tour of a human service worker at work.

Often several human service strategies are combined in one event. These students planned and are now conducting a Valentine's Day flower and cake sale. With the money raised, they will purchase books to use when they volunteer as tutors for women at a local prison.

SUMMARY

1. Solutions to social problems should flow from a diagnosis of the causes of the problems.

2. The uniqueness of people and their problems calls for diverse, tailor-made interventions.

3. Strategies of intervention are overall approaches to the helping process that have been identified by studying the tasks that workers do in their daily practice.

4. All of the intervention strategies are necessary and equally important. They are used at different times by the generalist worker. Some workers specialize in a few of the strategies.

5. The fourteen strategies can be divided into those that directly assist the person with the problem and those that maintain or change the systems within which the person interacts and services are delivered.

6. The direct-service strategies are caregiving, case managing/counseling, teaching/ training/coaching, and behavior changing. The mixed direct-service and systems-change strategies are group facilitating, outreaching, mobilizing, advocating, consulting, and assisting a specialist. The systems-change strategies are planning, administering, data collecting and managing, and evaluating/researching.

7. The seven worker activities used for each intervention are gathering data, storing and sharing information, negotiating contracts and assessing problems, building a trusting relationship, designing an action plan, implementing the action plan, and monitoring and evaluating the plan.

8. By looking closely at three strategies of intervention used in Ruth's work as coordinator of the Disability Resource Center, we can see how she follows a similar pattern, always starting with data gathering and progressing through the other activities that end with monitoring and evaluating the work that has just been done.

DISCUSSION QUESTIONS

1. In the discussion of multicausality we assert that just as there are no two identical faces in the world (except for same-egg twins), there are no two identical psychological profiles. What might account for the often enormous differences in the personalities and interests of two siblings raised in the same family? For example, one might be an honor student and school council leader while the other lives for sports and is content to be at the bottom of her class.

2. Ruth Bork provides many services for special needs students, the largest segment of which are learning disabled. How fair do you think it is for the "mainstream students" when their LD classmates are given extra time for tests or can have a person take notes for them in class? Discuss the differences between "equal treatment" of students and "equitable treatment" of students.

3. How might you explain to an engineering major the reasons why organizing a bake sale to raise money for a tutoring program is a valid educational experience for a human service class?

WEB RESOURCES FOR FURTHER STUDY

Students with Disabilities
www.dyslexia.com

The first site listed explores the positive sides of learning disabilities and suggests therapies and teaching methods suited to the dyslexic learning style.

www.makoa.org

The second site is a directory of every kind of disability resource and links leading to accurate, informative sources. Each disability has several of its own web sites.

Strategies
www.geocities.com/heartland/4862/cswhome.html
www.socialworksearch.com
www.gwbweb.wustl.edu/website.html

For more data on each of the strategies and problem areas mentioned in the chapter, see these comprehensive sites. They provide links to social service resources in a wide range of practice areas, problems, and populations.

CHAPTER 4

Attitudes/Values, Skills, and Knowledge

We begin this chapter by going on a quick tour of the human service agencies in a typical urban center. Based on the material presented in the previous three chapters, we should expect to find much diversity of title, role, agency setting, and strategies of intervention. But you might be surprised to discover that the people covering the phones at a hot line, conducting a neighborhood meeting, and working at a community residence also have very different levels of training, ranging all the way from a volunteer to a social worker with a graduate degree. The reader might now wonder what on earth all of these people have in common. In this chapter, we look at what it is that binds all of these human service workers together, despite the apparent differences in their agencies and backgrounds.

We assert that all competent human service workers are characterized by their ability to cre-ate a disciplined helping relationship that, though similar to a friendship, varies in essential ways. We describe the content of that professional relationship, which is composed of *attitudes* and *values, skills,* and *knowledge.* Together they form an integrated whole, with attitudes and values as the bedrock. They are the first aspects of professional education. Grounded on this solid base, we then learn about and practice human service skills and knowledge.

After describing many of these values and attitudes, skills, and knowledge areas that a helper must acquire, we reassure the reader that no person ever fully masters them all. These are pathways we travel, rather than destinations we will reach. Having a model helps us chart the course of our progress and our direction for future professional development.

If we were to go on an around-the-clock tour of the human service agencies in Urban Center, U.S.A., we might find:

1. A young college student and a middle-aged homemaker hunched over telephones in a church basement, listening with great care to the words of the people on the other end of the lines. One of the callers is a recently widowed elderly man talking about ending his life. The other caller is a frightened teenager pouring out an anguished account of date rape.

2. In a union hall on the other side of town, an articulate, angry woman is holding the rapt attention of her neighbors at the weekly strategy meeting of the Citizens United for Economic Justice. Though she had to quit school after the sixth grade, she is organizing a campaign to raise welfare benefits for the poor people in this community. They have been suffering from a recent upsurge in unemployment. The next speaker has a degree in political science. He is an outreach

worker for a legal services program. He explains the intricacies of lobbying at the state house in support of subsidized, affordable health care.

3. In an old but brightly painted two-story house, a young man, a rehabilitation counselor, is teaching a cooking class to four adults. Though totally blind, they are preparing themselves for the day when they will leave this community residence to move into their own apartments.

As we continue our tour, we will meet workers who have a dizzying array of titles, qualities, styles, backgrounds, and motivations. Most typically, they will be working as parts of teams or coalitions that combine lay persons and professionals. They are working as staff members or are serving on committees and boards, sharing their expertise and uniqueness. At times, this mixture of people from different backgrounds is cooperative and supportive; sometimes it is abrasive or adversarial. Often lay people and professionals work in different ways toward similar goals.

So far we have seen incredible diversity in the roles, titles, agencies, and interventions of the profession. Without a doubt, it *is* infinitely easier to describe the training of a doctor, lawyer, printer, chemist, or elementary school teacher. Each draws on a specific body of knowledge and skill. Each works in a limited number of institutions or roles. Usually there are great differences between the abilities of these professionally trained workers and the ordinary "man in the street." We wouldn't feel very safe having our tonsils taken out by a garage mechanic who did a little surgery in his spare time.

This is not true in the human services. The highly trained professional, the person with a recent degree from a community college, a hot-line volunteer counselor who makes her living as an insurance broker, and a fellow sufferer in a support group all can play pivotal helping roles.

The fact that many types of people are helpers—caregivers, counselors, organizers, group leaders, and activists—does not make our profession any less dignified or prestigious. In fact, this inclusiveness is its strength.

So, what is it that binds all human service workers together? We think it is the common core of attitudes and values, skills, and knowledge of the helping relationship. Although formal training in college is likely to increase the competence of a human service worker, many people from all walks of life can share some common attributes. *Effective helping is both an art and a science.* The artistic qualities are definable but we cannot always teach them in a classroom. Creativity, compassion, and warmth, for example, are attributes a person is likely to have *before* entering a training program.

Let's look first at the helping relationship and its common attributes.

THE PROFESSIONAL HELPING RELATIONSHIP

A key element shared by all human service workers is the **professional helping relationship** they build with their clients. It differs in both structure and content from the purely social relationship.

Professional helping relationship
A relationship between a worker and client(s) that follows a pattern determined by the goals and ethics of the human service field.

In our *personal* lives, we might accompany a friend to a nursing home to lend moral support as he visits a dying grandmother. We might take care of a child while her parents go out to vote or attend an open-school night. In our *professional* role, we might talk about a baseball game with the members of a foster parent group before their meeting begins. However much these interactions might seem similar, our friendships and our professional helping relationships are uniquely different and the competent helper is always aware of this.

The Structure of the Professional Helping Relationship

Five qualities distinguish the professional relationship from the purely social one.

1. *The professional helping relationship exists for a limited time, whereas friendships might last forever.* In a professional helping relationship, a time schedule may be agreed on at its inception. For example, a worker and a group of teenagers who are physically handicapped might agree to spend six sessions discussing issues of sexuality. Or a worker in a rehabilitation agency might say: "We shall work together until my client has found a job and seems to have settled into it."

Whatever its duration, we commit ourselves to ending the relationship just as soon as the client no longer needs it. We strike a subtle balance between setting someone adrift too soon and hanging on so long that we encourage dependency.*

Saul Alinsky (1969, 1971), a pioneering community activist, always stressed that the human service worker who built a strong neighborhood action group should expect eventually to be thrown out by the indigenous leadership. Once the group members develop skill and self-confidence, they are likely to view the outside professional as excess baggage. Strange as it sounds, the aim of all human service workers is to work themselves out of the professional helping relationship and maybe even out of a job.

2. *The professional helping relationship has a clear focus, whereas friendships have many purposes—some superficial, others profound—most of them vague.* Though the focus of a professional helping relationship may change as it progresses, both client and worker need to agree on an initial set of tasks, stated in action outcomes:

> "I am going to this vocational counselor because I want to find a job so I can leave the hospital and be on my own."

or

> "I came to Renewal House because I need a safe shelter from my husband, who has been beating me. As soon as I find an apartment, get some legal help, and sort out my finances, I will move out."

---

*Unfortunately, in an age of managed care and cost cutting, forces outside our own reasoned judgment may decide when the professional helping relationship must terminate. This will be discussed further in Chapter 9.

or

"I work for the Children's Protective Services and have been asked to visit you and your daughter to see if you can use any of our services for families."

The helper and helpee **negotiate a contract** in which tasks and goals are spelled out. Some of these initial goals are likely to change. Sometimes the contract is a grudging one. Perhaps the client has been forced to see the worker in order to earn extra privileges on the locked ward of a mental hospital or to gain early release from prison. (The concept and skills involved in contracting are discussed more fully in Pincus & Minahan, 1973; Shulman, 1979; and Zayas & Katch, 1989.)

Negotiate a contract An attempt on the part of the helper and the helpee to forge an agreement about what will be included in their work together.

3. *The professional helping relationship depends on a division of labor.* Although friends often complement each other in many ways, the division of roles and responsibilities in a social relationship is random. The professional helping relationship is a *collaboration* but each of the parties has specified tasks. The person being helped shares expertise about the problem—basic facts as well as fears, hopes, and expectations. The helper shares knowledge of resources, alternative strategies, obstacles, and the prospects of different courses of action. Each has the right to make certain decisions. Whenever possible, most of the decisions should be made by the client, who must live with the decisions.

4. *The professional helping relationship is disciplined, whereas in a friendship each person is relatively free to act on impulse.* Of course, friends learn what to do and what to avoid if they want their relationship to last. In the professional helping relationship, much of the informal trial and error is replaced by a set of *operating principles*.

Even when the human service worker appears to be horsing around in the locker room with the basketball team member or drinking coffee with her parents, she is behaving in a conscious manner. Workers can relax, but they cannot lose track of the tasks that need to be done. The role of the worker is not to solve the clients' problems but to be a *catalyst* in the problem-solving process.

Even in informal settings, everything the client says must be kept confidential. Throughout the book, we will discuss the realistic difficulties in maintaining absolute **confidentiality.** But as a general principle, workers accept this basic tenet of the helping relationship.

Confidentiality Keeping information that the client reveals to the worker secret.

Although a recreation leader might have a splitting headache or a devastating family problem, on the job his or her personal issues take a back seat. Disciplined workers can, to an amazing degree, ignore their own illness or personal troubles when working. Afterward, in the privacy of their own homes, these irritants might resurface, as annoying as ever.

5. *The professional helping relationship is built on acceptance.* A friendship without some degree of mutual attraction is likely to end as soon as a more appealing companion comes along. A professional helping relationship, however, is not built primarily on mutual attraction. Without judging (or perhaps even liking) a client, the worker tries to understand the person's problem, accepting feelings without

necessarily condoning specific acts. Of course, if a worker cannot emotionally connect on *any* level with the essential humanness of a client's predicament, the client should probably be reassigned to someone else (Keith-Lucas, 1972).

From the helpee's point of view, physical or intellectual attraction may make a counseling relationship more pleasant, but the ultimate success of the relationship will be gauged by how much help was received in overcoming the helpee's problems.

The Content of the Professional Helping Relationship

Although the structure of the professional helping relationship sets the stage for competent human service intervention, its content—words and acts—is, of course, most important. Figure 4.1 illustrates the three components of this content.

These three components are the threads that bind all human service workers into a profession, whatever their title, label, or academic certification. *Attitudes* are feelings or thoughts about people or things; *values* are the worth we place on them. A person might be described as warm and outgoing; these traits are expressions of attitude. How important others think these qualities are depends on how high or low a value they place on such personality traits.

It is not always easy to separate attitudes and values from skills and knowledge. All are inextricably interwoven in our work. We will separate them into categories only because it is easier to describe them that way.

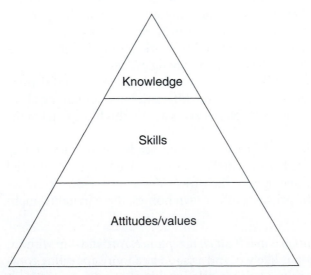

FIGURE 4.1   The pyramid model of the components of the helping relationship

THE PYRAMID MODEL

Professionals in every field require a combination of attitudes and values, skills, and knowledge, a constellation that has been dubbed the "ASK" concept (Schulman, 1991). In Figure 4.1, we represent the three components in the form of a pyramid. Any professional who lacks one of these components will be less than satisfactory. For example, a doctor who is a brilliant diagnostician (skills and knowledge) but also is cold and brusque (attitude) and lacks a comforting bedside manner might slow down the patient's recovery. The racetrack driver who has the bravado to compete (attitude) but has not carefully studied the engine in his new car (knowledge) is likely to lose the race or have an accident.

Of course, the constellation of specific attitudes and values, skills, and knowledge varies from one profession to another. Those of the engineer, for example, are very different from those of the typical human service worker. Vocational preference tests are constructed on the assumption that by studying the attitudes and values of members of occupations, a profile of the typical worker can be constructed. As students answer questions about their attraction or repulsion to different ideas or activities, they move closer to the norms of one occupation and further away from others.

Not only do the attitudes and values, skills, and knowledge areas vary from one occupation to another, but so too do the *relative importance* of each dimension. For example, in the training of doctors, knowledge and skill are stressed the most. That annoying doctor who lacks an empathetic bedside manner (attitude) can still be elected to high office in a medical society for her brilliance as a diagnostician. She's even likely to be sought out by anxious patients willing to put up with gruffness as the price of being cured.

With human service workers, however, all three dimensions have *equal weight*. Their work is very holistic, perhaps more so than any other profession. But each component of their work must be built on the base of appropriate attitudes and values.

For example, it is possible for a guidance counselor to be knowledgeable but be of no help to a student. Perhaps you have met Mr. Schroder. He knows all about college requirements and the Scholastic Aptitude Tests (SATs). But if he does not have the warmth to relax that shy, inarticulate student sitting before him, he may never find out what Eric *really* wants to do after graduation. Lacking empathy and insight (attitudes and values), he doesn't sense Eric's ambivalence about going to college. He rambles on. Eric barely hears him and will soon forget what he has been told. Mr. Schroder never notices that although Eric has ostensibly come for college counseling, he wants to take time off from school but is worried about hurting his parents.

Or consider Ms. Jorgensen, who announces to Alice at the start of their interview that her record indicates that she "isn't college material" or that "girls shouldn't go into airplane mechanics because it is a man's field." All Ms. Jorgensen's well-meaning advice about the advantages of secretarial school will fall on deaf ears. Alice withdraws, feeling labeled and pigeonholed. Perhaps she does need to think more carefully about her choices, but the abrupt judgment thrust on her by the guidance counselor is a setback to the vocational exploration that needs to get done.

These two workers giving vocational counseling do not show a grasp of key attitudes and values. They have not analyzed their stereotypes about the ideal college student or the proper occupational roles for women. They have not spent time getting to know the unique person who sits across from them. By not being self-aware and sensitive, they are likely to continue to discourage other students. Perhaps a young woman yearns to be a doctor or carpenter or a young man has an intense but self-conscious interest in nursing or early childhood education. How might they react to judgment-laden advice from counselors who are unaware of their own biases?

Attitudes and Values Form the Base of the Pyramid

Human service education and work must always start from a solid base of appropriate attitudes and values. On that base, knowledge and skill can then be added. Some people argue that human service work is based much more on profound faith than it is on theory and skills. The late Paul Halmos (1966), a British sociologist, carefully analyzed the literature of the field of counseling and concluded that:

> The literature of counseling is an inspired literature as much as it is a scientific one, and even in their ascetic disowning of inspiration the counselors testify to an inspired dedication.... They use a language of reverence, and even a theological language and imagery, as if they could not do their job effectively without their evocative power.... The counselor applies himself in a way which suggests a set of convictions, a powerful mood, a moral stance, a faith. (pp. 6–7)

Halmos went on to assert that counselors seemed rather ashamed of subscribing so outspokenly to humanistic values and relying so heavily on them. They feared that might make their theory seem less scientific. He urged them not to feel shame but to be proud to be the bearers of those values.

Although attitudes form the base of the pyramid, they are not in themselves sufficient to help the person who must take the next steps in solving the problem. The worker at the local mental health agency who is filled with empathy (attitude) for the family of a recently blinded child might be able to give appropriate emotional support, but if she does not know how to find the best resources for the education, recreation, and rehabilitation of children who are blind (skills and knowledge), she won't be of much assistance.

Bruno Bettelheim, an eminent psychologist, underscored this point in the title of his landmark book on working with disturbed children: *Love Is Not Enough* (1950). He asserted that human service work, like effective parenting, is a combination of love coupled with wisdom and the skills to communicate both.

The pyramid concept is especially important to understand as you begin your training. Most human service educators visualize the pyramid in their minds even if they do not draw this diagram for their students. Their teaching style assumes that the starting point is attitudes and values. They often use first names, encourage students to share their backgrounds, sit in a circle, and stimulate discussion to elicit students' ideas on controversial topics. Although they are using a method of interaction aimed at helping class members sharpen their self-awareness and self-confidence, students sometimes worry that the class is not academic enough. One faculty member expressed her surprise at the students' hesitant reactions to her teaching style.

> At each class session, I would come into the classroom hoping to find the students buzzing to each other about their fieldwork or the controversial speaker we'd heard the day before. Instead, they'd be sitting seats apart from each other in the vastness of the lecture hall. They waited for me to start, as if nothing could happen among them until I arrived. Every day I'd insist they get up, push the tables to the side, and form the chairs into a circle. Although they were much more animated when sitting in a circle, they still seemed to view the furniture moving as a pointless waste of energy. They resisted, and I got frustrated. I felt that they did not believe that listening to each other's ideas and experiences was an important part of their education.
>
> After that disappointing semester, I got the idea of starting off my first class with a discussion of the attitudes/values, skills, and knowledge pyramid. Once the students understood that we were exploring the attitudes and values at the base of the triangle—as we played name games or argued about capital punishment—they stopped worrying about memorizing my words to repeat back for the final exam. They even stopped resenting the work involved in moving chairs around into a circle.

These students realized, as we hope you do, that without a firm, broad base, a pyramid will topple over!

ATTITUDES/VALUES, SKILLS, AND KNOWLEDGE: AN OVERVIEW

Table 4.1 lists the attitudes and values, skills, and knowledge areas that are of vital importance to the professional helper. We have already warned you that the categories are bound to overlap. In addition, our list is neither definitive nor exhaustive. Your course instructor or field supervisor is likely to say of us, "They have missed this vital concept or given too much importance to that one.

It is easy to understand differences in emphasis. If you compare the catalogue description of the program you are enrolled in with a similar one at another college, you will probably find much variation in the courses offered and the competencies stressed. Because human service programs are relative newcomers on most campuses, they have grown out of, or remain under the wing of, more established behavioral fields. They take their coloration from the particular academic department that gave them life. If the program is under the wing of the Psychology Department, the course content stresses counseling and interpersonal skills, whereas course work

TABLE 4.1   The Content of the Helping Relationship

Attitudes/Values	Skills	Knowledge

Patience	Data gathering
	   Interviewing—active looking,
	   listening, and question asking
	   Observing
	   Researching
	   Attending conferences
	   Visiting
		Human growth and development

Empathy		Abnormal growth and development
Self-awareness		
Capacity to deal with ambiguity and take risks		The impact of society and culture on behavior

Willingness to ask for help and offer feedback	Storing and sharing information
	   Keeping records
	   Writing reports
		The dynamics of groups and organizations

Belief in people's and systems' capacity to change	Building relationships	The social and political forces that affect helping
Open-mindedness, skepticism, and rejection of stereotypes	Negotiating contracts	Social problems, special populations, and resources
Humor and a light touch	Forming action plans	Issues of research and evaluation

	Implementing action plans
	   Intervening
	   Referring	

	Monitoring and evaluating
	   Giving and receiving feedback
	   Constructing evaluations	

emphasizing social, cultural, and institutional elements of mental health and treatment might take a backseat.

The reverse is true of the programs that the authors of this book have taught in. Our academic backgrounds are more sociological. We stressed social change, social welfare policy, and group and community interventions.

Whatever their predominant focus, most human service programs incorporate many dimensions of human behavior and use methods that provoke active learning of concepts and skills. (See National Organization of Human Service Education on p. 85.)

Before reading the descriptions of human service attitudes and values, skills, and knowledge, rest assured that no human service worker ever masters all of them. Each of us understands, accepts, or integrates some areas better than others. As challenges occur, such as a new job or an unusual situation, we stretch ourselves to learn more, sharpen our skills, and explore the impact of our attitudes and values on our current tasks.

Most of us are likely to change direction several times in our careers. Sometimes the change is a response to political upheaval; sometimes it is a move to renew ourselves and avoid burning out as work becomes too draining. We may have

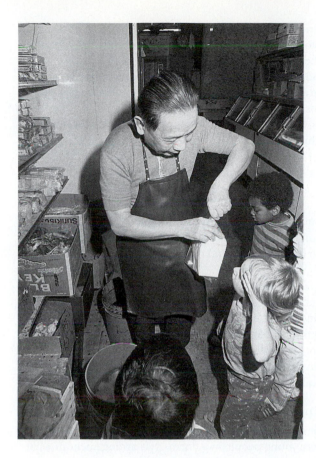

Our beliefs about the value of people of differing classes, ethnic groups, ages, and genders begin early. These nursery school children are learning to respect varying lifestyles by taking trips around the city and being exposed to differences and similarities in the families and cultural backgrounds of their classmates.

counseled individual clients for many years and then discovered that we enjoy managing or planning an agency. Some workers start their careers by doing recreation with children who have disabilities and then later engage in advocacy with the elderly or with troubled families.

In order to make the components of the model less theoretical, let's look at the work of John Torrente, a counselor at Sanctuary House. As you read about his work, see how many elements of attitudes and values, skills, and knowledge you can identify.

I N T E R V I E W

John Torrente, Outreach Counselor at Sanctuary House, a Shelter for Teenagers

Sanctuary is just what its name implies. It is a safe haven. Many of the teenagers have run away from their parents' homes. Maybe there was some abuse or they felt no one wanted them around. A few are running from the consequences of some of their own antisocial actions.

Some have left—with or without permission—from foster families, institutions, or community residences. There are as many stories as there are kids. You learn early on that you can't judge in advance why they left and how justified it was.

A few of them have had jobs and places to live, but something went wrong. Maybe they broke up with their lovers or their roommates, or the rent got raised and they had to leave. They come from all income brackets, races, and religions.

I am one of six outreach counselors at Sanctuary. This is my second year on the full-time staff. I go to college part time during the day. I've been working on and off at the house for four years. I began as a volunteer when I was in high school as part of a community service club. I used to go one evening a week with some of my classmates and we would help to cook dinner. In our high school, we put on dances to raise money and ran raffles and things like that.

Because of my excitement about the house, my father got involved too. He is now on the board of directors. He's an accountant, so he helps a lot. My mom and my girlfriend also volunteer here. My mother works in the thrift shop and my girlfriend comes with me when she is home from college.

It's easy to get hooked on this place. The woman who runs it is a sister from a Catholic religious order. She doesn't fit any of the stereotypes of a nun, though. She is one tough cookie and she has seen it all; nothing shocks her. She is a human dynamo who manages to rev us all back up again when everything looks particularly hopeless. She is a genius at wheedling money and donations out of people. It's mostly because of her that the house has grown so phenomenally. It started in a small storefront in Highland Heights, then moved to a big private house. Now we are located right in the middle of the downtown section in what was once a fancy hotel.

Starting out with three cots in 1983, we now can sleep about seventy teenagers, mostly in two-bedded rooms. In the middle of February, when it gets incredibly cold on the streets, we usually put up about twenty more young people in a dorm-style arrangement in what was once the ballroom of the hotel.

To do my kind of work, you have to be a night person. I start at about 8:30 or 9:00 P.M. three nights a week and work straight through until maybe 6:00 in the morning. Then I'm on a day shift one day over the weekend. The staff goes out in pairs, a male and a female, looking for kids who need shelter. Two teams cover the train station, the bus depot, and once in a while the airport.

We know the sections of town where the kids gather. They go in and out of the bars and fast-food places in what we fondly call "the combat zone." That's the district for cheap hotels, dirty book stores, and X-rated movie houses. We're always looking for the new kids. These are the ones who have recently left their homes. They are trying to hook up with somebody for a bed and a meal. We spot them in the Greyhound Bus terminal. They are hanging around the fringes of the groups of kids who congregate there to socialize. They usually don't have much luggage, no one meets them, and they seem hesitant. We try to make a quick assessment and then start talking to them. If we've guessed right and they have some kind of problem, we try to get them to come back to the house with us. Noreen, the nun I mentioned, welcomes them, gives them a meal, and tries to find out what's going on.

She never pressures the kids. If they don't want to talk, that's okay. They don't even have to tell us their names. Noreen and the other counselors let them know that what matters to us is that they are safe. When and if they are ready to trust us enough to tell us what pressured them to leave home, then we'll see what can be done. Sometimes kids open up the first night, and it will all come pouring out. They'll call their folks or the place they ran away from, and we'll put them on a bus home. There is a national program run by one of the bus companies that guarantees passage back home to any runaway kid if an agency verifies his or her story.

We try to assess the situation they came out of. If they tell us there was physical or sexual abuse, we let them know that they have options. They can stay for a while at Sanctuary House or find a shelter back in their own communities. No kid, no matter what he or she might have done, deserves to be hurt so badly that they have to run away. Sometimes we'll call an agency for them in their hometown and a counselor will meet their bus and start working with the kid and family. Often they call a priest or a friend who'll meet the bus when they get home. When kids first run away, they often think there is no other solution. Maybe we can help them see that there are people who can help them in their own communities. Maybe then they can slowly move back home.

It's possible, though, that what they were running away from isn't much safer than roaming the streets after dark in this town. A lot of the parents seem like very troubled people themselves. Of course, some seem like ordinary folks who are going out of their minds with worry and facing marital or employment problems of their own. Most of the parents we never meet, and we very rarely hear how things worked out, so all of this is guesswork.

If it seems they are deep into alcohol or drugs, we'll invite them to stay for the night and then link them up with a rehabilitation program the next day. We can't handle teens with active substance abuse problems at Sanctuary. It seems like a contradiction to say we are there for the kids and then reject some of them, but Sister Noreen learned early on that if the house was filled with drugs, then no one was safe.

The streetwise kids can often describe some sobering realities to the newcomers, but the reverse can be true also. Sometimes kids who have been out on the streets teach the new kids survival techniques we wish they wouldn't learn. We run groups every night in which we encourage the more mature teenagers to help the newcomers find safer solutions. Sometimes they'll take advice more readily from another kid than from an adult. Facilitating the group sessions is a tricky job, but when they work well, they are very effective interventions.

We tap into a broad network of services. If kids are determined to make it on their own, we can refer them to programs where they can complete their high school education. We also have counselors who try to find foster homes for them in their home city if that seems appropriate. We try everything we can to keep them from making a life on the streets.

Sometimes, though, life on the streets seems exciting and romantic to them, especially at first. You can make a quick buck and there are no adults around to tell you what to do. Once they are out there a while, they often change their minds. After a while, though, it's hard for them to leave. We have a saying around here that after two or three months on the street, "you can't go home again." In even that short time, the kids have seen so much human degradation and done so many things just to survive that they are not kids anymore. They feel like they wouldn't fit in with their friends back at their high school. They are often too embarrassed to face their relatives.

If a kid has already been on the streets for a while, sometimes he or she develops serious health problems. We have a clinic at Sanctuary and contacts with local doctors who volunteer to see our kids. Sometimes a young woman thinks she is pregnant. Often that's the case. Many of the kids pick up sexually transmitted diseases. They even have dental problems that have grown outrageously from being neglected.

The constant problem for us is that there are plenty of other people around the terminals and on the streets who have things to offer the kids. The pimps are doing some of the same things we are. They're also trying to spot the greenhorns. But they offer them a hot meal and a bed along with a line of cocaine. Their offers come with plenty of strings attached. They will be just so generous to the kids until they have them in their debt, and then they show them how to "repay." Usually it's by turning tricks, a young woman or young man having sex with a "john." The kids have to give the pimps a large part of the money they earn through prostitution.

Other people are offering the kids a chance to pick up money delivering drugs and running illegal betting slips. It's hard for us to compete with the kind of money these kids can make. At first, money means independence, not having to go back to a home that they hated or to grown-ups who order them around. But in the end, they trade one kind of confinement for a worse one.

Sometimes I go out with the Sanctuary van. It's a soup kitchen, infirmary, and office. Most nights we have a volunteer nurse. We park in a location where a lot of street kids congregate. There is an area down by the docks that is used as a pickup spot by men who want to buy teenage boys for sex. They come driving in from the suburbs. They have their suits and ties on like they just came from work. Sometimes they arrive in their work trucks. You wonder what is going on with their families while they are down here. They look over the line-up and invite a kid into their car, go off for an hour, and then bring the kid back to the dock.

We offer the kids coffee, medical help, and conversation. If they want to go back to the center for the night, we drive them there. You have to be careful not to pressure them or they just avoid you. If they think you will call the cops every time you see something illegal, they won't tell you anything.

Of course, we have limits as to what we can ignore. If we think they have a weapon, it's always a judgment call. Can you get them to give it to you? Do you call the police? If you do, will the word get out and then will all the other kids stay away from the van? It's never easy. You need to be a good listener, try not to judge them, and take it one step at a time.

One night a week I spend at the house just playing around with the kids who are living there. When they are there for a while we try to get them into a job or further education. We have link-ups with programs that train young people in computers. One kid is going to a community college. We have a terrific volunteer who teaches kids to lay carpets. He has gotten four of them decent-paying jobs.

The night I spend at the house I lead a rap group. We have a women's group to talk about special issues that concern them. We have a group for kids who have been sexually abused and a young parents club that some kids continue to attend even after they've left the house. I also work with the house council. We try to get the guests to take responsibility for running parts of the house.

I love the work, but I can see signs that I'm beginning to burn out. You have to focus on small successes. You can't think in absolute terms, like this kid went home and everything worked out fine. Life isn't that simple. The thing that keeps me going, in addition to Noreen, is the rest of the staff. We do a lot of social things together and rally around each other when there is a crisis. We are always celebrating someone's birthday or graduation or thirty days of sobriety.

I finish my courses next May. I think I want to get a master's degree in counseling. I'd like to get more skill working with groups of kids. I think maybe I will work in a high school. If adults could help teenagers talk about their problems *before* they get so serious, we could prevent running away, the date rapes, and depression, as well as teen suicides and the outbreak of violence.

I'm doing my senior seminar paper on teenage kids who are in crisis—runaways, suicides, addicts, etc. I'm looking at what it is that causes such serious problems and what teachers, counselors, and parents can do to try to head it off before kids hurt themselves or others. I've just finished two books that really impressed me. The one about boys and what society often does to help mess them up is entitled *Raising Cain: Protecting the Emotional Life of Boys* (Kindlon & Thompson, 2000),* and the one about the pressures that girls experience is called *Reviving Ophelia* (Pipher, M., 1998). Those recent school shootings were horrifying, but frankly, they didn't come as a surprise to many of us who work with troubled kids. We see those isolated, unhappy kids every day.

*See also Canada (1998); Evans, Fitzgerald, and Frantz (2000); Guetzloe (1999); Jenson and Howard (1999); Sheldrick (1999); Sourander, Heltstela, Helenrus, and Pina (2000); and Szyndrowski (1999).

ATTITUDES AND VALUES OF THE HUMAN SERVICE WORKER

Patience

The worker who thrives in this field understands and accepts the slowness, painfulness, and awesomeness of change. John sometimes feels annoyed when kids refuse the services he offers them. Sometimes he'll spend three or four nights without any of the kids on the docks coming back to the house. He's faced disappointment many times when a kid has dropped out of a job program or has broken his sobriety. But usually he manages to control his impatience. He sets small, achievable goals, taking comfort in any signs of progress.

When the frustration with two steps forward and one step backward becomes too overwhelming, he heads for a gym and works out. He spends time talking with his supervisor, and sometimes he asks to change his job assignment for a while. When he is really feeling burned out, he finds that raising funds for the house, instead of doing direct work, can renew his energy.

No matter how slow or discouraging the change effort, the effective worker deflects feelings of impatience *away* from the clients. They can't be punished for the worker's often justifiable sense of frustration.

We also need to be patient with ourselves. Our skills seem so inadequate when we watch young people nightly put themselves and others in danger and we cannot

Supporters and opponents of reproductive choice are unrelenting in their stands. They mount vigorous demonstrations, lobby legislators, and use all the other means of persuasion. So far the American public appears to be equally divided on this issue.

stop their downward slide. Rarely do we know all the facts; seldom can we control the many forces buffeting our clients. *We have no magic solutions.*

John has had to divest himself of the rescue fantasies he had when he came to Sanctuary. But as he learns to accept his own and his clients' limitations, he must also guard against drifting into callousness or complacency. He has seen kids and parents change, and he knows that his agency can make a difference.

Human service workers walk a tightrope between what is and what might be, between the reality of the moment and a vision of change for the better.

Empathy

Empathy An attempt to put oneself in the shoes of another person, to feel or think of a problem from another perspective.

John tries hard to understand the difference between sympathy, feeling sorry for another person, and **empathy,** putting himself in the shoes of another. Needless to say, no worker can ever really know precisely what it is like to occupy someone else's skin. It is especially hard when that other person is of a different race, gender, or age, or has a different set of abilities (see Rivera & Erlich, 1995, and Schram, 1971). But he tries hard to see the world as it might look through a set of eyes very different from his own. Empathy is a path we walk, not a destination we can ever be sure we have reached.

Empathy requires a finely tuned, intuitive sensitivity to other people, the kind that one finds in good fiction or poetry. Sometimes as we read a novel, hear a song, or look intently at a great painting, we have an amazing moment of recognition. We see our own thoughts reflected and are surprised that someone can touch us so deeply. It is this profound understanding of the human condition, with its complex and ambivalent emotions, that explains why the plays of William Shakespeare, written in the late 1500s and early 1600s, can still bring tears to our eyes today.

Small empathetic moments occur in the simplest of situations. On the playground, a group leader instinctively feels the momentary distress of a little boy who dropped his lollipop in the mud. He had licked it until it fit precisely into the roof of his mouth. Understanding the seemingly minor but significant disappointments of childhood, the worker does not rush in to offer a new lollipop, nor does he dismiss the tears as overreacting. He simply puts his arm around the child's shoulders and says, "What a shame that it fell!" Then perhaps they can try to find another treat.

To sharpen empathetic understanding, John taps the well of his own experiences. He hasn't been an alcoholic, but when he's counseling a compulsive drinker, he remembers how it felt when *he* tried to stop overeating, quit smoking, or disengage from an unhealthy love affair. Although he has never been discriminated against because of his race or religion, he can recapture the feelings of impotence he felt as a young child being unfairly scolded by his parents or teachers. He is not severely physically disabled but can remember a time when a broken arm or sprained ankle kept him from joining the gang for bike riding or playing ball.

All of us have distant memories of shoplifting, skipping school, lying, or disappointing our parents through fear, ignorance, or peer pressure. These memories can help us avoid rushing in to judge harshly a person with whom we are working.

The famous therapist Carl Rogers listed empathy as one of the three vital counselor attributes that can lead to positive change. The other two are nonpossessive warmth and genuineness (Rogers, 1951). These three attitudes are important in all major counseling theories. In fact, there is accumulating evidence that therapy is effective *only* when these attitudes are present at high levels, no matter what the particular school of psychology or counseling method used (Davis, 1994; Okun, Fried, & Okun, 1999; Truax & Carkhuff, 1967; Truax & Mitchell, 1971).

> The empathetic counselor must see beyond conventional facades, refrain from imposing personal interpretations and judgments, and be willing to risk understanding another person's private logic and feelings, which in superficial daily contacts the counselor might view as weak, foolish, or undesirable. (Hammond, Hepworth, & Smith, 1977, p. 3)

This kind of "unconditional positive regard" that flows from empathy may seem impossible.

> It may seem that we are requiring of the helping person a kind of "freeing love" which is a high spiritual quality unlikely to be possessed by a normally fallible human being.

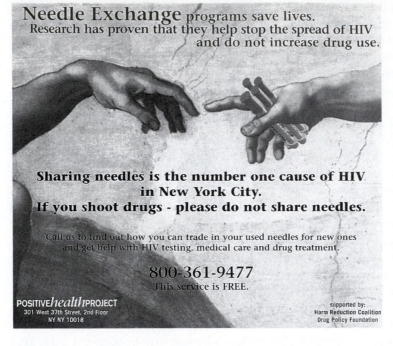

Needle Exchange programs save lives.
Research has proven that they help stop the spread of HIV
and do not increase drug use.

**Sharing needles is the number one cause of HIV
in New York City.
If you shoot drugs - please do not share needles.**

Call us to find out how you can trade in your used needles for new ones
and get help with HIV testing, medical care and drug treatment.

800-361-9477
This service is FREE.

POSITIVE*health*PROJECT
301 West 37th Street, 2nd Floor
NY NY 10018

supported by:
Harm Reduction Coalition
Drug Policy Foundation

There are arguments for and against this campaign to provide free hypodermic needles to narcotic addicts. Sharing needles spreads AIDS, but some people claim that distributing free needles encourages drug addiction. What are your attitudes toward this intervention?

In one sense this is true. It is only this kind of concern and the empathy which springs from it which brings the apparently impossible command to love one's enemies within the realm of practicability. It is only by transcending like and dislike that one could possibly "love" those one "dislikes." (Keith-Lucas, 1972, p. 107)

To test the strength of this value in yourself, consider how you would be able to work with a man who had murdered his own child. On most people's scale of values, that crime may be the most reprehensible. Could you work with such a man without being repelled by him?

A French filmmaker in the 1950s considered this question in a film called *We Are All Murderers.* At the time the film was made, France had the death penalty and executed people by the guillotine. A man was charged with murdering his own baby and confessed to the crime. Unemployed, he lived with his wife and baby in a tiny, cramped apartment. The baby cried constantly. The man was profoundly depressed by not being able to care for his family. He cracked under the stress and hit his baby. He did not intend to kill the child, but he did. He was convicted of murder and sentenced to die. The film raised the issue of individual guilt as opposed to the guilt that society must share in the provocation of such a crime.

Many times John has wondered how *he* would act if he had been the child or parent in one of the many hair-raising stories he has heard at Sanctuary House. Sometimes he even wonders what he would do if he found himself sexually attracted to young boys. Would he sneak down to the pier to buy sex in the dead of night? How would he feel on the drive back to his suburban home? Often he finds himself saying, "There, but for luck and chance, go I!"

Self-Awareness

John is genuinely fascinated by his reactions to the things he sees around him. He constantly wonders about the complex forces that have shaped these feelings. He has had to be willing to reexamine all of his attitudes and values. How does he feel about money, work, marriage, war, sex, homosexuality, and abortion? Each of his opinions has been challenged by things he has seen and heard. He has been provoked to explore whether the attitudes and values transmitted by his family are still valid for him.

He has had to find the courage to talk openly about emotion-laden topics such as rape and suicide. He believes that each woman should have a right to choose what to do about her body, so he supports legal abortion. Sister Noreen opposes it on religious and ethical grounds. They have agreed to disagree with each other on that topic. Both positions are defensible, but they must be openly acknowledged. If they are kept underground, they can direct or constrict the clients' own exploration of possible courses of action.

Effective human service workers need to be clear about where their own and their clients' problems overlap. Many young workers, for example, are still separating from their parents. When working with teenagers, these workers have to be alert to keep their own anger or ambivalence about dependence from influencing the way their clients feel or react toward their families.

The most important part of self-awareness is being able to sketch an increasingly accurate portrait of one's own strengths and weaknesses, likes and dislikes. John has been learning how to say, "I can do that task very well, but I don't feel competent in doing some other task. I need help."

Some of us can work with exquisite patience with a multidisabled person; others enjoy the liveliness of healthy children in a recreation center. Some workers cannot tolerate the slowness of the elderly infirm; others thrive on working with that population. The ability to live with other people's emotions and express our own is not something most of us can do automatically. We may need to undertake some personal-development work in this area. Nichols and Jenkinson (1991, p. 46), in discussing the preparation of support-group leaders, help workers assess their readiness. They suggest that you think about these questions:

- Do you think that you are aware of and open to the flow of feelings in your daily life—do others confirm this to be so?

- Are you able to say that you value your own feelings and allow their expression rather than striving to mask them?

- Are you able to share your feelings with a trusted companion without being defensive?

- Are you able to receive and experience the painful feelings of others in a relaxed, accepting manner without wanting immediately to placate, soothe, or distract them from expressing those emotions?

- Do you believe that if a person expresses or acts out feelings in a group you will be able to allow this to unfold without needing to take control and return the discussion to more matter-of-fact issues?

Finally, John tries to set limits on himself by learning his warning signals of fatigue and frustration so he can keep from burning out. Because they care profoundly, many of the staff members at Sanctuary House pay no attention to all the extra hours they work. But they cannot afford to neglect their own support network of friends and family. Ultimately, they serve the teenagers best if they nurture themselves.

Capacity to Deal with Ambiguity and Take Risks

None of us is comfortable with ambiguity. Uncertainty creates tension. Yet John has come to understand that when working with people, one is never sure of what has gone on in the past or will happen in the future.

The young people he works with are so complex that there can be no guarantees that a "correct" action will produce the "right" results. The expression "the operation was a success but the patient died" is often true in the human services.

Even when working with the general public there are many unknowns. Last month John organized a community meeting for prospective volunteers. He took enormous care with all the details. He double-checked the invitations for accuracy and clarity, made sure the meeting place was conveniently located, brought refreshments, arranged for child care, got a good speaker on the topic of runaway youth, and then waited expectantly for the crowd that never came. There were probably twenty different reasons so few people showed up. One person had a household emergency, another got tickets to a world series game. Everyone had a reason for not attending that seemed legitimate to them. So John swallowed his disappointment and did the best job he could with the few volunteers-to-be who attended the meeting. Next month he will try again.

Often John must close the book on a child's problem without being able to read the last chapter. How can he know if the addicted teenagers he worked so hard with for so long will stay off drugs for six months, one year, or a lifetime? Usually the staff loses track of the young people after they leave the program. When a young person returns to her family in a distant city, John often wonders if she was able to talk out the disagreement that made her run away. But he will probably never find out.

He has to act with very little and very inaccurate background information. Sister Noreen has been around homeless youth a long time and has sharpened her ability to distinguish the drug abuser from the occasional user. But even she cannot be sure if the teenager is telling her the truth about where his money went. Was it *really* lost, or did he spend it on cocaine?

When she was a protective service worker, she often had to decide whether to leave a child over the weekend with a family that had been accused of abuse. If she removed the child, there was no guarantee that the foster family she placed him in would be much better than the family he had just left. She learned early in her career that the human service worker has to be a *risk taker*.

Just last week John had to decide at six o'clock in the morning whether to cancel the buses he had leased for Sanctuary's annual family outing. At 6:00 A.M., the sky was overcast and the forecast was for rain. If it didn't rain and he cancelled, a lot of disappointed folks would be angry at him. If they went and it poured all day, the long-awaited event would be a disaster. He decided to risk it. They went, the sky was overcast and dropped a few sprinkles, but no major problems spoiled the day's activities. Was it good judgment or good luck? A little of each, perhaps!

The outreach counselors live with ambiguity because their job tasks are necessarily ill defined. They are required to make moment-to-moment decisions:

- Which park should they visit?
- What youngster should they talk to?
- At what point should they call the police when they witness a drug deal or a fight?

Each decision is a judgment call made in a split second. Phoning the police too frequently might make it impossible to build relationships with these volatile and troubled young people. Waiting too long to respond might result in another teenager or staff member getting hurt or even killed!

Capacity to Ask for Help and Offer Feedback

To increase his effectiveness while struggling with ambiguity, John has developed a positive attitude about asking for help. When he couldn't decide whether to cancel the trip, he woke up two other staff workers and made them help him. A burden is always lighter if someone else can carry it with you.

As he has matured and become more able to acknowledge his weaknesses, he is able to say, "I don't know that, but if you give me an hour, I'll find out," or, "I've tried to do that, but I wasn't able to; can you help me?"

Knowing when to ask for assistance or for an honest appraisal of her work is the mark of a self-confident human service worker. The less-secure worker needs to bluff, pretending false expertise. But the field is so vast and ever-changing that no one could ever know everything. Social welfare legislation, laws, and entitlements are evolving daily. New programs are added, old ones cut back. No matter how many years Sister Noreen has worked with homeless youth, if she were to shift to another problem area, perhaps working with the educationally or physically disabled, she would be a novice.

Sanctuary offers an orientation program for new staff and volunteers and in-service training for everyone. Even staff members who have been in the field for a long time need to keep learning about the ins and outs of this particular program, population, and community.

Just as important as asking for help is the willingness to give honest feedback to others. In our personal lives, much of our social interaction is superficial. We often give stock answers to standard questions: "How are you today?" provokes the anticipated neutral answers. We are hardly going to share our inner problems with all the neighbors or tradespeople we meet during the day. But at Sanctuary when someone asks, "How did I do?" or, "How could I have done it better?" they have a right to expect a thoughtful and honest reply. Sometimes a less than positive evaluation is momentarily painful, but if the person learns from it, then it is a gift.

Belief in the Capacity to Change

At the risk of stating the obvious, John has to be a person with a powerful belief in the capacity all of us have to grow and change. His clients need a lot of help, but most of them are not *permanently* stuck in destructive patterns. He knows they often resist change; they fear the unknown consequences that change may bring, no matter how painful their current reality.

As he tries to assess realistically how much growth is possible or how fast it can happen, he has to struggle to maintain his own delicate balance. On the one hand, John has energy and optimism; on the other hand, he sometimes feels rage and frustration. All the workers at Sanctuary juggle feelings of pessimism and optimism. The discouraging reality of the life they see on the streets exists side by side with their hopes for the futures of the young people. No worker ever has enough time or resources or skill.

Although our minds and bodies cannot tolerate perpetual rage, we should be intolerant of injustice wherever we encounter it. We need to hold firm to our convictions about equal opportunity and the potential of equal access (Pantoja & Perry, 1992). A veteran human service worker once said that she was an *optimist in her heart and a pessimist in her head*. What does that mean to you?

No matter how discouraged he gets, John still appreciates the astounding plasticity, flexibility, and resilience of people. Human behavior has an almost infinite range of possibilities. The brutality of the street pimps and child pornographers contrasts sharply with the altruism and decency of all the volunteers who give up their evenings to help out.

Because he realizes that *each* of us is capable of acts of cruelty as well as altruism, he rejects glib generalizations about human nature, such as:

"People are no damn good!"

"People are only out for themselves!"

"Nowadays parents don't care about their kids!"

When things are falling apart, he looks to see what forces in the environment might be inhibiting human potential. He struggles to understand the obstacles in people's paths rather than retreat into fatalistic conclusions about their inferior heredity, moral lassitude, or psychological deviance.

He also has to stop himself from feelings of hopelessness when he sees city workers who seem so overwhelmed with their caseloads that they appear to throw up their hands in defeat.

Open-Mindedness, Skepticism, and Rejection of Stereotypes

John has learned that being open-minded is a requirement of his job. Open-mindedness is often derided. A comedian once described the open-minded person as one whose head is so porous that the wind whistles through it. Others describe the open-minded person as someone whose two feet are firmly planted in midair.

Of course John has opinions, but by keeping his mind open to new information, he protects himself from casting his first impressions in concrete. He meets someone, forms a preliminary estimate of her situation, and then continues to change that impression as he learns more.

He must keep from generalizing about a whole group from the behavior of one person. Even though, for example, he sees many men who are homosexuals abusing young boys, he knows that most homosexuals, just like most heterosexuals, would never do that. Though he hears many horror stories of family indifference, he also knows that many parents have struggled long and hard to do the "right thing" against insurmountable odds. We live in a culture that encourages aggressive behavior and competition. Often peer pressure and the media have more power than the values of the parents.

Human service workers need to see beyond the simplistic bigotry of common stereotypes that declare that:

- The Irish drink too much and beat their wives on Saturday night.

- The Scots are thrifty to a fault.

- The Poles are stupid.

- The Jews are acquisitive.

- Women are passive, emotional creatures who yearn to be dominated.

- Men are like beasts when aroused and can't control themselves.

Each of these facile stereotypes must be questioned. Although the differences in behavior or attitudes among cultures or groups should be acknowledged—sometimes celebrated and sometimes regretted—shortcuts to understanding these variations should be rejected.

Ethnic background, race, class, and gender play significant roles in the social-ization of every child. Still, no two people, even those from the same background, are ever identical. The teenagers want the staff to understand their lifestyles and stresses, but they would resent being labeled as "suburban, middle-class, Christian white teenage underachievers with domineering divorced parents." Although that kind of labeling sounds like a caricature, John has heard a surprisingly large num-ber of workers referring to the teenagers at Sanctuary with shorthand labels that deny the humanness and uniqueness of the runaways. But categories and labels can be important in qualifying a client for a particular service or benefit. They must be used, but used with care and only when needed and accurate.

Humor and a Light Touch

John, like many of the young people he works with, finds that laughing, sometimes even at himself, is a great way to get rid of tension. A belly laugh, like a good cry, cleanses the system, putting a difficult situation back into perspective. One of John's favorite teenagers is a streetwise 18-year-old whom the kids have nicknamed "Flash." He is in perpetual, often impulsive motion. He is likely to say or do almost anything. John told him one day that he was going to get him a sweatshirt with his motto printed on it. In big, bold letters it would read:

READY! FIRE! AIM?

It took Flash a few minutes to understand the joke, but once he got it, he repeated it with obvious relish. And perhaps it slowed him down a little the next time he was quick to anger or become defensive.

Because working with these very troubled kids can be fraught with so much pain, humor might seem out of place. But John has discovered that many times a serious message can be effectively communicated through good-natured teasing. He uses tact and timing to moderate his wit. By picking up signals that he is being insensitive when he teases, makes a pun, or giggles at the absurdity of life on the streets, he can quickly back off or apologize.

Human service workers, especially in group or community settings, often so-cialize with their clients and coworkers at potluck suppers, holiday celebrations, and open houses and in the after hours of weekend workshops or retreats. They need to learn how to organize these occasions so they are not too threatening. Touchy issues will always surface when we cross the fragile boundary line between client and worker or worker and supervisor.

Traditional mental health practitioners such as doctors, psychologists, and psy-chiatrists often rigidly cling to boundary lines. Human service workers don't. When they work and when they relax, John, Noreen, and the other staff confront ambigu-ity, take risks, and individualize every situation.

SKILLS OF THE HUMAN SERVICE WORKER

Data Gathering

Every day John is asked dozens of questions that he has no answers for.

"Do you think Larry is telling the truth about where he got that money he has been flashing around?"

"If we send her home on that bus who will meet her at the other end?"

"Where did Gloria go? I haven't seen her in a week, but I heard she was badly beaten up. Is it a rumor?"

"Where can we get money to purchase a van?"

"Where can we find a volunteer to teach an Introduction to Computers class?"

"What do other centers do when guests are caught in each other's rooms in compromising positions?"

"What is herpes? Is it catching? Is it terminal?"

He often responds, "That's a good question; I really don't know." Then, because he is a conscientious worker, he goes on to say, "But I'll find out what I can and call you back on Tuesday [or in an hour]."

The process of finding out as much as possible about a topic is called *data gathering*. John has been trained to use a variety of methods. In some ways, he is rather like a detective on the trail of insight and information. These are some of the data-gathering skills he uses:

- Asking questions of clients, coworkers, and his supervisor
- Listening to answers and remembering what he has learned
- Systematically observing
- Going to the library to read newspapers and journals or surfing the Internet
- Attending workshops, conferences, and seminars
- Visiting homes, other agencies, and the like

INTERVIEWING

Throughout the time you work in human services, you will keep increasing your skill in phrasing questions that help people to think more clearly. You will learn a great deal about how to establish an atmosphere that helps the interviewee relax and become engaged in the process of information sharing. The counselors at Sanctuary must learn *how* and *when* to ask questions while preserving a young person's dignity and right to privacy.

When John conducts an interview with a young runaway's parents, he is trying to find out as much as he can about the family's situation and assess its potential resources. Each person needs the space to tell his or her own version of the crisis that precipitated the family breakup. He will listen to each family member and try to tune in to the emotions that might be surrounding the words. The counselor discovers that everyone has his or her own story to tell, and everyone has stories that never get told (Cottle, 1974). If John is lucky, he will have several interviews he can use to fill in the background.

Often John must act quickly in a crisis situation, condensing all his data collecting into a few hectic moments. A fight erupts on the docks and he must quickly decide how serious it is. Should he call the police or try to break it up himself? He reviews all he knows about these young men. He has a brief exchange with one of the leaders to see how seriously *he* is taking it. Based on his past experience, John makes an educated guess whether they are likely to have weapons and if they are likely to use them. To an outsider, it might look as though the fight will turn violent. But after a few minutes of this process, John is able to distinguish "dissing," a street game of trading insults, from the kind of genuine anger that will leave one of the participants dead or injured.

Whether talking to a public official over the phone or at a meeting, conferring with a parent or teacher, or sharing information with a coworker about a referral, John uses the following skills.

Active Listening

After asking questions, John uses his skills of active listening. Each guest at Sanctuary has a unique style of communication. He has to remember and file away for future reference precisely what has been said. He has to be able to rephrase the ideas and feelings of the speaker to make sure he has understood correctly. He counts on such data so that he can point out connections between what is said at one time and at another.

When actively listening, he also "hears" the emotion that surrounds words. He listens to the *sounds of silence:* words left unsaid, hesitations, pauses, small sighs. By checking back with the interviewee, he avoids the pitfalls of overanalyzing or over-interpreting (Wolvin & Coakley, 1992).

Active Looking

From his study of psychodynamics, John has learned about the theory of the unconscious mind. He knows that people do not always do and say exactly what they mean. It is not easy to put one's feelings into words. Careful scrutiny can often tell us more than any words can convey.

The workers at Sanctuary also use active looking to better understand their group or community. By absorbing the many small details of a neighborhood, for example, John can make educated guesses about the stresses and the quality of life of its residents. He can walk into the game room and notice the small signs that signal trouble is brewing.

READING, RESEARCHING, AND ASSESSING

Because John encounters his clients in random, often unpredictable ways, he usually starts out by knowing almost nothing about them. In most other agencies, workers have access to a variety of background information. Reading through a client's file is a form of research. A file might include:

- Notes from previous professionals
- Employment records
- Test scores
- Medical records
- Records of monetary grants
- The results of some type of investigation or a court case

Reviewing published material and web sites is also a form of research. When, for example, he is writing a proposal for a grant, John wades through the books in the library that list philanthropic foundations and searches the databases of funding sources. Then he collects evidence of the agency's need for a new or expanded service. For example, he read an article in the *New York Times* about a recreation center that conducted an all-night gym program in a high-crime neighborhood, believing that it played a role in the reduction of townwide crime statistics. He'll clip that article and attach it to his proposal to lend support to his assertion that recreation can have a positive impact on vandalism.

He has become adept at using directories of community resources so that he can make referrals to job training, housing, and medical services for his clients. He always wondered why he had to take subjects such as statistics and research in college; they seemed so far removed from the human service field. Now he realizes how much he depends on his skills of finding information. Recently he needed to find the most accurate material on AIDS for a client. Before that, he had to find out how an adopted child goes about seeking out his biological parents. He has to learn to wade through the endless amount of material his search engine produces, screening the material for accuracy and relevance.

ATTENDING CONFERENCES AND WORKSHOPS

At least three times a week John participates in a case conference. It might be held at Sanctuary, the local courthouse, the mental health clinic, or the Department of Social Services. At these meetings, the teenagers, their families, and a variety of mental health workers pool their perspectives about a young person's problem. Learning how to gather and present information at a case conference is an important set of skills.

Occasionally John has been able to attend a professional conference or workshop. He recently went to one organized by the Coalition for Homeless Youth. He networked with other workers and came back newly energized.

MAKING HOME OR AGENCY VISITS

John finds that visiting a young person's home or another social agency provides him with in-depth knowledge. Observing for himself helps him gain insights into the strengths and weaknesses in an environment. When he visits a local health center, a shelter, or school, he reads the graffiti on the walls and the notices on the bulletin boards. He can evaluate the atmosphere on first entering the front door or sitting in the waiting area. He forms initial impressions of the kind of service the agency might give his clients by the messages it projects to him.

Information Storing and Sharing

Once gathered, information about a particular client, problem, or program must be put into a useful format. John resists writing records and is often reminded by Noreen how important this skill is. At Sanctuary the workers enter a description of their daily activities in a computerized log book. This is used for continuity from one shift of staff to the next or from one period of time to the next. If good records have been kept, a young person won't be asked to summarize in a few sentences his or her complex set of problems when a new worker comes on staff.

At the end of any major event—a camping trip, parent workshop, or community fair—John writes an evaluation. He describes how the money was spent, what equipment was used, and what pitfalls he encountered. If he takes the time to sit down at the computer and write a full description, the next worker who repeats that activity can build on his successes and try to avoid his failures. To start again each time from scratch would be a misuse of everyone's scarce time and energy.

At Sanctuary the staff rotate taking notes on the decisions made at meetings. The meeting records help keep absent members in the mainstream of the group. Minutes act as reminders of significant deadlines, changes in laws or regulations, and other vital data. Behind every error—a name omitted from a list or a person who does not receive a meeting notice—lies a lost opportunity.

An entire program can rise or fall on the quality of its administrative detail. When a budget is reviewed, the bits and pieces of paper—bills, invoices, moneys taken out and brought in—can determine whether a program will be continued or terminated (Kettner, Moroney, & Martin, 2nd ed., 1999; Lewis, J. A. et al., 2nd ed., 2001; Schram, 1997).

Relationship Building

If John cannot build a relationship with a runaway child, he will never be able to help her. Gaining the trust of teenagers is especially hard. Even an adult as young as John still represents the adult world that these young people are busy rebelling against (Zayas & Katch, 1989).

John has found that there are no formulas for building a relationship. Stock empathetic phrases such as, "I can understand just how you feel," or reassurances such as, "I'm sure everything will work out fine!" are perceived by the teenagers as being patronizing and hollow. And they are!

Sometimes, with all his skills, John just doesn't connect with a particular teenager. The elusive element of "cohesion," the bond that develops between people, just isn't there. There are workers who cannot connect with certain clients and clients who find it impossible to trust anyone. John has had to honestly admit when he is having difficulty relating to a particular young person. If he can, he adjusts his approach. No one on the staff considers it a failure if a relationship does not gel. Of course, if John found that he couldn't build a relationship with most of the young people he worked with, he would obviously be in the wrong job.

Negotiating Contracts and Assessing Problems

This process of sorting out mutual goals, roles, and tasks is called negotiating the contract. At Sanctuary the contract between clients and workers is not actually written. Instead, it is discussed during the initial stages, when a client first begins working with a staff member.

A contract begins by stating mutual expectations. Global statements such as, "I am here to help you," "We are meeting to change the way the police act toward street kids," or, "I want you to make my son behave" are only starting points. The counselors break down large goals into small, do-able steps that can build, one on top of the other. The discussion of mutual expectations and consequences includes a description of who will do what in the change effort and which consequences will follow which actions. At Sanctuary the young people are not allowed to use drugs in the house. They need to know what will happen if a worker finds them shooting up in the bathroom. They also need to review the rules of confidentiality. Will their parents be called; if they have a weapon, will it be taken away; under what circumstances will the police intervene?

Some parents or young people expect John to solve their problems by giving advice or orders; others think he will sit back and remain mute, like the psychiatrists they have seen in movies. Of course, he does a little of both.

Constructing Action Plans

In most agencies, Individual Service Plans (ISPs) spell out the goals that will be worked on and the tasks that can accomplish them. At Sanctuary there are no formal, written action plans. The staff sets short-term goals with and for each resident. John tries to keep those goals in mind. They shape the choices he makes about how to spend his time.

Because so many of the teenagers have no ability to see beyond their next meal and warm bed, the staff tries to teach them how to chart a course and stick to it in a variety of ways. When planning a house dance or trip to a beach, John tries to help the residents make lists of the jobs that need to be done, when they must be completed, and who is responsible for doing them. If they don't keep careful track of their plans, the kids often backtrack over each other's trails, leaving important pieces of work undone or rushing to do a month's worth of work in a few hours. Lack of clarity creates conflict.

By teaching them how to use an action plan, counselors seek to enable their clients to accomplish two goals: organize a successful event and, more important, practice a method of systematic problem solving. Translating goals into concrete actions can help clients avoid emotional overload. All of these youngsters have had crises in their lives and have reacted by withdrawing or striking out. John tries to bring some order into their chaotic lives.

Implementing Action Plans

To translate plans into reality, John might meet with a youngster who is looking for a job. He offers encouragement and shows him how to use the job listings or locate an employment agency. Another of his clients has just moved into an apartment. He refers her to a day care center for her 2-year-old son and helps her apply for financial assistance. Another resident has a court appearance; John briefs her on her rights and offers to go with her. Helping clients make decisions, release emotions, and locate and use services are ways he assists them as they implement their action plans.

Although John might spend most of his time doing individual casework, he also has had to learn to run a group. Because Sanctuary is short of staff, he teaches a small class in word processing and coaches an occasional baseball game. All of these activities help implement Sanctuary's overall goal of helping each teenager survive the transition into adulthood. Like John, most human service workers are willing to do a little bit of everything.

Monitoring and Evaluating

John has learned how to use many techniques to elicit feedback. It is not easy to be objective about one's own work. He asks his clients and coworkers how he is doing but knows that most people have a hard time being constructively critical. The board of directors of Sanctuary has hired a professor from a local college to conduct a yearly evaluation. She interviews the staff and residents, summarizes the agency's progress, and then helps the board and staff set goals for the next year.

BASIC KNOWLEDGE OF THE HUMAN SERVICE WORKER

Human Growth and Development

All college human service curriculums are likely to include courses called Self and Society, The Person in the Environment, or, simply, Introduction to Psychology or Human Growth and Development.

These courses describe the major milestones and developmental tasks that face the newborn infant as he or she grows through childhood, adolescence, young adulthood, adulthood, and old age and finally faces death. They discuss the basic needs shared by all human beings, regardless of their particular culture or the era in which they live. Students are challenged to think about how human beings meet their needs for association and acceptance, for work, play, sexuality, and spirituality.

Many of the major theorists disagree with each other about what it is that causes people to think or act as they do. But the struggle to understand and synthesize their varying perspectives sharpens the intellect. It has provoked John to take a second look at many of his facile assumptions about the nature of human nature.

Abnormal Growth and Development

After studying "normal" or "typical" behaviors at different stages, most students learn about the forces that stunt development. They explore the ways in which biology, genetics, and family and social relationships contribute to mental breakdown, stress, family disorganization, and various forms of physical and mental disabilities. Through the study of nontypical or deviant behavior, they begin to understand the complex, intertwined issues of causality. Understanding how psychological problems develop has helped John to seek out the multiple resources needed to cope with or overcome them.

Sanctuary House does not base its work on one particular psychological theory. At John's internship in a community residence for developmentally delayed adults, the staff was expected to act in accordance with a rigid program of behavior modification. John is more comfortable working in an agency in which staff have the latitude to pick and choose from a variety of approaches.

Impact of Society and Culture on Behavior

While he was studying some of the psychological, genetic, biological, nutritional, and interpersonal forces that shape human behavior, John also had to understand the social context. While the family is an important influence on personality formation, so too are the many groups within which individuals interact.

The study of socioeconomic class, social role and status, ethnicity, peer group, family, church, school, and community—with their norms, myths, pressures, and subtle messages—has helped John to further understand why people act as they do. Realizing how cultures place expectations on behavior and mete out punishments for nonconformity, John begins to see order in the confusing crosscurrents of our pluralistic, heterogeneous society.

The Dynamics of Groups and Organizations

Once he recognized the ways in which groups influence attitudes and behavior, John was curious about how they form and maintain themselves. In studying small groups such as the nuclear family, the gang, or the clique, he discovered that they have much in common with larger, more diffuse organizations such as workplaces, schools, and social agencies. Groups develop patterns of predictable behavior, rules, regulations, and rituals. These eventually determine how well the members will accomplish the goals of the group.

Learning how bureaucracies form and how they can be changed has helped the staff of Sanctuary secure services and resources for clients from a panoply of often unresponsive city agencies. It has also helped them look critically at the house itself to figure out how it could be improved.

Social and Political Forces That Affect Helping

Although no human service worker can possibly absorb all of the political, economic, and sociological data about society, he or she needs a basic understanding of how communities are organized and how they are changed.

In anthropology and sociology courses, John has learned about variations in beliefs from one culture to another. He has learned that there are different definitions of how men and women should treat each other, how children should be socialized, and how the aged and the young should relate to each other.

These insights drawn from history and cross-cultural analysis prepare the human service worker to suspend quick judgments about what is right and wrong. They warn us that there are no carved-in-stone ways to run a world, a community, or an individual life.

Study in this area might also include knowledge about how laws are introduced, implemented, and amended. John still does not know enough about how the legislative and judicial systems affect the delivery of social services to homeless youth. He has some clear ideas about what he would like to see happen. He will need to keep on learning.

Social Problems, Populations, and Resources

John's human service courses and his internships introduced him to many social problems and special-population groups. He has learned a little about the problems of crime and corrections; mental and physical disabilities; hospitalized, neglected, and abused children; family relations; alcohol and drug abuse; death; suicide; survival in the rural or urban community; poverty; and discrimination. He has learned about discrimination based on social class, age, ethnic or religious status, and the tensions surrounding sexual identity. All are issues he sees played out in his work every day.

Although he has not learned in depth about all of these issues, he has begun to understand how social problems are identified, how new problems rise to prominence on the social agenda, and how new services to deal with them come into being. He has learned that mental illness, alcoholism, aging, childhood, and male–female relations, among other issues, have changed in dramatic ways in the past several decades. Mental illness was once considered a moral depravity, later it was treated as a wholly psychological disturbance, and now it is viewed as an illness with both psychological and biological roots. Definitions have shaped interventions.

He knows a bit about the general shape of the social welfare system. Now that he is a committed newspaper reader, he attempts to keep up with the ever changing legislation in the field.

Research and Evaluation

Although John is probably never going to have full responsibility for conducting formal research projects, he needs to understand the language of research. He has helped out in the formulation of projects and tries to read them as an alert consumer.

Research in the human services is particularly complex, controversial, and problematic. Human beings are infinitely unique and are perpetually bombarded with conflicting demands and environmental stressors. It is always hard to pinpoint the exact causality of any social problem or its solution. There are probably as many reasons for a youngster to leave home as there are residents at Sanctuary House.

Despite the limitations, research and evaluation studies need to be conducted in the social services. Results are sometimes used for increasing our knowledge base. More often, studies are used to decide whether funding of a particular program should be sustained, increased, or terminated.

SUMMARY

1. It is difficult to draw a boundary line between the lay-person helper and the professional helper.

2. The boundary lines between professional specialties in the human services are often unclear. Work roles overlap.

3. Regardless of formal credentials or titles, competent helpers share a commitment to the content and structure of the professional helping relationship.

4. The structure of the professional helping relationship differs from the purely social one. The professional relationship:
   Exists for a limited time
   Has a clear, agreed-on focus
   Has a division of labor
   Is disciplined
   Is built on acceptance rather than attraction or affection

5. The content of the helping relationship is composed of three components:
   Attitudes and values

Skills
Knowledge

6. The three components build on each other like a pyramid, with attitudes and values at the base.

7. Though all the components are of equal importance, the training of human service workers begins with attitudes and values.

8. The key attitudes and values are:
   Patience
   Empathy
   Self-awareness
   Capacity to deal with ambiguity and take risks
   Capacity to ask for help and offer feedback
   Belief in people's and systems' capacity to change
   Open-mindedness, skepticism, and rejection of stereotypes
   Humor and a light touch

9. The basic skills are:
   Data gathering, interviewing, and researching
   Information storing and sharing
   Relationship building
   Negotiating contracts and assessing problems
   Constructing action plans
   Implementing action plans
   Monitoring and evaluating

10. The basic knowledge areas are:
    Human growth and development
    Abnormal growth and development
    The impact of society and culture on behavior
    The dynamics of groups and organizations
    The social and political forces that affect helping
    Social problems, special populations, and resources
    Research and evaluation

11. No worker embodies or masters all the attitudes and values, skills, and knowledge described. They form a model that helps set goals for professional development.

DISCUSSION QUESTIONS

1. Reflect on the picture of the Statue of Liberty on the opening page of this chapter. What do you think the artist who did it was trying to communicate? What

do you think the authors might be trying to say—or might be trying to get the students to think about—by using this picture to introduce the topic of attitudes, values, and skills of human service work?

2. What do you think is meant by the statement, "empathy is a path we walk, not a destination we can ever reach"? How might you prepare yourself to try to empathize with one of your classmates who comes from a different ethnic or religious background than you do, or is of the other gender, or has a different sexual orientation, or perhaps who has a different set of abilities or disabilities than you do?

3. To what extent do you think you could work with homeless youth who often might appear angry at adults or might be sexually provocative or manipulative? How do you think you would react to having to deal with the "johns" or pimps that often prey on the youngsters, or the parents from whom they have run away?

WEB RESOURCES FOR FURTHER STUDY

Homeless and Runaway Teens
www.standupforkids.org

www.mockingbirdsociety.org/program

http://aspe.hhs.gov/homeless/index.shtml

For more information on the problems and program strategies of working with homeless and runaway teenagers these web sites should be very helpful. The second site is especially concerned with the teenagers who become homeless after "aging out" of the foster care system. The third site is the official Heath and Human Services site, and it has a section on homeless and runaway youth.

CHAPTER 5

Values and Ethical Dilemmas

In the last chapter, we described the attitudes and values, skills, and knowledge that are the hallmarks of the competent human service worker. But it is always easier to discuss them in abstract terms. When we look at the real-life situations that human service workers face, we discover that it is never as easy to follow these guidelines as it at first appeared. Value conflicts and dilemmas are inevitable in our work. Some serious clashes in what we believe we *should* do and what we *can* do stem from differences in the personal values, ideologies, class and ethnic backgrounds, and gender identities among members of the community and between workers and clients. The quality of service we are expected to give to our clients may be determined by the theories about human nature that our director or board subscribe to. The choices our clients make will often depend on their basic beliefs about the appropriate roles of men and women, how children should be reared, and who should control reproduction.

The values of self-determination and confidentiality, which are keys to building trust in the professional relationship, are often impossible to adhere to. This is especially likely when the client does not seek help voluntarily but has been forced to do so because he or she has committed a serious crime or has a severe disability.

The worker needs to be aware of and sensitive to the ethical and legal limits that are inherent in even the most admirable concepts. Human service workers also must be honest with themselves and their clients, lest they subtly manipulate them into making decisions they will later regret. In the last chapter, we asserted that human service workers must live with ambiguity and be able to take risks. In the several case examples we present in this chapter, you can experience both with dramatic intensity.

Lydia Carston, a psychologist at Morville Prison, is facing the worst moments of her long and distinguished career. She works in a special program for sex offenders that uses a variety of experimental techniques to try to rehabilitate these men. Most are repeat offenders convicted of seriously abusing children. Lydia leads group therapy sessions and counsels some of the prisoners individually. She has been working on an intensive basis with Don H., who is serving a second sentence for having beaten and sexually violated a 9-year-old child. In all the years she has worked at the prison, she has never had a client who seems as beyond rehabilitation as Don. Although he *says* he wants to stop being a pedophile, he seems to come alive when he describes what he has done to the children he violated and when he describes his fantasies and dreams about sexual violation.

Don has served his sentence, has been a model prisoner, and is going to be released in one more week. He plans to start his life over again in a new town. But

Lydia is absolutely convinced that he will attack another child. She would like to alert the police in the town he is moving to. She feels the neighborhood children need to be protected from this man.

Don's lawyer, convinced that Don has his problems under control, has pleaded with her to give the man a chance. If she tells the chief of police or lets the newspapers know about his past, he will be hounded out of town. He will never get a job or have a chance to prove he can live a life among ordinary people. A voice inside her says that the lawyer is right. She has been taught that a belief in change is one of the key attitudes of an effective human service worker. She has also been taught that a client has the right to have some assurance of confidentiality when he shares his thoughts with a counselor.

But what if another child gets hurt? Still worse, how will she live with herself if the next time he molests, he also kills the child? She is being pulled in two directions. Danger lies in each of the paths. What should she do?

Every attitude and value carries with it the seeds of conflict and insoluble dilemmas. Debates about the **ethics of helping** are not just mental gymnastics best left to university scholars or cloistered philosophers. Lydia's dilemma is an unusually difficult one, but human service workers face dilemmas or value conflicts of one sort or another every day, no matter what their role in an agency.

Sometimes there are conflicts between what we have been taught is correct behavior and what our clients do. For example, perhaps our parents, church, and school taught us that it is wrong for a woman to get an abortion; yet we may work with many people who do not share this value. Or perhaps, because everyone we knew *said* so, we might believe that most welfare recipients are lazy people avoiding work. Yet we find that assumption false when we read research on the subject. Which path do we follow when we must choose between our vision of life and our client's, between a long-held belief and research findings?

Value conflicts are often caused by the realities of our work. We know that our ethics dictate a certain path, but the efficiency needs of the bureaucracy that employs us or provides funds and the pressure of public opinion—especially in an election year—demand actions counter to our convictions. Human service workers know that whoever pays the piper calls the tune!

> **Ethics of helping**
> An ethical commitment to helping others rather than engaging in dog-eat-dog competition.

CAN WORKERS BE COMPLETELY UNBIASED?

Many of the values we hold have been shaped by our social class, ethnic group, or gender. These values may be very different from those of people from another group. This can create problems in the helping relationship.

Some theoreticians urge workers to be objective and "value free," which means being careful not to impose their own values on their clients. Yet in practice this is simply impossible. Even if one only grunts and says "uh-huh," the timing of the noises can reflect a value judgment about which of the client's statements warrant attention; inflections of the voice can give a sense of approval or displeasure. Inevitably there will be some differences between the client and the worker in attitudes toward politics, religion, sexuality, culture, social class, time orientation, or the environment, or in beliefs about human nature. Some of those **value conflicts** may not be very important. A Democrat can help a Republican, or vice versa, without needing to agree on the respective party platforms. But if the worker honestly believes that abortion is murder and the client wants help in terminating a pregnancy, that can create such a serious problem in their working relationship that special effort is required to soften or eliminate the conflict.

Value conflicts
Disagreement brought about by differences in values between people.

Florence Miller is a human service worker whose life and beliefs illustrate some of the value conflicts we will discuss in this chapter. As an African American woman who has dedicated her life to helping people deal with oppression, she has a keen awareness of the dilemmas that can arise from differences.

I N T E R V I E W

Florence Miller, Advocate at WINGS, an Agency That Helps Women Who Are Addicted

Florence Miller describes herself as an advocate–freedom fighter. Her job is to improve the way the social system works. She does this through writing to newspapers and talking to people wherever she goes—on trains, buses, at schools and colleges, and at work. She is one of the founders of WINGS (Women's Institute for New Growth and Support), an agency dedicated to the empowerment, education, and political awareness of recovering women addicts who need support to remain clean and sober.

WINGS started as an informal support group when a few women met in each other's homes. They expanded their circle to many members of their community and have rehabilitated an abandoned house to use as a community residence. It provides housing for women recovering from substance abuse, many of whom have had their children taken away by the Department of Social Services. When she was staff director, Florence wrote grant proposals for funds. She also worked with architects, lawyers, zoning boards, city officials, and contractors.

Florence's life experiences have given her an amazing understanding of the problems that poor people face. She describes painful memories of being taught by a white teacher that she was a "nigger" and could not aspire to go on in school. She has been a single mother on welfare, a foster mother, and a General Relief participant. She says, "The humiliation, frustration, and dehumanization suffered by those seeking help is atrocious."

Florence found that the social system doesn't work for black people, and that includes the social service system. She encountered some good workers in the state child-welfare agency, but many of them she found to be culturally insensitive; they want to acculturate black children to white norms. "If you take black children into white families, why can't black families take white children?"

Eventually she was able to obtain an education and was the class valedictorian when she graduated with an associate's degree from a community college in 1988. She went on to a private liberal-arts college for her social work degree and graduated at age 61 with a BSW degree with a minor in art.

In her first internship, Florence disagreed with her supervisor about making a mother leave her home because a father, who had been abusive and was out of the home, was allowed by the court to visit his children in the house. Florence didn't believe that the mother should leave her home, because it was the father who had been abusive. The conflict with her supervisor was so great that Florence was switched to another placement, where she found no major conflicts with her values.

In her BSW program, Florence was often the only black person in class, so when issues about poor people, black people, or people on welfare came up, students would look to her for answers. Florence says, "The kids told me they liked to hear me talk and we became very close. I learned no matter how rich or poor people are, we have to remember our commonalities, not our differences."

In addition to her work at WINGS, she is one of a group of eleven low-income women who are learning to publish a newspaper called *Survival News.* To do this, Florence attended a writing workshop and has learned word processing. Florence believes that in this information-based economy, it is important for everyone to learn computer skills.

Florence believes you should never stop learning. She speaks of Frederick Douglass, the great black leader. As a plantation slave, he was not allowed to go to school. His owner said, "Don't teach him, he will want more." She went on to say, "And that is what we need, to *want more.*" She urges people to avoid becoming clones. "We need critical thinking, using our own mind. We need equality and the ability to speak out."

Now at the age of retirement, Florence is receiving Social Security benefits. While that system is more dignified than welfare, the money is barely enough to live on.

As she looks toward the future, Florence is satisfied with where she has arrived and looks forward to continuing her human service work and her political activities. The two are inseparable. WINGS is a service agency with a political mission—to help women break the bonds of the addictions that enslave them, to help them reestablish healthy family ties, and to join with others in the community and nation to free us all.

Value dilemmas
A situation in which competing values make it difficult, if not impossible, to determine the correct choice.

In the following pages, we will look at some of the areas that can lead to **value dilemmas** and conflicts, either within us as workers or within society as a whole. Often the dilemmas or conflicts occur simply because human situations are by nature unclear and complex. The choices open to our clients are all imperfect, and each carries unknown consequences. "The horns of a dilemma" is an apt phrase. The very definition of a dilemma implies that it is an impossible situation with no solution. We shall give some case examples and ask you to think through the values and ethics involved in each example, using the questions in Figure 5.1.

Questions to Guide Decision Making

1. What values are promoted by the action?

2. What values are violated by the action?

3. Is the client competent to decide? If not, how should a decision be made? Who should make it? How should we define "competence"?

4. How does the social worker's position/power affect our evaluation of the action? How does the institutional setting affect our evaluation?

5. What alternative actions are possible? (Evaluate each in terms of questions 1 through 4.)

6. How do your own values affect the way you evaluate the action? Would your client or agency make a different evaluation?

In evaluating each course of action, consider the client's right to self-determination; such values as privacy, trust, honesty, and respect; the good or harm of the action for the well-being of the client/others/community.

FIGURE 5.1 Human service dilemmas

Source: Rhodes, 1989.

DILEMMAS SURROUNDING THE VALUE OF SELF-DETERMINATION

What happens when one person's right to control his or her own behavior clashes with another set of rights? **Self-determination** is a value held in such high esteem in the social work profession that the National Association of Social Workers' Code of Ethics puts it at the top of its list of professional values: "The social worker should make every effort to foster maximum self-determination on the part of clients."

Lynn Atkinson, a social work professor who believes that social workers should not force their services on clients, defines self-determination as follows:

> In working with people, social workers must respect the right of individuals to choose their own life paths. Although a social worker may disagree with the choices or the values of a particular person, the social worker must respect that individual's right to believe and do as he or she wishes and honor that right by not forcing the person to do something that is against that person's will. (Atkinson & Kunkel, 1992, pp. 159–160)

In a rejoinder to Professor Atkinson, another professor of social work, O. Dale Kunkel, points out that subsections of the Code of Ethics on self-determination "quickly hedge by characterizing the legal conditions under which client self-determination is not primary" (Atkinson & Kunkel, 1992). Kunkel argues that social workers often must work with clients who do not come to them of their own

Self-determination People's right to determine their own life plan without interference.

free will because they know they have a problem and want to solve it. Florence Miller, for example, works with women who have had their children taken away from them by the state child-protection agency because of their substance abuse.

Social workers must investigate complaints of child abuse and neglect with or without the client's consent; they counsel alcoholics and drug abusers who have been court-ordered into treatment; they work with juvenile delinquents and adult criminals who are incarcerated or who are on probation or parole; they treat mentally ill people who have been involuntarily committed to hospitals. Many of these people could assert that their self-determination is being abridged.

What happens to the value of self-determination when someone has or might be hurting themselves or others? Consider the following case reported in a local newspaper. If the judge asked you to give your professional opinion of what should be done, what would you say?

CASE STUDY

Social, Moral Issues in the Case of a 96-Year-Old Woman

KENNEBUNK, ME—It would be a cruel euphemism, a gross understatement, to say that Nellie Teach lives in squalor.

Neither words nor pictures can adequately capture the wretchedness in which this feisty and fiercely independent 96-year-old woman makes her home.

The kitchen resembles a dung heap. She sleeps and lives in this room; all others are barricaded by rubbish. The stench made at least one social worker ill. The three burners on her gas stove are fully ablaze to heat the room; cardboard containers sit precariously close to the flames. The floor beneath her bare feet is rotted away.

This is home to Nellie Teach, a home she has lived in for decades and which she adamantly refuses to abandon. The faded white two-story house is owned by a disabled, elderly nephew who cannot make repairs to it. "I don't want a nice apartment," she said last week. "I don't want something that belongs to someone else. I don't want people interfering with me."

People who look in on Nellie Teach—neighbors, nurses and doctors, state social workers—fear for her life. They want to clean her house or find her new quarters. But Ms. Teach will not clean up and she will not go. Doctors say she is mentally competent, so she cannot be

removed against her will. The town, as a last resort, went to court last month. They have asked for the authority to "cleanse, disinfect and fumigate" her home.

The conflict between a community that wants to help and a woman who refuses help has opened a panoply of social, moral, and legal questions that are neither unique to Nellie Teach's situation nor easy to answer. Officials in Kennebunk say there are other people in town just like her. Advocates for the elderly say every community in Maine has its Nellie Teaches.

Compassion seems to have dictated the actions of those who have tried to help Nellie Teach. Yet many people say the state and the town should leave her alone, that they are trying to evict a poor, hapless woman. Others say too little is being done to help her. "We're either blamed for being intrusive or not doing enough," says A. Ricker Hamilton, regional program manager for the Maine Department of Human Services.

"How do you intervene and still respect the rights of the individual?" asks Lee Tallion, community care director for Southern Maine Senior Citizens, Inc. "Nellie Teach has a right to do what she wants until legally she endangers herself or someone else."

Nellie Teach is a staunchly independent woman who reached adulthood long before welfare became commonplace.... The state is an institution that is feared by the Nellie Teaches of New England. It...engenders distrust, even contempt....

Some people question the town's suit, wondering whether a serious health hazard does exist. After all, her living conditions have been horrendous for years, according to neighbors and social workers. Nellie Teach is 96 and in excellent health, given her age, according to doctors who have seen her recently.

People wonder what will happen to Nellie Teach if the town should win its suit.... "This lady," says her physician, "has always found the cracks in the system to prevent anybody she doesn't want from coming into her house and changing the status quo. I think a person's independence is to be cherished. But there's a line somewhere that must be drawn." (Adapted from Berney, 1984)

This case is a vivid illustration of the complexity involved in making ethical decisions—individual rights versus the rights of the community. When they conflict, human service workers have to decide which takes precedence. Yet in Nellie Teach's case, officials disagreed about the danger she posed to herself or society.

On the surface, this case involved an issue of public health, but some of the unspoken issues may have involved deeper levels of anxiety about cleanliness and neatness and the moral implications of dirtiness and disorder. "Cleanliness is next to godliness" is an old saying from our Puritan heritage. Many of our ethical dilemmas come from conflicting moral standards. Sometimes the conflict is framed in terms of bureaucracy versus the individual. Bureaucrats who are removed from the life of the local community are often more likely to see issues in abstract, impersonal terms and in terms of the demands of their job. Nellie Teach's neighbor who took her food saw no problem, whereas the director of the public-health department saw a public-health problem that he had to do something about.

Human service workers employed in public welfare are confronted daily with ethical dilemmas. An especially painful one was posed during the 1950s and early 1960s when, in some cities, workers were ordered to make night raids on single-parent welfare recipients to see if an unauthorized male was living in their homes (in which case the males would be responsible for their financial support). Knowing that the Supreme Court had declared this practice unconstitutional, a social worker who lived by the values of the profession was faced with the choices of quitting the job, fighting the ruling powers, or violating the ethics of the profession.

One worker who sued the department of welfare for violating the rights of clients to privacy was, in fact, fired for insubordination, but that worker's courage eventually helped put an end to the practice.

Self-Determination and Child Abuse

Now consider a case that deals with the widespread conflict between a client's style of parenting and an agency's concept of what is appropriate child rearing. This case is summarized from a newspaper article.

CASE STUDY

Falsely Accused, a Mother Fights Back

SCITUATE, MA—The call that brought terror into Brenda Frank's life came on September 17, 1986. A social worker with the Department of Social Services informed Frank that an anonymous complaint of sexual abuse and neglect of her two young daughters had been filed against her.

"I was frozen. Shocked. It was beyond my comprehension," said Frank, during a recent interview in the living room of her modest two-bedroom apartment in this seaside town. "The allegations included the fact that my 4-year-old, Emily, was still being breast-fed occasionally and that both girls (Emily and Rebecca, or Becky, then 6) slept in my bed with me."

Where did such allegations come from? Did she have an unknown enemy out there somewhere?

"I felt so vulnerable," said Frank. "Everything you do is put under a microscope by DSS and you have to defend your every move. I stopped letting the girls sleep with me. I wouldn't let them go outdoors to play in case they fell and got hurt. It was all so very isolating. But I didn't know who to trust. I didn't want anyone to see me, the lady accused of abusing her kids, riding my bike around town or walking down the street...."

When Frank received the phone call from DSS, she had been separated from her husband for five years and was a stay-at-home mother living on welfare. Although finances were always an issue, Frank said she was grateful to have two healthy children, a roof over her head in a town with good schools, nearby stores that she could reach by bicycle, new friends and like-minded young mothers she met through La Leche League (a group advocating breast-feeding until a child naturally weans herself).

Frank describes what happened when the worker from DSS came to her home:

"I was very nervous and frightened and had my mother, a nurse, come for support," said Frank, who had read dozens of books on nutrition, childbirth and parenting during her two pregnancies. "But I felt sure that all I had to do was explain the La Leche philosophy of child-led weaning and give her some of their literature. I thought I would show her their literature and the stuff I've been reading about the concept of mother and child sharing a bed. I had a book by Tine Thevenin called "The Family Bed: An Age-Old Concept in Child Rearing."

I told the worker that I didn't agree with the fact that in our country children are expected to sleep alone at night in their own rooms behind closed doors. I told her my girls slept with me because I wanted them to feel safe at night."

Several days later...she got a letter from DSS ...telling her that the allegations against her had been substantiated. It said:

"You have neglected to guide your children in age-appropriate individuation development and have exposed your children to sexual stimulation with your belief in the concept of the 'family bed.'"

"In other words," said Frank, "I was found guilty of the way I had chosen to parent...."

[Frank] believes the person who anonymously reported her to DSS worked at her complex and might have been angered by Frank's advocacy against the use of pesticides on the grounds and for the ability of elderly residents to have pets.

Frank turned to a lawyer for help. They appealed to the commissioner of DSS for a review of her case. It was under this review that the allegations against her were dropped. But it would be 1989—two years later—before her name was finally taken off DSS's central list as an alleged perpetrator....

Frank may have won her own battle, but she has not remained silent. She continues to testify before state legislatures, to pore over books in law libraries and to counsel others.... (Doten, 1991)

Although Frank won her case, the politics at the Department of Social Services (DSS) did not change until a well-publicized case of a child being peremptorily removed from a foster home in September 1992 created a public furor. The governor ordered the creation of a special commission to investigate DSS policies and procedures. Several bills were introduced in the legislature to

> set specific guidelines for removing children from biological or foster parents, strengthen the rights of grandparents and other relatives in seeking custody of children and immediately clear the record of a parent falsely accused of abuse…and DSS has spawned Families United, a Weymouth-based support group for families having problems with DSS.…
>
> At the time of the Frank case, there was no mechanism by which a person could appeal a 51A (a complaint of abuse or neglect). If a complaint was filed and supported, a person had no recourse. Frank helped to change that. Now there is an automatic review process in place. (Doten, 1991, p. 31)

Child-welfare agencies across the nation are under fire from groups of all ideological points of view. About thirty states have had lawsuits brought against them.

- From conservatives objecting to the agency invading the sanctity of the family
- From advocacy groups claiming that the agency fails to protect children because it is understaffed and underfunded and does not adequately train workers
- From parents claiming that their rights have been abused by intrusive social workers
- From parents claiming that the agency doesn't give them the services their children need
- From foster parents claiming that the agency does not treat them like coprofessionals

The mothers with whom Florence Miller works complain that the Department of Social Services takes children away from parents rather than giving them the resources they need to keep their children. The mothers also complain that DSS often won't return their children to them even after they have recovered from substance abuse.

In May 1992, about two hundred aggrieved people held a rally in the parking lot of the Division for Children and Youth Services (DCYS) in Concord, New Hampshire. They were supporting Stephen and Joan DeCosta, both born-again Christians whose four children were placed in foster care during a highly publicized dispute with the division in 1989. The DeCostas were accused of child abuse when the children's grandmother reported that one of the DeCosta children had been spanked until he bled. The DeCostas are one of a group of parents who claim they have a right to decide how to discipline their children, while DCYS maintains it has an obligation to draw the line. "A district court judge found the DeCostas guilty of abuse, but the case was resolved by a consent decree between the family and the division. The family was reunited, which the division insists is always its ultimate goal" (Doten, 1991, p. 31).

The Frank and the DeCosta cases represent very different child-rearing philosophies. The DeCostas subscribe to the biblical injunction, "Spare the rod and spoil the child." The majority of parents in the United States probably spank their children, but child-welfare agencies seem to be moving in the direction of regarding spanking, especially severe spanking, as child abuse. They are concerned about the rise of violence in our society, and perhaps spanking sends the wrong message to the young child. Most shelters for battered women do not allow the parents to spank their children while they live in the shelter.

The City Council of Oakland, California, introduced a resolution in 1999 to make Oakland the nation's first official No Spanking Zone (Gorov, 1999). They planned to place stop signs with that message in libraries and other public buildings. "We want people to know it's not a good idea to hit kids. And when the government takes a stand against it, it helps them realize they're not supposed to do it," said Dr. Irwin Hyman, a psychologist who runs the National Center for the Study of Corporal Punishment and Alternatives at Philadelphia's Temple University (Gorov, 1999).

Opponents of the purely symbolic resolution countered that local government has no business telling parents how to discipline their children, and that laws already exist to protect youngsters from child abuse (Gorov, 1999). (The resolution did not pass.)

Dr. Hyman, author of "The Case Against Spanking," said that six countries, including Sweden, Norway, and Finland have abolished spanking, and Germany is considering it (Gorov, 1999).

GENUINE CHILD ABUSE VERSUS FALSE CHARGES

Parents of children in day care centers have been divided into warring camps over this issue. Day care centers have set up strict guidelines for touching children, making teachers cautious about physical contact. Parents have become more cautious about putting their children in day care centers. Ann Withorn, a professor of human services at the University of Massachusetts, believes that conservative officials consciously manipulate people's sexual anxieties in order to discourage parents from using day care centers, thus taking the pressure off of the government to provide funding for them (personal communication, 1994).

This conspiracy theory is, of course, quite controversial. False memories and false accusations occur, but so do actual cases of child abuse. Clearly, abuse must be treated as an outrageous and impermissible assault on children. At the same time, there is a great deal of hysteria about sexual abuse, and some innocent people, such as Brenda Frank, have been victimized by this hysteria.

This issue presents human service workers with the complex problem of differentiating between genuine sexual abuse and false charges. In Frank's case, her consulting psychiatrists judged that breast-feeding children to a late age and allowing children to sleep with her did not constitute sexual abuse. When experts disagree on the issues involving parenting styles and lifestyles, there are no easy answers for human service workers.

Self-Determination When Treatment Is Mandated

To get their children back, some of the mothers Florence Miller works with have been ordered to undergo treatment for their substance abuse and counseling for their personal problems. Under these conditions, it is very possible that a client will go through the motions of **mandated treatment** simply to gain the promised benefits or avoid punishment. But can people change if they are forced to accept help? Consider the following case, in which a mother did what she had to get her children back but never liked what she had to do. This is an actual case, described by Robert Ingram (1992), a social work therapist and one of the founders of Empower, a welfare rights group.

Mandated treatment
Treatment that is legally required by the courts or by government officials.

CASE STUDY

Alice

"I was working in a nursing home as a nursing assistant. I didn't want to ask welfare for anything. It felt good. I worked from 7 to 3. My 12-year-old daughter was supposed to take my 6-year-old son to nursery school and then go to school herself. They were mad because I was working so the kids didn't go to school. They fooled around and they set the house on fire.

"They (social service department) took the kids. I was missing work, and I lost the job. They said the kids were emotionally upset. Any kid would be if he was taken out of his home. They wouldn't let me see the kids. They told me that if I go to therapy, I'd get my kids back. They didn't say anything about how long I'd be in therapy. They told me it would be up to the therapist to say when the kids could come home. The therapist was like a judge. [I] went to the therapist.

"All he wanted to do was talk about the past. What the…does the past have to do with it? The therapist said it was up to the judge when I'd get the kids back. The judge said it was up to the protective worker, and the worker said it was up to the therapist. It took me a year and a half to convince the therapist that I was well enough to have the kids at home. I was calmer because I had a job and had something to do with my time."

Ingram asked her if the therapist said anything to her or gave her medicine that helped her to be calm, and she said, "No." She went to the therapist once a month at first. Ingram asked her if it wouldn't have been better to go more often to learn or do whatever it was to get the kids back.

[Alice said], "I don't know. That's the way it was set up. I used to tell him, 'I'm doing good.' There was nothing to talk about. It got to be boring. I told him, 'I'm not trying to be rude, but I have better places to be.' He'd sit there and shake his head yes. He had no suggestions at all. After a year and a half, the therapist sent a letter to the judge, suggesting that [my] younger child should be returned home and that the therapy should continue. Then I had to go twice a month, with my son. It was a pain. I had to get him out of school early. It was messing up his school work. [My] employer was concerned that I was taking time off work to go to therapy. The therapist told me I didn't have to work but he wouldn't help me get SSI (Supplemental Security Income)…."

[Ingram] asked her how she finally stopped seeing the therapist. She said that he resigned from his job. He tried to persuade her to continue with another therapist but he let her go when she insisted that she did not need to continue in treatment.

Ingram treats mandated clients, leaving the decision about whether to submit to the therapy up to the client, and recommends developing a contract with the client in the beginning. The contract certifies that the client is in treatment if he or she at least shows up regularly for interviews. "Once the therapist demonstrates his or her trustworthiness by adhering to the contract, the client may begin to work on the issues that attracted the attention of the mandating agency" (Ingram, 1992, p. 96).

Sometimes treatment is not mandated by an agency but is forced on a client by his or her family or friends. One drug treatment program, for example, occasionally kidnaps addicted adolescents at the parents' request and physically forces them to remain in treatment. Some of these adolescents later thank their parents for doing it, believing that they would not have kicked the life-destroying habit on their own. Others are still angry at their parents for violating their autonomy.

Parents of mentally ill children are often eager for their children to be hospitalized and to take psychotropic medication, even while the children resist both hospitalization and medication. In our interview with Judi Chamberlin in Chapter 2, Judi talks about how parents in the Alliance for the Mentally Ill often push for hospitalization and medication against the wishes of their children. The Mental Patients' Liberation Front believes in complete freedom of choice. Its members develop self-help support groups and alternative treatment methods and hope they can win voluntary membership.

Aversive behavioral treatment
A form of behavior modification based primarily on punishment rather than reward.

Some therapists advocate the use of **aversive behavioral treatments** that employ harsh methods of discipline as a training technique for clients who have been given up as hopeless by other agencies. A residential treatment institution for autistic children in Rhode Island came under fire in 1991 for such a treatment. The Massachusetts Office for Children filed suit against the institution, charging that it treated children cruelly with "white noise" and physical punishment. Many of the parents supported the institution, saying that the treatment helped their children control their behavior. In the course of the debate, some psychologists came forward with testimony claiming that there are more advanced and humane methods of treatment that are just as effective. However, the Office for Children lost the suit, and the institution continues this form of problematic behavior management.

Self-Determination Is Undermined When Clients Are Manipulated

Manipulation
Trying to influence someone's behavior or thoughts by covert, unstated methods rather than open, explicit methods.

Although it is not easy to know how to handle the ethical dilemmas of mandated treatment, at least both client and worker openly acknowledge that there is coercion in the relationship. But there is another kind of coercion that undermines self-determination. **Manipulation** by the worker is subtle and harder for a client to detect and to defend against. For example, before the 1960s, social workers were so convinced that unmarried mothers should give their babies up for adoption that they often subtly manipulated the clients into accepting that choice. By presenting no other options and services, unmarried mothers were geared to giving babies up for adoption. Homes for unwed mothers offered no opportunities to learn parenting skills, and no day care was provided. Unable to visualize any other path, young women, whether they had worked through the issues or not, simply agreed to give up their children even before they were born. Often that might have been the best course of action, but manipulation violates the tenet of self-determination.

In discussing the philosophical implications of manipulation, Rhodes argues that manipulation should usually be avoided and needs always to be carefully monitored. If [the worker believes that] coercion is necessary, it should generally be undertaken *with the client's knowledge.* Otherwise, social workers may be able covertly to force actions on clients that society and clients would not allow if these actions were made explicit (Rhodes, 1989, p. 118).

Rhodes argues that, because it is impossible to be ethically neutral in human service work, workers should be open with clients about their ethical commitments so that clients can make an **informed choice.** "*How much* a therapist reveals must depend upon the relationship and the client's ability to process such information" (Rhodes, 1989, p. 120).

> **Informed choice**
> A choice that is made after being given all the relevant information about the issue.

SOME CURRENT ETHICAL CONFLICTS

Conflicts Surrounding AIDS

The issues that surround AIDS are fiercely debated. Some children with AIDS have been excluded from nursery schools and public schools because of parents' anxieties about contagion. Other school directors, principals, and parents have welcomed those children into their schools, convinced that they are not a danger to the other children and that the youngsters need to live as normal a life as possible, despite such a traumatic illness.

AIDS has also raised debates about whether medical personnel should be routinely tested; whether prostitutes or other prisoners with AIDS should be held in prisons for periods longer than their sentences to protect the public; whether condoms or clean hypodermic needles should be distributed; and even whether AIDS victims should be quarantined.

Many of those debates contain more heat than light. It is important for human service workers to base their thinking about AIDS on the most up-to-date medical information, which will be willingly provided by local public-health agencies or AIDS action groups.

Conflicts Surrounding the Right to Die

Some conflicts between the individual and the community spring from conflicting interpretations of morality. For example, does an individual have a right to choose to die, or does the state have the right to forbid that choice? If a terminally ill person wants to die, should a doctor help her or him do so? Do parents have the right to decide on **euthanasia** (also called mercy killing) for their terminally ill child?

> **Euthanasia**
> Active intervention in hastening death, usually made by a doctor with the permission of the dying person or the family.

DUNAGIN'S PEOPLE

"DON'T WORRY. WHEN SEX EDUCATION IS PRESENTED IN A CLASSROOM SETTING, IT WILL BECOME AS FOREIGN TO THE STUDENTS AS MATH AND SCIENCE."

There is a fierce debate today about sex education, with the government advocating "abstinence only" programs and others arguing that young people should be told about all the options. This cartoon suggests that any sex education program given in school will not be relevant to students' actual life experiences.

The following case is reported by the Hastings Center, an organization founded in 1969 to study issues raised by the advances in medicine, the natural sciences, and the social and behavioral sciences. The Hastings Center studies "organ transplants, human experimentation, prenatal diagnosis of genetic disease, life-extending technologies, recombinant DNA research, health policy, and control of human behavior" (Hastings Center, 1979, p. 1).

CASE STUDY

Andrea

Andrea was a 9-year-old girl who had been diagnosed as having cystic fibrosis at the age of 13 months. Since then she had been hospitalized twelve times, eight times during the last year.

When admitted for the last time she was already receiving an experimental antibiotic, which was being administered in an attempt to control a resistant pneumonia superimposed on severely damaged lungs, a result of her underlying disease. She was at that time a severely ill, emaciated child with moderately labored breathing. She seemed to have no interest in her environment and refused to communicate with anyone but her mother.

The parents indicated that in the event of a cardiac or respiratory arrest, they did not want their child to be resuscitated and the appropriate medical order was written. The child was not involved in these conversations or subsequent decision making.

As this child's condition continued to decline, the parents asked the doctor how much longer she would live and how she would die. At one point the father said: "Watching your own child die is worse than dying yourself." This comment led to a discussion of active euthanasia utilizing intravenous potassium chloride or a similar drug. The physicians pointed out that no matter how hopeless a

situation or how much suffering the patient and family were enduring, the law prohibits the active taking of a patient's life. They refused to consider this option.

The following day, Andrea's heart began to fail. Her condition became progressively worse, and she died approximately forty-eight hours later. During these last two days her parents were in great despair because of her steadily deteriorating condition. They felt helpless and impotent to alleviate their daughter's distress. Medical treatment was continued to the end, and no measures were taken to hasten Andrea's death.

Approximately two months after her death, the mother was asked if she would still have given permission for active euthanasia if she had been offered that option. She replied, "Yes."

Should active euthanasia be permitted to spare the patient and family from suffering when death is inevitable? Does it make a difference if you are deciding about a child, a young adult, or an elderly person? Do you think you would think the same way if it was your relative? What if the doctors were wrong, what if a new medication were about to be discovered that could have saved Andrea's life a few months later? How can we be sure?

In the commentary on this case, James Rachels (1979, p. 19), a philosophy professor, points out that the American Medical Association (AMA) says that active euthanasia is not only illegal but immoral as well. The AMA condemns mercy killing as "contrary to the most fundamental measures of human value and worth." However, the AMA statement goes on to say that allowing patients to die by ceasing treatment is in some circumstances all right. Rachels argued that the doctors should have given a lethal injection to end Andrea's suffering. The doctors chose not to prolong Andrea's life by aggressive treatment, so evidently they felt that prolonging Andrea's life was pointless. "If it was pointless for her to endure, say, a four-day period of dying, why should we choose a course that requires her to endure a two-day period of dying?" (Rachels, 1979, p. 19).

Another philosophy professor, Philippa Foot (1979), disagreed with Rachels. She thought that active euthanasia was risky in this case because of Andrea's inability to decide for herself. She believes that "we are apt to think about [active euthanasia] in a confused and superficial way. This is one reason why there is so much danger in supporting any kind of active euthanasia, never mind its extension to children and noncompetent adults" (Foot, 1979, p. 20).

Since the Nazi death camps, decisions about euthanasia have taken on an ominous cast. No one can afford to be casual about taking human life for any reason or under any circumstances. Dangers lurk behind what seems to be an otherwise logical and compassionate policy. We don't honestly know how we would decide the case of Andrea, but we can understand the reasoning of all the people involved.*

Conflicts Surrounding Reproductive Choice

Fierce battles have raged over the issue of abortion for over two decades. In this deeply personal and intimate area, most people have firm opinions. Because social science is never value-free, we should state our biases on this hotly contested issue. Along with most feminists, we believe that women should have the right to choose whether or not to have a baby, a right that the Supreme Court affirmed in its 1973 *Roe v. Wade* decision.

This decision protects a woman's right to privacy regarding what she does with her own body through the second trimester of pregnancy. Both the decision and the right have been contested ever since. The pro-choice faction fights to retain the right to an abortion for all women. The anti-abortion faction works to make it illegal in the same way that murder is outlawed.

The *Roe v. Wade* decision was modified in July 1992 in a case entitled *Planned Parenthood v. Casey.* This case involved a Pennsylvania law that required physicians to give counseling that encouraged childbirth to women seeking abortions. After the counseling, women would be required to wait for twenty-four hours before receiving an abortion. The law also required that the woman's spouse be notified, as well as the parents of a minor teenager.

The Supreme Court upheld all of the Pennsylvania requirements except spousal notification. A narrow five-judge majority held spousal notification to be unconstitutional because it was "unduly burdensome," particularly to women in abusive or otherwise dysfunctional marriages. It did not, however, consider a twenty-four-hour wait to be unduly burdensome to poor women. Yet many view this waiting time as burdensome: "The 24-hour waiting period can require extra travel, lodging and child care costs beyond the financial means of poorer women. For these women, such extra costs can turn a burden into a veritable ban on access to abortion" (Boston Women's Health Book Collective, 1992, p. 379). Access to abortion for poor women had already been limited by the Hyde Amendment passed by Congress in 1976, which banned using publicly funded Medicaid money for abortion unless a woman's life was in danger.

---

*The commentaries on the case of Andrea and others in the *Hastings Center Report* are more complex than our brief summary indicates. We suggest that it would be worthwhile for students to read some of this material at length, as the discussions give an excellent frame of reference for thinking through ethical issues. The address of the *Hastings Center Report* is 360 Broadway, Hastings-on-Hudson, NY 10706.

Following the federal government, many states stopped funding "medically unnecessary" abortions. The result was immediate in terms of harm and discrimination against poor women. In October 1977 Rosie Jiminez, a Texas woman, died from an illegal abortion in Mexico after Texas stopped funding Medicaid abortions. (Boston Woman's Health Book Collective, 1992, p. 377)

Other Supreme Court decisions have weakened the *Roe v. Wade* decision. Several states have passed laws restricting abortion in various ways. Restrictions include waiting periods, informed consent, parental notification, and allowing abortion only in cases of rape, incest, and risk to a woman's health. Many of these restrictions are now being contested in the courts. In March 1993, the Supreme Court upheld a lower-court decision that prohibited Louisiana from virtually outlawing abortions. This affirmed that states have no constitutional right to outlaw abortions. A Colorado law that prohibited Medicaid funding for abortions in cases of rape or incest was struck down by the Supreme Court in 1995, leaving intact a federal law that forces states to provide Medicaid funding of abortions for victims of rape or incest.

The anti-abortion activists have succeeded in intimidating doctors and clinics through the use of militant, often frightening demonstrations. Doctors and clinic workers have been murdered. Most doctors now do not want to risk doing abortions. Only 13 percent of medical schools require doctors to receive such training, and 83 percent of the counties in the nation do not have a clinic or hospital that performs the medical procedure of abortion (Schreiber, 1993).

People who oppose abortion made a further assault on the right to abortion through their efforts to ban what they called "partial birth abortion," a term that doctors considered medically meaningless. This ban, passed by Congress and signed into law by George W. Bush in 2003, was declared unconstitutional by Federal District Court Judge Phyllis J. Hamilton in 2004. Kim Gandy, president of the National Organization for Women praised the judge's action:

> The court in San Francisco acknowledged that the Bush Administration passed extreme legislation with complete disregard for women's health and the law. The law bans abortions as early as 13 weeks, prohibiting a procedure that doctors regard as safe and among the most effective in preserving a woman's health. Judge Hamilton wrote, "The act creates a risk of criminal liability during virtually all abortions performed after the first trimester." (NOW, 2004, June 1)

This decision, in *Planned Parenthood v. Ashcroft*, applies only to Planned Parenthood clinics and doctors. The law is also being challenged in three other federal courts.

Another hotly contested issue in the abortion fight was RU 486 (mifepristone), the drug regimen that terminates pregnancy within the first five weeks, which can be taken by women at home. Anti-abortion forces tried to prohibit it; pro-abortion forces fought to have it legalized. After much research, it was finally approved by the Food and Drug Administration (FDA) in 2000. It is marketed by Danco under the trade name of Mifeprex. During his 2000 campaign, George W. Bush pledged to sign any legislation that restricts mifespristone. In August 2002, anti-abortion groups petitioned the FDA to ban mifepristone. However, it continues to be sold legally and Danco announced in 2002 that since FDA approval, 100,000 women have used it to terminate pregnancy (Feminist Majority, 2004).

The "morning after pill," called "Plan B," has also been a hotly contested issue, even though pro-abortion forces insist that it is not an abortion since it prevents the fertilized egg from being implanted in the wall of the uterus. It can be obtained by prescription, but is not always easily available. Feminist organizations such as NOW and NARAL offer information about how it can be obtained.

Whether or not abortions are legal, women will continue to get them. One researcher says that the real public policy question is not *whether* we will have abortions but *what kind* of abortions we will have (Schreiber, 1993, citing Miller, 1992).

The kind of abortions performed while they were illegal were often very dangerous. In his 1955 survey of female sexual behavior, Alfred Kinsey reported that 22 percent of his married respondents said they had had at least one abortion. Kinsey claimed that illegal abortion in the 1960s was estimated to be the third largest moneymaker for organized crime, exceeded only by narcotics and gambling, and he pointed out that most large public hospitals had septic abortion wards to treat the large number of life-threatening infections from abortions performed under non-sterile conditions.

In the face of this massive right-wing assault on abortion rights, all of the feminist organizations in the nation joined in the March for Women's Lives in Washington, D.C., on April 25, 2004. Over a million people marched for reproductive rights, for justice, and for equality. It was probably the most diverse of the many women's marches that have been held in Washington, D.C., with many women of color, welfare rights activists, gays and lesbians, and social justice activists.

THE FETAL PROTECTION MOVEMENT

A recent tactic of the anti-abortion movement has been the campaign to protect the fetus from harm. Anti-abortion activists claim to care only about the health of the fetus, but as columnist Bob Herbert (1998) pointed out, they have a hidden agenda.

> The underlying goal of the fetal protection movement is to have the fetus defined as a person in as many venues as possible, thus, in the long run, undermining a woman's right to have an abortion. If a developing fetus becomes legally identical to a person, with all the rights of a person, then a woman's right to an abortion necessarily collapses. Abortion under those circumstances would logically become, under the law, murder. (p. 17)

In 1998 Governor Tommy Thompson of Wisconsin signed into law a bill that will permit the state to take into custody pregnant women who exhibit a serious and habitual "lack of self-control" in the use of alcohol or drugs. The bill defines "unborn child" as a human being from the time of fertilization to the time of birth and would give the state the right to appoint a legal guardian to represent the interests of the fetus.

March for Women's Lives, Washington, D.C., April 25, 2004. Over a million people marched for reproductive rights and economic justice for women.

The fetal protection movement has not made any serious effort to provide women with the alcohol and drug treatment they need, or even adequate prenatal care. That is not part of their agenda. "When South Carolina began locking up pregnant addicts for criminal child abuse, there was no residential treatment for pregnant addicts in the entire state. Wisconsin still has long waiting lists of pregnant women seeking addiction services" (Herbert, 1998, p. 17).

Anti-abortionists succeeded in getting a law passed declaring it a crime to harm a fetus, called The Unborn Victims of Violence Act. It was passed by Congress and signed into law by George W. Bush in 2004. This law gives a fetus the same rights as the pregnant woman. Kim Gandy made the following observations on the law:

> The sponsors of this cynical bill have devised a strategy to redefine the Fourteenth Amendment, which guarantees equal protection of the law to "persons," which has never been defined to include fetuses. The inventive language of this bill covers "a member of the species *homo sapiens* at any stage of development." Such a definition of "person" could entitle fertilized eggs, embryos and fetuses to legal rights—ultimately setting the stage to legally reverse *Roe v. Wade.* (NOW, 2004, March 26)

"CRACK BABIES"

It is hard to be clear about our values when we are bombarded by the agendas of so many different individuals, organizations, and the media. Newspapers want to sell papers; TV shows want to get a large audience, and they often sensationalize stories in order to do this. The "crack baby" story is a good example.

The development of crack significantly reduced the price of cocaine and increased the availability of the drug, expanding its use from the middle and upper classes to urban minorities. Once cocaine abuse became crack abuse, the problem became sociopolitical rather than medical (Musto, 1988). The rate of substance abuse among African American women and among European American women was about the same, according to a study of pregnant women in Pinellas County, Florida, although black women used cocaine more often than white women. However, despite similar rates of substance abuse, African American women were ten times more likely to be reported to the authorities (Chasnoff, 1989). For the media, the demonization of drug-abusing parturient women made better copy than did detailed elaborations of the complexity of the germane issues (Lyons & Rittner, 1998).

It is true that using substances such as crack, alcohol, cigarettes, and amphetamines can be harmful to a developing fetus. Yet the media seized on the issue of crack babies and created an atmosphere of hysteria with news about a problem of "epidemic" proportions. It exaggerated the numbers involved. "Despite efforts to collect reliable information, exaggerated estimates of an annual incidence of 100,000–739,200 pregnant women or newborns with drug diagnoses persist in the scientific and the popular literature; furthermore, it is often suggested that the figures solely represent cocaine exposure" (Dore, Doris, & Wright, 1995, p. 533). In fact, a careful research study estimated the number of drug-using pregnant women as 88,000 per year and about 48,000 per year for drug-affected newborns (Dore et al., 1995).

It is difficult to assess the causes of damage to a newborn. If the mother used any cocaine, the assumption is often made that all the damage to the child was due to cocaine when in fact there may have been multiple causes, including malnutrition. Most of the mothers are poor and some are homeless. One researcher asks, "What would be the public implications if…we learned that what we thought were drug effects were actually due to poverty and not to drugs per se?" (Lester & Tronick, 1994, p. 118).

The media created the impression that any baby whose mother had used crack was ruined for life. Yet recent research suggests that the damage done to the newborn may not necessarily be permanent. This "new research on the effects of prenatal exposure to cocaine challenges the popular notion of a lost generation of children, permanently damaged by their mothers' drug use" (Sege, 1992, p. 20). The research suggests that many babies can recover from the effects of crack-cocaine *if given adequate treatment and support*. The permanent damage some of them suffer may be the result of the family's *poverty and lack of adequate health care, housing, and other social supports.*

Some of the findings of this later research have begun to find their way into the popular media, but the earlier scare stories had a profound effect on politicians and officials. Record numbers of single mothers are in prison for first-time drug offenses, and the number of women in federal and state prisons more than doubled from 1984 to 1994 to 55,000 nationwide, with almost the same number in local jails. More than two-thirds are mothers (Bernstein, 1996a). More than 200 women in thirty states have been prosecuted on some theory of "fetal rights" (Goodman,

2001a). Many states have enacted legislation making it possible for pregnant women to be charged with child abuse or endangerment if they gave birth to babies who tested positive for certain substances, especially cocaine (Bernstein, 1996a). Many of these same states have cut welfare benefits, and probably none has enough treatment facilities for pregnant women who are substance abusers.

South Carolina jailed two drug-using pregnant women by redefining a state child-abuse law to include a viable fetus. The American Civil Liberties Union appealed, arguing that it will hurt those women who, because of fear of arrest, may not seek the prenatal care that could improve maternal and fetal health. The Supreme Court denied the appeal, without any comment or dissent.

In 1989 the hospital of the Medical University of South Carolina tested the urine of patients who fit a certain police "profile" and turned over the results of those who tested positive to the police (Goodman, 2001). Over a few years, women with the same "profile"—all but one of them African American and all of them poor—came for maternity care and ended up in police custody. Later the hospital added drug treatment as an alternative, but thirty women were jailed during pregnancy or were shackled in the delivery room or arrested in recovery.

The Center for Reproductive Law and Policy challenged this practice all the way to the Supreme Court, and were supported by seventy-five medical associations who argued that when doctors doubled as cops, they violated the doctor–patient relationship, and also frightened women from receiving medical care. A 6 to 3 majority of the Supreme Court ruled in 2001 that a hospital can't secretly test a pregnant patient for evidence. Without a warrant and without the woman's consent, the drug test amounted to an unconstitutional search (Goodman, 2001a).

However, the ruling was not a clear victory for women. Justice Anthony Kennedy said that while this practice was unconstitutional, "There should be no doubt that South Carolina can impose punishment upon an expectant mother who has so little regard for her own unborn that she risks causing him or her lifelong damage and suffering" (Goodman, 2001).

In fact, South Carolina still imposes punishment on some pregnant women by applying the law against child abuse to viable fetuses.

As we sort out our values, we need to be careful not to be swept up in popular hysteria about a problem, and we need to distill the true facts from all the myths and stereotypes.

ATTITUDES TOWARD ABORTION ARE DEEPLY ROOTED BELIEFS

When does life begin? This is an abstract philosophical question, which most of us probably answer according to our value system and not by scientific evidence. Catholic theology holds that life begins at conception, although some believe that the Catholic hierarchy does not represent the views of most American Catholics on this issue nor the practice of Catholic women who have abortions at the same rate as the national average for all women. Some orthodox Jews believe that life begins with the sperm, even before it meets the egg. Other religious groups, such as the Mormons and fundamentalist Christians, oppose abortion on religious grounds.

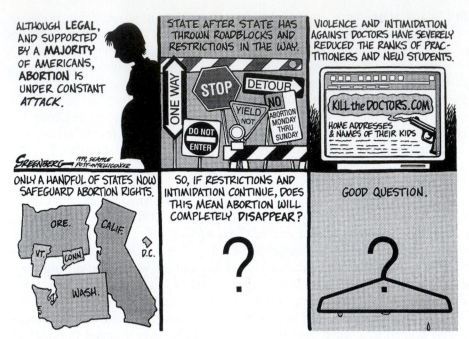

The Supreme Court has ruled that the termination of an unplanned pregnancy is a matter between a woman and her doctor. But since this landmark decision, many states have placed limitations of this right. Pro-choice supporters fear a return to the days when desperate women used crude devices such as unfurled coat hangers to end their pregnancies.

Many of the most militant anti-abortion demonstrators have come from the ranks of fundamentalist Christians with conservative politics. Although they sponsor a few social service agencies geared to helping women keep their babies, as a group they pay little attention to the policies that make it easier for poor women to raise children—adequate TANF grants, affordable housing, good wages, child care, and so forth. One of the authors of this text (Mandell) circulated a petition to raise AFDC grants at an anti-abortion demonstration. No protestors signed it, and some expressed their opposition to or ignorance of welfare. Many pro-choice counter-demonstrators, on the other hand, eagerly signed the petition.

Despite our own pro-choice stance, we have the greatest respect for those who oppose abortion because of their deep commitment to preserving life, and who express that commitment after the children are born by working for a more equal distribution of tax money and an end to war. The Catholic Workers are one such group of dedicated pacifists and social activists who oppose abortion.

Human service workers need to inform themselves thoroughly about the issues, be as clear as possible about where they stand, and make their position known to clients so that their biases do not subtly influence clients to make choices they may later regret.

STEM CELL RESEARCH

If a fetus deserves the same protection as an existing child, does a stem cell also deserve that protection? Is using embryonic stem cells for research equivalent to an abortion? This is the subject of fierce debate between pro-abortion and anti-abortion forces.

Embryonic stem cells, harvested from 5-day-old fertilized eggs, may offer the best hope for curing some serious diseases such as Alzheimer's, Parkinson's, juvenile diabetes, and arthritis. Scientists believe that embryonic stem cells can be regenerated into customized replacement organs that resist rejection. Research suggests that these cells can become insulin-producing cells that would ease the burden of diabetes (Rosen, 2001).

Federal research guidelines allow only the use of excess embryos stored at fertility clinics, a byproduct of the widely accepted practice of in vitro fertilization, and then only with permission of the parents producing the embryos (Rosen, 2001). Although the issue has been framed as an abortion issue, even the opponents of abortion are split on this. Congressman Orrin Hatch, an anti-abortion stalwart, is open to the possibility of stem cell research and defends his position: "People who are pro-life are also pro-life for existing life" (Goodman, 2001c).

President George W. Bush, who had received a good deal of support from opponents of abortion, agonized over the decision and in the summer of 2001 he compromised by allowing research on what he described as sixty self-sustaining colonies of embryonic stem cells that existed in the United States and abroad. Researchers objected that there were far fewer than sixty, but seemed to accept President Bush's decision as better than nothing. However, researchers expressed doubts about the usefulness of the existing colonies, which used material from mouse cells and bovine serum. Critics of Bush's policy say this contaminates the colonies. Debate continues on the issue. This is a good illustration of how ideological positions can affect the direction of scientific research.

NONTRADITIONAL METHODS OF REPRODUCTION

While some women seek abortions because they have chosen not to have a baby, many people cannot conceive children. Reproductive technologies now make many new choices available. Some of them present ethical dilemmas.

In the past, many people who could not conceive chose to adopt. However, there are now many fewer babies available for adoption because of the legalization of abortion, the increased use of birth control, and the fact that many single women now keep their babies.

Nontraditional ways of having children include artificial insemination by a donor, surrogate parenting, and in vitro fertilization.

Artificial Insemination

In **artificial insemination,** semen from a donor is injected into a woman's genital tract. Most children conceived in this way have not been told about the circumstances

Artificial insemination
The practice of implanting semen into a woman's uterus by a method other than sexual intercourse.

surrounding their birth. Indeed, hundreds of thousands of children "have been unknowingly deprived of the basic facts about their origins, an enormous violation of their rights" (Holbrook, 1990, p. 334), as well as an ethical issue of immense proportions.

In 1983, the Sperm Bank of California in San Jose became the first in the nation to ask donors whether they would be willing to be contacted by their offspring after the children reached adulthood (Bergstein, 2002). The first of these meetings occurred in 2002 when an 18-year-old woman contacted her biological father to thank him and to learn more about their shared genetic history.

Men who refuse to release their identity are still allowed to donate at the Sperm Bank of California, but those who say yes cannot reverse the decision. Now 80 percent of the bank's clients request a donor willing to release his identity. The director of the sperm bank commented that this development is happening at the same time as the open adoption movement because people want to know their father's identity. Some other sperm banks also release donor identities. Estimates of the number of American children born each year through artificial insemination range from 30,000 to 75,000 (Bergstein, 2002).

Surrogate Parenting

Surrogate
parenting The
procedure in which
a fertile woman
conceives and bears a
child for an infertile
woman by being
impregnated with
the husband's sperm.

Surrogate parenting involves a fertile woman conceiving and bearing a child for an infertile woman by being impregnated with the husband's sperm. Generally the surrogate mother does it for a payment. Perhaps the best publicized case was the 1987 case of "Baby M," a baby conceived and borne by a working-class woman in the pay of an affluent couple. Although she initially contracted to give the baby up, she changed her mind after the baby's birth. This created legal and ethical problems and was the subject of much public debate. Some people, particularly certain feminists, were of the opinion that such transactions should be outlawed because they constitute exploitation of poor women. Other people argue that a woman has a right to determine what she wants to do with her own body. Some people are concerned about the ethics of buying and selling children like merchandise in a department store.

In Vitro Fertilization

In vitro fertilization
Fertilization of a
woman's egg outside
her body in a petri
dish.

In the process of **in vitro fertilization,** "a doctor stimulates a woman's ovaries with medication, and puts her eggs in a petri dish. The fertilized eggs become embryos and are then implanted into the womb" (Holbrook, 1990, p. 335). The average cost is about $7,800 per attempt, and failure is frequent. The first government survey of fertility clinics was done by the Centers for Disease Control in 1997. Based on data from 281 clinics around the country, the survey showed that the overall success rate (the "take-home-baby" rate) of assisted reproductive technology is 19.6 percent (Foreman, 1997).

Some clinics give out misleading information about their success rates. Many people worry that creating life outside the womb will upset the natural order of things or violate God's intent. There have also been legal and ethical questions about the practice of freezing embryos. This problem arises when several eggs are fertilized in the lab. What should be done with these "embryonic orphans"?

Cloning

The cloned lamb Dolly stunned the world in 1997 when its existence as the first mammal cloned from an adult cell was publicly revealed (Saltus, 2001). This raised the possibility that human beings can be cloned. Some researchers and biotechnology companies want to use "clonal embryos," that is, genetic duplication of existing individuals, to do stem cell research. The company Advanced Cell Technology in Worcester, Massachusetts, announced that it has already moved forward with producing clonal embryos using methods similar to those used to clone Dolly the sheep (Norsigian & Newman, 2001).

However, many scientists and physicians oppose bringing clonal embryos to term. They cite the hazards that have led to fetal and postnatal deaths, birth defects, and health problems with advancing age in the majority of cloned animals to date. (Dolly the sheep, for example, developed early-onset arthritis when she was 4 years old.) In the first birth-to-death study of cloned animals, Japanese scientists reported in 2002 that cloned mice die significantly earlier than their naturally born counterparts, the first clear evidence that cloning causes life-shortening biological abnormalities (Mishra, 2002).

Beyond these risks, opponents of human cloning believe that social and ethical considerations should lead to banning the practice. A group of 100 pro-choice advocates and organizations signed a statement calling for an effective ban on human reproductive cloning. They are concerned primarily with the risks to women's and children's health and do not want women and children subjected to mass experimentation of the sort we are now seeing with cows, sheep, and pigs (Norsigian & Newman, 2001). Some signatories emphasize that cloning would violate deeply and widely held convictions about human individuality and dignity.

Any person produced in this fashion would be an experiment, someone designed to possess specific characteristics of a preexisting genetic prototype—not the normal genetic "roll of the dice" that has led to each of us being a genetically unprecedented individual.

It will be all but impossible to enforce a ban on the creation of fully formed human clones if clonal embryo research is allowed to proceed. In the current climate, with several maverick researchers already moving forward with efforts to bring cloned humans to full term, it is critical that public policies actively thwart such efforts—at least until international agreements that would effectively ban the cloning of genetic duplicate humans are firmly in place (Norsigian & Newman, 2001).

These opponents of human cloning emphasize that a ban on creating clonal embryos would not foreclose the use of human embryos resulting from in vitro fertilization procedures for valid medical research, including their use to generate embryonic stem cells (Norsigian & Newman, 2001).

CONFLICTING VIEWS ON THE NATURE OF HUMAN NATURE

The Declaration of Independence states that people have an inalienable right to life, liberty, and the pursuit of happiness. But in daily life, no one is guaranteed a job, and no one is guaranteed an income or a home or food. No matter how compassionate a worker in a welfare department is, he or she is forced to convey the message to clients that society does not place them in high enough esteem for even a poverty-level income.

Although welfare recipients' taxes have already paid for some of the money they receive, they probably didn't pay for all of them. Money must come from the haves to help the have-nots. This is also true of Social Security. Most people get back a good deal more than they paid into the fund. *Yet the crucial question is not whether people should get back only as much as they paid, but whether society as a whole has a responsibility to care for its members when they are having a hard time.*

Your values about the kind of society you want to live in are partially shaped by your beliefs about human nature. Each of us has a mental picture of the "normal" child or adult, even if we have never articulated it. If we are program planners, administrators, or food stamp clerks, our basic view of people will be expressed in many direct and subtle ways as we plan or implement social programs.

These are some of the most common views of the nature of human nature. Which ones come closest to yours? In what ways do your views differ from your parents', your peers', or your neighbors'?

The Belief That People Need to Be Civilized

Some people believe that human beings are born basically evil—born in sin. Although they may be redeemed by the grace of God, they must be kept under control by the rules and regulations of society and civilization.

Hobbes, Thomas
A seventeenth-century philosopher who believed that people need a strong authority in order to regulate their desires.

For **Thomas Hobbes,** a seventeenth-century English philosopher, the human condition was characterized by both desire and rationality. If everyone pursued desire fulfillment, that, according to Hobbes, might lead to conflict with others and to lives that are "nasty, brutish, and short." But every rational person wants to live and to live in peace. Thus he or she accepts authority to regulate, perhaps curb, desire. Considering the times in which he lived, a period of constant war, Hobbes's conclusions are understandable.

Some people have interpreted William Golding's widely read novel *Lord of the Flies* (1959) as a Hobbesian allegory. In this story, a group of English schoolboys, stranded by an airplane crash on a desert island, create a social order that looks very much like the Hobbesian scenario of dog-eat-dog survival, with restraints of authority removed. (Others point out that the boys were simply duplicating the authoritarian society of the supposedly civilized English private school from which they came.)

People who subscribe to a view of human nature similar to Hobbes's are likely to advocate a strong authority and favor "law and order" approaches to human problems. Clearly, Hobbes doesn't believe in self-regulation. A social worker sharing Hobbes's distrust of self-regulation might give clients vouchers rather than cash, keep careful watch over their behavior, and invoke strong punishment for deviations.

The Belief That People Are Basically Rational

While Hobbes was propounding his theories, **John Locke,** another English philosopher and scientist, had a different view. He believed that if people followed their own self-interest, a rational, just society would result. Locke rejected the traditional view that babies were born with fixed selfish ideas or brutish characteristics. He believed instead that a child came into the world with a tabula rasa (blank tablet) on which the world could inscribe itself through the experience of the five senses. People in the helping professions who follow a philosophy similar to Locke's would be likely to subscribe to a more environmentally oriented psychology such as that of the **behaviorist** B. F. Skinner (1974). The assumption in his work is that with the appropriate stimuli, correctly administered, human social behavior can be positively shaped and changed.

The Belief That People Are Corrupted by Society

Jean-Jacques Rousseau, an eighteenth-century Swiss-French philosopher, put forth the idea that people were good by nature but corrupted by civilization: "Man is born free, but is everywhere in chains." He believed that education should draw out the knowledge that people are born with, in contrast to the "banking" theory of education, which holds that knowledge should be deposited in people's empty heads. Education, according to Rousseau, should allow the free development of human potential. Paolo Freire (1970), the Brazilian adult educator, subscribed to a theory of education called "conscientization," which is similar to Rousseau's theory. According to Freire, people's education should begin by raising questions about why they are so poor and why they have been kept from getting the education they need.

The Belief That People Need to Be Connected to Each Other

Several nontraditional and feminist psychologists suggest that, in contrast to the individualistic and competitive orientation commonly found in men, women are socialized to place value on nurturing, cooperation, and nonviolence. Carol Gilligan (1982) asserts that women choose their actions when faced with a moral dilemma according to what effect their choice will have on the others who are involved, rather than by referring to abstract concepts of justice. Caring and responsibility for others are central to their moral concerns.

Locke, John
A seventeenth-century English philosopher and scientist who believed that if people followed their own self-interest, a rational, just society would result.

Behaviorist
A theorist who believes that behavior can be shaped or changed by the systematic application of rewards for behavioral compliance with the demands of the caregiver or therapist.

Rousseau, Jean-Jacques
An eighteenth-century Swiss-French philosopher who believed that people were good by nature but corrupted by civilization.

Counseling Theory	Beliefs about Human Nature
Rational-emotive	Humans subject to powerful biological and social forces have potential for being rational; can rid themselves of emotional difficulty by maximizing rational thinking.
Freudian analysis	The individual is both animalistic and human, shaped by biological needs, sexual drives, and aggressive instincts; behavior primarily determined by unconscious processes that are motivational and goal-directed.
Client-centered counseling	The individual is rational, good, trustworthy; moves in self-actualizing directions or toward growth, health, self-realization, independence, and autonomy.
Existentialism	The individual is required to shoulder tasks set by life and hence to define meaning of life; strives for freedom from instincts and environment; individually unpredictable, free, and responsible to self.
Gestalt therapy	Human beings are not independent from their environment but work as a whole; individual not sum of parts but a coordination.

FIGURE 5.2   A comparison of beliefs about human nature in five counseling theories

Source: Shertzer & Stone, 1980, pp. 236–237.

Psychologist Jean Baker Miller (1976) says that these "feminine" traits that have been traditionally regarded as weaknesses are, in fact, strengths. They take us beyond the "macho" succeed-at-any-cost attitude. She suggests that men as well as women need to strengthen their ability to empower each other without needing to dominate or control.

Figure 5.2 compares the beliefs about human nature of five different counseling theories.

CONFLICTS CAUSED BY BUREAUCRATIC DEMANDS

Most human service workers, unless they are in private practice or a small independent agency, will be employed by bureaucracies that have organizational needs that may be contrary to the needs of workers and clients. In fact, they often pit workers against clients. A welfare worker, for example, may be convinced that a TANF claimant needs more money than the grant allows but is unable to help the client because of complex regulations.

According to Max Weber (Gerth & Mills, 1958), the nineteenth-century sociologist, bureaucracy is supposed to make work more efficient, to substitute dependable rules for arbitrary decisions, to treat people more fairly, and to judge workers on merit rather than favoritism. But bureaucracies also depersonalize and objectify people. They divide work into specialized components so that no one has the satisfaction of seeing a job through to completion. They set up hierarchies of authority that take away the autonomy of workers. One of the most pervasive problems of modern society is **bureaucratization** of work and of relationships. In human service work, this is especially serious because our work requires warm and genuine relationships between people.

The occupational hazard for workers in a bureaucracy is the tendency to "go along to get along." Most workers want to keep their jobs and do what is required, even when it is not in the best interest of clients. You have seen in the interview with Florence Miller that while she was a senior intern, she challenged her supervisor over the issue of whether a mother should have to leave the home when the father visits the children. It was not easy for her to endanger her internship and graduation, but her commitment to justice was too strong to allow her to buckle under.

The tendency to go along willingly with authority has been studied by social psychologists. One of the most famous of these studies is the Milgram experiment (Milgram, 1974) in blind obedience, which explored the conditions under which people would refuse to obey immoral commands. Milgram asked people to "shock" subjects with varying amounts of "electricity" each time they made an error on a task. (Subjects were not actually shocked, but were trained actors who simulated being shocked.) Far more people obeyed the commands than either Milgram or others predicted. Milgram concluded that a person's conscience is diminished in a hierarchical system and in authority systems, people are more likely to see themselves as agents who carry out other people's wishes rather than as autonomous decision makers.

Another classic study that revealed people's willingness to go along with authority was the prison experiment done by Zimbardo, Haney, and Banks (1982) with healthy college students. Half of the students were instructed to be "prisoners," the other half "guards." In a very short time, the students were adopting the behavior they had been assigned. The experiment had to be discontinued because of the sadism of some of the "guards" and because some participants, especially the "prisoners," were breaking down emotionally.

Bureaucratization Increased organizational centralization, hierarchical control, larger workplaces, and decreased autonomy for workers.

Guidelines for Dealing with Conflicts in a Bureaucracy

The task of debureaucratizing society is an enormous one that requires the best creative thoughts and efforts of all of us. We need to accept responsibility for the ethical and political dimensions of our work. Rhodes (1989) suggests workers can do that by:

- Speaking out about their beliefs, showing the politics behind alternative courses of action, and pointing out inconsistencies in the way the agency does its work. Speaking out is a skill that requires as much planning and thought as the most carefully planned case presentation.

- Forming alliances with other workers and with clients to organize social action on policy issues.

- Questioning the rationale behind rules and regulations rather than docilely implementing policies with which the workers disagree.

- Offering expertise on legislative committees, pushing for legislative action, and educating the public about human service issues. (pp. 154, 156)

The Client as Our Employer

The concept that the client is our employer is closely related to the value of self-determination—the belief that only clients can decide what is best for themselves. Even when the client does not pay a fee for our service, we subscribe to the belief that the service should be responsive primarily to his or her needs, not to the workers' or agency's needs. Yet clients are rarely asked to evaluate our services, make suggestions for improvement, serve on boards, or attend case conferences. Overworked agencies are under pressure to "process" people through the system in as short a time as possible.

Some workers who have undergone long and arduous training in the profession may not understand why their clients' opinions about what they need should be valued. This is especially true when their clients are poor, incarcerated, or mentally unstable. Nevertheless, just as in a relationship with an architect, real estate agent, or lawyer, the client has the right to decide which problems are most pressing and which treatment methods are most acceptable.

Professionalization creates built-in conflicts about how to behave with clients. Social work comes out of a nineteenth-century paternalistic tradition. Gratitude was expected from "deserving" clients. Help was refused to the "undeserving." Although twentieth-century professionals no longer hold such expectations, old attitudes linger on. When money or services are defined as everybody's right, as with Social Security, beneficiaries feel entitled to the benefit and do not feel any obligation to be grateful or behave in a certain way. However, when a service is not presented as an automatic entitlement, there are ambiguous behavioral expectations. Both the giver and the recipient resent a relationship in which one person does all the giving and the other does all the taking. Self-help groups derive much of their attraction from the fact that power is shared equally among the members. *The relationship of a human service worker to a client is inherently unequal because of the power differential. The worker is in a position to give or withhold benefits.*

In the chapter on diversity, we suggest that some cultural groups expect a very personalized helping relationship, and therefore it is important to structure the relationship to meet their expectations. A classic study of helping relationships in child abuse and neglect (Berkeley Planning Associates, 1978) concluded that two of the most important factors in helping parents were a more friendly, personalized relationship and the down-to-earth assistance given by parent aides. This was true for a wide variety of cultural groups. Rhodes (1989) concluded, after reviewing four studies of client satisfaction, that

> client satisfaction and client change depended to some extent on clients' perceptions of their workers as "friends." And such friendship had the following qualities: empathy, caring, flexibility, patience, suggestions rather than advice, reciprocity in the form of sharing aspects of one's personal life, and immediate concrete help *in the mode requested.* In addition, many small social activities were viewed as important to befriending: "calling in for a cup of tea, accepting an invitation to a party, sending cards while on holiday, extending a home-visit to play with the children…." (p. 164)

These clients did not seem to make a sharp distinction between "friend" and "professional" when they liked their worker. If a worker was only a professional and not a friend, the worker was usually viewed with hostility or at least distrust (Rhodes, 1989).*

Studies of clients' opinion of human service workers are rare, and the few that Rhodes cited are not necessarily the last word on professional practice. Some of the findings, such as the importance of "many small social activities," are contrary to much of the advice that the professional literature gives caseworkers.

We would understand much more about client satisfaction if every agency regularly asked for feedback. The fact that this is done so rarely suggests that professionals have not yet fully accepted clients as their *employers,* whom they are obliged to satisfy.

Social Class Differences between Workers and Clients

Human service workers are often of a different social class than their clients. A large proportion of agency clientele are poor, and the social class of workers generally ranges from lower to upper middle class. Sometimes workers impose their class-based values on their poorer clients. This was evident in one study of adoption workers. It showed that middle-class workers selected adoptive parents who were "shockingly similar" to themselves (Maas & Engler, 1959, p. 374). The typical husband and wife were white and Protestant, had strong inner controls and little personal flexibility, placed a heavy emphasis on education and ambition, were task oriented, lived in a single family home, earned much more than the average income, and had at least a high school degree. Yet there are surely other kinds of people who can be excellent parents.

---

*Studies that Rhodes reviewed included John W. Mayer & N. Timms, *The Client Speaks: Working Class Impressions of Casework,* New York, Atherton, 1970; E. Sainsbury, *Social Work with Families: Perceptions of Social Casework among Clients of a Family Service Unit,* London, Routledge and Kegan Paul, 1974; S. Rees, *Social Work Face to Face,* New York, Columbia University Press, 1979; T. Keefe & D. E. Maypole, *Relationships in Social Service Practice: Context and Skills,* Monterey, CA., Wadsworth, 1983.

In the 1960s, some research showed that caseworkers believed that people should not rely too heavily on their relatives for help (Leichter & Mitchell, 1967). Caseworkers at that time were mostly white, upwardly mobile, and middle class. They tended to discourage dependence on extended-kin networks. Their attitude has changed somewhat because later research showed that networks play a major role in the lives of poor and working-class families. In fact, we have come to realize that these networks constitute a source of strength for all families. Yet, despite agencies' professed goal of strengthening the family, the bulk of state child-welfare money is spent on foster care rather than on homemaker service, respite care, parent aides, and day care for hard-pressed families. All of these could strengthen a crumbling family, so that the child would not have to be placed in a foster home with strangers.

CONFLICTS DUE TO THE VARIATION IN NATIONAL VALUES IN THE UNITED STATES

Although it is as hard to generalize about national values as about individual or ethnic-group values, some dominant themes stand out in each nation. At times these themes conflict with one another. In the United States, the democratic and humanitarian values expressed in our Constitution stand side by side with the Protestant ethic, which says that all people who work hard enough can "pull themselves up by their own bootstraps." Social Darwinism maintains that in society, as in the jungle, only the most fit can and should survive.

These contradictions help us understand the mixture of progressive and surprisingly punitive legislation that makes up our social welfare system. The values implicit in the punitive legislation often strongly influence public opinion and misconceptions about welfare assistance. In the United States, people in need of financial assistance often receive less help and are more stigmatized than they are in several European countries.

It is interesting to see how these values of competition, individualism, and a belief that people are in control of their own destiny affect the view of people in the United States toward the mentally ill. Anthropological studies of cultural attitudes toward mental illness show that many other cultures are more tolerant of mental illness than the United States and other Western societies. Schizophrenics actually seem more likely to recover in less-developed countries, such as Mexico or India (Bass, 1992).

Anthropologist Janis Jenkins found that Mexican and Indian families are more likely to believe there are forces *outside* each person's control that influence their ability to ward off disease. They are, therefore, much more likely to believe that the person suffering from mental illness deserves sympathy, support, and special treatment. Hispanics are also more likely than Anglo-Americans to believe that even severe mental illness is curable. When people *believe* that they will be cured, they are more likely to be cured. In the United States, on the other hand, we are more likely to stigmatize mentally ill people because of the dominant belief that people are autonomous and in control of their own destiny (Bass, 1992).

Jenkins (1981) found that Hispanic families seem to be more tolerant of unusual behavior, such as hearing voices or having delusions of grandeur, because of the way Hispanic cultures view religion. Jenkins speculated that in the Hispanic culture, people often talk to Jesus and the saints and feel close to spirits, so family members are not as concerned about a patient hearing voices as they are by disruptive or disrespectful behavior (Jenkins, 1981).

In contrast to the greater tolerance of Hispanic cultures toward mental illness, Anglo-American adults are more likely to see mental illness as a personal weakness.

Age and Aging

Increasing awareness of race and sex discrimination has been followed by an increased awareness of age discrimination. Robert Butler (1975), former director of the National Institute of Aging, coined the term **ageism.** In a culture that values youth, attractiveness, productivity, and activity, older people are often devalued. Professionals who work with them sometimes share society's dominant attitudes. Many professional psychiatrists feel inadequate treating older people (Cyrus-Lutz & Gaitz, 1972). Some human service workers have misconceptions about the inevitability of the degenerative process. Although there is no evidence suggesting there must always be a decline in the mental activity, responsibility, and even sexual prowess of the elderly, it is hard not to be influenced by these widely held misconceptions.

Ageism
The practice of discriminating against people because they are old; attitudes associated with the practice.

Sexual Orientation

The lesbian folk singer Betsy Rose sings a song about a lesbian telling her mother for the first time that she is a lesbian. In contrast to the shock and consternation that most mothers would express, Betsy Rose's imaginary mother in the song is delighted and says, "Darlin', I'm glad you're gay!" The song is presented humorously and the audience laughs, because it is so contrary to what happens in real life.

Homophobia (the irrational fear and stigmatization of homosexuality) is deeply ingrained in society, and human service workers are not immune to it. It was not until 1973 that the American Psychiatric Association declared that homosexuality was not a mental illness and removed it from its list of psychiatric disorders. Two years later, the American Psychological Association followed suit.

Despite the lack of scientific evidence for regarding homosexuality as an aberrant or degenerative disease, homosexuals have been a stigmatized minority in many societies. They were one of the first groups the Nazis forced into concentration camps in Poland and Germany. They were required to wear a pink triangle as an identifying symbol, in the same way that the Jews had to wear a yellow star. It is important to remember that the mentally ill and retarded were also locked up in the concentration camps, as well as Gypsies, Masons, Seventh Day Adventists, and

Homophobia
An unreasoning fear or loathing of any person who has an intimate sexual relationship with a person of the same sex.

In 2003 the state of Masschusetts legalized marriages between two persons of the same gender. In response to this break with tradition, some legislators are attempting to amend the U.S. constitution to make such unions illegal.

others whom the Nazis viewed as less than human. When we define anyone as being less human than we are, we have taken a step toward the death camps.

Because they are stigmatized, gays and lesbians often stay in the "closet," that is, they pretend to be heterosexual. It is often traumatic for them to publicly acknowledge their sexual orientation. It may be especially hard for older people, because the stigma was even more severe in their times.

As early as 1948, the Kinsey study reported that among men between the ages of 16 and 55, 13 percent were homosexuals for at least three years, 25 percent had more than incidental homosexual experience for at least three years, and 37 percent had at least some overt homosexual experience to the point of orgasm (Kinsey, Pomeroy, & Martin, 1948).

It is a safe bet that, whether you know it or not, you work with, learn with, or are taught by a gay person, whether or not they identify themselves as such. The homeless mother in a battered women's shelter, the undocumented immigrant from El Salvador in an English as a Second Language program, the man in a nursing home with Alzheimer's disease, the runaway teenager on the street, your supervisor—any of them could be gay. They are not likely to tell you until they trust you. It is important not to make any a priori assumptions about a person's sexual orientation. If, for example, you are a hospital social worker and are called to help a man who was brought to the hospital because of a bicycle accident and someone needs to be notified, you might ask him, "Could you tell me the name of someone who is close to you who could come to help you?" rather than asking, "Do you have a wife I should phone?"

Because even long-term gay couples cannot legally marry (except in Massachusetts), they do not have the same rights as married heterosexuals. Gay companions are not automatically consulted about their mates' welfare, as are husbands and wives. Occasionally one reads in the newspaper about a gay or lesbian who has had an accident and is seriously disabled. Although the lover has on a day-to-day basis acted as a legal spouse and would logically be the one to care for his or her mate, the parents of the disabled person insist on gaining custody, and the wishes of the accident victim are ignored.

At some point, you might be asked to make a recommendation to a judge in a custody case. As a human service worker, you are more likely to be concerned with the capacity of parents to nurture their child than with that parent's sexual orientation.

Several stereotypes exist about gays and lesbians as parents:

- That they will sexually abuse children in their care
- That the children will grow up with a gay orientation
- That children will be psychologically harmed by being raised by two parents of the same sex
- That children will be harmed by the social stigma

Research has not shown that any of these stereotypes are supported by the facts. Most sexual abuse of children is done by heterosexual men. Children of gay parents are no more likely to grow up gay than are children of heterosexual parents. (Remember, the vast majority of homosexuals were raised by heterosexual parents.) Studies that compare children of lesbians and gays with children raised by heterosexuals show that gay men and lesbian parents do not differ in child-rearing practices or lifestyle from other parents. Apparently their children have no more adjustment problems than do other children. "In fact, there is some evidence that children of lesbians have a greater appreciation for diversity of all kinds and value tolerance more highly than others, having seen first-hand the toll that prejudice like homophobia can take" (Appleby & Anastas, 1992, p. 360). For example, the lesbian singers Betsy Rose and Holly Near show appreciation for diversity by signing their concerts for the benefit of deaf people. As for stigma, there is no clinical evidence of stigma or unusual emotional problems in these children (Kirkpatrick & Hitchens, 1985).

The new reproductive technologies, especially artificial insemination, have opened up the possibilities for childbearing for younger lesbians. Some gays and lesbians also want to become foster or adoptive parents. "Social workers in medical and child welfare settings increasingly find themselves dealing with lesbian clients as they give birth, and with gay and lesbian clients seeking adoptive or foster children or who come for help with the vicissitudes of parenting" (Appleby & Anastas, 1992, p. 359).

KEEPING VALUES STRAIGHT IN A TIME OF WAR

The 9/11 attack on the United States and the subsequent war on Iraq have created value dilemmas for everyone in the country. Human service workers share in the world's grief and bewilderment as we try to sort out the issues. How do our core values shape our reactions to this crisis? Does our profession have anything special to offer the world?

Frederic Reamer, a social work professor, looks to the core values of social work as guidance for these times, and his advice is appropriate for all human service workers (Reamer, 2001). He helped to write the Code of Ethics for the National Association of Social Workers, which included a list of six core social work values. Following are those values and Reamer's suggestions of how they can be applied to these times.

1. *Service.* The primary goal of social workers is to help people in need and to address social problems. Our clinical skills, especially our ability to help people cope with trauma and loss, are crucial in these times.

2. *Social justice.* Social workers have a long-standing commitment to social justice. In relation to 9/11 and its aftermath, we must help to facilitate constructive dialogue, self-examination, and, "where warranted, criticism in an effort to promote social justice and confront injustice." (p. 22)

3. *Dignity and worth of the person.* Social workers (and all human service workers) have a strong belief in human dignity and worth. But what about our response to the terrorists? Should we also be expected to respect their dignity and worth? "As an analogy, must social workers who help rape victims respect the dignity and worth of rapists? Must social workers who help abused children respect the dignity and worth of the abusers? What, if any, are the limits of social workers' long-standing commitment to being nonjudgmental? In an abstract sense, some social workers argue, practitioners can feel angry toward the rapist or child abuser and still respect that individual's basic human worth and dignity and right to assistance. It is this respect that gives these social workers the strength, stamina, and fortitude to work with offenders and help them achieve the insights and behavior change that can prevent future misconduct and harm." (p. 23)

    Social workers are also called upon to respect individual difference and cultural and ethnic diversity. At the same time, social workers sometimes struggle to distinguish the ethical from the unethical. "At what point does a culturally accepted child rearing practice, such as physical beatings, become an ethically unacceptable form of child abuse?… By extension, at what point does the Taliban government's treatment of its citizens—especially its women—become ethically intolerable? Cultural relativism and tolerance have their place in social work, but they also have their limits. There is a bottom line in social work ethics. The challenge, of course, is deciding where to draw that bottom line." (p. 23)

4. *Importance of human relationships.* Social workers must recognize the key role that relationships play, not only among people in their family but also relationships within and between social and ethnic groups and communities. Social workers must work to prevent international and global conflict.

5. *Integrity.* Trust is the key element, not only in day-to-day dealings with clients and colleagues, but also in response to the terrorist attack. "Social workers must engage in good faith efforts to mediate disputes and facilitate diplomatic conversations among people who disagree with each other and view life and the world through radically different lenses. This does not mean that social workers must suspend any semblance of moral judgment in the face of what may be ethically abhorrent ideology or conduct." (p. 23)

6. *Competence.* "Social workers cannot be effective without being fundamentally competent.… Social workers cannot afford to be isolationists or parochial. The world is our stage, and more so with each passing day." (p. 23)

Reamer concludes with important advice to all of us: "Social work's core values can ground us during these frightening times as we seek to regain our balance and equilibrium. If we're not careful, our understandable outrage, fear, and anguish can lead us to view the enemy as a dehumanized demon that must be annihilated no matter the cost to our own soul. As much as possible, we must resist the temptation to retaliate in a way that compromises our fundamental values and principles. Our core values can help guide us down a more productive and judicious path" (p. 23).

FINDING YOUR WAY THROUGH THE MAZE OF ETHICAL CONFLICTS

How do we find our way through this thicket of ethical dilemmas and ambiguity? The first thing we need to do is learn to tolerate ambiguity. Rhodes (1989) says that resolving ethical dilemmas is not a hopeless undertaking. First, we need to separate them into those that can be solved and those that demand action but can't be solved. Human service workers are under pressure to believe that all problems are solvable, yet they are called on to work with problems that nobody has yet been able to solve—poverty, alcoholism, and drug addiction, as well as problems that are an inevitable part of life—old age, disabilities, and death. Rhodes cautions us to "recognize the immensity of the task we are expected to do and the inevitable failures that must result" (1989, p. 9).

Rhodes recommends that we set aside time to focus on the ethical dilemmas we face every day. If we avoid the issues, we will "muddle through," assuming that we are helping others when we may not be. Agencies could help workers with this by setting aside time for workers to discuss ethical issues. Rhodes says,

Dialogue is central to ethics. Only through sustained and open dialogue can we develop ethical positions.

This assumes:

(1) that we can communicate across different views;

(2) that we can be open to each other; and

(3) that we need other views in order to fully reexamine our own. (1989, p. 19)

SUMMARY

1. No one is value-free. Our values are shaped by many influences: families; friends; school; church; the workplace; and by our social class, ethnicity, and gender.

2. The value of self-determination is important in the human service professions.

3. Despite its importance, self-determination is difficult to follow in practice, especially in work with involuntary clients.

4. Decisions about self-determination must weigh the good of the individual against the good of the community.

5. Child-welfare agencies are under fire across the nation. Complaints come from biological parents, foster parents, and advocacy groups.

6. Human service workers disagree about treating clients who are ordered to receive treatment. Some refuse, believing that the client's right of self-determination is

an overriding value. Others believe that they can often overcome resistance and their help will be accepted.

7. Self-determination can be violated by manipulation as well as by overtly coercive methods. Manipulation should be avoided.

8. Some current ethical dilemmas center on the treatment of AIDS patients, the right to die, and reproductive choice.

9. One's view of human nature shapes the service one gives. Three views of human nature were proposed by Thomas Hobbes, John Locke, and Jean-Jacques Rousseau.

10. Bureaucracies often conflict with meeting the needs of clients and workers.

11. Workers need to take responsibility for their own beliefs and speak out about them.

12. Clients are our employers, though they are seldom asked their opinion about our services. Feedback from clients improves practice.

13. Social class and other differences between workers and clients often interfere with giving and taking help.

14. There are misconceptions about the process of aging.

15. Dialogue is central to dealing with ambiguity. Only through dialogue can we carve out the most ethical positions.

DISCUSSION QUESTIONS

1. Although self-determination is an important value in human service work, it is often hard to follow in certain kinds of work. In what ways could self-determination be maximized in the following situations if you were the human service worker?
   a. A parent has been reported as being abusive to a child.
   b. A person who was driving while drunk has been mandated to get treatment.
   c. A delinquent is on probation.

2. A woman says she would rather die than go through the debilitating processes that are inevitable with her illness. She is 50 years old and has early-onset Alzheimer's disease. What are your thoughts on this?

3. You are given the job of leading a discussion between pro-choice and pro-life people. How do you structure this discussion?

4. In some open adoption arrangements, the biological parent and the adoptive parents continue to have contact with each other after the adoption, and the biological parent is allowed to have frequent contact with the child. What are the possible advantages and disadvantages of this arrangement? Do the same issues

that apply to open adoption also apply to artificial insemination, when the child that is born as a result of the insemination is allowed to contact his or her father?

5. Why do you think that few social agencies have institutionalized a process to get regular feedback from clients?

WEB RESOURCES FOR FURTHER STUDY

The Hastings Center
www.thehastingscenter.org/

The Hastings Center is an independent, nonpartisan, and nonprofit bioethics research institute founded in 1969 to explore fundamental and emerging questions in health care, biotechnology, and the environment.

National Association of Social Workers (NASW)
www.socialworkers.org/

NASW is the largest association of professional social workers in the United States. With more than 155,000 members in 56 chapters, NASW promotes, develops, and protects the practice of social work and social workers. NASW also seeks to enhance the well-being of individuals, families, and communities through its work and through its advocacy. The NASW *Code of Ethics* is intended to serve as a guide to the everyday professional conduct of social workers.

CHAPTER 6

The Social Welfare System

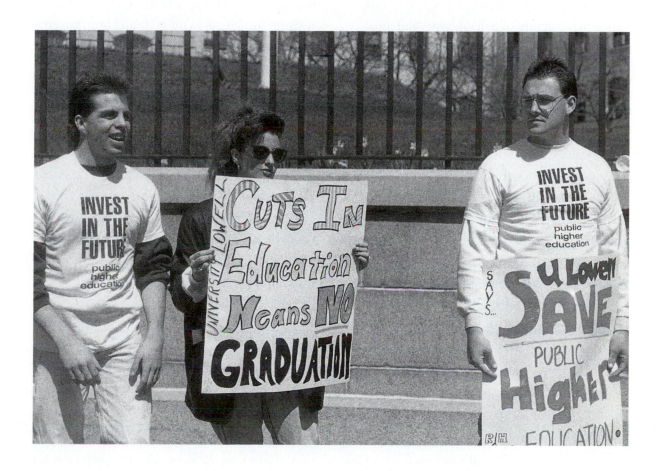

When we were describing the knowledge areas of human service work, we made sure to include the necessity of understanding the social and political forces that affect helping, social problems, and the issues of research and evaluation. In this chapter, we ask you to begin using what you have already learned about these areas and we challenge you to struggle to understand the realities of the sociopolitical and economic system in which we must do our work. Without this superstructure of federal, state, and local laws and monetary appropriations, there would be few services for people in need and few agencies through which human service workers could implement strategies of intervention.

But understanding the crazy quilt that is our social welfare system will not be an easy task. The system, composed of legislative mandates, judicial decisions, agency regulations, and alphabet-soup entitlements such as SSI and TANF, can confuse even the most experienced human service worker. Imagine the anxiety it causes the person who is desperately in need of food, clothing, shelter, job training, or rehabilitation.

Our social welfare system has grown large and complex since the great economic depression of the 1930s. But the growth has been chaotic, often marked by the street-level protests of the disenfranchised poor and most recently by taxpayer revolts in the election booth, anti-welfare sentiment, and conservative political officials. We are currently in a period of sweeping cutbacks in social benefits and what has come to be called "devolution," a shifting of responsibility from the federal to the state and local government. Some view this as reform, while others see it as a throwback to a harsher era.

As a worker coming into the field, you will need to be knowledgeable about proposed changes and will be expected to form opinions about what should be done to improve social conditions for your clients. You may be called on to testify at hearings and to interpret the arcane language of legislation to your clients. You will surely be expected to exercise your obligations as a professional and as a citizen to let your informed opinion be heard.

Surveying the Current Scene

Sandra remembers standing in line at food pantries last year thinking, "I'm working and here I am in a food line. It's hard." Those were the worst times for Sandra and her three children. She was driving a van for elderly and handicapped people, but not making enough to pay her rent ($600 a month) and buy food. "We had a meal every day but it wasn't enough. I didn't eat," she says. "Joey [then 11] was always hungry" (Project Bread/The Walk for Hunger, 1991).

It is a warm July evening. Through the windows, a mother and her two children listen to the sounds of a carnival in town. They walk up the street. Standing on a small hill, they watch the Ferris wheel go around and spot the glow from the new rocket ride. The mother and the children walk slowly back home. The children look over their shoulders at the lights from the rides. Their mother does not have the money for the entrance fees. (Schein, 1995)

What can a human service worker do for these two families? To answer that question, we must look not only at the social welfare programs that might help them, but also at the kind of society they live in and whom that society chooses to help. We describe the major social welfare programs in the United States and the social context of those programs.

THE SOCIAL WELFARE SYSTEM

Social welfare programs encompass those goods and services that a society believes to be a collective responsibility. They include Social Security, public assistance, food stamps and food vouchers, medical care, housing and housing subsidies, child care, unemployment and workers' compensations, veterans' benefits, and personal social services.

The major health and welfare systems in the United States are patchy, uneven, and scanty. The term social welfare system implies a sense of order, comprehensiveness, and rational planning. But that is not the way things are. In fact, the social welfare system is more like a patchwork quilt. Bits and pieces of theories, interventions, and funding are patched together to form programs and helping agencies.

Of course, this system differs from a quilt. A quilt comes together as a whole piece to keep someone warm in bed on a cold night. The system does not serve everyone's needs equally. It is always in the process of being pieced together and also increasingly being ripped apart.

In this age of satellites and space stations, we are all in instant communication. The world is shrinking. Corporations have factories and stores all over the globe. Globalization is affecting every facet of our lives. In such an age, it is helpful to compare the social welfare spending of the United States with other industrialized countries.

Comparing the United States to Other Countries

The United States has the highest poverty rate and the highest rate of inequality of income and assets compared to seven other industrialized countries—Canada, United Kingdom, France, Germany, Japan, Italy, and Sweden (Goldberg and

Rosenthal, 2002). Thirty-four countries have lower infant mortality rates than the United States (Geography IQ, 2004). In contrast to the universal public health care systems of Canada and the United Kingdom, the United States has a private system that costs more than the public systems in Canada and the United Kingdom and does not provide any health insurance for about 45 million people.

Forty percent of female-headed families lived in poverty in 2002, compared to a national poverty rate of 12.1 percent (Children's Defense Fund, 2004, p. 4). The picture is quite different in Sweden, Finland, and France, where both married and single mothers have the lowest poverty rates in the world, and those countries have by far the most generous employment supports for mothers. They are also nations that have a high participation of women in political positions. France and the Scandinavian countries have universal day care; the United States does not (Mandell, B., 2004).

Conservatives and neoliberals around the world want to cut back or eliminate social provisions so that they can use more money for investments and profit making. They want private businesses and private charities to run social programs. They resent the strong European welfare states and hold the United States up as a model for cutting back, claiming that they need to do this in order to become economically competitive. Sometimes they have been able to cut back social provisions even in strong welfare states, but they have met with resistance because people depend upon their social protections. When people are accustomed to national health care and day care, paid parental leave from work, generous unemployment compensation, a good pension, free college tuition, and family allowances for the care of children, they fight against cutbacks in these programs. Here are two examples of those fights:

> When England's Prime Minister Tony Blair proposed in 2004 to charge a $5,400 tuition fee at public universities, a system with a proud tradition of public funding, he met severe opposition from the ranks of his ruling Labour Party. This, along with opposition to his joining the U.S. in the war on Iraq, came close to toppling the government. (Mandell, B., 2004)

> When France's Prime Minister Juppé announced cutbacks in pensions and the nation's health system in 1995, over 2 million people demonstrated and forced Juppé to retreat on most of his proposals. When President Chirac proposed cutbacks in the pension system in 2003, over a million workers and students waged a massive strike of protest. Although they did not immediately win most of their objectives, President Chirac and his ruling conservative party suffered a crushing defeat in regional midterm elections in 2004, and the victorious Social Party vowed to repudiate Chirac's policies. (Mandell, B., 2004)

Despite its status as what has been called a "reluctant welfare state," the U.S. programs of assistance have raised millions of people out of poverty, given medical care to the poor and the aged, provided compensatory education, and provided food, housing, and cash assistance to the poor, the elderly, and the disabled. We discuss some of these programs below.

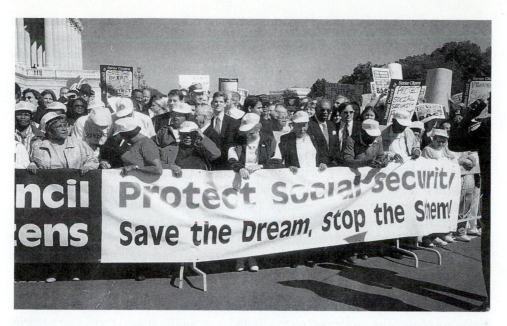

Members of the Gray Panthers lobby to protect and expand health and welfare benefits for older Americans. Their assertive strategies fly in the face of stereotypes that depict the elderly as passive grandparents glued to their rocking chairs.

Social Security

If you ever had a job, you no doubt noticed that money was taken out of your pay check for FICA (Federal Insurance Contributions Act). That is your contribution to Social Security (officially called Old Age, Survivors, and Disability Insurance, OASDI). The program is funded by employee and employer taxes. In 2004, employees paid 6.2 percent of their wages for Social Security and 1.45 percent for Medicare, and employers paid the same. In May 2004, there were 47,378,000 people on OASDI, receiving an average payment of $843.40 a month (Social Security Administration, Table 1, 2004). Included in this number were 4,067,000 children who received Social Security payments. These children and their widowed or retired parents receive little or no media attention, in contrast to the enormous amount of media attention paid to families who receive TANF assistance.

In 1935, the federal government for the first time took responsibility for helping needy families, the aged, and the disabled when Congress passed the Social Security Act. That act included Old Age Insurance for the aged, and later included insurance for the disabled and medical insurance for the aged (called Medicare). Social Security has been a hugely successful antipoverty program. In 1959, more than 35 percent of old people lived in poverty. With the expansion of Social

Security, poverty among the elderly was about 8 percent in 2001 (Social Security Administration, 2001). Despite the success of the program, however, there are efforts to dismantle it as a public program. For the last decade, conservatives have sought to privatize the program by having people invest some or all of their savings in the stock market. They raised the alarm that the system will go broke as the aging population increases and the number of younger working people decreases. They proposed various ways to cut back the program such as raising the retirement age and taxing benefits. The one thing they didn't propose was to raise the cap on the amount of money that is taxed. In 2004, the cap was only $87,900 of wages that was subject to taxes for Social Security, although there is no cap on Medicare. (In other words, all income earned over $87,900 is not taxed by Social Security. A billionaire like Bill Gates pays the same amount of Social Security tax as someone earning $87,900.) If the salary cap were removed and all wages were subject to a payroll tax, there would be more than enough money to keep Social Security solvent. And if the newly hired state and local government workers were brought into the system, the two measures together would easily solve the long-term financing problems (Mandell, M., 1997).

In her book *Pitied but Not Entitled,* Linda Gordon (1994) argues that the deserving/undeserving, universal/means-tested split was built into the Social Security law at its inception because of the differing philosophies of the men who developed the universal parts of the act and the women who developed the means-tested ADC (later called AFDC and now replaced by TANF). The women were social workers who directed the Children's Bureau. Although they had been heavily influenced by the suffrage movement and helped to create many programs for mothers and children, they shared the elitism and racism of many in the Progressive movement of the early twentieth century. They felt morally superior to immigrants and blacks, and as social workers they felt it their duty to supervise these people on an individual, case-by-case basis. They envisioned a small program with "deserving" women, mostly widows and their children. They thought of it as a temporary program, presumably until women got married again. They ignored the large numbers of single mothers who could not—or would not—rely on a husband for support.

The people who built the social insurance program, on the other hand, wanted a program that workers were *entitled* to. They were not interested in people's character flaws. They developed the unemployment compensation system, workers' compensation, and old-age insurance. But they shaped a program that responded to the needs of working men and to the elite of the working class, those with steady jobs with major employers and professionals. It left out single mothers, the working poor who had low wages, and workers who were not wage earners, such as farmers, sharecroppers, and small-business owners. African Americans were not included initially because they worked at jobs that were not covered, such as domestic and agricultural work. Only much later were those people included. Female homemakers were never included in their own right, only as dependents of their husbands. Wives were expected to stay home and depend on their husbands' wages. Men were expected to earn a "family wage" to care for their families.

Because it is a universal program and therefore politically protected by middle-class voters, Social Security has so far been relatively protected from large cutbacks, although there have been cutbacks for college students, the disabled, and the very poor. Its administrative costs are remarkably small—only 0.5 percent of total benefits paid out.

Aid to Families with Dependent Children/ Temporary Assistance to Needy Families

Politicians score points by being "tough on welfare" and "tough on crime." Sometimes they link the two issues, as if being on welfare were a crime. AFDC, Aid to Families with Dependent Children (now called Temporary Assistance to Needy Families—TANF—on a federal level), drew the fiercest fire in the anti-welfare war. It is a program that provides income to families with dependent children, generally headed by a single parent but also available on a limited basis to two-parent families. About 95 percent of the single parents are women.

The AFDC program was part of the Social Security Act of 1935.* Until 1996 the federal government set guidelines and shared program costs with the states; the states set benefit levels. Everyone who was eligible was *entitled* to assistance. That is no longer true. The Personal Responsibility and Work Opportunity Reconciliation Act of 1996 (PRA) ended federal control over AFDC, and gave the states block grants to run their own programs. By ending the entitlement status of AFDC, the federal government, for the first time in sixty years, no longer guaranteed that it would help families in need. Conservatives in Congress proclaimed a victory; liberal senator Edward Kennedy, who voted against the bill, proclaimed it "legislative child abuse" (Edelman, 1997). Journalist Bob Herbert called it "officially sanctioned brutality" (Herbert, 1996).

The state programs that were held up as models for other states to copy were the more punitive ones. The most outspoken advocate of dismantling welfare was Governor Tommy Thompson of Wisconsin, who was appointed director of the federal Department of Health and Human Services by President George W. Bush in 2001 (and resigned in 2003). He implemented the "W-2" program in Wisconsin, which called for replacing welfare with work, and ended authorization for the TAFDC program in Wisconsin on January 1, 1999. Women are required to work when their children reach 12 *weeks* of age. There is a two-year time limit for supported work or community service, with extensions permitted on a case-by-case basis (Miranne & Young, 1998, p. 163).

Thompson bragged that his program was a success because it reduced the rolls by 22 percent over a decade. However, much of the reduction was due to a restriction of

---

*The program was first called ADC (Aid to Dependent Children) because parents were not included. Mothers were not included until 1950, and unemployed fathers were not included until 1965, when the name of the program was changed to Aid to Families with Dependent Children.

eligibility and benefits. The goal of W-2 "is to place welfare recipients in a job—not necessarily a good job, or a satisfying job, or one on the first rung of the career ladder. Rather, any job will do" (Miranne & Young, 1998, p. 166). Many of the people who found jobs in the early stage of the program would have found them even without the program because of a strong state economy, and many of the jobs they found did not pay enough to support a family. Those who did not find a job were still kicked off the rolls when they reached their two-year time limit. Since welfare reform, there has been a sharp rise in foster care placements and the reversal of long-term downward trends in black and Hispanic infant mortality (B. Mandell, 2004, *Journal of Progressive Human Services,* p. 89).

TIME LIMITS

There was no time limit on AFDC until the Personal Responsibility Act set a life-time time limit of five years in which people could receive assistance. Peter Edelman, who resigned his position as assistant secretary for planning and evaluation at the Department of Health and Human Services in protest against President Clinton signing the welfare bill, said that Clinton used anti-welfare rhetoric that he himself may not have really meant in order to get votes for his reelection. President Clinton signed the bill, despite the study by the Urban Institute (commissioned by the Department of Health and Human Services before the bill was passed), which estimated that it would move 2.6 million people into poverty, including 1.1 million children (Urban Institute, 1996).

The states can now do almost anything they want. Some have set shorter time limits than the federal limit. Connecticut set a twenty-one-month time limit; Massachusetts set a two-year time limit. On the other hand, states are free to set no time limit at all if they want to pay for the program out of state funds after the federal time limit is up, and Maine has done that. The law does not require that assistance be in the form of cash. It can be in the form of vouchers. States can even turn over the program to counties (Edelman, 1997, p. 50).

WORK FIRST

When AFDC began in 1935—during the Great Depression—there was vast unemployment, and officials wanted women out of the labor market and at home caring for children so men could fill the jobs available. This policy began to change in the AFDC program when the Work Incentive Program (WIN) was instituted in 1967 as a mandatory work and training program that provided monetary incentives to get a job. As more mothers entered the waged labor market, the philosophy that a woman's place is in the home began to change, and there was less public support for allowing mothers on welfare to stay home to care for their children.

The main thrust of the Personal Responsibility Act is to get recipients into the paid labor market. (Taking care of children is also work, of course, but proponents of the bill do not believe that low-income mothers should be considered "employed" by their caretaking role.) "Work first" is the bill's mantra. Mothers of newborn babies could be subject to the work requirement, although states are allowed to exempt recipients whose youngest child is less than 1 year old. States are allowed to exempt 20 percent of the caseload from the work requirement, but they are required to have a growing portion of their caseloads in work or training activities over several years.* States can meet their quotas by knocking people off the rolls, and that is what many states have done (Edelman, 1997, p. 50).

When the law was passed, about half the caseload was composed of people who had been on the rolls longer than five years. About 70 percent of recipients leave the rolls within two years but, because their jobs don't pay enough to support a family and pay for health insurance and child care, many return to welfare. Another study that tracked recipients for ten years found that 60 percent left welfare within the first year of receiving AFDC, but half of them without a high school diploma who left welfare for a job returned within a year. Half of the women with high school diplomas who left welfare for work returned within two years (Greenberg, 1993).

In effect, welfare recipients have always been in and out of the workforce, often because of their child care responsibilities. They have traditionally used AFDC as a substitute for unemployment insurance, for which they are usually ineligible because much of their work is temporary or part-time. Unemployment insurance is popularly thought to be for "deserving" workers who are out of work for no fault

*Single parents were required to work at least thirty house per week by 2000 (twenty hours per week for single parents with a child under 6). Two-parent families must work thirty-five hours per week. President George W. Bush has proposed to increase that requirement to 40 hours a week.

of their own. Some people believe that if unemployment insurance were expanded to include those low-wage workers who are not now eligible for it, it could provide a more dignified income supplement to women who would otherwise have to go on welfare (Handler & White, 1999). At least nineteen states have already put programs on the agenda to extend either temporary disability insurance or unemployment benefits to workers with care-giving needs (Gornick, 2001, p. 17).

WORKFARE

After two months of being on welfare, recipients are required to find a community service job if they have not found paid employment. Community service work is usually menial work such as raking leaves, picking up garbage, or washing dishes in a school cafeteria. In some cities, workfare workers have replaced regular workers. Although the law prohibits the direct substitution of welfare recipients for currently paid workers, some localities have circumvented this requirement by not renewing expired employment contracts with paid workers. In many localities, low-wage workers have been displaced by workfare "trainees" working off their welfare benefits at less than the minimum wage—sometimes as little as $1.50 an hour (Cooper, 1997). In Baltimore, a thousand workers had lost jobs to welfare trainees by mid-1997, despite the fact that city workers had only two years before won a city ordinance guaranteeing a living wage to anyone employed under contracts with the city (Cooper, 1997, p. 12).

In New York City, thousands of workfare participants have done the work once done by higher-paid city workers (Greenhouse, 1997).They have been exposed to hazardous working conditions, including limited or no access to protective clothing, toilets, and drinking water. They sued the city and in August 1997, a state Supreme Court justice ruled that the city was obligated to provide these necessities (Greenhouse, 1997). In July 2001, the federal government sued the Giuliani administration in New York City, charging it with doing too little to protect women in workfare jobs from sexual and racial harassment by their supervisors. The Giuliani administration said that welfare recipients in the city's workfare program were not employees and had no legal right to protection from sexual discrimination or sexual harassment in the workplace (Greenhouse, 2001). Unions have fought this discrimination, and workers won some rights given to regular employees.

Four *New York Times* reporters looked at the Work Experience Program (workfare) in New York City and found the following: workfare didn't lead to full-time jobs (Finder, 1998); many participants took the place of full-time workers (Greenhouse, 1998); mothers faced acute lack of day care (Swarns, 1998); and tough workfare rules were used as a way to cut welfare rolls (Toy, 1998).

CHILD SUPPORT—"DEADBEAT DADS"

Many of you have probably seen a poster of "deadbeat dads" in the Post Office or subway. States have always tried to get child support money from the fathers of children on AFDC, but in the 1990s they become more aggressive about it.

The Personal Responsibility Act required states to impose harsh sanctions on families where the parent does not "cooperate fully" in collecting child support and establishing paternity. The definition of "cooperating fully" is subject to various interpretations. For a time, Massachusetts was dropping families from the rolls if the mother was unable to provide such information as the father's Social Security number, his whereabouts, and place of employment, even when the mother did not have this information. A class action suit brought by legal services stopped the practice (Mandell, B., 1997, p. 35).

The *"cooperate fully" requirement may be life-threatening for women who are fleeing from battering husbands or boyfriends.* They may be in great danger if they give information about their batterer to the welfare department, because there is no guarantee that the welfare worker will not inform him of her whereabouts.

It is certainly reasonable to expect children's fathers to support them, but it is not reasonable to expect to recoup large amounts of money from men who have little or no money. In 1989, the average *annual* child support award for poor mothers was only $1,889 (Bassuk, Browne, & Buckner, 1996, p. 62).

A high proportion of mothers on welfare have been subjected to domestic violence. In the general population, about 22 percent of women experience domestic violence at some point in their adult lives, while most studies estimate that 50 to 60 percent of welfare recipients experience violence in their lives (Lawrence, 2002). The percentage of TANF recipients who have experienced recent violence is estimated to range from 15 to 25 percent (Raphael, J., & Tolman, R. M., 1997). Children are also likely to be abused when the mother is abused.

There are several aspects of the welfare law that could be harmful to battered women. Time limits may not give a woman enough time to stabilize her life. The law permits states to have a residency requirement, which would penalize women who flee to another state for safety (Gonnerman, 1997, p. 22). About half the states have some program to identify and help victims of battering, yet even the states that have a program are often reluctant to grant women waivers from oppressive regulations. NOW, the National Organization for Women, has organized a campaign to get all states to adopt the Family Violence option (Gonnerman, 1997, p. 21).

Men who batter women often prevent them from working or attending education and training programs, as illustrated by the following story:

When Bernice Haynes tried to get off welfare by enrolling in a job training program, her boyfriend tossed her textbooks in the trash. He refused to watch their two children while she was in class. And he would pick fights with her when she tried to study.

"Before the final exam, we fought all weekend from Friday to Monday morning," says Haynes, 31, who lives on Chicago's West Side. Haynes never got the chance to open her books over the weekend. "When I went in that Monday, I was exhausted—from the constant verbal abuse, the putdowns, from trying to keep myself alive—that test wasn't on my mind." She flunked. Haynes, who had been attending classes for a year and was trying to become a licensed nurse, was kicked out of the program—just twelve weeks before graduation. (Gonnerman, 1997, p. 21)

People disagree on the child support issue. Many people, including some middle-class feminists, believe that the state should force all fathers to pay support, regardless of the mother's wishes. They assume that this would help to lessen the need for welfare. Others believe that the choice of whether to enforce a support decree should be left up to the mother. Many mothers have begged the state to collect child support and have given all necessary identifying information, but the state has done nothing. In Sweden and Finland mothers have no anxiety about getting child support from their husbands because the government pays child support advance payments when the absent parent cannot or does not pay child support (Mandell, 2004).

Voicing her opposition to mandatory paternity establishment and child support provisions, Gwendolyn Mink says that they

> mark poor single mothers as a separate caste, subject to a separate system of law. The system of law under which they live penalizes their moral choices, prescribes intimate associations that may be unwanted, and infringes rights guarded as fundamental to the personhood of all other citizens. (Mink, 1998, p. 73)

In their zeal to make fathers pay, many believe that Congress and the president subjected all fathers whose children are on welfare to police state tactics. "They are subject to liens, withholding of wages, credit investigations, and exposure to employers, among other sanctions. They further indenture poor fathers (as well as irresponsible ones) in work programs ordered by courts and state agencies" (Mink, 1998, p. 91). Depending on what state he lives in, a delinquent father may lose his driver's, occupational, and recreational licenses (Valentine, 1997). If he owes more than $5,000, he may lose his passport.

BEHAVIORAL REQUIREMENTS

Welfare reform not only aims at getting people to work, but also to enforce certain behaviors. Even before the federal law was passed, states received permission (called waivers) to enforce certain behaviors on welfare recipients. These rules reveal a profound distrust of the parenting abilities and sexual behavior of the poor. As of 1998, twenty states had implemented a "family cap" policy, which prohibits benefits from being increased when a recipient has another baby while she is on welfare and for some months after she gets off welfare.

Many states have imposed laws to control parenting and child behavior, including "Learnfare," which reduces the grant if a child truants from school and "Shotfare," which reduces the grant if parents do not get their children immunized.

In a misguided effort to control substance abuse, the federal law stipulates that people convicted of drug felonies are prohibited from receiving a TANF block grant or food stamps *for life*.

The Personal Responsibility Act said that promoting marriage was one of the major purposes of welfare reform, and states have used some of their TANF money for marriage programs. The House of Representatives in Congress has proposed to spend $1.6 billion over five years to promote marriage, including matching funds that states must provide (Children's Defense Fund, 2004a, p. 2). The PRA also aimed to reduce illegitimacy, and gave bonuses to states that reduced their illegitimacy rates (without increasing their rates of abortion).

State officials seem so doggedly determined to defend these restrictive policies that they ignore research showing that they accomplish little. Wisconsin was the first state to institute a program popularly called Learnfare, which penalizes families by reducing the grant when a child is truant. The intent of the program was to encourage school attendance. Yet, despite a study of the program that showed that the program "had no detectable effect on school participation" (Johnson, 1996), Wisconsin continued the Learnfare program.

New Jersey was the first state to implement a family cap program, but when a study by Rutgers University showed that this had contributed to an increase in abortions, officials tried to ignore the study by calling it a "draft." Catholics and anti-abortion groups in New Jersey were upset about the increase in abortions. The American Civil Liberties Union (ACLU) and the National Organization for Women (NOW) sued the state in 1997 because they believed that interfering with a woman's decision about whether to have a child violates her privacy and reproductive rights. Lenora Lapidus, legal director of the American Civil Liberties Union of New Jersey, said, "The state is saying on the one hand to women, 'We will not give you child support. However, we will pay for an abortion.' A poor woman faced with that choice is left with very little option" (Fitzgerald, 1998, p. 7).

There is little evidence that marriage will pull substantial numbers of people out of poverty. A national study of unmarried parents "highlights the fact that for unmarried mothers living in poverty, economic stability is seen as a prerequisite to marriage. Helping single parents succeed requires policies aimed at boosting their educational and economic prospects. Once economic stability has been achieved, marriage may become a more attractive option" (Children's Defense Fund, 2004, p. 5).

As for the illegitimacy bonus given to states, three of the five states that received the bonus didn't even have policies or programs to achieve these goals. In effect, they received a bonus for demographic changes that they had nothing to do with. And "abstinence only" programs were found to be ineffective in changing sexual behavior (Mandell, B., 2004, *Journal of Progressive Human Services*).

LIMITED TRAINING

The current welfare reform law uses a narrower definition of work and training than the previous program did. It does not allow higher education to count as work, and allows only twelve months of vocational training. Officials prefer really short training programs; as short as six weeks. States can allow more education to count for training, but by 1998, thirty-five states did not count education and training as a work activity, or counted it on a very limited basis.

A few states do use state money to support higher education for recipients. Maine, for example, subsidizes parents to go to four-year colleges under their "Parents as Partners" program. But in most states, funds for education and training have been largely redirected from substantive training to brief resume writing and mock interview "job readiness" programs. Recipients are discouraged from pursuing programs that might lead to increased skills and higher earnings and are instead pressured into taking any job that comes along (Cahill, 2000, p. 12).

The job search program is sometimes used as punishment. Here is the story of a woman living in a family shelter for the homeless. She has a part-time job, but the state welfare department (Department of Transitional Assistance) complicates her life enormously by imposing housing and job search requirements.

CASE STUDY

It's Not Because We Made Bad Choices

I work as a home health aide and have to get up at 4:45 in the morning to be to work by 6:30, three days a week. I'm also trying to finish a program to get my Associate's degree in nursing, and looking for an apartment so I can get out of the homeless shelter where I live. I'm looking for a place, but it's hard to find anything. I only make $200 a week, and most two-bedrooms are $700 a month. I tried to find a studio, but most landlords don't want kids in a studio. I also need to buy a car to be able to get back and forth to school (I've been borrowing a friend's car but can't for much longer) and welfare keeps giving me a hard time— telling me I don't need a car and I should be saving money. But I live in Lowell and go to school in Lawrence, and I have a 4-year-old! Do you know how

hard that would be to get back and forth without a car and still do the housing search and all the other things we have to do at the shelter? We have to turn in forms that list where we looked for housing each week, and we have to have twelve—no matter what. If the landlord doesn't return your call, it doesn't count. Even if there are only six listings in the paper, they tell you that's not enough—that you have to try harder. It's so degrading. You know, besides being homeless, we have other issues, and we should be treated with respect. I have low self-esteem, and it's really hard to keep myself going, but they just keep piling more things on us. There are all these mandatory meetings—that you have to go to even if they don't have anything to do with you. Like going to these employment sessions—on how to get a job. I already have a job! But I still have to go—because it's mandatory. You know, anybody could end up in this predicament—it's not because we made bad choices. That's the way life is. Some people are lucky, and some are not. And a pat on the back would be so much better than constantly putting us down. (Massachusetts Coalition for the Homeless, 2000)

Only former recipients with at least a two-year postsecondary or vocational degree are likely to escape poverty by earnings alone, according to one study (Children's Defense Fund, 2000). Since the PRA was passed, there has been a precipitous drop in college enrollment among welfare recipients. *This massive exodus of recipients from college does not bode well for their future ability to climb out of poverty.* People with college degrees have less than a 1 in 50 chance of being poor, compared to 1 in 5 for those without. One study of six states found that 87 percent of recipients who graduated from two- or four-year colleges were still off welfare six years later. A study by the University of Wisconsin at Milwaukee found that as of 1998, only one out of six women forced off welfare had a job that lifted her out of poverty. Meanwhile, the average salary of someone with a one-year or two-year degree from Milwaukee Area Technical College ranged between $20,000 and $24,000 (Jackson, 1998).

> Stories are emerging of women who were forced out of college to become minimum-wage bartenders, waitresses, and sales clerks. One such woman in Wisconsin, who wanted to become a police officer but was forced into a $6.25-an-hour retail job, said: "In class I was so confident and proud because I was going to do this. It's strange. I've gone from this positive, happy person to—I don't know, I'm just so sad." (Jackson, 1998)

Charitable Choice

The Personal Responsibility Act contains a "Charitable Choice" provision that requires states, if they contract with nonprofit organizations to provide social services, to include religious organizations as eligible contractees. Many faith-based organizations have been receiving government funds for decades for social service programs such as emergency food service, child care, youth programs, counseling, and housing. However, prior to the passage of the PRA, they were required to set up a nonprofit 501(c)(3) organization separate from their religious activities. Now, religious organizations that provide welfare services funded by the government can display religious symbols, use religious language, and use religious criteria in hiring and firing employees. Funds flow directly into the church budget (although they must be used exclusively for the provision of social services and not for religious activities).

Republicans and Democrats have both talked a lot about religion in their campaigns for office and have supported legislation for faith-based social services.

President Bush has long been a devotee of religious social services. When he was governor of Texas, he set up the first Christian-run wing inside a state jail, and he even supported making Christian conversion an "explicit goal" (Ridgeway, 2001, p. 13).

President Bush often talked about *compassionate conservatism,* a term that was coined by his advisor Marvin Olasky. Olasky was the author of *The Tragedy of American Compassion* (1992), which argues that history shows that religious institutions are the best vehicles of compassion. He held up the colonial era as a model of effective social care, a period which "stressed man's sinfulness, which only God's grace could change" (Press, 2001). He argued that the rise of the welfare state and the Great Society programs of the 1960s replaced true compassion with government handouts. This book was influential with conservatives and contributed to their efforts to dismantle the welfare state. Historian David Hammack challenged Olasky's statements, saying that

> Olasky's "Early American Model of Compassion" was never uniformly accepted and nowhere put comprehensively into practice. Colonial towns often "warned out" people who could not demonstrate a right to "settlement," leaving the poor to fend for themselves, and established churches frequently mixed "compassion" with oppressive and exclusive policies that many colonists bitterly denounced. (Press, 2001, p. 23)

Charitable Choice has become a hot political issue. President Bush wants religious organizations to be exempt from antidiscrimination laws in hiring. The opponents of Charitable Choice fear that it will lead to religious proselytizing, discrimination in hiring, a lowering of professional standards, a loss of tax money, and further erosion of public social welfare provisions. They fear that it will undermine the strong U.S. tradition of separation of church and state. Its proponents claim that faith-based social services are more effective, but there is no research evidence to support this claim. Mark Chaves, a sociologist at the University of Arizona who has conducted numerous national surveys of church-based social programs, says, "It can't be said strongly enough how little we know about whether religion makes a difference in the effectiveness of delivering services" (Press, 2001, p. 20).

The Charitable Choice bill exempts faith-based programs from the state education and training requirements applied to all secular providers. Many people fear this will create a dangerous two-tiered system. The former director of the National Association of Alcoholism and Drug Abuse Counselors, expressed his concern about this:

> When you come at alcoholism not as a disease but as a moral issue, and your counselors are saying, "These people can withstand temptation if they just pray," and they are not subject to the state licensing and regulatory standards that everyone else must meet, that is troubling. Because this is a disease, and it is in the proper domain of public health, and if you are out there promoting what you are doing as treating addiction, you should be properly licensed. (Press, 2001, p. 24)

Although Congress has mandated that there must be a nonreligious alternative offered to recipients of services who don't want faith-based services, states need not inform beneficiaries of their right to seek an alternative. Some areas may not have any alternatives. Already there have been lawsuits that raise constitutional questions. Among these are a case involving state funding for a Bible class in Texas and another involving a Christian twelve-step course for addicted fathers in Wisconsin (Press, 2001, p. 25).

On the national level, conservatives have largely backed Charitable Choice and liberals and progressives have expressed deep concern about the provision. At the grassroots level, however, there is a confusing set of alliances. One study of more than 1,200 churches shows that congregations that are already engaged in social outreach programs seem more likely to apply for government funds, while those that keep to themselves are less likely to apply. Overall, politically conservative congregations are much less likely to apply for government funds than are middle-of-the-road or liberal congregations. "There is clearly a disconnect between national conservative policy groups and conservative congregations and national liberal and progressive policy groups and liberal congregations" (Baker, 2001, p. 8).

In addition, race and class affect which congregations are most interested in applying for government funding. Predominantly minority congregations are

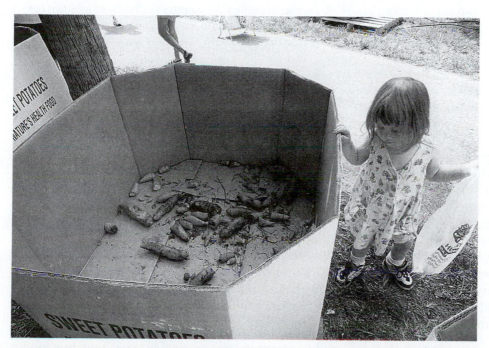

Homelessness and hunger wreak havoc on lives. This little girl lives in Florida where hurricanes wiped out vast stretches of already substandard housing. For her, the food cupboard, like this box of surplus potatoes, is often empty.

substantially more likely to be willing to apply for government funds than are white congregations. "It is no surprise that African American and Latino churches, which have historically served their own community in an effort to augment limited government services, would be more comfortable taking on broader social service responsibilities" (Baker, p. 8). However, because their resources are limited they are not likely to extend themselves to serve a broad range of people. Minority congregations are likely to be poor and poor congregations have a far more limited access to money, volunteers, and social capital. They are unable to help welfare recipients to find employment because none of their members are in a position to hire anyone or know anyone who does.

The Effects of Welfare Reform

Officials who supported the PRA point to how well it has been working because it has drastically reduced the welfare rolls. Welfare rolls have shrunk 54 percent between August 1996 and September 2003. There were 2,006,597 families and 4,880,037 individuals receiving assistance in September 2003 (*U.S. Newswire*, 2004, March 30). *But are the families who left being lifted out of poverty by their work? Other statistics draw a distressing picture.* Peter Edelman summed it up:

> Two out of five former welfare recipients around the country neither have jobs nor currently receive cash assistance.... More than a million women and more than 2 million children have been forced off welfare or denied help when they went to the welfare office to ask.
>
> Children are at a grave risk. One out of six children is poor, but only 7 percent of children receive welfare now, half the number who were getting cash help six years ago. (Edelman, 2001, p. 16)

"Work first" isn't lifting most families out of poverty. Women leaving welfare earn an average of $6.75 an hour, not enough to support a family ("Welfare reform's uncounted failures," 2001). Most of the jobs are not full-time and full-year and do not provide benefits. Fifty-eight percent of employed former recipients have incomes below the poverty line (*The American Prospect*, 2001). The incomes of 10 percent of homes headed by single mothers *have dropped 14 percent since the 1996 law was signed.* Virtually every other group in the nation has seen its income rise during the economic boom (*New York Times*, 2000). Although some welfare mothers are better off when they work than when they were on welfare, most are not. Low wages and the added expenses of working such as child care, transportation, and health care guarantee that. Income gains among former recipients generally came from working more hours, not from higher wages.

- More than half of employed former recipients are unable to pay rent, buy food, afford medical care, and/or pay for phone or electric service (Children's Defense Fund, 2000).

- Employed former recipients of welfare and recipients combining work and welfare earn, on average, between $8,000 and $10,800 a year (Sard & Lubell, 2000, p. 3).

- The maximum TAFDC grant for a family of three in Massachusetts is about $7,000 a year, and that is a higher grant than in most states. A study by Wider Opportunities for Women showed that a mother and two children in Boston needed to earn $51,284 a year to meet basic needs in 2003 in order to make ends meet (Pearce, D. & Brooks, J., 2003).

What has happened to the unemployed? No one knows for sure because the federal law did not require follow-up studies.

- Youth workers report that children are going hungry and begging has increased (Cahill, 2000, p. 29).

- Soup kitchens and food pantries are swamped, often unable to give food to those who need it. Requests for emergency food assistance increased in 88 percent of the 25 cities surveyed by the U.S. Conference of Mayors in 2003. Forty percent of cities said emergency food assistance programs were not able to provide an adequate quantity of food in 2003, and they predicted an increase in requests for emergency food assistance in 2004 (U.S. Conference of Mayors, 2003).

- Child abuse and neglect have increased. Between 1995 and 2001 there have been steady increases in the number of children with substantiated reports of abuse and neglect and in the number of children referred to foster care services. An increasing proportion of children remained in foster care for more than one year. Family income is related to the speed with which children return home; children whose mothers had higher incomes went home more quickly than did children whose mothers had lower incomes (United Press International, 2004).

- As many as 1 in 7 families who left welfare from 2000 through 2002 had no work, no spousal support, and no other government benefits. That is up from 1 in 10 in a 1999 study (Kaufman, 2003).

- Census Bureau figures for 2002 showed the number of people living in severe poverty—with incomes less than half of the poverty rate—had grown by 600,000 over the previous year (Kaufman, 2003).

- The number of people in poverty rose for three years from 2000 to 2003 to 35.3 million, or 12.5 percent of the population. The number of people without health insurance also rose during that period to 45 million, or 15.6 percent of the population (Knowlton, 2004).

LOW WAGES AND POVERTY

One way to alleviate poverty is to raise wages. Economists and public policy scholars point out that because welfare reform has brought so many poor mothers into the workforce, any discussion of child poverty must now shift to the less popular matter of wages. During the Congressional debate about reauthorizing the Personal Responsibility Act in 2004, Democrats proposed to raise the minimum wage to help lift families out of poverty. Republicans opposed this proposal and instead proposed to increase the work requirement to 40 hours a week.

Barbara Ehrenreich, author of *Nickel and Dimed: On (Not) Getting By in America* (2001), decided to find out how anyone could live on the $6 or $7 an hour that will be earned by the roughly 4 million women about to be booted into the labor market because of welfare reform. She worked undercover—as a maid in Maine; a waitress in Key West, Florida; and a Wal-Mart clerk in Minneapolis—to get material for her book. Although she took the same kind of jobs and lived in the same kind of housing as welfare mothers, she was better off than they were because she had no children to support and had a car. Ehrenreich found that she couldn't afford even basic needs such as housing or food on her salary. She was surprised and distressed to learn about people's dire poverty, such as the maid in Maine who eats hot dog rolls for lunch. She commented, "I was shamed by that. There are all kinds of levels of ignorance. I've talked to people who thought everyone was getting $15 an hour because that's what they pay their housekeeper" (Dougherty, 2001, p. D4).

Ehrenreich says that we shouldn't use the word "unskilled." She says, "Every job requires a lot of concentration, memorization, quick thinking. Those things take intelligence and skill" (Dougherty, 2001, p. D4). A common misperception is that low-wage earners are stupid; that if they were smart enough, they'd be able to better their situation. Ehrenreich does not believe this. She says,

> The implication is that they have some terrible problem, or made awful mistakes to get into that weird position. But about 30 percent of the workforce is in this position. It has increased since the mid-80s with the elimination of high-paying union jobs that a high school graduate could get. More and more people who might have been in manufacturing 20 years ago are driving a forklift or something like this, so it's not that the person is stupid. (Dougherty, 2001, p. D4)

REDUCING THE ROLLS BY SANCTIONS

One of the most common reasons for closing cases during welfare reform has been sanctioning welfare applicants and recipients for some bureaucratic reason, resulting in reducing or cutting off benefits. A study by the General Accounting Office showed that in an average month in 1998, 135,800 families (or 5 percent of the average monthly caseload) were being sanctioned, with about 23,100 under a full-family sanction and receiving no cash assistance ("GAO Report Reviews State Sanction Policies," 2000).

Clients are sanctioned for failing to return a form on time, for failing to fill a form out correctly, for not coming to a meeting with a worker (even when the meeting conflicted with required community service activities), for not cooperating with work or community service requirements, and because of the worker's mistake.

Recipients report that workers across the nation regularly harass and intimidate clients, and withhold information about benefits to which they are entitled.

Workers are rewarded for getting people off the rolls, not for helping people get the supports they need to care for their family. Many clients feel that they are the victims of a war against the poor.

The laws are complicated, and welfare workers often don't understand them and often give clients wrong information. Welfare departments close offices, forcing clients to travel large distances for appointments. Most offices are not open evenings or weekends. New York City requires clients to submit to two eligibility reviews, which requires travel of over an hour each way from many parts of the city.

In the face of such barriers, as well as the increasing stigma against being on welfare, many mothers who are eligible for benefits do not want to apply, and many do not appeal unjust decisions.

REDUCTIONS IN MEDICAID AND FOOD STAMPS

States have stripped more than a million low-income American parents, mostly single women, of health insurance. When removed from the welfare rolls, they were dropped from the Medicaid rolls as well. The PRA did not impose penalties on states for failing to follow the law. Texas, under the governorship of George W. Bush, had one of the biggest declines in the Medicaid rolls—46 percent, as compared to the average of 27 percent in the major welfare states included in the study (*International Herald Tribune*, 2000).

Welfare reform has also reduced the number of people who receive food stamps. Workers often neglect to tell people that they are still eligible for food stamps when they leave the welfare rolls, and many people who have not been on welfare don't realize that they could receive them. An Urban Institute study found that only 42 percent of families that left welfare but had incomes below the food stamp eligibility limits continued to receive food stamps (Greenstein & Horney, 2000, p. 22).

IMMIGRANTS AND LINGUISTIC MINORITIES

The current anti-immigrant sentiment has resulted in repressive immigration laws and severe cutbacks in funding for welfare. The PRA was most severe toward legal immigrants, cutting off their access to any benefits except emergency health care. They were denied SSI, food stamps, and Medicaid. (Illegal immigrants never had access to those benefits.) Several states pay for immigrant benefits out of state funds, but state benefits are usually lower than federal benefits. In July 1997, Congress voted to change the law to restore some of the benefits to people who entered the country before the law was passed in August 1996, but they did not restore food stamps or Supplemental Security Income (SSI) to most immigrants, and legal immigrants have to wait five years after they enter the country in order to receive free medical care. The number of legal permanent residents subject to that restriction on medical care reached some 4 million by 2001 (Newman, 2001).

This law has resulted in severe hardship for immigrants, forcing them to forgo medical care and even food. Despite working full time, immigrant families cannot take part in programs that were created for working poor families, and immigrant women's weekly earnings have been falling since 1970 (Moran, 2000).

Immigrants who are applying for a green card (a permit to work and reside here) must document a constant work history during their stay in the United States, making it all the more imperative that they find work (Cahill, 2000, p. 37). Many are in a bind because they couldn't get authorization to work due to the multiple-year backlog at the Immigration and Naturalization Service (p. 38).

Many welfare offices and other social service and health agencies do not provide translators. Human service staff of community-based organizations often have to accompany clients to appointments at the welfare office, where waits are long and language barriers high. Workers often do not refer people to ESL classes. One community service worker said, "We have a lot of clients who don't know English so that they're not able to complete forms and attend training and things so they're not really at a level where they're even able to take advantage of the few things welfare is offering" (Cahill, 2000, p. 38).

BARRIERS TO WORKING

Not Enough Jobs

After about six years of dramatic decline, the number of Americans on welfare has begun to rise significantly in several states and has stopped falling in most states. Since March 2001, the economy has slowed down. During the recession in the early 2000s, 9 million workers were unemployed and only one job existed for every three people looking for work (Mandell, B., 2004, *Journal of Progressive Human Services*).

In some areas of the country, there simply are not enough jobs for all the women who are required to work, especially in states that have high concentrations of poverty and large welfare caseloads. Even when public service jobs are created for welfare recipients, it is costly to provide the training and support needed for women who have few marketable skills and little employment history. A well-designed project in Kansas City was able to put 1,409 out of 15,562 welfare recipients to work. After two years, only 730 were still at work (Edelman, 1997, p. 53).

Not Enough Child Care

The law does not provide enough money for child care for working parents, and most states do not add enough of their own money to provide the necessary child care. Under the new TANF program the federal government sends child care money to the states in a block grant. There is no longer any *entitlement* to child care, even though it is an absolute necessity if parents are to enter and stay in waged work. The cost of child care is a major drain on a working parent's income.

The day care issue has become even more crucial now that Congress is expected to increase the number of hours that welfare recipients must work in exchange for benefits. Only one in seven, or 15 percent, of eligible children are now receiving assistance with the cost of day care. The Bush Administration objected to increasing child-care spending in a 2004 bill to reauthorize the Personal Responsibility Act, but 31 Republicans joined 46 Democrats "in an overwhelming affirmation that families trying to move from welfare to work need a helping hand with child care" (*The Daily Review*, 2004). Senator Olympia Snowe, Republican from Maine, proposed to increase allocations for child care by $6 billion.

Parents report that patching together safe, reliable, and child-positive care is "a job in itself" (Dodson, Joshi, & McDonald, 1998, p. 10). Many of the jobs the mothers get require part-time, before-school, after-school, evening, swing-shift, and weekend schedules.

> Child care is seldom taken care of with one arrangement, rather it often requires many arrangements: a combination of family, neighbors, formal care, and sibling care. Of course, any of these arrangements can break down, and often do. Then child care becomes, in the words of one young mother, "giving that child the rules, locking the door, and praying while you're at work."(p. 10)

Many of the older girls in families are pressed into service to care for the younger children while their mother works, which of course impedes their own schooling and development.

Quality of child care is another problem. Parents who are unable to find or afford good quality child care are often forced to make do with inadequate arrangements. A study done by the Families and Work Institute of children cared for in about 225 homes of relatives and nonrelatives in Los Angeles, Dallas, and Charlotte, North Carolina, rated only 9 percent of the home-based care as high quality. More than half, or 56 percent, of the care was rated as merely custodial and 35 percent was judged harmful to the children's social and educational development ("Workfare's Missing Link," 1996).

Not Enough Transportation

Under the Family Support Act of 1988, anyone in education and training was provided with transportation costs. This is not required under the new law, and lack of transportation is a major barrier to getting a job. The majority of recipients do not have cars, and those who do have unreliable ones.

Two-thirds of all new jobs are in the suburbs, but three-fourths of welfare recipients live in rural areas or central cities. A study of transit service from a point in Boston in which a high population of welfare recipients lived to the high-growth areas for entry-level employment found that more than 66 percent of existing jobs could not be reached within two hours—even though most of the city's welfare recipients live within one-half mile of public transit (Lacombe, 1997). Furthermore, public transportation services offer inadequate hours of operation and infrequent service. And it is expensive.

The problem with transportation in rural areas is also severe. In many parts of Maine, for example, there are no buses. One woman regularly hitchhikes nine miles to a training program.

> Poor women…find themselves stranded, unable to scrape up enough money to buy or maintain cars. Pressed by welfare deadlines to seek employment outside their home,

they are relying on bicycles, or squandering their money on taxicabs, or walking for miles in the dead of winter, or missing their appointments. (Barry, 2000, p. A26)

Not Enough Health Insurance

Many of the jobs that welfare recipients get do not provide health insurance. Although they and their children are eligible for Medicaid for a year after they leave the welfare rolls, many of them are not aware of this, and even those who do get Medicaid for a year are left without any insurance after the year is over.

Some of the children dropped from the Medicaid rolls because of a parent's employment are eligible for coverage under the Childrens' Health Insurance Plan, but 40 states have failed to use all their funds under that plan and will have to turn the money back to the federal government. California and Texas account for more than half of the unspent money—$590 million and $446.3 million, respectively. Together, they have 29 percent of the nation's 11 million uninsured children (Pear, 2000).

A recent study showed that up to 1.6 million impoverished and working-poor Americans—at least a third of them children—have been deliberately knocked from publicly financed health care programs in 2002 and 2003. "Officials in 34 states are opting to slash Medicaid and poor children's health insurance coverage as a path of least resistance to the balanced budgets mandated by law" (*New York Times,* 2003).

Disabilities

Poverty is very bad for your health, both physical and mental. Poor children are at a higher risk for any number of health problems, including attention deficit disorder, asthma, dental disease, and injuries resulting from accidents or physical abuse and neglect. They score lower on developmental tests, and they have a higher mortality rate (Aber, Bennett, Conley, & Li, 1997). They also have higher levels of depression and antisocial behavior, particularly under conditions of persistent poverty (McLeod & Shanahan, 1996). Low-income adults are also at greater risk for health problems. Predictably, both the mothers on welfare and their children have a high rate of disability. This interferes with the mothers' ability to get a paid job, both because of their own health problems and because they need to stay home to care for disabled children.

The General Accounting Office found that over 40 percent of TANF recipients have at least one physical or mental impairment or they have a child with a disability, and 8 percent of TANF families have both an adult and a child with a disability (*U.S. Newswire,* 2004, March 11). Some states exempt disabled parents and parents caring for a disabled child from the work requirement, but there are stiff requirements for proving disability. Emotional and cognitive disabilities are especially hard to prove.

Most of the parents have disabilities that do not qualify them for Supplemental Security Income (SSI) but still restrict their ability to work. If the TANF program used the definition of disability included in the Americans with Disabilities Act, many more women would qualify for assistance. The federal welfare law expressly provides that the ADA applies to all activities funded with TANF funds, and these standards are the ones that states should use. The definition of disability under ADA rules is: a physical or mental impairment that substantially limits one or more major life activities of the person, while SSI is for severe disabilities that are expected to last at least twelve months or result in death and which prevent substantial gainful activity (Sweeney, 2000, p. 14).

An Urban Institute study showed that almost half of parents receiving welfare either said that they were in poor general health or scored low on a standard mental health scale. One-third said that their health limits their ability to work (Sweeney, 2000, p. 5). Of those parents dropped from welfare because of failure to comply with rules, from one-fourth to one-half say that they were unable to comply with the rules because of their health condition (Sweeney, 2000, p. 5).

The most common mental health problems are depression, post-traumatic stress disorder, and general anxiety disorder. According to one study, about 42 percent of heads of households receiving TANF meet the criteria for clinical depression—more than three times the national average (Solomon, 2001, p. 112.) What appears to many people as "laziness" is actually a sign of depression.

Many parents have learning disabilities, up to one-half of recipients in Washington state. In many cases, women are not aware of their learning disabilities and in most states there are few attempts to diagnose and help women to overcome their disabilities.

STATES ARE NOT SPENDING FEDERAL MONEY

Under the 1996 law, big sums of money went to the states in the form of five-year, fixed block grants. Much of it was to be spent to help with the many difficulties in moving people off welfare and into work. Some states have used the funds to help people, such as making higher education possible and using TANF funds to establish programs to provide housing assistance to families attempting to make the transition from welfare to work. Some states have expanded health care for the working poor, and some others have spent federal dollars to increase education and transportation opportunities for the poor. Most states, however, have done little, except get tough (Warren, 2000).

States that have been faced with a fiscal crisis have drastically cut back services and benefits for the poor. California, which had helped welfare recipients with education and training, transportation assistance, child care, and counseling and treatment through its CalWORKS program, has dropped many of these special services (Scripps Howard News Service, 2004).

FIGHTING BACK

The Personal Responsibility Act had an expiration date of October 1, 2002. By then—five years after states were required to have new welfare policies in place—Congress was supposed to decide whether to reauthorize the existing law or replace it. Congress had extended the law several times, but "the reauthorization effort became trapped in a political tug of war between Republicans (who wanted tougher work requirements added to the law) and Democrats (who wanted increased federal money for child care)" (Besharov, 2004). Grassroots welfare activists were in the odd position of fighting to keep the existing law, which they don't like, because they feared that a new law would be worse. Some people hoped that John Kerry would be elected president and would help to shape a better law. There was little basis for this hope since Senator Kerry voted for the welfare reform law in 1996, although Democrats in Congress say that increased work requirements must be accompanied by increased spending for child care.

TANF was extended until April 2005 without changes. After that, Congressional debate will continue. President Bush proposed to cut $1 billion from the TANF program in his 2005 budget (Jackson, D. Z., 2004).

Organizers agree that the first step toward getting a more humane law is to change attitudes toward the poor. Peter Edelman says,

> We have been reduced to the politics of the waitress mom. She says, all too legitimately, "I bust my tail. I don't have decent child care. I don't have health coverage. Why should 'these people' get what I don't have?" (Edelman, 1997)

Advocates say to this waitress, "You are right. You deserve to have a job that pays enough to support a family, and you deserve good child care and health coverage. Join us in working for these things for *everybody.*"

As Gwendolyn Mink says, we do indeed need to end welfare—"but as poor mothers experience it, not as middle class moralizers imagine it" (Mink, 1998, p. 134). The means-tested AFDC/TANF program has always been stingy and punitive. Whatever programs we work for should be universal ones, inclusive of *all* people; otherwise they take on the stigma that is always directed at poor people. Examples of such universal programs are:

- A family allowance granted to every family with children

- A guaranteed annual income for all citizens

- Refundable tax credits for children

- Individual Development Accounts for families and children, which give money or goods to individuals with the goal of helping them to accomplish life goals such as getting an education, buying a house, or starting a business

We need to create a real safety net, including restoring entitlement to financial assistance; establishing a minimum level of cash assistance that is high enough to meet basic needs; restoring food stamp cuts; and providing all benefits to immigrants, including undocumented immigrants.

We also need to work on improvements for all workers—an increase in the minimum wage, paid family leave, guaranteed child care, comparable worth policies, decent unemployment compensation, universal health care, a full employment policy, investment in education and vocational training, and aggressive enforcement of anti-discrimination laws. "This end to welfare will take us down many paths, all leading to gender justice" (Mink, 1998, p. 139).

Most Americans don't believe that it's a good idea to move people off welfare into jobs as quickly as possible if the jobs offer little chance of advancement, and they would not feel that welfare reform has been a success if people were still in poverty after leaving the welfare rolls. The public might be ready to support stronger job supports and removal of time limits that are forcing large numbers of people into poverty if they are better informed about the effects of welfare reform (Sen, 2000, pp. 20–21).

Universal welfare programs such as Social Security have powerful constituencies who fight to retain their benefits and have won major victories against government cutbacks. Means-tested programs such as TANF have little political support and must join with powerful allies. The National Welfare Rights Organization achieved significant victories in the 1960s and early 1970s because they were allied with the Civil Rights and anti-war movements. The women's movement would seem to be a logical ally for welfare recipients today, since the majority of welfare recipients are women. Countries where women have strong political power, such as Sweden and France, have strong women-friendly services such as universal day care and generous family leave provisions.

The leadership of the National Organization for Women (NOW) has been exemplary in their resistance to welfare reform, but they have been unable to bring along large numbers of their constituency. Some feminists, preoccupied as they are with getting ahead in the work world, think there is nothing wrong with requiring welfare recipients to work, even if the work is flipping burgers for the minimum wage.

The March for Women's Lives in Washington, D.C., on April 25, 2004, presented an opportunity to give welfare issues national attention and to mobilize the support of feminists. The National Network of Abortion Funds formed the Access and Equality Contingent to broaden the focus of the march from an exclusive focus on reproductive rights to a broader focus that includes the right to have children and to have the resources to care for them. The March leadership and the sponsoring organizations gave significant attention to low-income women's issues. The March, attended by over a million people, seemed more diverse than any previous women's march and more attentive to issues affecting low-income women. Several welfare rights groups around the nation came to the March and enlisted the support of other women's groups.

Labor is another potential ally for welfare recipients who have entered the paid work force. (We purposely specify "paid" work force because mothers are working for no wages when they care for their children.) Welfare recipients have always been in and out of the paid work force. Now that there is a five-year lifetime limit to welfare benefits, they will have no other source of subsistence but paid work, and workplace organizing will be crucial. Resistance to welfare retrenchment needs to focus on full employment as well as on the welfare programs themselves. Living-wage campaigns in the U.S. are an important part of the struggle, as are union struggles to keep jobs, wages, and benefits. Unions have occasionally become involved in welfare issues, as in New York City where workfare took away jobs from unionized workers. Many unions have won family friendly benefits for their members. Service Employees International Union (SEIU) organized 604 former welfare recipients in Milwaukee, Wisconsin, who care for their parents, employed by the nonprofit agency New Health Services (NHS). These workers were paid at the rate of $7.10 an hour, with no benefits of any kind. After their union was certified, they went on to negotiate a contract for higher wages, improved training, health insurance, and pension benefits (Glenn, 2001).

Churches have also given strong support to the welfare struggle, especially the Catholic Church, Unitarian Universalists, the American Friends Service Committee, and the United Church of Christ.

Our strongest ally may eventually be the middle class. Many middle-class people are only one paycheck away from welfare. When enough of them realize that they too are deserving of a safety net, we will have a powerful constituency to struggle with us for a more humane welfare state.

Supplemental Security Income and Social Security Disability Insurance

Supplemental Security Income (SSI) is a federal means-tested program for the aged, disabled, and blind, including children. It was created as part of the Social Security Act in 1974, consolidating two former programs called Old Age Assistance (OAA) and Aid to the Permanently and Totally Disabled (APTD). OAA and APTD were structured in a way similar to AFDC in that states provided matching funds, but SSI federalized these programs.

Social Security Disability Insurance (SSDI) is the part of Social Security that pays benefits to disabled workers and their dependents. In May 2004, there were 69,000 disabled workers who received an average monthly benefit of $936.30. There were 4,000 spouses who received an average monthly benefit of $232.00, and 41,000 children who received an average monthly benefit of $240.70 (Social Security Administration, 2004c).

In May 2004, there were 6,970,366 SSI recipients (Social Security Administration, 2004b). Federal monthly payments in 2004, without state supplements, were $564 for an individual and $846 for a couple. Several states supplement the federal SSI payment. Some states provide a cost-of-living allowance for SSI, but some do not. Although the federal government assumed all administrative costs for the first twenty years of the program, in 1993 Congress ordered the government to start billing states for its services (Murphy, 1995).

CUTBACKS IN SSI AND SSDI BENEFITS

Disabled people faced severe cutbacks in their benefits in 1980 when President Ronald Reagan and Congress pushed 491,000 people off the rolls of SSI and SSDI (Social Security Disability Insurance), arguing that some people were taking advantage of the system and could go to work. As a result of protests by beneficiaries and their advocates, laws were passed that required medical proof of improvement in the condition of beneficiaries before they could be terminated from SSI. Half of the people who fought back, about 200,000, were put back on the rolls (Blau, 1992, pp. 56–57).

Although the mentally ill made up just 11 percent of those receiving SSDI, they constituted almost one-third of the cases terminated in the first year. "Mentally disabled people possessed neither the skill nor the resources to appeal termination of their benefits. As a result, many joined the homeless population" (Blau, 1992, p. 57).

The second large-scale onslaught on SSI came with the Personal Responsibility Act of 1996, which cut off all legal immigrants from SSI.

The definition of SSI eligibility for disabled children was also narrowed, which has resulted in removal from the rolls of 100,000 to 200,000 of the 965,000 children who received SSI (Edelman, 1997). Lawmakers believed that many of the children did not have severe disabilities. As a result, the Social Security Administration put together a complex set of standards to determine who still qualified. In New York, about 60 percent of children with attention deficit disorders were disqualified, as well as 84 percent of children with learning disorders or speech and language problems and 28 percent of children with mental retardation (Sexton, 1997b).

> While waiting anxiously to hear whether her child would be cut off of SSI, Paula Schmecer, the mother of a 9-year-old boy who suffers from heart disease, hyperactivity and severe myopia, said, "They are trying to cut as much as they can. They think people and their problems are illegitimate. I have an expensive boy who I try and build up as much as I can. How can I do that without funds?" (Sexton, 1997, p. 9)

The law also cut off benefits for about 40,000 people with drug or alcohol addictions. Conservatives argued that SSI checks were fueling addictions. George McGovern, one-time Democratic presidential candidate and father of Terry McGovern, who died of alcoholism, said, "It means that members of Congress who voted for that legislation still don't understand that alcoholism is a disease, and a fatal disease if it's not treated. I regard it as the number-one health problem in this country" (Conklin, 1997, p. 25).

> Bonita Brooks, a thirty-eight-year-old mother of three grown children, first received SSI in 1992 because of a bipolar disorder that causes manic depression, and at the time she was addicted to crack. She kicked the drug habit, but still has depression for which she needs medication, and has been unable to find a job. Because of the drug addiction, she was cut off SSI since then and hasn't been able to get medication. She says her drug habit was closely linked to her depression, but lengthy waiting lists have kept her out of free group counseling. (Conklin, 1997)

General Assistance

General Assistance (or General Relief) programs give cash grants to people who do not qualify for TANF, SSI, or Social Security. Eligibility varies among states, but in general the program is for single individuals or childless couples, including individuals who are disabled for less than a year or who are awaiting a determination of whether they are sufficiently disabled to qualify for SSI. Elderly people who do not qualify for SSI or Social Security are generally eligible. Some states give general assistance to people who have exhausted their unemployment insurance, but others don't. Some families who are not eligible for TANF receive general assistance.

General Assistance programs are funded entirely with state or local money, without any federal matching funds. Benefits are very low, and these programs are generally the first to be cut when states cut welfare programs. Not all states even have the program. During the 1991–1992 recession, Michigan abolished its General Relief program, ending benefits for about 82,000 recipients, and Illinois cut off benefits for about 66,000 GA recipients. Rhode Island abolished its program. Ohio ended aid after six months. Several other states cut back the program in various ways. Follow-up studies in Michigan and Ohio showed that relatively few former General Assistance recipients became employed after their benefits were ended, and those who did were in low-wage and often temporary jobs. In Michigan there was a 50 percent increase in homelessness. In Ohio the ranks of the homeless increased substantially (Nichols & Porter, 1995). Massachusetts cut all able-bodied people from its General Assistance rolls and changed the name from General Assistance to Emergency Assistance to the Elderly, Disabled, and Children.

In cutting General Assistance programs, states assume that large numbers of the recipients can obtain and keep a job. They often cut those they define as employable, whether or not there is any realistic prospect that such "employables" can really obtain employment.

Food Stamps

Food stamps aren't really food stamps any more. Electronic credit and debit cards replaced coupons for food stamps across the nation in 2004, and the federal administration is inviting the public to suggest a new name for the program (Pear, 2004).

The food stamp program is paid for by the U.S. Department of Agriculture. Administered by state welfare departments, its purpose is not only to feed low-income people but also to provide subsidies to farmers. Stores and banks also receive money for participating in the program.

People can buy most foods with the cards, but they cannot use them for paper goods, diapers, toiletries, cigarettes, and so forth. Food stamps are not intended to provide anything more than a minimally nutritional diet, but they have substantially reduced hunger and malnutrition in this country. When food stamps are cut back, people need more emergency food assistance such as food pantries.

In March 2004 there were 28,815,664 persons receiving food stamps. That represented a rise of more than 2.8 million persons compared to the March 2003 level and nearly 6.6 million persons since July 2000 (when program participation reached its lowest level in the last decade). Increases are due partly to a weak economy and partly to improved access to the program in states. Legal immigrants who have lived in the United States at least five years and all those under 18 became eligible for food stamps in 2003. Yet, nearly one in four eligible people still do not receive food stamps (FRAC, 2004a).

Cutbacks in the food stamp program began in 1981, when the Reagan administration and Congress cut funds used to advertise the program for outreach. Then, between 1982 and 1986 they cut $6.8 billion from the budget, eliminating 1 million hungry people and reducing benefits for the remaining 20 million (U.S. Department of Commerce, 1997, p. 475).

The next major onslaught against the food stamp program came with the Personal Responsibility Act of 1996. The Republicans had hoped to eliminate entitlement to food stamps, but the agribusiness lobby stopped that. Yet Congress made deep cuts, including making legal immigrants ineligible, and cutting the amount of benefits.

> *Perhaps the most troubling cut is the one limiting food stamps to three months out of every three years for unemployed adults under age fifty who are not raising children.* The Center on Budget and Policy Priorities describes this as "probably the single harshest provision written into a major safety net program in at least 30 years." (Edelman, 1997, p. 48)

CASE STUDY

Two Families Lose Food Stamps

In Brooklyn, a 42-year-old mother of four from Trinidad spends her rent money on food, buying grape Kool-Aid instead of orange juice and canned tuna instead of fresh beef, and edging ever closer to eviction.

And in the Bronx, a 40-year-old woman from Peru rides the subway from food pantry to food pantry, pleading for groceries to fill her refrigerator. One turns her away because she lacks a referral. Another runs out of rice, spaghetti, and green apples while she waits in line.

"I'll keep looking," the woman, Rosa Dolone, said wearily as she walked out of the crowded church into the cold winter morning. "My children have to eat." (Swarns, 1997, p. B1)

In the first wave of welfare cuts to hit New York City under the federal welfare law, more than 50,000 able-bodied legal immigrants between the ages of 18 and 59 have been denied food stamps since September. (Swarns, 1997 p. B1)

One of the most disturbing aspects of life in this very wealthy country is the persistence of hunger. In 2002 there were 34.9 million people living in households experiencing food insecurity, 11.1 percent of all U.S. households. Of the 12.1 million households that were food insecure, 3.8 million suffered from food insecurity that was so severe that the United States Department of Agriculture's very conservative measure classified them as "hungry." Since 1999, food insecurity has increased by 3.9 million individuals: 2.8 million adults and more than one million children. (Food insecurity refers to the lack of access to enough food to fully meet basic needs at all times due to lack of financial resources) (FRAC, 2004b).

Special Supplemental Food Program for Women, Infants, and Children (WIC)

> Betty Khlanoyan, 33, a mother of four from Clinton, Massachusetts, said that she has been helped by the federal food supplement program for women, infants, and children (known as WIC). Her husband lost his job when his employer went bankrupt, and without the WIC payments, "I would have had to cut back on formula for the youngest child," she said. (Yenkin, 1992, p. 3)

The WIC (Women, Infants, and Children) program is sponsored by the U.S. Department of Agriculture. It provides vouchers to purchase specific foods, such as baby formula, milk, eggs, and fruit juice. It also gives nutrition screening and nutrition counseling to pregnant and postpartum women, infants, and children under 5 years of age. They are eligible for the program if their family income is below 185 percent of the poverty line and are at nutritional risk. (From July 1, 2004, to June 30, 2005, 185 percent of the poverty line amounted to $34,873 for a family of four.)

In March 2004, there were 7,908,416 people who received WIC benefits each month (U.S. Department of Agriculture, 2004). WIC is not an entitlement program. Federal funding is determined annually by Congress. Some states supplement the WIC program. Although most eligible infants are covered, about 20 percent of eligible women and children are not covered.

WIC has proven its value by reducing low birth rates, reducing the number of infants who die, and reducing the number born with developmental disabilities. WIC has encouraged greater use of prenatal and pediatric care. It saves Medicaid money because fewer low-birth-weight infants require hospitalization after birth.

This cartoon points up the discrepancy between the unpaid labor of women who prepare Christmas dinners and the paid labor of restaurant workers.

WIC is more popular than TANF with legislators, even though both programs feed children. Some states have expanded their WIC program even as they cut back on TANF. Yet even this popular program has not been immune to cutbacks as both the states and the federal government face fiscal crises. President Bush proposed to cut $122 million from the WIC program in his 2005 budget (Jackson, D. Z., 2004).

School Breakfast and Lunch Programs

School lunch and breakfast programs are sponsored by the U.S. Department of Agriculture, which provides states cash to administer the programs and supplies 20 percent of the food. Children at or below 130 percent of the poverty level are eligible for free meals, and those with income below 185 percent of the poverty level are eligible for reduced-price meals. (For the period July 1, 2003, through June 30, 2004, 130 percent of the poverty level was $23,920 for a family of four; 185 percent was $34,040.)

During the 2002–03 school year, more than 27.8 million children in more than 97,000 schools and residential child care institutions participated in the National School Lunch program. About 16 million of the 27.8 million children, or 57.5 percent, were receiving free or reduced price lunches. Over 7 million children participated in the school breakfast program, including 6.7 million low-income children (FRAC, 2004c). For low-income children, these meals are often a lifeline. School lunches provide one-third or more of the key vitamins and minerals children need; school breakfasts provide one-fourth or more.

There has been some criticism of the nutritional value of the food served in these meals. Studies show that school lunches are higher in fat and sodium content than the government's recommended guidelines.

There has also been a great deal of criticism of competitive foods offered at schools through vending machines, school stores, or snack bars. These include carbonated sodas, fruit drinks with low percentages of juice, salty snacks, and high-fat baked goods. School cafeteria "a la carte" lines most commonly sell desserts, ice cream, chips, and fruit drinks. Major beverage companies have exclusive contracts with half of all school districts. These high-calorie foods, low in nutritional value, are contributing to high obesity rates among children and adolescents.

The Bush administration claimed that more than a fourth of the children who eat free or discounted school lunches might be ineligible, and they implemented rules to tighten the eligibility process. Studies by the U.S. Department of Agriculture found that tightened income verification not only does not increase the accuracy of verification, but also keeps low-income children out of the program. Increasing verification caused a 20 percent drop in the percentage of children eligible for free meals (FRAC, 2004d).

As poverty and hunger increase, school lunch and breakfast programs are more important than ever. One study found that only about one-half of the children who needed the school breakfast program received it, and fewer than one-half of the states' schools offered it. Children often do not want to take the meals because they feel ashamed. Federal regulations prohibit any separation of the free-lunch students from all the others, but schools still do it, fueling the children's understandable resistance to being stigmatized. Some school systems avoid this stigmatization by offering "universal" School Breakfast Programs, programs that serve breakfast at no charge to all students. These include New York City, Cleveland, and Kansas City (MO). "Because universal programs reduce administrative burdens and costs, draw no lines between students based on income, reduce the stigma some students feel in a means-tested program, and rapidly increase participation so that every child can do better in school, the idea is gaining popularity" (FRAC, 2003).

Medical Aid Programs

MEDICARE

Medicare is a federal universal program; *Medicaid* is a means-tested program. Everyone on Social Security, whether rich or poor, is eligible for Medicare, but only low-income people can receive Medicaid. In 2003, there were 40.8 million enrollees in Medicare (CMS/OACT, 2003).

Medicare helps pay the hospital and medical costs for people ages 65 or older, as well as for disabled Social Security recipients. If medical expenses exceed what Medicare pays for, some elders pay private insurance to cover the balance, or they might seek Medicaid. Medigap is the part of Medicare that pays for things that Medicare doesn't cover, including doctor's bills and some prescriptions. There is no long-term care provision in Medicare for either nursing home care or in-the-home assistance. Because coinsurance rates are rising and many parts of their bills are not covered, the elderly are now paying more for their health care than before Medicare began. Enrollment in traditional Medigap plans has been declining while enrollment in HMOs has been increasing, but most of the HMOs do not cover prescriptions.

In 1983 the Reagan administration and Congress tried to limit Medicare expenses under a program called Diagnostic Related Groups, or DRGs. The hospital is paid a set fee for each particular diagnosis. Many people were concerned that hospitals were releasing patients sooner than was medically advisable. "Periodically, newspaper accounts surface regarding elderly patients who die shortly after what appears to have been a premature hospital discharge" (Popple & Leighninger, 1990, p. 446).

Some people have complained that their managed-care plans refuse to pay for treatments ordered by doctors, and two patients sued. The suit went to the Supreme Court, which ruled in June 2004 that patients cannot sue in state courts when their managed-care plans refuse to pay for treatments ordered by doctors. Patients can still sue in federal courts, but they can seek only reimbursement for the benefits they were denied, not compensation or punitive damages for any additional costs or harm stemming from such denials (*New York Times*, 2004, June 23).

Medicare did not cover prescriptions until 2003, when Congress passed a Medicare bill that pays part of the costs of some prescriptions. George W. Bush took credit for it and thought it would help him get votes from seniors, but the bill "is now the subject of intense scorn among many seniors" (Washington, 2004). Most aspects of the law don't start until 2006, but seniors were invited in May 2004 to sign up for drug discount cards. Seniors became confused when they tried to sort out which plan was best. There are seventy-three different types of cards available. They offer different discounts based on what types of medicines are purchased and where they are purchased. Millions of seniors called special hotlines set up by the Centers for Medicare and Medicaid Services, or CMS, which administers those programs, but were subject to long waits and often couldn't get the information they needed.

Ron Pollack, executive director of Families USA, said, "The more seniors learn about the new Medicare law, the more unhappy they are" (Washington, 2004). The new law prohibits Medicare from negotiating for lower drug costs, as the Veterans Affairs administration is able to do for veterans. Drug companies lobbied hard against allowing Medicare to negotiate lower prices. Representative Sherrod Brown, an Ohio Democrat who voted against the bill, said that seniors he has talked to have "an intuitive understanding that this bill was written by the drug and insurance industries" (Washington, 2004).

The new drug benefit is the biggest expansion of Medicare since creation of the program in 1965, but patients will still face substantial costs, and the bill prohibits the sale of any Medigap policy that would help pay drug costs after January 1, 2006. The plan further limits coverage by establishing a list of preferred medicines and refusing to pay for any drugs not on the list. Congress defended its ban on the sale of Medigap drug policies, saying they wanted beneficiaries to bear some of the cost because health economists claim that when beneficiaries do not have to bear the costs, they tend to overuse medical services (Pear, 2003).

There is no limit placed on what pharmaceutical companies can charge for prescription drugs in the United States, as there is in Canada. As a result, drugs in the United States cost two to three times more than they do in Canada. Some people are getting prescription drugs from Canada, and pharmaceutical companies have lobbied to make that practice illegal. In Amherst, Massachusetts, seniors are teaching each other how to order cheap prescription drugs from Canada on the Internet, a practice that federal officials say is both against the law and dangerous. Rosemary Morgan, age 66, who orders her breast cancer drug from Canada Rx for $44—a 90 percent discount from U.S. prices, says, "My understanding is it's legal, but if it's not, you can chain me to a fence with all the other bald-headed ladies" (Kowalczyn, 2001).

MEDICAID

Medicaid started as mostly a welfare program for the poor, but during the boom years of the 1990s many states took advantage of rising revenues to cover the near-poor and working poor and added benefits. Congress started a Children's Health Insurance Program (CHIP) in 1997, which extended coverage to more low-income children. Recently, however, as the economy slowed and states faced fiscal crises, many states have reduced payments to hospitals and nursing homes, eliminated many services, or found ways to discourage enrollment. The most severe cutbacks were in Mississippi, which ended Medicaid eligibility for some 65,000 low-income senior citizens and people with severe disabilities in 2004 (Herbert, 2004).

There were 9 million children in the United States without health care coverage in 2004, 5.8 million of whom were eligible for either CHIP or Medicaid. About 90 percent of those uninsured children had at least one parent who worked, but for many of those families, affordable health coverage was not offered through their employer. Most states have set the eligibility level for CHIP at 200 percent of the poverty level, which means that children under age 19 in a family of four with income up to $36,800 a year may qualify (Children's Defense Fund, 2004).

Despite all the cutbacks, state Medicaid rolls have continued to rise because the needy population is expanding. By 2005, 45 million people had no health insurance at all. Many more are uninsured for a portion of a year but not for the entire year. One in three people below the age of 65, 81.8 million, were without health insurance for all or part of 2002 and 2003. Of those 81.8 million uninsured individuals, two-thirds (65.3 percent) were uninsured for six months or more (Families USA, 2004). Medicaid insured 14 million people in poverty in 2002, but another 10.5 million people—representing 30.4 percent of those in poverty—had no health insurance in that year (U. S. Department of Commerce, 2003).

If people on Medicaid need false teeth or eyeglasses and are lucky enough to live in a state in which the Medicaid program pays for these items, they will be able to chew food and read. If, however, people who need dental care or eye care have the bad luck to live in a state without this Medicaid coverage, they will have to eat strained food and stop reading. Hard as this may be, those Medicaid recipients without dental or eye-care coverage are still better off than an unemployed 56-year-old who is in a General Assistance program in a state that provides little medical care for the unemployed.

Since President George W. Bush took office, Secretary of Health and Human Services Tommy Thompson approved more than 900 Medicaid program changes and waivers (Kirchhoff, 2001). President Bush has proposed to turn Medicaid over to the states in the form of block grants, but Congress has not yet acted on that proposal. Medicaid has a more powerful political constituency than does TANF because large numbers of middle-income people have elderly parents in nursing homes whose bills are paid by Medicaid. It is the Medicaid program, not Medicare, that pays for the bulk of nursing-home care. In addition, hospitals and physicians receive Medicaid payments, and they all have substantial political clout.

Officials sometimes label Medicaid a "budget buster" because as medical costs have skyrocketed they have taken a large chunk of state budgets. Although TANF recipients make up 65 percent of the Medicaid caseload, they account for only 30 percent of the spending (U.S. Department of Commerce, 1995). About three-fourths of Medicaid dollars are spent on the elderly and disabled, who have exhausted most of their life savings in paying nursing-home bills (McNamara, 1995). The following story is similar to thousands recounted in the nation today.

C A S E   S T U D Y

Nursing Home—An Agonizing Decision

In the mythical American family, Grandma never soils the bed sheets. Or wanders into traffic. Or slips her nightgown over her dress at bedtime.

She lives in her own home. She cooks Sunday dinner for a table full of children and grandchildren. When her health fails, she moves in with a daughter who cares for her without any disruption to the younger woman's work or family life. When she dies, she goes peacefully in her sleep.

It is hard to pinpoint the exact moment when the myth began to unravel for Judy Keane. It might have been the year her sister died of cancer and her brother-in-law of a brain seizure, leaving Judy—a widow herself—to care for her mother, Mary, just as Mary had cared for them when Judy's father died young.

It might have been the winter morning Judy slipped out of work to check on Mary, only to find her outside barefoot, in night clothes, while the home health aide lounged in front of the TV.

It might have been the night an ambulance carried Judy away from Mary's relentless needs on a stretcher, her heart racing with anxiety.

Or it might have been the tearful afternoon when she and her mother finally said the words "nursing home" out loud.

"Unless you have experienced it, you can't understand it," Judy said yesterday, after her regular visit with her 88-year-old mother at Marian Manor in South Boston. "You wonder how many of his mother's diapers Newt Gingrich has changed." (p. 28)

The fastest growth in welfare spending has been on medical care. Part of the reason for that growth is the increase in older people, but a large part of the reason is the inflated profits of doctors, hospitals, and drug companies. The health care crisis continues to get worse. Some key findings:

- Health care costs are escalating and it is projected that by the year 2007 the United States will be spending 20 percent of its GNP for health care.

- Many people are self-employed and unable to afford the cost of health insurance. Millions of people work for employers who don't provide health insurance. Many workers can't afford health insurance, but are not poor enough to qualify for Medicaid (Anderson, 2004).

- The Institute of Medicine has estimated that 18,000 adults in America die every year because they are uninsured. Women with breast cancer who don't have health insurance are twice as likely to die as those who are covered (Anderson, 2004).

The Clinton administration tried to implement a national health insurance plan, but it was defeated by the Congress. Many people, including the present authors, believe that even the Clinton plan was flawed because it relied on private insurance companies and managed health care. We think that a single-payer plan run by the government, similar to that in Canada and most European countries, would provide the best universal coverage at the lowest expense.

Unemployment Insurance

Unemployment insurance is administered by the U.S. Employment and Training Administration and each state's employment security agency. It is funded by a federal unemployment tax levied on the taxable payrolls of most employers. State laws vary concerning the length of time benefits are paid and their amount. In most states, benefits are paid for twenty-six weeks and, during periods of high unemployment, extended benefits are paid by matching federal and state funds to people who have exhausted their regular state benefits. The amount of benefits varies widely between states, with some states giving over twice as much as others. Some states supplement the basic benefit with allowances for dependents.

There have been cutbacks in Unemployment Insurance, a federal–state program. The automatic extension of benefits by the federal government when unemployment is high was eliminated during the Carter and Reagan regimes and replaced by emergency extensions when unemployment is high.

As unemployment has increased and unemployment benefits have been cut back, millions of workers have used up their unemployment benefits without finding work. In July 2003, 44 percent of workers ran out of their state employment benefits, the highest figure since the statistics were first published in 1972 (Unemployed Workers, 2004). Unemployment insurance does not help many low-wage single mothers when they become unemployed. Eighty percent of unemployed women did not meet the eligibility criteria in 1995, as opposed to 74 percent of men (Yoon, Spalter-Roth, & Baldwin, 1995, p. 30).

In their efforts to cut costs, businesses have pressured the states to cut unemployment insurance. The value of the benefits has also dropped, as states tightened their benefits to reduce the unemployment tax on employers and to make states more attractive for executives looking for places to open businesses (Blau, 1992, p. 59).

Earned Income Tax Credit

The Earned Income Tax Credit (EITC) is a refundable federal income tax credit for low-income working individuals and families. Congress originally approved the tax credit legislation in 1975 in part to offset the burden of Social Security taxes and to provide an incentive to work. The credit reduces the amount of federal tax owed and can result in a refund check.

Income and family size determine the amount of the EITC. Families with one child who earned less than $29,555 in 2003 (or less than $30,666 for married workers) were eligible for a credit of up to $2,547. Families with two or more children who earned less than $33,692 in 2003 (or less than $34,692 for married workers) were eligible for a credit of up to $4,204. Workers without a qualifying child who earned less than $11,230 (or less than $12,230 for married workers) were eligible for a credit of up to $382.

Most increases in social welfare in the United States since the 1970s have been done through the tax system. EITC now spends more federal money than was budgeted for AFDC in the late 1990s or than its successor TANF is actually using. It raised more children out of poverty in 1996 than all other government programs combined, although it provides less money to the very poor and nothing to those without money. Employers like the program because it subsidizes wages and may reduce the incentive of workers to fight for higher wages. It has functioned more to offset the decline in wages than to better workers' conditions. However, in 2003 the government began an attempt to cut back the EITC through stricter eligibility requirements and investigation of claimants (Mandell, B., 2004).

An estimated 3 million families with children—about 15 percent of the total eligible families—did not receive the EITC in 2003. If the number of families receiving EITC were increased by 10 percent, about 2 million families would receive benefits of as much as $3.2 billion (Children's Defense Fund, 2004d).

The Child Tax Credit

The Child Tax Credit is designed to help families offset some of the cost of raising their children by reducing or eliminating their income taxes. Parents or caretakers of a child under age 17 who is claimed as a dependent on their tax return may claim the credit. In 2003, families must have earned at least $10,500. The credit begins to phase out when a family's income exceeds $75,000 for a single parent and $110,000 for a married couple (Children's Defense Fund, 2004c). Nearly 612,000—about 25 percent of—low-income taxpayers with children did not claim the Child Tax Credit in 2001, losing $238 million (Children's Defense Fund, 2004d). Human service workers will do a great service to working people by telling them about the EITC and the Child Tax Credit.

Personal Social Services

Government programs that spend the most money are those for education, health, income maintenance, housing, and employment. Expenditures for other personal social services account for only 6 percent of total expenditures. Even though they account for a small percentage of total expenditures, they are very important to both human service workers and recipients. In fact, many graduates of human service programs will work in these programs, which include such services as:

- Day care for children of working parents
- Homemaker service and home health care for children, the disabled, and the elderly
- Respite care, to provide a breathing spell for overburdened parents, foster parents, or caretakers of people with disabilities
- Foster care and adoption
- Community residences for the mentally ill, mentally retarded, and delinquents
- Shelters for battered women and runaway teenagers
- Community mental health centers
- Children's institutions
- Protective services for abused and neglected children
- Community services for the aged
- Recreational programs
- Family planning counseling
- Correctional and penal programs
- Care of the handicapped, frail, and retarded
- Veterans' programs
- Drug and alcohol programs
- Legal assistance
- Counseling in various settings for various kinds of problems
- Information and referral services

The personal social services make up a diverse collection of programs that grew rather haphazardly in response to various social needs. They can be crucial to the person needing help. Here are some examples:

- George Silva has a severe mental illness and cannot work. He needs counseling and perhaps medication supervised by a psychiatrist or psychopharmacologist in order to function again.
- Laurie De Simas needs help finding day care for her child so she can take a job outside the home.
- Mary and George Smith are unable to bear children. They need the help of an adoption agency to get a child.
- Mr. Longo is frail but may be able to stay out of a nursing home if he has a homemaker and a home health aide to look after his needs.
- Cheryl Rezendez was totally disabled by a stroke. She will need nursing care or intensive home care.
- Ann Rice works nine to five, and her school-age children need a community center to care for them after school.

These are important services used by the middle class as well as the poor. Most of us will need some social services in the course of our lifetime.

Vital-Service Delivery Programs

SERVICES FOR THE AGED

Kris Bentley recently graduated from college with a degree in psychology. She is a case manager in a Home Care Corporation—an agency that works with older people. She visits people in their homes, when they cannot get to the home care office, and helps them figure out what services they need and how to get them. She can arrange for meals on wheels, homemaker service, home health service and chore service, as well as recreation. If her agency cannot provide a service, she refers her clients to agencies that can. The part of the job that Kris likes best is listening to people's stories about their lives. She also likes counseling people about the problems they are facing.

THE AGING POPULATION

One of the most dramatic changes in the country has been the rapid rise in the numbers of older people. There are now nine times as many people 65 years old or older as there were in 1900. The fastest growing segment of this population is people 75 years old or older.

Despite the success of the Social Security program in raising people out of poverty, many older people are still very poor. Elderly minority women are the poorest; about two-thirds of older black women living alone are poor. Although the SSI program established a national income floor for the aged, it still averages only about 75 percent of the poverty level. Seventy percent of SSI recipients receive such low Social Security benefits that they are also eligible for supplemental SSI payments. The burden of poverty falls disproportionately on those with an employment history of low wages, especially widowed black women and, to a lesser extent, white widows. The number of elderly in poverty increased from 3.4 million in 2001 to 3.6 million in 2002 (U.S. Census Bureau, 2002). Discrimination follows minorities into old age. Of those over 65, whites had a 9.1 percent poverty rate, while 23.8 percent of blacks and 21.4 percent of Hispanics were poor (U.S. Census Bureau, 2003b).

THE OLDER AMERICANS ACT

The Older Americans Act of 1965 created a new federal agency, the Administration on Aging, within the former Department of Health, Education, and Welfare. It established or encouraged many new services for elderly people:

- Nutrition programs
- Housing and transportation assistance

- Homemaker and home health care
- Legal services
- Chore services
- Senior citizen centers
- Day care centers
- Telephone reassurance
- Job training and placement

These services are delivered through area agencies on aging. But the funding is insufficient and many old people are not receiving the services they need, either to remain at home or, for the 5 percent of the people who need it, to secure appropriate institutional care.

Housing for the elderly is often built by local sponsors with financial help from the federal Department of Housing and Urban Development. The War on Poverty also created some service programs for the elderly, including:

- Retired Senior Volunteer Program (RSVP), which seeks to match work and service opportunities with elderly volunteers.

- Foster Grandparent Program, which pays the elderly for part-time work as mentors, tutors, and caregivers for at-risk children and youth with special needs.

- Service Corps of Retired Executives (SCORE), which provides consulting services to small businesses.

FAMILY CARE

You may have heard people say that families do not care for their elderly as they did in the "good old days." Studies show that this is not true. Almost one-quarter of American households provide home-based care to friends or relatives age 50 or older. Nearly three-quarters of these caretakers are women. They provide an average of 50 percent more hours per week of informal care than men (Young, 2002).

When most workers take time off from work because of caretaking responsibilities, they feel the pinch. Three-quarters of caregivers for older people work full or part-time, and half of those who work are making some sort of work-related adjustment such as going to work late, leaving early, or taking time off from work. Some give up work entirely. These work adjustments take a large financial toll.

A substantial number of adults who provide care to a parent, age 65 or older, report symptoms of depression. Two out of three informal caregivers are in ill health. Routine caregiver tasks can cause acute and chronic physical strain, particularly when caregivers lack appropriate training. Although most caregiving is short-term, prolonged responsibilities take a toll on the emotional and physical health of caregivers. Caregivers worry about not having enough time to spend with their spouse, partner, or children, or by themselves (Young, 2002). These people need supportive services such as respite care.

FOSTER CARE AND ADOPTION

Kathleen is a caseworker in a child welfare agency where she is responsible for foster care and adoption placements. She investigates reports of child neglect and abuse and determines whether foster care placement is indicated or whether she can help a family stay together. This is very rewarding work, but it is sometimes stressful. Kathleen sometimes feel that she needs the wisdom of a Solomon to make the decisions that will change children's lives. She works in a well-funded and supportive private agency, where she has help with these decisions and with her work from her supervisor, colleagues, a psychologist, and a psychiatrist.

There were 155,355 nonrelative foster homes in 2001, caring for approximately 542,000 children. Each year, more than 20,000 young people age out of foster care. Children of color are disproportionately represented in the foster care system by a margin of more than two to one. In 1990, for the first time, there were more African American children than European American children in foster care (Child Welfare League of America, 2004a).

One of the most recent stunning changes in the child welfare system has been the major growth in the number of children in state custody who are living with their relatives. About a third of all children in foster care are living with relatives. According to the 2000 U.S. Census more than 2 million grandparents are raising 4.5 million children, and other relatives are raising an additional 1.5 million children. Some factors that attribute to these increases are:

- Increased reporting of abuse and neglect
- A change in drug usage related to the spread of crack cocaine addiction and other drugs
- Increased levels of poverty
- More children are affected by HIV/AIDS
- Parents struggle with physical and mental health problems
- Family violence and parental incarceration
- Decline in the availability of traditional foster homes (Child Welfare League of America, 2004b)

Approximately 2 percent of all U.S. children are adopted. Forty-two percent were adopted by stepparents or other relatives; 5 percent were intercountry adoptions; 16 percent were adoptions of children from foster care completed through public agencies; and 37 percent were either private agency or independent adoptions of children from the United States (Child Welfare League of American, 2004c).

In 1997, President Clinton signed the Adoption and Safe Families Act into law. The law was intended to promote adoption or other permanent arrangements for foster children who are unable to return home, and to make general improvements in the nation's child welfare system. The law was a response to a concern that children were remaining in foster care too long without a permanent plan. It resulted in terminating parental rights sooner, but it also has resulted in depriving many parents of their parental rights. Advocacy groups say "there have been heartbreaking consequences for some mothers who deserve to keep their children" (Crary, 2003). The act directs state governments to start termination proceedings once the parent of a child in foster care has been in prison at least 15 months. It is an inflexible time limit and once parental rights are terminated, it is usually impossible for a mother to reverse that judgment. "'Even if women have relatively short sentences for nonviolent offenses—if they don't have family members to step in, they lose their kids,' said Joanne Archibald of Chicago Legal Advocacy for Incarcerated Mothers" (Crary, 2003).

Federal investigators have found widespread problems in child welfare programs. Some states, including New Jersey and Florida, received national attention because of scandals in their child welfare programs. But no state was found to fully comply with standards established by the federal government to assess performance in protecting children and finding safe, permanent homes for those who have suffered abuse or neglect. Some of the charges included: significant numbers of children suffered abuse or neglect in foster homes; caseworkers did not visit children often enough to assess their needs; and children were not provided promised medical and mental health services. A report on child welfare in Texas was even more negative than the federal report. The comptroller of Texas, Carole Keeton Strayhorn, said, "Some of these children are no better off in the care of the state than they were in the hands of abusive and negligent parents.... Some children have been moved among 30 or 40 temporary homes. Some have been sexually, physically and emotionally abused while in the system. A few have even died at the hands of those entrusted with their care" (Pear, 2004, April 26).

Mental Health Services

Fred is a psychologist in a community mental health center, one of the almost 2,500 mental health outpatient clinics in the nation (Callicutt, 1987, p. 126). He is a member of a clinical team that includes social workers, psychologists, psychiatrists, and mental health nurses.

Before 1981, the clinic got its funds directly from the federal government, but after the passage of the Omnibus Budget Reconciliation Act of 1981, it had to compete for its share of the block grants that the federal government gave the states. Fred has a varied caseload. He counsels people who have been recently discharged from a mental hospital. Some live at home, some in a community residence. Most are comfortable with their living arrangements, but one has consulted a lawyer about suing the state for placing her in a group home rather than in a private apartment. The lawyer believes that because the Americans with Disabilities Act protects people with disabilities from discriminatory treatment, a person who is placed in a group home is being treated differently than a person who can choose to live in his or her own apartment.

Fred's clinic is getting more and more patients who have been "dumped" by private hospitals on to financially strapped public hospitals and community services. A study showed that hospitals with managed care plans are particularly likely to reject uninsured patients and discharge patients when their insurance runs out, whether or not they are better (Kilborn, 1997). Fred's clinic is in a state that has privatized its mental health care. Public hospitals used to take everyone, but private hospitals eager to make a profit are less likely to accept seriously ill or uninsured patients.

Most of the long-term patients are receiving medication for mental illness, supervised by the clinic psychiatrists. Some check their patients often to see how they are responding; others seem casual about checking. Part of Fred's job is to alert the psychiatrist about any unusual symptoms he observes. Fred took a course on drugs in graduate school and keeps up-to-date on the literature. He has mixed feelings about drugs, feeling that they do some good but are overused. He prefers to emphasize talk therapy. Not all psychiatrists agree with him, and they have most of the power in the clinic. Since Fred does not have a medical degree, he is not authorized to dispense drugs or to give any official advice about them.

Some of Fred's clients suffer from what some psychiatrists call *free-floating anxiety.* They are able to function fairly well at their work and with their families, but need Fred's support to help them function. Fred also does family therapy.

Fred knows, almost by memory, the American Psychiatric Associations' *Diagnostic and Statistical Manual of Mental Disorders IV* (1995) because every patient has to have a diagnosis in order for the clinic to get reimbursed by private insurance, Medicaid, or Medicare. He wishes that he did not have to label everyone, and he does not agree with all the labels, but he knows that is the way the clinic gets paid.

Fred is aware of the power of self-help groups. He often refers his clients to a local group for manic depressive and depressive patients, a widow-to-widow group, the Alliance for the Mentally Ill, or the Mental Patients' Liberation Front. Fred feels that the state Department of Mental Health has not vigorously recruited minority staff or trained the present staff in cultural sensitivity. He takes courses and reads a lot about different cultures. He also tries to get to know people from different cultures. Not all the staff are as concerned as he is. He has winced at episodes of cultural insensitivity. It does not surprise him that some people of color do not return to the clinic after their first visit.

Medical Social Work

Dorothy is a medical social worker in a hospital. She graduated with a BSW, and she considers herself lucky to have this job, because many hospitals only hire social workers with an MSW degree. Medicare legislation in 1966 stipulated that if a hospital sets up a social work program, it should be under the direction of an MSW. That same legislation expanded the number of hospital social workers. More were hired after the

1978 amendments to the Social Security Act, which provided expanded benefits for patients with end-stage renal disease. To qualify for that funding, hospitals had to hire MSW social workers to treat those patients (Rossen, 1987, pp. 816–817).

Dorothy works with a multidisciplinary team of doctors and nurses, psychologists, nurse clinicians, physical therapists, occupational therapists, and patient advocates. She helps make living arrangements for patients after they leave the hospital. This is called *discharge planning*. In child-welfare agencies, social workers are almost always in charge, but the social worker in a hospital is sometimes the low woman or man on the hierarchical totem pole, unless the hospital administration establishes clear role divisions.Dorothy also helps victims of domestic violence, including victims of rape, child abuse, spouse abuse, and elder abuse. She was trained in crisis intervention and continues to receive in-service training. She has friends who work in other medical settings, such as:

- Home health care
- Hospice services
- Nursing homes
- Employee assistance programs (working with the employees of a corporation or organization)
- Health Maintenance Organizations (HMOs)
- Visiting-nurse associations
- AIDS clinics
- Health education
- Private practice

All states and the District of Columbia had some form of legal regulation for social work practice (Edwards, 1995). Because insurance companies grant third-party payments to licensed social workers, programs are eager to hire licensed workers.

Services for the Disabled

Disabled people won a landmark victory when the Americans with Disabilities Act (ADA) was passed in 1990, which outlaws discrimination against people with disabilities. The ramps you see on buildings, the leveled sidewalks for wheelchair access, the signer for the deaf at an event—are all in compliance with the ADA. Celebrating the tenth anniversary of the ADA, the Department of Justice has listed some of its victories on its web site. Here are two of them:

- Jackie Okin is now in law school studying to be a civil rights attorney because the ADA forced the Educational Testing Service and College Entrance Exam to schedule more dates in 1994 for people with disabilities to take the new SAT. People without disabilities were given several dates to take the exam, while over

20,000 people with disabilities were given only one date. Jackie said that the ADA gave her an equal chance to take the SAT and it has made a huge difference in her life.

- Kevin Holmes served successfully for ten years as a police officer in Aurora, Illinois. But because he had diabetes, he was excluded from the state's pension fund. He would not receive the retirement pension available to other officers and if he was impaired in the line of duty, he would not receive any disability benefits. In response to a suit filed by the Department of Justice, Illinois enacted legislation to eliminate discriminatory provisions in its police and fire pension code. (Department of Justice, 2001)

There are other laws, in addition to the ADA, that cover the developmentally disabled. The term most commonly used for mental retardation since 1975 has been *developmental disability,* which describes the level of functioning that makes people eligible for federally funded programs. The Developmental Disabilities and Bill of Rights Act of 1975 and an amendment of 1978 have defined developmental disability as a severe, chronic disability of a person that results from mental and/or physical impairment; begins before the age of 22; is likely to continue indefinitely; results in substantial limitations in functioning in self-care, language, learning, mobility, self-direction, and economic self-sufficiency; and results in the need for individually planned and coordinated services of lifelong or extended duration (Golden, 1990, p. 49).

Because the law covers only severe disabilities, many mildly disabled people are not eligible for these services. The legal limitation affects the poor disproportionately because there is a high correlation between poverty and disability, yet often poor families have the fewest services made available to them.

The diagnosis of mental retardation used to be determined solely by scores on intelligence tests, such as the Wechsler or the Stanford-Binet. In the 1980s, the American Association of Mental Deficiency decided that adaptive-behavior tests, which showed how a person actually performed, should become a part of the diagnostic criteria for mental retardation (Grossman, 1984).

The Developmental Disabilities Act of 1984 and changes in 1987 strengthened the Education for All Handicapped Children Act of 1975. These bills have encouraged independence, productivity, and community integration for adults. They have encouraged the phasing out of sheltered workshops, which segregated the mentally retarded into low-paying work, and the placing of people into regular jobs. The work of one human service worker exemplifies these bills:

> Tricia Doherty works in a community residence for four retarded men. She teaches them the skills they will need to function in life. In fact, it took her three years to teach them to walk around the block without kicking stones, bothering strangers, or wandering off the route. She needed three more years to train the three most advanced residents to go to a nearby supermarket by themselves. She showed them how to observe traffic lights and look both ways at intersections.... Today the three men shop by themselves and have jobs that pay almost as much as Doherty's. (Golden, 1990, p. 50)

These men achieved success through this painstaking process because they were able to learn from one staff member over a long period of time. Unfortunately, there is a high rate of staff turnover in community residences. "Few workers are willing to stay more than a year or two in a draining job that pays just above the poverty line" (Golden, 1990, p. 50).

Community residences throughout the nation vary. Even in the same state, there are vast differences among them. The lack of start-up capital keeps many patients who could live in the community languishing in hospitals. Because of exclusionary zoning practices, it is usually difficult to open a residence in the pleasant tree-lined streets of affluent communities. Many must be located in poor neighborhoods and in run-down buildings. The NIMBY syndrome—Not in My Back Yard—is the perennial complaint of people concerned that bringing in people whom they consider "undesirable" will lower the value of their property.

Disabled people won a victory when the U.S. Supreme Court in 1999 made a landmark decision, *Olmstead v. L. C.,* which held that unjustified isolation in an institutional setting was discriminatory under the 1990 Americans with Disabilities Act. Many disabled people have been confined in nursing homes because the current Medicaid reimbursement system allocates more money to institutional service providers rather than community-based programs. This Supreme Court decision forced states to provide care and treatment in "the most integrated setting" possible. The Court noted in its decision that the Americans with Disabilities Act includes language which states, "historically, society has tended to isolate and segregate individuals with disabilities" and "discrimination against individuals with disabilities persists in such critical areas as… institutionalization" ("Equal choice for the disabled and seniors," 2001).

WHERE THE MONEY COMES FROM

If you work in a human service agency, you will want to know who pays your salary and how secure it is. If, for example, you were working in the JOBS program placing welfare recipients in jobs, when the federal government abolished that program, you would join your clients in the ranks of the unemployed.

Funding comes from different levels of government—county, city, state, and federal—and from private sources. In theory, some agencies are public and others are private (voluntary, nonprofit), but in practice there is a complicated mix of public and private agencies. Some agencies that call themselves "private" get most of their funds from the government, and public agencies sometimes hire personnel from "private" agencies to do some of their work. Sometimes when agencies are privatized, workers find themselves making less money for doing the same job they did when they were state workers.

Most private, nonprofit agencies were historically organized under religious auspices and were a major source of charity. Now most of them are more public than private, sometimes getting as much as 90 percent of their funds from public sources. Even programs that decide not to take government funds get a subsidy in the form of a tax exemption.

Private Enterprise and Social Welfare Programs

Since the 1960s, state and local governments have been hiring more and more private corporations to do some of the work that state bureaucracies used to do themselves. This is called **contracting out.** Corporations want to make profits on human service. Public officials and corporations want to reduce the growing power of public-employee unions, and they weaken unions by contracting services to private corporations.

Corporations have continued to enter the social welfare field, particularly since the inception of Medicare and Medicaid in 1965, when the government began paying large sums to doctors and hospitals. This **privatization,** as it is often called, has occurred on a large scale in health care, especially in hospitals, nursing homes, and group medical care. Hospital chains such as Hospital Corporation of America and Humana sprang up in the 1970s and are making large profits. Nursing homes had become a $25-billion-a-year industry by the early 1980s, when 70 percent of them were under proprietary, for-profit management (Stoesz & Karger, 1991). By the 1980s, human service corporations had established themselves in child care, ambulatory health care, substance abuse care, psychiatric care, home care, assisted living facilities, and continuing care. Even some prisons have been privatized.

Unable to break their dependency on government funds, corporations are crying for profits from the 1996 welfare law. Small corporations were already in the welfare business before the 1996 welfare law was passed. Curtis & Associates "supplements its successful welfare-to-work jobs clubs with accessories like 'motivational fortune cookies' at $3.99 a dozen. A sample message is, 'The way to control your future is to work hard today'" (Bernstein, 1996b, p. 1). Maximus Inc., a consulting company in McLean, Virginia, did $100 million in business in 1996, including $7 million in welfare-to-work programs in Boston, two California counties, and Fairfax, Virginia (Bernstein, 1996b).

Lockheed Martin, the $30 billion giant of the weapons industry, began in 1995 to sell its Texas Integrated Enrollment System as a newer, better, privatized public assistance program. The defense giant's proposal promised to save the state up to 40 percent on its welfare program. The designers included a veritable roll-call of former state and congressional officials. It took a massive fight back in Texas by the Texas State Employees Union and others to stop it at the state level, but Lockheed didn't give up. Congressional leaders immediately proposed a "welfare flexibility bill" that would allow Texas to privatize its entire welfare system. A national battle ensued in Congress, with leadership from Service Employees International Union (SEIU) and other unions only narrowly defeating the "Lockheed Martin" legislation (Bill of Wrath, 1998).

Contracting out
A system whereby a government agency contracts with a private agency to do some specified work for pay.

Privatization
Changing the funding and administration of social welfare programs from the public to the private sector.

A survey of privatized programs by the SEIU showed that the for-profits' current management of human service programs reveals fraud, embezzlement, massive cost-overruns, extremely high error rates, technical incompetence, improper benefit denials, and "revolving door" hiring (Service Employees International Union, 1997). In Wisconsin, the two largest work-to-welfare agencies in Milwaukee were found to have misspent welfare funds. Maximus admitted to inappropriately billing the state for $411,000, and the Legislative Joint Audit found an additional $1.6 million that wasn't well documented. Maximus spent the money on disallowed meals, parties, and attending conferences (Gowans, 2000).

The corporations also have used welfare reform to get into the child-welfare business. Lobbyists managed to persuade legislators to delete the word nonprofit from an old section of child welfare law. Before the law was changed, only foster families or nonprofit institutions could get child welfare money to care for children who are removed from homes judged unfit. Children can no longer count on government help to stay in their own families, but if they are placed in an institution or

Cutbacks in public funding for medical assistance programs and limitations imposed by private managed care companies have drastically altered the health care field. Hospital workers often resort to direct action to maintain their own working conditions and standards of patient care, as Suzanne Dennehy is doing here.

foster home, an open-ended stream of federal revenue covers up to 75 percent of the cost of placement (Bernstein 1996b).

WHO IS POOR?

In the richest country in the world, there are more poor people every day. In 2002, there were 34.6 million below the official poverty line, a figure 1.7 million higher than the 32.9 million in poverty in 2001. The official poverty rate in 2002 was 12.1 percent, up from 11.7 percent in 2001. Although more whites are poor in terms of absolute numbers, the groups who are most poor as a proportion of the population are people of color, children, and women. The poverty rate for African Americans in 2002 was 24.2 percent; for Hispanics 21.8 percent; for children 16.7 percent; for female-headed families 26.5 percent (U.S. Bureau of the Census 2002).

The situation is particularly devastating for young people. Among people age 16 to 19 the total rate of joblessness in the United States was 16.5 percent in 2003. The rate for African Americans was 29.8 percent; for Hispanics 20.1 percent (Bureau of Labor Statistics, 2003). These figures understate the actual picture because people who have stopped looking for work are not counted in the unemployment figures.

Since 1973, average American wages and salaries are down (after adjusting for inflation) $50 a week, while the wealthiest Americans have seen their share of the nation's after-tax income more than double since 1977 (United for a Fair Economy, 2001, p. 1). Twenty-eight million working Americans, or one in four workers between the ages of 18 to 64, made less than $9.04 an hour in 2004, putting them below the federal poverty level for a family of four (FRAC, 2004, June 4).

The wages of human service workers have also fallen and benefits have been cut. Some workers are fighting for better working conditions and wages. Following are the observations of a Bridgewater State College student who did her social service internship with a union at Cape Cod Hospital in Massachusetts. This is a militant union that has not only fought for better benefits for workers but has also fought for better care for hospital and nursing-home patients.

INTERVIEW

Suzanne Dennehy, Hospital Workers' Union Intern

At the union I've done every kind of thing, from attending eighteen sessions of contract negotiation between Cape Cod Hospital (CCH) and the hospital workers' union (Local 767, SEIU, AFL-CIO), to actually making the picket signs and marching, and so forth.

Both sides of the table are stalling, waiting to see what Medicare changes are going to occur. At the midnight hour when the contract ran out last week, CCH finally took subcontracting off the table. It had, of course, threatened jobs. CCH will reopen the issue in one year, though.

About four weeks ago, CCH gave us all a presentation on the new health insurance they're trying to force on the workers, who are not happy about this. They've grown fond of their Blue Cross Health+ gold card and don't want to switch. This is the second and most important issue, after subcontracting. I thought, "We're all acting like it's normal to be here (talking about insurance benefits and plans) but if we had the right to national health coverage, none of us would be sitting here debating this issue. All the gatekeepers and primary-care physicians infantilize us, but in this day and age we ought to be taught to take care of ourselves. Since who cares more about one's health than oneself?"

I have no love for big business and insurance companies. I see how workers stay job-locked just to keep their health insurance. I see how the health care industry names the tune to which we all dance....

It feels natural out there on the picket lines and in the march, for me. I wonder what all this means later when I drive home alone. When I arrive home, I crank up Pete Seeger's "We Shall Overcome" on my new powerful stereo system that my son bought me. I stare at the miraculous march, at all those workers in the photograph...and get goose bumps. Yeah, we shall overcome. Justice as a theme to ponder.

Playing with Statistics: The Poverty Game

With all this talk about poverty, we need to be clear about how we define it. This is as much a political game as a scientific one. Government officials often minimize the extent of poverty or try to deny it altogether. In fact, they sometimes even stop doing research that would make the problem look more serious. In 1981, the Reagan administration stopped the Bureau of Labor Statistics (BLS) from compiling statistics on how much it actually costs to live at various standards of living. Those figures were always far higher than the poverty guidelines put forth by the U.S. Department of Agriculture. In 1981, their "lower standard of living" budget ($15,323 for a family of four) was 65 percent higher than the official poverty line set by the Department of Agriculture. By BLS standards, over a third of U.S. citizens were poor in 1981.

The way in which poverty is measured is enormously important, particularly to poor people. Many government programs base eligibility on the poverty level. Administrations are judged on their success or failure at reducing poverty. Many people object that the government's poverty line is too low and that the government therefore underestimates the number of poor people.

The poverty line is outdated. The U.S. Department of Agriculture used data from the 1950s in setting the poverty line. They figured that the average family spent one-third of its budget on food, and they multiplied the food budget by three to arrive at the poverty line. Today, however, the average family spends less than one-fifth of its budget on food, partly because of higher rents, medical care, and child care costs. If the Department of Agriculture's least expensive food plan were multiplied by 5, the poverty line would be 68 percent higher than the government's poverty line (O'Hare et al., 1990, p. 6).

People are malnourished at the poverty line. Two-thirds of the people who spend the amount of the Economy Food Plan on food get less than 80 percent of the recommended dietary allowance for all major nutrients (O'Hare et al., 1990, p. 6).

The official 2004 poverty line for a nonfarm family of three in the mainland United States was $15,670 a year, $18,850 for a family of four (U.S. Department of Health & Human Services, 2004). When you read any discussion of how many people are poor, remember our warning that these figures are too low.

IMPACT ON CHILDREN

In her impassioned introduction to a study of child poverty in the nation, Marion Wright Edelman, president of the Children's Defense Fund, expressed her outrage at the country's neglect of children:

> We are an under-developed nation when it comes to caring for our children and ensuring them the Healthy Start, the Head Start, the Fair Start, and the Safe Start the American dream envisages. (Sherman, 1994, p. xviii)

Edelman goes on to talk about the high cost of poverty to children:

> Poverty stacks the odds against children before birth and decreases their chances of being born healthy and of normal birth weight or of surviving: it stunts their physical growth and slows their education development; frays their family bonds and supports; and increases their chances of neglect and abuse. Poverty wears down their resilience and emotional reserves; saps their spirits and sense of self; crushes their hopes; devalues their potential and aspirations; and subjects them over time to physical, mental, and emotional assault, injury, and indignity.
> *Poverty even kills*. Low-income children are

- 2 times more likely to die from birth defects.

- 4 times more likely to die in fires.

- 6 times more likely to die from diseases. (Sherman, p. xvii)

IMPACT ON WOMEN

In recent years, poverty has increasingly taken on a female face. Some scholars describe this process as the **feminization of poverty**. The lower wages that women earn, compared to those of men, is partly because of discrimination against women in the job market, and partly because women are tracked into the low-wage jobs that are traditionally defined as female jobs. Another reason for women's growing poverty is that fewer women are getting and staying married. Currently over 40 percent of all adult women in the United States are not married. One result of the trend toward nonmarriage is that *one woman out of six is a single mother* (Albelda & Tilly, 1994, p. vi). A family with only one wage earner has a much higher risk of being poor than does a family with two wage earners.

Feminization of poverty The phenomenon of increasing poverty among women, particularly among female heads of families.

Single mothers also face a poverty of *time*. All working mothers are under pressure to juggle child care with work, but single mothers must do it alone. Affluent people can buy many of the services a wife used to do at home. But routine household tasks take even more time for poor families. A well-off family buys new clothes, sometimes from catalogs or online (which saves time but is often more expensive), buys food at the most convenient market or eats out, does laundry at home with its own washer and dryer or takes it to a dry cleaner, and drives one of the family's new, well-maintained cars. A financially pinched family, on the other hand, combs through second-hand clothes and mends clothes, searches for food bargains or stands in line at a food pantry, takes clothes to the laundromat, relies on public transport, nurses a clunker car, or arranges a ride. The well-off family has enough savings to "splurge with the urge," using a checking account, credit card, or ATM to pay bills conveniently. The financially pinched family struggles to figure out how to make the money last through the week (or month), robs Peter to pay Paul, pays bills in person, and purchases money orders (Albelda & Tilly, 1997, p. 55).

THE LOSS OF HOUSING

Increasing poverty has resulted in increasing homelessness. In 2001 there were 4.7 million more low-income households that needed housing than there were affordable housing units (Alexander et al., 2003).

Some of the factors that have contributed to the rise in homelessness are:

• *Renovations and evictions.* Millions of apartments where poor people used to live have been renovated (gentrified) for upper-income people and the low-income people have been evicted. They face a housing squeeze because demolitions and conversions have removed much of the old housing that they used to be able to afford.

• *Lack of housing for the marginal worker.* The single-room-occupancy (SRO) hotels have almost disappeared, where many elderly people, casual laborers, and recently deinstitutionalized patients formerly lived. As these old buildings were razed by the bulldozer, new condominiums and high-priced rentals took their place.

• *Lack of affordable subsidized housing.* Government-subsidized housing has been taken away. Federal subsidies have never provided much housing for poor people, unlike subsidies granted in western European countries. Yet, even the small housing subsidies given by the federal government were dramatically cut back during the Reagan and Bush Sr. administrations, from $32.1 billion in 1978 to $9.8 billion in 1988 (Blau, 1992, p. 71). Rather than constructing new housing, both the Reagan and Bush Sr. administrations and Congress preferred giving low-income people vouchers (Section 8's, as they are commonly called).

Section 8 "has survived the generation-long assault on public housing because it is based partly in the private sector.... Families, most of them living at or below the poverty level, pay 30 percent of their incomes toward rent, and Section 8 vouchers pay the remainder. Developers used the Section 8 guarantees as backing when they raised money for low- or mixed-income developments" (*New York Times*, 2004, May 22). This has helped many families, but it does not add to the limited housing stock, leaving large numbers of people without a place to live. Nationwide, 650,000 rental units were lost between 1985 and 2001 (Washington, 2001).

The George W. Bush administration cut housing funds further. Section 8 vouchers, which give rent subsidies to 2 million of the country's most vulnerable families, were frozen for some time in 2004. The president's 2005 budget proposed $1.6 billion less than is needed to continue helping the people who are now served, according to the Congressional Budget Office (National Alliance to End Homelessness, 2004).

The Bush administration emphasized home ownership over rental assistance, which would scale back funding for low-income tenants and would intensify the shortage of rental housing.

• *Abolition of rent control.* Some cities and states that had rent-control laws did away with them. This often resulted in evictions and homelessness because people could not afford to pay the increased rents.

Although the government has cut back its housing support for low-income people, it has maintained a tax break for middle-class and wealthy people, with mortgage interest. Home-ownership tax breaks amount to more than four times what the government spends on poor families.

The Homeless

The decades from the 1980s to the present are often described as a time of greed and insensitivity to the poor. How can one explain the shocking presence of millions of homeless people in one of the most affluent nations in the world?

It is hard to know how many homeless there actually are. The late homeless advocate Mitch Snyder compared the attempt to count the homeless to counting the grains of sand on the beach. The numbers change from day to day. Not all the homeless are on the streets or in places where they can be counted. Some sleep in campgrounds, automobiles, on the roofs of tenements, or other places where researchers can't find them. Some are doubling up with relatives and friends and will be homeless when the crowding becomes intolerable. Many will lose their jobs and be unable to pay the rent. Women will leave their battering husbands when they fear for their lives or their children's lives. Many people are so ashamed to be homeless that they lie about it to researchers. Some lie about it because they are afraid of what officials might do to them if they admitted their homelessness.

As with the definition of poverty, counting the homeless is a political issue. Conservatives want the numbers to be low and they minimize the problem; liberals want action to alleviate the problem, so they opt for the high figures, sometimes being accused of "lying for justice." Debates rage about the numbers. In most cases, homelessness is a temporary condition. A count of the homeless at a single point in time does not give an adequate picture. A more appropriate measure of the magnitude of homelessness is the number of people who experience homelessness over time.

The Urban Institute estimates that as many as 3.5 million people experience homelessness in the course of a year (Burt, M. & Aron, L., 2000). A national telephone survey conducted in 1990 and a follow-up study done in 1994 found that 12 million adults nationwide had been homeless at some point in their lives, and that 6.6 million adults nationwide had experienced homelessness (literal or doubled up) between 1989 and 1994 (Link et al., 1995). That study was done in the early- to mid-1990s, at a time when homeless rates were lower and affordable housing was in greater supply.

The questions about how people experienced homelessness drew responses that are painful to read. Over 60 percent reported not having enough food, and 26 percent reported other deprivations, such as no access to a toilet, their possessions being stolen, and being unable to bathe or shower. Physical assaults were common—42.2 percent had been assaulted, mugged, robbed, or burglarized. Although those people who stayed with friends or relatives had less severe experiences, 25.6 percent of them reported at least one extreme condition of deprivation or victimization.

The homeless population is diverse. It includes individuals and families who cannot afford the rent, some of them formerly middle-class people who lost their jobs. Although they are better educated than the homeless of the 1930s and 1940s, the new homeless are without the technical skills required in a high-tech job market. About half have high school diplomas, compared to those from the past who had only an eighth-grade education. Families with children are the fastest-growing group among the homeless (Blau, 1992, p. 25).

The high cost of housing combined with low wages and welfare grants has increased homelessness. The median cost of a two-bedroom apartment in Boston in 1999 was $16,000 a year. The minimum wage is not adequate to afford the fair market rent anywhere in the United States (Massachusetts Coalition for the Homeless, 2000). Current TANF benefits and food stamps combined are below the poverty level in every state; in fact, the median TANF benefit for a family of three is approximately one-third of the poverty level (National Coalition for the Homeless, 2001).

By 1997, 5.4 million working people in the nation paid over half of their income on housing or lived in severely substandard housing, but received no government housing assistance (Greenstein & Horney, 2000).

In twenty-five major cities surveyed by the U.S. Conference of Mayors in 2003, the average demand for emergency shelter increased by 13 percent in a year and requests for shelter by homeless families increased by 15 percent. An average of 30 percent of the requests for emergency shelter by homeless families were unmet dur-

THE HOMELESS

Some take shelter in silence,
huddling fetally,
their only home that one remembrance.

Some speak uncontainably,
having no walls to hold the words in.

Some rage at each other,
having no space to save rage for those
who are anyhow too sheltered
from their own hearts to care.

—Chris Mandell

ing the past year. People remain homeless an average of five months. The length of time people are homeless increased during the past year.

The Mayors' report said that lack of affordable housing leads the list of causes of homelessness. Other causes cited, in order of frequency, include mental illness and the lack of needed services, low-paying jobs, substance abuse and the lack of needed services, unemployment, domestic violence, poverty, and prison release.

The Mayors' report estimates that, on average, single men comprise 41 percent of the homeless population, families with children 40 percent, single women 14 percent, and unaccompanied youth 5 percent. The homeless population is estimated to be 49 percent African American, 35 percent white, 13 percent Hispanic, 2 percent Native American, and 1 percent Asian. In 60 percent of the cities, families may have to break up in order to be sheltered. In 48 percent of the cities families may have to spend their daytime hours outside of the shelter they use at night (U.S. Conference of Mayors, 2003).

Some studies show that a large number of the homeless spent some of their childhoods in foster care. Many children are placed in foster care because of their families' homelessness. A New Jersey study of 690 foster children showed that 40 percent of the families were homeless at the time of placement. Some surveys also show that as many as 22 percent of homeless mothers have been investigated on charges of neglect or abuse (Blau, 1992, p. 30).

Many of the homeless have AIDS—10,000 in New York City alone. In Chicago, 25 percent of the 50,000 to 70,000 HIV-infected drug users said they were homeless. San Francisco and New York City are the few cities that have any supportive housing, and even they do not have nearly enough beds to meet the need (Blau, 1992).

Responses to Homelessness

THE PERSONAL RESPONSE

Most of the poor are hidden away in poor neighborhoods. But we see the homeless every day. Blau (1992) calls them the "visible poor." As suburban commuters walk through a large bus terminal, they see the homeless sleeping in the corridors, washing up in the bathroom, asking to carry their luggage, and asking for change. The commuter may wonder what to do. Do we give them money? If we do, do we select out some as being more deserving than others? Do we separate out the "worthy" from the "unworthy" homeless? Do we salve our consciences by deciding that the homeless man or woman asking us for money is really into a scam, and is actually very well off?

People make their own choices and form their own rationale about these encounters. We all wish we did not have to face such dilemmas. But the very visibility of the problem forces us to make some decision, if only to pass by and do nothing.

There are basically two approaches to helping the homeless. One is to take care of the immediate needs for food and shelter. This approach treats the problem as a private issue. The other is to try to make basic social and political changes that will prevent the problem from happening. This approach treats the problem as a public issue.

BEYOND THE PERSONAL RESPONSE

Many charitable organizations offer free meals, food banks, temporary shelters, and used-clothing distribution. This has been the major response to homelessness. But although these are necessary, they are only stopgap measures.

Thousands of activists and lawyers have gone beyond the private approach to build a movement to affirm housing as a human right. "While they have not progressed very far in gaining recognition for this right, their lawsuits, demonstrations, and political campaigns have nonetheless gotten enough attention from the government to propel homelessness to the first rank of policy issues" (Blau, 1992, p. 93).

The best known of the advocacy groups is the National Coalition for the Homeless, which was founded in 1980 when the police tried to remove the homeless from the vicinity of the Democratic National Convention at New York City's Madison Square Garden. It has since broadened into a national organization with headquarters in Washington, D.C., and affiliated groups in thirty-four states.

Legal services lawyers for the poor have been in the forefront of advocating for the homeless. Although they have not established a constitutional right to housing on the federal level, they have won some major victories. The most significant of these resulted from a class action suit in New York City, *Callahan v. Carey*, which resulted in the New York State Supreme Court establishing a right to shelter. This inspired many similar suits in other states, with varying success. Lawyers have fought for and won many victories for the homeless.

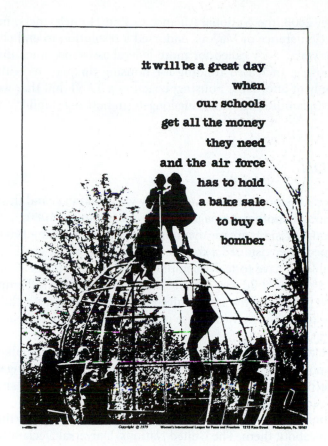

it will be a great day
when
our schools
get all the money
they need
and the air force
has to hold
a bake sale
to buy a
bomber

Why do cities put so much money into shelters rather than building affordable housing for people? Shelters are anything but homelike. Many people refuse to sleep in them because they are dangerous. Forty-three percent of residents report that they have been robbed. Many emotionally disturbed people are housed there, as well as people with criminal records. In such tense conditions, any remark can trigger a violent response (Blau, 1992, p. 145).

Shelters may ultimately be more expensive than permanent housing. Many people believe that in spite of that, cities rely on shelters because building housing would compete with the real estate industry and would establish government responsibility to provide housing for people. And there is money to be made in the **shelter industry.** "In the mid-1980s, one-third of New York City's welfare hotel business went to two separate business partnerships that together grossed $25 million in rents" (Blau, p. 159). New York City sold some welfare hotels that the city owned, and contracted with the owners to house the homeless, "paying them $1.2 million a year to house families in a hotel that it had owned outright just four years earlier" (Blau, pp. 159–160).

Shelter industry
The system of using private hotels as shelters for the homeless. It has become a profitable industry in the last several decades.

In summer 2000, the National Alliance to End Homelessness, in partnership with the U.S. Conference of Mayors, endorsed a resolution to end chronic homelessness in ten years. They called for more federal assistance, including: increased subsidized housing; increased funding for housing for persons with HIV/AIDS; increased supply of affordable housing; enacting a TANF bill that would provide more support to families; and ensuring long-term housing stability for youth.

OUR VISION

Most of us have a vision of the kind of society we would like, and this vision varies from one person to another. Some people say that from the 1980s to the present is "the mean season." Visions are meaner now than they were in the 1960s. During the 1960s, many people envisioned a compassionate society that would assure people that they would not have to fear unemployment, hunger, homelessness, or going without health care or child care. People made proposals for full employment, for national health insurance, for a guaranteed annual income, for a childrens' allowance. But they did not get any of those proposals, and some people even stopped dreaming about them.

We believe that it is important to keep the vision, to keep on talking about our vision of the good society, and to keep working to realize it. Knowing what we want helps us to recognize windows of opportunity when they arise and to put our weight on the side of forces that may do some good.

Practical politicians label some visions as "pie in the sky." Nevertheless, it is important to think about them. The United Nations' Universal Declaration of Human Rights presents a vision that we subscribe to. It states (in part):

- Everyone has the right to a standard of living adequate for the health and well-being of himself and family, including food, clothing, housing, medical care, necessary social services, and the right to security in the event of unemployment, sickness, disability, widowhood, old age, or other lack of livelihood in circumstances beyond his control.

- Mothers and children are entitled to special care and assistance. All children, whether born in or out of wedlock, shall enjoy the same protection.

The United States has not signed this statement. It is up to the citizens of the country to work for the kind of compassion for people that the statement reflects.

Many European countries do not view single mothers as a "problem." In Sweden and Finland single mothers are often privileged in social programs such as subsidized child care programs, housing allowance, and child support advance payments (in which the state pays child support when the absent parent cannot or does not). Sweden's child-care system is universally available. Parental leave for birth or adoption replaces wages for 360 days, if each parent takes at least 30 days' leave.

Parents can also take up to 60 days of leave per year for the care of a sick child under the age of 12, compensated at 80 percent of wages.

Sweden has been a pioneer in public programs to enable the elderly to live in their own homes as long as possible. Homelessness is rare and substandard housing is virtually unknown in Sweden. Affordable housing has been assured through public ownership and financing of large portions of the housing stock and income-tested housing benefits for families and the elderly. Sweden has universal health insurance, and universal allowances for families with children, as well as a national pension.

Finland does not have shelters for homeless families because they believe that families should not be in shelters. Rather, they help families obtain public or subsidized housing. Finland gives all mothers of newborn babies a layette or the equivalent value in cash. Single mothers are not stigmatized; in fact, they are considered to be doing valuable work by caring for children (Mandell, B. 2004).

SUMMARY

1. Some of the government income maintenance programs are: Temporary Assistance to Needy Families (formerly Aid to Families with Dependent Children); General Assistance; Social Security; Supplemental Security Income; Emergency Assistance; Medicaid; Medicare; Women, Infants, and Children food program; food stamps; unemployment insurance; and Earned Income Tax Credit.

2. Other social services use a small proportion of government spending for social welfare, but are important to rich and poor alike.

3. Some of the fields of service described include services for the aged, foster care and adoption, mental health services, hospital social work, and services for the disabled.

4. Funding for social services comes from local, state, and federal government, as well as from private sources.

5. Social services are becoming increasingly privatized. Corporations are taking over services that were once run by the state.

6. The official poverty line is based on an underestimation of the number of poor people.

7. Children are the hardest hit by poverty, especially children of color.

8. There has been a rise in single-parent families, which are much poorer than families with two resident parents.

9. Increased poverty has resulted in increased homelessness.

10. The main reason for homelessness is lack of affordable housing. Apartments have been turned into expensive condominiums, single-room-occupancy hotels have disappeared, and government-subsidized housing has been slashed.

12. The fastest growing segment of the homeless is families.

13. Most of the response to homelessness has treated surface problems by providing shelters and food, rather than getting to the root of the housing problem.

14. Our vision of a future society includes a guarantee of adequate income, housing, health care, child care, and full employment.

DISCUSSION QUESTIONS

1. If you were put in charge of developing an ideal system of social supports, what would your system look like?

2. Discuss the attitudes toward welfare recipients that you have encountered in your family, school, and community. How were these attitudes developed? Does your attitude differ from other attitudes you have encountered?

3. Discuss the attitudes toward the homeless that you have encountered in your family, school, and community. How were these attitudes developed? Does your attitude differ from other attitudes you have encountered?

4. Legislators in Congress voted to restrict payments for prescriptions for the aged on the grounds that people overuse the medical system when they don't have to pay for it. What do you think of this reasoning? Do you think you would overuse medical care if you got it free?

WEB RESOURCES FOR FURTHER STUDY

Poverty USA: Budgeting for Poverty
www.nccbuscc.org/cchdpovertyusa/tour2.htm

A brief (two-and-a-half minutes) slide show that very effectively breaks down what a federal poverty line income does (and doesn't) buy. Prepared by the U.S. Conference of Catholic Bishops.

Children's Defense Fund
www.childrensdefense.org/

CDF provides a strong, effective voice for all the children of America who cannot vote, lobby, or speak for themselves. They pay particular attention to the needs of poor and minority children and those with disabilities. CDF educates the nation about the needs of children and encourages preventive investment before they get sick or into trouble, drop out of school, or suffer family breakdown.

Food Research and Action Center (FRAC)
www.frac.org/html

FRAC is a leading national organization working to improve public policies to eradicate hunger and undernutrition in the United States. FRAC is a nonprofit and nonpartisan research and public policy center that serves as the hub of an anti-hunger network of thousands of individuals and agencies across the country.

Center on Budget and Policy Priorities
www.cbpp.org/index/html

Center on Budget and Policy Priorities does thorough research on public policy, particularly policy affecting low-income people. Their areas of research include tax policy, food assistance, health policies, low-income immigrants, labor market policies, low-income housing, poverty, social security, fiscal policy, unemployment insurance, and welfare reform/TANF.

National Coalition for the Homeless
www.nationalhomeless.org/

The mission of the National Coalition for the Homeless is to end homelessness. They focus their work in the following four areas: housing justice, economic justice, health care justice, and civil and voting rights. Their approaches are: grassroots organizing, public education, policy advocacy, technical assistance, and partnerships.

Child Welfare League of America
www.cwla.org/

The Child Welfare League of America is the nation's oldest and largest organization devoted entirely to the well-being of America's vulnerable children and their families. The site provides information about CWLA advocacy tips, action alerts, and child welfare statistics.

RESULTS: Ending Hunger and Poverty
www.resultsusa.org

RESULTS is a nonprofit, grassroots citizens' lobby that identifies sustainable solutions to the problems of hunger and poverty, nationally and worldwide, and works to generate the resources necessary to make those solutions succeed. The site features information about the organization, action alerts, background on hunger and poverty issues, Capitol updates, articles about the organization, and links to other web sites.

CHAPTER 7

Working with Diversity

As we move into the second section of this book, we zero in on the nuts and bolts of human service practice. We will be reading about the specific ways in which human service workers go about the tasks of interviewing, counseling, leading groups, and planning and organizing programs and social change campaigns. To implement each of these strategies, the competent worker must bring to his or her tasks empathy for the clients and their special problems. This deep empathy must be based on an accurate understanding of the cultural context in which the client lives and interacts with his or her family, peers, and the larger society. All of our actions and attitudes have been shaped to some degree by the beliefs, traditions, and history of our ethnic, religious, and class groups.

Yet, as we have grown through childhood and into adulthood, we probably encountered different and often conflicting sets of beliefs. Most of us (with the exception of Native Americans and some Mexican Americans who originally lived on land conquered by the United States) are from another soil: African Americans, Italian Americans, Irish Americans, Chinese Americans, Nisei or Issei (Japanese Americans). So we have been socialized into our own blended culture while still being influenced by the larger society, composed to a great extent of the values and history of the predominately white, Anglo-Saxon, monolingual, upper-class, able-bodied men and women who settled in the "New World" and left their stamp on it.

Our sex roles, gender identity, and mental or physical disabilities also shape how we think and act and how others react to us. How has this process of acculturation shaped our clients, and what impact has discrimination had on those clients who are members of minority groups? This chapter will raise many questions to ponder as you venture into working with people who may be different from you in many ways. It will then propose some guidelines to help you perform ethnic-sensitive practice.

The comedian Chris Rock asked, "What does it say about America when the greatest golfer in the world [Tiger Woods] is black and the greatest rapper [Eminem] is white?" While much of Rock's comedy targets the racism that is directed against black people, in this statement he was celebrating the fact that in the United States today "no role or occupation (at least in sports and music) is now determined by skin color" (Gallagher, 2003, p. 31).

We celebrate the progress that this nation has made in combating racism. The civil rights movement of the 1960s ended legal segregation. White people and people of color now eat together in restaurants, sit together in public transportation, go to school together, play on the same sports teams, and even get married. Advertisements show black models in yachting clothes. Jimi Hendrix and The Who sell Apple Computers, designer shoes, and SUVs. "Du-Rag kits, complete with bandana headscarf and elastic headband, are on sale for $2.95 at hip-hop clothing stores and family centered theme parks like Six Flags. Salsa has replaced ketchup as the best selling condiment in the United States" (Gallagher, 2003, p. 21). Black families in the media are doing well. The Huxtable family in the Cosby Show is solidly upper middle-class. But do these media pictures give the true picture of race relations in the United States? Have we finally ended discrimination against people of color?

Many people think so. National polls show that a majority of whites believe that discrimination against racial minorities no longer exists. They believe that blacks have as good a chance as whites to find a job and are as well-off financially and educationally as whites. When people are asked to explain why so many blacks aren't doing well, "the most popular explanation is that of black people's lack of motivation or willpower to get ahead" (Schuman 1997).

Most black people don't see it that way. Author bell hooks writes about her childhood as a black girl. She learned as a child that to be safe it was important to recognize the power of whiteness, even to fear it, and to avoid encountering it. She remembers walking from her home to visit her grandmother:

> It was a movement away from the segregated blackness of our community into a poor white neighborhood. I remember the fear, being scared to walk to Baba's, our grandmother's house, because we would have to pass that terrifying whiteness—those white faces on the porches staring us down with hate. Even when empty or vacant those porches seemed to say *danger*, you do not belong here, you are not safe.
>
> Oh! that feeling of safety, of arrival, of homecoming when we finally reached the edges of her yard, when we could see the soot black face of our grandfather, Daddy Gus, sitting in his chair on the porch, smell his cigar, and rest on his lap. Such a contrast, that feeling of arrival, of homecoming—this sweetness and the bitterness of that journey, that constant reminder of white power and control. (hooks, 1997, p. 175)

Times have changed since black folks had little intimate contact with whites, but bell hooks believes that feeling of impending danger has never completely left black people, even when they have adopted the values, speech, and habits of white people. She says that even though it was a long time ago that she visited her grandmother, she still has associations of whiteness with terror. "All black people in the United States, irrespective of their class status or politics, live with the possibility that they will be terrorized by whiteness" (hooks, 1997 p. 175). She says that most white people don't understand this terror.

Let's look at some facts about inequality between whites and people of color:

- *Home ownership.* In 1999 over 73 percent of white households owned their own homes compared to 46 percent for blacks, 45 percent for Hispanics, 53 percent for Asians, and 56 percent for American Indians (U.S. Census, 1999).

- *Median family income* in 1998 was $42,439 for whites, $25,351 for blacks, and $27,330 for Hispanics.

- *Assets.* In 1993 whites had about ten times more in assets than blacks or Hispanics (U.S. Census, 1993).

- *College attendance.* In 1997 almost 25 percent of whites over the age of 25 had four years of college or more compared to less than 14 percent for blacks and Hispanics (Gallagher, 2003, p. 35).

- *Poverty.* In 2000, 9.8 percent of white people were in poverty, compared to 23.6 percent of black people, and 22.8 percent of Hispanics (U.S. Department of Commerce, 2001).

- *Health.* Whites have lower rates of diabetes, tuberculosis, pregnancy-related mortality, sudden infant death syndrome (SIDS), and are more likely to have prenatal care in the first trimester than blacks, Hispanics, or Asians.

- *Health insurance.* In 1997, 15 percent of whites did not have public or private health care coverage compared to 21.5 percent for blacks, 34 percent for Hispanics, and 20.7 percent for Asians (U.S. Department of Health and Human Services, 1998).

- *Professional advancement.* Blacks and Hispanics are underrepresented as lawyers, physicians, professors, dentists, engineers, and registered nurses. In Fortune 1000 industrial and Fortune 500 service industries, 96.6 percent of the executives are white males. White men comprise 90 percent of the newspaper editors and 77 percent of television news directors (Feagin, 2000).

- *Police apprehensions and convictions.* A Department of Justice study in 1999 found that blacks and Hispanics were twice as likely as whites to be subjected to force when they encounter a police officer, were more likely to be subjected to car searches during a traffic stop, and were more likely to be ticketed than whites (Gallagher, 2003, p. 35). A 2004 Northeastern University study found that of the 366 police departments in Massachusetts, one of four engaged in racial profiling of minority drivers (*Metro*, 2004).

- *Political representation.* In 2000 the House of Representatives was only 9 percent black, 4 percent Hispanic, although both blacks and Hispanics comprised over 12 percent of the population. The Senate was 97 percent white with no black or Hispanics members (Abrams, 2000). There are no black or Hispanic governors.

- *Voting rights.* Blacks who lived in Florida in the 2000 presidential election were four times as likely as whites to have their ballot invalidated (Parker & Eisler, 2001).

AN OVERVIEW OF THE STRUGGLE FOR EQUALITY

The founding fathers of the United States—all white and Christian—did not grant the vote to women or to black men. In fact, they gave the vote only to people who owned land. Those excluded from having a say in how the country was run have had to gain their equality by long, hard struggles. Frederick Douglass, an African American leader who literally fought his way out of slavery, said, "Power concedes nothing without a struggle. It never has and it never will."

A look at history shows this to be true. The Civil War freed the slaves, and the Fifteenth Amendment of 1870 gave blacks the vote. But they were kept from using it until the civil rights movement that began in the 1950s struck down segregation laws (called Jim Crow laws) in the South. Then the Civil Rights Act of 1964 prohibited racial and sexual discrimination, and the Voting Rights Act of 1965 banned practices that disenfranchised African Americans.

The first wave of the women's movement in the late nineteenth and early twentieth centuries fought long and hard for the Nineteenth Amendment of 1920, which gave women the right to vote. The second wave of the women's movement, beginning in the 1960s and continuing to the present, renewed women's struggle for equality on many fronts. Gays and lesbians began to fight for equal treatment when they resisted police repression in 1969 at the Stonewall Club in New York City, and their struggle continues. The struggle reached a new level when Massachusetts legalized gay and lesbian marriages in 2004. Vermont paved the way for this victory by recognizing spousal rights for same-sex couples through "civil unions."

Many stigmatized groups began their struggles for equality and self-esteem in the 1960s, giving birth to advocacy groups such as the National Welfare Rights Organization, Mental Patients' Liberation Front, Disabled People's Movement, and others.

But power does not yield easily. The backlash against the liberation movements of the 1960s and early 1970s bubbled up in the mid-1970s, picked up steam in the 1980s, and led to a volcano of conservative repression with the Republican takeover of Congress in 1994 and their Contract with America, which essentially dismantled many of the social gains of the previous decades.

Conservatives oppose affirmative action programs that were established in the 1960s and 1970s. There are fierce fights against immigrants, bilingual education, multicultural curricula, sex education in schools, gay and lesbian rights, and abortion. In the past decade, laws have passed to deport illegal immigrants, cut off welfare benefits and food stamps for legal immigrants, end affirmative action for minorities, and end bilingual education. Since the 1980s, women's progress in narrowing the gap between women's and men's wages has ended, with women still earning only 72 percent as much as men with the same level of education (National Organization for Women, 2004). The wage gap between women and men has even been widening for women under age 45. Dr. Heidi Hartmann, President of the Institute for Women's Policy Research, characterizes the period since 1993 as "a disaster" for recent women graduates, ages 16–24, who are entering the labor market at lower pay rates than they would have ten years ago (*PR. Newswire*, 2004).

Where does the human service worker fit into this political maelstrom? When the battle enters directly into the social service field, the worker has to make choices about implementing restrictive policies. For example:

- If you work in the welfare department in a state that has an English Only law and you don't know Spanish, how do you explain the regulations to a Spanish-speaking client? Policies won't be printed in Spanish, and the agency might not employ a Spanish-speaking worker.

- Massachusetts passed a law prohibiting the placement of foster children with homosexual foster parents, but after years of organizing work by homosexuals and their allies, then passed a law forbidding discrimination against homosexuals. If you are a worker in a state child-welfare agency and the legislature passes a law saying you can't place foster children with homosexual foster parents, what will you do if you disagree? Do you obey the law, even against your convictions? If you do, how do you resolve the internal conflict this is likely to cause? Do you oppose the law, and if so, how? Do you work with the movement that is fighting against it by joining demonstrations, writing letters to the editor, lobbying your legislators? Do you simply place a child with a foster parent whom you know to be homosexual but tell the foster parent to keep his or her sexual orientation a secret?

- If you are a human service worker in a state that has passed a law denying services to legal immigrants, what would you do? In California some workers could not in good conscience obey the law, and they vowed to continue to give services. Many teachers in California refused to obey the law that eliminated bilingual education and continued to teach as they had done before the law.

Some legislation may not require you to make such agonizing choices but will nonetheless affect your work environment and agency practice. If affirmative action is ended, your agency may become less diverse. If you are white, you will have fewer opportunities to work with people of color. African American, Hispanic, Asian, and Native American clients will have less chance of getting a worker who shares their culture.

Regardless of what you do about the politics of diversity, you will always need to understand how the issues affect your clients or you will be shortchanging your clients and shortchanging yourself as an effective worker. If you belong to a group that has been discriminated against, you probably have already had personal experience that will help you to identify with a client who has also faced discrimination. If, on the other hand, you have never experienced discrimination, it may be hard for you to identify with people's reactions to it.

Understanding Oppression and Privilege

Individuals can be dominated by other individuals for a variety of reasons. Siblings often oppress each other; parents sometimes oppress their children. In this discussion, however, we are talking about social forces that hold people down, hem them in, and block their ability to lead a good life. "Oppression and dominance name social realities that we can participate in without being oppressive or dominating people" (Johnson, 2001, p. 13). Oppression occurs because of structural inequalities in society.

Privilege is the other side of the coin of oppression. If Group A has something of value and keeps Group B from having it, Group A is privileged and Group B is oppressed. Any individual, however, could be privileged in one respect but oppressed in another. One way to look at this was devised by Patricia Hill Collins (1990) who constructed a "Matrix of Domination" which integrates categories such as gender, race, class, sexuality, age, and ability. This matrix assumes that everyone is shaped by some combination of interacting social categories; and everyone experiences varying degrees of privilege and oppression depending upon her or his social location or place. In the African American community, for example, there are vast differences in lifestyle and outlook between affluent professionals and executives and the people on the bottom rung of the income and status ladder, yet the color of their skin ensures that both groups will face some discrimination.

In all ethnic groups, women have less power than men (although the patriarchal tradition is stronger in some cultures than others). But wealthy women have more power than poor women. A rich woman who is abused by her husband is unlikely to go to a shelter for battered women. She can afford to leave and rent an apartment or buy a house, provided she has access to the checkbook or charge account and her psyche has not been battered to the point of helplessness.

Ethnicity is only one of the many factors that determine people's standing in society and feelings about themselves. Social class and gender are also powerful influences. Anthropologist Oscar Lewis (1966) maintained that social class was a more powerful determinant of behavior than ethnicity. He believed there was more similarity between poor people in the barrios of New York City and poor people in the favelas of Sao Paulo than between the poor Puerto Rican and the rich Puerto Rican. Although both the poor and the wealthy might share certain cultural beliefs and behaviors, their differing social class positions would result in different self-identities.

Psychologist Robert Coles (1977) studied many children in different groups, including children from wealthy families. He said that one of the most outstanding attitudes of the rich children is their "sense of entitlement." They know they will inherit the country. Most poor people don't expect to inherit anything. All they can hope for is to win the lottery.

Since we all participate in a racist, sexist, homophobic society, it is inevitable that we have internalized some of these cultural beliefs. We don't need to feel guilty about that, but we do need to examine our own position in society and our own attitudes. Battling discrimination is a life-long process in which the authors of this book are also engaged. We provide two exercises at the end of this chapter that will give you and your fellow classmates an opportunity to examine oppression and privilege.

COLORBLIND PRIVILEGE

Some people say, "I don't treat people any differently no matter what their color is. I don't care if they're black, brown, or purple—it's all the same to me." The good part about that attitude is the commitment to treating everybody with equal dignity and respect and the belief that everyone is valuable. The problem with that attitude is that people *do* come from different cultures, and those cultures affect how people think and behave. To ignore a person's culture is to ignore an important aspect of that person's uniqueness.

The sociologist Charles A. Gallagher maintains that colorblindness "maintains white privilege by negating racial inequality" (2003). The belief that America is free of **racism** and discrimination and that people get ahead only on their merits allows whites to believe that being white or black or brown has no influence on their economic situation. It allows whites to believe that their material success was gained only by individual hard work, determination, thrift, and investments in education, and has nothing to do with institutional racism. It also allows whites to avoid feeling any guilt about institutional racism.

People who are reading this book are likely to be college students. It hasn't been easy for many of you to get to college and to stay there until graduation. Many of you work part-time, or even full-time. Many of you have been poor and are trying to work your way out of poverty. If you are white and someone suggests that you are privileged because of your white skin, you may think that is ridiculous. You don't feel privileged. You have worked hard to get to where you are. Yet we suggest that you examine some of the things that made it possible for you to get to where you are. You might discover that you did in fact have some privilege because of your white skin. One of the authors of this book, Betty Reid Mandell, did that examination of her own life and found that despite her growing up poor she did indeed enjoy certain privileges that were denied to people of color. She began this exercise when she was doing outreach work at a welfare office to give people information about their rights. Here is the description of her self-examination:

Racism Hatred or intolerance of another race or other races. Beliefs that one's own race is superior.

CASE STUDY

You've been well cared for*

I was sitting in the Homeless Unit of the Grove Hall Department of Transitional Assistance (welfare department) chatting with some women. One was living in a homeless shelter in Saugus, a town on the north shore of Massachusetts; the other was applying for shelter. They were ashamed to be here. They said that they had worked and held responsible jobs. Life had dealt them raw blows. One had to leave her job because of an injury to her spine which seemed to require endless treatment, and she didn't know when she could return to work. The other had various

This article was published in *New Politics*, Vol. IX No. 4, Winter 2004, pp. 136–137.

medical problems. She was infuriated because the DTA worker was "jerking her around." She had an appointment for 9, and it was now 11 and they still hadn't seen her.

They cared deeply about their children. The woman who lived in Saugus was driving her daughter to Boston every day so the child would not have to switch schools. I told her that a recent federal law requires the home school district to provide transportation from the shelter to the child's home school. I pointed to the sign on the wall that told about this and urged her to call the number.

The woman who was being "jerked around" said in a resigned voice, "It's all down hill when you get old. I'm 45 and I don't think things will get any better." I protested, "Come on, I'm 78 and I'm not going down hill. I'm still here fighting." The women were amazed. "You're 78?" they said. "You've been well cared for. We've been battered around all our lives."

I've been thinking about that a lot. I think the women were implying that I had been treated better in life because I am white, while prejudice and discrimination against African-Americans had given them harsher treatment than I had faced. Was that true?

As a child, I didn't feel privileged. My father was one of the last homesteaders to get free land from the government, but he got the worst land—dry land in the prairies of Colorado where it seldom rained and the dust storms were so fierce that you literally couldn't see your hand in front of your face if you were outside, while the wind whipped sand through the cracks of the windows and doors. On a freezing winter day the car broke down coming home from the school, which was 7 miles away, and we froze our fingers and toes walking home for 2 miles.

My parents lived in constant dread of the bank foreclosing on the mortgage, and one day they held an auction to sell off cattle and machinery so they could pay the mortgage. We were eager to watch the auction, but my parents made us go to school so we would not witness their humiliation.

Still, we kept the farm and somehow all four of us children went to a public college where the tuition was cheap. My sister and I raised and sold prize 4-H steers and saved the money for college. I pumped gas at a filling station during World War II, helped with bookkeeping at the gas station, typed letters for a local cattle rancher, and when I went to college, had a work-study job and a scholarship. I paid for my graduate school by part-time secretarial jobs and stints as a group work leader at the YMHA and Community Church in New York City. I didn't mind working, even enjoyed much of it, but I never felt that I had a privileged life.

Yet as I thought about it, I did get better breaks in life because of my white skin. When I read the history of the Homesteading Act, I learned that African-Americans were discriminated against and didn't get even the poor land that my father got.

The Mexican-American children whose family came to town to pick sugar beets attended my school, but they had to leave because their family moved on to other migratory work when the beets were pulled. My family were permanent residents and I could stay in school.

When I went to Grange Hall dances, I noticed that the two sons of the only African-American farmer in our neighborhood stood on the sidelines and never asked any of the white girls to dance. I would have been shocked if they had asked me to dance, but I think I would have been pleased too because they were handsome and I had secretly wanted to get to know them. An unwritten community prejudice had kept us from getting to know one another. That was not privilege for me—that kept me from living as full a life as I could have.

At college I joined a sorority that I later discovered did not allow African-Americans to become members. I tried to resign, but was told that no one was allowed to resign. Their racism was mandatory!

The parents of one of my best friends in college were living in a Japanese-American concentration camp, having been put there during World War II. I gave speeches against the injustice, and I knew that my parents were never under suspicion of being spies because their skins were white.

I taught at a state college and since I retired I have lived on the state pension, as well as Social Security. Many African-Americans weren't covered by Social

Security because it did not cover domestic workers or agricultural workers for many years. Even when they were covered, they often received less money because the work had paid so little.

I have had health problems too, but the state health benefit, combined with Medicare, pays for almost all of my medical care and I can choose any health care provider I wish. I can afford to pay for massages, acupuncture, and weight training classes, and to buy both prescription drugs and herbal medicine. I know that I am privileged in this compared to Medicaid recipients, who have a limited choice of doctors and cannot get all the services they need, and compared to people who work in low-wage jobs that don't provide health insurance.

So yes, I have been privileged. Those women in the DTA office asked why I came to the office and did this kind of work. I told them that I had been a social work professor at Bridgewater State College, and I be-

lieved in not only talking about my knowledge and beliefs, but acting on them. They commended me and said that it was good to stay active and involved. "It's sure better than sitting on the couch and clicking the remote."

I agreed. I am privileged to be able to use my knowledge to come to the DTA office and tell a homeless woman that she does not have to drive her child 20 miles to school and back every day, and that the school system is breaking the law if they don't pick the child up. I am privileged to know enough to go into a fair hearing with a woman and point out to the worker and the hearing officer that they are breaking the law by cutting off the woman's welfare benefits. I am privileged to help a woman apply for food stamps. And I am privileged to know the brave mothers who come to the DTA and keep their spirits up for the sake of their children.

The playwright August Wilson talks about attitudes toward blackness:

> When you go to the dictionary and you look up black, it gives you these definitions that say, "Affected by an undesirable condition." You start thinking something's wrong with black. When white people say, "I don't see color," what they're saying is, "You're affected by this undesirable condition, but I'll pretend I don't see that." And I go, "No, see my color. Look at me. I'm not ashamed of who I am and what I am." (Lahr, 2001, p. 52)

Overt racism is easy to spot, but covert racism is more subtle. In his discussion of unintentional racism, Charles Ridley describes how both color-blindness and color consciousness can lead to unintentional racism in counselors:

> Color-blind counselors relate to minority clients as though race is unimportant. Their denial disregards the central importance of color in the psychological experience of the client. These counselors tend to overlook the influence of racism and discrimination upon the attitudes, feelings, behaviors, and personality development of minority clients. Color-blind White counselors also disregard the undeniable influence of their whiteness upon the client. (1995, p. 68)

Color consciousness is the opposite of color blindness. It is based on the premise that the client's problems stem essentially from being a person of color.

The color-conscious counselor places too much weight on the color of the client and assumes that all problems are due to the client's ethnicity.

Impact of Prejudice on Self-Esteem

Positive self-esteem is at the core of mental health. In the following anecdotes, consider how prejudice and discrimination might negatively affect people's feelings about themselves.

• A 70-year-old person recounted the following incident: "I was driving into a parking lot and a youngish woman was driving out. She evidently didn't like the way I was driving, because she screamed at me, "Where do you think you're going, you old bat?"
The 70-year-old woman had never considered being old as the most important part of her identity, but here she encountered a woman who saw her age as the most important part of her identity, and as a degraded status. The yelling woman combined her anger about a person's driving with her contempt of old people. Because the older woman was secure in her identity, and in her driving ability, she was able to pass this incident off with a shrug. But this example of ageism is representative of the mountain of insults that older people face, insults that can wear down a shaky self-confidence.

• A lesbian student is told by one of her teachers that she has no right to wear a necklace with a cross on it because lesbianism is against God's will. The teacher forces her to "come out of the closet" to the class about being a lesbian, and when she does, some class members turn on her angrily. The student is hurt and angry, feeling that she has been emotionally violated.

• Battered women are not only physically abused, but they also face a barrage of emotional insults from their batterers, often to the point of agreeing with the batterers who tell them that they are worthless.

• Two social psychologists, Claude Steele and Joshua Aronson, tested the effects of expectations on students' performance. They gave graduating black high school students GRE exams. When they told the students that white students get better scores on those exams than black students do, the students' self-confidence went down and, true to the prediction, on average their scores were lower than the scores of white students. But when they were told that the exam was not being used to evaluate ability or qualification, their scores went up and were as good as the scores made by white students (Steele & Aronson, 1995). When their anxiety about performance was removed, black students worked up to their full potential, which is as great as that of white students. This study is one of the many that disprove the premise of the widely publicized book *The Bell Curve,* that the intelligence of black people is consistently lower than that of white people (Herrnstein & Murray, 1994).

Steele and Aronson also conducted a similar experiment with women, using math tests, and the results were the same.

How can a human service worker combat prejudice and discrimination? We need to work on three levels—with the larger community, with small groups, and with individuals. Working for community-wide social change will involve social activism. Causes that might be embraced include the women's movement, gay and lesbian liberation, welfare rights, antiracism, immigration issues, ageism, disabled patients' liberation, mental patients' liberation, or body-image liberation.

The most effective change in social attitudes is brought about by large-scale movements. Liberation movements not only change public attitudes, but they also can raise the self-esteem and self-confidence of oppressed people. People often internalize their oppression and come to believe that they are like what the oppressor says they are. When they join with similarly oppressed people, the very fight to free themselves raises their self-esteem. "Say It Loud: I'm Black and I'm Proud" is a slogan to counter the demeaning belief that black people are inferior. Gay Pride marches help restore pride to gays and lesbians. The women's movement has had a profound effect on women's self-esteem, giving support to women's quest for equality with men. The welfare rights movement helped welfare recipients feel themselves to be worthy and productive people.

On an individual level, the most important job for human service workers is to understand the culture of their clients. We use the word *culture* broadly. In a sense, every individual you work with is from a different culture. But in this chapter, we will focus particularly on groups that have been oppressed because of their ethnicity, social class, gender, sexual orientation, or physical or emotional status.

UNDERSTANDING ETHNICITY

The Definition of Culture

There is no one agreed-on definition of *culture*. We will use the term to connote a group of people who share history, language, traditions, and networks. They may also share a minority social status. More important, they see themselves and others see them in a special way, although their ethnic and cultural status may have slightly varied meanings for each individual (Lukes & Land, 1990).

Theories about cultural identity have changed over time. The melting-pot theory, popular among the "Establishment" of the 1960s, implicitly assumed that the white, Anglo-Saxon culture was the ideal that other cultures should aspire to. The theory proved to be inadequate. Ethnic groups never totally assimilate into the majority culture, and they have asserted their right to be unique.

During the War on Poverty, some sociologists proposed a "cultural deficit" theory (Moynihan, 1965), which assumed that minority cultures were inferior to the

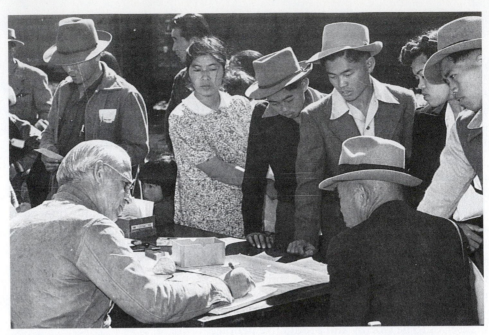

During World War II the United States government forcibly interned thousands of U.S. citizens of Japanese ancestry. The official reason was that they might spy for Japan, our enemy. Yet the German Americans and Italian Americans, both of whose ancestral countries also opposed us, were not harassed. Why do you think Asian Americans were treated so much more harshly?

mainstream. This theory called for socializing minorities into the mainstream culture. That was one of the guiding principles of the Head Start early-childhood program.

Through the organized efforts of those supposedly deficient cultural groups, the cultural-deficit theory yielded to a theory of cultural difference, which focused on the uniqueness of each minority culture but implied that each was separate from the dominant culture. However, that too was inadequate, as there is much overlap between the minority and dominant cultures.

A current theory is called **bicultural theory.** It states that, although people are socialized into their minority culture through family and ethnic community, they are also influenced by the dominant culture through social institutions and the mass media. No one is quite sure how people incorporate cultures. Each person goes through the process with varying degrees of success. The totally bicultural person moves easily between two cultures, feeling at home in each, to the extent that the dominant culture allows this (Lukes & Land, 1990, pp. 155–156).

Some anthropologists say that your ethnicity is situational, asserting itself according to the situation you are in (Green, 1982). An African American person might speak Black English with other African Americans, but when with white

Bicultural theory
A theory asserting that although people are socialized into their minority culture through family and ethnic community, they are also influenced by the dominant culture through social institutions and the mass media.

people, will speak the dominant form of English. It is important to know how people deal with ethnicity in cross-cultural interactions as well as within their culture.

It is absurd that the amount of melanin (pigment) in one's skin or the tightness of the curl of one's hair should cause another person to do anything more than casually notice these features as two of the many that distinguish one person from another. Yet the social meaning of these features in the United States has built up over three centuries, beginning with the arrival of the first slave ship from Africa. Since its arrival (and the thousands that came after), no one in this country has been casual about color. Ever since the arrival of those three fateful ships that Christopher Columbus led to the American continent in 1492, the rulers of this country have subjugated native populations and constricted them with minority status in their own lands.

Advances in genetics and biotechnology in the past few decades have caused a dramatic shift in thinking about race. Most anthropologists now agree that race is not a biological reality at all. It is nothing more than a social, cultural, and political invention (Chandler, 1997). But that is not how the general public sees it. A biological anthropologist at Yale University, Jonathan Marsh, said that changing most people's minds about race is "like convincing someone in the 17th century that the Earth goes around the sun and not vice versa. What you think is out there is different from what's really out there" (Chandler, 1997, p. A30).

The mapping of the human genome provided scientific proof that human beings are not divided into separate biological groups. J. Craig Venter, whose company, Celera Genomics, mapped the human genome, said, "It is disturbing to see reputable scientists and physicians even categorizing things in terms of race. There is no basis in the genetic code for race" (Stolberg, 2001, p. 1 wk).

While we agree that there is only one race, we go on to discuss race as a social construct because it is a concept deeply embedded in people's ideas about themselves and others.

The actress Lonette McKee, who played the role of Alice in the TV series *Queen*, has both African American and Finnish-Swedish ancestry. Her mother told her that she had the best of both worlds. But McKee does not agree.

> The world doesn't tell you that when you're out there looking for a job. The world doesn't tell me that when I've got the job and then they don't want to pay me what I'm worth. It's a political, social reality—one drop of black blood, you're black. To look at yourself any other way is a lie. And we're involved in a system designed to weed us out, to keep us out of the mainstream. (Smith, 1993, p. 30)

Media Stereotypes

The media has a powerful influence in shaping our attitudes. A comparison of how the media presents black and white people shows that black people are likely to be shown in a more unfavorable light than white people. For example, consider the media treatment of six fatal schoolyard shootings over eight months by white youths in American small towns.

Kip Kinkel, 15, the boy who allegedly killed his parents and two classmates in a gun rampage in Oregon, was "skinny," "slight," "diminutive," or "freckle-faced." A *Newsweek* story described him as having "an innocent look that is part Huck Finn and part Alfred E. Neumann—boyish and quintessentially American." A Roxbury judge, Milton Wright, said, "Quintessentially American? That always means white" (Dowdy, 1998, p. E1).

Luke Woodham, convicted in Mississippi of killing two students, was described as "the chubby, poor kid at Pearl High School who always seemed to get picked on," a "nerd," and "intelligent but isolated" (Dowdy, 1998, p. E1).

Michael Carneal, who allegedly killed three students in West Paducah, Kentucky, was "thin" and "a solid B student." Mitchell Johnson and Andrew Golden, who allegedly killed four girls and a teacher in Jonesboro, Arkansas, were "little boys." Andrew Wurst, who allegedly killed a teacher in Edinboro, Pennsylvania, was a "shy and quirky eighth-grader with an offbeat sense of humor" (Dowdy, 1998, p. E1).

Contrast these benign descriptions with the media treatment of young African American and Latino killers. They have been called "maggots," "animals," and "super predators." Julian Bond, chairman of the National Association for the Advancement of Colored People, comments, "If this were black kids doing this, you'd see op-ed pieces…talking about a pathology of violence loose in the community, about some dangerous elements being unleashed, about the breakdown of family values" (Dowdy, 1998).

News accounts of young black killers in court often describe them as "blank-faced," "dazed," or "showing no emotion." "Unlike the more human terms given the white school killers, young black suspects often are not described physically at all. Often, the first description of them is whether the youth was in a gang" (Dowdy, 1998, p. E1).

Boston District Attorney Ralph Martin says that many young black suspects are "seemingly sweet of countenance, and lacking in obvious bravado" (Dowdy, 1998, p. E1), but he rarely sees black youth described that way in the newspapers.

Alvin Poussaint, a Harvard Medical School psychiatrist, notes that although there is wide media discussion of mood disorders and depression for the white teenage killers, "there is little of that for low-income African-American and Latino youth killers who suffer at higher levels of the kind of depression that precedes violence" (Dowdy, 1998, p. E1).

Julian Bond comments that it is time that the United States looked at factors behind youth violence that cut across race and class. He said, "It seems to me there's kind of a pathology out there, some kind of love of guns, a gun culture out there that's dangerous and insidious" (Dowdy, 1998, p. E1).

The following is an interview with two women of Puerto Rican heritage who work in a shelter for battered women. This interview illustrates some of the interconnections between ethnicity, social class, and gender.

INTERVIEW

Oly Reid and Inez Figueroa, Counselors at a Battered Women's Shelter

Oly Reid and Inez Figueroa work in a shelter for battered women and their children in a medium-sized city. Because the women whom they serve need to hide from their abusers, the location of the shelter is a secret. We interviewed them in an office that had no name on the door.

Some people have compared the battered women's shelters to the Underground Railroad of slavery times (a network of secret hiding places for runaway slaves). Oly entered this work out of the same passion for justice that motivated the abolitionists in the Underground Railroad. She has a fierce commitment to helping free women from abusive husbands. She says, "Women have been abused since the beginning. It is time to put a stop to it. We have to stand up for our rights."

Oly does bilingual counseling in Spanish, conducts house meetings and support groups, supervises volunteers, and does administrative work. Inez is the legal advocate. She helps women with their court appearances and works with people in the community. The shelter is a one-family house with three bedrooms that houses ten women. The residents can stay six weeks if they have children, four weeks if they are single.

About 30 to 35 percent of the women they serve are Spanish-speaking. Both Oly and Inez are from Puerto Rico, so they are fluent in Spanish. If no one in the shelter speaks a woman's language, they can generally find another shelter where a worker does.

Most of the abusers are men, although, as Oly says, "We are all human and anyone can be an abuser"—mothers, sisters, lovers (both heterosexual and homosexual). Lesbians have double trouble when they are abused by a lover. Society rejects them because they are lesbians, because they are women, and because stereotypes dictate that women are never violent.

Most women are ashamed to ask for help, but women of some cultures are more ashamed than others. Two or three Chinese women have used the shelter, but, in general, the Chinese culture discourages revealing one's troubles because it would bring shame on the family. They are taught that "whatever their husband says, goes."

Puerto Rican women have experienced oppression from white people in their native land. It is hard to expose their most intimate problems to white Americans because of shame and pride. Puerto Rican women often drop charges against their husbands because they are afraid of them. They live a very isolated life. They have to stay home and often don't learn English, while the man goes out to work and learns the language. When the women call the police, they are usually unable to express themselves clearly. But their husbands can. So the police believe the husbands.

Generally, women who are hiding from an abuser want to go to a shelter in another city because their abusers are less likely to find them there. Sometimes they even go to another state. Shelters communicate to help each other place women. If the abuser lives in the same city, the women can't go out of the shelter at all. They have to stay in the house twenty-four hours a day.

Women may minimize the abuse they have experienced, justifying the actions of the men and feeling themselves at fault. They think that if they don't make the men mad, the men won't hit them. They excuse men "because they are drunk and don't know what they are doing." Oly said, "That is no excuse. If they don't know what they are doing, why don't they beat up a big man [instead]?"

Inez thinks that abusive men should get a mandatory jail sentence of one year. "The judge often gives a year's sentence, but the time gets cut through good behavior in jail and other reasons so that he is often out in three months and on the woman's doorstep again."

Most of the women have their kids taken from them, often unjustly. Even though they didn't abuse the children, the men will often get revenge on the women by complaining to the welfare department or the Department of Social Services that they have men living with them and supporting them or that men are going in and out of the apartment all the time, doing drugs, and so forth. One man wrote to the landlord saying that the woman was dealing drugs and that people were living in the apartment and not paying rent.

Sometimes abusive husbands are given visitation rights, but it is the women who have their children taken from them, and they have to prove themselves fit mothers. When the Department of Social Services (DSS) investigates, it often accuses the mothers of not protecting the children. Oly says, "But how can a woman in that situation find housing, pay a baby-sitter, pay the rent, heat, food, transportation, and so forth, without any help? DSS should help her get settled and support the family rather than taking the children away." Sometimes women feel overwhelmed and place their children voluntarily, expecting to get them back when they have their lives together. But when they go to DSS to get them back, DSS may refuse to return the children.

Children need help too. Even if they have not been directly abused, they may have witnessed their mothers being attacked and this is very disturbing. One child said to her mother in the shelter, "You're not scared anymore. You were always scared at home." The mothers sometimes claim that the children weren't aware of what was happening, but the children always know.

The advice that Inez and Oly give to human service students is, "Be sympathetic. Let the woman know it's not her fault. She doesn't deserve it. She's not alone. Tell her, 'There is always help, someone who will listen to you.' If a woman says, 'My husband is going to kill me,' believe her."

Inez and Oly are always themselves in their work, never putting on a false front. When a woman cries, sometimes they cry with her. They hug the women and get angry along with them. Having gone through some of the things that the residents are going through, they are able to empathize with them.

Ethnic Identity

It is risky to generalize about ethnic traits. There is much variety within each culture. For example, some of the literature on working with ethnicity points out that although the usual advice in interviewing technique is to look someone straight in the eye, that would be the wrong technique for some Asian, Latino, and Native American groups, who might interpret that as hostility. In her autobiographical novel *The Woman Warrior*, Maxine Hong Kingston shows that this advice would be wrong for an older woman, Moon Orchid, who was newly arrived from China, but

Of course this cartoon is an exaggeration, suggesting that police use a device to spot the race of a motorist instead of their speed, but it does point out that racial profiling is too often a reality on our nation's highways. Civil rights groups have lodged protests against this practice.

right for her nieces, who were acculturated to the American tradition of looking people straight in the eye:

"Good morning, Aunt," they said, turning to face her, staring directly into her face. Even the girls stared at her—like cat-headed birds. Moon Orchid jumped and squirmed when they did that. They looked directly into her eyes as if they were looking for lies. Rude. Accusing. They never lowered their gaze; they hardly blinked.... Sometimes when the girls were reading or watching television, she crept up behind them with a comb and tried to smooth their hair, but they shook their heads, and they turned and fixed her with those eyes. She wondered what they thought and what they saw when they looked at her like that. She liked coming upon them from the back to avoid being looked at. They were like animals the way they stared. (Kingston, 1977, p. 133)

The most important guideline for a human service worker is to seek to understand how each individual person is affected by his or her ethnicity. To do that, there is no substitute for asking the person. If you are working with many people from a culture different from yours, you would be wise to read as much as possible about that culture, including the literature of the culture. That will enrich your life as well as help you in your work. If their language is different from yours, it would also help you to learn their language. We are the first to admit that this isn't easy. One of the authors of this book, Betty Reid Mandell, has been struggling to learn Spanish so she can talk with Hispanic people who come to the welfare office where she does outreach. She has been taking Spanish courses for many years, but she is still far from being fluent. Yet even her halting attempts to communicate with Hispanic women are appreciated, and the women help her with the language.

The Power of Names

When we discuss ethnicity, we need to explain some terms. You may wonder sometimes what you should call a particular group of people. Do you call old people *elderly, senior citizens,* or simply *old?* How do you designate people who do not have all possible physical or mental functions? Are they *handicapped, disabled, differently abled, physically challenged, developmentally disabled,* or *people with disabilities?* Are American people of African descent called *African Americans, black,* or *Negro?* Are American people with Mexican ancestors called *Mexican Americans* or *Chicanos (Chicanas)?* Are people whose native language is Spanish called *Hispanics* or *Latinos (Latinas)?* Are indigenous people *Indians, Native Americans, First Nations,* or a specific tribal name?

The name that a group chooses to be known by is important because it reflects that group's self-identity. When a group is oppressed, the name it chooses becomes a political as well as a linguistic issue. For example, people with disabilities generally do not like to be called simply "disabled" rather than "people with disabilities," because the former term implies they are deficient in some way and not whole people.

In the course of their liberation struggles, American people of African descent said they no longer wanted to be called *colored,* because that term carried connotations of lower status, so they changed their designation to *Negro.* During the civil rights movement of the 1960s, they proudly declared that their skin color should be a source of pride rather than shame, so they called themselves *blacks.* Later on, as they proudly claimed their African heritage, politically active people used the term *African Americans.* Recently the trend seems to be to return to the term *black,* partly out of consideration for West Indians, who do not consider themselves African Americans, and partly because *black* is an easier term. The term *people of color* is often used to describe people of ethnic groups that are not considered *white* or *Caucasian,* but some people point out that these are not entirely accurate terms because Caucasians are not actually white, and many Hispanics are white, even though they may be considered under the rubric of people of color. Similarly, some politically active people of Mexican descent changed the old term *Mexican American* to *Chicano* (for males) and *Chicana* (for females).

As these name changes take place, not everyone in the group adopts them, and often the old names linger on alongside the new ones. For example, the word *colored* is still part of the name of the National Association for the Advancement of Colored People (NAACP). Many people still call themselves *Mexican Americans* rather than *Chicanos (Chicanas)*. Although many indigenous people prefer the term *Native American* to *Indian,* some activists are now saying that both terms are reminders of colonialism. They prefer the term *First Nations* or *First Americans,* or their tribal names. "American Indian" is also an accepted term. The Census Bureau calls all Spanish-speaking people *Hispanics* but makes it clear that "persons of Hispanic origin may be of any race."

As authors, we use the terms that we believe are in current usage by people who are in the forefront of their particular group's liberation struggles. When more than one term is in current usage, we use both. *When in doubt about the term a particular person prefers—ask that person!*

BROAD CATEGORIES DISGUISE LARGE DIFFERENCES

Many different nations are lumped under the categories of "Asian American" or "Latin American," but these broad categories obscure enormous national differences. One could no more speak of a "typical Asian" than of a "typical European." Immigrants from Japan, China, Korea, Cambodia, Vietnam, Laos, and the Philippines all speak different languages and come from vastly different cultures. Immigrants from Colombia, El Salvador, Argentina, Guatemala, Mexico, and Puerto Rico all speak Spanish, but they too come from very different national cultures. Although Haiti and the Dominican Republic share the same Caribbean island, their people speak different languages and have different histories and cultures.

The Census Bureau has finally recognized the reality that many people are of more than one race and for the first time in 2000 allowed people to select more than one racial category. The Census Bureau records "race" and "Hispanic ethnicity" as separate questions. Thus, a Hispanic person can be of any race. Officially, the proportion of ethnic groups in the United States in 2000 was as follows: Caucasian 69.13 percent; black 12.06 percent; Hispanic 12.55 percent; Asian 3.60 percent; American Indian and Eskimo 0.74 percent; Hawaiian and Pacific Islander 0.13 percent; two or more races 1.64 percent; other 0.17 percent (Censusscope.org, 2000).

The Hispanic population has surpassed the black population recently, and there is a trend toward an increasing Hispanic population.

Discrimination Hurts Everybody

The college students who scrawl JAP (Jewish American Princess) on a dorm door have been infected with a contagious, chronic virus. Having learned how to hate one group of people, they are likely to turn on others from backgrounds they do not understand or feel threatened by.

Prejudice and discrimination have economic, psychological, and political causes. In recent years, as the job market has contracted and wages have gone down, people's anxieties and fears about competition for jobs have increased. Many working people look for scapegoats, and we have seen a frightening increase in hate groups such as the Ku Klux Klan, American Nazi Party, Aryan Nation, and right-wing militias. The bombing of a federal building in Oklahoma City in 1995 was an example of these groups' potential for violence and the danger that hate inspires.

Prejudice is widespread and is directed against many kinds of people. The comedian Tom Lehrer satirized the pervasiveness of prejudice in his song "National Brotherhood Week." Following are some excerpts:

> Oh the white folks hate the black folks;
> And the black folks hate the white folks.
> To hate all but the right folks is an old established rule....
>
> Oh the poor folks hate the rich folks,
> And the rich folks hate the poor folks.
> All of my folks hate all of your folks;
> It's American as apple pie....
>
> Oh the Protestants hate the Catholics;
> And the Catholics hate the Protestants.
> The Hindus hate the Moslems,
> And everybody hates the Jews.
> During National Brotherhood Week, National Brotherhood week,
> Its National-Everyone-Smile-at-One-Anotherhood Week.
> Be nice to people who are inferior to you.
> It's only for a week, so have no fear.
> Be grateful that it doesn't last all year.*

In his classical study of prejudice, psychologist Gordon Allport described a racist as a person who is suspicious and distrustful of anyone perceived as "different" and who is a "super-patriot," believing that all newcomers or those who are different from the mainstream pose a threat to an idealized and more secure past (Allport, 1954, pp. 69–72). Allport's study discovered that bigoted people go through life feeling threatened. They are insecure, cannot live comfortably with themselves or others, and are burdened by guilt. They insist on a strict code of morality in order to try to control their own instinctive feelings, which they mistrust.

Prejudice generally leads to discrimination against the feared group. It is a way to shore up the prejudiced person's weak ego by feeling that he or she is better than other people. It is also a way to protect privileges, by keeping other people out of jobs, housing, or other benefits they need.

Sociologist Robin Williams says that "Racial ideologies developed to rationalize the social, economic, and political domination initially developed to enhance

---

*From *Too Many Songs*, Tom Lehrer. Copyright © 1965 by Tom Lehrer. Used by permission.

the resources and privileges of white Europeans" (1966), a domination that persists to the present day. Discrimination harms all workers. Discrimination against people of color and women enables management to pay workers low wages and to rationalize cutbacks in social spending. Anti-Semitism enables the power elite to use Jews as scapegoats to deflect anger away from those in control. As long as they are fighting with each other, minority groups cannot unite to bring about equality and equity for everyone.

The closing off of equal opportunities to people of color has not only caused incredible hardship to them and to their communities, but it has also created social instability that threatens all of society. Rising unemployment in the black community has affected the structure of the black family. Sociologists have pointed out the relationship of black male unemployment to the rise in single-parent families. Although he does not claim that this is the only reason for the rise in female-headed families, sociologist Robert Staples says that "the percentage of black women heading families alone…corresponds closely to the percentage of black males not in the labor force. Men want to help support their families and lose self-esteem when they cannot find work" (1988, p. 321).

Until the problems of unemployment and low income are solved, none of the other problems of the African American community can be solved. Slavery, and the decades of racism that followed, created a workforce in which "blacks still predominate in those occupations that in a slave society would be reserved for slaves" (Ezorsky, 1991, p. 74).

There is also a correlation between the numbers of unemployed young men and the crime rate. The official response to crime has been to build more prisons, at great expense to the taxpayer, but as the director of the American Civil Liberties Union points out,

> Crime rates correlate, not with how many prisons are built, but with the proportion of young people in the population and the percentage of those young people who are unemployed, uneducated and face a bleak future. Most violent crimes are committed by alienated young men, who have no reason to hope and nothing to lose—a dangerous mix. (Glasser, 1992, p. 16)

Institutional Racism

How does institutional racism or sexism differ from individual racism or sexism? Imagine a situation in which no worker in an agency holds strong racist (or sexist) views, yet the policies of the agency are constructed so that minorities don't receive fair treatment. Such a situation is an example of **institutional racism (sexism)**. It is larger, more powerful, and harder to change than one person's attitudes, because interconnected systems and policies perpetuate it. Even if a policy may appear fair and neutral on the surface, it can become racially discriminatory in the way it is practiced. Institutional racism is pervasive in all of society's institutions, including human services. The following are two examples of institutional racism.

Institutional racism (sexism) Discrimination against a racial group (or gender) practiced by an organization or an institution, usually perpetuated by an interconnected system of policies and practices.

A 10-year-old African American girl was living with warm, stable African American foster parents who wanted to adopt her. The girl's relatives lived close by and frequently visited her. Even though the girl wanted to stay, the child-welfare agency tried to place her for adoption with strangers, a white couple from an affluent suburb. The relatives feared they would lose contact with her because none owned a car. They felt this move was motivated by the social agency's elitism— "money equals a more loving family." The aunt said, "A child belongs to people who love it, even if they are not rich" (Matchan, 1992, p. 1).

Research has shown that adoption workers favor affluent parents over low-income parents. We don't know enough of the details of the above case to assert that social class biases were *all* that influenced the agency's decision, but there *is* a solid body of research that makes one suspect the aunt was correct. When agency policy blindly gives preference to adoptive applicants because of a high salary, a home in the suburbs, and a professional occupation, these criteria will necessarily discriminate against minority applicants. Treated unequally by the society they live in, they are less likely to make a high salary, live in a well-serviced neighborhood, and have a stable work history in an occupation that requires long and costly training. *This adds up to institutional racism.*

Institutional racism can be attacked through changing social policy and legislation. One of the purposes of a practice called "subsidized adoption," which was given federal support in the Child Welfare and Adoption Act of 1980, was to make adoption financially possible for those prospective parents who had been denied access to the chance to earn the money that qualified them to adopt. Now, more people of color and of low income are able to share their lives with those children who need a home, many of whom because of unequal opportunities are themselves from low-income and/or minority groups.

Another example of institutional racism occurs in the criminal justice system. The hypothetical stories that follow are based on research that contradicts the widespread belief that drug use is primarily confined to the black ghetto. In actual fact, white youth sell and use drugs at *higher* rates than black youth. Institutional racism seems to be at work here.

> William Greer, an African American youth, was picked up by the police while he was using crack on a ghetto street corner. He was unemployed and could not afford a lawyer to represent him in court. The legal aid lawyer appointed to defend him was overworked and could not spend much time with William; in fact, he talked with William for just a few minutes before court began. He advised William to plead guilty and plea bargain rather than ask for a jury trial. The judge, known to be "tough on drugs," sentenced him to a mandatory five-year prison sentence.

> Jack Clifford, a white college student, was sniffing cocaine at a party. He had purchased the drug in the suburbs from another student who was known as someone who always had drugs for sale. The party got wild and a neighbor called the police. Jack had to appear in court on a drug charge. His parents hired a skilled lawyer. She asked the judge to allow Jack to get psychiatric treatment for his drug habit rather than go to jail. The judge agreed, knowing that the parents were successful professionals in the community.

Generally, the deviant behavior of poor urban people (minorities are overrepresented among the urban poor) is more likely to be defined as criminal and handled in the criminal justice system. Conversely, the deviant behavior of whites is more likely to be defined as a mental health problem and handled in the mental health system (Morales, 1978, p. 387). To explain this difference, researchers look to the dynamics of institutional racism.

Institutional racism is pervasive in the criminal justice system. Black and Hispanic youths are treated more severely than white teenagers charged with comparable crimes at every step of the juvenile justice system, according to a comprehensive report sponsored by the Justice Department and six of the nation's leading foundations (Butterfield, 2000, p. 1). The report found that minority youths are more likely than white youths to be arrested, held in jail, sent to juvenile or adult court for trial, convicted, and given longer prison terms. At each additional step in the juvenile justice system, things get worse for minority youth than for white youth. Here are the shocking facts:

- Among young people who have not been sent to a juvenile prison before, blacks are more than *six times* as likely as whites to be sentenced by juvenile courts to prison.

- For those young people charged with a violent crime who have not been in juvenile prison before, black teenagers are *nine times* more likely than whites to be sentenced to juvenile prison.

- For those charged with drug offenses, black youths are *forty-eight times* more likely than whites to be sentenced to juvenile prison.

- White youths charged with violent offenses are incarcerated for an average of 198 days after trial, but blacks are incarcerated an average of *254 days* and Hispanics are incarcerated an average of *305 days*.

Mark Soler, the president of Youth Law Center, said, "These disparities accumulate and they make it hard for members of the minority community to complete their education, get jobs and be good husbands and fathers" (Butterfield, 2000, p. 2).

In the past, when studies have found racial disparities in the number of adult black or Hispanic prison inmates, critics have said that it was because members of minorities committed a disproportionate number of crimes. Mark Soler said while that may be true, it does not account for the extreme disparities found in the report, nor for disparities at each stage of the juvenile justice process. He said, "When you look at this data, it is undeniable that race is a factor" (Butterfield, 2000, p. 2).

The nation's war on drugs unfairly targets African Americans, who are much more likely to be imprisoned for drug offenses than whites even though far more whites use illegal drugs than blacks, according to a report by the advocacy group Human Rights Watch (Fletcher, 2000). African Americans accounted for 62 percent of the drug offenders sent to state prisons nationwide in 1996, although they represent just 12 percent of the U.S. population. Overall, black men are sent to state prisons on drug charges at thirteen times the rate of white men. The report said that drug transactions among blacks often are easier for police to target because they more often occur in public than do drug transactions among whites. Human Rights Watch recommended the repeal of mandatory sentencing laws for drug offenders, increasing drug treatment, and eliminating racial profiling as a police tactic (Fletcher, 2000).

"We've spent a lot of money and we've wasted a lot of lives," said James Alan Fox, a criminologist who teaches at Northeastern University. "The war on drugs was a failed policy which resulted in the overincarceration of drug offenders, most of whom are not dangerous" (Rodriguez, 2001).

In 2003, there were 2.1 million people in U.S. prisons and jails, and the numbers continue to rise despite a fall in the crime rate. The Justice Department's Bureau of Justice Statistics attributes much of the increase to get-tough policies enacted during the 1980s and 1990s, such as mandatory drug sentences, "three strikes and you're out" laws for repeat offenders, and "truth in sentencing" laws that restrict early releases. The nation's incarceration rate tops the world. Members of racial or ethnic minorities made up 68 percent of prison and jail inmates in 2003 (Cass, 2004). This figure is higher than previously believed because until recently prisons were counting Hispanic inmates as white (Rodriguez, 2001).

The "get-tough" sentencing laws adopted by the federal government and most states have forced judges to impose prison terms for certain crimes, including drunk driving and selling drugs. These laws have resulted in a disproportionate number of arrests of black men. The possession of 5 grams of crack results in a five-year mandatory minimum jail sentence, whereas it takes 500 grams of powdered cocaine to get the same penalty. Ninety-five percent of those convicted of crack offenses are black and Hispanic, although almost two-thirds of crack users are white. The prison sentences of blacks convicted on cocaine charges are 41 percent longer than those for whites (Wideman, 1995). These harsh sentences for crack users do nothing to solve the problem of drug abuse. There is a 68 percent recidivism rate for those who go to prison, compared to only an 11 percent rate of recidivism for those who get treatment (Wideman, 1995).

The racial inequalities of the war on drugs also disproportionately affect pregnant women of color. "Despite similar or equal rates of illegal drug use during pregnancy, African American women are ten times more likely to be reported to child welfare agencies for prenatal drug use" (Drug Policy Alliance 2003).

Some states are beginning to soften their stand on long mandatory sentences for minor drug offenses and policies that forbid early parole. Budget constraints are forcing states to reconsider the enormous amount of money they have spent on building prisons. After a two-decade boom in prison construction that quadrupled the number of inmates, states by 2001 were spending a total of $30 billion a year to operate their prisons. Crime is down, and voters are saying they are more concerned about issues like education than with street violence. A voter initiative in California provides for treatment rather than prison for many drug offenders. State legislators are finding they must cut the growth in prison inmates to satisfy the demand for new services and to balance the budget (Butterfield, 2001). Every year an inmate spends in prison costs taxpayers an average of $22,000. A study by a Stanford University professor estimated that the cost of a life term for an average California prisoner is $1.5 million (Zimbardo, 1994).

Discrimination against Arab Americans

Discrimination against Arab Americans has been around for a long time, especially in the work place, but since 9/11 it has risen at alarming rates and spread into many other areas of life.

CASE STUDY

What a human service worker needs to know about Arab Americans: *Meet Luby Ismail.*

Lobua "Luby" Ismail awoke before dawn in her hotel room near Orlando, Florida, knelt on the floor and bowed low in the direction of Mecca to say her morning prayers. She finished dressing, wrapped her Muslim headscarf, or *hijab*, snugly around her dark features and, after a light meal, headed off to lead a cultural training session at Walt Disney World Resort.

Ismail sat in silence in the front of the room while the trainees, all of them Disney World employees, arrived. She then scrawled a message on the blackboard: *"The first part of this session will be nonverbal, OK?"*

As the students nodded in agreement, she wrote another message asking the trainees to share with their training partners, in writing, some assumptions that society—or the class members themselves—might make about a woman who looked and dressed like she did.

To the student who is reading this book: *Put this book face down on the table and write down five words that come to your mind as you picture this Arab woman!*

Now read the responses that Luby got and compare them with yours.

The responses her trainees came up with ranged from *"submissive"* and *"uneducated"* to *"foreign"* and *"someone who is not my friend."* Other responses she might have heard—especially if she had been accompanied by an Arab man—might have been *Ali Babi, Sinbad, The Thief of Baghdad, white slaver, abuser of women, slave owner, polygamist, sheik, oil millionaire*—images drawn from books and the media…and since 9/11, *religious fanatic and bomber.* Even Sesame Street, the children's educational TV program, has one character dressed in stereotypical Arab garb and he always teaches negative words like *"danger."*

Ismail then broke the silence by proclaiming in perfect English that she is a born-and-bred American who was the pitcher for her ninth-grade softball team and student body president in high school and who today is a wife and business owner. She is one of many advocates engaged in a campaign to pierce the stereotypes about Islam and its followers, called Muslims. These advocates want to help employers make their workplaces more comfortable for the country's growing numbers of Muslims, who may be of any race or from any part of the world (Panaro, 2004).

Some basic facts that will help you avoid simplistic assumptions (a.k.a. stereotypes) (Adams, 2000; Deen, 2004):

- According to the 2000 Census, there are 1,189,731 Arab Americans in the United States.

- There are twenty-one separate Arab nations, but the United States only recognizes 16 of them.

- There is no simple definition of who an "Arab" is. That word refers to those who speak the Arabic language—but almost every country's version of Arabic is different from another's and several Arab countries have internal ethnic groups who speak a totally different form of Arabic or some non-Arabic language.

- There are two more terms often used to describe people like Luby (or her ancestors): *Middle Easterners* and *Muslims* (not Moslems). The first refers to geography and the second to religion. BUT—not all persons who consider themselves Arabs or Muslims come from the Middle East (some countries are in Africa, for example)…and not all Arabs are Muslims. Many are Christians, some are Hindus, and a few are atheists (they have no religion). Just to keep things complicated, there are three countries in the Middle East that are not Arab or wholly Muslim: Iran, Israel, and Turkey.

- While some Arab Americans are very wealthy, many others are extremely poor, and there is a small middle class. Arab Americans as a whole are more highly educated than are many other ethnic groups (except for Cubans).

- Arab Americans, very family oriented and often from large families, tend to shun social service intervention into private affairs. While conversation is very important and often close, many do not accept public touching of the opposite sex.

- Religious discrimination is currently at an all-time high. Most Americans know very little about the Muslim faith and the importance of articles of clothing, such as head coverings, scarves, as well as beards. Often the wearing of these is prohibited in schools and workplaces, and practicing Muslims may not be given the time or space for the daily prayers that are fundamental to their religion. Yet these observances are protected under the U.S. Constitution and Section VII of the Civil Rights Act.

What should a human service worker do to stop discrimination again Arab Americans?

1. Learn more about the religion and customs of the many Arab countries, and whenever you encounter others who are spreading misinformation, try to set the record straight.

2. Support your clients or fellow citizens who are being denied their rights to practice their religion (as long as such practice does not endanger others) in their school or work place by suggesting accommodations that administrators might make. When helpful suggestions fail to make changes, encourage per-

sons who feel their rights are being abridged to file complaints with the top level of administration or the town or state Commissions Against Discrimination. Of course it is always more effective if the complaints come from other members of the affected population and if coalitions are built with like-minded individuals outside of the ethnic group or religion.

3. Remember that while it is important to learn about groups other than the one you belong to, be aware that there are enormous differences both among various populations and within groups who share some characteristics. For example, some very observant Catholics oppose abortion rights and work to repeal *Roe v. Wade,* while others who consider themselves co-religionists, reject abortion for themselves but support the legal right to choose. Similarly, some Jewish people eat only kosher foods and wear special clothes, while others feel free to eat what they wish and dress like the mainstream population, while still attending synagogue or organizing special celebrations for Jewish holidays.

Some useful resources include:

- American Arab Anti-Discrimination Committee (www.adc.org)
- The Middle East Network Information Center (MENIC, http://link.lanic.utexas.edu/menic/). Gives information about twenty-six Middle East countries.
- Council on Islamic Education (www.cie.org/)
- Encyclopedia of the Orient (Lexic Orient) (http://i-cias.com/e.o/). The only encyclopedia for North Africa and the Middle East
- Massachusetts Institute of Technology Arab student organization (http://web.mit.edu/arab/www/)
- Search on Google, using the words *Arab American* or *Arab American Directory: Who's Who in the Arab-American Community*
- The web site www.findarticle.com gives you access to 3.5 million articles from over 700 publications.

Anti-Semitism

Is Mel Gibson's film "The Passion of the Christ" anti-Semitic? This question was hotly debated when the film was shown in the spring of 2004. Some people saw it as a powerful Christian message; others said the film unnecessarily paints Jews as most responsible for Jesus' death, "thus repeating a charge that led to anti-Jewish violence and feelings for centuries" (Diamant, 2004). When an interviewer asked six Christian and five Jews what they thought of the film, all of the Christians said the film was emotionally compelling and a significant religious experience, but the main reaction of the Jews "was that the movie was insensitive to valid concerns about anti-Semitism" (Diamant, 2004). Reaction to the film showed that anti-Semitism is still a potent issue in the United States.

There is a long history of discrimination against Jewish people. They have been persecuted and punished simply because they were born of Jewish parents. Six million were exterminated in death camps by the Nazis in the 1940s. Jews are still arbitrarily excluded from neighborhoods, job promotions, or social clubs in many parts of the United States, causing personal pain and damage to their self-esteem. There has been an upsurge in vandalism to synagogues and Jewish cemeteries. Nazi skinheads, the Ku Klux Klan, and militia groups spread their virulently poisonous anti-Semitic message.

In Terre Haute, Indiana, on November 17, 2003, a Holocaust museum was destroyed by an arson attack. A hate-filled anti-Semitic extremist left a note venerating the Oklahoma City bomber, Timothy McVeigh. In Beverly Hills, California, in 2003, anti-Semitic graffiti defaced Jewish institutions during the High Holy Days. In the same year, in the New York City boroughs of Brooklyn and Queens, congregants coming to services found their synagogues spray-painted with swastikas and a sukkah (religious enclosure) torched (Foxman, 2003).

As of 1990, the United States had the largest population of Jews of any country in the world (Schaefer, 1989), although Israel, because of the recent influx of Jews from the former U.S.S.R. and other Eastern European countries, may soon have the largest Jewish population. Yet Jewish people constitute only about 2 percent of the entire U.S. population, and their numbers are diminishing because of low birth rates and intermarriage.*

In contrast to people of color, no physical characteristics distinguish a Jew from a non-Jew, because they have come here from every corner of the world. American Jews have no common language, other than English (although Hebrew is spoken in Israel and in orthodox religious practice, and Yiddish was often spoken by an earlier generation of Eastern European Jewish immigrants). There is enormous variation in their involvement in Judaism and their identification with its practices and culture.

Currently, most people of Jewish ancestry are clustered in urban areas, primarily in New York and New Jersey, and in white-collar professions, although this was not so in their early immigrant days (Schaefer, 1989). They are not, as a group, economically deprived. Yet prejudice and discrimination have the same devastating effect on Jews as on other minority groups.

Affirmative Action

Affirmative action, a policy that gives some preference in admissions, hiring, or promotion to equally qualified members of underrepresented minority groups, is

---

*The U.S. Census Bureau no longer asks questions about religious affiliation; therefore, statistics have had to be estimated since 1957, the last time this question was asked. The Gallup Organization estimates that about 2 percent of the U.S. population (5.6 million) identifies itself as Jewish (The Gallup Organization, 2004).

one of the mechanisms that attempt to redress the inequalities that minorities have historically encountered. African Americans have not only suffered from slavery, but also from many forms of discrimination since slavery. In housing, for example, the Federal Housing Administration, which underwrote one-third of all new housing construction from 1937 to 1972, required that all properties "continue to be occupied by the same social and racial classes" (Chappell, 2004). The Interstate Highway Act of 1956 directly displaced 330,000 poor families, mostly black. State laws and local zoning ordinances artificially concentrated both poverty and wealth and sharply segregated people on the basis of ethnicity and social class (Chappell, 2004).

Federal support for affirmative action has weakened since the 1980s and the policy continues to be under fierce attack. White people who feel they have been denied opportunities because of affirmative action have fought it in court on the grounds that it violates the equal protection clause of the Fourteenth Amendment. In a case brought against the University of Michigan, the Supreme Court in 2003 ruled that colleges can consider race in admissions, but must also treat students as individuals, and not accept or reject them solely on the basis of their skin color. Soon after this decision was handed down, Ward Connerly, a member of the University of California Board of Regents who led successful ballot initiatives in California and Washington State that ended racial preferences, took his campaign to Michigan to put a similar measure on the ballot there. In Colorado the bill that would have banned affirmative action in the state was defeated by one vote in the Republican-controlled state senate. That one vote was cast by State Senator Lew Entz, a Republican, who crossed party lines to deliver the deciding vote. Senator Entz had a large constituency of Hispanics, who favored affirmative action (Klein, 2004).

Not surprisingly, women and minorities are more likely to support affirmative action than are white males. A 2003 Gallup poll found that one in three white male teens favor college affirmative action programs, while two-thirds of female and minority teens favor them. A 2001 survey found that 43 percent of white men favored college affirmative action programs, compared to 64 percent of women and minorities (Jackson, 2003).

While affirmative action is often divisive and cannot by itself achieve racial equality, we believe it is still an essential device to counteract institutional barriers to minority advancement. Ezorsky reports, for example, that 80 percent of executives find their jobs through *networking,* and over 86 percent of available jobs do not appear in the classifieds.

> Historic patterns of discrimination and segregation which exclude blacks from white neighborhoods, business and social clubs have locked blacks out of a remarkably high percentage of job opportunities simply because they do not have the necessary white contacts to learn of the jobs or to be considered for them. (Forman, 1992, p. 172, reviewing Ezorsky, 1991)

Furthermore, some hiring criteria such as diploma requirements or standardized tests often work against minorities. Many tests have been shown to be culturally biased, drawing material from the white middle-class world. This bias can be overcome either by constructing culturally sensitive tests or by giving training in test taking. For example, the highest pass rate on the National Teachers' Exam is by graduates of Grambling University, which has a primarily African American student body. That is because the university requires its students to take a test-taking course (Hacker, 1992).

Even when they are hired, blacks are discriminated against because of seniority-based promotion, layoff plans, and the "glass ceiling" (an invisible but real barrier to advancement) of tradition. Because they are the last to be hired, they are the first to be fired and among the last to be promoted (if ever).

Many universities have admission practices that favor upper-class people. Critics say that a policy of "legacy admissions," which gives preference to children of alumni, amounts to affirmative action for upper-class whites. Ivy League schools have admitted about 12 percent of their student body through legacy admissions, while Notre Dame's legacy admissions make up 24 percent of their student body. President George W. Bush was admitted to Yale through a legacy policy, as he himself has admitted that he was not accepted to Yale on the strength of his grades. The legacy policy at Texas A&M University helped more than 300 white students qualify for admission every year but only about 30 blacks and Hispanics. After Texas A&M did away with affirmative action for minorities, they decided that it was inconsistent to keep a legacy policy that favored white students and did away with that policy. Georgia and California have also ended legacy policies in their state schools (*Talk of the Nation*, 2004, January 15).

Affirmative action has become a lightning rod that attracts people's anxieties about race. It "dominates the nation's obsession with race relations" (Holmes, 1997, p. 1) and seems to have become magnified out of all proportion to its real significance in people's lives. When public opinion polls ask whites whether they ever lost a job or a promotion or were denied college admission as a result of affirmative action, few say yes.

Affirmative action costs little, in comparison with social services. It hardly affects the majority of Americans. Most students who are eligible for college are accepted, regardless of affirmative action (Holmes, 1997).

We can get some idea of what will happen when affirmative action is done away with by looking at what has already happened in California, where Proposition 209 spelled the end of affirmative action in that state in 1997. There has been a dramatic decline in minority applications to medical and law schools at the University of California. Most applicants who were accepted did not enroll because they felt unwelcome. Just one of the fifteen blacks accepted to Berkeley's Boalt Hall law school enrolled in the fall of 1997. Only fourteen of the forty-six Hispanics admitted did. The two Native Americans who were accepted turned the school down (Gorov, 1997). Hashona Braun, a black student at the law school, said, "We really don't feel welcome here anymore, and the people who aren't here yet feel even more unwelcome" (Gorov, 1997, p. A1). Michael Rappaport, dean of admissions at UCLA's law school, said, "Another way of looking at it is that there are fewer blacks in Boalt than at the University of Alabama in the days of George Wallace. That's what's so frightening" (Gorov, 1997, p. A1).

One of the many programs that was ended because of Proposition 209 was a state-funded program called CAL-SOAP, or California Student Opportunity and Access Program. Its math classes aimed to give minority students an edge in math when applying for college. CAL-SOAP recruited about 200 seventh-graders a year who scored at least a 2.4 grade point average and then worked with them until they went to college. It also mentored and trained college students to work intensively with the teenagers. The program had a 100 percent college attendance rate. Norma Lara, a former CAL-SOAP participant and a student at the University of California at Berkeley, was the first in her family to attend college. She now worries about her 13-year-old twin sisters.

Lara says that Proposition 209

"says we're all one big happy family in California. We're all equal. Our education system is great. But it's obviously not true. We don't have a level playing field. In order for everyone to have the same opportunity, the education system has to be equal. They have to reform the school system before they can take that away." (Katz, 1997, p. L7)

Some people argue that economic diversity is as important as racial diversity, and we need to refocus on a new kind of affirmative action based on social class.

On a day when many of us celebrate our Thanksgiving festival, two children from the Wampanoag Nipmucs look across at the Mayflower replica. Native Americans gathered for a day to mourn together over the plight of their people since the Pilgrims landed.

Affirmative action helps middle class more than low-income minorities. Low-income white people as well as low-income minorities are also disadvantaged in college admissions. In the 146 most selective universities, low-income students make up only 3 percent of the student body. In two-year colleges generally, about two-thirds of those from the top economic quartile go on to a four-year college, while in the bottom economic quartile, only about one-fifth do (*Talk of the Nation,* 2004, April 15). This economic stratification is getting worse as colleges increasingly grant scholarship money on the basis of merit rather than need. As college tuition becomes more expensive, low-income students are increasingly priced out of college.

Immigrants

As our country celebrated the 500th anniversary of Columbus's "discovery" of the nation, people from the First Nations reminded us that *they* had already "discovered" this nation and had been living in it for a long time before Columbus appeared at their shores. All the rest of us emigrated here from another country or, in the case of some Mexican Americans, came with the territory when the United States won the Mexican American War in 1848 and annexed Mexican land in the

Southwest. Here are vignettes about three children who recently immigrated and what it was like for them:

A twelfth-grade Lao Mien* boy who immigrated at age 14 tells an interviewer:

> The school was so big! There was no one who could speak Mien and explain to me. My uncle had told me if I needed any help to go to the Dean. My teacher asked me something and I didn't understand her. So I just said "Dean, Dean" because I needed help. That is how I got my American name. She was asking me "What is your name?" Now everybody calls me Dean. It is funny, but it is also sad. My name comes from not knowing what was going on.

A ninth-grade Filipino girl who immigrated with her parents declares:

> Our parents don't come [to school functions] because they don't know any English. I don't even tell them when they are supposed to come. They dress so different and I don't want our parents to come because the others will laugh at them and tease us. We are ashamed.

A Cambodian boy who immigrated is reminded of his past:

> In an elementary school in San Francisco, a teacher is playing "hangman" with her class as a spelling lesson. One "Limited-English-Proficient" (LEP) student, a Cambodian refugee, bursts into tears and becomes hysterical. Later, through an interpreter, the teacher learns that the student had witnessed the hanging of her father in Cambodia. (Portes & Rumbaut, 1990, pp. 180–181)

FLUCTUATIONS IN IMMIGRATION POLICY

The first wave of immigrants was predominantly white and European; the recent wave is, to a large extent, Hispanic or nonwhite and from third-world countries, especially Asia and Latin America. The immigration policy of the United States has fluctuated between the country's need for labor and people's xenophobia and fear of losing their jobs to foreigners; it has also been influenced by foreign policy. When the country needed workers in the nineteenth and early twentieth centuries to build the railroads, work the mines and the steel mills, and weave cloth, it especially welcomed European immigrants for these jobs. African slaves were brought in primarily to work on southern cotton plantations. Chinese immigrants were brought in to help build the railroads in the West, especially for menial work that white men refused to do.

After the railroads were built, the country no longer wanted Chinese people and passed restrictive legislation to keep them out. They didn't even allow the Chinese men who had built the railroad to be present when the golden spike was driven to mark the joining of the two railroads (Hsu, 1971, p. 104). This was one example of the rising tide of racist fears that led to the United States excluding people of color.

---

*One of the tribes in Laos.

Some of the fears were fueled by competition for jobs. Organized labor feared that Chinese laborers would be used as strike breakers, which did sometimes happen.

Immigration policy in the United States has always made distinctions by race, ethnicity, and socioeconomic class. Japanese people were excluded in 1907, except in Hawaii where they were needed as agricultural workers. In 1921, the United States adopted a national-origins system that limited admissions from each European country to 3 percent of the foreign-born population here as of the 1910 Census. That resulted in favoring northern Europeans over southern and eastern Europeans for nearly half a century. Most Asians were still excluded, but there were no limits on migrants from the Western Hemisphere (Schmitt, 2001b).

The civil rights movement helped to achieve more fairness in immigration policy. The Immigration and Naturalization Act of 1965 eliminated racial criteria and replaced country-by-country quotas with a system that awarded green cards (permits to work) based largely on family or employer sponsorship. The author Calvin Trillin, a connoisseur of ethnic food, is grateful for the Immigration Act of 1965 because it brought in a rich variety of ethnic food. He says, "I have to say that some serious eaters think of the Immigration Act of 1965 as their very own Emancipation Proclamation" (Trillin, 2001, p. 42). Immigration policy before 1965 "reflected not simply bigotry but the sort of bigotry that seems to equate desirable stock with blandness in cooking. The quota for the United Kingdom was so high that it was never filled. Asians were, in effect, excluded" (p. 42).

But the pendulum swung again in the 1980s. The Immigration Reform and Control Act, passed by Congress in 1986, was a response to increasing concern about illegal immigration, particularly across the Mexican border, but also from other war-ravaged Latin American countries. Now, for the first time, employers can be fined and sentenced to prison for hiring illegal aliens. That is why, if you start a part-time job at a restaurant or store, your employer will ask you to give proof of your citizenship.

The act has contributed to discrimination against both legal immigrants and illegal immigrants. Many employers hire and then exploit illegal immigrants, forcing them to accept substandard wages and working conditions because they fear deportation. Employers also sometimes assume that anyone who has a Spanish name or speaks English with an accent is an illegal immigrant, and so they refuse to hire immigrants who actually have valid work permits (Schaefer, 1989, p. 126).

The Immigration Act of 1996 provides for "expedited removal" of immigrants and represents a major change in the country's treatment of immigrants. Columnist Robert Kuttner sees it as one aspect of a growing police state. Kuttner says that under the provisions of the act,

> legal permanent residents who make innocent technical mistakes face Kafkaesque nightmares. Hundreds of U.S. married couples have been separated for years because a foreign-born spouse neglected to fill out paperwork.
>
> People guilty of only technical lapses have been led off in handcuffs and jailed. Legitimate Canadian and Mexican business people, including corporate board members,

have been barred from entering the United States and treated like common criminals because they lacked some immigration form.

Other long time legal residents have been deported abruptly because of minor legal problems decades ago. The law disdains due process, makes judicial appeal almost impossible, and reinforces the thuggish tendencies of the Immigration and Naturalization service. (Kuttner, 1998, p. F7)

The 1996 law changed the rules for about 300,000 refugees from Nicaragua, El Salvador, and Guatemala who fled civil wars in the 1980s and were given temporary protection from deportation. The law increased the residency requirement from seven years to ten years, eliminated hardship to the refugee as a basis to fight deportation, and limited the number of immigrants who could seek permanent residency through this avenue to 4,000. The law also imposed a ten-year bar to reentry on those who leave the country and forced them to return to their home countries to obtain permanent visas ("Flaws," 1997). Under the old law, there was no income test for sponsors, just a requirement that incoming immigrants show they would not need public aid, but the new law imposed a legally enforceable income requirement. Advocates say this law needlessly divides hard-working husbands and wives from each other and their children. A study by the Urban Institute found that 40 percent of immigrant families in the United States and 26 percent of American-born people in the United States would not make enough to sponsor an immigrant under the new standards (Dugger, 1998).

The law also stipulates that legal immigrants who leave the country and then return—even after a brief vacation—may be subjected to harassment and imprisonment without due process if they have any criminal record. This includes the most minor infractions. Theft of cable television service, for example, can be treated as an "aggravated felony" under the new law, and the Immigration and Naturalization Service (INS) may detain legal immigrants and begin deportation proceedings against them for it (*The Progressive*, 1997).

One person who was caught in this web was Jesus Collado-Munoz, who was born in the Dominican Republic but has lived in the United States for more than twenty-five years as a legal permanent resident. He married and raised his family here. His wife and daughters are all U.S. citizens. Because of the "aggravated-felony" provision in the new immigration law, Collado was jailed for sixteen months in a maximum-security prison in Pennsylvania, under threat of deportation, because of a twenty-two-year-old misdemeanor conviction (*The Progressive*, 1997). He had visited the Dominican Republic for two weeks, but on his return, INS agents detained him. He admitted that he had had a brush with the law when he was 19 years old. The mother of his then-15-year-old girlfriend brought statutory sexual-assault charges against him for having consensual sex with her daughter. The two teenagers were dragged into court. Collado pleaded guilty to a misdemeanor and was convicted.

Twenty-two years later, the mother of Collado's old high school girlfriend pleaded for his release, to no avail. The federal courts could do nothing about this injustice because with the new law, "Congress stripped federal judges of their power to review cases like Collado's and to grant waivers of deportation" (*The Progressive,* 1997). A lawyer for the ACLU Immigrant Rights Project said that "The situation of Jesus Collado is the most compelling example of everything that's wrong with the immigration law. The Supreme Court has said again and again that due process applies to everyone" (*The Progressive,* 1997). The case drew national attention because Collado's ordeal highlighted the effects that tougher immigration laws could have on the lives of ordinary citizens who committed crimes long ago (Ojito, 1998b).

In October 1998, an immigration court judge in New York dismissed the deportation case against Mr. Collado. While he was relieved, Collado said he still cannot rest easy. While he was detained, he almost lost his restaurant in Washington Heights. He has large debts, as both his wife and daughter had serious health problems. He sleeps fitfully and visits a psychologist once a week (Ojito, 1998b).

The Justice Department's attempt to speed deportations of thousands of immigrants convicted of crimes in the United States was dealt a setback in 1999 when the Supreme Court let stand appeals of court decisions that gave those immigrants the right to judicial review of their cases (Vicini, 1999).

The Immigration Act of 1996 and the benefit-cutting effects of the Personal Responsibility Act created panic in the immigrant community. Immigrants and their advocates fought back through both legal and political means. There have been many legal challenges to the law. Lawyers in California challenged the law's income requirement as unconstitutional and discriminatory (Lewis, 1997). The twenty members of the Hispanic Congressional Caucus mobilized their resources to fight both the immigration law and the cuts in benefits of the Personal Responsibility Act. Congress and the president decided that they had gone too far in attacking immigrants. House and Senate Republican leaders "who are trying to improve their tainted image with immigrants in states with large immigrant populations, like California and Florida" (Schmitt, 1997, p. 10) decided in 1997 to ease some of the immigration curbs of the 1996 law. Congress passed a law in 1998 that allowed about 40,000 Haitians who applied for political asylum before 1996 to stay in the country. The changes to the law exempted about 400,000 Cubans, Salvadorans, Nicaraguans, Guatemalans, and even some Eastern Europeans from the new deportation rules. However, it did not exempt thousands of Haitians who fled after a military coup in 1991.

The fierceness of the anti-immigration sentiment was beginning to abate before the 9/11 attacks. The AFL-CIO, in an 180-degree policy turn, shifted from denouncing illegal immigrants as a threat to American workers, to calling for a general amnesty for them all (meaning they could stay and join a union) (Pertman, 2001, p. D2). Some states have granted drivers' licenses to illegal immigrants. Virtually no business owners worry at all about being fined for hiring illegal immigrants, because they almost never are. Cecilia Munoz, vice president of policy for the National Council of La Raza, the largest Hispanic civil rights organization, says, "Frankly, they'll take anybody they can get and undocumented workers are often the only ones willing to accept such poor wages" (Pertman, 2001, p. D2).

Much of the shift in attitude stemmed from the need for workers. Offering driver's licenses to illegal immigrants so they can get to work benefits not only the workers, but also the employers who need them (Pertman, p. D2). In 2000, high-technology employers facing labor shortages persuaded the Republican-controlled Congress to nearly double the annual quota for temporary, high-skilled immigrants, to 195,000. Most of those visas go to immigrants from China and India. They are paid less than U.S. workers, and are often deported when their services are no longer needed. In 2001, a broad coalition of employers from restaurant and hotel owners to landscapers and meat-packing plants lobbied to expand a temporary worker program to include lesser-skilled laborers in their fields (Schmitt, 2001b).

After the attacks on the World Trade Center and the Pentagon, fears about terrorist attacks led the White House and Congress to move rapidly toward making immigration laws tighter. The reversal, which came just as the administration had considered loosening its policies, sent a chill through legal and illegal Hispanic immigrants. Maria Blanco, national senior counsel for the Mexican American Legal Defense and Educational Fund, said, "People are very disappointed that, so soon after the debate seemed to be moving forward on immigration, it has taken a few steps backwards. Latinos don't want to be tainted by this broad brush" (Sterngold, 2001, p. 00).

Before the September 11 attacks, Mexican President Vincente Fox and President George W. Bush discussed the possibility of granting legal status to millions of undocumented Mexicans living in the United States. However, after the attacks, President Bush no longer talked about how hard-working immigrants seeking a better life should be given a chance. Instead, there is now a more mistrustful view of immigrants. The immigration debate has been recast to focus on border security and homeland defense (*New York Times*, 2001).

In 2004, President Bush proposed a "temporary worker" program that would allow undocumented immigrants living in the United States and workers abroad to obtain a three-year work permit with the employers' sponsorship. Although the work permit would be renewable for an unspecified number of years, participation in the program could not lead to normal permanent residency and citizenship. Workers would still have to return to their home countries when their permits expire, they fail to maintain steady employment, or "break the law" (Northeast Action, 2004). Most of the major Hispanic advocacy organizations (including National Council of La Raza, the League of United Latin American citizens, United Farm Workers, and the National Immigration Law Center) oppose the president's immigration policy, while welcoming his willingness to discuss immigration policy (Goldstein, 2004).

Both Republicans and Democrats tried to use the immigration issue to get votes. After President Bush proposed his plan, the Democrats put forward a bill that would make it harder to import so-called guest workers, but would open the path to citizenship for illegal immigrants already in the country and would loosen quotas that prevent many immigrants from bringing relatives into the United States (Alonso-Zaldivar, 2004, May 2).

The U.S. Immigration Service (formerly the INS, or Immigration & Naturalization Service) held some 23,000 people in custody in 2004. Many of these prisoners are contracted out to private prisons and local jails because the federal government lacked detention space and the local officials needed the revenue. More than half of the prisoners are held in county jails around the country as "administrative detainees," not serving sentences. The local and federal custodians use the arrangement to evade accountability, and many incidents of torture have been reported.

At Florida's Jackson County Jail in 1998, INS inmates described the regular use of "shock shields" against INS and state prisoners. One inmate witness told the Florida Immigrant Advocacy Center (FIAC) that the inmates were tied down "in the position of a crucifix" and left in that position for over nine hours with no food or drink. The guards would administer electric shocks to the inmates while they were tied with an electric shield and a stun gun. As a result of persistent complaints filed by FIAC, the Civil Rights Division of the Justice Department finally investigated and concluded that the Jackson County Jail was violating the U.S. Constitution by using excessive force and denying prisoners access to courts. The INS inmates were transferred out of the jail; state prisoners were left behind (Dow, 2004).

Immigrants and their advocates have mobilized to resist their discriminatory treatment. Inspired by the freedom riders of the civil rights movement, thousands of immigrants participated in an Immigrant Workers Freedom Ride in October 2003. With organizing support from the AFL-CIO and other groups, they marched and demonstrated in 116 cities across the country, including New York City, where over 76,000 rallied to publicize a host of immigrant rights issues from equal rights in the workplace to immigration reform (*Northeast Action,* 2004, p. 4).

Undocumented immigrants were guaranteed access to a free public K–12 education by a 1982 Supreme Court decision, but the 1996 Immigration Act prohibits undocumented immigrants from accessing any post-secondary education benefit unless a citizen or national of the United States is eligible for such a benefit. As a result, many states have blocked access to in-state tuition for undocumented students. An estimated 60,000 undocumented students graduate from the nation's high schools each year, and most are unable to pay in-state tuition at their public college, except in the few states that allow them to. A bill has been introduced in Congress called the DREAM Act, which would make it possible for immigrant students to pay in-state tuition, and would also make it easier for them to become legal permanent residents (Lazarin, 2003).

People's fears about the costs of providing social services to immigrants may be exaggerated. Studies show that new immigrants, especially undocumented immigrants, make little use of health and welfare services, because of both fear and not knowing about the services. The only large groups of immigrants to use such services are *political* refugees invited in by the U.S. government, principally Laotians, Cambodians, and Russians.

A study by the National Academy of Sciences that came out in 1997 concluded that immigration added about $10 billion a year to the nation's economic output. Although the job prospects of low-skilled workers, particularly high school dropouts, were sometimes hurt by competition with immigrants, the effects are relatively small and are not concentrated in the areas where immigrants live but are dispersed across the United States. The study concluded that immigration is neither a panacea for the nation's economic problems nor a source of huge costs. The fiscal impact of immigrants overall is positive because they tend to arrive as young workers and "will help pay the public costs of the aging baby boom generation" (Pear, 1998a).

The people who benefit most from immigration, aside from the immigrants themselves, are businesses and the wealthy. David Card, an economist who studies immigration, said that when he moved to San Francisco, he noticed some changes from his lifestyle in Princeton. "In California, a professor has at least a gardener and maybe two, someone who cleans his house, and two or three day-care workers," he said (Cassidy, 1997, p. 41–42). The study by the National Academy of Sciences said that in the six states where immigration is highest (California, New York, Texas, New Jersey, Florida, and Illinois), 78 percent of the male cooks and 62 percent of the female housekeepers are immigrants. The Academy report concluded that "benefits from lower prices are higher for households with very high levels of wealth and education" (Cassidy, 1997, p. 42).

Many undocumented immigrants are hired by the rich, despite the law prohibiting that practice. Two prominent cases involved people who were nominated for federal attorney general—Zoe Baird and Kimba Wood. President Clinton withdrew their nominations because it became known that they had employed illegal immigrants as nannies.

Although it is important to know the economic facts about immigration, economics is not the only factor to use in evaluating the benefits and costs of immigration. We can't forget that immigrants built this nation and continue to enrich it in many ways.

> Much of the anti-immigration sentiment seems to reflect a belief that there are "good" immigrants and "bad" immigrants. People whose ancestors arrived in the late nineteenth and early twentieth centuries believe that this qualifies them as real Americans. The early immigrants are remembered as good, hardworking assimilators, while the new ones are "inferior, parasitic, and implacably foreign." (Walker, 1995, p. 62)

Discussing the repressive Immigration Act of 1996, a *New York Times* editorial ("Hard Times," 1997) warns of the threat to all of us:

> This law won political passage by attacking an unpopular group. That, historically, is how more widespread deprivations of rights have started. The law is not just an assault on vulnerable people who deserve protection from abuse, but a threat to the liberties of all Americans. (p. WK14)

CUTBACKS IN BENEFITS FOR IMMIGRANTS

The Personal Responsibility Act created widespread panic among immigrants. A 51-year-old Cuban immigrant, diagnosed as schizophrenic, hanged himself after learning he would no longer qualify for public assistance because he was not a U.S. citizen (Conniff, 1997).

Many elderly and disabled noncitizens who have been in the United States for a long time and lack the mental capacity to do what is necessary to become citizens were thrown out of their homes or out of nursing homes or other group residential settings that were no longer reimbursed for their care. (Edelman, 1997, p. 48)

Cuts in programs for immigrants were predicted to save about $22 billion, about 40 percent of the savings in the bill. Almost 800,000 legal immigrants received SSI and most of them would be cut off. In response to protests and lobbying by immigration advocates, Congress restored $11.4 billion in immigrant benefits (Alvarez, 1997). It restored SSI benefits to most legal immigrants in 1997, but not to all. It restored food stamps to some immigrants, including the elderly, disabled, and children, but not to all. By the end of 1997, the law had pushed about 770,000 immigrants off the food stamp rolls across the nation.

In a suburb of Boston, a Latina woman told hunger researchers that she was so desperate to feed her two young children after using up her allotment of groceries from the local food pantry that she had no choice but to gather scraps from the garbage (Kong, 1998).

ELIMINATION OF BILINGUAL EDUCATION

Although elimination of bilingual education programs was also an attack on immigrants, in California it was supported by some Hispanics. California's Proposition 227, a voter initiative, was sponsored by Ron Unz, a California multi-millionaire software developer and former Republican candidate for governor. Unz launched a national movement called English Only to eliminate bilingual education across the country by amending state constitutions, with the ultimate goal being to amend the Constitution of the United States. He spearheaded the defeat of bilingual education in California, Arizona, and Massachusetts, but met fierce resistance in Colorado, where it was voted down. While Unz has funded many anti-bilingual education ballot initiatives, the English Only movement is led principally by a multi-million dollar conservative organization called U.S. English (DePass, T., 2003, April).

Unz scoffed at research that says it can take up to seven years for students to become fully fluent in academic English, and proposed that, except in charter schools, they be given just one school year—180 days—to learn the language intensively before being mainstreamed into all-English classes. This program, called "English immersion," has eliminated most bilingual education programs, which helped limited English proficient (LEP) children keep up with all their required academic competencies, such as math, history, and science, while they are learning English through ESL (English as a Second Language) classes. Many LEP students learn to speak conversational English within the first two years, but research consistently shows that it takes four to seven years before most students are able to use English to learn academic subjects and perform on a par with native English-speaking peers (Massachusetts English Plus Coalition, 2003).

There is heated debate on the efficacy of bilingual education nationwide. Unz and his supporters argue that the offspring of earlier immigrant groups were forced

Tibetan women, recent arrivals in the United States.

to learn English and, therefore, succeeded in America. Speaking for the opponents of Unz, Massachusetts State Representative Jarrett Barrios, a Hispanic, said, "There's no way you can construe what Ron Unz is doing as anything less than anti-immigrant and anti-children" (Lupo, 2001). Opponents of English Immersion have argued that the initiatives are too punitive because teachers could be personally sued for speaking Spanish in the classroom, and too restrictive because they would eliminate dual-language programs and parent choice. Hispanic opponents argue that the attack on bilingual education is an attack on their cultural identity. Many African Americans joined the struggle to save bilingual education, remembering their own struggles to become literate, being able to vote, and having equal access to education. A 2003 Gallup poll showed that the views of Hispanic Americans are quite different from those of white Americans, with nearly three-fourths (72 percent) of Hispanics favoring it, compared to just over half (53%) of whites. Black Americans hold nearly identical views to Hispanics on the issue. Political affiliation also influences people's views, with 69 percent of Democrats favoring bilingual education, compared to 46 percent of Republicans. Support for bilingual education also drops sharply among advancing age categories. Seventy-five percent of 18- to 29-year-olds favor bilingual education, compared to 61 percent of 30- to 49-year-olds, 49 percent of 50- to 64-year-olds, and just 44 percent of people aged 65 and older (Mason, 2003).

Guidelines for Ethnic-Sensitive Human Service Work

People who have been discriminated against because of their skin color have reason to be mistrustful of white-dominated organizations, including (and sometimes especially) human service agencies. Unfortunately, agencies have a poor track record in eliminating discrimination. After the Civil War, such agencies were almost always segregated and poorly funded. The Charity Organization Society served very few people of color. In her autobiography, *The Woman Warrior,* author Maxine Hong Kingston (1977) gives an example of the feeling of alienation created by discrimination.

> Lie to Americans. Tell them you were born during the San Francisco earthquake. Tell them your birth certificate and your parents were burned up in the fire. Don't report crimes; tell them we have no crimes and no poverty. Give a new name every time you get arrested; the ghosts* won't recognize you. Pay the new immigrants twenty-five cents an hour and say we have no unemployment. And, of course, tell them we're against Communism. Ghosts have no memory anyway and poor eyesight. (pp. 184–185)

The distrust that discrimination creates affects all of us. An individual white person may never have discriminated against anyone, but the climate of fear that prejudice has created in a society may make *every* white person seem like a potential enemy until she or he proves to be trustworthy.

Of course, people of color can also express prejudice against white people when they believe that all white people are alike. And some light-skinned black people are prejudiced toward dark-skinned black people. In Boston, a light-skinned Cape Verdean teacher was prejudiced against dark-skinned children in her class. She seated pupils by skin color, with lighter-skinned children at the front of the class and darker-skinned children at the back. The darker-skinned children always got the worst treatment. She shamed the children, hit them, and humiliated them. Some other teachers in the school protested and sparked an investigation by the U.S. Department of Education (Gaines, 2000).

GUIDELINES TO BUILD TRUST

1. *Learn the culture.* You can learn a lot about a person's culture by asking sensitive questions. No matter how much you have read about a group's culture, you won't know how it affects the specific person you are talking with until you ask.

Here is an example of an incorrect assessment of a person based on a lack of understanding of the culture.

> A young Southeast Asian woman was ordered by the court to attend therapy for repeatedly shoplifting merchandise from a neighborhood grocery store. The young woman

---

*In this story of Chinese people in San Francisco, the Chinese regarded *all* non-Chinese people as "ghosts" because they seemed as alien as ghosts. Interestingly, her protagonist saw black ghosts as more friendly than white ghosts.

These legal immigrants are among the hundreds who lobbied Massachusetts legislators in April 2004 to get health care. The Personal Responsibility Act of 1996 cut federal funds for health care for immigrants.

had been in this country less than a year and spoke minimal English. She was assigned to a white therapist who after several failed attempts to get the young woman to communicate her reasons for shoplifting informed the court that the client was withdrawn, uncommunicative, and appeared depressed.

A young Asian paralegal working in the office at the time read the case and was able to shed some light on the problem. The Asian paralegal related that the item, repeatedly stolen from the store, sanitary napkins, was not openly displayed, or sold in public markets in the country of the Southeast Asian woman....In the woman's country, it was considered highly improper for women to publicly acknowledge their monthly menses. Purchasing the pads outright or explaining her reasons for taking this product would have caused this woman great embarrassment and public shame, not to mention a breach of her ethnic and cultural values on proper conduct. (Boyd, 1990, p. 160)

2. *Create a welcoming atmosphere.* As soon as they walk in the office, people should receive the message that they are welcome. If the agency's clientele includes people who speak a language other than English, posters on the wall and informational brochures should be written in that language. The magazine rack could include local African American and Hispanic newspapers. Gays and lesbians will be reassured to see their own newspaper or magazine.

3. *Acknowledge the validity of their suspicion of you.* Research has shown that people from minority groups are less likely to return to a human service agency after the first interview than are people from the dominant culture.

Maxine Hong Kingston (1977) talks of the reticence about discussing intimate affairs within the traditional Chinese culture, but she indicates that it was a much more serious offense to share secrets with the "ghosts."

> They came nosing at windows—Social Worker Ghosts; Public Health Nurse Ghosts; Factory Ghosts recruiting workers during the war (they promised free child care, which our mother turned down); two Jesus Ghosts who had formerly worked in China. We hid directly under the windows, pressed against the baseboard until the ghost, calling us in the ghost language so that we'd almost answer to stop its voice, gave up. (p. 98)

The person who suffers from discrimination feels a dreadful wound, a humiliating degradation, and if he or she is strong enough to feel it, tremendous rage. (Most tragically, the individual may turn the rage inward against him- or herself.) *The Autobiography of Malcolm X* (Malcolm X & Haley, 1966) presents a vivid literary description of these feelings. An outstanding leader of the American Muslims in the 1960s, Malcolm X was assassinated in 1965. He gives us a personalized account of his disillusionment as he writes bitterly about the state welfare workers who claimed to be "helping" him. In the course of his life, he encountered a good many helping agents of the state and found them wanting. When he was a young

This woman's strength shines through her face. If she came for help, a worker would need to recognize that strength and help the woman draw on it.

boy, his father was killed by whites, and his mother had to struggle to keep the family together, eking out a living by cleaning houses. She hated to accept welfare assistance, but when she finally gave in, she was harassed by welfare investigators. They termed her "crazy" for, among other behaviors, refusing to eat pork, even though she was a Seventh Day Adventist and it was against her religion to do so. They also opposed her seeing a male friend, even though this made her happier than she had ever been before. Malcolm X held them partially responsible for his mother having to go to a mental hospital, and he said they were as vicious as vultures (Malcolm X & Haley, 1966).

Malcolm was placed in a foster home, and this is what he thought about that.

Soon the state people were making plans to take over all of my mother's children....[A] Judge McClellan in Lansing had authority over me and all of my brothers and sisters. We were "state children," court wards; he had the full say-so over us. A white man in charge of a black man's children! Nothing but legal, modern slavery however kindly intentioned....I truly believe that if ever a state social agency destroyed a family, it destroyed ours. We wanted and tried to stay together. Our home didn't have to be destroyed. But the Welfare, the courts, and their doctor, gave us the one-two-three punch. And ours was not the only case of this kind. (pp. 20–21)

When Malcolm was about to enter the third grade, an English teacher asked him what kind of career he wanted. Malcolm said that he wanted to be a lawyer, to which the teacher replied:

You've got to be realistic about being a nigger. A lawyer—that's no realistic goal for a nigger. You need to think about something you can be. You're good with your hands—making things. Everybody admires your carpentry shop work. Why don't you plan on carpentry? (p. 36)

By raising people's consciousness about discrimination and pressuring organizations to change, Malcolm X and other civil rights activists helped reshape social services as well as other institutions of society. Since the 1960s, many ethnic groups have developed their own agencies and professional organizations, creating changes in the policies and hiring practices of white-dominated agencies. The National Association of Black Social Workers was formed in 1968 to improve the provision of social services to blacks and to spur the recruitment of black social workers (McRoy, 1990, p. 11).

4. *Emphasize strengths in individuals and communities.* In the game of bridge, the person who plays the first card often plays to the strength of the partner. The same is true when working with people, especially with minorities, because people have already focused so much on their weaknesses.

Emphasizing people's strengths is equally important when working with communities as it is when working with individuals. John McKnight (1992) believes that some professionals who claim to help others actually harm them by focusing on their weaknesses. He has developed a questionnaire designed to discover people's talents and a map called the Neighborhood Assets map designed to highlight a community's strengths. It lists strengths—cultural organizations, individual capacities, religious organizations, citizens' associations, home-based enterprise, social service agencies, and so on. McKnight also designed a map called the Neighborhood Needs map, which lists pathologies—slum housing, crime, mental illness, teenage pregnancy, alcoholism and substance abuse, illiteracy, and so forth. The Neighborhood Needs map is the one that people use most often, but it ignores the strengths of a neighborhood.

The liberation movements of oppressed people have revealed their enormous strength and courage. Thousands of people have literally put their lives on the line to win their freedom. And there is the quieter but enduring strength they show by protecting their families and communities in the face of constant oppression and discrimination.

5. *Find sources of power.* Lorraine Gutierrez (1990) recommends that the worker and client together engage in a "power analysis" of the client's situation to assess the structural barriers a client faces and the potential strengths available to the client.

> Clients and workers should be encouraged to think creatively about sources of potential power, such as forgotten skills, personal qualities that could increase social influence, members of past social support networks, and organizations in their communities. (Gutierrez, 1990, p. 152)

6. *Use the network of family and friends.* The first strength of any group is family and friends. Many minority groups rely heavily on this support. Some students of Native American culture say that it is hard for Native Americans to accumulate resources, not only because of their low-wage work and unemployment but also because of their ethic of sharing with other family members.

African American communities have a long tradition of mutual help. Carol Stack (1974) showed that although many families in a poor black community in the Midwest were officially designated "single-parent" families, they were actually extended-kin networks, sharing in child care. This was more typical among the very poor. As families became upwardly mobile, they were less likely to share their resources. Urbanization and industrialization have weakened extended-family networks for all of us. But the African Americans who shared their resources despite their poverty were expressing a higher value of caring and compassion than more affluent people, who were more preoccupied with "getting ahead."

7. *Use the community networks.* The ethnic neighborhood itself is a support system in which people can share their language, religion, food, memories, and experiences. Networks include neighbors; churches; political, social, and service organizations; newspapers; stores; restaurants; and bars where people gather. The church is an especially important support network in the African American community. In Hispanic communities, the spiritualist is an important support to many people, and many Native Americans turn to the tribal medicine man or woman for

support and guidance. In her study of ethnicity in the social services, Shirley Jenkins (1981) found that, in general, minority people prefer going to services in their own community staffed by bilingual and bicultural workers.

8. *Understand patterns of informality and friendliness.* Pedro de Cunha, a Portuguese-American social worker, tells of common complaints among Portuguese immigrants regarding social agencies: "The social workers are too cold, too distant. They are never there when we need them; They don't really help; They never found us a job or an apartment" (de Cunha, 1983, p. 15). One of the problems, says de Cunha, is that the Portuguese come from a country that has not developed specialized helping agencies; instead, people tend to turn to the priest for help. The priest has many roles. Not only does he minister the Word and the sacraments, "but he is also the financial adviser, the marriage counselor, the funeral director, the father, the judge, the social worker" (p. 15). The grocer not only sells groceries; he "would not sell any groceries if he did not listen to the problems of his patrons, if he did not extend credit to those who cannot pay immediately, if he did not read the illiterate their mail" (p. 15).

People from an agrarian society expect help to come in the context of a personal relationship. They expect helping roles to be diffuse rather than specific. De Cunha recommends that workers be trained to understand their clients' background and expectations and become more comfortable being less formal and more friendly.

9. *Be willing to share yourself.* Workers need to be willing to share something of their own lives with clients, to make the atmosphere of the agency warm and nurturing. Perhaps you could serve refreshments or coffee, be willing to accept small gifts, be flexible about time, be willing to make an occasional home visit, and have at least one worker for walk-in clients.

10. *Understand clients' lack of resources.* People's poverty affects how they use social services. They may not even have the carfare or gasoline to get to the agency. If they do have a car, it is probably in poor repair and often breaks down. Clients may not be able to keep appointments because they can't afford baby-sitters or fear losing their job if they take any more time off from work. They may not have a checking account, so cashing a check might be costly and time-consuming.

11. *Give concrete services and information.* Because of their lack of resources, poor people need concrete help. Whatever your agency's activities, your knowledge of benefit programs might be more important than any mental health counseling. One formerly homeless woman said that she was in homeless shelters for four years because the workers there did not tell her about housing vouchers or how to get welfare benefits. It was not until she discovered a welfare rights group that she learned about her rights from other welfare recipients.

12. *Learn how to empower.* Oppressed people are relatively powerless. A large proportion of poor families are headed by women, who have less power than men.

Women of color make up a large proportion of the clientele in human service agencies. They are more than twice as poor as white women. They are overrepresented in low-status occupations and have on average a low level of education. The stress of having poor housing or no housing, insufficient food and clothing, and inadequate access to health services takes a toll on their physical and mental health. Human service workers need to deal with the psychological effects of their clients' powerlessness and provide concrete resources to better their lives (Gutierrez, 1990, p. 149).

The literature on empowerment indicates that small-group work is the ideal method for empowerment. In these groups, members receive support, reduce self-blame, learn new skills, and provide a potential power base for action (Gutierrez, 1990).

WORKING WITH WOMEN

Many college women, even those who do not call themselves feminists, are benefiting from the gains won by the women's movement, even though they might not be aware of the struggles that other women went through to win them. Although women have many struggles to endure before they achieve equality with men, the gains of the women's movement have been enormous. The women's movement has touched every aspect of women's lives. Women have fought for equal pay and advancement and have often won. They have defined some lower-paying jobs as equal in worth to higher-paying men's jobs, even though the jobs may be different, and won some major **comparable worth** lawsuits. They have entered fields previously defined as men's work, and some have argued that housework and caretaking, traditionally defined as women's work, should be paid wages and shared equally by women and men.

Comparable worth Describing and paying wages for jobs according to their inherent difficulty and worth in order to help equalize women's wages with men's.

The Women's Movement and New Social Services

Some of the most dramatic changes in the helping process were brought about by the women's movement. By 1994 shelters for victims of domestic violence had been established in more than two-thirds of the 3,200 counties in the United States (Carden, 1994). Women also created rape crisis centers; women's health centers; feminist mental health services; and services for displaced homemakers, women substance abusers, older women, single parents, and ethnic minority women (Gottlieb, 1980a, 1980b).

Feminists created new social services because they believed that traditional social agencies were not in tune with women's needs. Drawing on Freudian psychology, traditional workers said that a woman who is battered by her husband might have a sadomasochistic need to be beaten. But feminists would assert:

• The husband is committing a criminal act by beating his wife and must be legally restrained.

- No one has the right to beat her for any reason.

- She might be staying with him because she has:

    no place to go
    no money
    children to care for
    no marketable work skills
    shame because of the stigma of being abused

- She might need supportive therapy, but she also needs:

    a court order
    a shelter
    a support group
    a job or an adequate welfare grant
    decent, affordable child care
    help in finding an apartment

Feminists also redefined rape. Traditional common wisdom assumed that women inadvertently "asked for it" by their behavior. Feminists defined rape as an act of violence used to control women. They told women that they didn't ask for it or deserve it. They taught them how to struggle against it and how to do the healing grief work to recover from the assault. They told women that there is no "allowable" rape—forced sex by a date or by a husband is rape. They also lobbied to change the laws that made reporting of rape another form of assault on self-esteem. In fact, feminists looked at *every* aspect of services to women and suggested new ways to view old problems.

Feminists took a new look at depression, menopause, and premenstrual syndrome and critiqued the way the medical establishment deals with them. Depression, for example, is much more prevalent among women than among men. Feminists believe this is due to the socialization of women rather than to any inherent female characteristics. This socialization includes:

- A stress on self-effacement, which leads to low self-image

- A sense of powerlessness and of lack of control over one's life

- Difficulty in asserting oneself

- An inability to cope with stress (Gottlieb, 1980a, 1980b)

Women, socialized to be passive rather than assertive, have a much greater tendency to turn their aggression on themselves than do men. This is generally considered to be one of the dynamics of depression.

Understanding New Theories about Women

There has been a flowering of feminist theory since the late 1960s that has had a profound effect on the human services. Feminist psychologists challenged some of the traditional Freudian theory that claimed women were "naturally" masochistic, passive, and envious of men. These psychologists helped women to feel comfortable with the assertiveness they had been taught to repress since childhood.

Feminist research has helped women reclaim their sexuality by rejecting the Freudian assertion that the only "healthy" orgasm is a vaginal one (Koedt, 1971). Ann Koedt showed that the vagina has few nerve endings and that the clitoris is more sensitive to sexual stimulation than is the vagina. (Kinsey had also shown this in his research on sexuality in the 1940s, but it was not until feminists focused on female sexuality that these findings became more widely understood.)

"Women's intuition" and emotionality, which had been ridiculed as inferior to the male world of "hard facts," won a new respectability when feminist researchers, in comparing women's ways of learning about the world and relating to people with men's ways, concluded that women's ways were different but might make for a more peaceful world.

How Feminist Theory Influences Our Practice

Feminist theory shaped Oly's and Inez's work in their shelter for battered women. They see themselves as comrades to the women they work with, struggling together to stop the abuse of women. They have shared their experiences and are living proof that it is possible to survive an abusive experience and to become strong, confident, and independent. *This feeling of engaging in struggle with your clients as equals is one of the hallmarks of feminist social services.*

Feminist therapy introduced a sociological and political perspective that had been lacking in most traditional therapy, helping women as well as men to realize that their problems were not just personal troubles but also social issues. The women's movement was built through consciousness-raising groups, a model that was adopted by other self-help groups.

Yet much of feminist theory and practice has been focused too narrowly on middle-class white women, neglecting issues of social class and ethnicity. Women of color have written a wealth of literature and contributed research about their lives, and some white feminists realize that the assault on poor women is an assault on all women, particularly at a time when the middle class is eroding. However, although the leadership of the National Organization for Women has been militant in fighting against repressive welfare policies, most NOW members have not been involved in welfare rights struggles. That may be changing. When over 1 million people attended the March for Women's Lives in Washington, D.C., on April 25, 2004, there was the largest representation of women of color and low-income women that has ever attended a women's march. Cheri Honkala, a welfare recipient and leader of the Kensington Welfare Rights Union in Philadelphia, gave a moving speech about welfare and emphasized that choice for women involves not only the right to have an abortion, but also the right to choose to have children and the resources to care for them. Toni Bond, a low-income woman who had been helped to get an abortion by the National Network of Abortion Funds, spoke powerfully about the importance of financial help to women who can't afford an abortion. (There has been no federal funding for abortions since the Hyde Amendment was passed in 1974.)

Feminist scholars have analyzed social policies and social services, exposing institutional sexism. Abramovitz (1988) described how Social Security regulations discriminate against women. By giving larger pensions to those who earned more in their work, women, who almost always earn less than men, receive lower pensions. Thus gender inequality is perpetuated through the life cycle. Further, by not including caretaking work as wage earning, homemakers are unable to draw a pension of their own but must rely on their husband's record of earnings.

A Gender Analysis of Child Welfare

Over thirty advocates in New York City, employing a feminist perspective, challenged the way the child-welfare system treated battered women and their children in New York City (Coalition of Battered Women's Advocates, 1988). This group mobilized after the widely publicized death of a child, Lisa Steinberg, and the battering of her mother, Hedda Nussbaum, by the child's father, an affluent attorney.

The coalition pointed out that women are often afraid to cry out for protection to the police or social service agencies for fear that they will lose their children or that the batterers/child abusers will retaliate against them or that no one will believe them. Often, service providers remove battered children from the home where a man is abusing his wife rather than force the abusive husband to leave. This can result in children being victimized a second time by the trauma of foster placement (Coalition of Battered Women's Advocates, 1988). Many of these women and their children become homeless when they leave the batterer. Subsequently, many mothers are charged with neglect, and their children are taken from them and placed in foster homes.

The advocates demanded that the police and judges take women's complaints seriously, removing the batterer from the house rather than the nonabusive mother and her children, and doing everything possible to prevent further harassment. They call on agencies to provide more safe, short-term emergency refuges for women and children and ask that funds used for foster home placement be used instead to provide violence-free homes for the children. Advocates also ask that service providers receive training in domestic violence, as few know even the basic facts about it.

The advocates lobby for more affordable housing, more community-based services such as day care, legal assistance, health care, substance abuse prevention, child abuse prevention, and job-training programs. They point out that undocumented abused women are especially at risk for fear of deportation, that lesbian mothers fear losing custody of their children if they ask for help, and that women of color face racist assumptions that their children are at a higher risk of abuse.

Domestic violence affects women of every race and class, yet the poor, who are disproportionately non-English speaking and/or black, are most often victims of involuntary intervention by police and child protective workers (Coalition of Battered Women's Advocates, 1988).

WORKING WITH GAYS AND LESBIANS

In Chapter 5, we discussed the value judgments people make about gays and lesbians. Here we will put forward some guidelines for human service workers in their work with this particular population.

Betty Carter, a feminist therapist and director of the Family Institute of Westchester, tells the story of how her awareness was raised about the needs of lesbians:

> My awareness was…raised by a trainee…who was an out lesbian. At the end of the training, she told me what a wonderful experience she had because we had all been so open to her sexual orientation. "But can I tell you something?" she asked. I said, "Of course," knowing I didn't want to hear it. "You know, there is nothing that would let anyone like me know that I would be welcome here." I was totally startled because I had never thought about how stigmatized groups do need a sign that they are welcome. She pointed out that we had no featured course on gay or lesbian families. (Carter, 1995, p. 12)

Since then, Carter has instituted a training program on lesbian and gay family issues. She seeks the expertise of lesbians, who understand the complex issues of being marginalized because they experience it in their lives. After hearing the personal experiences of women in lesbian families, heterosexual workers who used to wonder why they needed to spend so much time and attention on lesbians and gays "had an awakening: 'Oh, I never thought of how heterosexism would have affected someone that way'" (Carter, 1995, p. 14).

Carter uses what she calls a "gay lens" to take special notice of the effects of stigma. She says, "Until you tell me otherwise, I will assume everyone in your family and work system takes a dim view of your not being straight" (p. 15). The gay lens helps to define the task of therapy, which is empowerment. Carter tries to help them deal nondefensively and strategically with the way in which they are pushed to the margins of society, and she helps them to recognize it as a product of ignorance and fear that has almost nothing personal to do with them.

The gay lens not only helps Carter and other therapists work with lesbians, but it also helps them work with heterosexuals. Every new way of viewing issues has far-reaching implications for human service work. Carter describes how she uses the gay lens:

> The "gay lens" challenges the way roles in relationships have become gendered. For example, if you ask about the division of chores in a heterosexual couple, it becomes clear who is in charge of the emotional life of the relationship and who will fix the boiler when it breaks. When we therapists are working with couples in a heterosexual rela-

tionship, most of us have stopped even questioning the fact that it is 99.9 percent of the time the woman who is in charge of emotions and the man who is in charge of the boiler. But when we look at lesbian and gay couples, it becomes clear that this isn't inevitable, because here you have two people of the same sex who have ungendered these roles. The emotional life still gets taken care of; the boiler still gets fixed. So how do they decide who does what, if it's not based on gender?

…The gay lens gives you a way to look at how same-sex couples manage to work these things out, and you can apply it to straight clients. This is no small matter. A fair division of housework and parenting would make life much more harmonious for heterosexuals. Most of our clients come in with some irritation or larger complaints about these matters, and I know I had started to believe it was impossible to achieve equity between men and women around the house. But then I'll see a gay or lesbian couple and suddenly realize it's not impossible for people to be total partners. Or, just as I'm about to give up on men for being exasperatingly unemotional, I'll work with a gay couple and be amazed by how open and tender they can be in expressing their feelings. (Carter, 1995, p. 14)

Gays and lesbians won a major victory in 2004 when the Massachusetts Supreme Court declared that the equal protection clause of the Massachusetts Constitution called for full-fledged marriage rights—and nothing less—for same-sex couples. Massachusetts became the first state in the nation to legalize same-sex marriages. Conservatives fought the legalization of gay and lesbian marriages by trying to introduce a constitutional amendment to prohibit same-sex marriages, the Federal Marriage Amendment. However, the Senate voted 50 to 48 against the amendment. Some Senators who are personally opposed to same-sex marriage were nevertheless opposed to a constitutional amendment to prohibit it (NOW, 2004, July 14).

WORKING WITH PEOPLE WITH DISABILITIES

People with disabilities are an oppressed group because they have not been allowed equal access to society's benefits. They are a minority both in absolute numbers and in the political meaning of the term.

People with disabilities have an acronym for people who define themselves as nondisabled: They call them TABs—Temporarily Able-Bodied. This word vividly reminds us that being able-bodied is only a temporary condition. Any one of us could get hit by a car when crossing the street or get hurt when skiing or diving. The recognition of our own vulnerability helps to lower that psychological barrier between "them" and "us," which is the biggest handicap of all.

The liberation movement of the disabled population challenged the arbitrary distinctions people make on the basis of differences in physical or mental functioning. Members declare that the *real disability* lies in society's unwillingness to structure its architecture, public facilities and space, cultural offerings, and so forth to open up the entire society to everyone regardless of their level of functioning.

New Definition of Disability Influences Our Practice

Psychosocial model of disability
A model that looks at the entire environment of the person, including social attitudes, attitudes of other individuals, and the society that the able-bodied have created.

Traditional models of disability focused on labeling each "disease," defining what people can do in the job market, and what functions a person can and cannot perform. The new model is a **psychosocial model of disability.** It looks at the entire environment of the person, including social attitudes, attitudes of other individuals, and the society that the able-bodied have created (Roth, 1987). The psychosocial model of disability was recognized in public policy by Section 504 of the Rehabilitation Act of 1973, the first civil rights act for disabled people, as well as by the Education for All Handicapped Children's Act of 1975. That law required disabled children to be mainstreamed with able-bodied children as much as possible. The most sweeping civil rights law for disabled people was the Americans with Disabilities Act of 1990.

At different times in history and in different places, certain disabilities could be or were viewed as somewhat of an asset, not as a liability. Dostoyevsky, who had epilepsy, describes the aura preceding an epileptic seizure as a route to cosmic clarity. Julius Caesar had epilepsy in Roman times, when it was considered to be a holy disease. During the nineteenth century in the Western world, people with tuberculosis were considered especially refined, sensitive, and wise. If a character in a nineteenth-century novel was described in Chapter 1 as refined, sensitive, and wise, it was sure to be revealed by Chapter 8 that the character was dying of tuberculosis or consumption.

Obtaining an accurate count of how many disabled people there are is especially tricky because the number depends on whom you define as disabled. Some deaf people do not consider their deafness a disability because they are totally immersed in the deaf culture and take great delight in it. They would consider it a handicap to be deprived of that culture. When the deaf students at Gallaudet College for the Deaf successfully rebelled against a hearing person being chosen as president of the college, some of them declared that their deafness should not be defined as a disability and that they were as "normal" as anyone else. Neurologist and author Oliver Sacks (1989), who described that rebellion so vividly, tells of a community on Martha's Vineyard in Massachusetts in which so many significant citizens were deaf that everyone learned sign language. With no communication barrier, life was the same for the hearing and the nonhearing.

The 2000 census found there are about 50 million people with disabilities in the United States, of which some 70 percent—35 million—are unemployed (*LRP Publications,* 2004). There is a disproportionate number of disabilities among older people, poor people, people of color, and blue-collar workers. Disabled people are more likely to be unemployed or underemployed, and if they are employed, are more likely to earn less than able-bodied workers. They face discrimination in the job market and often have to navigate buildings not designed for their needs.

Six disabled Tennessee residents achieved a victory in 2004 when the U.S. Supreme Court declared that states can be liable for not making courthouses accessible. One of the people who sued was a man who refused to crawl or be carried up to a second-floor courtroom in a county courthouse to answer a criminal traffic complaint. He sued after the state charged him with failing to appear for his hearing (Greenhouse, 2004).

People with disabilities and their dependents who were covered under Social Security when they worked are eligible to receive payments from Social Security Disability Insurance (SSDI). If their income is low enough, they might also qualify for Supplemental Security Income (SSI). Recipients of SSDI whose grants are lower than the SSI grant often receive both. Although it is possible to do some work and still receive SSI, in general, both programs require recipients to be unable to work in the same way or as much as able-bodied people. "This definition of disability reflects how government perceives disability, administers its remedies, and sometimes can even be said to create it" (Roth, 1987, p. 67). Human service workers who work with people with disabilities need to be informed about the eligibility guidelines for both programs, as well as for workers' compensation, to make sure their clients get the benefits they are entitled to. Legal service lawyers who specialize in disability law can help with this.

Because applying for these benefits requires people to see and define themselves as disabled and thus unable to work, many people do not apply. This is a dilemma for both the client and the worker. On the one hand, clients are refusing needed income; on the other hand, people's self-definition and self-esteem are critically important to their mental health. Some people will accept General Assistance even when the grant is much lower than SSI because they regard General Assistance as short-term temporary help until they get a job.

SUMMARY

1. There is a widening gulf of distrust between people of color and white people in the United States today.

2. The issue of diversity has stirred up public passions. There are fierce fights against immigrants, bilingual education, multicultural curricula, sex education in schools, gay and lesbian rights, and abortion.

3. Prejudice and discrimination may negatively affect people's feelings about themselves.

4. In order to fully understand people, we must understand their culture.

5. The current theory about culture is bicultural theory, which assumes that people are socialized into their own culture and influenced by the dominant culture.

6. Having limited access to power defines a "minority group."

7. The United States has been run predominantly by white, heterosexual, Anglo-Saxon, English-speaking, middle- and upper-class able-bodied men. Those who differ have often suffered discrimination.

8. "White-skin privilege" refers to the fact that people with a white skin are awarded privileges not available to people of color.

9. Hispanics face discrimination sometimes on the basis of skin color and often because of not speaking English, or speaking with limited fluency and an accent.

10. Acculturation is stressful, causing conflict between the older and younger generations in families.

11. Ethnicity, social class, and gender must be considered together.

12. In order to understand any group, we must understand its history.

13. Because minorities have been discriminated against, they are likely to be distrustful of white-dominated organizations.

14. Institutional racism is harder to change than individual racism because it involves interconnected systems and policies that perpetuate it.

15. Affirmative action has become a lightning rod that attracts people's anxieties about race.

16. The immigration policy of the United States has fluctuated between the country's need for labor and peoples xenophobia and fears of losing their jobs to foreigners.

17. The 1996 Immigration Act, which provides for "expedited removal" of immigrants, represents a major change in the country's treatment of immigrants.

18. A study by the National Academy of Sciences concluded that immigration added about $10 billion a year to the nation's economic output.

19. The Personal Responsibility Act of 1996 denied federal help to legal immigrants in the SSI, food stamp, and Medicaid programs. In 1997 some SSI and food stamp benefits were restored.

20. The elimination of bilingual education programs was an attack on immigrants, but in California it was supported by some Hispanics.

21. It is important to emphasize people's strengths rather than their weaknesses.

22. Family and friends are the most important supports for people.

23. Most minority groups are poor and therefore need concrete supports from human service agencies. Telling people about the benefits to which they are entitled empowers them.

24. Workers need to be willing to share themselves, be informal, be flexible about time, and be willing to make home visits.

25. Feminists have created alternative social agencies and new theories.

26. Feminist practice tends to be less hierarchical and more egalitarian.

27. Understanding issues that affect gays and lesbians not only helps them but can also give new insights into heterosexual behavior.

28. The new definition of disability does not accept the medical model; rather, it sees the problem as the reluctance of society to accommodate the needs of the disabled population.

29. The Americans with Disabilities Act of 1990 requires sweeping changes in accommodations for people with disabilities.

DISCUSSION QUESTIONS

1. What do you think is a good immigration policy for a nation? What guidelines would you use in setting up such a policy? The National Catholic Social Justice lobby, NETWORK, calls for "just reform of immigration policy" and "just U.S. foreign policy that fosters economic equity and alleviates global poverty." What do you think would be a just reform of immigration policy and a just U.S. foreign policy?

2. The Massachusetts Supreme Court ruled that there was no "constitutionally adequate reason" why same-sex couples should not enjoy the same legal rights as others. Opponents of that rule say that it will destroy traditional heterosexual marriage. On what do they base that argument? What do you think are the pros and cons of same sex-marriage?

3. Exercise: In group discussion, students name several social identity groups that they think influence people's lives. This could include race, ethnicity, gender, sexual orientation, class, physical ability, religion, age, and any other. Each person should identify where she or he fits in those groups in a notebook. During class discussion, students should share this information to the extent that they feel comfortable doing so. Discuss how (or whether) people are oppressed, or feel oppressed, because of their social identity. (No one should feel under any pressure to share personal information.)

4. Exercise: In group discussion, students share information on neighborhoods they grew up in and organizations they belonged to. How diverse were these neighborhoods and organizations? Discuss the reasons for their diversity or lack of diversity.

5. France has passed a law saying that Muslim girls are not allowed to wear head scarves in school, as this violates the principle of the separation of church and state and erodes national identity. What do you think of this law?

WEB RESOURCES FOR FURTHER STUDY

NETWORK
www.networklobby.org

A National Catholic Social Justice Lobby that educates, lobbies and organizes to influence the formation of federal legislation to promote economic and social justice.

MoveOn.org
www.moveon.org/

MoveOn was started by Joan Blades and Wes Boyd, two Silicon Valley entrepreneurs, with their family and friends. MoveOn is working to bring ordinary people back into politics, charging that the system today revolves around big money and big media, and that most citizens are left out. MoveOn is a catalyst for a new kind of grassroots involvement, supporting busy but concerned citizens in finding their political voice. MoveOn builds electronic advocacy groups around issues such as campaign finance, environmental and energy issues, impeachment, gun safety, and nuclear disarmament.

National Clearinghouse for Bilingual Education
www.ncela.gwu.edu

News, discussion groups, and resources for educators working with linguistically and culturally diverse students.

Drug Policy Alliance
www.drugpolicy.org

Provides information about drug policy in states, the nation, and worldwide. Works to promote drug policies based on science, compassion, health, and human rights.

Betsy Leondar-Wright
www.classmatters.org

Betsy Leondar-Wright is the Communications Director at United for a Fair Economy. Her recent book, *Class Matters: Cross-Class Alliance Building for Middle-Class Activists,* helps activists collaborate better across class lines to build stronger movements for social change. Her web site gives advice that she has gleaned from interviews with activists, resources, and information about class and how it intersects with other identities such as race, gender, disability, and sexual identity.

SisterSong: Women of Color Reproductive Health Collective
www.sistersong.net/

The SisterSong Women of Color Reproductive Health Collective is made up of local, regional, and national grassroots organizations in the United States representing four primary ethnic populations/indigenous nations in the United States: Native American/Indigenous; Black/African American; Latina/Puerto Rican; Asian/Pacific Islander. SisterSong does community organizing, self-help, and human rights education on reproductive and sexual health and rights.

Abortion counseling or referrals
www.prochoice.com

National Abortion Federation Hotline (English/Spanish): 800-772-9100

National Network of Abortion Funds (NNAF)
www.nnaf.org

NNAF provides support and technical assistance to local abortion funds, aids in the creation of new abortion funds in areas where they do not exist, and provides visibility and voice for women facing financial barriers to abortion. NNAF's member funds directly help over 19,500 women a year with a combined total of over $2 million in financial assistance.

CHAPTER 8

Interviewing

Because all of the interventions begin with collecting relevant data, it is clear that the process of interviewing is the bedrock skill of human service workers. The interview is an interaction between people—a client and a worker, a worker and a legislator, a supervisor and a trainee—that has a consciously planned purpose, structure, and goal. An interview can take place anywhere that people interact, although, of course, some atmospheres provide more privacy and comfort than others. Wherever it is held, and whoever the partners are, an interview requires the mastery of specific insights and skills. These enable the interviewer to ask clearly focused questions, to observe reactions, to summarize and share information, and to listen attentively to what is being said. When the interview has ended, the painstaking work of recording what has transpired begins.

Through case examples we see how worker behaviors can encourage trust and sharing or create barriers to communication. Blockages in building a trusting relationship occur when we focus on the interviewee's weaknesses rather than strengths, jump in to "rescue the client," or sit back in an overly passive way. But when workers learn to encourage the expression of emotion in an atmosphere of respect and cultural sensitivity, the ground is prepared for a productive interview. By phrasing open-ended questions, we encourage maximum expression of ideas and feelings. These enable the interviewee to gain perspective and summon up courage to face the problem at hand.

By giving examples of very specific interview leads and responses, we begin to answer the human service student's question, "But exactly what do I do and say when someone tells me about a problem?" Interviewing skills need to be continually strengthened through classroom role-plays and on-the-job supervision.

The following are excerpts from an interview conducted by Karen (K), a first-year student in an MSW program. Fran W. (FW) is the client, a 26-year-old white female, mother of 6-year-old Ann (A) and girlfriend of George (G).

K: You look sad.

FW: I am. I am angry with myself because G and I did coke on Friday.

K: What happened?

FW: Well, he was upset and we were on our way home and we just did it…I am so stupid. I can't believe that I did that. And I am having these dreams. I am in this slum with really sleazy people and I am looking for coke, but I never get any.

K: First of all, I think that you should not be so hard on yourself. You were sober for two weeks when you were using every single day. You should give yourself credit for that. This has been an issue with you for a long time. You are addicted. Obviously, you are not going to be able to just stop and you may slip a few times. What do you think the dream means?

FW: Well, like I said, it is the frustration of wanting it and not getting it. Morning and around dinnertime are real hard. I go to bed and my leg starts shaking…

FW: I get angry with A. When we are playing a game, I will snap at her. I love A. I would do anything for her. I love G too but I would not give up my life so that he could live.

K: Have you ever done coke in front of her?

FW: NO! I don't think she knows…. I close the door, but I don't know.

K: Children are very perceptive. When you get angry and you take it out on her, you may want to say that it is not her fault.

FW: Yeah, but she must get sick of hearing that I am not angry with her, I am just going through a hard time.

K: I think that it would be beneficial for her to hear that it is not because of her. If you said it a million times it would be fine.…

CHARACTERISTICS OF AN INTERVIEW

In the above interview, the counselor, Karen, is engaged in purposeful communication with the goal of helping the client, Fran. A counseling interview is only one of the many kinds of interviewing that human service workers do. Every intervention that a human service worker uses—whether counseling one client or mobilizing a group to take social action—requires interviewing. All our work is built on planned, careful communication: talking and listening, making nonverbal gestures, or writing. In this chapter, we will discuss the basic elements and skills of interviewing.

Because we are writing for the beginning human service worker, we will not focus on long-term counseling or psychotherapy interviews or on specialized treatment of children. Nor will we discuss the skills specific to research interviewing (though many of the skills we will talk about also apply to this area). These topics require experience and training beyond the beginning level.

We define a human service interview as an interaction between people that has a consciously planned purpose, structure, and goal and requires specific communication skills.

Purposeful Communication

Social conversations need not have any conscious goal. When we are having a casual chat with a friend, we generally don't have a fixed agenda about what we discuss. The conversation often ambles at a leisurely pace from one topic to another: the weather, what happened on the way to work, how we feel, the party we went to last night, gossip about friends, and so on. You talk because you enjoy being with each other.

An interview, on the other hand, has a purpose and a goal. You may engage in some small talk with clients to establish rapport, but usually a person comes to you for a specific service, or you reach out to them.

Focus and Structure

Each person involved in a conversation expects more or less equal attention. But in an interview, the focus is on the needs of the client. We would feel neglected or angry if a friend talked endlessly about his or her problems without bothering to listen to us in return. In an interview, however, skilled workers know how to stay in the background and encourage clients to say what is on their minds. This does not mean that interviewers never reveal anything about themselves; in fact, research suggests that it is useful to share a moderate amount of information about one's own life (Hepworth & Larsen, 1987, p. 998). Of course, the interviewer is responsible for keeping the interview focused on the client.

The structure of an interview varies according to the context in which it takes place, the individual client, and the phase of the helping process. Each interview is unique, but initial interviews always include (1) the beginning process of establishing rapport (which continues to some degree throughout the helping relationship); (2) opening the interview and making the contract; (3) exploring the issues; and (4) closing the interview and looking forward to the next steps in the helping process.

SPONSORSHIP

The **primary purpose** of the social agency shapes the focus and content of the interview. The focus of the Department of Welfare, for example, was broader before 1974, when workers were called "social workers" and could offer help for problems beyond financial need. Now workers are called "investigators" or "eligibility workers." Their function is narrowly focused on a client's financial situation. However, a multifunction agency, such as Child and Family Services, can have a broader focus in the interview because it is authorized to offer counseling for a broad spectrum of clients' needs. When an agency has a narrow focus, the worker can refer a client whose needs fall outside its scope to one that serves those needs.

In agencies that work with involuntary clients, interviewers need to be particularly skilled in helping people express anger or resentment, yet they must be able

Primary purpose
The main goal of an agency that determines the work it does.

to stay on course with the main purpose of the interview. A worker also needs to be skilled in sorting out the issues inherent in situations that limit self-determination and in dealing forthrightly with those issues.

Image of an agency
The reputation that a social agency has established in the community.

The public support and **image of an agency** also influence interviews. For example, because welfare benefits are kept low and the agency is chronically underfunded and understaffed, a Department of Welfare office often does not provide the privacy that people should have when discussing their personal affairs. Understaffing means that clients must often wait for long periods for an interview, and sometimes the interview is more rushed and mechanical than it should be. Such working conditions can be demoralizing to both clients and workers. Even though a dedicated worker can conduct a superb interview in a stigmatized or underfunded agency, the pressure of the work and the drabness of the surroundings can encourage joyless and dehumanizing treatment of claimants. As a general rule, agencies that serve the poor are understaffed and poorly housed and do not give as much privacy or time to the clientele as do agencies that serve more affluent people.

SETTING

The focus and content of an interview are also affected by the setting in which it takes place. Interviews can happen anywhere—in a locker room, on a street corner, in a living room. Ideally there should be a logical relationship between what you are going to talk about and the place where you do the talking. For example, if you are chatting with a member of the women's basketball team in a locker room after a basketball game and she blurts out that her father beat her mother the night before during an alcoholic binge, you might suggest she go with you for a cup of coffee or a walk so you can talk in privacy.

Sometimes interviews take place in the home of a client with the television set blaring and the children within earshot as the parents talk about them. Even in our offices, we must often ask personal questions with little more privacy than a room divider. Although we can try to improve these conditions as a long-range strategy, we must deal with them from moment to moment the best way we can.

The following suggestions can help make an awkward situation more private and comfortable for the client:

- Try to assess the emotional state of the client to see what behavior would be appropriate. Lower the tone of your voice, lean forward, and listen intently so the client does not have to shout his information.

- If you are in an office with no privacy, apologize to the client or comment that you know she might feel uncomfortable in such a setting. Say that you're sorry about it and wish there were a more private space.

- Move your chair to the side of the desk so that it doesn't separate you from the person you are talking with. Have a plant at your desk, or some objects that make it as attractive and personal as possible.

Skill and Awareness

Conversations and interviews differ in the level of skill each require. It is true that people vary enormously in their interpersonal skills, and therefore some people carry on more creative conversations than others. Yet, as long as we can make ourselves understood, most of us don't think we must train ourselves to carry on social conversations. In order to become skilled interviewers, however, we need to learn a great deal about how people interact with each other. We need to assess behavior: to listen carefully not only to words but to shadings and nuances of tone, pitch, and volume; and to communicate our understanding of what we have seen and heard in a clear and concise way that shows we genuinely care about that person. Indeed, much of the skill in interviewing comes from awareness:

- Awareness of your own personality and the personality of the interviewee
- Awareness of your own expectations and those of the interviewee
- Awareness of your own cultural background and that of the interviewee
- Awareness of your own attitudes and values

We will discuss each of these separately, but remember that in practice no one factor can *really* be separated from all the others.

AWARENESS OF PERSONALITY AND STYLE

Because each interviewer and interviewee has a unique personality and style, there is no magic formula for interviewing. An outgoing person may be a more assertive interviewer than a quieter one, but both can be equally skillful. Fortunately, people are not programmed robots. Precisely because of our human capacity for spontaneity, there is always an element of uncertainty in what we will say and what others will say to us. Therefore, interviewing, depending as it does on words and gestures, can never be totally systematized in a scientific way and will always remain—to some extent at least—*an art*. We believe, however, that we can all learn to become more sensitive to others through studying ourselves and our interactions and through continual practice in self-discovery and effective communication techniques.

Self-discovery continues for each of us until we die. Unquestionably, however, some people are more sensitive than others, and a certain level of sensitivity is an absolute requirement in human service work.

Certain kinds of interviewer behavior that could create barriers to communication include:

- Focusing on weaknesses rather than strengths
- The need to "rescue"
- Overly passive behavior
- Discomfort with emotion

- Anger
- Condescension

Focusing on Weaknesses

Some interviewers see the glass as half empty rather than as half full. These interviewers are less helpful than those who look for strengths. *At the core of mental health is self-esteem,* so we look for genuine ways of enhancing the interviewee's self-esteem. Sometimes we can find an interviewee's positive intentions even in undesirable actions. Then we can emphasize the intentions, not the undesirable actions. For example, you might say to a man who stole money in order to feed his family: "Although your stealing gets you in trouble, I understand that you are very worried about your family and want to help them. Let's discuss ways of supporting your family that won't get you into trouble."

Need to "Rescue"

An occupational hazard of human service workers is their need to rescue people, whether or not the clients want to be rescued. *We are supposed to be "doing with," not "doing for."* "Doing for" implies that the helper is superior and knows what is best for the helpee. "Doing with" implies a mutuality and equality. J. D. Salinger captured this distinction in his novel *The Catcher in the Rye* (1951). The hero, Holden Caulfield, wants to straighten out the world—erase all the obscene graffiti and rescue everyone. His desire is expressed in his interpretation of a poem by Robert Burns, set to music. First Holden hears it as, "If a body *catch* a body, coming through the rye." After much life experience, he is reminded by his younger sister Phoebe that the words are "If a body *meet* a body, coming through the rye." The point is not to rescue, but to meet. At the end of the story, Holden realizes that he is connected to everyone he ever knew—even people he disliked—and he misses them.

Rescue fantasy
A fantasy that envisions saving someone from his or her fate.

Children and extremely dependent people are especially likely to evoke **rescue fantasies** in us. We often have strong feelings about what is acceptable parenting, and when working with children, we must curb any tendencies to be in rivalry with the children's parents.

Overly Passive Behavior

The amount of the interviewer's verbal activity will vary from one situation to another. Some interviewees talk easily and with little prodding; some need help in limiting or structuring their verbosity; others do not talk easily and need more encouragement from the worker. A worker who sits like a bump on a log gives the appearance of being uninterested in the interviewee or of having no structure or goal for the encounter.

Discomfort with Emotion

Some interviewers are uncomfortable with emotions, which makes it harder for the interviewee to express powerful feelings. This characteristic can show itself whenever the interviewee cries or expresses anger. To avoid dealing with the emotion, the interviewer changes the subject, talks about superficial things, gives false reassurance, intellectualizes about the problems, or becomes emotionally detached.

Anger

Because an interview is a human encounter, there will be times when the interviewer will feel angry with the interviewee. There could be many reasons for the anger. Perhaps something the interviewee said triggers some old resentments, or perhaps some personality trait annoys the interviewer. An articulate, assertive interviewer may become impatient with a passive interviewee; a laid back interviewer may feel annoyance at an interviewee who is a compulsive talker.

Whatever the reason, it is important for interviewers to be aware of their anger and come to terms with it. When this happens, anger can be a useful tool. It is not helpful to express the anger impulsively and thoughtlessly to the interviewee, but anger can be used helpfully if the interviewer understands it. One author recommends recognizing "the inward side of a feeling."

> If the counselor feels bored with or angry toward a client, rather than express these feelings (the outer edge) that imply criticism or blame, he seeks to determine and to express deeper aspects of the feelings by asking himself, "Why do I feel this way?" In seeking the answer, he will discover that behind the boredom lies a positive desire to hear more personal and relevant information that can facilitate progress. Likewise, behind the anger lies disappointment in being unable to be more helpful to the client. If we similarly analyze such feelings as impatience, irritation, criticism, or disgust, we will discover that the inward side of these feelings will consist of a desire that the client have a better and more fulfilling life, a desire that can be shared safely and beneficially. (Hammond, Hepworth, & Smith, 1977, p. 224)

Condescension

Condescension implies that the worker feels superior to the client. Workers are generally unaware of these feelings, but clients have their antennae attuned to them. A condescending attitude gives the message, "I know what is good for you. The fact that you are a client automatically guarantees that you don't know as much as I do about human behavior in general, and your behavior in particular. You came to me because you want my expertise, and I intend to give it to you."

AWARENESS OF MUTUAL EXPECTATIONS

When two people come together for an interview, they bring with them the sum total of their past experiences and current expectations. This is their mental set. They bring anxieties, knowledge, misinformation, and hopes to the interview. They may be from different social classes, races, or ethnic backgrounds. Their ages, gender, physical capacities, or sexual orientation may be different. All these qualities have shaped their attitudes and will help shape the interview. Each might have a drastically different agenda for the interview. A depressed person may hope for a pill to cure the depression immediately, and the worker may have been trained to believe that medication must be supplemented by a lengthy counseling process.

A study of working-class clients who came to a family service agency in England revealed that clients and workers had differing expectations of each other. Some clients who were having trouble with their husbands expected the worker to give the husband a good talking to to straighten him out. Some resented personal questions and only answered when pushed continually to do so. Some assumed that workers asked personal questions because they were nosy, interested in gossip, or trying to annoy (Rhodes, 1989, p. 71).

The researchers were amazed by the mutual lack of awareness of the reasons for the other person's behavior (Mayer & Timms, 1970). Workers and clients seemed sometimes to be in two different worlds. The solution to such divergence between client and worker expectations is to clarify expectations and bring them into convergence by changing either the worker's or the client's expectations or by changing the treatment methods. At times, perhaps all of these changes may be necessary.

Both the interviewer and interviewee come to the interview with anxiety, particularly if they are meeting for the first time. Everyone feels anxious in a new and untested situation. For example, remember how you felt at the beginning of a semester during the first session of your classes. Perhaps you wondered how the teachers would treat you or what they would expect from you. You might have wondered whether the teachers would be tough or easy graders. Would the classes be boring or interesting? Would the teachers humiliate you or be sarcastic if you gave a wrong answer? Would the teachers respect your individual needs and ideas?

Remember, too, how you felt when you were about to be interviewed by a prospective employer. You probably wondered whether you would measure up to the employer's expectations. Would you say the right things? Were you dressed correctly? Would the employer like you? Would you be asked questions you'd rather not answer? What parts of your experience and personality should you emphasize, deemphasize, alter, or conceal?

Inexperienced workers usually wonder whether they will ask the right questions: "What if I ask the wrong question? Will it send the client into a tailspin? What if the client doesn't talk? What if the client talks too much? What if the client talks about the wrong things, or what if I talk about the wrong things? How can I keep the interview on target? Will the client like me, or will I like the client?"

To move the interview along toward its goal, the anxieties of both the interviewer and the interviewee need to be dealt with. The interviewer can practice certain techniques through role-playing and can deal with personal anxieties through supervision and peer support.

AWARENESS OF CULTURAL BACKGROUNDS

Cultural issues are related to expectations because people from various cultural backgrounds might have different expectations of each other and might even literally speak different languages. Even when the language *seems* to be the same, people who belong to a subculture within an English-speaking culture will probably have developed their own language variations.

Sometimes words convey different meaning to different people. Slang is one example of this: *straight* means "very proper" in one person's vocabulary; to another it means "not crooked." To another it means "heterosexual." In a discussion of the relative merits of surplus foods, someone said, "The cheese was smokin'!" He was not referring to smoked cheese; he meant it was a very tasty cheese. We should try to use language that the interviewee understands, which means that we have to learn the interviewee's particular idiom if it differs from ours. However, we should not use slang that is unnatural or uncomfortable to us. Trying to act hip in a forced way with a teenager in order to be part of the gang is more likely to reap ridicule than trust.

George Esber Jr., an anthropologist, gives an interesting example of differing cultural expectations between workers and clients in a program for teen parents (1989, p. 4). At the conclusion of a two-year program for teen parents, the director concluded that the program was not really needed. The teens went through pregnancy with little trouble and were able to do a reasonably adequate job of mothering. The program was begun for a group of people that had a higher rate of teen pregnancy than the dominant culture. However, "in that particular subculture, teen pregnancy was normative, and teen parenting practices were a part of institutionalized behavior patterns" (p. 4). Thus, teen pregnancy was seen as a problem by members of the dominant culture but not by the youths themselves, who "were conforming to norms in their own subculture" (p. 4).

Learning about a Client's Culture

Anthropologists have a lot to teach human service workers about interviewing and about how to relate to people. Their job is to learn how a culture works, how people relate to each other, what kinds of organizations they create, and what their strengths are. When anthropologists do ethnographic interviews, they are the students and the interviewees are the teachers. The anthropologists make some decisions about how to structure the interview, but they have no preconceptions about people's problems or the way to solve them. They are curious about people's lives and their relationships to others in the family and the community.

Human service workers are more likely to think they need to be in control of an interview and to have some thoughts about the nature of the problems and ways to solve them because they believe that they are the experts. Anthropologist James Green (1982) challenges social workers' emphasis on empathy, openness, and getting in touch with feelings. He suggests that social workers could develop a deeper understanding of their clients if they think less about those emphases and strive instead to develop real knowledge of the client's world view. He says:

> The real trick in cross-cultural social work, as in any kind of cross-cultural learning, is to comprehend what it is that the client knows and how that knowledge is used in the mundane traffic of daily meaning, client meaning, and not contrived, a priori "caring responses." What clients say—literally—is a crucial source of data, which must be carefully gathered, using such simple ethnographic interviewing techniques as will elicit in the client's own terms…the meanings attached to personal, family, or other problems typically brought to social workers. (p. 74)

Although Green downplays the importance of empathy, the seriousness of an anthropologist's respect for the client's view and the intensity of his or her search for understanding can result in genuinely empathetic understanding. The worker who glibly responds, "I know how you feel," without actually having any idea how the client feels pays only lip service to the concept of empathy.

Social work professor Irene Glasser uses these ethnographic methods in teaching students interviewing techniques. She considers any situation to be cross-cultural when the worker "is working with someone who views the world, defines reality, and organizes behavior differently than the worker does. This means that practically *all* of my social-work students are engaged in cross-cultural work whether they are working with poor people, young parents, people on probation, children in a class for emotional problems, or shelter residents" (Glasser, 1989, p. 5).

Glasser suggests that students become the "learner" of each person's culture. Some questions that might be helpful are to ask people to talk about:

- Their daily routine
- A critical period in their lives
- Their childhood
- Common expressions and jokes friends tell each other

Listen carefully to people's words and ask for clarification when necessary. Don't be too quick to "understand." An admission of ignorance might be more productive than a facile claim to understanding. Look for recurring themes in people's conversation or behavior (Glasser, 1989).

James Spradley (1979) gives guidelines for ethnographic interviewing that emphasize three skills: (1) asking global questions; (2) identifying "cover terms" (explained below); and (3) eliciting descriptors for the terms they choose to explore.

Global Questions

Global questions
General, open-ended questions about some aspect of the interviewee's life.

Global questions are "general, open-ended questions about some aspect of the interviewee's life, something personally or professionally puzzling to the worker and potentially salient to the presenting problem" (Green & Leigh, 1989, p. 8). Green and Leigh give the example of interviewing a Native American. The worker, who knows little or nothing about this group but knows that the Native American is newly arrived to a large city from a nearby reservation, asks (after preliminary introductions) the following global question: "I don't often meet people from the American Indian community in this office; can you tell me why some of the people you know leave their reservations to live in this city?"

The worker does not start with the "presenting problem" or by taking a social history. While he is partly concerned with warming up and establishing rapport, he is also inviting the person to volunteer information about his experiences and his culture. The way the question is phrased puts the interviewee in the role of expert—a cultural guide. The goal is to generate discourse and to understand the context of his behavior, to see how normative it is in terms of *his own* reference group. The goal is not to jump right into a person's problem as would the question, "Why did *you* leave the reservation?" The ethnically competent interviewer takes the interviewee's language seriously, rather than "reading through" language to see what is *really* behind what is being said (Green & Leigh, 1989, p. 8).

Cover Terms

Cover terms subsume, or cover, some aspect of culturally significant meaning and experience. To illustrate, Green and Leigh continue with the above example. The interviewee's response might be: "A lot of people leave. They need money, some kind of work, and they have families to help. But I know several who just wanted to see Seattle, to get away from it all, you know." There are at least six cover terms in this response:

1. "a lot of people"
2. "some kind of work"
3. "families"
4. "to help"
5. "just wanted to see Seattle"
6. "get away from it all"

The worker could choose one that seemed significant and might ask: "You say 'a lot of people'; does everyone you know leave at some time, or just some people?" By asking such global questions, the worker would in time elicit the cultural context of an interviewee's behavior, information that would also be applicable for work with future clients of similar background.

Descriptors

"Descriptors are simply blocks of descriptive information, systematically collected, used to build a composite portrait of selected cultural characteristics more or less shared by a set of clients" (Green & Leigh, 1989, p. 8). Compiling **descriptors** requires careful recording, which could present a problem to workers already pressed for time. Green and Leigh suggest that the process recording that agencies use to train workers could also be used to compile ethnographic descriptions of even a few paragraphs in length, which could then be used as training aids and for staff discussions. Green and Leigh list the following areas for focusing on the interviewee and his or her presenting problem:

1. The client's own definition and evaluation of an experience as a problem.
2. The semantic elements of the client's discourse in reference to the problem.
3. Indigenous strategies of problem resolution, including the identity and procedures of indigenous healers and advisers.
4. Culturally based criteria of problem resolution.

Cover terms Terms that describe some aspect of culturally significant meaning and experience.

Descriptors Blocks of descriptive information, systematically collected, used to build a composite portrait of selected cultural characteristics more or less shared by a set of clients.

5. Contrasts in worker–client and agency–ethnic community views of the problem and articulation of how those contrasts can be positively used in problem solving. (p. 8)

Awareness of Attitudes and Values

Interviewers set the stage for a worthwhile interview by their attitudes of active observation, physical attentiveness to the interviewee, and active listening. These attitudes are essential to productive interviews.

ACTIVE OBSERVATION

The 1950 Japanese movie *Rashomon* tells the tale of a bride and her samurai bridegroom who were traveling through the woods when a bandit set upon them and may have raped the bride and murdered the bridegroom. We say "may have," because the only thing the film tells us for certain is that the bridegroom is dead. A woodcutter was the only witness at the scene. During the trial of the bandit, the audience hears four different versions of the incident: the bride's, the woodcutter's, the bandit's, and (through a clairvoyant speaking to the husband's ghost) the husband's. The bride's alleged rape and the manner of the husband's death are disputed by all the witnesses; each saw the events differently. This movie is a vivid reminder that each of us brings our selective filters to every event we observe.

Active observation is different from the kind of looking we generally do in our everyday life. It is like the difference between being a passenger on a bus and the driver. The driver is aware at every moment of the conditions of the road, the traffic, the passengers, and the fare box. But although they might glance casually about, noting some people and incidents with mild interest, the passengers are generally preoccupied with their own thoughts.

Observing Nonverbal Messages

In a similar fashion, interviewers get clues about the people they are listening to from their nonverbal messages. Suppose, for example, you are a human service worker in a nursing home. A middle-aged couple comes to see you about placing the husband's mother in this home. As you show them through the halls, you notice that they get quieter; their voices drop; their speech slows; they glance significantly at each other as they look at the seriously ill residents in wheelchairs, walking with walkers and canes, staring into space. They look away from you and decline your invitation to see the wing of the home where the more seriously ill residents live. Observing their behavior and knowing how much stress people are under when making decisions about their sick or aged parents, you'd want to help this couple talk about their feelings about placing their mother, as well as their impressions of what they have just seen.

Interviewees can give nonverbal clues about feelings: rigid posture, trembling, yawning, wringing hands, sweating palms, trembling voice, blushing, a sad look, moistening of the eyes, sighs, clenched jaws and hands, pursed lips, lowered head,

Interviews are conducted with people who are struggling to cope with many problems in diverse settings. This man is incarcerated. His worker will need to be especially sensitive to the limitations on his self-determination and the feelings they provoke.

and other gestures. Workers also communicate with clients through nonverbal behavior. They can express warmth by a handshake, by leaning toward the interviewee rather than sitting back, and by facial expressions. Workers can also express disapproval, contempt, or disinterest by glancing off into space, fidgeting, coming to an interview late, looking at their watches, forgetting important names or facts about the interviewee's situation, and interrupting the interview to answer the phone or talk to others.

There is disagreement in the field about how much physical contact is appropriate between the interviewer and the interviewee. Although we cannot go into a full discussion of this issue, we do believe that touching can send both positive and negative messages. When touching becomes sexualized by either the interviewer or the interviewee, it can be abusive. Some people's natural style of relating to others involves touching. However, before you touch a client (except for a handshake), you should ask permission. Even if it is natural for you to touch people, it might make some interviewees uncomfortable. It takes experience and skill to know when, how much, and with whom physical contact will help build rapport. Few doubt, however, the usefulness of using some reassuring touch when it seems appropriate.

To illustrate this, we return to the case of the elderly woman whose son and daughter-in-law were choosing a nursing home for her. The woman was terrified of going into this institution, imagining it was a type of prison, even though her son and daughter-in-law saw it as a gracious, well-run home. During the intake interview, the worker in the nursing home took the woman's trembling hand in her own. Afterward, as the elderly woman recounted the interview to her children, she said, "She put both of her hands around mine and made me feel not so alone."

Looking for nonverbal clues to feelings is not a parlor game! Some people jump to quick, simplistic conclusions based on one gesture. Yet you can't tell much about the significance of a gesture if you don't know what a person's typical body stance is like. A crying child may tell you, when you ask, that nothing is wrong, but his uncharacteristically sad face and quietness tells you that something is upsetting this usually bouncy youngster.

Although intuitive understanding is important, your first reaction to a scene may not always give you accurate information. For example, you might see able-bodied men hanging around on a street during working hours and assume they are shiftless or chronically unemployed. In fact, the men might be construction workers who have just been laid off because a project is finished and are looking for a new job. Or perhaps they might be migrant workers waiting for the grape harvest to begin. To arrive at any valid understanding, your observations of any one person or incident must be put in social and historical context.

ACTIVE LISTENING

> In every human self there is the universal longing at times to be understood intuitively, by a gesture, by silence, in short, by no effort of language, since language at best is always felt initially as separating rather than uniting.... Yet...only through the willing use of language, that universal means of conveying both thought and feeling—can any substantial relationship develop. (Faatz, 1953, p. 98)

Much as we long for that perfect nonverbal understanding, we communicate our thoughts and feelings through language. Yet our attempts to communicate with one another often seem doomed to failure. Why is this so? One reason is that language itself is too frail to carry our full meaning. In the novel *Madame Bovary*, nineteenth-century French author Gustave Flaubert expressed his tragic awareness of this fact. Madame Bovary had told her lover Rudolph that she loved him, and she meant it sincerely. Rudolph, however, felt the words were being used in a phony way, perhaps because he himself had used them that way so often that he no longer believed them. Madame Bovary could not get through to him. This is what Flaubert (1856/1959) writes:

> He [Rudolph], this man of great experience, could not distinguish dissimilarities of feeling between similarities of expression...as though the fullness of the soul did not sometimes overflow into the emptiest phrases, since no one can ever express the measure of his needs, his conceptions or his sorrows, and human speech is like a cracked

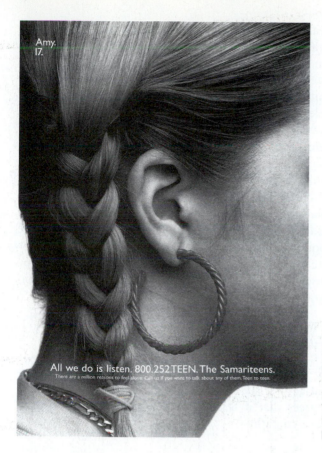

Amy.
17.

All we do is listen. 800.252.TEEN. The Samariteens.
There are a million reasons to feel alone. Call us if you want to talk about any of them. Teen to teen.

The teenage years can be very stressful, leading to anxiety and depression. The Samariteens, part of a suicide prevention program, trains young adult volunteers for its hotline, which lets young people discuss problems in total anonymity.

pot on which we beat out rhythms for bears to dance to when we are striving to make music that will wring tears from the stars. (p. 165)

In many of our conversations we are faced with the awareness that our words may not carry our full meaning. Perhaps it is because we have not chosen the right words or because the listener is not really receiving our message or because we are not sure of what we mean ourselves.

An interviewer needs to master the crucial skill of active listening to be able to grasp the complex personality and the complex situation of each person. In order to "read" the emotion behind the words of the speaker and get closer to the real meaning, we must listen carefully to each word and then remember what has been said. Careful, active listening is not a usual occurrence.

Try to remember the last time someone gave you their absolutely undivided attention and listened to you talk about your concerns, without interjecting any of their own. Few people are capable of giving their undivided attention to everyone they meet. Most of us are preoccupied, worrying about a test, a dentist's appointment, or a troubled friendship.

Although some people reveal themselves easily, most of us do not pour out our innermost thoughts to total strangers. In fact, we have been taught caution. Even with good friends we are often reluctant to speak about what is on our minds. Many people feel a special reticence when they must ask for help, embarrassed to admit that they can't handle some aspect of their lives without help. Many people raised in the United States have learned the individualistic "pull yourself up by your own bootstraps" ideology. So when a person comes into an interview at a human service agency, we need to be alert to any feelings of anxiety about asking for and receiving help.

Recurrent references to a subject may indicate great concern about that topic. The way ideas are associated with each other can give hints and feelings. For example, if a woman tells about her daughter's beauty and then shifts to her own concern about her appearance, we might wonder if the woman's feelings about herself are mixed up with her feelings about her daughter. Sometimes people conceal their meanings by saying the opposite of what they mean. A man whose fiancée has broken the engagement may say angrily that he's glad it's over, because his ego is too injured for him to admit the opposite.

Core Values of the Interviewer

Many counselors and psychotherapists regard the values of empathy, warmth, respect, and genuineness as essential for a successful helping relationship. However, although everyone probably agrees that it is essential for a helper to respect a helpee, not everyone agrees about empathy.

EMPATHY

Empathy is the capacity to identify yourself with another person's feelings and thoughts, to suspend your own judgment for the moment and feel with another. It differs from sympathy, which involves feeling sorry for someone but not necessarily suspending one's own feelings to try to identify with another person.

Empathy is an ongoing process rather than a state that is achieved once and for all. Some people object that because it is not measurable or observable, one should concentrate on training helpers in skills of communication that can be demonstrably improved. Others argue that empathy is not important when a helper is dealing with environmental concerns, such as helping someone to find housing.

We believe that empathy, without knowledge of how to work the system, would be useless in helping people with environmental concerns. Yet it is also essential to identify with people's feelings about their environmental concerns in order to understand fully how to help them. For example, a person may need to file a complaint against a landlord in order to get heat. The helping person needs to understand that person's personality in order to know whether she will actually file the complaint or be too frightened to do so.

In working with a welfare rights group of TANF recipients, the prime goal may be to increase the TANF grant; yet, on the way to doing that, we must feel the linkages between the personal and the political. We must be able to:

- Identify with the recipient's rage against an arbitrary system or a mean-spirited worker

- Identify with feelings of powerlessness

- Understand a recipient's need to identify with the oppressive welfare system when she acts superior to other recipients

- Stretch our capacity to understand when, as club treasurer, the recipient is tempted to steal the club funds

- Plumb the depths of the recipient's feelings of deprivation

- Understand the female recipient's feelings of frustration when the welfare functionaries watch her like a hawk to try to suppress her sexuality

- Understand the recipient's capacity to fight the system in order to know how to buoy that capacity

Empathy springs out of our common humanness. Although no two people have *precisely* the same experiences, we all go through the same life cycle and share similar feelings. This could be considered as a kind of universal kinship. Kinship is not only relatedness to one's family, but "also a type of connection—biological, spiritual, emotional, social, between people" (Cottle, 1974, p. xii). Using our imagination, we form connections to our interviewees that help us to experience what they are experiencing. Empathy requires a finely tuned intuitive sensitivity to other people. This kind of sensitivity is often found in good fiction or poetry. In his character Seymour, author J. D. Salinger (1965) portrays an intensely empathetic person. Seymour is so attuned to others that he sometimes gets burns from touching them. In *Raise High the Roof Beam, Carpenters,* Seymour writes in his diary:

> If or when I do start going to an analyst, I hope to God he has the foresight to let a dermatologist sit in on the consultation. A hand specialist. I have scars on my hands from touching certain people. Once in the park, when Franny was still in the carriage, I put my hand on the downy pate of her head and left it there too long. Another time, at Loew's Seventy-second Street, with Zooey during a spooky movie. He was about six or seven and he went under the seat to avoid watching a scary scene. I put my hand on his head. Certain heads, certain colors and textures of human hair leave permanent marks on me. (p. 75)

The burns on Seymour's hands are Salinger's metaphor for a sensitivity to people so fine that it is almost mystical.

Empathy may be essential for survival, according to Dr. Steven Hyman, professor of neurobiology at Harvard Medical School. He says that "from an evolutionary point of view, we're probably hardwired for empathy, which confers 'selective advantage,' allowing the young—and the species—to survive" (Foreman, 2003). An infant is at greater risk of perishing if the parent is not empathic.

The capacity for empathy probably grows, at least in part, out of a baby's inborn ability to mimic facial expressions, according to psychologist Andrew Meltzoff, at the University of Washington in Seattle. Through mimicking adults, the infant "constructs a worldview that says, in essence, that other people are 'like me.'... Empathy, including the sophisticated talent for treating others as you would like to be treated, 'builds on primitive imitation'" (Foreman, 2003).

For people in the caring professions, there are potential pitfalls when experiencing another person's pain can lead to "empathic over-arousal," according to Nancy Eisenberg, a psychologist at Arizona State University. "In this unpleasant state, the focus then becomes one's own feelings of stress rather than the other person's need. The over-aroused person may have to leave the room or emotionally withdraw to feel better" (Foreman, 2003). Human service workers need to learn how to empathize with a client's feelings without drowning in those feelings and without accepting the person's assumptions that led to those feelings.

RESPECT

Respect is a quality that most people understand in their social relationships. It involves regarding others as important and being concerned about their welfare. It acknowledges their uniqueness and their rights to feelings and needs. Respect requires that the helper be **nonjudgmental** when trying to understand the helpee.

Nonjudgmental
Refers to an attitude that withholds moral judgments on another person's behavior, attitude, or values.

GENUINENESS

Genuineness is also a quality that people understand in their day-to-day relationships. When people use slang expressions such as "He's a stuffed shirt," or "She's a pompous ———," or "White man speak with forked tongue," they are expressing contempt for a person who puts on airs or is hypocritical. We want to know that the person to whom we entrust our thoughts and feelings actually cares. This quality has come to be more highly valued by many helping professionals than it used to be. Classical Freudian psychoanalysis established a helping model in which the therapist acted as a "blank slate"—sitting passively behind the patient, seldom interjecting an opinion or showing strong emotions. This model was always inappropriate for helping people who had concrete environmental problems and is increasingly seen as inappropriate for most therapeutic relationships. Counselors and therapists nowadays are more likely to express appropriate feelings openly. "By being willing to discuss personal feelings, the helper encourages the helpee to respond similarly. The helpee opens up and learns to be genuine, too" (D'Augelli, D'Augelli, & Danish, 1981, pp. 58–59).

Genuineness also involves "being non-defensive and human enough to admit errors to clients.... [Practitioners] must be models of humanness and openness and avoid hiding behind a mask of 'professionalism'" (Hepworth & Larson, 1987, p. 998).

CASE STUDY
Jean

A woman named Jean was out of money. Her husband had been unemployed for many months, and their relatives were equally poor and couldn't help. She set out for the welfare office to apply for TANF for herself and her two small children.

SPONSORSHIP AND SETTING

The welfare office had once been within walking distance of Jean's apartment, but because of fiscal cutbacks, the intake departments of several neighborhood welfare offices had been consolidated and centralized in a downtown office. Jean borrowed the $5.00 round-trip transit fare from a friend and, with two young children in tow, set out in the pouring rain for an address that rang no familiar bell in her memory. Asking her way as she went along, by trial and error, she finally found the office, marked by a sign chiseled into the stone facade: OVERSEERS OF THE PUBLIC WELFARE.

Jean entered the lobby and winced as she saw a security guard with a gun in his holster. Because it was Monday morning, the lobby was filled with people, many of them standing, since there were not enough chairs. The once-white paint on the walls and ceiling was peeling, and it was hard to see what color the floors had been, as they were threadbare in many spots. Faded posters describing long-defunct job programs lined the walls.

The receptionist sitting behind a thick glass partition ignored Jean, continuing a conversation with the other receptionist about a party she had gone to the night before. Finally she shoved a piece of cardboard with the number 20 scribbled on it and an application form to fill out through the half-moon in the glass. Jean filled out the form and waited—and waited—and waited. The children whined—and whined—and whined. There were no toys for them and few diversions.

PERSONALITY AND STYLE OF THE INTERVIEWER

After about an hour, an assistance payments worker came into the hall and shouted, "Number 20!" Jean meekly followed the worker into a room where four other workers sat at their desks, a room as dingy as the lobby, devoid of any of those objects that personalize an office.

There was a shaky coat rack, but the worker didn't suggest that she hang her wet coat there, so she simply left it on. Although the worker did not invite her to sit down, Jean assumed she was expected to do so. The worker did not smile, nor did she introduce herself. Jean remained "Number 20" in the worker's mind, and the worker was simply an animated function in Jean's mind. These two people were to talk with each other for at least half an hour, perhaps longer.

CLIENT EXPECTATIONS

Jean had been raised to believe that any interchange that took this long called for an exchange of names. Feeling that some deep social taboo was being violated and wanting to set it right, Jean introduced herself and made a few comments about the driving rain outside. The worker looked up briefly from the application form, which had been absorbing her attention since she sat down and mumbled, still unsmiling, "I'm Marie Klausner."

ATTITUDES AND VALUES OF HELPERS

The interview could have been conducted by a computer. In fact, Jean amused herself by turning Marie into a blinking, chiming computer in her fantasy as the questions and directives flew at her:

- How much money do you have in the bank?
- What is your bank account number?
- What is your Social Security number?
- What are your children's birth dates?
- Bring in verification of their birth dates.

- Bring in bank statements for the past twelve months.

And so on and on.

The worker was annoyed by the children's interruptions. After she filled out the intake form and listed the many verifications that Jean would have to bring back before she could be accepted for TANF, the worker finally asked if Jean was in immediate need. On hearing the she was, she gave her some food stamps. Frantic and depressed, Jean went back home in the rain, the children begging to stop for a hamburger each time they passed a fast-food restaurant.

Jean lived in a large city, and her welfare office reflected the poverty of the inner city. Jean's friend Marian, however, had a very different experience.

CASE STUDY

Marian

Marian lived in a smaller town where most people knew each other and the director of public welfare had some personal contact with many of the clients or their families. The director was supportive of workers' efforts to experiment with innovative ways of getting the job done. Although the department had limited funds, the workers pooled their resources to set up a modest child care center in the lobby. They brought in plants to create a more cheerful atmosphere, and when they couldn't convince the town council to paint the office, they held a raffle to buy paint and organized a painting party. Workers, clients, and members of the welfare advisory board painted the lobby themselves.

On the same rainy morning that Jean visited her welfare office, Marian came to this office to apply for TANF for herself and her child. The receptionist smiled at Marian when she came in and pointed out the rack where she could hang her coat. She took the children to the volunteer who cared for clients' children, and in a short time she escorted Marian to a worker's office. After introductions and a sociable comment about the weather, the worker asked Marian how she could help her and learned that she had come to apply for financial assistance because her husband had died recently.

ACTIVE LISTENING, EMPATHY

As she explained what benefits Marian was entitled to and what the application process involved, the worker, having learned that Marian's husband had died only a week ago, kept her emotional radar tuned to Marian's distress signals. The worker knew that her main job was to process an application for TANF; she also knew that a human being was in pain and might need solace on the way to getting financial support. She obtained the same kind of information that Jean's worker had gotten; yet she led Marian gently into the application process, taking time to let Marian talk about her grief when she needed to.

Why did Jean and Marian receive such different treatment from their respective workers? A comparison of Jean's and Marian's encounters illustrates some of the factors that shape a human service interview.

FOCUS

The focus of both interviews was to find out if the applicants were eligible for benefits and, if they were, to start the process of obtaining them. Both workers were clear about their primary purpose and did not allow other issues to distract them from the task. In that respect, they were on target. Marian's worker was skillful enough to achieve the primary goal while not ignoring the other needs of her client. Jean's worker, in her single-mindedness, accomplished her goal but with a high cost to her client's sense of self-worth.

CLIENT EXPECTATIONS

Jean's attitude about applying for welfare was shaped by all the negative publicity she had heard through the media and the grapevine. She came to the welfare office with a mental set of shame. The dingy, crowded, impersonal setting of the office heightened it. The interviewer was in no mood to reach out to Jean and put her at ease.

SPONSORSHIP OF THE INTERVIEW

Jean's worker was burned out. The entire office seemed demoralized. Demoralization is not inevitable, even in an organization with limited resources. The welfare office Marian went to was able to treat clients with respect and dignity because it was located in a small community where there was no sharp social division between the affluent and the poor. Most people knew each other, and the director and workers lived in the community and regarded their clients as "one of us" rather than as "one of them." The director was a warm and imaginative person who, working with limited resources, tried to bring out the best in workers and clients.

Both Jean and Marian were entitled to dignified treatment. Yet Jean went home with a hollow, angry sensation in the pit of her stomach. She had gone through what one sociologist has termed a "successful degradation ceremony" (Garfinkel, 1965). Marian, although still worried about a future with a diminished income and scared of loneliness, did not feel such degradation. She felt less alone and was reassured that the worker at the welfare office would process her claim as quickly as possible.

Interviewing skills are needed for many aspects of group work as well as for ongoing individual relationships. Before she began the school bully project, the worker described below interviewed teachers, parents, children, and the principal.

I N T E R V I E W

Madeleine K. Jacobson, Director of a Bully Project

Madeleine Jacobson, a licensed social worker in private practice, directed a Bully Project at an inner-city Catholic elementary school. Two senior students in the Regis College Social Work program did their internship with her in the project.

Madeleine has an MSW degree from the University of Chicago and has completed training at the Boston Psychoanalytic Institute. She started her private therapy practice when she had a family, because it gave her flexible hours so that she could combine family responsibilities and work. Yet the work is isolating, and she felt the need to get into some work that broadened her contact with the world. She became a part-time field instructor at Regis College, where she supervised two students.

Bully programs with school children began in Norway under the direction of Dan Olweus, who made major theoretical contributions to the program. Madeleine uses his theories, as well as behavior modification techniques, John Bowlby's attachment theory, and object relations theories.

In the wake of the student shootings at Columbine High School in Colorado and shootings at other schools, bully programs have been initiated in many schools in the United States. The two boys who did the shooting at Columbine had been bullied themselves.

The kind of bullying that children engaged in at the Catholic school where this project took place did not involve violent behavior such as carrying guns, sexual harassment, or physical assault. Catholic schools tend to expel children for that kind of behavior. The behavior that Madeleine observed was psychological bullying. Sometimes it involved a clique of children taunting a vulnerable child. The girls used gossip, exclusion, isolating, and rumor-spreading as their method of bullying. They would direct this behavior at girls who they viewed as more vulnerable. The boys made fun of each other openly.

Children cannot learn unless they feel safe. Unfortunately, many of our children do not come from positive, safe home environments and communities and therefore the school needs to be safer than homes. The presence of bullying indicates that the school is not a safe environment.

While school administrators may see the bully problem as a problem of several individual children, this program identifies the school as the client and looks at the whole system first. Everyone must be involved—the administration, teachers, parents, and even the custodial staff. All members must be committed to working towards a bully-free environment, which is then declared through posters, letters home, and within each class. The children need to know that bullies will not be tolerated.

After involving the entire system, the second phase of the project is for the social worker to go into each class on a continuous basis, ideally once a week. The goal is to inform the students about bullying and to distribute questionnaires about the existence of bullying. Writing assignments are then assigned on a variety of topics such as:

- Describe a bully situation that you have observed.
- Who are your heroes?
- What are your goals for the future?
- Describe your family and country of origin.

Children are told that privacy will be respected. The social worker can communicate with individual children via their written work, which leads to many students asking to talk with the social worker. Thus, children become self-referred clients. Of course, parental permission is required.

Students read their papers on a volunteer basis only. As they read, some of the other students engage in bullying behavior through taunts, snickers, and rudeness. The social worker uses this "in-the-moment" aspect of the process to help children see for themselves their own behaviors. The social worker maintains a position of neutrality and acceptance. She does not express disapproval, but tries to help the children explain their feelings behind their actions. Many of the children are impulsive, have never been spoken to about "how they feel," and welcome this new and strange opportunity. Many come from homes where bullying behavior is encouraged as manly, and an "eye for an eye" retribution is encouraged.

Bullies lack empathy. Therefore there are many lessons about empathy and what they can do about developing it. Obviously, in the lower grades these techniques are modified in accordance with developmental needs.

Once information about bully patterns is established, the social worker is free to use her creativity in devising smaller groups. For example, Madeleine developed a group of bullies from the seventh grade and told them they were to be in charge of explaining bullying to the lower grades and acting as a tribunal in which they could "hear bully problems" from other classmates. These bully children wanted to be the center of attention but lacked the necessary social skills to know how to channel their needs.

If racism appears to be behind many bully problems, the social worker can create programs to encourage awareness of cultural differences. In the school where Madeleine worked, there was some tension between Haitians, Hispanics, and whites. Both children and staff tended to deny racism. When asked about racism, one child said what she thought adults wanted to hear, "We're all God's children, and the color of our skin doesn't make any difference."

One exercise that the children enjoyed was a "Chicken Festival." Madeleine had asked the children to name some of the things that people say about Haitians or about white people. One child said, "White people can't cook chicken. Their chicken is all bloody." With the consent of the parents, Madeleine asked each child to bring in the best chicken that their parents cook. Children enjoyed tasting each other's chicken, and of course the white-cooked chicken wasn't bloody. Madeleine used this as an example of how people hold false ideas about each other. However, one white parent was furious at the assignment and wrote a scathing letter saying the idea was stupid and ridiculous.

Madeleine said the project was sometimes frustrating, but rewarding. When children develop some awareness of their emotions and feel secure and contained in their environment, they will have positive attachments with the school and their friends. Bullying does not exist in safe schools. Children who can develop a thinking process that includes self-awareness and empathy for others have less chance of becoming either victims or bullies.

STRUCTURE OF AN INTERVIEW

Like a story, an interview has a beginning, a middle, and an end. It takes place within a specific time frame. The span of interviews varies enormously, from a ten-minute hot-line conversation, to the more traditional "fifty-minute hour" at an agency, to an interview that could take an entire day (for example, when a worker places a child in a new foster home).

Unfortunately, there never seems to be enough time. The interviewer needs to tell the interviewee in advance what the time limits are so that both can use the time to the best advantage. Although it is difficult to know just when to move on to another topic or return to a previous one, the worker is on safest ground when being up front and open. For example:

- "I think we'd better spend a few minutes talking about John's summer plans because we only have one hour, and I know that the deadline for camp registration is April 12th."

- "I plan to catch the 5:10 train back to the city, so perhaps you'd like to use the time between now and 5:00 on any questions you have about the vocational tests you'll be taking on Monday."

There are various ways of looking at the stages of an interview. From a broad view, the interview has three stages: (1) **opening the interview,** starting to build rapport and making a contract; (2) exploring the issues and making an action plan; and (3) closing and reviewing the actions to be taken.

In actual practice, these phases blend together, and elements of each phase can be found in the others.

Stage 1: Opening the Interview and Building Rapport

At the first point of initial contact, two people begin to play out their expectations of each other and begin to develop a way of working together. The purpose of the interview is set by either the interviewer or the interviewee; most often it is a joint process. If the interviewee has asked for the interview, she or he generally takes the initiative, stating, for example, "I have come to find out about job training." Sometimes, even when the interviewee has requested help, the interviewer needs to find out exactly what *kind* of help is needed. If the interviewer has asked for this time, he or she takes the initiative in explaining its purpose: "Your foster child's teacher says that Ollie Belle isn't paying attention to her studies. I'd like to discuss this with you."

Building rapport is a crucial part of the beginning stages of interviewing. A warm-up period of small talk is one way to foster rapport and is particularly important with some ethnic minority clients for whom such periods of informal exchange are the cultural norm. Most people require only a short warm-up period and expect to get right to the business at hand.

It is particularly important to convey respect in this first interview. Begin to establish rapport with introductions and by shaking hands, and either use surnames or ask how clients prefer to be addressed. It might be insulting, for example, to call an older woman by her first name rather than use "Mrs., Miss, or Ms." before her last name. African Americans are particularly sensitive to being called by the wrong name because that has traditionally been a sign of disrespect, especially in the South. Yet a teenager might be more at ease on a first-name basis.

A first principle in all human service work, including interviewing, is to begin by exploring the agenda of the person who seeks help. The much-repeated advice in our training is, "*Begin where the client is.*" If the interviewee doesn't want to come at all, then beginning where the client is will involve dealing first with any feelings of resentment or entrapment.

MAKING THE CONTRACT

The interview begins by the interviewer finding out what the interviewee thinks the purpose of the interview is and what he or she feels about it. If the client's purpose is different from the agency's purpose or capacities or from what the interviewer has in mind, then interviewer and interviewee will be working at cross-purposes.

Opening the interview The first stage of an interview, when worker and client begin to play out their expectations of each other and develop a way of working together.

Those differences must be aired and negotiated. It is important for both people to understand clearly what might be accomplished in their time together and what the whole process may look like.

This process is called **building the contract**—the agreement two people make, whether verbal or written, about the purpose of their work together. There is a contract for the entire working relationship, which we discuss in the chapter on case management, and there is a contract for each interview. This contract helps to clarify what the interviewer is prepared to do and what the interviewee will have to do for him or herself.

If someone is applying for a benefit, such as food stamps, the purpose of the interview may be self-evident (although not necessarily; there may be other needs that the person is hesitant to admit to or other help for which he or she might be eligible). Once it is established, for example, that obtaining food stamps is the most pressing need, the beginning of the interview consists of the interviewer asking a few questions to establish whether the interviewee is potentially eligible. If, for example, the interviewee says that she is a college student, then the interviewer will save time for both of them by asking right away if the student meets a set of criteria. If not, there is no point in continuing. The interviewer then should politely explain the requirements, and ask the student if she would like to be referred to some other resource (or, if the student is interested, to some group that is seeking to improve food stamp benefits). Workers should also tell clients that they have the right to appeal the decision the worker has made.

Although most of us recoil from long, complex official forms, some forms are necessary. Yet an interview need not become machinelike. Sometimes the claimants already filled out the form while waiting to be interviewed. Then the interviewer can go over it, helping the interviewee provide additional answers. The worker can further explain the program, finding out if the interviewee needs other kinds of help.

If the form is to be filled out during their time together, an interviewer can use it as the basis for a structured conversation rather than as a script for a third degree. If information pertaining to a particular question on the form has already come out in the opening conversation, the question need not be asked again. If, however, the interviewer's time is limited and there are others waiting, then the interview will probably have to be more constricted. In general, workers should ask questions precisely as written *only* when the answers are needed for a very structured research project or for a medical history.

Consider how a food stamp application might be taken. Here is the beginning of an interview using the mechanical approach.

Name?

Address?

Who is in your household?

How much money do you have in the bank?

Do you have a checking account?

Do you have any insurance?

Building the contract   Making an agreement, whether verbal or written, about the purpose and goal of the work that the helpee and helper do together.

Any boats, camping trailers, land?

The following interview uses the more human approach. After the initial pleasantries, the interviewer says to the applicant, Guy LeBlanc:

> Mr. LeBlanc, the food stamp program has a lot of rules about who can get food stamps and who can't. I hope you qualify, since you must need them or you wouldn't be asking for them. Yet I have to know a lot about your living arrangements and your resources before I can determine if you are eligible. Could you tell me about who you live with, how you make your living, and things that you own, such as a car, bank account, et cetera?

This question is broad enough to set Mr. LeBlanc off on a discussion of his circumstances, from which you will probably be able to get most of the information you need. You can ask questions about the things he left out, but you have given Mr. LeBlanc initiative in the interview rather than making him feel as if he were on a witness stand.

The following two principles are useful guidelines for *all* stages of the interview: seeking concreteness and focusing on the here and now (immediacy).

SEEKING CONCRETENESS

Someone once said, "God resides in the details." It is life's details that are important, and a good interviewer knows how to go after those details. This is called *seeking concreteness* or *specificity of response*. When someone says, "She's an awful parent," you could ask them to clarify exactly what she does that is awful. In this way, you help the client to be clearer, get details about significant interactions and events, and make sure that you and the client understand each other's meanings.

To help an interviewee be more concrete, the interviewer can ask about specific examples or stories as a follow-up to a general response. If the interviewee says, "I really liked it when I first got here," you can ask, "Can you give an example of something you really liked?" Or, "What was most surprising about…?" "What was the worst disappointment in…?" (Martin, 2001, p. 179).

IMMEDIACY

The interview should focus on the present concerns of the interviewee rather than on past or future events or concerns. This characteristic is called *immediacy*. The concerns may involve the interviewee's life situation or something happening in the relationship between interviewer and interviewee. Following is an example of the former:

> INTERVIEWEE (separated from her husband for three months):   When he first told me that he was going to leave me, I was very angry, but now I'm managing by myself without his help.
>
> INTERVIEWER: You're really proud that you have managed by yourself.

This response focused on the interviewee's present feelings of pride in her ability to manage her life, the most important issue at the moment. If the interviewer had chosen to focus on the past, she might have said, "You were really angry when he first told you." Or, if the interviewer had chosen to focus on the future, she might have said, "In the future, you'll be glad it worked out this way" (Evans, Hearn, Uhlemann, & Iveg, 1979, p. 74). Both of those comments would have deflected the interviewee's attention from her main concern at the moment.

Stage 2: Exploring the Issues

The exploration stage is the main body of the interview, but much of the productivity will rest on the clarity of purpose and atmosphere established in the opening phase. If an interview concerns an application for some benefit, the main body of the interview will deal with establishing eligibility and processing the claim. If the interviewee is asking for help with employment, housing, child care, marriage, children's behavior, or emotional depression, then you need to learn more about the problem. Although workers tend to categorize clients into broad, often stereotypical, classifications (e.g., delinquent, retarded, permissive parent, culturally deprived, hard to reach, multiproblem), each person has a unique perception of his or her problem. The challenge for the interviewer is to ferret out the uniqueness so that it can be matched to the appropriate services and resources.

The principle of self-determination guides a worker to leave as much initiative as possible in the hands of the interviewee. Your job is not to *tell* people how to run their lives, but to help them discover the strengths in themselves and the alternatives or options they have. All of our questions, responses, and comments should be directed toward those goals.

QUESTIONS THAT HELP PEOPLE TALK

The techniques of the ethnographic interview, such as asking global questions, are useful in helping people to explore problems. **Open-ended questions** begin conversations but leave the choice of direction to the client.

If an interviewer asks a lot of closed-ended, or yes/no, questions, the interview becomes a question-and-answer period in which the interviewee passively responds. Experienced interviewers try to avoid asking too many questions, which can destroy a client's initiative. Asking the right question at the right time is an important interviewing skill. Beginning workers sometimes take refuge in the question-and-answer format as if it were a security blanket, perhaps fearing loss of control with a looser structure. One guideline to use in deciding how to ask a question is: The question should help to further the process of discovery, either of an interviewee's inner self or the outer world.

Even a question aimed at finding out if a person is eligible for a government benefit can, if combined with information, help interviewees understand the program and their place in it.

Open-ended questions Questions asked in such a way that they allow for a variety of responses.

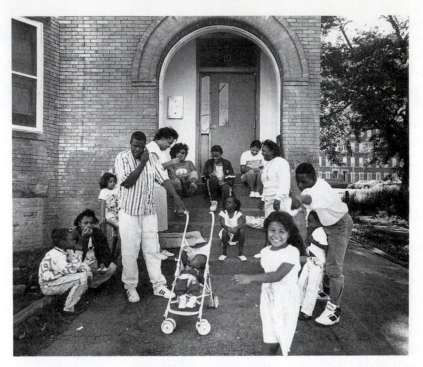

Counselors try to understand an interviewee's ideas in the context of his or her neighborhood. Then they assess the systems of support that the community can offer.

INTERVIEWER (to a TANF recipient who has applied for the job training program): Mrs. Leavitt, the job training program doesn't require a parent to enroll in it if she has a child age 2 or under. How old are your children?

MRS. LEAVITT: I have a 1-year-old.

INTERVIEWER: Then you don't need to apply, but you still can if you want to. How do you think the job training program might help you?

Some kinds of questions keep control in the hands of the interviewer; others give more freedom to the interviewee. The closed question allows for few options and gives minimal information.

CLOSED: Do you like your teacher?

OPEN: What's your teacher like?

CLOSED: Do you shop for bargains and use dried skim milk?

OPEN: It's hard to make a TANF grant stretch. How do you manage?

CLOSED: Do you get enough sleep with the new baby?

OPEN: How is the baby's schedule affecting you?

Another controlling question that is hardly ever helpful is the question "why?" Think about how your parents, teachers, and other authority figures frequently scolded by saying, "Why did you do that?" You probably answered, quite honestly, "I dunno," and the conversation ended. It is almost always perceived as a threatening question.

The **indirect question** gives the interviewee more options and elicits more insight than the direct question. It is phrased like a statement, without a question mark, but actually asks a question. Here are some examples:

DIRECT: What jobs have you held in the past?

INDIRECT: I'd be interested to hear about your previous jobs.

DIRECT: Has your new foster child adjusted well?

INDIRECT: I imagine a lot has happened since I placed Billy here. What kind of a week did you and he have?

Door openers, a term coined by Thomas Gordon (1970, pp. 47–49) are an invitation to say more about something the interviewee has brought up. Although sometimes done by questioning, door openers are best done in the form of an open-ended request for more information:

Tell me more.
I'm interested in hearing about that.

The concept of funnel sequences is another way of looking at ways to encourage interviewees to talk (France & Kish, 1995, p. 21). Funnel sequences begin with a broad probe or question, continue with reflection and possibly some open questions, then end with closed questions to fill any gaps in information you must gather.

Inverted funnel sequences take the opposite path. They begin with easily answered closed questions, then move to broader responses such as reflection and open questions. This technique is a good way to encourage a client to talk when the person is reluctant to speak with you. Here is an example of an inverted funnel sequence, used in an interaction with a 16-year-old who was hospitalized following a drug overdose suicide attempt. In response to an initial open question of "How are things going?" the patient said nothing and turned away from the interviewer. But he started to talk when the interviewer used the following inverted funnel sequence:

INTERVIEWER: Did Dr. Matthews see you this morning?

CLIENT: Mmhmm.

INTERVIEWER: Have they brought you breakfast?

CLIENT: Yeah. (Turning toward the interviewer with a disgusted look.)

INTERVIEWER: You didn't like the food.

CLIENT: It was awful. Everything was cold, and the fried eggs were all runny. It was almost as bad as that stuff they had me drink last night to make me throw up. I just want out of here.

Indirect question A question or statement that encourages the fullest possible expression of the interviewee's thoughts and feelings.

Door openers   An invitation to say more about something that the interviewee has brought up, preferably in the form of an open-ended request for information.

INTERVIEWER: You'd really like to go home.

CLIENT: But they're making me stay, even though I've told them I want to go home. This place is terrible. It's boring and there's nothing to do.

INTERVIEWER: What do you think would need to happen in order for Dr. Matthews to discharge you?

Initially, this client was reluctant to talk. But two easy-to-answer closed questions evoked short responses. Then two reflections elicited animated descriptions of thoughts and feelings. Finally, an open question led the interaction toward a discussion of positive change (France & Kish, 1995, p. 22).

FURTHERING RESPONSES

Furthering responses Responses that encourage clients to continue talking.

A number of techniques can be used to explore a problem. Often they can be used in combination. One skill, called **furthering responses,** encourages clients to continue talking (Hepworth & Larsen, 1987). These include:

1. *Physical attending.* This is part of active listening and involves being there physically.
2. *Silence* (when used to indicate thoughtful attention).
3. *Minimal verbal or nonverbal responses.* A minimal response such as an attentive look of interest, a nod of the head, or a verbal "uh-huh" is often all the encouragement the interviewee needs. Whatever is natural to the listener is usually appropriate as long as it does not interfere with the interviewee's message.
4. *Accent responses.* This involves repeating, in a questioning tone of voice or with emphasis, a word or short phrase that the client has just said. For example, "if a client says, 'I've really had it with the way my supervisor at work is treating me,' the practitioner might respond, 'Had it?' to prompt further elaboration by the client." (Hepworth & Larsen, 1987, p. 1000)

VERBAL FOLLOWING RESPONSES

There are a number of responses that let clients know they have been heard and understood and provide immediate feedback (Hepworth & Larsen, 1987). These are called *verbal following responses* and include paraphrasing or restating, clarifying, and reflecting.

Paraphrasing or restating Putting the interviewee's words in another form without changing the content in order to encourage the interviewee to go on.

Paraphrasing or Restating

Paraphrasing or restating what the interviewee has just said is similar to a minimal response in that its purpose is to let interviewees know their messages have been understood. They encourage clients to continue. There is literal restatement, such as:

INTERVIEWEE: I felt terrible.

INTERVIEWER: You felt terrible.

But there is paraphrasing or summarizing, such as:

> INTERVIEWEE: The baby cried a lot, and I've never taken care of a baby before. I just didn't know what to do.
>
> INTERVIEWER: It was a new experience and you were confused.

Clarifying

Clarifying goes beyond a minimal response. The interviewer now seeks further understanding of what has been said or tries to clarify for the interviewee something hard to express. A question designed to help the interviewer understand might be (1) I don't understand that very well. Could you explain it again? (2) Are you saying that…? or (3) Do you mean…?

The following is an example of clarification used to help interviewees articulate their thoughts:

> INTERVIEWEE: When the baby cries, I feel like I'm falling apart. I don't know what to do, I'm so mixed up. I want to be a good father, but I don't know how to. It's all so confusing.…
>
> INTERVIEWER: The baby's crying seems to scare you. You feel mixed up and unsure of how to care for your baby.

Clarifying
Seeking further understanding of what has been said in an interview.

Reflecting

Compared with restating, which deals with what the interviewee *said,* **reflecting** deals with what an interviewee *feels.* Adding nothing of their own, interviewers say what they empathically sense the interviewee might be feeling.

> INTERVIEWEE: There's sure a lot of red tape I have to go through to apply for welfare, isn't there? Why can't you people get together? I go from one person to another answering the same old questions all over again.
>
> INTERVIEWER: I guess you feel like you're getting the runaround, don't you? Are you pretty mad at us by now?

Reflecting   An interviewer response that puts into words what the interviewer thinks the interviewee might be feeling.

OTHER WAYS OF RESPONDING

Some responses are not specifically geared to drawing the client out but can be useful when timed correctly and given sensitively. However, some of them are controversial. They include giving information, encouraging and reassuring, suggesting, advising, confronting, and interpreting.

Giving Information

Clients need to know everything we can tell them about the services and benefits to which they are entitled. This information should be given when clients are ready for it, in a way that doesn't overwhelm or confuse them.

Encouraging and Reassuring

Encouraging and reassuring responses are too often used insensitively. In our everyday relationships, we often encourage our friends by saying, "Oh sure, you can

Encouraging and reassuring
Providing a message of hopefulness in an attempt to inspire confidence, often without regard to what a person is actually feeling.

win the race," "…you can get that job," "…you can get her to go out with you." Such statements may not always be helpful, especially if they are not true. We say such things because we can't think of anything else or because we don't have the time, emotional energy, or courage to explore the real possibilities.

Such seemingly reassuring statements can actually leave clients feeling even more frightened if they don't feel strong or qualified. We all need permission to feel weak and vulnerable and to anticipate failure, and sometimes we need someone to remind us of our strengths. It takes a great deal of sensitivity, however, to recognize when encouragement is appropriate.

The following is one example of helpful reassurance given by a foster parent to a biological parent:

> BIOLOGICAL PARENT: I always felt low. Like I was kind of an outcast. I don't know why. This is just my nature…. I know people think I'm a drunkard. I was in a mental hospital for two weeks, and this had a bad effect on me. So I felt both insane and poor. I had no money. And you don't look nice, and you don't feel nice, you don't perform well.
>
> FOSTER PARENT: …anybody who has done what you did and let your children go is a big person.
>
> BIOLOGICAL PARENT: Well, I'm glad you feel this way.
>
> FOSTER PARENT: And you yourself said you felt this way.
>
> BIOLOGICAL PARENT: I don't think my child would have ever made it to college. At least she has the chance…. (Mandell, 1973, pp. 167–168)

The following is an example of reassurance that definitely can't help anyone cope with reality:

> INTERVIEWEE: I'm feeling awful about my job. Nothing seems to work right.
>
> INTERVIEWER: Oh, don't worry. We all have job problems. It will work out all right.

Suggesting

Suggesting is a mild form of advice. If a suggestion is made tentatively, without any coercion, it can pose alternatives that the interviewee may not have been aware of.

> INTERVIEWER (to a college student):   Since you are a junior with a 3.0 average and need money, you might consider the co-op program, where you could work for a regular salary and get six credits.

Advising

Giving advice assumes that one person knows what is best for another, and that is a risky assumption. An interviewer should be cautious when **advising** a client. When an interviewee asks for advice, the interviewer should first find out what the interviewee *already* thinks about the problem and what alternative paths are being considered. This process by itself may help the interviewee to clarify his or her problem.

Suggesting Giving a mild form of advice, generally made tentatively.

Advising Telling a client what to do. Used with caution, if at all, in interviews, because it incorrectly assumes that one person knows what is best for another.

Although many experienced interviewers try to avoid giving direct advice, when they feel it is appropriate, they do so tentatively. They make it clear that their feelings won't be hurt if the interviewee rejects it. Then they ask for feedback on what the interviewee thought about it. The following is an example of an interviewer talking with a student who is considering dropping out of college because he finds his workload too heavy and boring:

INTERVIEWER: Maybe next semester you might want to take a lot of courses in your major with teachers whom you like and pick up the rest of your required courses later. You seem so discouraged about school that some "fun" courses might get you interested again. What do you think?

Confronting

One of the most emotionally loaded debates about interviewing centers on the issue of the usefulness and timing of confrontation. **Confronting** is a tactic used to call interviewees' attention to discrepancies, inconsistencies, or self-destructive tendencies in their words or behavior. It aims to help interviewees view their behavior in a different light, perhaps unmasking distortions, rationalizations, or evasions. Confrontation can be used gently, with a great deal of empathy, or it can be used in a cruelly assaultive way. There are many gradations along the gentle-to-harsh continuum. Here is an example of a gentle confrontation:

Confronting
A tactic used by the interviewer to point out to the interviewee discrepancies or inconsistencies in an interviewee's words or behavior.

INTERVIEWEE: I don't mind that my husband insults me and says I look like a fat pig [tears in her eyes].

INTERVIEWER: You say you don't mind, yet you have tears in your eyes. Most people I know mind a lot when someone insults them. I know I do.

This is a mild confrontation, pointing out the discrepancy between the client's words and behavior. It was followed by a supportive statement, which gives permission to be upset and is concrete and descriptive ("You have tears in your eyes") rather than abstract and judgmental ("You must be a masochist"). It "universalizes" the issue by helping a person realize her feelings are common to many people.

Some counselors routinely use a high level of confrontation and intrusiveness, justifying it as a high-risk but high-yield method. One study, however, declared that this justification is a myth (Lieberman, Yalom, & Miles, 1973). It found that highly challenging and confrontive encounter group leaders were destructive in their impatient pressuring of clients to change and ignored the need to individualize treatment. Another researcher warned against the assumption that everyone benefited by "letting it all hang out." Some may, indeed, need help "tucking it all in" (Parloff, 1970, p. 203).

Another study showed that counselors whose confrontations focused on the clients' weaknesses were less effective than those who focused on strengths (Berenson & Mitchell, 1974). It also showed that more effective counselors initiated sensitive confrontation more than did less effective ones.

Some human service workers who work with street people report that a more confrontational style is expected and appreciated on the streets. A human services professor in Minneapolis says, "On the streets here, it is known as 'tough love.'... Many of our students are street people. They understand 'tough love,' and they believe it works" (D. Foat, personal communication, 1982).

Interpreting

Interpreting
A form of response that speculates on the meaning of an interviewee's statement or behavior.

Interpreting is one of the most controversial responses. It originated in psychoanalytic practice. Client-centered, gestalt, and some existential theories avoid this technique. Ethnographic interviewers would also not use it because it puts the interviewer in the position of being the expert:

> Whatever information the client offers must be taken at face value, even if it seems outrageous or even false. Careful follow-up of the cover terms offered will quickly reveal if this is the case. It will also demonstrate to the client that the interviewer takes the discussion seriously, almost literally, and that dissembling will be difficult to sustain. (Green & Leigh, 1989, p. 9)

Others believe that interpretation is essential. They argue that it "encourages clients to see their problems from a different perspective, with the desired effect of opening up new possibilities for remedial courses of action" (Hepworth & Larsen, 1987, p. 1008).

The other responses we've described, if done correctly, do not go beyond what the interviewee says or feels. Interpretation, however, *speculates* on what the words might *actually* mean. If the interviewee accepts a response as an accurate interpretation, it can be helpful. However, the "expert's" interpretation is often rejected with irritation, or worse, swallowed whole without reflection. The interviewee's response is the best guide to deciding whether a worker's interpretation has been helpful. The following is an example:

> INTERVIEWEE: I don't know why the baby's crying makes me feel so helpless. My mother always knew what to do when my baby brother cried.
>
> INTERVIEWER: When you compare yourself to your mother, you feel inferior to her.
>
> INTERVIEWEE: Maybe that's what it is.

SELF-DISCLOSURE

Interviewers often have a hard time deciding when they should reveal elements in their personal lives and attitudes. At one time, that was considered strictly a no-no. Now, most researchers and helpers believe that appropriate self-disclosure can be supportive to the interviewee and creates a more honest relationship. Most of us find it easier to share thoughts and feelings with someone who is willing to risk similar sharing. When the interviewer does this, she is modeling desirable sharing behavior and showing that she, too, is human.

The guideline for deciding when the worker should disclose something about her personal life is the extent to which it brings clarity rather than burdening the client with the interviewer's concerns. *Sharing can illustrate the universality of human concerns.* The interviewers who spend too much time discussing their families, hobbies, or worries are obviously more interested in themselves than in the client. The following are two examples of an appropriate use of sharing personal experience:

INTERVIEWER: You seem to be wondering if I can understand the problems you're having with your foster child. My wife and I cared for a friend's child for a couple of years while she was ill. I know that's not exactly the same as your situation, but the child did show some of the same problems you're having. I'm not sure that means I can understand the problems you're having, but I'd like to try.

INTERVIEWER: I just listened to you telling how hard you worked on the paper— reading books on research and style, spending days in the library, and doing everything in your power to do a good job. Then you described how the teacher scribbled sarcastic comments all over the paper and ridiculed it in front of the class. You apologized for doing such a bad job and say you feel like a failure. Yet, while listening to you, I found myself feeling indignant about the teacher's behavior. Didn't you feel some anger yourself?

Rather than pretend to an interviewee that you have no values or that you agree with the interviewee's values when you don't, it is better to be honest. This leaves both you and the interviewee free to hold on to values that are important without needing to impose them on each other. The following is an example of an appropriate use of disclosing values:

COUNSELOR: Can you try to tell me what you see as the worst problems in this marriage?

HUSBAND: Yes, that's easy. She's out fooling around with her art groups all the time and the house is a mess. I don't have clean socks and underwear in the morning and dinner is never ready on time.

WIFE: You never say anything nice to me, you never talk to me, and now that I finally, after twenty years, found interests and friends of my own, you resent it and you're continually carping at me.

COUNSELOR (to husband):   It's important to you that your laundry be done, the house cleaned, and dinner prepared when you come home.

HUSBAND: Damn right it is! That's what wives are supposed to do.

COUNSELOR: I have a hard time with this because I do not agree with your definition of a wife's obligations. However, I do see that in your view, she is not meeting the terms of the marriage contract under which you are operating (Okun & Rappaport, 1980, p. 185).

The counselor expressed her views without deriding or punishing the husband. This seemed to help both husband and wife begin to acknowledge and evaluate some of their own values and beliefs about sex roles and marriage.

AUTHORITARIAN LEADS AND RESPONSES

Although giving advice may *sometimes* be helpful, authoritarian leads and responses in interviewing are *never* helpful. They are generally harmful because they do not take the feelings and thoughts of the interviewee into account. They assume that the interviewer is superior, which makes the interviewee feel inferior. These leads and responses include:

- Urging
- Threatening
- Moralizing
- Contradicting
- Arguing
- Commanding
- Scolding
- Punishing
- Criticizing
- Denying
- Disapproving
- Rejecting
- Ridiculing
- Putting words in someone's mouth

When the interviewer takes a high and mighty moral tone, the interviewee has a choice of mindless submission or stubborn defiance. Either way, the interviewee has not been helped to grow in awareness or independence. We have all been lectured to or preached to at some time in our lives, and it's a safe bet that we have resented it! The following are some examples:

INTERVIEWER: I thought you were smart enough to know you should use birth control.

INTERVIEWER: Stealing is wrong, so the teacher had a right to suspend you.

Stage 3: Closing

The crucial final stage of the interview takes thought and practice. There are three important principles for a constructive closing:

1. Both people should be clear about when the interview is coming to a close and accept the time limitation. The interviewer usually is the one who takes more responsibility for closing.

2. No new material should be discussed toward the end because the closing should summarize what has already been discussed. If new or unfinished material is brought up, another interview should be scheduled to discuss it.

Sometimes a client is not ready to talk about controversial or emotion-laden subjects until the last moments. There is no hard-and-fast rule that says you should never continue an interview longer than planned, and sometimes it makes sense to do so. Usually, however, you will have other things you must do, so if the material is not about an immediate crisis, schedule another interview. If you are constantly looking at your watch, you are only half available. Consider this interchange and its analysis:

INTERVIEWER: You know, Helen, I'm very glad we had this talk today. We'll have to stop now, as I've got to catch my bus.

INTERVIEWEE: I still haven't told you what Dad said when he came to see me last week. I didn't know he was coming, and I was in the middle of…

INTERVIEWER: I'm glad you want to talk about that, but if you continue now, I won't be listening very well because I'll be worried about missing the bus. So why don't we meet on Thursday at the same time and discuss this the way we both want to. Is Thursday all right? OK, see you then.

You had long wondered whether Helen would ever mention her father; in fact, you had even hoped she would. Therefore, when she finally did, you were torn between the desire to hear her out and the necessity to catch your bus. However, knowing that missing the bus would complicate the rest of the day, and suspecting that you might feel that Helen was to blame, you decided it was preferable to stop and arrange a new appointment (Benjamin, 1981, pp. 29–30).

3. Time at the end of an interview should be used to review material you have both covered, making sure each of you has the same understanding and knows clearly what the next steps will be. Either person can summarize what has been said in their time together, giving the other a chance to correct or clarify any point. Both should agree on what is to happen next. If any commitments have been made, they should be written down so that both remember the date and time of that appointment for testing, the class in parenting, the senior citizen social, or whatever.

The general rule of thumb in the closing stage is that there should be enough time left at the end so that the interviewees do not feel rushed but rather feel that they have had a chance to express themselves fully.

RECORDING

Many workers would much rather spend their time on interviews than on recording interviews. Yet, because memory is notoriously unreliable, human service agencies would be in deep trouble if they did not require workers to record interviews.

1. *Recording provides continuity from one worker to another and from one session to the next.* Suppose as a worker in a halfway house you learned from Mary that

she planned to go home next week and needed to be driven to a job interview from her home on Wednesday of that week. If you did not record this, the staff member who came on duty after you might not learn of these plans, and Mary would not get to the interview.

2. *Recordings of interviews can document progress or lack of it in each particular situation.* If you are working with a woman in a nursing home who is losing her memory, your periodic notations about her mental state help to assess whether her memory loss is getting worse over time, staying about the same, or getting better. Or suppose you need to show your funding source the quality and quantity of the services you have given clients. Only if you have kept careful records of referrals and interviews can you do that.

3. *Recording provides documentation of a client's eligibility for service.* If done according to previously agreed on and uniform procedures, recording can also be used for research and evaluation of programs and for researching the history of programs.

4. *Recording can provide important evidence in legal suits.* Workers who have been accused of negligence in child abuse cases have been able to prove, through records of visits and phone contacts, that they had done everything in their power to prevent the abuse.

5. *Recording is used by some agencies as a therapeutic tool.* In a few states, patients and ex-patients of mental hospitals are permitted to read their own records. "One state mental hospital in Washington has for several years allowed all patients to examine their own records and has found that policy to be therapeutic." (Ennis & Emery, 1978, p. 177)

Recording and Privacy

Even when an agency does not allow clients to read the record, a curious and ingenious client may sneak a look. A poignant example of the devastating effect this can have on a person's self-esteem is given in a *New Yorker* account of a mental hospital patient, Sylvia Frumkin:

> On March 20th, Sylvia Frumkin started therapy with Dr. Sheila Gross, a child psychiatrist at the Jamaica Center. That afternoon, when she arrived to see Dr. Gross..., she saw a sheaf of papers on the doctor's desk. The top piece of paper was the first page of Mrs. Schwartz's report. Sylvia has always been able to read upside down. She was stunned by the first line on the page—the one that read "She is a tall, unattractive girl." She decided to test Dr. Gross, and asked her to read the page to her. Dr. Gross glanced at Mrs. Schwartz's report, read aloud, "She is a tall girl, not unattractive," and then changed the subject. Although Sylvia went to see Dr. Gross once a week from the end of March to the end of June, she didn't trust her, because the doctor hadn't been honest with her. (Sheehan, 1981, p. 66)

When workers know that interviewees can read their records, they are likely to be more careful about what they write. They are much less prone to make global evaluative statements such as "The child is in danger of neglect" and more likely to make concrete descriptive statements such as "The fourth-floor windows do not have window guards and the mother has four small children to look after so cannot always keep watch over each child to prevent them from falling out the window. The landlord has not provided enough heat, so the mother turns on the gas stove for heat. This is a fire hazard."

Instead of saying, "The child appeared malnourished," a more verifiable statement would be: "Medical exam showed the child to be fifteen pounds below the normal weight for that age and anemic."

You should strive in your recording to let a future reader see what you saw. Concrete, descriptive statements are not only more accurate, but they also force workers to be more precise, avoiding moralistic, judgmental statements. Some workers discuss with clients what they think should go into a record, using this as a tool to help clients articulate their problems and progress.

Kinds of Recording

NOTE TAKING

The simplest form of recording is taking notes during an interview to help remember what was said. This should be done as unobtrusively as possible so as not to disturb the interviewee's flow of conversation. Some workers prefer not to take notes, believing that it impedes the spontaneous flow of conversation. The number of notes you take will vary, depending on the nature of the interview and how well you trust your memory. An interview to determine eligibility for a government benefit may require a great deal of note taking, and a less structured interview about a personal problem may require less precision.

PROCESS RECORDING

Detailed recording of everything said in an interview is time-consuming but helpful to a beginning worker learning to improve interviewing skills. On occasion, an experienced worker who needs consultation on a challenging case also finds the method helpful. The same purpose can be achieved, probably more effectively, by tape-recording or videotaping interviews. However, such electronic aids are not available in most agencies, and they may also be intimidating to a client. If used, the client must give informed consent.

Process recording has the advantage of giving a worker practice in remembering an interview. It is read primarily by a supervisor in preparation for supervisory conference. It should be summarized before being placed in the permanent record. Ethnographic interviewers recommend some process recording for discussion and training purposes.

SUMMARY REPORTS

Most case recording is done in summary form. Because a summary includes only the most important facts, the worker must organize and select the material carefully under appropriate headings. Summary recording can take many forms: a summary of one interview; a periodic summary of case activity; an intake summary; a transfer summary of the entire case when one worker turns the case over to another worker; a referral summary when the case is to be transferred to another agency; a closing summary when the case is to be closed; and specialized summaries, such as social histories and court reports.

Summary recording contains the information and inferences that the worker obtains from interviews with clients. These inferences are based not only on data collected in the interview but also on the worker's experience, insight, knowledge, and theoretical framework.

OTHER FORMS OF RECORDING

Other forms of recording include the following:

1. *Assessment summary.* An **assessment summary** is an analysis of the observations and information that the worker has obtained through interviews.
2. *Intervention plan.* An **intervention plan** contains the decision for intervention or nonintervention and the methods of intervention. It is based on the assessment analysis. It could also be called "goals" or "objectives." Ideally, the worker and the client decide on the intervention plan together.
3. *Goal-oriented recording.* A **goal-oriented recording** is a specialized form of summary recording used especially in government agencies that are concerned about accountability and effectiveness. It is sometimes used in agencies where setting goals is an especially critical part of the work, as in foster care agencies where foster children cannot be allowed to drift without a permanent plan, or in work with the mentally disabled to help workers assess progress in an individualized service plan.
4. *Computerized recording.* Some agencies have introduced **computerized recording** to store essential facts on each case. This is often done to standardize information for research projects or for reporting to funding sources such as the government. It is also used when each worker has to write daily behavioral records for large numbers of clients.

SUMMARY

1. The interview is defined as an interaction between people that has a consciously planned purpose, structure, and goal and requires specific communication skills.

Assessment summary A summary recording that analyzes the observations and information that the worker has obtained through interviews.

Intervention plan Specific acts or words aimed at moving persons or programs toward their goal.

Goal-oriented recording A specialized form of summary recording that focuses on the goals in a case and the proposed methods of reaching those goals.

Computerized recording Recording in a computer contacts with, and information about, clients.

2. Important elements of all interviews include the location or setting; the personality, expectations, cultural background, and style of both the interviewer and the interviewee; agency sponsorship; and the attitudes and values of the interviewer. All of these are interrelated.

3. The structure of the interview includes three stages: opening, exploring the issues, and closing.

4. During the opening phase, the interviewer and interviewee work out a formal or informal contract to plan their work together.

5. The exploratory stage involves negotiating the contract, which clarifies what the interviewer and interviewee agree to work on together.

6. In the closing stage, material covered in the interview, as well as future action that was decided on, should be reviewed.

7. Attitudes that are essential for good interviewing include active observing, physical attention, and active listening.

8. Important values include empathy, warmth, respect, and genuineness.

9. Recording interviews is important for continuity of work between workers, for helping the worker remember essential facts, and for legal reasons.

10. Forms of recording include note taking, process recording, summary reports, diagnostic summary and treatment plans, goal-oriented recording, and computerized recording.

DISCUSSION QUESTIONS

1. *Humanizing the eligibility interview.* Obtain an application form for food stamps or TANF and study the form with the goal of humanizing the interview. How can you ask questions that will give the interviewee some initiative in the interview? How can you keep some warmth and genuineness in the interview? How can you get the information you need and, at the same time, make the clients feel that they are important and deserving of respect? After studying the questions and deciding on your strategy, role-play the interview with someone, and complete the application form. After the interview, ask the interviewee for feedback on the strengths and weaknesses of your interview.

2. *Active observing.* Two students should go together to a railroad station, a store, the street, or around the campus with a notebook. Observe for fifteen minutes. Then write up a one-page summary of the observation. Bring it to class without conferring with each other. Note the differences in the pair of observations.

3. *Analyzing an observation.* In the presences of several other people—on a bus, in a subway, in a waiting room, or at a party—observe people's behavior

closely. Note the relationship of elements in the environment to behavior and the interrelationships among people. Make notes on your observations, write them up, and discuss them with other students.

4. *How well can you listen?* One student takes the role of listener and another of talker, and a third student observes. For three minutes, the talker speaks about any topic she or he chooses. Then the listener repeats what has been heard. The observer judges how accurately the listener has heard the speaker. Switch roles until each has had a chance to be talker, listener, and observer.

5. *Asking questions.* Decide on some information you want from another person. First, ask the person six controlling or closed-ended questions and write down the answers. Next, ask six noncontrolling or open-ended questions about the same subject and write down the answers. Which questions gave you more information? Talk to the interviewee about how he or she felt about the two kinds of questions.

6. *Learning to deal with anger.* Two students role-play and one student observes an interview in which the interviewee imagines being very angry with the interviewer, feeling the anger as genuinely as possible and expressing it heatedly. For two or three minutes, the interviewer should react defensively; then for two or three minutes the interviewer should react empathetically. Both interviewer and interviewee should observe and contrast the difference in reactions to the two kinds of responses. The interviewer should note how he or she felt about the angry attack and how the two different responses felt. The interviewee should note how the two interviewer responses felt. The observer should note carefully the nature of the feelings expressed by the two role-players, as well as nonverbal behavior that gives clues to feelings. Change roles so that each person has an opportunity to play all the roles (Hammond, et al., 1977, pp. 202–203).

7. *Dealing with a "helpless" person.* In a group, ask a volunteer to play the role of Mrs. Jones, an interviewee. All but Mrs. Jones close their eyes and imagine they are in an office and Mrs. Jones is seeing them for the first time. Their job is to help Mrs. Jones. She sits down (adopting a slightly helpless tone of voice and a dramatic presentation): "I am so glad you have time to see me. You are absolutely my last hope! I can just tell you will be able to help me. I've been to four other places, and they all have waiting lists, or no time, or just were not interested. I am feeling absolutely desperate and I was so relieved when you could see me right away! The others did not understand me at all; they didn't even take the time to listen to my difficulty; I only need someone to help me sort out the problem and I am sure you can do that. I am grateful that you are spending time with me." Change roles so that each person has an opportunity to play all the roles (National Center for Child Abuse and Neglect, 1979).

WEB RESOURCES FOR FURTHER STUDY

Interviewing in Social Work
www.questia.com/Index.jsp?CRID=interviewing_in_social_work

The online library called Questia.com contains a list of nine books on social work interviewing, plus related resources.

Social Work Skills Demonstrated: Beginning Direct Practice CD-ROM with Student Manual

by Judith Sevel, Jim P. Cummins, and Cesar Madrigal. Boston: Allyn & Bacon, 1999.

This CD-ROM is designed as a practical guide to teaching basic 21counseling skills. It offers video segments showing three different social worker–client interactions. The student can view the video, stop the action and respond to questions, look up references, or obtain more in-depth information about each skill segment. Common pitfalls are noted for each skill set, as well as examples of appropriate and inappropriate uses of skills and outcomes.

CHAPTER 9

Case Management/
Counseling

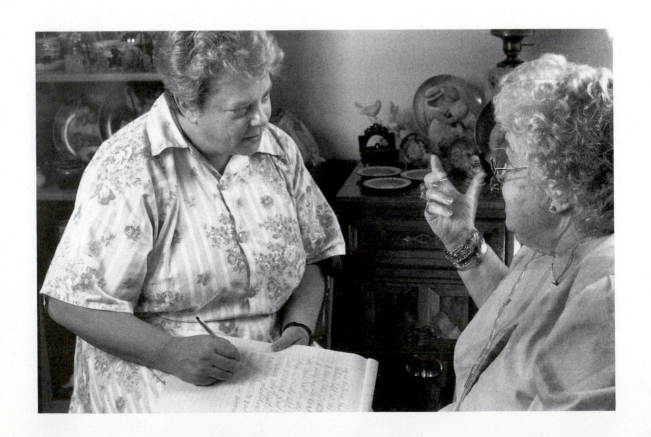

Now that we have read about the philosophy and techniques of the interview process we can look at the goals and steps of the casework process. Although agencies assign many different job titles to those who do this kind of human service intervention, common threads run through all their direct-service work.

We choose to refer to all of these workers by the generic title case manager/counselor. You will find workers doing the same types of tasks who are called family resource workers, advocates, social brokers, and even therapists or social workers. Whatever their title, these workers help clients to find and use resources that aim at alleviating their painful situation.

Problems are an integral part of life. Although the people facing a troubling divorce or the loss of a long-held job may feel alone in their pain, they are in fact facing the ordinary problems that are likely to occur in most of our lives. Human service workers help them release their strong emotions, increase their understanding of themselves and their situation, make important decisions, and implement the decisions once made.

To do this important work, they help clients break down big tasks into small steps, refer them to specialized agencies and income maintenance programs, model appropriate problem-solving behavior, and offer them emotional support.

As we read about the work that has been done by Carmen Mejia in her three case manager/counselor positions, we can see how she prepares for a case by reviewing both objective and subjective background data. Then, in concert with the client, she works to build a supportive relationship, negotiates a working contract, decides on priority problems, and creates and follows through on an action plan. If the person is in crisis, she uses a more time-limited set of techniques to help reestablish an equilibrium so that he or she can benefit from a more thorough casework process.

Finally, we learn about the ways in which case managers/counselors seek evaluative feedback on their work by using both formal and informal evaluation techniques.

Since the phenomenal upsurge in managed health care programs, case manager/counselors have had to master a whole new system with its unique language and regulations. We provide a brief background to managed care and a glimpse into its jargon, assets, and liabilities.

Reading this excerpt from a human service student's journal is a very appropriate way to begin a discussion of case management/counseling:

> I was having a real hard time studying and I was sure I was going to flunk my courses. I couldn't concentrate because my family was going through a divorce. I felt like I was being pulled apart by my parents. Who was I supposed to be loyal to? I knew I was getting

to depend on cocaine too much. I was stoned most of the time. I figured I better talk to someone soon before I blew my stack. I started asking my friends and my dorm supervisor for the name of a good therapist. People would ask me if I wanted to see a psychiatrist, a psychologist, a social worker, a family therapist, a drug and alcohol counselor, or what. I'd ask what the difference was but no one gave me a clear answer. So they didn't know and I didn't know! I felt more confused than when I began looking for help.

Thus far in this book you have met many human service workers. The majority of them were delivering direct services and spending most of their day working one-on-one with clients. Although doing similar work, they were likely to be referred to variously as:

- Case workers
- Social workers
- Counselors
- Advocates
- Therapists
- Case managers
- Clinicians
- Therapists

All this semantic fuzziness can be confusing to the client who must figure out whom to go to with a problem. And a worker searching the job listings in the newspaper or a web site can never tell from the title of the position exactly what tasks or problem areas it will include. The general public, accustomed to name brands, finds it difficult to understand how a middle-aged woman with a doctorate in psychology and a young man with an associate's degree in human services can both assert that they do "counseling."

In an effort to make job titles uniform, some professionals in the human service field have suggested that a distinction in title should be made according to how much a human service worker deals with highly charged emotional material rather than with the ordinary problems of daily life. They might say:

> "A social worker or therapist who has an advanced degree helps clients deal with deep-seated intrapsychic problems. A case manager or counselor (a less academically trained person) helps clients make decisions and then use social resources to implement them."

But we don't think that is a sensible distinction! *All human service workers, regardless of their backgrounds, job titles, or their clients' problems, must inevitably deal with inner emotions as well as external pressures.* Of course, with more study, experience, and training, a clinician can work more effectively with the deep emotions that surround problems.

Human service problems stem from the interaction of biological, emotional, and environmental stresses. If we ignore one set of forces, we get a lopsided view of a problem. And lopsided views lead to inadequate interventions.

For example, Timothy, a counselor in a residential prison-diversion program, has been asked by Barry, one of the residents, for a change of roommates. Before the counselor began to juggle rooms to accommodate Barry's request, he encouraged him to clarify the problem he was having with his present roommate. Timothy asked Barry about:

1. His expectations of his present roommate and what he thought his roommate's expectations were of him.

2. The similarities and differences in their habits, routines, and lifestyles.

3. The extent to which they both tolerated differences in styles.

4. The methods of conflict resolution they had already tried when they had a disagreement.

5. The stresses of study, family, work, or social life that may have been aggravating their problem.

After several conversations with the two men, some separately and some together, Timothy suggested that the tension between them might lessen if they set up a more workable system for cleanup. He offered to help them design a chore chart. They also agreed to make some mutually acceptable rules about playing the radio and going to bed. Through their sessions, one of the young men realized that some of his anger at his roommate probably stemmed from his past irritations with his brother and that, in fact, there were many parts of living together that he enjoyed. They agreed to try to use the chore chart and a few rules they both could agree on for two weeks. They also agreed to check in with Timothy for ten minutes each day. Thus, both young men found possible solutions to a relationship problem that at first seemed insurmountable.

There might have been other root causes for the tension. Perhaps Barry brought home a great deal of anger from his job and that was the primary source of tension between the roommates. If that had been the case, Timothy could refer him to a vocational counselor and a youth employment agency to help him change jobs or cope better with the one he had.

Although the counseling assignment of beginning human service workers might involve helping clients find and use resources, they should never lose sight of the fact that a client's unexplored feelings can subtly sabotage even the simplest solution.

ALL PROBLEMS ARE SERIOUS YET ORDINARY

Some people assert that the differences in the roles of professional helpers lie in the gravity of the problems they are assigned. But this is also an oversimplification. Human problems can never be divided up on a scale ranging from very serious to less serious and then be parceled out to different workers.

All problems appear overwhelming and unique to the people who have them and to the workers who deal with them. However, Laura Epstein (1980, 1992), in

Task-focused casework
A method of helping a person with a problem by focusing on the immediate priorities of the client and the small steps involved in realizing, or seeking to realize, the ultimate goal.

discussing her concept of **task-focused casework,** argues that just the reverse is true. In reality, most human problems are mundane and ordinary. No one goes through life without facing many serious, painful problems. Someone we love will die or become disabled, someone we need will leave us, barriers will be thrown up in our paths at many junctures. In making this surprising assertion, Epstein does not mean to trivialize human problems or suggest they are easily overcome. She is simply pointing out that all human service problems have similar characteristics:

The person lacks the specific resources to alleviate a painful situation.

The person lacks the skills to cope with or overcome a painful situation.

The difficulty of a problem-solving process depends on how well the necessary techniques and resources can be mustered. All human service workers are likely to encounter a variety of life's problems. On a first fieldwork assignment, for example, you might be coaching a basketball team in a suburban after-school program. That might seem like a pretty simple assignment until the day you take one of the youngsters home and are told that her mother has just been critically injured in a car accident.

We will resist the temptation to offer simple definitions for the titles and roles human service workers carry, and we urge you to tolerate a certain amount of confusion in the titles and roles themselves. In the rest of this chapter, the term "case manager/counselor" will be used. But everything we say could apply to any mental health worker regardless of the title a particular agency chooses to use.

Let us listen in on a conversation with a counselor named Carmen Mejia. In the eleven years since she graduated from college, she has been employed by three different agencies. In each she has been assigned a different title and has worked with a different population. First we will read about her current position. Then she will re-create a scene from each of her two previous jobs.

INTERVIEW

Carmen Mejia, Family Resource Worker, Coordinated Approach to Partnership in Parenting (CAPP)*

I'm really excited about talking about my current job. I've been here for four years, but my position keeps changing. I was hired as a foster care worker on a special grant from the Community Council Foundation. The child-protection social workers at the Department of Social Services (DSS) designed my position and then fought to get it funded. There were never enough appropriate places to send children when they had to be taken out of their homes on a temporary basis.

*For further insights into permanency planning projects, see Hampton, Senatore, and Guillotta (1998); Kelly and Blythe (2000); Kinney et al. (1998); Lloyd and Bryce (1984); and Schneider (1991).

My first assignment was to recruit more foster parents, especially for Latino children. When children can't speak English or they are dark-skinned, it is especially hard to place them. This county has a rapidly growing population of immigrants from El Salvador, Nicaragua, Panama, and the Dominican Republic. The families come here to escape discrimination and poverty but find a whole new set of problems. They have difficulty obtaining the "green cards" from the federal government that permit them to legally stay here. Even when they have the legal status, jobs are hard to find and pay very little. The housing they can afford is very run-down. They get frustrated from all the pressures and they lack the family support they were accustomed to in their countries. Frustration can turn outward into violence or inward into drug and alcohol abuse.

Before I started, they often placed Latino children in any home available. The kids weren't understood, the food was strange to them, and they were often ridiculed or rejected. They went from one bad situation at home to another in foster care.

For months I went around the community speaking at churches and meeting with residents at their social clubs. I had to explain about how someone applied to be a foster parent and reassure them they wouldn't be rejected because they didn't speak perfectly. I recruited a lot of new foster families. But it was obvious that just putting kids in foster homes isn't enough. It was often like a revolving door. Either the foster parents didn't get enough help from us, or their situations changed and they had to move to another town or focus on their own children.

No matter how good their foster parents were, the kids still suffered from having too many transitions in their lives. Most of the time they wanted to return home and their folks wanted them back. Both the foster and the birth parents were pretty much ignored by the system. Sometimes children did get sent back, but it would tear your heart out to hear stories of how nothing had changed; the same abuse or neglect would start all over again.

I think both the birth parents and the foster parents felt unsupported by DSS. The social workers felt they were being unfairly pressured by lawyers and the media. Nothing seemed to get resolved and children lived in limbo year after year. Every once in a while there would be a big newspaper article about some terrible mistake we made when we took children out of their homes or returned them to a dangerous situation.

I was about ready to leave the agency from sheer frustration. Then a new program was initiated. It's called CAPP, Coordinated Approach to Partnership in Parenting. It grew out of the mayor's task force on **permanency planning** and **family preservation.** The aim is to reunite families when that is possible or to free children for adoption and a new permanent home. All along the way it offers help to all the parties.

I am now called a Family Resource Worker. I am part of a team composed of the foster parents, the birth parents, and the social worker. If the child is old enough and is able, he or she is included also. The first step in CAPP was a ten-session training program for workers. They also invited prospective foster parents to join so they could be trained and screened at the same time. We did role-plays and guided imagery and talked about our own childhoods and parenting styles. We discussed child development and alternative discipline techniques. We learned how to look for signs of learning disabilities, mental illness, depression, drugs, and sexual abuse.

This wasn't the first time there has been training, but this was special. For once, we were all sitting down *together.* Maybe some of the presentations were a little elementary for the social workers with master's degrees, but for me it was eye-opening. I think that the morale and

Permanency planning
An attempt to create, in a timely fashion, a plan for a child that will return him or her safely to the family of origin or legally frees the child to be adopted.

Family preservation
A commitment to provide the resources and supports that can hold together or reunite a family unit, especially to provide stability to the children.

the understanding of this new batch of foster parents is better than most of the older ones. For the birth parents it is very supportive. They are encouraged to think of us as helpers, not as snoops who are punishing them. Some of them had pretty rough treatment when they were kids. They need new models of discipline and more understanding of children's needs.

One of the big parts of my job is to visit the birth parents and foster parents on a regular schedule. I ask them to make an agenda—things they want to talk about so we can be sure to cover what is going on and what they need from me. Whenever there is a crisis—a child runs away or a parent goes off the deep end—I hang in with the family for as long as it takes to get the situation ironed out.

I had one case of a father who was removed from his home because he sexually abused his two sons. He was attending counseling regularly, so the team suggested that he be allowed to come home for visits as long as the children could be protected. I worked with the whole family on this. First we put locks on the younger children's door. Then I arranged for respite care—a child care worker so the mother didn't have to watch the children all the time. I spent a lot of time with the family talking about what was okay touching and what is sexual or physical abuse. I go back often and monitor the arrangement. If our plan works, the father can stay in touch with his family while he continues his individual counseling and group therapy. He needs to figure out what drove him to be an abuser and how he can stop. Some people disapprove of this plan, but our goal is to reunite this family *and* extinguish the destructive behavior that led to its breakup.

The program is still new and there is never enough time and energy. We do endless paperwork. Every contact has to be documented, partly for the research but mostly in case there is a legal problem down the road. We have to prove that we did everything possible if we recommend that parental custody be terminated. We have to keep records so that we don't just keep trying the same things over or lose track of something important.

I still get frustrated by the lack of resources for the kids despite the fact that research shows that most clients benefit more from things like day care or homemaker services than just counseling alone. But we are always hustling to obtain summer camp placements, transportation to school tutoring programs, and competent therapists, especially ones who speak Spanish. With all the talk about family preservation, child-welfare agencies spend only 10 percent of their budgets on concrete services for the families. It makes you wonder how serious they are about keeping families together.

Carmen Mejia as Case Manager/Counselor for Youthful Offenders

The following is a scene from Carmen's previous case manager/counselor position at St. Joseph's Home, a program for youthful first-time offenders:

> On a blustery, cold winter afternoon, Carmen drove up to the courthouse on Beel Street, parked her car, and rushed in to keep her 2:00 P.M. appointment with Mr. Creavey, a youth probation officer. As an advocate employed by St. Joseph's Home, she implements service plans for juveniles convicted of serious but nonviolent crimes.

LEGACY OF AN ADOPTED CHILD

Once there were two women
Who never knew each other.
One you do not remember
The other you call mother.

Two different lives,
shaped to make yours one.
One became your guiding star
The other became your sun.

The first gave you life
And the second taught you to live in it.
The first gave you a need for love
And the second was there to give it.

One gave you a nationality
The other gave you a name.
One gave you the seed of talent
The other gave you an aim.

One gave you emotions
The other calmed your fears.
One saw your first sweet smile
The other dried your tears.

One gave you up
It was all that she could do.
The other prayed for a child—
And God led her straight to you.

And now you ask me through your tears
The age-old question through the years
Heredity or environment—which are you the product of?

Neither, my darling,—Neither.
Just two different kinds of Love.

—Anonymous

This poem is a powerful reminder that parents can be defined both by biology as well as by the nurturing role they take in a child's life. It also poignantly asserts that neither guilt nor blame should be attached to a birth parent who cannot raise a child she has conceived. Most people are doing the best they can.

She carried extensive notes on Sal, a 15-year-old boy found guilty of car theft. His case file included reports from the house parents at St. Joseph's where he had been living since convicted, from the guidance counselor at his high school, and from the therapist who worked with him and his family. During the next half hour, Carmen and Mr. Creavey reviewed the progress Sal had made toward the goals they had all agreed on three months earlier. Toward the end of their time together, she stated her arguments in favor of Sal returning home to live with his parents. They agreed to continue his family therapy; Sal had promised to attend school regularly. He was to get special-education services, which would hopefully make school a more successful experience than it had been in the past. He also would be enrolled in a teenage violence prevention program to help him learn more constructive ways of expressing his angry feelings with his peers and his family. The course used a curriculum developed by a public health expert (Prothrow-Smith, 1987).

That evening at St. Joseph's, Carmen met with Sal, his family, and the therapist to report on the meeting with Mr. Creavey. They reviewed the Individual Service Plan (ISP) agreed to by the probation officer. Carmen answered their questions and encouraged them to see this as a new start under better conditions.

Carmen Mejia as Case Manager/Counselor for the Elderly

The following is a scene from Carmen's first case manager/counselor job at Elder Care, a private, for-profit agency that helps to arrange supportive life services for aged infirm adults:

Carmen had been on the phone for almost an hour calling local geriatric agencies to find out what services they offered and if they had space available. She looked over her notes and heaved a sigh of satisfaction. She had finished just in time and had located several resources. She placed them in her **referral file**.

Referral file
An updated list of all available resources in a human service area with notations about the special characteristics or qualifications of each.

In ten minutes, she would be meeting with Mr. and Mrs. Knopf who were coming to consult about Mr. Knopf's elderly aunt. They were concerned about her living arrangements and wanted to make some plans for her future. She lived alone and they checked on her every few days. She had begun a rapid slide downhill in her ability to take care of herself. She could no longer feed or dress herself adequately or keep her apartment in reasonable order. They were planning a long trip to England and were her only close relatives. They wanted the agency to help them find a nursing home or assisted-living facility or perhaps a reliable personal-care attendant who would visit regularly.

In this first interview Carmen wanted to understand the medical and social background of the aunt. She would find out what kind of services the Knopfs had already used and how those had worked. She would explain the services her agency offered and would strongly suggest that the next visit include the aunt. If the aunt was not able to come into the office, Carmen was prepared to set up a meeting in her home. Carmen was convinced that any referral she made would fail unless the client was involved in making the decisions about her care.

Carmen sees herself as a matchmaker, a person who brings people together with the services they need and then makes sure they are right for each other. She now understands how painful and stressful it can be for the whole family when a loved elder enters institutional care (Peek, 2000).

GOALS OF THE CASE MANAGER/COUNSELOR

Carmen has the same goals and employs the same skills, whether she is talking with a foster mother at her kitchen table, reporting to the young man and his family after the conference with the probation officer, or interviewing the couple who are planning care for their elderly relative. She asks questions and gives information and support in a way that allows the clients the space and time to clarify their situation and explore alternative courses of action. Because she believes in client self-determination, Carmen does not tell people what to do or how to do it. She knows she might be able to influence or manipulate a pregnant teenager into giving up her child; she knows she could pressure a young offender into going back to school. But she also suspects that as a result of that kind of worker interference the teenage girl is likely to carry around a heavy emotional burden of loss for many years and the young man coerced back into school is likely to drop out.

Often she must set aside her own convictions. When she is working with the criminal justice system or the child-protective systems, her actions are dictated by certain rules and regulations that conflict with her concept of the importance of self-determination. Whether the clients come to her agency on their own initiative or are mandated to do so, she works to accomplish four outcomes:

1. The clients will be able to express or change a negative emotional state.
2. The clients will increase their understanding of themselves and their situation.
3. The clients will be better able to make important decisions.
4. The clients will be better able to implement a decision once it is made. (See *Helping Others Help Themselves: A Guide to Counseling Skills*, Loughary & Ripley, 1979, p. 9.)

Releasing or Changing a Negative Emotional State

As Carmen encourages her clients to express their negative feelings, she assures them that *there are no right or wrong feelings*. When 14-year-old Kim is angry at her foster mother for not allowing her to go to a party, Carmen does not tell the youngster that she should or should not feel angry. *Feelings are valid and need to be respected*. Well-meaning people often say to someone who is in a rage or a deep depression:

> You should be ashamed of yourself for being so angry (or depressed) when you have so much to be thankful for.

or

> You think *you've* got problems, let me tell you what happened to me.

These kinds of responses are likely to make the person feel worse! People do not want to be told that their feelings are trivial, self-pitying, or irrelevant. Carmen knows that when Kim is in pain, she desperately needs someone to listen. Sometimes she does not even need anyone to agree with her. Later, as the intensity of the feelings lessen, Carmen can discuss the problem in a more objective way.

Workers should not try to talk people out of their feelings. Their job is to help them figure out why one particular issue provokes emotion. After Kim is allowed to express her feelings, perhaps then she can figure out how to avoid another confrontation. And if her rage at her foster mother causes her to get into a fight with her teacher at school, Carmen needs to help her find a less destructive way to express her feelings.

Understanding of Self and Situation

After Kim expresses her feelings, Carmen tries to get her to put herself in the role of her foster mother or teacher. It is not easy for Kim, or any high school students struggling to find their own identity, to tap into the feelings of powerlessness a caretaking adult might have. Perhaps her foster mother is immersed in a midlife crisis, job transition, or a marriage problem. Perhaps her desire to protect Kim is an expression of love. Empathy is a difficult skill for a client to develop. It is, however, the cornerstone of communication. Carmen has participated in workshops to learn how to utilize role-play techniques to increase her clients' ability to empathize with the other actors in their family dramas.

Carmen also tries to provide Kim with insights into the nature of her specific life crises, developmental issues, and social problems. She encourages her to ask questions. Together they might explore:

- What is alcohol really doing to my body or mind?

- How realistic is the notion that I'm going to flunk all my courses, or does it just feel that way at the moment?

- What are the phases most kids go through when they lose their home and parents?

- How much am I similar to other people who have faced this? In what ways am I unique?

- Why are adults so controlling?

Carmen helps clients gain perspective on their fears, hopes, and plans by sharing what she has learned from other young people and from college courses.

She is always adding to her storehouse of information. From each of her jobs she has learned information to take to the next one. She knows a great deal about the ins and outs of the juvenile justice system from her time at St. Joseph's Home. She received a crash course in special-education services as a foster care worker. And because of elder care, she knows about meals on wheels and different levels of nursing homes.

It is easy to assume that "of course, everyone knows the services available in this town for the unemployed, handicapped, elderly, depressed, or alcoholic." But often low-income as well as more affluent people do not know precisely how to connect with an agency once they have found it (Haas, 1959; Hall, Smith, & Bradley, 1970).

Making Decisions

When people are in crisis they often desperately need to make a decision. Yet that is precisely when they are immobilized. Any actions they take are bound to have negative as well as positive consequences. To make the best possible decisions, they need to sort out inaccurate or conflicting bits of information about each possible choice, get in touch with their feelings, anticipate possible consequences, and then try to decide what is in their best interest. Solving problems and making decisions can be a reasonably systematic process or a frustrating and chaotic one.

Carmen works with her clients to help them make one specific decision and to develop decision-making skills that can be used again and again as new problems arise.

Implementing Decisions

BREAKING A BIG TASK DOWN INTO SMALL STEPS

The most carefully thought out decision is little more than an exercise in futility if action does not follow. When a decision is arrived at, Carmen helps her clients break a big decision into small steps. Then each small step is discussed, practiced, and evaluated.

Carmen has been working with Lila Parsikian, a mother recently released from a drug rehabilitation program. Lila seems stuck. She has said that she wants to eject her abusive lover from her home. But even thinking about confronting him with her decision makes her break out in a cold sweat. Implementing a decision involves personal risk. The possibility of failure lies close behind each new move. Carmen and Lila have been rehearsing what she will say. They also have discussed her sources of protection. Lila thinks that her brother would be willing to stay with her for a few days. Carmen encouraged Lila to finish the paperwork for Transitional Assistance so she could get immediate financial support and break her economic dependency on her lover.

GIVING EMOTIONAL SUPPORT

Carmen has to be careful as she treads the fine line between reasonable encouragement and false reassurance. She can encourage her client to feel that she is a worthy person and does not deserve to be beaten. She can explain to the young woman that she has the right to get a legal restraining order that prohibits her boyfriend from harassing her. She can promise to call her each day and refer her to a shelter if she wants to go that route. But she also must be honest about the fact that a restraining order does not guarantee her safety. Women have been battered and even killed by violent mates as they clutched a restraining order in their hand.

MODELING BEHAVIOR

When they discussed Lila's growing frustration with her very aggressive child, Carmen found out about the discipline techniques Lila uses. After suggesting some methods that avoid physical punishment, she visited Lila's home to work with her and her child. By modeling a disciplining behavior, such as a short "time-out," and then staying there as the parent tries it, Carmen teaches while giving emotional support (Kernberg et al., 1991; Webster-Stratton & Martin, 1994; Zeilberger, Sampen, & Sloan, 1973).

MAKING REFERRALS

Sometimes Carmen refers clients to support groups or training programs. Assertiveness training helps hesitant young women put their good sense into action. Perhaps she will tell Lila about a parenting group at a local mental health center or a shelter for women who are in abusive relationships. She might make the phone call with her to find out where it meets.

Her clients' needs for hand-holding, reassurance, and rehearsing vary enormously. Sometimes a little push in the right direction can set the top spinning on its own. But sometimes, resistance to taking the next step masks real discontent about a decision. If Lila is not ready to take the first step to go back to school, maybe Carmen needs to spend more time working on building her self-confidence through taking some small steps with a high probability of success. Maybe attending a one-day workshop on career choice or opportunities in computers would be a good start.

OVERCOMING BARRIERS

Clients often get stuck moving a plan into action because barriers block their path. Kevin, a young man who is blind, is ready to graduate from a residential school and attend college in his community. But the college does not provide up-to-date braille texts, special library equipment, and enough note takers. He will not be able to succeed without those supports.

When barriers keep her clients from getting the services they are entitled to, Carmen uses her organizing skills. She suggested that Kevin file a complaint to the dean and to the department in the state bureaucracy that oversees special educational services. If that does not work, he might need to go to court. Carmen is with him every step of the way. She might refer him to an agency that does legal advocacy on behalf of students with disabilities.

THE PROCESS OF CASE MANAGEMENT/COUNSELING

Getting Prepared for the Client and the Problem

Even before clients walk into her agency, Carmen has begun working with them. Perhaps she has spoken to them briefly over the phone or a worker from another agency has sent a written referral about their situation.

Even though she never has enough time in her day, Carmen always takes a few moments to quietly and systematically think about her next appointment before he or she arrives. During the initial encounter (and each subsequent one) she will face many unknowns, but the more carefully she has prepared herself, the more she will be able to meet the challenge of each unique personality and situation. She prepares herself by tuning in to the clients and their problems both emotionally and intellectually.

USING PREPARATORY EMPATHY

We have already stressed the critical importance of empathy, putting oneself into the shoes of another person and seeing the world out of another person's eyes. Now we introduce the concept of **preparatory empathy** (Gitterman & Shulman, 1994; Shulman, 1979, p. 14). Of course, it would be arrogant to think that we can ever predict what another human being will feel. We *can*, however, sensitize ourselves to listen and watch intently for the emotions that might lie below the surface of a client's words and actions. Tuning in helps us to respond accurately to the garbled, often ambivalent messages that people send when they are experiencing a high level of stress.

Preparatory empathy An attempt to put oneself in the shoes of another person, to feel or think of a problem from another perspective, even before encountering a client, to sensitize the worker.

To sharpen her preparatory empathy, Carmen collects and then sifts through all she knows about the emotional baggage that often accompanies a particular set of problems. Carmen has been preparing for a home visit to Laurel Schultz, the mother of a 5-year-old girl who is enrolled in a day care center affiliated with a large teaching hospital. She has never met Ms. Schultz, but was asked by the center director to try to get her to agree to having her daughter evaluated. The director suspects that the youngster has attention deficit hyperactivity disorder (AD/HD), which is a biological condition that makes concentrating and following rules very difficult (Barkley, 1997, Wender, 1987). Because so few people understand this disability, children like Ms. Schultz's daughter are likely to be high-risk students when they go on to public school. They appear to not care, not listen, or not be trying hard enough, so they are frequently punished by authority figures and rejected by their peers.

The following "Q and S" section shows how Carmen prepared herself for her meeting with Laurel Schultz. "Q" stands for Carmen's questions and "S" stands for her speculations. Some of this preparation she role-played with her supervisor.

Q: What kind of emotions might I anticipate from a parent at this day care center?

S: *Well, I will be visiting the mother of a preschooler, so I'll need to review what I've learned about the parents of toddlers in general and about the parents in this particular center. One thing that stands out is that many of the parents feel that they are being blamed by the staff when their child has a problem. Most parents, especially of small children, have dreams for their youngsters. It can be devastating to be told that the experts suspect there is something that isn't quite normal.*

I find most of the day care staff very supportive. They don't usually sound the alarm until they have a strong sense that the problem isn't going to work itself out.

Many of the parents have a love–hate relationship with the doctors at Morgantown Hospital, which works with the center. Some parents are so intimidated by experts that they don't question them about anything. Others are suspicious and bitter toward them. Many feel that the doctors use their kids as guinea pigs to train interns, who graduate and then practice in more affluent communities.

There are so many drugs around this community that the very mention of a medication such as Ritalin, which is sometimes used for AD/HD, may be met with instant resistance.

Q: What kind of emotions might I anticipate from this family?

S: *The staff has told me that the Schultzes have already asked them for help in figuring out how to cope with their daughter's impulsive and oppositional behavior. So they might really welcome the evaluation. They have three other children who have not had problems in school, so they are not likely to feel they are being singled out unfairly. They can be reminded of how successful their parenting has been. Both of the Schultzes have attended meetings and potluck suppers at the center, so the staff thinks they are very motivated.*

When I phoned Ms. Schultz she sounded welcoming, but she did indicate that her husband thought his daughter's problem is due to the school's permissive discipline. She might be feeling pulled between him and the teachers. I'll need to try to engage his cooperation.

Q: What are my own feelings about this situation? How would I feel if a worker from my child's day care center came to visit me to tell me about a potential learning problem with my child, especially one that might not be easy to deal with?

S: *I remember my mom would complain about my younger brother but hated it when anyone else said anything negative about him. I know she felt guilty about having a job. Ms. Schultz works outside the home. I wonder if she might have some of the same feelings?*

I hate it when my supervisor is too critical about something I've done; it's hard to be told that things are not going well. But I appreciate it when she starts by talking about all the good things I do.

Q: What do I know about impulsive and oppositional behavior in young children?

S: *I'd better call a therapist at the School Function Clinic at Children's Hospital and get some clues about techniques and referrals. I'll need them.*

ANTICIPATING MISUNDERSTANDINGS AND TENSION BETWEEN WORKER AND CLIENT

Preparatory empathy is not a parlor game in which the worker tries to outguess the client! Rather, it is a process that alerts a worker to issues that *might* turn out to be important. If feelings are not brought up by the parents, then Carmen sends up a trial balloon. She might say:

Some people have heard a lot of conflicting information about hyperactivity and attention deficit disorders. I'm wondering what you might have heard and if you have any feelings about the way it is diagnosed and treated.

If Ms. Schultz shrugs off the question, Carmen lets it drop. Perhaps she has no questions or isn't ready yet to ask them.

In the following, Shulman (1979) describes a home visit that goes sour very quickly because the worker did not use preparatory empathy.

> A young human service worker visits a parent in her home. This is their first meeting. The parent, a middle-aged mother of seven, had been struggling for years with a multitude of serious problems with her children. Over the previous several months, the mother had developed a good relationship with her last case manager/counselor. She was a woman close to her own age who was suddenly transferred to another office. After a few minutes of rather tense introductory chatting, the parent interrupted the worker and asked in a brusque tone of voice: "You got any children of your own?"
>
> After suppressing a gulp and an internal "Oh my goodness, what do I say now?" the young worker answered: "No, I don't have any children, but I have had child psychology courses in college and I know a lot about parenting." The client laughed derisively, and essentially ended the interview by withdrawing into silence. (p. 15)

Shulman states that if the worker had anticipated this question, she might have been prepared to respond to the mother's possible feelings of:

- Defensiveness
- Fear of being judged a "bad" parent
- Fear that this new worker couldn't understand how hard it is to parent when one is poor, lonely, and lives in a neglected neighborhood
- Anger at being abandoned by her former worker
- Sadness for the loss of a relationship that was helpful

If she had tuned in to these feelings, she could have answered with a more supportive, less defensive statement. She might have said:

> No, I don't have any children, but I'll try very hard to understand what your family situation is all about.

or

> No, I don't. I also have wondered if this will get in the way of my fully understanding you and being of help. I hope you'll tell me what it is like for you and what kind of help I can give.

or

> No, I don't. I wonder if you're worrying if this will make it hard for us to work together? Let's talk about that. (Shulman, 1979, p. 15)

Reading and Evaluating Referral Materials

When Carmen starts working with a client, she usually has some background information about the person and situation. Sometimes it is a bulging file; often it is just a brief note or verbal statement from another worker.

When she worked with young people who had trouble with the law, a file was likely to contain some of the following:

- An official record of the arrest and a description of the precipitating incident

- A report prepared by the probation officer on the youth's school achievement, family background, and work history

- A summary of tests that the public school administered and the school transcripts

- The results of a vocational test administered by a rehabilitation agency that was working with the youth before the arrest

- A medical report on the youth's physical condition

- Notes taken at a family interview with the court social worker

Objective data
Data based on unbiased facts, not affected by personal feelings or prejudice.

Some of this information is **objective data.** It states facts such as the dates of events, medical findings, court dispositions, work history, or any public benefits that have been received. Other pieces of data might *appear* objective but are open to judgment and bias. For example, the results of a battery of personality tests, although useful, are open to varied interpretations according to who administered or scored them.

Subjective data
Personal opinions about the client's attitude, situation, and behavior that may or may not be objectively true.

Other documents are filled with clearly **subjective data.** They state opinions about the client's attitude, situation, and behavior. Carmen is always careful to be a little skeptical of this kind of data. In the Shulman (1979) example of lack of preparatory empathy, the worker might have written that the client was "aggressive" or "hostile." But if Carmen had been the worker and had tuned in to the client's feelings, she might have interpreted her behavior as "appropriately anxious." Emotions are often in the eyes of the beholder.

Reports can be riddled with diagnostic labels that do not have hard data to support them. Phrases like *mentally disturbed child, overprotective parent, hyperactive child,* or *juvenile delinquent* will frequently crop up in a client's file. We have no way to evaluate the credentials, skills, or sensitivity of the people who affixed the labels. These terms are often used imprecisely and should not be automatically accepted as an accurate depiction of a client's personality or background.

Referral statement
An initial verbal or written statement that explains the reasons a client is being sent to or has chosen a specific resource, person, or agency.

As long as Carmen is a bit skeptical, the **referral statement** can still be very useful. She learns about the client's previous experiences, which might give clues to his or her expectations. If it is not clear from the referral statement exactly why the client is coming to the agency, a few direct questions early in the first interview may bring clarity.

POINTS TO KEEP IN MIND WHEN REVIEWING REFERRAL MATERIALS

1. *Background records generally exclude the views of the client.* The reports on a client's attitudes, behavior, or progress are written only from the perspective of the workers. To round out the picture, we need to hear how the *clients* evaluate their experiences. Unfortunately, their reflections, even when included, are often given little credence.

2. *Background records can lead us to prejudge clients.* Carmen tries to guard against tunnel vision. But without realizing it, another worker's opinions can color her initial judgments, which might have been different if she had started from scratch.

3. *Background information can lead to shaping the client's behavior.* Once we have formed preconceptions, we might slip into a pattern of treating the client in a certain way. Treated that way, clients might reciprocate by acting as we assumed they would. That is called a *self-fulfilling prophecy.*

4. *Background data can be based on dubious measures.* Through the years, professional opinions about various test measures have shifted, and many questions have been raised about the extent to which some instruments unwittingly reflect only the ideas or styles of the test designer or the dominant cultural group. Intelligence tests, vocational tests, and even reading tests are believed to give inaccurate assessments of women and members of ethnic minorities. In addition, when clients are tested against their will, they are not at their sharpest or most optimistic, and thus inaccuracies may occur.

Methods of Collecting Additional Data about a Case

When we review the file of a new client and evaluate the quantity and quality of material in it, we appreciate the critical importance of careful recording. When records are well organized, including all the pertinent information about critical events, Carmen starts out many steps ahead. When records are vague and inaccurate, Carmen wastes valuable time hunting down the details of a hospitalization, an application for a program that was refused, or a court sentence that was suspended under specific conditions. Clients understandably resent telling their story again and again.

Information gathering must be focused. Human service workers often fall into the trap of assuming that more is better. Yet, random information gathering can muddy the waters. Although it is often true that the sources of current problems lie in past experiences, the case management/counseling process generally focuses on the here and now. Worker and client need to systematically gather data about the times, places, and circumstances surrounding the client's most immediately pressing problems.

The client should be told what information is needed and how it will be gathered and used. Many human service agencies have standardized procedures and time lines for gathering information. For example, if Carmen is helping a young mother apply for health care or for subsidized day care, she explains what documentation will be needed to support the request. She also explains why it is needed. She tells clients whether the law stipulates a time frame or an appeals process if they are denied benefits.

As with all the explanations workers give, clarity and honesty coupled with sensitivity are vital. When she calls to set up a visit, she might say, for example:

> Mrs. Tryforo, the social worker from school, has called me to say that she is very concerned about the bruises on your son's face. I need to visit with you, preferably in your

home, and talk about those bruises. I will then have to visit his school and talk to his doctor and your neighbors. I have to submit my report to my supervisor within three days.

There are many ways we go about collecting data. Here are some of the methods we use.

INTAKE INTERVIEWS

Intake interview
An interview (form) soliciting relevant information before the delivery of a service begins.

In the CAPP program, all the counselors take turns doing initial **intake interviews.** They write up the information gathered and decide whether the person's needs fit into the agency services. If they do and there is room in the agency's caseload, the worker decides which staff member might "fit" best with that client. For example, one worker has the reputation for being especially effective with angry teenagers and another worker is known to do well with very shy, inarticulate people.

The intake interview zeros in on the immediate problem situation—how it came about, what has already been done to deal with it, and what specific actions the client wants to or is required to take. Though usually conducted on a one-on-one basis, CAPP has experimented with group intakes both for efficiency as well as to provide prospective clients with emotional support.

HOME VISITS

CAPP includes a home visit as an integral part of its regular data-gathering process. The home visit provides an opportunity to gain greater understanding of the patterns of interaction, support, and stress that daily confront clients and their family systems. Carmen has a few clients whom she sees regularly in their homes. Many clients welcome the less formal atmosphere, but others resist and resent it. Perhaps it makes them feel intruded upon.

Carmen usually has the flexibility to let clients choose the interview setting. When clients have little choice because they are mandated to receive services in their home, she helps them express any negative feelings they might have about her visit. She reassures them that their angry or apprehensive feelings are understandable.

Client resistance usually lessens if a counselor makes advance appointments, sticks to a time schedule, has a clear sense of the purpose of each encounter and explains it clearly, encourages expression of feelings, and is respectful.

STAFFINGS OR CASE CONFERENCES

Often several different workers and agencies are involved with the same client or family. For example, Lila Parsikian has been seen by:

- A hospital staff person who evaluates her youngster's behavior problem
- A recreational specialist who works with her child in the after-school play group
- The teacher and guidance counselor who work with her child at school
- A rehabilitation counselor who runs an AA-type postrelease group

- The family therapist who meets with Lila, her boyfriend, and her child one evening a week

- The foster parent who provides respite care on the weekends

Carmen tries to weave all the strands into one supportive rope. All these people need to sit down together (preferably with the client) and pool information and ideas. CAPP organizes a conference when a new case is opened or when a new worker is assigned to an ongoing case. Conferences are also convened periodically throughout the service period as action plans are reviewed and revised. Carmen, the generalist among all the specialists, is the logical worker to chair these sessions.

An evaluation or information-sharing conference may be required under the mandate of a legislative act. Under Public Law 94.142, which governs the services given to pupils with special learning needs, a formal time schedule dictates how often staffing conferences are to be held. Everyone who attends must sign a form to show they participated. These reports are monitored by the regional or state education agency.

DIRECT OBSERVATIONS

Observations are usually informal. Carmen might visit the recreation room of an institution, drop into a child's classroom, or go on a trip with a client or foster parent. Here too, she tries to be sensitive to signs that the client might be feeling invaded or spied on. It is important that she has a clear idea of what behaviors to observe and has formulated questions for which answers are being sought. The clearer the focus of the observation, the more useful the data she gathers will be.

BUILDING SUPPORTIVE RELATIONSHIPS

As we have stressed, the vital work of building a trusting relationship with each client starts immediately after Carmen has been assigned to a case. When she schedules the appointment for the initial interview and greets the client for the first time, she knows that her words, tone of voice, and facial expression all communicate. Through her warmth, openness, humanness, and honesty she shows her clients that she respects them and considers their problems important. She continues to cement the relationship by:

- Listening, observing, and accurately reflecting back feelings and thoughts

- Encouraging the full expression of emotions and ideas by helping to put them into words

- Keeping clear about the purposes of each encounter

- Raising questions for thought and suggesting alternative actions, resources, and services

Often, the case management process has a happy ending. Both of these parents were adopted at birth, the father by a single parent and the mother by a couple. Now they are raising a family of their own and are active in an adoption support program.

- Admitting the limits of her own expertise and seeking additional help
- Protecting confidentiality or being clear about why it cannot be kept

No matter how competent she is, Carmen's relationships with her clients are likely to be stressful and volatile. At no point can she sit back and say, "Well, that's done. Now we have a trusting relationship!"

At times, a particular relationship seems very strong, but within minutes it can swing to mistrust or conflict. Carmen has to keep reminding herself that frustration, anger, and tension are inevitable when people grapple with difficult decisions.

Her ability to pay close attention to details strengthens her relationships. Returning phone calls promptly, being on time for appointments, remembering the details of what has been said, and following through on promises are all concrete demonstrations of the verbal caring that she professes. Leaving a client's record carelessly lying on a desk where it can be read by anyone or missing a special event in a client's life without telephoning are actions that communicate just the reverse. Being able to count on caring that is consistent with their cultural backgrounds can give clients that extra measure of emotional support they so desperately need when facing overwhelming personal distress. (See Ariel, 1999; Okun, Fried, & Okun, 1999.)

Negotiating and Refining the Working Contract

When Carmen begins an encounter with a client, she does not make any assumptions about who knows what or who wants what. All the parties in the process—client, worker, family members, or other professionals—must negotiate and then refine their own special mutual working agreement. Although contracting has long been part of the business and entertainment world, it has been widely used in casework and counseling only within the last three decades (Epstein, 1980, 1992; Kravetz & Rose, 1973; Schwartz, 1971; Shulman, 1979, 1993). Perhaps it was the civil rights struggles of the 1960s that made clients aware that they should be included in making the significant decisions that affect their lives.

Contracting grows out of the basic principle that the case management/counseling process is a *collaborative endeavor* between client and worker. Through mutual agreements and joint commitments, the worker tries to minimize the helpee's fear of being case worked, psyched out, or manipulated by a powerful, controlling professional.

If clients do not acknowledge problems or are not convinced that they have the strength to overcome them, any change effort is likely to prove futile. According to the tenets of AA, no change effort can begin until the person with the problem stands up and says, "I am Susanne, and I am an alcoholic. I am an alcoholic, and I want to stop drinking."

The word *negotiating* implies that Carmen and her clients might disagree on the work that has to be done. Sometimes they start out agreeing on all aspects of their working contract, but as they gain new insights they are likely to change their initial contract. If there are many issues to be worked on, they must set priorities.

The word *refining* acknowledges that our goals and tasks are very imprecise. They must be broken down into many smaller components with specific meaning. If, for example, Carmen and Ms. Schultz agree that they will work together on her daughter's problems in school, that still leaves the parent unclear about what she is expected to do and what services Carmen can offer her.

PROBLEMS WITH CONTRACTS

No matter who has started the ball rolling, the goals of an encounter always need to be clarified. When workers fail to do so, the relationship can begin with tension. Shulman (1979, p. 26) illustrates this in the following passage about a hospital social service worker who visits the bedside of a woman who recently had a hysterectomy. The worker introduces himself by saying, "Good day, Ms. Tunney. I'm Mr. Franks from the social service department. Your doctor asked me to find out how I can help you."

Although the worker thought that was clear, the patient did not have the foggiest notion of what a hospital social worker had to do with her. Her first terrified thought was that the social worker was softening her up for some bad news. She wondered if she was sicker than the doctor had told her or if her husband was neglecting their children.

To reassure herself, the woman asked the social worker if he routinely visited all patients. But the worker, still not realizing that he was making her anxious, kept on talking in generalities about giving help. He asked her many questions about her family situation. She answered in a guarded fashion, wondering how her answers would be used.

Actually, the doctor had told the social worker that although the operation had been completely successful, Ms. Tunney required a long period of bed rest. Because she had several children and a working husband, she might need some referrals for homemaking and child care assistance. Shulman suggests that phrases such as *giving help* or *offering services* are so unclear that they have little meaning to most people.

By being very specific and giving an example of what *help* might mean in this particular situation, it could have become clearer. The worker might have said:

> Your doctor told us you have several small children at home and your husband works long hours. He wondered if perhaps your husband needed some additional help in keeping your household running smoothly while you're away and when you're recovering. Sometimes people ask us for help in locating homemakers or in arranging for temporary day care. I'm wondering what concerns you have at this time.

In the above example of contracting, the worker not only proposes some items for the contract but also tries to determine the client's priorities. Perhaps she has enough assistance from her neighbors for child care and housecleaning but is very confused about how to apply for disability compensation. Helping her file the proper forms would then become Task Number 1 in their working contract.

TASKS THE WORKER WILL DO

Some clients resist working with human service workers, but others do just the opposite; they impute magical powers to them. Without being cold or rejecting, we need to be honest about what actual activities we can undertake as well as our limitations. If it turns out that the client's needs are greater than our time or resources, we try to refer them to other agencies.

In the example of the hospital encounter, it is important that the worker let the patient know from the start that the hospital does not actually provide homemakers or day care. He can, however, refer patients to community agencies that do. Perhaps he is willing to make phone calls to these resources. But if he has a ward full of patients with urgent needs for postrelease planning and cannot realistically do the phoning, then he must say so.

TASKS THE CLIENT WILL NEED TO DO

Many of Carmen's cases are mandated by the courts or the Department of Social Service. Agency regulations dictate what each party is expected to do. Carmen always makes sure that these regulations are discussed and understood early in the encounter. If clients are required by law to attend a counseling session, find a job, or do some other activity, it is important that they know what the consequences will be for them if they choose not to do so.

When clients are voluntary referrals, they should know that they have the right to shop around for social services and that it is best that they do. That is what an alert consumer does when choosing a home or buying a major appliance. If the agency employs a particular theory or philosophy of helping or if it uses behavior modification, psychoanalysis, or group therapy, certain demands will be made. The client needs a chance to say "No, thank you" without feeling guilty.

If the worker is aware of programs that use other approaches, clients should be encouraged to consider them. Then, hopefully, their decision to choose a particular helping process or social program will be made with the conviction that it suits their needs. Unfortunately, these choices are not as available in social service programs as they are in consumer products. The sad reality is that our finances usually determine the nature of our choices. This might be fair when choosing a couch or TV set, but it might be disastrous when picking a physican or nursing home.

DECIDING ON THE RULES OF THE ROAD

Early in their encounter, worker and client must agree on the following rules that will govern their working together:

1. A reasonable projection of how much time or how many sessions the overall process will entail and which special activities it will include (such as testing, home visiting, or case conference)

2. A schedule for sessions, visits, and so forth

3. The names and addresses of places where the encounters will occur

4. A decision about the kind of note taking or recording the worker will do and the rules of confidentiality

5. Information about the client or the worker that might help or hinder their working together

6. Information about fees and how they will be billed and should be paid

Deciding on Problems and Priorities

Human service workers have often been criticized for having goals so grandiose that they can never be achieved (Richan & Mendelsohn, 1973). It is certainly true that it is an unrealistic aim to "save a marriage" or "improve someone's self-concept." Those goals are too global and diffuse for case management/counseling. We can, however, help the person with marital problems or low self-esteem figure out how to find better ways to settle arguments with a spouse, find a job or living situation that makes life less stressful, try out a new support group, or practice a form of self-relaxation.

Critics have long accused workers of choosing clients' goals *for* them rather than *with* them. To avoid that trap, Laura Epstein (1980, 1992) stresses that the skill of workers lies in their ability to help clients articulate their priorities. She asserts that even very troubled people can be helped to state their most pressing problems in action-oriented, concrete terms. To do this, the worker helps the clients decide on the priority of their needs, ranking them by importance or feasibility.

By working on those problems that the *client* defines as critical, the worker captures the client's positive energy. If a definition of the problem is made primarily by the worker, client energy can be squandered in resisting the worker and protecting against being controlled. There are no right or wrong priorities in this task-centered and client-focused approach.

Conducting an Assessment Study for an Agency

Most often the extensive data that the worker has been collecting is in preparation for the work that client and case manager/counselor will undertake together to work through a specific problem. But sometimes the data gathering is an end in itself or the major role the worker will play in a casework/counseling encounter. For example, if Carmen were employed by the department in her agency that arranges foster homes for children, her role would be to gather data that could be used by the agency to assess the suitability of a potential foster home. In order to do this, she would seek answers to a specific set of questions. She would use a form designed by the agency, which would be used as the basis of a final placement decision and an after-placement plan.

Some of the data collected will be factual information; much of it will be the applicant's feelings and thoughts. Some of the material in the assessment report will require Carmen's professional judgement of this applicant's capacity to parent and the kind of help they will need in order to thrive as a foster family.

QUESTIONS A WORKER MIGHT SEEK ANSWERS FOR IN A FOSTER CARE ELIGIBILITY ASSESSMENT

Part I. In this section of the form (or interview schedule) she seeks specific information about each member of the family—their ages, occupations, health status, ethnic background, schooling, etc. Questions are also asked about their neighborhood and its accessibility to schools, churches, hospitals, its level of safety, etc. The worker probes to establish what kinds of people constitute the support network of the family—their neighbors, extended kith and kin. She tries to ascertain what changes they might need to make in their employment and other life arrangements in order to foster a child.

Part II. In this section the potential foster parents are presented with a checklist of the types of children they would accept—what gender, ages, disabilities, or past history (perhaps of abuse or neglect) they feel they could work with. And, most important, why they have made those choices.

Part III. In this section she asks questions that help assess the relationships among family members, the way decisions get made in the family, the type of discipline used on their own children or with other foster children. She probes to clarify their attitudes towards people of different ethnic backgrounds and their exposure to people with physical handicaps or emotional problems.

Part IV. In the final phase, the worker estimates how open this family is to further training and to seeking out resources and support from the agency. Finally, Carmen would give her judgement of how successful she thinks this family can be with the type of child they have expressed a willingness to parent and with the resources the agency can offer.

The assessment process is not solely about establishing suitability for foster parenting but is just as much concerned with providing the potential parents with information and helping them decide if and what type of fostering would be right for them. (For further resources on conducting an assessment, see Holland, 2004, and Jordan & Franken, 1995). A useful resource for preparing the final assessment or case study report can be found in Papadopoulos, 2003.

Creating the Action Plan

All the work we have done so far has prepared the soil for our action plan. Now the worker and client use the following techniques.

DIVIDING MAJOR PROBLEMS INTO THEIR SMALLER COMPONENTS

When they were negotiating their working contract, the most challenging task facing Carmen and the client was to state, in action terms, the exact nature of the problems and the hoped-for outcomes. When people are overwhelmed by life's demands and feel buffeted by circumstances, it is hard to see the small stumbling blocks that contribute to their overall problems of poverty, rage, or depression. Understandably, clients are impatient to tackle the problem head-on. In the action plan we take the goals and figure out how to get to them *one step at a time.*

For example, Ms. Lugo is a recently widowed mother who complains of profound depression. She is overwhelmed by the prospect of parenting alone. Carmen helped her decide which component parts of her current situation troubled her the most. Then they could begin to work on them one at a time. Together, they reviewed her:

- Financial situation
- Social situation
- Living arrangements
- Work role
- Parenting role

Every widow experiencing the loss of a mate has different priorities, depending on her socioeconomic status, interests, age, location, and support system. All problems can, with skill and patience, be broken down into smaller parts.

VISUALIZING ALTERNATIVE PATHS, STRATEGIES, AND RESOURCES

Once the larger problem is seen in its component parts, we move on to choosing one piece of that larger problem to work on. Carmen encouraged her client to articulate exactly what she needed in order to cope with her sense of financial deprivation. They agreed that Carmen would meet with her at home. Beforehand, the widow would gather all the bills and receipts she could find. Carmen would go over them with her and together they would construct a budget. Once they figured out the family finances, Ms. Lugo might need to visit a legal services center or a consumer credit counselor to deal with any debts, inheritance, or documents that needed to be transferred into her name.

The second high-priority problem identified was the burden of parenting her little girl who had serious emotional upset. They began working on finding:

- Specific programs, social agencies, or "people resources" that would give her some time off from parenting and her daughter additional adults to relate to

- Appropriate agencies or benefits that could pay for some respite care, camp placements, and so forth

- A counselor, support group, and network of family and friends who could be a sounding board for her questions about discipline now that there is no other adult in the home to talk things over with

CONSIDERING THE CONSTRAINTS

After thinking creatively about the many possible strategies and resources they could tap into, Carmen and Ms. Lugo reviewed the options to see how feasible each one was. For each possible program or resource they had to find out its:

- Location
- Costs
- Availability
- Eligibility requirements

Together they weighed the pros and cons of each.

CHOOSING THE ACTION ALTERNATIVES

After the pros and cons of each option were analyzed, it became apparent that some action plans had more chance of success than others. For example, if enrolling in a support group for widows seemed helpful but the meetings were held in a building that was far away from public transportation, Ms. Lugo would not be able to use that resource.

Often, as resources are looked at and found to be inappropriate, Carmen is able to identify significant unmet service needs in the community. Although she might not be able to single-handedly start a new support group that is accessible for inner-city residents, perhaps some other agency or worker might have the expertise to start one or obtain a van to drive people to one. (The chapters on program planning and systems change describe the skills workers need to undertake these tasks.)

MAPPING OUT STEPS IN AN ACTION PLAN

Once major problems have been broken into smaller issues and likely strategies chosen, Carmen and her client must put a time frame on each step. If Ms. Lugo's daughter is to enroll in a summer camp, they must find out when the application and medical forms need to be turned in. Then Ms. Lugo will have to find time to gather up camp clothes, label them, and arrange the time off from her job to take her child to the bus depot.

Ms. Lugo might decide that she wants to find a smaller apartment now that her income is reduced. Before rushing out to look for one, she needs to decide which steps in the apartment-hunting process must be done first, how long each will take, and where she will get the extra money for moving expenses, security deposit, and the last month's rent.

Implementing the Action Plan

Often Carmen's major contribution to the problem-solving process is to act as a sounding board. As she listens to the client's plans, she plays devil's advocate, raising questions to think about. At other times she is like a coach, helping to recharge someone's emotional batteries. Worker and client can divide up the work. Ms. Lugo will find out about the town day camp while Carmen finds out how much money her agency might be able to contribute to the fees. They can share the work that needs to be done so that the client will not be overwhelmed. Yet Carmen should not infantilize Ms. Lugo by solving all of her problems for her. Each time Ms. Lugo takes one small step she begins to feel more confident about her capacity to sucessfully raise her child without her husband.

Because she has worked with so many families, Carmen is frequently asked to suggest a specific program. Linking a person to such a resource is called the *process of making a referral.*

MAKING REFERRALS

Making a successful referral is a much more complicated process than simply supplying the name of an agency and trusting that it and the client will connect. Research has indicated that many clients fall through the cracks after being referred by one agency to another (Kirk & Greenley, 1974). Perhaps the client's needs and the agency's services were mismatched. Or perhaps the client and the agency failed to make a solid bond with each other. To avoid this, workers try to obtain accurate data about agency services and entitlements. They also need to learn to build firm linkages with both the client and the prospective agency (Feltham & Horton, 2000).

CREATING A RESOURCE FILE

Our referrals can fail when our information about the agency or service is wrong or incomplete. There are often vast differences between the official description of an agency in a resource directory and the actual service it is able to deliver. Anticipating this kind of discrepancy, Carmen has constructed her own personal resource file. Alongside the official facts about the agency's fees, waiting period, and eligibility requirements, she notes her own observations. Perhaps it states in the agency brochure that all clients are seen within a two-week period, but she has heard from many clients that the waiting time is more like two months. She jots this down so she can warn the next client. Optimally, she has seen the agency in action. If that has not been possible, she relies on feedback from other workers and clients.

When Carmen has not taken the time to double-check on her referrals, she has sent clients on wild-goose chases. Once she sent a client to a legal services program for assistance in obtaining a legal separation from her husband; the agency had run out of rent money two years before. The client making that futile trip was rightfully annoyed and she then missed her next appointment at CAPP.

If Carmen finds out that there is a long waiting list for a service, she warns clients about it. Armed with an accurate understanding of its limitations, clients can then decide whether to wait their turn or shift gears.

Her referral file also includes resources that she has simply read about or heard of. Though potentially useful, the client needs to be warned that they are unknown quantities. A client who decides to use those services should be armed with a host of questions to ask. Role-playing the questions in advance prepares a client for an ill-defined encounter. Soliciting impressions after the client visits feeds valuable data back to Carmen's resource file.

CEMENTING A REFERRAL

After reviewing the official and informal data about a resource and deciding to suggest it, several acts can prevent the client—especially the very troubled or disorganized one—from falling through the cracks. Weissman (1976) has identified worker acts that constitute what he calls **linkage technology.**

Linkage technology
The acts involved in referring a client to another agency, worker, or resource.

1. *Write down the referral for the client.* Carmen always takes an extra moment to write down an agency's address, how it can be reached, when it is open, and any documentation that must be brought on a first visit. Then she hands the paper to her client. In the midst of an emotionally intense session, it might be hard for the client to take accurate notes or remember details.

2. *Connect the client to a particular person at the agency.* If possible, Carmen tries to find out the name of the worker at the referral agency whom the client will be seeing. She often writes or e-mails an introductory note preceding the visit. This can build a valuable bridge for the client. Sometimes the referral can be set in motion by the client's phoning for an appointment from Carmen's office.

3. *Determine who might accompany the client.* In certain cases Carmen might decide to go with her client to the referral agency. If she cannot go but thinks that

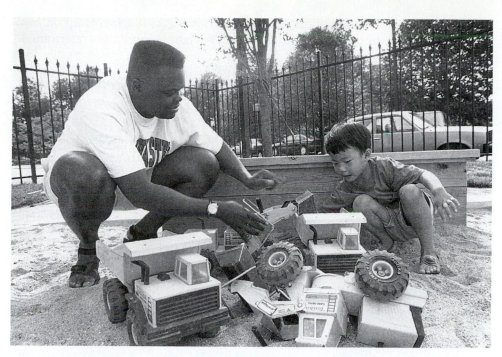

To build a supportive relationship, we try to find common ground. We work on developing trust according to the age and abilities of each client. Even the smallest child will hesitate to reveal a painful feeling until the worker has created an atmosphere of acceptance and safety.

extra support is necessary, she helps clients think about who in their own network of friends and relatives might be able to accompany them.

4. *Determine what other resources the client needs in order to use the referral.* Sometimes her clients need money for transportation, a specialized vehicle, child care, or another resource in order to use the referral. Carmen helps them to think through potential stumbling blocks and negotiate them in advance. If left to chance, these stumbling blocks can undermine a referral.

5. *Check back on how the referral went.* Carmen always asks her clients for feedback. She often arranges an interview after their visit to an agency so they can talk it over. Then she can find out if there were any unanticipated obstacles that need to be dealt with.

6. *Advocate for high-quality service.* As she solicits feedback from her clients, Carmen discovers instances of inadequate service. Because of red tape, bureaucratic inertia, worker turnover, or misunderstanding, clients often do not get the services they need. Clients need encouragement to take the next step to overcome obstacles. That might entail switching to another resource or finding ways to pressure that agency to meet their needs.

It is best if clients advocate on their own behalf, but if they cannot, then an outside advocacy group, Carmen, or her supervisor push a complaint higher up the power structure of the agency. If Carmen does not follow up on complaints, all her future referrals to that agency might be similarly undermined.

Evaluating the Work and Deciding on the Next Step

INFORMAL EVALUATION TECHNIQUES

There are many moments during a counseling session when both Carmen and the client step back and review the work that they have done. If Carmen has just finished explaining the complex steps involved in applying for a job-training program—or if they have role-played a job interview—she does not move on to another issue without making sure that the client has understood the process. Carmen might say,

"I know this red tape can be hard to figure out,"

and

"Are there any steps in the application process that aren't as clear as they should be?"

or

"If any questions come to mind, I'd be glad to review what I've said."

Each time she asks the client for feedback or shares her own reflections on their work together, she is evaluating. In addition to these moment-to-moment evaluations, she also sets aside five minutes at the end of each session to review the progress that has been made in the last hour. If the session runs too long and there is no time remaining for thoughtful evaluation, she phones the client before the next session.

Carmen has found that it is not easy to get honest feedback. Many of the foster and birth parents she works with are accustomed to doctors, lawyers, or school principals who rarely solicit or welcome client opinions about their services. When the clients *have* complained to authorities, they might have been ignored or punished for doing so. To convince them that she *really* wants to hear their opinions—negative as well as positive—and will seriously consider what they say, she needs to reassure them again and again. She might say:

I really appreciate it when you stop me and ask me to explain a term or abbreviation. I am so accustomed to using them that I forget that most people haven't the vaguest idea what they mean. Please stop me again if I forget, okay?

Carmen demonstrates how much she values feedback by trying, whenever possible, to act on criticism. If she has kept a client waiting for a long time, she not only apologizes but makes a point of rearranging her schedule so it is less likely to happen again. She also demonstrates the value of criticism by not becoming defensive when clients point out something she has said or done that upsets them. That does not mean that she accepts and acts on every evaluative comment, but it does mean that she listens attentively and thinks seriously about any she receives.

FORMAL EVALUATION TECHNIQUES

In addition to ongoing informal feedback, CAPP undergoes a formal evaluation of its services by an outside consultant once each year. The public who fund this agency have a right to know if their tax money is being carefully used.

The field of human service evaluation is very challenging. It is almost impossible to verify success or failure of case management/counseling encounters. Optimally we should be able to measure the progress of our programs by charting changes in the mental health or functioning of our clients. But rarely are we able to make cause-and-effect conclusions with a high degree of scientific accuracy.

When Carmen works to keep a family functioning, her efforts are only one factor in a vast constellation of shifting pressures. There are so many variables at work that her best efforts can be wiped out by forces well beyond her control. A poor economy makes job placement almost impossible for her low-skilled clients, so money pressures mount. Money pressures often lead to increased family tension, and so it goes.

Most personal and social problems resist arbitrary definitions of *cure*. How can we be sure that the improvement in the way the parents cope with their child is permanent? How can we know if any improvements we observe are a direct result of our work?

A recognition of the obstacles that keep us from fully evaluating our work should not, however, stop us from trying to do so. On a day-to-day basis, Carmen can see enormous changes in a few of her families and a little bit of change in most of them. The outside evaluation has helped to reshape the CAPP program by stimulating staff members to think about how they could do their jobs better.

CRISIS INTERVENTION

The word *crisis* is used frequently in daily conversation—so often, in fact, that it has lost precise meaning. In human services, however, both the terms *crisis* and *crisis intervention* apply to a specific body of theory and techniques of counseling.

Defining a Crisis

Counselors assert that there are several types of potentially hazardous events that can precipitate a total upheaval in a person's life, such as:

1. An unanticipated situational event, such as hospitalization, sudden death, rape, robbery, or loss of a job.

2. An unusual widespread cataclysmic event, such as a flood, war, hurricane, or plane crash. The destruction of the World Trade Center in the United States and the tsunami in Southeast Asia are recent examples of such events.

3. Unusually severe reactions to normal developmental stages or events, such as the birth of a child; the onset of adolescence; retirement from work; or the

emptying of the nest or the return of adult children to the nest. (Frisch & Kelley, 1996; Golan, 1978; Hendricks, 1995)

Distinct periods mark a crisis. First there is the *vulnerable state* coming right before or after a hazardous event such as those listed above. People in a vulnerable state feel a heightened sense of stress and tension and a threatened loss of balance. They might experience a threat to their personal integrity and the fulfillment of their needs. Perhaps they fear the loss of an ability or a challenge to survival, growth, mastery, or self-expression (Golan, 1978).

The second period is the *precipitating factor,* the proverbial straw that breaks the camel's back. When the weak link in a chain of stresses is reached, anxiety rises to a peak, shattering one's sense of normalcy, well-being, and predictability.

Finally, there is the *active state of crisis.* Each of us reaches it at a different time and expresses crises in a unique manner. But generally we experience both emotional and physical turmoil. The head throbs or the belly knots in pain. There may be aimless activity, loss of cognitive functioning, and too much or too little eating and sleeping. There may be suicidal thoughts.

Helping the Person in Crisis

Crisis intervention draws on some basic theories about the way all of us maintain our balance, or *homeostasis.* It assumes that we are all mutually dependent on each other for support, nurturing, guidance, and communication. Our day-to-day behaviors are influenced by responses and feedback we get from others in our environment. All of us are part of many interdependent groups: family, friends, class, or work group. Each of these is a system of relationships.

A change in any one part of a system reverberates and can change everyone else in the system. Sometimes this change comes in unexpected ways. Sometimes the change comes in very negative ways. The case of the Knowles family that Carmen worked with helps to illustrate this.

> The Knowles family, consisting of George and Myra Knowles, a couple in their mid-forties, and their three teenage daughters, was referred to her by a guidance counselor at one of the children's schools. Carmen found out in the first interview that Myra Knowles, who had long been a chronic alcohol abuser, had recently stopped drinking. But now that Ms. Knowles was assuming her parenting and homemaking role, the girls, who had become used to managing the household themselves, were suddenly doing poorly in school. At home they were surly and disrespectful just as the family seemed to be pulling itself together.
>
> Carmen worked with a consultant to her agency to understand what might be going on in this family. She realized that in order to maintain their family balance, the Knowles had organized their behaviors around coping with the mother's addiction. The sudden move into sobriety changed the way the whole system functioned.
>
> Although this case is unusual, it illustrates one way in which a disturbed system copes with change, even when it is for the better. In this case, perhaps the Knowles chil-

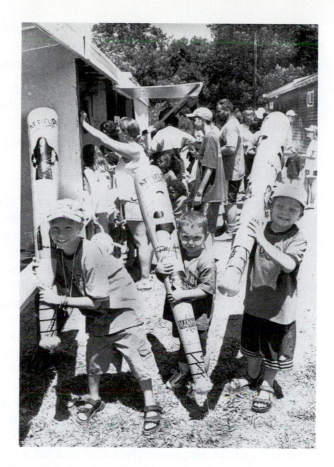

These youngsters are participating in a Portuguese festival. Staying in touch with one's cultural roots and neighbors provides strength when problems in the family, community, or society threaten one's sense of confidence or self-esteem.

dren, dealing with sudden unpredictability, developed more negative patterns, scapegoating their mother and each other. Perhaps they were able to be strong when it seemed important to be, and now they could let out their rage at all the years of tension. Perhaps they resisted believing that this change would last, in order to protect against the pain of more dashed hopes. The whole family needed to achieve insights and develop new, more appropriate coping mechanisms, perhaps taking some risks and experiencing success.

Carmen felt intuitively that if they did not integrate their mother's positive changes into their family system she might become so discouraged that she would return to drinking. *Life would be once again in balance, but everyone would suffer in the long run.*

Lee Ann Hoff (Hoff, 1995; Hoff & Kazimiere, 1998) suggests that the following acts help people move to a new integration (see also Greenstone & Leviton, 2002; Hendricks, 1995; Van Ornum, 1990).

• Spend time listening actively and tuning in to feelings.
• Encourage freedom of expression, no matter how painful the feelings or memories.

- Help the client make connections between the active state of crisis and the events that have led up to it.

- Move toward a realistic understanding of the situation.

- Encourage ideas and suggest new ways of coping.

- Find the sources of immediate support within the client's social network and community.

- Review progress frequently and point out positive developments.

EXAMPLE OF A SITUATIONAL CRISIS

Karen Siloe is a counselor at a community college. She had just started eating her long-deferred lunch when the receptionist phoned to say that a very agitated student wanted to talk with someone immediately. Karen put down her sandwich and went into the reception room to escort the student to her office.

The young woman slumped down in a chair opposite Karen and dissolved into tears. Little by little she told her story. Over Christmas vacation her boyfriend of two years was killed in a car crash as they were driving home from a party. She received minor bruises, which have now healed. But she finds it impossible to study, has bouts of nausea, and cannot sleep at night or pick up the threads of her life. She has a vial of pills in her hand and says she feels like taking them.

Karen moved closer to the young woman and put her arms around her, holding her for a few minutes as she sobbed. Gently, Karen began to ask some questions, searching to discover the people who could give her some immediate support. She obviously needed help getting through the rest of that day and night. So she phoned the people the young woman told her she was close to. A sister said she would leave work and pick her up. Karen also called and left a message for a professor, stating that the young woman would not be in class that afternoon. Karen suggested that her family doctor might also be a resource if she needed some medication to get through the next few days.

They made an appointment to meet first thing the next morning. They would begin the process of grief work, sorting out her feelings of loss and guilt. Karen also knew of a support group she might refer her to. And she would also suggest a full physical examination to make sure that the young woman was not suffering from any undetected physical problems as a result of the accident (France, 1996).

9/11: The Human Service Response to the World Trade Center Crisis

There are many human service agencies—both public and privately financed—whose primary job it is to respond rapidly when disasters occur that destroy a significant amount of property and cause widespread human suffering. Typically, the events that propel these agencies into action have been airplane crashes, shipwrecks, wars, and crime sprees, as well as natural disasters like hurricanes, tornadoes, floods, and fires. Crisis response teams rapidly arrive on the scene of disasters with temporary food, shelter, and medical resources, as well as with financial and mental health assistance.

But the events of September 11, 2001, when the World Trade Center and four airliners went up in flames, taking thousands of lives and impacting on many more thousands of relatives and neighbors, were surely the most complex of all the events the crisis management agencies in our country ever had to cope with. It is impossible to imagine what the aftermath of such an event has been on the people left physically impaired by the blasts, the occupants of the buildings, and the families, neighbors, and spectators. All of these people are likely to spend years restructuring and rebuilding their careers, families, and sense of security. Almost equally as difficult, all of us must find a way to cope with the memories of the human suffering 9/11 engendered. Words such as Posttraumatic Stress Disorder (PTSD), flashbacks, sleep disturbances, and survivor guilt will crop up in discussions of the mental health aftermath of this unique episode in American history.

Two major constellations of groups have taken on the gigantic task of providing mental health assistance to those who were directly or indirectly traumatized by this disaster. One program, Project Liberty, is the federally financed agency that offers free of charge, short-term crisis counseling for anyone experiencing distress related to 9/11. It is intended to help individuals return to their predisaster levels of functioning, especially to regain their sense of security. The project offers individual and group counseling. It also sends human service workers into schools and workplaces to offer educational services. One of its workers, for example, might visit a New York City day care center to help its children and staff talk about what they experienced during the blasts, what they have seen on TV, and what their fears are now about their own sense of safety. The counselors work primarily in the community, but they will also meet with people in their homes. They operate a toll-free phone line that connects the caller (in English, Spanish, and several Asian languages) to a counselor with whom they can ventilate feelings while perhaps choosing to remain anonymous. Callers can also obtain a referral to a mental health service that can work with them in a more long-term or face-to-face counseling process.

The other major group offering a wide range of mental health services is the 9/11 United Services Group. USG is a coordinating body composed of over thirty-eight social agencies that supplement what Project Liberty can offer. Member agencies represent a wide range of existing nonprofit groups including the American Red Cross (traditionally the largest and most experienced of crisis management agencies in the country) all the way to smaller special-interest agencies such as Filipino American Human Services, Inc., the Hispanic Federation, Jewish Board of Family and Children's Services, and The Council on Adoptable Children.

As time passes and there are fewer governmental resources available to meet 9/11-related needs, the USG services will become more critical to the long-term recovery process. USG has not only energized and coordinated the crisis counseling work of its various constituent agencies but it has also trained hundreds of service coordinators who can help guide people through the complex maze of 9/11-related services and benefits. Most important, USG is recording all that has been learned from this disaster, so it can, in a systematic way, pass on this wisdom to hundreds of other social service agencies in other parts of the country and the world.

PROBLEMS THAT HAVE OCCURRED WITH THE DELIVERY OF 9/11 MENTAL HEALTH SERVICES

Only 642,710 people had asked for short-term, one-on-one counseling through March of 2003 (Gittrich, 2003), while officials had expected 2.5 million people to use the services they offered. Surely many New Yorkers continue to suffer from the trauma of 9/11. Opinions vary as to why this number is low compared to the one predicted.

Of course, no matter how well-intentioned, there are always gaps between the services that human service agencies offer and those the clients feel that they need. There are also wide gaps between what human service workers plan to offer and what they can actually deliver. One major problem with the short-term immediate approach offered by Project Liberty may be that many of those affected by the trauma of 9/11 might require many more counseling sessions extending over several years. Symptoms of depression, aggravated grief, severe anxiety, phobias, alcohol and drug abuse, family disintegration, etc., may not occur or be recognized until years after the traumatic event. Additionally, often the people who most need the help resist using it, held back by the cultural and social resistance to counseling or the illusion that their adjustment has been fine.

The traditional crisis model of short-term therapy might be effective after earthquakes and floods, but living under the threat of future terror attacks tends to cause more prolonged psychological problems that cannot be addressed through quick interventions. Recognizing these problems, the government has recently allocated more money and extended the deadline of its own efforts. Private agencies, which will be around for many years to come, have tuned up their services to meet what is bound to be a growing need. In the human services we are always evaluating our work and making informed guesses about how best to fit our model of crisis intervention with the needs of those we are counseling.*

CASE MANAGEMENT/COUNSELING IN THE ERA OF MANAGED HEALTH CARE

At a recent public forum on managed health care, audience members lined up in front of the microphone to tell their legislators what was on their minds. A local real estate agent came up to the microphone and said:

---

*For more information on 9/11 mental health services, see www.4therapy.com and www.9-11usg.org/service.asp.

I had a blocked valve in my heart and they had to do extensive surgery. I was in the hospital three times, the last time for seven days. When I was released, they put me in cardiac rehab. I see a physical therapist and do stress management three times a week now. My bills must come to thousands of dollars but I have paid almost nothing out of my pocket. Without my managed health care plan, I would be dead or totally bankrupt. I am so damned grateful for the plan.

An elderly man faced the audience and stated with strong emotion:

I absolutely refuse to give up my regular Medicare and be forced into a private managed health plan, even though I could probably get some financial help with my prescription costs. I have a friend who died waiting while his plan argued about whether he needed a certain procedure. My internist is very independent and doesn't belong to any of the plans. I won't give him up! He knows me and my health conditions so well. And I want to go to the specialists *he* recommends, not be forced to choose a doctor from some impersonal list.

Health care delivery is a much debated subject that no reader of this book can afford to ignore. It is vital—for both your personal and professional life. But if you are a young person whose parents have reasonably high incomes and jobs that offer them health insurance, paying medical bills probably hasn't been much of a worry. If you are in college now, although you may not be thrilled with its services, your school most likely has a free health clinic funded by the fee you paid along with tuition.

But if you took time off between high school and college, worked at an entry-level job, and turned 19, you might have been surprised to discover that you had been dropped from your parent's health insurance and your entry-level job didn't offer any medical insurance. As a young person—with the illusion of invulnerability—that probably wouldn't have bothered you very much until:

- You came home from a camping trip with a strange rash that wouldn't heal.
- You broke your leg in a waterskiing tumble.
- You faced the stark reality that you needed help controlling your drinking or drugging behavior or your starving and bingeing behavior.
- You wanted to try some new techniques like acupuncture or hypnosis for an intractible sports injury. (Becvar & Pontious, 2000)

Recent Developments in Health Care Delivery

Throughout most of this century, medical care has been delivered by independent, private doctors along with a mix of private and for-profit hospitals. The bills for medical care have been paid by the patient who received the treatment. Only very poor people (or those who are currently in or have served in the armed services) received free or subsidized care in clinics.

Health Maintenance Organization (HMO) A health care institution or association of doctors that contracts with its members to collect a fixed sum of money monthly or yearly in exchange for doctor visits, tests, medications, hospital care, and preventative services as needed.

During the second half of this century, hospitalization insurance, paid for by individuals, sometimes with the help of their employers, became part of the funding picture. As early as the 1920s there were a few scattered small-scale experiments that offered prepaid doctor visits with a panel of medical practitioners. But it was not until the Depression that a large-scale innovative program, the nonprofit Kaiser-Permanente—the grandparent of all **Health Maintenance Organizations (HMOs)**—came into being (Lowman & Resnick, 1994). This early HMO had a populist flavor to it. The designers of the plan wanted to deliver accessible, high-quality care to a large portion of the neglected population. This experiment and others patterned on it were enthusiastically received years later, as health care costs and the demands for services spiraled out of control. Congress passed the Federal Health Maintenance Organization Act (PL 93-222) of 1973, which established nationwide standards and offered financial incentives to fledgling HMOs.

While employer-supported and private health plans expanded their reach, social activists were prodding Congress to pass health care legislation that would cover everyone in the country and be paid for from income taxes—the kind of universal coverage that Canada and several European countries already had. After many years of acrimonious debate between the social service establishment and organized associations of medical doctors, Medicare, prepaid health care for those 65 years of age and older, was finally passed by Congress. It still wasn't universal coverage, but it was a beginning.

By the 1980s, at least six or more innovative arrangements in health care delivery were gaining momentum:

- Group practices of medical practitioners
- Panels of medical practitioners
- Building-based Health Maintenance Organizations
- Prepaid medical plans
- Employer-assisted plans
- Government-managed, tax-based medical insurance

The Rise of For-Profit Managed Health Care

During the first two years of the Clinton administration, tax-supported universal health insurance looked as if it had a good chance of passing. But it suffered major political and public relations setbacks. Fearful of more "big government," Congress wiped it off its agenda.

However, it was clear to everyone that health care options were multiplying along with health care costs and that some type of managed system was vital. For-profit managed health schemes incorporating many of the previously mentioned features and promising to keep escalating health care costs under control arose to fill the gap. As they grew in number, they formed what is now admiringly referred to by stockbrokers as the *health care industry,* the fastest-growing sector of the economy. In 1997, between 100 to 150 million people (about one in eight) were enrolled in an HMO or some other form of managed health care. That number continues to rise (*Psychotherapy Finances,* 1998; Vallianatos, 2001).

Some Problems with the Expansion of the Health Care Industry

Although more people have prepaid health care coverage than ever before and many are receiving care they never dreamed of in the past, both human service practitioners' and the public's attitudes about for-profit care are conflicted (Corcoran & Vandiver, 1996; O'Neill, 2001b). There is an odd mix of negatives and positives; there are more medical options available; people are living longer, but health plans still need to turn a profit.

As one anonymous critic summed it up, "The doctor's credo of *'Do no harm!'* sometimes seems to have evolved to *'Do no harm—to the stockholders!'*" A review of the issue published by the National Association of Social Workers is entitled "Humane Managed Care?". The report suggests that those words might be an oxymoron! (Schamess, Gerald, & Lightburn, 1998). The following criticisms are the ones we hear discussed in human service agencies, by patient advocacy groups, and even the medical establishment.

- Some plans offer doctors financial incentives to keep costs down by *not recommending* expensive tests or procedures that might be of critical importance.

- Panels of approved health care providers are not necessarily screened for quality but simply for their willingness to accept the **fee-for-service** stipulated by the company. Often a limited list of providers means long waits for medical procedures or visits.

- Many plans have been accused of rationing or denying requests for respected experimental or complementary medical procedures.

- Most plans have **gatekeepers** (often untrained in the particular medical specialty) who have the power to veto a doctor's choice of a treatment plan.

- When a requested service is rejected, some plans have no genuine appeal mechanism for the consumer's protest.

- By congressional fiat, plans are protected from being sued for malpractice when a service is withheld, although individual doctors can be held accountable.

- Mental health practitioners are often forced to affix a diagnosis or label that they do not believe is accurate, in order to obtain approval for counseling sessions with a person in crisis.

- Computerization of personal health and mental health information might be used to reject a prospective enrollee or it might be divulged to a current employer without the patient's knowledge or consent.

Fee-for-service
A prearranged amount of money that will be paid to a health care provider each time he or she delivers a specific service to a plan member in accordance with the plan's criteria for that service.

Gatekeeper
A person in the health plan organization who decides whether a prescribed medical service will be paid for based on its set of criteria for care.

EMPLOYEE ASSISTANCE PROGRAMS (EAPs)

The terms *EAP* or *Employee Assistance Programs* may not be as familiar to most people as the terms managed health or HMOs, but EAPs are becoming increasingly more important in the provision of mental health services, often for people who have no other resources. EAPs have actually been in existence about as long as managed health plans, and as both types of program expand, it is often hard to tell where one begins and the other leaves off.

EAPs are structured, separate plans (independent from health insurance) provided by employers (usually of mid-size to large nonprofit and profit-making businesses) that provide employees with referral and counseling services covering substance abuse, mental illness, marital difficulties, financial and legal problems, and the like (Sciegas et al., 2001; U.S. Dept. of Labor, 1998). These are all problems that could adversely affect the productivity of employees. In Chapter 1, we read about the worker from the human resource department of Kathy's dad's brokerage firm who made a referral and even arranged payment so her father could enter an alcohol rehabilitation program. His employers didn't want to lose this employee, one with many years of service in whom they had invested the time it took to train him to do his work well.

If you attend a large university, it is likely that there are EAP personnel available to help a staff member who is in serious crisis. They might provide services in the personnel department or counseling center or contract with a local mental health agency, hospital, or other social service program.

There are scant hard data on the effectiveness of these programs, but since they continue to proliferate, one might assume that employers find them a useful tool to cut down on the attrition, absenteeism, and distraction of employees, especially those in the upper echelons of the enterprise.

Yet EAPs, like managed health plans, have their downsides, also. In a study of several companies, Ian E. Butterworth (2001) found an interesting paradox. On the one hand there was consistent support among participants for the services provided. But, unfortunately, this enthusiasm appeared to apply only when it related to a fellow employee or a supervisor's problem, not their own. Butterworth found that many employees attached a great deal of stigma to using the services the EAP provided. They feared that supervisors or colleagues would lose respect for them if they admitted having a problem. They felt that they would be embarrassed to be seen, for example, walking into an AA meeting.

Of course this finding is not at all surprising. The researcher proposed that employees, both the current and new ones, be given an orientation to the EAP program. In that orientation the staff should openly acknowledge the existence of stigma in using human services, especially in the workplace. Perhaps open discussion of this issue would encourage employees to use the services before they arrive at a critical point. Not surprisingly, many employees who had previously avoided the "stigma" of EAP services embraced them gratefully after the attacks at the World Trade Center on September 11, 2001 (9/11). Whether that will have a permanent effect on worker receptivity to their firm's EAP services in the future is open to conjecture.

Implications for Human Service Workers

There is no doubt that for-profit managed health care is here to stay and is expanding. More and more employers—even in the low-wage service sector—are providing some form of health insurance via an HMO or managed health care plan. That is good news for many clients, who in years past would have had no funds to obtain physical and mental health services. That is the upside of the picture.

But there are serious downsides. The news from the financial sector is that many of the for-profit health care companies are merging, forming a few megacorporations that can exert more decision-making control over which patients will receive what kinds of services.

Recently, the complaints of health care consumers and advocates have grown louder and have reached the halls of Congress (O'Neill, 2001a). There is momentum to pass a consumer's bill of rights, which would provide protection from the arbitrary power of the gatekeepers and the cost cutters. Proposed legislation is also aimed at providing consumers with some legal redress if they feel mistreated (Grillo, 1997; Weinstein, 1998).

Although all issues of a client's well-being are of concern to human service workers, it is the cutbacks in the area of mental health services that affect our ability to help clients. Many mental health workers complain that reimbursement for the "talking therapies" is becoming almost impossible to obtain. Routinely, patients are offered only the more economical, quick-fix medication solutions. While medication can be vital for a person in a psychological crisis, many causative factors in a person's depressed or addicted behavior also need to be explored (Hoyt, 1995; MacKenzie, 1995; Schreter, Sharfstein, & Schreter, 1994).

What Can the Individual Human Service Worker Do to Improve Health Care Delivery?

Here are some suggestions for workers to help human service clients benefit from the advantages of expanded health care while avoiding some of its pitfalls:

1. Keep yourself informed about the issues of patients' rights in health care by reading periodicals and professional articles. Share this information with your clients.

2. Write to your own legislators, encouraging them to support consumer protection legislation in health care.

3. When a client has a choice of health care providers, help him or her review questions to ask about the benefits and procedures of each plan that will lead to an informed decision. If necessary, make the phone call with them or for them, according to their language fluency and general capabilities.

4. If you believe that a client is being denied a necessary service, encourage him or her to get a full explanation (in writing) of the grounds for the refusal and the qualifications of the person who made the decision. Then file an appeal on the decision and alert others in the agency about the appeal. If all other channels fail, the client usually has the right to go to arbitration.

5. If a particular company routinely denies appeals, it might be necessary to notify the state agency that oversees insurance carriers and health plans as well as your local legislators. This is especially important if there is a pattern of egregious practices that come to light.

All of these acts might seem very difficult for the beginning worker. But when you read the chapter on organizing strategies, you will discover that most beneficial changes happen when a lot of people get together, do their homework, and mobilize public opinion (Jarmon, McFall, Kolar, & Strom, 1997; Urdang, 1999).

SUMMARY

1. Terms such as *case manager, counselor,* and *advocate* are often used interchangeably. There are no universally agreed-on definitions of their roles or training. We choose the term case manager/counselor.

2. Arbitrary distinctions might be made on the basis of the worker's academic degree, the gravity of the problems, or whether the worker deals with emotions or resources. We do not think that this kind of distinction is useful. All workers deal with emotions and resources.

3. All case manager/counselors work to help clients:
   a. Release negative feelings
   b. Increase understanding of themselves and their situations
   c. Make plans and decisions
   d. Implement plans and decisions

4. The case manager/counselor performs seven steps in each case process. He or she does the following:
   a. Prepares for each encounter by using preparatory empathy and evaluating referral data. (Referral data are both objective and subjective.)
   b. Gathers information in a planned and focused way through conducting intake interviews, home visiting, holding case conferences, and doing direct observation. This is often called the assessment phase.
   c. Builds supportive relationships
   d. Negotiates a written or verbal contract
   e. Creates an action plan that translates overall problems into smaller ones, visualizes alternative paths, considers constraints and consequences, sets priority tasks, maps out steps, and sets time frames
   f. Implements the action plan through giving emotional support and making referrals to resources
   g. Evaluates the process through informal requests for feedback and through more formal surveys and questionnaires

5. Crisis intervention is built on systems theory. The worker must quickly and directively help mobilize the person in crisis and his or her resources until the immediate danger period passes. Long-range work on the precipitating problem can then begin.

6. Case management in the era of managed health care offers both assets and liabilities. It can provide many more physical and mental health services now than in the past, but HMOs and insurance companies often arbitrarily ration

or limit that care. Caseworkers must learn strategies to assist clients in choosing and navigating health care programs.

7. Employee Assistance Programs (EAPs) also are sources of mental health services for workers in many businesses and nonprofit organizations. The stigma involved in using these services in the workplace needs to be openly acknowledged and worked with. We suggest that since the widespread trauma of 9/11, this stigma may have lessened, as many employees and family members involved in that tragedy have already sought help.

DISCUSSION QUESTIONS

1. Think back to when you have been in a dispute with your parents over issues of spending money, curfew, use of the car, your choice of friends, etc. In what ways have you tried to understand their point of view? How might you apply the concept of "preparatory empathy" before embarking on what might be a very tense encounter with your parents or in the future with a client who presents a very troubled picture of perhaps child or spousal abuse?

2. When you think about a class that you are now taking (either this one or another) as a form of human service encounter with the student as a client and the instructor as the worker, try to visualize the contract between the parties. What are the rules of the road in that class, both the formal ones and the informal ones? How clear are the expectations the students have of the instructor and those the instructor has of each of the students? How might this contract be made clearer or more realistic, if you think it needs to be changed?

3. What kind of health care arrangements do you and your family have right now? What kind of comments have you heard your parents make about their coverage situation? Would you be willing to pay higher taxes if it meant that every citizen would be given health insurance through the government (just as Medicare now covers most people over the age of 65)? What are the upsides and downsides of a government-sponsored health care program as opposed to the current free-market approach where coverage depends on your employer or your ability to buy a private plan?

WEB RESOURCES FOR FURTHER STUDY

National Center on Child Abuse and Neglect
http://nccanch.acf.hhs.gov

American Foster Care Resources, Inc.
www.afcr.com

For more information on the issues and resources available for children who have been abused or neglected and for foster care in general.

Mental Health
www.mentalhealth.org

Many resources for information on children and families who face mental health problems either with their birth children or with foster or adopted children.

Managed Care
www.naswil.org/mc/managedcare.htm

For materials about managed care plans and for explanations of terms, etc.

CHAPTER 10

Facilitating Groups

As we have read, many people seek out a casework/counseling intervention when they need help coping with a problem. But at some point they are likely to realize that many others have the same problem. Perhaps they would benefit from interacting with those people, giving and getting support from them. So they might be referred to a group or find one themselves. It might be a therapy group, a recreation group, or a self-help group led by a human service worker or by a person who has lived with that problem but is now in recovery.

We point out in this chapter that many human service workers hesitate before starting or leading a group. The patterns of interaction can be hard to follow and even harder to control. They fear that confidentiality might be breached and that they cannot guarantee each member's safety. But while those are real hazards, group interventions have been on the rise for the last four decades. With the deinstitutionalization of mentally and physically disabled people and escalating budget cuts, group interventions are likely to continue to expand. So workers must prepare themselves to master the leadership skills this intervention demands.

From reading the log entries of a human service worker in a community residence, we observe how she moves in and out of the interaction among the members, helping them plan an activity and then resolve conflicts that occur along the way. She helps them take responsibility for their behaviors as members of a group.

Before a worker like Beth begins a group, she must ask and try to answer ten basic questions. She must ponder why the group is needed, what its goals will be, and what phases it is likely to pass through. She must think about who the members should be, where the group should meet, and what activities and structure will help it do its work. She must think through issues concerning a suitable environment for the group and consider the leadership it will need at different junctures in its life history. She must reflect on the kinds of interactions the members and leader will experience among themselves and what feedback mechanisms will help the group members work together most effectively to meet their goals.

WORKERS AS GROUP MEMBERS

Few people have neutral feelings about being in a group or working with one. Groups elicit strong feelings.

"Oh, no, not another meeting!" groans Arlene, an overworked drug abuse counselor. "All we do when the staff gets together is waste time arguing. We listen to dull reports or the administrator asks our opinion about decisions she has already made. I'd rather be at my desk catching up on my paperwork or be out in the field visiting a client!"

"Although I never have enough time in my day, I look forward to our agency meetings," says Ernesto, a family worker in an early-intervention program for developmentally delayed preschool children. "When we get together, we pool our ideas, share information, and really encourage each other. Sure we argue sometimes, but at least when a decision finally gets made, I know that I put my two cents' worth into it."

It is not surprising that there are such sharp differences of opinion about the usefulness of working in groups. When members are interacting productively, a group can be an invaluable tool for solving problems, receiving and offering emotional support, and building self-confidence. When conflict rages or goals and procedures are unclear, a group can be a seething cauldron of tension and inefficiency.

Regardless of how *you* feel about groups, as a staff worker in a human service agency, you will probably spend a surprisingly large percentage of time interacting in groups. You will be expected to be an active participant in workshops, case conferences, and staff meetings. Eventually you might find yourself:

1. Facilitating a meeting of new staff or perspective clients
2. Leading a support or training group
3. Mediating a staff gripe session
4. Chairing a committee that is planning the agency open house
5. Becoming active in your agency union or professional association

After your workday ends it is likely that you will interact with members of your family, the nuclear unit as well as your extended network of relatives and intimate friends. At some time in our lives all of us have been members of peer groups: the Scouts, a 4-H club, the "Y," a sorority or fraternity, a church, a choral group, a civic association, or sports team.

Some groups are formal organizations conducted according to by-laws, rules, and codes of conduct. Friendships, cliques, or gangs are informally organized, but they also develop a structure and unwritten rules called **norms**. Both types of groups play a role in our early socialization, and some will continue to influence us throughout adult life.

Groups are sources of emotional support and help shape each member's attitudes and behavior. Sociologists call the ones that influence us the most profoundly our **primary reference groups**.

Norms Mutually acceptable rules, regulations, and standards of behavior.

Primary reference groups Groups in which a person is intimately involved, including family and friends who influence one's attitudes and values.

Group Leadership Roles Have Been Increasing

In the past, workers who felt uncomfortable assuming group leadership roles used to be able to keep them to a minimum. As counselors in a hospital or a mental health agency, they traditionally conducted most of their work on a one-to-one model. The person coming for help was seated across the desk from the "expert" human service worker who knew the resources. Because workers rarely interacted with clients in groups, the skills of group leadership received scant attention in the mental health literature and in college courses. But now the need for skilled group leaders has risen dramatically. Several factors have accounted for this increase. Let us review these, as they will undoubtedly continue to exert pressure to expand the use of group interventions.

THE IMPACT OF THE "WAR ON POVERTY" PROGRAMS

As noted in Chapter 2, Congress passed a landmark piece of legislation in the 1960s, the Economic Opportunity Act, which launched the "War on Poverty." This bill mandated that all programs for the unemployed and underemployed must include the "maximum feasible participation" of the client population. For the first time in our history, poor people were not to be seen as simply the recipients of services. They were recognized in federal legislation as resources who had ideas about what they needed in order to improve their life chances. No longer would *they* be considered passive supplicants and professionals the sole experts. The legislation assumed that clients and mental health professionals, by collaborating, could solve the pervasive problems of poverty.

The War on Poverty programs stressed the need to search out and eradicate the social roots of personal problems. During this period of energy and creativity there was a growing use of the "each-one-teach-one" model of helping. Community activists were encouraged to organize, inspire, teach, and assist their neighbors at churches, in recreation centers, and at the meetings of tenants, unions, and hometown clubs.

Many of these activists were hired by neighborhood-based **grass roots programs.** The styles of these indigenous workers grew out of neighborhood life. They talked, ate, and lived like the client population. They felt at home with the pace and closeness of group interaction, which felt much like that of their extended families.

Although most of these programs have long since been terminated and maximum feasible participation is fast disappearing from the scene, the informal group interventions it birthed left an imprint on the field. The concept and style of client participation still persist in the ethical codes of most human service workers.

Grass roots programs
Programs started by those persons who do not hold the official decision-making positions within a system but have a stake in the outcome of its services or policies.

THE RISE OF THE SELF-HELP SUPPORT GROUP

During this same last four decades, the self-help group model, pioneered by Alcoholics Anonymous (AA), has grown tremendously. The support group, in which members use each other as resources for problem solving, has spread from one area of addiction and dysfunction to many others. The twelve-step model of recovery designed for alcohol abuse has been adapted to help people who smoke, overeat, gamble too much, or use physical violence in relationships. It has grown at such a tremendous pace that there are now self-help groups for virtually every social and medical problem one can imagine (Riessman & Gartner, 1977, 1980; Wuthnow, 1994). They have proliferated all around the world (Madara & Meese, 1998; White & Hadara, 2004).

A variation of this self-help model has been used to further the work of the civil rights movement and for the liberation struggles of feminists, homosexuals, and people who are physically and emotionally handicapped. Unquestionably, support groups will continue to spread in response to the increasing disintegration of the traditional extended family and workplace, as well as the decreasing role of many religious, civic, and fraternal associations.

THE IMPACT OF DEINSTITUTIONALIZATION

The community mental health movement begun at the end of World War II has continued to gain momentum and has firmly lodged itself in the field. It was propelled by the belief that mental patients and developmentally delayed adults were being made even more dysfunctional by being segregated in impersonal institutions. The road to health lay in moving them out of the back wards of state institutions and back into community life.

Small community residences or group homes were opened to receive them and integrate them into the mainstream. There, the residents performed many tasks of daily life together. These groups became natural arenas for emotional support and behavioral change. Group leaders had to be recruited and trained to staff these houses. The need for staff continues to this day and many students are likely to do their internships and accept employment in these programs.

After being deinstitutionalized, some former patients moved back to their family homes. To avoid isolation and stagnation, day-activities programs and sheltered workshops were organized. In these settings, group interaction is prescribed as a vehicle for acquiring socialization and independent-living skills.

THE DEVELOPMENT OF SYSTEMS THEORY

The development of systems theory has also spurred interest in groups. Systems theorists assert that when any member of a group—a family, for example—has a serious emotional, physical, educational, or vocational crisis, all members of the group are intimately involved. They are part of the problem and thus must be part of its solution.

The group member who is identified as the troubled person might be acting out tensions that can be traced to the faulty interaction patterns of the whole family. The mother who drinks too much, for example, might be either the scapegoat or safety valve who keeps other family members from facing the seriousness of their own problems (Okun, 1996; Okun & Rappaport, 1980). Systems theorists warned us that working with one family member in isolation from all the others is pointless. All of the members must struggle together to deal with the problem and readjust to a new way of interacting. The extensive use of family and network therapy (the web of significant people in one's life) plunged human service workers into the center of groups (Nelson & Tripper, 1998).

THE IMPACT OF BUDGET CUTS

After most periods of expansion there is belt tightening. This certainly has happened in the social services. After the War on Poverty limped to an inconclusive halt in the 1970s, there were a series of cutbacks in social service budgets. Downsizing began in earnest in the 1980s and escalated through the 1990s. By working with people who share similar problems in groups, rather than in a series of one-to-one encounters, agencies try to more efficiently use the shrinking time and energy of trained staff. In schools, for example, as education budgets are trimmed, the guidance counselors and social workers are the first to experience a reduction in force. That lone counselor, facing a caseload of hundreds of teenagers and their families with many special needs and life transitions, is forced to utilize group meetings and orientations. In many settings, the one-to-one interview has become a rare luxury!

Thus, from both professionally sound considerations about the utility of groups as well as from practical necessity, the group model of problem solving continues to expand. Let's look at some moments in the life of the residents of a group home by reading the journal entries of one worker.

Example of a Human Service Worker in a Community Residence

Beth Soline is a night-shift counselor at Transition House, a community residence for ten adults who were released from a state mental hospital (after spending many years vegetating on the back wards). Transition House's primary goal is to provide a supportive home environment in which life survival skills can be strengthened. It is hoped that the residents will eventually rejoin their families or move into their own apartments and perhaps into the workforce. The residents have Individual Service Plans (ISPs) that describe in detail the life skills they need to work on. For example, these are the priorities for two of the residents:

1. For Eileen it is travel skills, learning to locate the correct buses, making change, and staying calm during rush hour.
2. For Miriam it is improving her social skills and learning to express feelings with words rather than through withdrawal or verbal abuse.

The counselors at Transition House spend the last hour of their shift carefully recording what transpired on the job. In the agency log book they note any commitments they have made to clients. They describe problems that occurred on their shift and any unusual circumstances that might have future repercussions.

The log book maintains continuity from one shift of workers to the next. By reviewing the logs periodically, the agency director assesses the progress of both the clients and the staff. Troubling episodes or behaviors that are described in the log book often become agenda items at weekly staff meetings. These notes also help the director decide on topics for their monthly staff training sessions.

Beth records in more detail than many of the other staff members because this position is her human service internship. By reading these recordings, her supervisor helps her expand her understanding of what is going on in the group and how she can best use her skills.

TRANSITION HOUSE LOG BOOK

Worker: Beth Soline

Time: Night Shift

Date: Tuesday, May 3

Arrived at 4:10 P.M. Found Miriam, Carlos, Michael, and Viet in the den trying to decide where to go for their social activity that evening. Helped them sort through the choices. Movies, bowling, and eating out were their first three. Got them to consider the costs, time schedule, dress requirements, and behavioral demands of each.

Carlos, Viet, and Michael wanted to eat out, but Miriam kept insisting on going bowling. She got pretty agitated when they wouldn't budge, raised her voice, and began pacing. Viet started mimicking her. I stopped the action and tried to get them to talk about what was going on. Everyone finally agreed that if we ate out tonight, we'd go bowling next Monday. Miriam accepted that, but she got very quiet, curled up on the couch, and looked tense. I'd like to use that episode as a role-play for the house meeting next week. We need to help them all talk about what it feels like when you're on the losing side. Let's see what ideas folks have about why this always seems to happen when those particular four people try to plan an event together.

Went to dinner at Charlie O's Tavern. Atmosphere got more relaxed. In fact, it was so easygoing that ordering food, eating, and conversation came naturally. I began getting that old feeling of how-am-I-earning-my-salary? But then I remembered the time Carlos threw up on the waiter the evening he changed medications. I reminded myself that I never know when I'll be needed, so that's why I'm there. Decided to enjoy myself and skip the guilt trip.

Spent the next hour sitting in on group therapy session led by Dr. Kreger. Michael, Viet, Yolanda, Tricia, and Vikki were discussing last weekend. They had each gone home, and they needed to get a lot of stuff off their chests. I didn't say much. Afterwards I spent a half hour with Dr. Kreger comparing notes on what we'd both seen and heard. I feel like he appreciates my observations. Sitting in on these sessions helps me understand the moods of the residents much better. I hope we decide to make co-leading the group a permanent arrangement.

At 8:00 P.M. I went into the living room to visit the meeting of the Mental Patients' Liberation Front. They are using the house for their meetings for the next three months on a trial basis. Made sure they had enough chairs, a working VCR, and the coffee fixings. Talked for a while with Viola who was running the meeting that night. She complained about poor attendance. I suggested she write an article for the local newspaper about MPLF. She thanked me for the coffee and suggestions but said she'd prefer it if I didn't stay through the meeting. She thought my presence might intimidate some of the participants. They have several serious complaints about conditions at Twin Oaks Hospital and are preparing to testify at the State House hearings. I wished them well and left.

I think one of our staff should also give testimony. We have been hearing about problems at Twin Oaks for a while. I have been given the runaround several times when I've tried to get in touch with staff members about medication prescriptions for some of our residents. I am scared to speak in public, but I need the experience. If the other staff agree, I'm willing to represent the house.

At 8:30 P.M. I got together with the four residents who are employed at the sheltered workshop. We went over the schedule for the morning and decided who would cook breakfast, do wake up, and call in any absentees. There have been problems getting out on time, so we're going to try a new system for speeding up breakfast and cleanup. Tyrone worked out a plan for getting breakfast things ready the night before. He got a lot of support for his idea. We agreed to try it for a week and reevaluate next Tuesday.

Spent the rest of the evening in the lounge, helping ease in the two new work-study students from Ryder College. Gloria Nywand brought in a cake for Terry's birthday. Terry played the recorder and a bunch of us had a cutthroat game of Scrabble. Evening ended with everyone but Carlos pitching in with cleanup.

When I went to Miriam's door to say good night, she wanted to talk about the blowup at dinner. She wondered if being the only woman in the group was why she was never listened to. She wanted to talk more about the male–female tension. I suggested she bring it up at house meeting. She asked me if I would do it for her. Do you think I should? Maybe we could have a discussion group for the women residents. Would it make for more or less division? Let's talk about it. Left at 11:45 P.M.

ESTABLISHING AND FACILITATING A GROUP: TEN KEY QUESTIONS

It might seem from Beth's journal that she was simply doing what comes naturally. But establishing and facilitating a group is not a random process. Before starting out and at many junctures along the way, Beth, the residents and the self-help group leaders of the Mental Patients' Liberation Front must ask ten key questions about their proposed or functioning group. The answers guide their actions as they organize and conduct the group meetings. These are questions that you will need to ask before you start a group. Each of these questions will be discussed in more detail:

1. What positives and negatives should we anticipate before beginning to work together as a group?

2. What phases or cycles is the group likely to pass through?

3. Why is this particular group needed? What is its central purpose? What are its secondary purposes?

4. What kinds of activities will help this group accomplish its purpose?

5. Who should be included in this group? What kinds of people and how many?

6. What kind of structures will help this group do its work?

7. What will be the role of the designated leader? What other kinds of leadership roles will the group need?

8. In what kind of environment will this group flourish?

9. What kind of interaction will the members have with the leader and with each other?

10. In what ways can we keep evaluating how well the group is doing?

What Positives and Negatives Should the Group Anticipate?

After a long discussion at staff meeting and then at the residents' council, Beth decided to start a women's discussion group at Transition House. She will need to think about the positives and negatives of her plan. Should she be dealing with issues of gender and role in a group, or might it not be better to talk things out with individual members? Would a mixed gender group be more useful? Would the women speak up if the men were present? Even though she might be comfortable interacting in a group, she knows that groups can be enormously intimidating places. Each member will need protection and there is no guarantee that the group will be productive.

As soon as a new issue surfaces as a problem for several members, this human service agency explores whether a new group is needed and estimates how many people might want to join.

Before they get started, she and the other women need to sketch a well-rounded picture of potential **trade-offs.** What might they have to give up for the benefits they get in return?

During one of the early sessions, Beth and the members will review the pros and cons of working together as a group. Through sharing their past successes and failures in groups, they may be able to figure out traps to avoid. Although every group is a unique entity, we learn by analyzing our past experiences.

Here is a list of the positives and negatives of working in a group format rather than in the traditional lecture-hall format. It was composed by the members of Beth's human service class at their first session.

Trade-offs Those things that must be sacrificed to obtain another hoped-for benefit.

Positive Factors	Negative Factors
1. In a group interaction class you are figuring things out by getting involved. You learn a lot about how you react when dealing with different people and moods.	1. It's hard to do solid work in a group. People use the group for their own needs rather than for learning about the subject. When a few people take over, the person in charge can lose control.
2. You hear a lot of opinions and relate to many different personalities. You can pick and choose the people and ideas that are helpful.	2. It's hard to stick to the topic or task. There's a lot of side conversation and people go off on tangents, especially if they don't have much in common.
3. When you work in a group, sitting in a circle, you feel an emotional linkage with the other members, not just with the leader (teacher). You can see that you are not the only one who thinks a certain way.	3. People can make you feel a lot of pressure. If they disagree, you can read it all over their faces. It's hard to speak when everyone's eyes are on you.
4. The attention of the person in charge isn't always focused on you; yet, it's easy to get into the discussion when you are ready.	4. People can avoid responsibility in a group. They can sit back and complain about the others who talk too much or won't cooperate.

What Phases or Cycles Is the Group Likely to Go Through?

If you were to reconstruct the history of any group you have been in for a long time, you would discover that just like a human being, the group has gone through childhood; adolescence; adulthood; old age; and, inevitably, retirement. Researchers who study group behavior in experimental situations and in natural settings have tried to describe and put labels on the most typical phases or cycles through which most groups are likely to pass. Like their counterparts who study the growth and development of humans, they do not all affix the same labels to each phase or agree on where one ends and the next begins. Some do not even think it is useful to label them at all. But most agree that basic tasks must be worked through at different points in a group's maturation. Earlier stages often reoccur, particularly when new members join the group.

Two models often used to describe these stages were created by Tuckman (1965) and Garland, Jones, and Kolodny (1965). Even though they use different terms, they are similar. The focus of the Garland et al. model is on how intimate the group members are willing to get with each other. Tuckman focuses on the interaction of the group as it goes about its business. Here are the phases they each describe.

Phases of Group Life

Tuckman	Garland, Jones, and Kolodny
Forming	Pre-affiliation
Storming	Power and control
Norming	Intimacy
Performing	Differentiation
Adjourning	Separation

FORMING, OR PRE-AFFILIATION

As it is being born and moving through infancy (forming), every group must, of course, work on negotiating its contract. Decisions need to be made about its purpose. What activities will implement its goals? Who should be a member? What type of structure, environment, and leadership will it need? Essentially, the "baby" is being named and is exploring the nursery and getting to know the rules of its own family. This is a period of tentative questioning. Members are probably asking these kinds of questions:

What's in this for me?

Is this group going to be worth the investment of my time?

Who in this group might be my friend, ally, or adversary?

How much can I share with these people? What about the leader?

Whom can I trust?

At the end of this pre-affiliation stage, members are beginning to feel fairly safe in the group and are willing to make a commitment to it. The leader gives the members freedom to explore, gently invites trust, and helps the group set up activities and group structure (Zastrow, 1993, p. 163).

STORMING, OR POWER AND CONTROL

In the storming stage, members are struggling to carve out their territory in the group. Each member seeks power, both for self-protection and to get the most he or she can from the group. Members want the approval of the leader and may vie with each other to get it. Cliques may form. Members begin to figure out ways to accomplish tasks. They test the leader and each other. Sometimes they become rebellious. Perhaps a few members decide the group is not working for them and they leave. This is the stage at which members are most likely to drop out. Some of their thoughts and questions might sound like this:

- Damn it, I seem to be the only one who gets here on time. Why shouldn't I come late also?

- We said we would throw people out if they missed three meetings, but is that fair?

- Boy, is that a relief. We agreed we could say anything we wanted, and when I told them I was gay they didn't seem to be blown away. But can I continue to trust them?

The group has to discover how well it can handle tension and resolve conflicts. During this tumultuous period, the group is beginning to establish rules. If members keep coming in late, for example, they can decide to be realistic and change the meeting time. If the bonding of the group members has developed well and they find ways of resolving conflicts, the group will be much stronger for having weathered this turmoil. If the group cannot achieve adequate **conflict resolution,** it probably will never be very productive.

For the worker this is a particularly difficult period as his or her role, compared with other members, goes through much transition. The worker should help members understand the power struggle they are going through, give them emotional support, and assist them in establishing norms that are productive.

Conflict resolution
The way in which a group handles sharp differences in opinion or digressions from accepted standards.

NORMING, OR INTIMACY

In the **norming** stage, the group becomes more like a family, complete with sibling rivalry. Members are more able to discuss feelings about the group and their place in it. They are more comfortable with the rules they have carved out and they begin to work on group tasks together. They see the group as a place where they can grow and change. "There is a feeling of oneness or cohesiveness within the group. Struggle or turmoil during this stage leads the members to explore and make changes in their personal lives, and to examine what this group is all about" (Zastrow, 1993, p. 164).

Norming
A process of arriving at mutually acceptable rules, regulations, and standards of behavior.

PERFORMING, OR DIFFERENTIATION

Having had a few successes and having survived disagreements and personality clashes, the members should now be able to spend less time on organizational tasks and on testing each other and the leader. Now the group is able to devote more energy and skill to program activities—to performing. It should be ready to take on more challenging tasks. Members recognize individual rights (differentiation), and leadership is more evenly shared.

If Beth starts a women's group and it gets this far, members may now be ready to take on more leadership in the residence. Instead of withdrawing from disputes, they might support each other during a house discussion, reminding the men that their needs have equal importance. Miriam might take a risk and agree to coordinate a celebration for Women's History Month.

If Beth does start a women's discussion group, she also may discover that her thinking about the phases of group life outlined by Garland et al. (1965) needs to be readjusted. Linda Yael Schiller (1995, 1997) suggests that there are special qualities in the phases of development of groups composed solely of women. If the group is composed predominately of African American women, she would be wise to read *Images of Me: A Guide to Group Work with African American Women* (Pack-Brown & Whittington-Clark, 1998). This is one example of why we always do research before beginning any intervention or when trying to understand why an intervention is not going as well as anticipated.

As it moves through its adulthood, new activities or shifts in membership might provoke other periods of tension and reorganization. But the group should be able to fall back on a reasonably workable structure, an appropriate division of labor, and some mutual trust. Now, the group has a history and a shared vision of its capacity to survive and perform.

ADJOURNING, OR SEPARATION

As the group comes to an end, hopefully its purposes have been achieved "and members have learned new behavioral patterns so they can move on to other social experiences" (Zastrow, 1993, p. 164). Ending is not always easy. Some members may not want to move on, and some go back to earlier behavior patterns to try to retain the feeling of safety of the group.

To help the members let go, the worker must be able to let go. Workers can help the members evaluate the experience, express their ambivalence, and take pride in the progress that they have made. If members need other sources of support, the leader can make a referral or bring in a guest facilitator.

How long any group will keep working together and whether it will need to change its direction will depend on its unique circumstances. Some groups never survive the storming stage and some perform for a while and then enter old age, becoming stagnant and eventually dying. If, for example, the women's issues group needs to reorganize or decides to go out of business, it is not necessarily a negative outcome. Perhaps it served its purpose and to keep going would be an exercise in hollow ritualism. It is always better to terminate a group on a high note than to let it simply wither away.

THE NEED FOR AWARENESS OF THE PHASES OF GROUP LIFE

Being aware of the phases of group life keeps everyone alert to their impact. Often, group members and counselors like Beth are unaware of the patterns of growth and renewal that groups are likely to go through. Each group moves at its own pace "and may eventually arrive at the same destination. Groups that skip stages or whose development is otherwise thwarted will often return to a previous stage where business is yet unfinished" (Zastrow, 1993, p. 165). A wise worker will allow the natural process to evolve and not try to force it.

It takes time and patience to build a solid group, and, once built, it may need to be frequently "renovated." Although deciding on a contract and negotiating conflicts can be very stressful, workers and members can be buoyed up during those hard times by realizing that periods of struggle are often precursors to periods of productiveness. The expression "no pain, no gain" is true for many human service interventions; it is especially true for groups.

Why Is This Group Needed? What Is Its Central Purpose?

We have stressed that no one should undertake a project without a clear purpose. Now we add that when a collection of people join together to form a group, they must articulate their goals and commit themselves to this shared purpose. This is easier said than done. Perhaps you can remember the feelings of annoyance and frustration that churned up your stomach when, after you had hurried to be on time to a meeting of your sorority or social club, someone else asked:

> *Hey, does anyone know what we're supposed to be doing here?*

Mild feelings of annoyance turn into rage when, after an hour spent working out the details of an event, someone says:

> *Hey, wait a minute, it's not our job to do that. It's the job of the program committee.*

Beth has noticed that when the members are not clear about the work their group is supposed to be doing, the members drift off. They start chatting with each other and arguing about trivial issues.

Each time a new activity or organizational arrangement is proposed, everyone should be able to answer the question:

> *In what way will this bring us closer to our group goal?*

SECONDARY PURPOSES OR GOALS

A mutually agreed-on purpose is the cornerstone on which the worker begins to build a group. But even after the group has articulated its central purpose, members might still come to a meeting with some different agenda items. Tyrone attends this meeting of the Mental Patients' Liberation Front because he is genuinely angry about the overprescribing of psychotropic medications, which have left many of his friends with facial tics. But he is also hoping to get a date with a young woman who captured his fancy at the last meeting.

Socializing can be a legitimate secondary purpose of this social action group. Recognizing this, Beth provides name tags and refreshments. A few minutes at the end of the meeting is always left for informal chatting. But socializing cannot fill too much of the time of this group. If it does, their goal of improving the mental health system will get lost in the shuffle.

In order to blend the group's central purpose with all those other purposes members bring with them, we need to remember two rather contradictory principles:

(1) A group must be able to convince its members to put their own individual purposes aside to advance the central purpose of the group. (2) A group will be most effective if it is able to work on its own central purpose while still helping to meet some of the other needs of its members (Knowles & Knowles, 1959; Rose & Edelson, 1990).

Sometimes the secondary goals for joining a group are so important to some of the members that they cannot simply be put on the back burner. Tyrone's desire to expand his social contacts is perfectly legitimate. If the Mental Patients' Liberation Front is not helping him meet that purpose, Beth might suggest two alternative pathways. Tyrone could try to get the group to expand beyond its political action goals by organizing some purely social events where members could get to know each other better. Or he might get together with some of the members who share his priorities and start another group whose main goal is socializing. Many new groups have begun as spin-offs from previous ones.

Experienced group leaders often begin a meeting by devoting a few minutes of time to the members' own immediate concerns. One welfare rights group always starts its meetings with a quick go-around in which everyone can tell the group about a tragedy or triumph that happened since they last met. The Society of Friends (the Quakers) begin their religious gatherings with a group participation time they call "goods and news."

GROUPS CAN BE CLASSIFIED BY THEIR CENTRAL PURPOSE

Although we are once again warning the reader that categories in the human services always have fluid boundary lines, it is useful to know the basic types of groups that can be organized to deal with an issue. Then, when you are in an agency and identify a new problem area, you can carefully think about which type of group seems most appropriate to deal with it. Of course we would all like to choose the model that seems most immediately important, but we might end up having to choose the model that is within our ability to deliver. For example, you may be able to organize a task-focused social action group for Tyrone and his peers or you may be able to help them organize a purely social club, but you are not likely to have the skills to be able to lead a therapy group.

Here are brief descriptions of each of the basic group formats.

Therapy Groups

Therapeutic or rehabilitative Types of groups whose members usually have in common a mental or physical problem of some magnitude. Usually led by a professionally trained leader.

Beth looks back with great satisfaction at the camping trip she went on with the residents of Transition House. The director commented on the sense of self-worth and competence that radiated from the campers on their return. In the fullest sense of the word, all successful group experiences can be **therapeutic or rehabilitative** for their participants.

But when we use those terms to describe a mental health group, we apply it more precisely. The term *therapy group* describes a group that is composed of people who have specific emotional and/or physical problems that seriously interfere with their work, education, or social relationships. At Transition House, for example, therapy groups are led by two trained professionals using a specific model of intervention. One of the psychologists describes herself as a behaviorist. She focuses on concrete methods of helping members extinguish nonproductive behaviors and create more positive ones. The other psychologist is more of an eclectic, using a variety of different psychological techniques, including art and music therapy, to stimulate insights that ultimately might change the members' behaviors.

Although the content of each therapy session grows out of the current and past experiences of the members, the focus of this type of group is in the hands of the counselor or therapist. The professional leader selects the participants and sets the ground rules. Most counseling or therapy groups encourage a great deal of interchange among the participants, but the leader is responsible for encouraging change in the attitudes or actions of each member.

These groups are usually quite small—six to ten members is most typical—and they frequently continue meeting over long periods of time (although current members might leave and new ones take their place) (Feltham & Horton, 2000; Jacobs, E. E., Masson, R. L., & Harvill, R. L., 2001).

Support or Self-Help Groups

Members who participate in a support or self-help group usually share at least one characteristic or experience that is troubling or challenging them. In Chapter 1 we saw Kathy's family becoming involved with AA (Alcoholics Anonymous) for those who drink too much, Al-Anon for their families, and Alateen and ACOA (Adult Children of Alcoholics). Within the mental health field there are many similar groups, some based on the specific AA twelve-step program and others that develop their own unique pattern.

Beth helped George and Irma Castro, Yolanda's parents, to start a family support group that meets at Transition House once a month. The relatives of several of the residents of Transition House share their pain, disappointments, hopes, and resources. They call each other between meetings when a crisis looms large and in many ways act as an extended family for each other. The group is very member-focused. Leadership rotates among the members. Every aspect of it is shaped by its participants.

Sometimes support groups are led by a professionally trained worker in their start-up phase. Beth withdrew after this group was launched. It has gone from being a support group to being a genuine self-help group with an indigenous leader and a self-generated agenda.

Support groups frequently form in response to the sense of alienation or dissatisfaction that many people encounter when enmeshed with faceless bureaucracies or unresponsive schools or social agencies. They provide desperately needed human services in the least threatening, most flexible manner. Through informality and dependence on each other, members vividly experience their own power to heal.

Both support and self-help groups typically meet in a wide range of settings. One can find them in hospitals, schools, churches, women's centers, shelters, living rooms, on park benches, and around kitchen tables.

Groups range in size from a handful of people to fifty or more members at one meeting. They are low-cost or free, easy to get into and out of, and have few screening mechanisms. Like the parent support group at Transition House, some are home-grown. Others, like AA and its offshoots, are chapters of a worldwide organization.

Although most of the AA-type groups stick to a narrow focus, the Mental Patients' Liberation Front offers both emotional support and advocacy activities. Many support groups find these two goals compatible. You may know someone who is a member of a DES support group. This countrywide network of groups is composed of women whose mothers took a drug called diethylstilbestrol (DES) to prevent miscarriages. Many of these women become infertile. In small groups they help each other cope with the deep feelings of loss engendered by not being able to conceive a child. They also plan strategies for their class-action lawsuit seeking monetary compensation from the drug manufacturer who marketed DES. In *Self-Help Sourcebook: Finding and Forming Mutual Aid Self-Help Groups,* Madara and Meese (1988) and White and Madara (2004)* offer valuable insights on the nuts and bolts of this format.

Training and Orientation Groups

Training and orientation groups have a clearly stated purpose and content that is established before any members are recruited. Although their goal is to educate the participants and perhaps to change their attitudes and actions, they are different from traditional classes. They use experiential learning techniques. Participants can test new attitudes and behaviors in the safety of the group.

Transition House regularly conducts training groups for their new volunteers and staff. They have also organized workshops for the police department and for counselors of the local family service and vocational placement agencies. Through role-plays and other simulations, participants try to understand the barriers of self-doubt and discrimination that the Transition House residents must cope with. Workshop members also receive accurate information about mental illness that punctures their stereotypes about this population.

Transition House staff members use the same techniques to train residents in job-hunting strategies, interviewing, and on-the-job survival skills. Training groups are usually time-limited but intensive. They might meet every Tuesday afternoon over a period of six weeks, last for a whole weekend, or occur several days in a row.

Beth's roommate, a graduate social worker, is employed by a private nonprofit adoption agency. Because there are so many complex issues to ponder before an individual or a couple can decide to start down the often torturous path to sharing their home with a child, her agency requires that all prospective parents attend an eight-week orientation/training course. Psychologists, social workers, medical personnel, and adoptive parents share a wealth of information on what to expect and strategies to deal with problems. They provoke the participants to think realistically

---

* An updated version of this book by Kerrin and Rothblatt is on the Web. See final page of chapter for Web address.

about the potential problems of taking on a child who is likely to be older, handicapped, of another race, or from another country.

These groups have proliferated in the last few years because many Americans have expressed a desire to adopt children from the former Soviet Union and Eastern Europe. Some of these children, virtually abandoned in warehouse-style foundling homes for the first years of their lives, have great difficulty bonding to their new families. There have been an alarming number of disrupted adoptions, a tragedy for parents and children. Responding to this, the social workers have organized many postadoption groups providing information on the cultural background and sociopolitical situation the children came from, and offering emotional support and referrals.

In the most focused training workshops, the leader sets up the tasks, assigns exercises, and runs the discussions. In more generalized human relations training—sensitivity or encounter groups, for example—the leader frequently sits quietly and challenges the members to carve out their own learning methods and find ways to resolve conflicts.

Task-Focused or Problem-Solving Groups

The task-focused or problem-solving group has both a clearly specified purpose and an end product. Staff, board members, and residents at Transition House volunteer (or are drafted) for these groups on the basis of their interests or special skills.

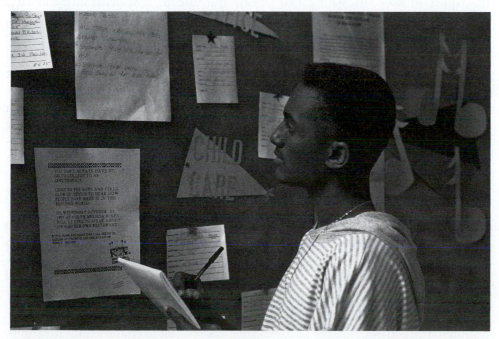

Keeping members informed is an ongoing challenge for every group. Bulletin boards, both actual and electronic, can do that. They must be kept up to date and relevant.

Committees, task forces, and study groups are formed when there is a job to be done. They disband when the task is completed, perhaps to be called back into action as needed. Right now, one group of staff and board members is writing grant applications to obtain money to expand the job-training capacity of the residence. Once they have written the program proposal, they will begin sending it out to foundations and corporation executives.

Last year Beth worked on the committee that obtained funds to send five of the house residents to a special camp program. Now she serves on another ad hoc committee to recruit and screen applicants to fill a counselor position. An ongoing task-focused committee of staff and residents publishes a monthly newsletter, *Transition Times.* Another group is organizing a holiday fund-raising event.

Task-focused groups work best when kept small so that everyone can share a portion of the work and keep moving at a brisk pace. Once formed, these groups select a leader, or one person is asked to coordinate. Coordinators help to delegate work and keep track of the group's progress.

Although task groups can be therapeutic and supportive to their participants, that is not their primary focus. Because they have highly specific output goals, they are ultimately judged by how close they come to accomplishing what they set out to do (Fatout & Rose, 1995).

Social or Recreational Groups

While task groups have very specified goals, social and recreational groups tend to have quite diffuse goals, stating their original purpose in broad generalities: to have fun, play a sport, socialize, encourage moral development, or do good works.

After working together for a while, some groups carve out a series of smaller purposes—putting on plays, conducting tournaments, sponsoring concerts, giving awards—and each event has its specific goal and tasks.

Social groups at Transition House, like those at neighborhood community centers, Y's, or residences for the elderly, might be led by paid workers, college students, or volunteers. The activities or programs that these groups conduct vary enormously, depending on the interests of the members, skills of the leader, and resources available. For example, there used to be a bowling club at Transition House, but the neighborhood bowling alley closed and now the nearest one is too far away.

What Activities Will Help This Group Accomplish Its Purpose?

Every group, regardless of purpose, sophistication, or stage in its organizational life cycle, must plan and carry out two kinds of activities: *maintenance activities* and *program activities.*

MAINTENANCE ACTIVITIES

Maintenance activities are the housekeeping chores that keep the group functioning so that it can accomplish its goals. These activities include:

- Finding and setting up a meeting space
- Sending out notices
- Electing officers
- Arranging for child care, transportation, or refreshments
- Raising money and keeping financial records and distributing minutes

Although these might seem like tedious chores to the impatient residents at Transition House, Beth has learned that if a group ignores these tasks, it rarely progresses beyond the initial stages. When maintenance tasks are taken care of, the group is free to pursue its primary reasons for being.

PROGRAM ACTIVITIES

Program activities are, of course, the primary reason for a group to exist. They include trips, plays, speakers, discussions, role-plays, and other special tasks or events through which members accomplish their goals. When Beth first began working with the residents' house council, she was not clear about what activities would be appropriate. Her supervisor told her that the acid test of any program activity was its logical connection to the primary and secondary purposes of the group. If the

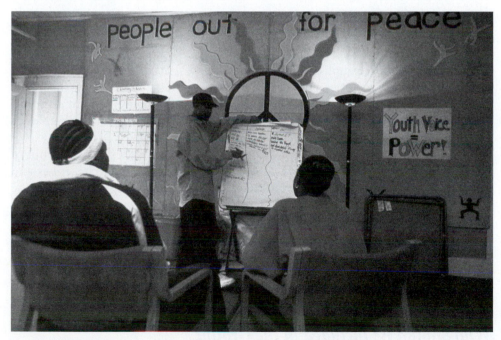

To achieve their group goals of reducing dependence on drugs, alcohol, and gang violence among their peers, these members of Teen Empowerment share their ideas about activities they might sponsor.

members could not explain in a few words why they voted to work on a particular task, it probably did not make sense to undertake it.

This advice came in handy when Beth was assigned to the World of Work Orientation group. When she took over from a previous worker, she discovered that the members had done little more than socialize and complain about their lack of jobs. They enjoyed coming to the meetings, but none of them had gotten much closer to their stated purpose of making money and moving toward independent living.

Beth suggested that they construct a long-range plan of activities to help them find work and keep a job. They could get started by inviting a speaker from the Downstate Rehabilitation Service to their next meeting. The employment specialist, Lionel Parker, could videotape them role-playing typical job interviews. When Beth first suggested it, they groaned, but she assured them that they would still have time for socializing if they started the meeting a half hour earlier. With that assurance, they agreed.

Beth learned in her course on group work that even programs that are very important to the lives of the participants might not be enough to ensure their regular attendance. Rose and Edelson (1990) suggest that group sessions, especially the initial ones, include high-interest activities, such as games, sports, dramatics, photography, and trips, in combination with the activities directly related to the more specific goals of the group. Beth has learned that delicious refreshments, especially made by one of the members, also make a group meeting so memorable that participants eagerly anticipate the next session.

COHESION

Cohesion is vital to accomplishing a group's purposes. In addition to their maintenance and program activities, effective groups must develop trust among the members and between members and leaders. Trust leads to the development of **group bond or cohesion.** This is the glue that keeps members coming to the group even when the going gets rough.

Group bond or cohesion
A complex set of forces that welds each member to the group and to each other.

Trust and cohesion are not built through any single activity. They grow out of the accumulated good feelings that come from weathering small challenges and successfully completing activities and tasks. The key to building them lies in the choice of activities. The skillful worker tries to assess accurately where the group is at any point in time. Both program and maintenance activities are chosen to be challenging without being overwhelming.

Failures that result because the group bit off more than it could chew hinder the development of trust and cohesion. The choice and pacing of activities is a matter of trial and error followed by careful reflection.

Who Should Be Included in the Group?

Most of us have a vague feeling that there is some perfect formula for the composition of a group, some numerically correct mix of males and females, introverts and extroverts, leaders and followers. Even if such a formula could be found, circumstances beyond our control usually determine the composition of our groups. The nature of the setting will most often dictate exactly who will be recruited and who will be excluded. For example:

> The Orientation group at Transition House is composed of all the new staff and volunteers who have started there during the month.

> The Mental Patients' Liberation Front and the World of Work Orientation groups are self-selected.

> New members of the Transition House board of directors are chosen for their political clout, economic resources, expertise in mental illness, and willingness to give up time and energy for scant tangible rewards.

With membership chosen by administrative fiat, chance, or self-selection, all of the groups at Transition House have imbalances. One week the MPLF had only one woman out of eight participants and no racial mix. The Parent Support Group had a preponderance of aggressive, outspoken people during its first year and the shyest of people the next.

When the family therapy group has several names on the waiting list, Dr. Kreger, the consulting psychologist, is able to make some thoughtful decisions about which members he thinks would do well together. Most of the time, though, he accepts any of the residents' families who are willing to attend.

In some groups in the community, members are voluntary participants; in others, members are mandated to attend. Perhaps a judge requires participation in a program as an alternative to a monetary fine or jail sentence. Or perhaps a spouse has dragged his or her partner to the meeting. There is profound disagreement in the field as to whether a human service worker can or should work with a group member who has not freely negotiated a contract. In any event, there is bound to be resistance, anger, and preconceived notions brought to the group by members who are being forced to attend. These resistances must be brought out into the open.

STARTING FROM SCRATCH

Occasionally workers have the opportunity to start a group by selecting its members. Then they can test their hunches about the optimal composition for that particular group. First, they will have to decide if in this instance it would be better if "birds of a feather flock together," or if "opposites might attract each other."

They will need to decide if the more articulate members should be spread among all the subgroups and committees to stimulate discussion, or if the more assertive members should be kept together so that they can stimulate and challenge each other (and keep from overwhelming the shyer members).

Whatever choices are made, the elusive quality of personal chemistry will ultimately play the most decisive role in how well the group will click. Effective working together can be encouraged through a careful matching of people and activities. But just like setting up a blind date, chemistry between people can never be predicted or guaranteed.

When deciding on the optimal *size* for a particular group, we are on firmer but still not solid ground. The sociology of numbers, long a fascination of sociologists (Simmel, 1955), as well as the practice wisdom of experienced group leaders, provide some guidelines (Bales & Borgatta, 1955; Hare, 1976).

Generally, when the tasks of a group are emotionally intense and highly focused, size should be kept small. Typically such groups have four to eight members. If they are much larger than that, members can be frustrated waiting a turn to speak. With too many opinions, decision making is cumbersome. When group purpose and tasks are less focused or the membership is transient, it is best to include more members. An open-ended support or social group might lack stimulation if it is too small.

Decisions about the composition of a group must also be related to the characteristics of the members. Age, past group experience, and communication disabilities are important factors in deciding on the optimal size of the group.

What Structure Does This Group Need?

Group structure
The sum total of rules and regulations that govern how a group organizes itself to do its work.

Whenever people assemble to achieve a common purpose, a **group structure** or a way of working together evolves. Even a very transient group—for example, a collection of volunteers who come together to rescue flood victims—quickly develops a division of labor and a leadership pattern. If the group stays together for any length of time, the routines and rules they initially establish will probably undergo change.

No matter how small or unbureaucratic the group is or how diffuse its purpose, all groups should decide on basic elements of structure. If they do not articulate their structure, one will emerge anyway. But if it has not been planned and acknowledged it will be unclear. Lack of clarity creates terrible tensions. Freeman (1972) aptly termed this the *tyranny of structurelessness.*

Over time, all groups develop rituals and norms, which are the rules, regulations, and methods of going about their work. The meetings of twelve-step groups like AA and NA (Narcotics Anonymous), for example, usually begin with the reciting of the Serenity Prayer. The meetings of the Transition House board of directors always start with the reading of the minutes of the previous meeting and a preview of the agenda for that meeting. The Parent Support Group never starts until a certain pivotal member arrives or until someone finally shouts, "Hey, gang, settle down!" The starting time in that group is officially 8:00 P.M, but the insiders know that they never begin before 9:00 P.M.

The structure that a group evolves must be reviewed from time to time. Sometimes members realize that a particular rule or norm stands in the way of getting their work done. Hopefully, they can then change either the rule or the way it is being administered.

Group purpose also determines structure. Training and task-focused groups often have a prearranged format that has proved workable in the past. Mutual-support groups and social clubs create their own. Counseling or therapy groups often have a structure dictated by the leader's psychological or theoretical orientation.

The secret of carving out a useful structure is to find a middle ground between mindless rigidity—"We start at 8:00 P.M no matter who is here"—and total chaos— "Who was supposed to bring the key to the clubhouse this week?"

What Kind of Leadership Does This Group Need?

Over many years the study of leaders, the kind of people they are, and what they do to mobilize others has captured the imagination of sociologists, historians, political scientists, philosophers, and biographers (Andrews, 1995; Bertcher, 1994; Stogdill, 1948; Stogdill & Coons, 1957). The nature of leadership is an intriguing topic.

Three different perspectives on leadership have held sway at different historical periods. All are still around today.

THE TRAIT THEORY OF LEADERSHIP

What historians call the "great man/woman theory" assumes that the unique, often **charismatic** qualities needed to lead others lie within the character and personality of outstanding individuals. Gifted with natural capacity to inspire and organize others, these leaders will, in virtually any situation, leave their imprint on a group. Implicitly accepting this trait theory of leadership, many people in the United States believe that the economic reverses and national drift of the last decades result from the lack of outstanding leaders and statesmen. They indulge in the always-intriguing "what if" game: "What if President John F. Kennedy and Martin Luther King Jr., both outstanding charismatic leaders, had not been assassinated?" or "What if the Supreme Court had decided in favor of Gore instead of Bush in the closest presidential election in our history?"

Charismatic leader A person who profoundly influences others through the dynamism of personality.

The house counselors at Transition House who accept this view of leadership keep their antennae out, looking for "natural" leaders among the residents. When they spot a likely candidate, they encourage him or her to take a position of responsibility on the house council.

THE SITUATIONAL THEORY OF LEADERSHIP

Proponents of the situational theory of leadership argue that dependence on a natural or charismatic leader encourages passivity in other members. It denies them the chance to develop their own leadership capacities. Eugene Debs, a founder of the American labor movement, told his co-unionists that he would not lead them into the promised land even if he could. He warned them that if he led them in, someone else could surely lead them out!

Nichols and Jenkinson (1991) assert that some of the behaviors thought of as desirable in a leader of a governmental or business enterprise may be counterproductive in a support group. For instance, a firm insistence that one's view is the correct one is not always helpful, nor is the tendency to take control.

Situationalists assert that it is not so much the great leader who shapes the times but rather the times that make the situation ripe for the emergence of a gifted leader.

They point to studies of temporary crisis situations when people who had never been viewed as leaders emerged out of the crowd. They took command during the flood or airplane crash, blending back into the background when the crisis abated.

Situationalists would argue that the Montgomery, Alabama, bus boycott was not so much the result of the charismatic leadership of Rev. Martin Luther King Jr. but that the situation following World War II was ripe for the emergence of a civil rights movement. Reverend King and Rosa Parks, the tired black woman who refused to give up her seat on the bus to a white man, were instruments of change, the situationalists say. They were expressing widespread discontent and a readiness to take action that already existed in the black community. Ms. Parks's refusal to yield to an unjust law ignited a spark that galvanized others. Had the times not been auspicious, the anger they expressed about racial segregation on public buses would have fallen on deaf ears.

Beth has a mostly situational view of leadership. She consciously varies the activities at the house, so that each member has an opportunity to become a leader at a particular time in the group's life. Each resident has some unique capacity. She tries to set up a situation in which each member can gain status by teaching or exhibiting that specialness.

THE FUNCTIONAL OR TASK-CENTERED VIEW OF LEADERSHIP

Leadership acts and roles   Influential behavior (feelings, acts, or words) that move a group toward its primary purposes and/or maintain the group.

The functional or task-centered theory of leadership does not focus attention primarily on the leadership person or selection, but concentrates on **leadership acts and roles.** It assumes that there are a series of leadership acts that are necessary for a group to maintain itself and achieve its goals. These tasks can be achieved by all the members working together. This concept of shared leadership focuses attention on the ways in which members interact with each other in pursuit of the group purpose.

Bales (1950), Bass and Stogdill (1990), and other group dynamics researchers carefully studied many groups both in laboratory settings and in real life in order to describe specific leadership acts. Typical leadership acts they identified included:

- Giving information
- Offering suggestions
- Seeking support
- Releasing tension
- Clarifying
- Elaborating
- Energizing
- Compromising
- Opening channels of communication
- Orienting
- Reminding the group of constraints

Bales and others visualized leadership as a series of functional acts. Thus, a group need not rely too heavily on outstanding personal qualities or auspicious circumstances. Leadership acts can be taught, practiced, and strengthened in a planful way in virtually any group.

Although human service workers find the functional theory the most useful to their work, all three theories help us understand and nurture leadership. By utilizing the task-focused concept, the staff at Transition House can help the group members understand that no one member, even the president or chair, should feel responsible for the successes and failures of the group.

The counselors at Transition House view themselves as **facilitators,** helping each of the group members improve their constructive leadership skills. Thus, when Brian loudly complains about members who consistently arrive late to meetings, they do not react as if he is a negative force. They assume that he is performing a constructive leadership act by trying to get others to live up to the group contract or to change it if it is not working.

Facilitators People involved in helping to move group members in the direction of their goal.

This perspective encourages workers to design program activities and training exercises that increase teamwork and cohesion. The role of the counselor/leader is constantly changing. If someone else is clarifying a point or asking a useful question, there is no reason for Beth to intervene. She jumps into the discussion only when no one else in the group seems able to. Hopefully, everyone's leadership skills will improve as the group matures. The worker's role thus becomes less and less active over time.

Many members might be fearful if told that Beth's aim is to share the leadership of the group with everyone in it. They need reassurance that their worker will be there when they get stuck and will help them grow into leadership roles. Each time a worker encourages members to analyze critically what needs to be done and figure out why some things have not worked, he or she demystifies the group process. When Beth helps the members reshape a rule, routine, or activity to better meet their needs, she models a problem-solving method that can be transferred from this setting to any other.

THE NEED FOR A VARIETY OF LEADERSHIP STYLES

Classic group dynamics research has shown that a democratic group leadership style is more satisfying and productive in the long run than an authoritarian or **laissez-faire style** (Lewin, Lippett, & White, 1939). But the nature of the situation will modify Beth's usual democratic leadership style. In the middle of the night when a sudden storm threatened to overwhelm the members on a camping trip, they had to quickly pack up and move into a shelter. It was not the correct time for shared decision making. Beth assumed an appropriately authoritarian "you-do-this and you-do-that" style.

Laissez-faire style A leadership style in which the worker allows the process of the group to flow with a minimum amount of leader direction.

After the storm ended, everyone sat down and pooled their thoughts on what to do next. Should they stick it out another day as planned, or go back to the house to dry out? During that discussion, Beth sat back, in laissez-faire style, letting the group make it or break it on their own. Switching styles is a matter of subtle timing that develops with experience.

What Kind of Environment Will This Group Need?

Groups, like flowers, must be planted in soil that has the right nutrients. Although the surroundings are not the critical factor in deciding whether a group will flourish, they can significantly impede or encourage communication, trust, and cohesion.

Try to visualize a meeting of your college's student council being held in a 300-seat lecture hall. Thirty students are spread throughout the hall, and the president is on the stage behind the lectern. Trying to form committees or conduct an open discussion about school problems in such an atmosphere would challenge the skills of the most experienced leader. If the council president is sensitive to the impact of environment, he or she is likely to invite everyone to come up to the first two rows or sit on the stage.

It would probably be much better to meet in a medium-size room with comfortable chairs arranged in a circle or horseshoe shape. A meeting place does not have to be beautifully furnished, but it should encourage members to talk easily without having to overcome barriers of space or noise.

Setting a good atmosphere entails common sense. If child care is provided at a parent meeting, the room for it should be convenient, but not so close that one can hear the noise of children at play. If there is inadequate ventilation, people will need to decide whether to permit smoking. If the group is doing a long-range project, it needs a safe place to store materials between meetings.

When Beth thinks about choosing a place to hold a meeting, she anticipates the problems each site presents. Then she tries to overcome them. Unanticipated obstacles are bound to emerge because every place has its limitations. The challenge is to find a creative way to manipulate the obstacles we find in the spaces that are available.

What Kind of Interaction Will the Members Have with the Leader and with Each Other?

All of us communicate our thoughts through our words (verbal communication) and our body movements (nonverbal communication). Even during silences, *something* is always going on. Whether she is interviewing a client or leading a group, Beth attempts to see and hear everything that transpires.

When she was talking with Miriam, for example, there was a pattern to their communication. Miriam spoke about how she felt when she lost the vote and Beth reflected back her feelings or made a suggestion. But in the group meeting earlier in the evening, the ebb and flow of communication was so fast-moving and complex that Beth could barely keep track of what was happening and often could not react before the topic changed. It was like a fast volleyball or basketball game without any rules.

Communication flows in all directions during a meeting as members look at and talk to the worker, whisper to their neighbor, or address their words to the whole group while staring intently at one particular person. While the worker is responding to a question that one member has asked, the others are out of her line of vision. The grimace on the face of one and the smile on another are messages that she probably has not received and cannot respond to.

As we get more experienced, we begin to discern the subtle patterns that have emerged among one particular group of people. We notice them and respond to the many barely audible messages crisscrossing the circle. As the residents get to know each other, they will (if they have practiced their interaction skills) begin to take on more of the responsibility for responding; they, too, will pick up a look of distress or another sign that help is needed. Then, Beth need not be in every place at once.

After working for a while with a group, Beth begins to identify alliances and antipathies that emerge whenever the group is making a decision or working on a task. Protective relationships emerge also, and so, too, do destructive patterns, such as scapegoating.

In many ways Beth is both a member of the group as well as its designated leader. She is distanced from it by virtue of the professional relationship. But she continues to play a central role in helping the members figure out which interaction patterns help or impede them as they work toward their goals. If no one else brings the issue up, she might say, "How come we can never make decisions without someone storming out of the room?" or "Does it bother you, Candice, that George always seems to disagree with you?"

The following are some of the acts the worker performs to help members understand and improve their interaction.

1. The worker watches to make sure that all members are part of the flow of ideas and opinions and are included in the activity if they want to be. If they are not, the worker helps members figure out what is blocking them. Perhaps the worker starts a discussion on how things might be organized better so people can move in and out of the action when they want to.

2. When conflict or confusion seem to be immobilizing the members, the worker helps them figure out where the trouble is, why it is there, and how it might be overcome.

3. The worker supports verbally and nonverbally those acts that increase cooperation, acceptance, and group bond.

4. Workers teach a repertoire of successful communication techniques drawn from previous groups they have interacted with.

Some surprisingly simple techniques can help a group get over seemingly insurmountable communication blockages. At the start of the women's movement, for example, many consciousness-raising groups experimented with ways to encourage members to participate equally. Some tried a system in which all the members began the meeting with the same number of poker chips. They had to use all of them by the end of the meeting. They spent one chip each time they spoke. Although the method seems very contrived, many groups found that it helped the more aggressive women sit back while the painfully shy ones took a larger role.

Similarly, breaking one large group into several subgroups of four or five members for a particular activity or discussion helps people speak more easily than they would when watched by twenty sets of eyes. Subgroups also permit members to experience working with everyone in the group at one time or another. Increased comfort in communication leads to more productive or satisfying meetings.

Beth has gained insight into group processes and patterns by co-leading groups with a peer or supervisor. Through their lively postmortem discussions she has learned more than any course can teach.

In What Ways Can We Keep Evaluating How Well the Group Is Doing?

Feedback Both positive and negative critical comments on particular actions, statements, or other factors.

Just like a spaceship, every group needs a **feedback** mechanism so it can keep correcting its course. If feedback is left to chance, it develops like a fast-growing vine filled with the distortions typical of one-way communication. An informal grapevine rarely includes everyone, so complaints are never aired fully enough to be acted on in a rational manner.

By using open-ended questions, which do not constrict or channel the members' reactions, Beth tries to elicit useful feedback on how each member views group interactions and activities. Examples of open-ended questions are:

- What worked best for you in the meeting this evening?

- What were some of the things that may have gotten in your way this evening?

- What parts of this meeting were most and least useful for you?

- To what extent did we include everyone in the discussion this evening?

- How much progress do you think we made on listening better to each other?

- What are two or three tips you have for Beth on how she might run the meeting even better next time?

PRINCIPLES OF CONSTRUCTIVE FEEDBACK

Before asking for feedback, it is important that the members discuss and accept these five basic principles:

1. With enough help, every member is capable of changing a specific pattern of behavior. All groups are capable of changing a rule, regulation, or routine if it hinders their work.

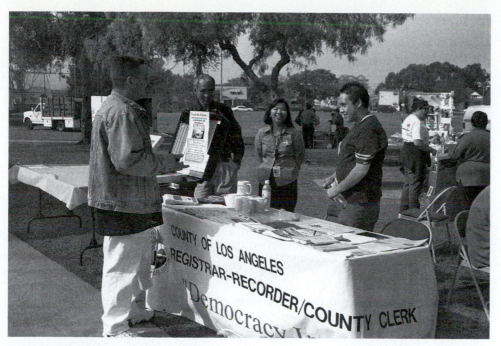

These politically active young people are staffing a table for a voter registration drive.

2. The goals of the group should be important enough for members to risk exposing themselves.

3. Criticism is not intended to provoke guilt but to help plan strategies for change.

4. Members need reinforcement for positive behaviors and help in changing less positive ones. Positive feedback should always come before the less positive.

5. It is important to criticize yourself constructively. It is also okay to give yourself a pat on the back.

These basic principles also apply to human service workers. As they evaluate their roles in the group's process and progress, workers need to constantly grow in their capacity to sensitively facilitate the development of the members and the accomplishment of the group goals (Fetterman, Kafterian, & Wandersman, 1996).

TECHNIQUES OF GIVING FEEDBACK

• *Be concrete.* Give feedback only on specific sorts of behavior that were exhibited during the meeting of the group. When our whole personality or character is judged, we become understandably defensive. Members cannot be expected to suddenly change their style of acting and reacting. They can, however, change small bits of behavior in little steps. Compare:

> I found it very disruptive to our work when you didn't show up for the meeting with the paper we needed to make the banner.

to

> You're the kind of person who always takes on a task and leaves others holding the bag.

- *Describe feelings or opinions in "I" statements rather than in "you" statements.* Most of us automatically interpret other people's behavior. Yet, we really do not know for sure what they meant; we know only how it felt to us. When we start a criticism with "You did…," we can put people on the defensive. Compare:

> You ignored me!

to

> I really felt ignored when you spoke to George and didn't say anything to me.

The "I" message in the second sentence gives a person a chance to explain why they acted as they did or to explain that they did not intend to do it. Often we do not want to hurt someone's feelings and welcome being given a chance to clear the air. It takes a bit of practice to use "I" sentences in place of "you" sentences, but it is worth the effort if it stimulates honest communication.

- *Offer suggestions for change.* When something makes us feel bad or we sense things are not going well, most of us have an alternative vision of what we would like to have happen. It is not always easy to find a concrete suggestion that puts that vision into words, but we need to try. When discussing that thorny issue of meetings not starting on time, the following sentences capture the spirit of the search for the constructive change of a negative behavior:

> I think if we all brought our coffee into the meeting room perhaps we could start on time.

or

> Maybe it just isn't possible for Gloria to be here at 8:00, so how about starting the meetings at 8:15?

- *Make sure you have heard a criticism correctly.* When we hear a criticism, no matter how hard we try to be receptive, we may still feel embarrassment, anger, or defensiveness. As the flush rises on the cheeks and the belly tightens, it is easy to misunderstand what someone is trying to say. So, after he or she finishes, it is helpful to put what was just said into one's own words. This is the process of "reflecting" back.

  For example:

> I think what you're saying is that several of us didn't do our committee work and that messed up the dance.

or

Are you saying that you actually heard me say those things about you or that you heard from someone else that I said them?

* *Keep reminding members that change is difficult and slow.* Even if we follow these rules meticulously, there are no guarantees that feelings will not be hurt. Some of us are bound to feel attacked and defensive. We are not used to giving and getting constructive feedback. It is important to remind the members that everyone is probably doing their best and that they can expect the process of feedback to improve as group trust and cohesion increase. Of course, if over time a group cannot improve its feedback mechanism, it has little chance of maintaining itself.

When she first started working with groups, Beth had a hard time soliciting criticism from group members about her own behavior. When she listened to people who had mental illness talk critically about the way she conducted an activity, it threatened her professional self-image.

Beth has begun to work herself out of the rut of self-doubt and recrimination that each criticism would plunge her into. Now she can take each critical comment, examine it, and, if she thinks it has validity, design strategies to overcome it. If someone says, for example, that she took over too much of the leadership at a meeting, she tries to think of specific parts of the next meeting in which she can delegate a task or ask for opinions.

Her group strategies must be constantly evaluated and redesigned. By sharing her efforts to act positively on criticism with the group, she demonstrates a model of self-growth. The process also shows them that human service workers are fallible creatures who, just like everyone else, struggle to improve their skills and insights.

SUMMARY

1. Groups can be powerful arenas for problem solving, giving emotional support, and building self-confidence. Groups can also be filled with tension and frustration.

2. In both professional and personal life, reference groups help to shape our behaviors and actions.

3. Workers are both group participants and leaders. Group work has expanded because of the War on Poverty; civil rights movements, community mental health, and self-help movements; and deinstitutionalization. Systems theory, family counseling, budget cutbacks, and managed care companies withholding resources make the use of group interventions a practical necessity.

4. Organizing and facilitating groups is a systematic process built on asking and answering ten key questions.

5. The positives and negatives of a particular group need to be anticipated.

6. Groups have phases or cycles of growth.

7. Members must share a central or primary purpose as well as a limited number of individual secondary purposes.

8. The five categories of group purpose are:
   Therapeutic or rehabilitative
   Mutual support and self-help
   Training and orientation
   Task-focused or problem-solving
   Social/recreational

9. All groups must work on maintenance activities and program activities. They must develop trust and cohesion, or group bond.

10. Group size and composition are not dictated by a formula. The more intense and focused the group goals, the fewer members it can accommodate. The more diffuse the goals, the more members can be absorbed.

11. The structure of a group must be articulated clearly and reviewed from time to time.

12. The three theories of leadership are the trait theory; the situationalist theory; and the functional, or task-focused, theory. All have validity, but the functional theory is the most useful for human service workers.

13. A group needs a system of evaluation to receive and utilize ongoing constructive criticism. Feedback must be phrased in "I" rather than the more accusatory "you" statements.

DISCUSSION QUESTIONS

1. Beth Soline, the counselor at the residential treatment house whose log you read, is planning to have a support group for the women members. How good an idea do you think that is? Do you think it is fair to the men to be left out of the discussions? Do you think it might increase communication among the male and female house members or create a wider gulf between them?

2. In small groups (about five or six members) each participant is required to give his or her personal reactions to the May 2004 decision by the Massachusetts Supreme Court to issue marriage licenses to couples of the same sex. If there is no disagreement among the members (an unusual situation given the American public's very split opinions on this subject), then the group members should assume roles with two students arguing for the rightness of the Supreme Court's action and two students arguing that the action is wrong and should be stopped, perhaps by the passage of the proposed amendment to the constitution that defines marriage as between one man and one woman. After a certain amount of time the group is required to reach a joint decision. One or two

members of the group should remain out of the discussion and take notes on how the discussion proceeded and how the joint decision was reached. Referring to the leadership acts described in the text, see if you can pinpoint who performed each of them. The whole group can then assess the kind of job each member did at articulating his or her position and how well they listened to each other.

3. How do you think a worker should handle episodes of scapegoating in a group of teenagers? What about bullying? Do you think a young person needs to find his or her own ways to combat being a victim—which would make him or her stronger in the future—or do you think an adult should intervene and put an end to the situation? Have you seen episodes of scapegoating or bullying in your own high school? What did adults do about it?

WEB RESOURCES FOR FURTHER STUDY

Haworth Press
www.haworthpressinc.com/store/product.asp

For articles on residential treatment, see *Residential Treatment for Children and Youth,* a journal, and for working with small groups, see the Journal of Social Work with Groups. Both have useful articles and can be accessed in hard copy or on-line at this site. Click on the Journal directory to find an index of a large assortment of other journals in many specific areas of human service intervention.

Self-help Groups
www.mentalhelp.net/selfhelp/

For a useful resource for work with self-help groups, visit this site.

For specific help in working in small-training or task groups refer to the following sites:

http://writing.colostate.edu/references/processes/group/index
http://writing/processes/group/index.cfm
www.wcer.wisc.edu/nise/cl1/cl/doingcl/finerpt.htm

CHAPTER 11

Program Planning

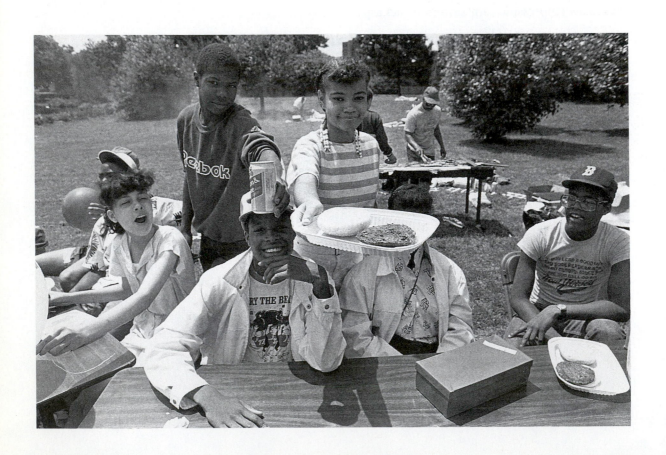

It was difficult to make the decision about precisely where to place this chapter in the book, since program planning is both a strategy of intervention as well as a method of systematic problem solving, and it should be used in all of the other strategies.

Human service work, because it involves people and their problems, is frequently chaotic and hectic. There are never enough hours in the day to spend with clients or enough workers to prepare a lobbying campaign or look for funding. Many of our jobs have intentionally vague job descriptions that are expected to change as we discover more about the needs of our group or community. Finally, we must often structure and prioritize our tasks with little help from our busy supervisors. We are constantly challenged to strengthen our repertoire of planning skills to create order out of chaos or ambiguity.

This chapter describes the tools of the planning process—the calendar and memo books, computers, files, task lists, flow charts, and agendas—that help us lay out the work that must be done and make sure that we fulfill our commitments. The chapter is organized around the three major phases of the planning process. The first phase is *troubleshooting*. It is during this initial period that a problem, or GAP, in services begins to be defined and studied and public support to fill it is generated.

In the second phase, the planner *magnifies* the area around the problem by visiting other programs, interviewing knowledgeable experts, and talking with the clients who need the service. It is during this period that new ideas are brainstormed. Proposals are then written for events such as workshops, conferences, or fundraisers.

Whether the worker is suggesting an addition to an existing program or a whole new approach to a problem, he or she then proceeds to the third stage. Now the worker, armed with support and budget for his or her program plans, begins the painstaking task of moving the program from a vision to a reality. In this final phase, *microscoping,* the worker breaks big tasks into small steps, delegates the work to be done, and then carefully evaluates each act so that future work can be improved.

A human service worker who was conducting a workshop on planning for several managers of group care facilities started the day with this anecdote:

> Years ago when I worked with after-school groups at a recreation center, I was cornered in the game room by an 8-year-old boy insisting that I try to guess the answer to his favorite riddle. Knowing when retreat was impossible, I graciously yielded.

"What is the most important fish in the ocean?" he asked me. After a few feeble guesses, I gave up. With a triumphant grin he announced, "The most important fish in the ocean is the porpoise, because no one goes anywhere without one!"

Out of the mouths of babes come words of wisdom! This silly riddle has stuck with me all these years because it is true for most things and especially for the planning process. It gives us a good rule of thumb with which to begin this chapter. The human service interventions we plan and implement—all our words and actions—must have behind them a clear purpose. Planning is the process that helps us to accomplish these purposes in a rational way. It is a systematic method of thinking through our words and actions so that they move clients and workers along in the direction of their goals.

Planning is an activity that is already very much a part of our daily lives. Think back to the last time you moved into a new apartment, looked for a summer job, or hosted a party. Before you started packing books into cartons or sending out résumés or invitations, chances are you had already decided on a plan of action. You might not have written down a step-by-step plan, but you must have had some overall map in your mind that would take you from point A to point B.

You probably gave some thought to which of the tasks needed to be done right away and which could be put off until later. You estimated how much time each task would take and figured out whom you could ask for help. If you are a good instinctive planner, you probably thought about what you would do if the apartment did not have enough closet space, if the job you were offered did not pay enough, or if the guest of honor could not make it to your party on the date you had chosen.

Without consciously realizing it, you probably evaluated your planning process after your goal was reached. Once you had settled into the apartment, you might have looked around your living room and said, "What a mistake I made scraping the floors before I painted the walls," or, "I should have checked with the neighbors before I moved in; then I'd have known that this landlord really scrimps on the heat," or, "Next time I move into a new apartment, I'm going to start packing boxes two weeks in advance rather than leave everything to the night before."

When urged to think back over a major planning endeavor in our lives, most of us will confess we have made some monumental blunders.

I can remember at least one hot summer day when, after reminding myself over and over again to fill up the gas tank, I realized I had neglected to do it when I stalled on a lonely highway miles from the nearest garage.

or

I designed and printed this great advertisement for the big concert of the year. Then I stuffed and sealed 600 envelopes, and brought them to the post office. On the way home I showed one to a friend. He noticed immediately that I'd left the date off my fancy flyer. What a disaster!

At a party it may sound winsome to say, "Oh, I never can remember anyone's name!" But a human service worker cannot afford to forget. Behind each name left off a list stands a flesh-and-blood child left alone on a street corner waiting for a bus that will never arrive to take her to an after-school program. Behind each forgotten name is a parent stung by your apparent indifference when you are not sure just which boy is her son Joshua, even though he has been coming to your recreation group for two weeks.

It is hard to imagine a human service job that does not require **problem-solving skills** and systematic planning. In his book on management in social agencies, Robert Weinbach (2002) asserts that even caseworkers, therapists, or social workers who spend most of their day in direct services still will be required to spend some time on management functions. Central to all those management functions is the skill of planning. He goes on to say that it is not true that managers manage, supervisors supervise, and caseworkers should be left alone to see clients. It is not "us" versus "them."

Even in an agency that uses the one-on-one, direct-service model, a worker might be assigned to:

- Compile a list of agencies that assist people with AIDS
- Design an outreach campaign to recruit volunteers
- Help clients put on a holiday celebration
- Assist clients who are starting a support group for eating disorders
- Organize an open house
- Plan a staff retreat
- Prepare a public information campaign
- Set up a child care corner in the waiting room
- Gather data to be used in an application for a grant to buy new computers

Although planning is a common act of daily life, the human service worker does it in a more disciplined fashion than the ordinary citizen is likely to. In this chapter we will start by describing the basic tools and attitudes of the **program design** process. Then we will describe some of its models, which can be adapted for use in an infinite number of situations.

BASIC TOOLS OF THE PLANNING PROCESS

No plumber or carpenter would go to a job without a bag of tools. Program planners also have their essential tools of the trade. The major ones are:

- Pencil and paper and a word processor
- Computer, e-mail, and planning software
- Directories, schedules, and other resource materials
- Calendar or memo book and a clock
- Large sheets of newsprint, a chalkboard, and markers

Problem-solving skills Systematic techniques that aid in achieving a goal in the most efficient and effective manner.

Program design The thoughtful mapping out of a program so that it includes an analysis of tasks, strategies, resources, responsibilities, schedules, a budget, and an evaluation plan.

Pencil and Paper and a Word Processor

Proposing that writing instruments are the basic tools of the planning process seems like a very simplistic statement. Yet, surprisingly, many people do not approach planning tasks with these in hand. Lakien, an organization development specialist, asserts that systematic planning is an act of writing, not simply one of thinking (Lakien, 1974). We heartily concur.

When engrossed in planning an event, we think about it almost constantly. Before falling asleep at night or when waiting at a bus stop, the mind races, buzzing with details. But although our thoughts may be profound, they are often fleeting insights, half-forgotten when we wake up the next morning. Plans that are not committed to paper and later double-checked for accuracy have a way of drifting out of our grasp. One supervisor we know lamented,

> "When I supervised graduate community organization students in a large public agency, I lost count of the number of times I had to stop a staff meeting in midsentence to point out that I was the only one in the group taking notes on the decisions we had just made. Knowing they lacked their own record of what happened at the meeting, I found myself constantly calling them during the week to make sure they remembered the details of the task they had been assigned."

In the course of our busy lives we cannot depend simply on our memories. Our heads are filled with the conflicting demands of home, school, and job. A worker who is careless about the details of tasks, names, times, dates, locations, or costs often fails to accomplish the overall goal of the helping encounter despite other excellent skills.

When conducting a meeting, even the most enthusiastic beginner can forget to circulate a lined pad with the words: NAME, ADDRESS, PHONE NUMBER (work and home), E-MAIL, and FAX NUMBER written across the top of the page. Lacking an accurate list of who attended the meeting and where those people live or work, the organizer cannot send everyone the minutes of that meeting or the notice of the next event. Without accurate records, it can take several days of diligent detective work to track down the person at the meeting who volunteered to print the flyers or staff the food booth for the neighborhood fair. All the people who do not receive the next mailing or phone call confirming their assignment are left to wonder why they were neglected. A minor omission can snowball into a major problem.

Pencil, paper, and a word processor actually accomplish much more than simply guaranteeing that we remember important names, addresses, or commitments; they are also analytical tools. By forcing ourselves to commit statements to paper about our problems and our proposed solutions, we visualize the planning process as it might unfold. Each time we write a list of tasks that must be done, the amount of time each should take, who will do what, and what help they will need, we fill in more details in the road map of our journey to a goal. Although the shortest distance between two points is a straight line, we often need to construct a visual image to see exactly where the straight line lies. The sorting and listing process also gives us some level of predictability, alerting us to potential roadblocks we might encounter along the way.

It is a good practice to keep a small notebook (or computer organizer) in your hip pocket, purse, or knapsack. Into this you can list those fleeting ideas that occur to you at unexpected times, and each time someone hands you a business card or tells you their phone number you have a ready receptacle for them.

Computer, Internet, and Planning Software

Although most of us still rely on the old-fashioned pen and pencil to help us remember bright ideas, commitments, and bits of information we have collected as we go about our work, computers, e-mail, and several types of planning software are also becoming vital tools in the planning process. In fact, it is difficult to remember how we managed to go about our jobs before these modern aids became widely available.

The computer should be the trusty repository for the jottings in your pocket notebook. If they are transferred at the end of each day to your computer, placed in the logical file folder on the hard drive, and, of course, backed up on disks, they guard against the loss of the notes you have taken. They also change your scribblings into solid bits of data that can be used now or in a future project and easily shared with other planners.

We do not need highly sophisticated computer equipment to order our notes into logical categories and help us build a database of people, agencies, suppliers, and so forth. Even in the most resource-poor agency or group, at least one person is bound to have access to a computer, if not in his or her home, then perhaps at a workplace or public library. In many towns there are stores that sell time on a computer.

Later in the chapter we will describe several charts that assist us in moving through each step of the planning process. These charts are also available on several software programs.

When available, e-mail and the Internet are invaluable tools for networking with others who are working in similar areas of the human services to generate ideas, secure resources, and build support. Through the Internet we can cast our net wide, bringing in ideas from diverse communities. E-mail (and the fax machine as well) is a marvelous tool for keeping members in touch with the progress of each piece of the plan and for sending out a request for assistance when a planner has hit a roadblock.

Directories, Schedules, and Other Resource Materials

The telephone book for your town and specialized directories of services and brochures are the planner's trusty companions. In the words of the advertising department of the phone company:

Let your fingers do the walking!

Perhaps you are working with a group of teenagers at a mental health center. They are trying to decide whether to go on a camping trip or to a country music concert in the next town. You suspect that both activities are too expensive. Before they get too deep into planning the details of either outing, you suggest they pick up the phone and obtain answers to some key questions.

- How much will each of the activities cost?
- Are camping sites or tickets available?
- How can they get there?
- How long will it take to get there?

Armed with facts rather than speculations, they can then go on to discuss whether they will be able to obtain the time, money, transportation, and permissions they will need. Then you can help them weigh the trade-offs of each option—what they might have to give up in order to get something they want.

One worker described how she used this technique of matching facts with wishes with a group of teenagers she worked with on a summer work camp.

Several years ago I took a group of twenty older teenagers to Mexico on an eight-week work project. The members were very mature but they often pushed against the limits of their independence and my sense of caution. During the first few weeks several of them made requests that frankly overwhelmed me. "We've been invited to a wedding next weekend three towns away. Please can't we go?" "Some people have asked us to join them in an expedition to climb a mountain. Is that okay?" Although many of their requests seemed risky, I didn't want to arbitrarily say "no." After a while we arrived at a program planning technique that worked wonderfully for the rest of the trip. At a group meeting we hammered out a set of basic questions: how, what, where, when, and what if? They were not to come to me with a request until they had the facts to back up their answers to those questions.

If, for example, they planned to travel by bus, I wanted to know the exact schedule and the exact cost, where it left from, and how they would get there. Many grandiose schemes were quickly put to rest after a call to the bus station made it clear that in this country you simply couldn't get from point A to point B in two days on a shoestring budget. By the time a request actually came to me, it was quite feasible and I was likely to agree to it.

Another worker reported using this same kind of reality-testing technique with a much younger age group:

When I ran a day camp in an inner-city housing project, the telephone was my best friend. On cold and rainy mornings the littlest children would crowd around me begging to go swimming even though I knew it probably wasn't going to be warm enough. Finally, one of the camp counselors taught her group members the phone number for the local weather report. Each day one child took a turn calling. If WE6–1212 said it was above 70 degrees and it wasn't going to rain, they went swimming. If it was going to rain and was below 60 degrees, we went to a movie, to the bowling alley, or planned an indoor crafts activity. It wasn't *me* making the decision. It was the objective fact of the weather forecast.

In each of these experiences, clients practiced systematic problem-solving skills that helped them to formulate current plans and equipped them to plan in the future. If the worker had access to the Internet, this would be a wonderful opportunity to show the children a practical way in which information retrieval can be done easily and used wisely. Yaffe and Gotthuffer, in their book *Quick Guide to the Internet for Social Work* (1999), describe a multitude of ways in which the Internet can help us in every intervention we make (Yaffe & Gotthuffer, 1999).

Calendar/Memo Book and Clock

Watch a group of human service workers at a case conference trying to arrange a date for their next meeting. All of them will dig into a briefcase, handbag, or back pocket and produce a well-thumbed appointment book or PDA. In it will be listed daily meetings and all the details surrounding them: who is to be seen, where the encounter will take place, and any driving or public transportation directions needed. Human service workers often list the home and work phone numbers of the people with whom they have made appointments. Then if they must cancel a meeting because of an emergency, even from home at 6:00 A.M., they are prepared. Another opportunity to demonstrate our caring for clients and colleagues!

A calendar book right at hand also helps a worker visualize what needs to be done, define priorities, and fit them in. Thus, "Stop by and see me sometime about those new regulations," or "We'll have to get together and talk about the Kramer child some day soon," become definite half hours on a specific day. If a worker cannot make an appointment with the foster parent who mentioned she was having a hard time with the Medicaid office, a note in the calendar book is a reminder to phone her the next day and arrange a time to talk.

Most human service encounters require some type of follow-up activity. The calendar book is a logical place to list the many small tasks that will need to be done before the next interview with a client or before a deadline expires on an application for an entitlement.

Finally, the calendar book can be a device to set self-limits, guarding against burnout. It should help workers to space out their tasks at realistic intervals, with times in between for reflection or paperwork.

A watch or unobtrusive desk clock can also help set a realistic pace. Although sensitive workers do not mechanically follow arbitrary time limits, they rarely have the luxury of unlimited time. Other clients are waiting for them, groups must begin on time, forms have to be submitted by deadline dates, or clients must be reminded to get to their jobs or interviews on time. Because every method of intervention has its own rhythm and flow, we need to establish and confirm with the clock an adequate time for a beginning, middle, and end to each encounter. Endings of meetings and interviews often sneak up on us, robbing us of the time we need to decide on subsequent steps, evaluate, or wind down emotionally. Setting a comfortable pace for our interventions is both an art and a skill.

Large Sheets of Newsprint, a Chalkboard, and Markers

To prod our memories or map out our ideas about a project, a pocket or desk pad or computer will do quite well. But when we are planning in concert with colleagues or clients, it is more helpful to use a large writing surface. A chalkboard, an erasable board, or large sheets of newsprint propped up on an easel work well. As members suggest an idea or take on an assignment, it can be written large enough to be seen by everyone. If there are disagreements about specific points, they can be quickly noticed and clarified.

An erasable surface communicates the message that ideas are to be played with. They can be listed, rubbed out as the members reject them, and raised to the top or dropped to the bottom of a list of priorities. This encourages experimentation and the free flow of ideas. Newsprint sheets lack that kind of flexibility, but they can be kept intact after a meeting ends. When a group is involved in a planning process over a protracted period, members can save the sheets with their initial ideas. Looking back at them, they can analyze how far they have progressed or notice initial ideas that were forgotten in the flurry of activity.

Black felt-tip markers, as opposed to regular pencils or pens, are part of the standard tools of the planner. They can be easily read from a distance. Thus, members of the planning group are not excluded from considering an idea simply because they cannot read it. Markers used for attendance lists, name tags, and meeting notes have the additional advantage of being easy to photocopy, avoiding excessive clerical work.

Clearly Focused Questions

When planning an intervention, you might be able to manage without a pad and pencil, a computer, a calendar, a directory, a clock, newsprint, a chalkboard, markers, and a phone, but you could not function without the questions:

- Who?
- Where?
- How?
- Why?
- Why not?
- How else?
- What if?

Planning is first and foremost a process of *asking and answering questions*. Sometimes the questions workers ask have definite answers. Often the questions are more speculative and have several alternative answers. Workers anticipate an interview with a client or a meeting with a budget committee by asking themselves and everyone else logical, hard questions about the topic under consideration.

Keith, a staff worker at the Larkin School, which provides services for children who are deaf, blind, and have emotional problems, has designed an expanded summer camp program. Now he is preparing himself for the much anticipated but equally dreaded moment when he must appear before the annual meeting of the board of directors to justify his plan. To prepare his answers to the questions the board members are likely to ask, he puts himself in their shoes (he uses his capacity for anticipatory empathy). Then he rehearses his answers to the questions that he would ask if he were a member of the board. He makes sure that he has the data to back up his answers. Most board members receiving a proposal for a new program are likely to ask the following questions:

Why isn't our existing summer program adequate?

What did you find the problems to be in last summer's program?

How do you know that the parents want a more extensive camp program?

What have you done to make sure there will be sufficient enrollment to cover most of the costs?

What makes you think that this new program can fill in some of the GAPs (necessary services or programs that are lacking) in the last one?

How safe and adaptive is the facility you plan to use for the program?

How much will the whole program cost the agency?

He knows there will be many more questions. They have a right to ask them, and he must be prepared to answer them. The meeting will be like a tennis or fencing match with questions flying at him from all quarters.

Asking questions is like shining a flashlight in a dark cellar instead of simply stumbling around looking for the fuse box. *Questions direct our thinking and protect us from jumping to wrong or incomplete conclusions.* Even after he has designed his action plan, this process of asking, finding answers, acting, and then raising more questions continues. It creates an information loop that looks something like Figure 11.1.

FIGURE 11.1   The information loop

Before we look at the specific techniques for moving a plan into action, we present the following interview with a young human service worker who has a great deal of experience in using these tools and techniques. Raquel Rosenblatt is the program coordinator of the Fenway Project, a student volunteer program at a large urban university.

INTERVIEW

Raquel Rosenblatt, Program Coordinator, Fenway Project

I have been working at this job for three years while I've been a student. The Fenway Project is our university's vehicle to get college students involved in volunteer work in the neighborhood. I am part volunteer and part paid worker. Though the work-study program pays my salary for 10 hours a week, this job takes a lot more time than that.

I can't imagine a better way to learn planning skills than this job. The first year I worked as the senior citizen coordinator. I met with the senior advisory committee composed of representatives from the seven senior citizen residences in the area. The members suggested trips and activities. Then I would recruit the sororities, fraternities, and other clubs on campus to run them. I'd get the nursing or physical therapy students to conduct exercise classes. I'd try to find a political science or government major to run a current-events discussion group or maybe a seminar.

One year we ran an all-day workshop on the crisis in prescription drug coverage. I invited the speakers and moderated the panel discussion. Another year we had one workshop on AIDS awareness and another on the political changes and globalization that so many young people are talking about. Our faculty members enjoy being asked to give mini-lectures to the seniors. It's a change from college students. I have found the elders to be a very alert group of people who want to keep up with current events.

We also invite the seniors to the campus to speak in classes. Faculty who teach about issues involved in aging, for example, like to have them give firsthand accounts of growing old in this country. A history professor who was teaching about the Depression era asked if we could set up a panel of seniors to talk about what life was like then. It was a major success.

Each Wednesday I organized a senior citizen trip, using the university buses and vans. We've gone to discount malls for shopping, to outdoor concerts, and to many of the historical places around the city. Few of the seniors still drive and for many of them we are their only source of mobility.

Once a month we sponsor a dinner at one of the centers and each year we have a dinner and dance. Sometimes a class or club sponsors them. I work with the students to make sure the event is done well. I've made up checklists of items they need to think about and a step-by-step how-to-do-it guide. I sensitize the student volunteers to the dietary requirements of many of the elders. We encourage the groups to do interactive programs like sing-alongs, bingo, charades, or pictionary so they can interact comfortably.

I also work out the logistics of our friendly visitor program. Many of the elders are well enough to live alone but are essentially housebound unless they have help. We'll send a student over to walk someone to the beauty salon or accompany someone on the train to a doctor's appointment. Some of the visitors just read mail to the shut-ins or pass the time of day.

We try to connect the senior citizens to the university resources. The adult education section of the university gives free tuition to senior citizens if there is an empty slot in a course. We can obtain tickets for them to sports events, plays, and concerts. Whenever possible, we'll transport groups of seniors in the university vans. Before Thanksgiving and Easter we recruit students to deliver meals to shut-ins; we also ran a project with Hillel that delivered baskets of special foods for the Passover holiday. There aren't many Jewish elders in this neighborhood, so they feel isolated on their special holy day.

There are two new programs I hope we'll get started even though I won't be here to run them. There are a few senior citizens who do volunteer work in neighborhood social agencies, but it could be better organized and widespread. This is an urban area with a lot of problems. They have kitchens in the Senior Residences, so we could organize a once-a-week cooking session and bring the food to one of the shelters for people who are homeless. I also think we should link up the elders with the children in the projects. They often live far away from their grandchildren and vice versa. I'd like to formalize an "adopt a grandchild" program.

Now that I am more experienced, I have been given more responsibility. I work closely with the faculty advisers on budget, office maintenance, supervising the work-study students, running staff meetings, and keeping the records. I organize the Volunteer and Work-Study fair on campus, where agency representatives try to recruit students for youth programs, the Red Cross, community improvement projects, teen sports programs, and the like.

Currently, I'm contacting faculty and convincing them to incorporate a relevant volunteer experience into their classes. I'll tailor a placement for a class. For example, for the criminal justice students I refer them to a prerelease center for nonviolent offenders or to the Safe Streets program. I also represent the Fenway Project at COOL (Campus Outreach Opportunity League). That is a national coalition of student volunteer groups.

I am beginning to think about both geriatrics and administration as possible career options. I plan to go to a school of social work.

I don't like administration as much as working with clients, but I'm good with details. I am very aware of how hard it is for women to get to the top of this field, even though there are plenty of women in it. I am not going to be stopped by the glass ceiling—I want to go as high as my skills will carry me!

PHASES AND STEPS IN THE PLANNING PROCESS

Planners wear many hats, a different one for each phase of the planning process. In the first phase, donning the peaked cap of a Sherlock Holmes detective, the planner is a gadfly, or **troubleshooter.** He runs around finding problems and noticing when the emperor has no clothes on. In the second phase, the planner replaces the peaked cap with a cowboy-style, ten-gallon hat and takes a giant step back from the

Troubleshooter
The person who is alert for signs or symptoms that indicate the existence of an actual or potential problem.

problem, looking at the *big picture.* In the last phase, the peaked cap and ten-gallon hat are put aside for the green visor of the accountant. Now, the planner looks at each part of the plan in depth, figuring out exactly what must be done. Now he or she is a nitpicker, a list maker, and a rule maker and keeper.

In the following section we will look more closely at each of these three phases of the planning process: *troubleshooting, magnifying, and microscoping.**

Phase 1: Troubleshooting

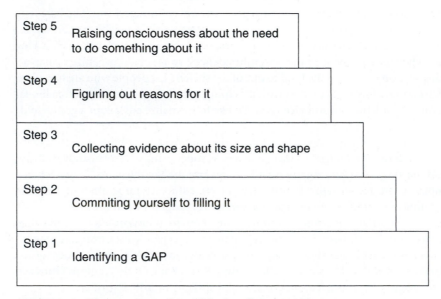

Step 5	Raising consciousness about the need to do something about it
Step 4	Figuring out reasons for it
Step 3	Collecting evidence about its size and shape
Step 2	Commiting yourself to filling it
Step 1	Identifying a GAP

FIGURE 11.2   The process of troubleshooting a problem

STEP 1: IDENTIFYING A GAP

As shown in Figure 11.2, the planning process begins as soon as Raquel or another Fenway Project staff member says:

> Something is wrong with how that is done!

or

> Something is missing from....!

*To read more about the steps involved in the three phases, see American Association of University Women, 1978; Dale, Magnani, and Miller, 1979; Dale and Mitiguy, 1978; Frame, 1995; Kettner, Moroney, and Martin, 1990; and Schram, 1997.

or

Wouldn't it be wonderful if….!

or

There oughta be a law about….!

Often we identify a **GAP,** without realizing we are doing so, when we are having a good gripe session. Listen in as Lowell, a Fenway Project volunteer, complains about the difficulty he had finding the appropriate social services for his elderly aunt.

> Over Easter break I spent a lot of time with my Aunt Elsie, who is 82 years old. She's in the hospital with a broken hip. I knew she would need some homemaking help and maybe some emotional support when she returned home. She lives alone in a small house. I don't know my way around this city. The social worker at the hospital was either too busy with more serious cases or really didn't know much about the resources for elderly people. Boy, was that frustrating! There really ought to be a place where elderly people or their relatives could go to get current information on home-care services. Even more important, I could use someone to steer me to the good programs and warn me about the ones to avoid.

Lowell was describing *what now exists* and then visualizing *what ought to happen.* In between the two, the *what is* and the *what ought to be,* there is a yawning cavern that a person is likely to fall into. We call that hole a GAP.

Sometimes a GAP is identified by a person who has a desperate need for a resource that he cannot locate, that does not exist, or that is functioning poorly. At other times a professional human service worker notices an unmet need and brings it to the attention of her supervisor or board.

In Figure 11.3 we have listed a few examples of people describing "what is" and visions of "what ought to be." In between the *is* and the *ought* lies a GAP that needs to be bridged by social service planning.

Example: A Professional Identifies a GAP

A doctor working in rural Alabama was surprised at how few patients came into the hospital with AIDS or HIV. Although AIDS is often thought of as an urban phenomenon, she knew that was not accurate. She had a hunch that people in southern rural towns, where everyone knows everyone else's business, were afraid to even ask for AIDS testing. The strong fundamentalist religious values of the region attach an especially noxious stigma to AIDS, with its implications of homosexual behavior. So, dipping into her own wallet for start-up funds, she began a public education program called ASK, which stood for AIDS Support through Knowledge. These are some of the outreach strategies she used:

- She set up an anonymous information telephone hot line.

- She convinced a popular disc jockey to play a rap song about AIDS over the local radio station.

GAP   A necessary service or resource that is lacking in a program or in services that might help solve a problem.

WHAT IS	THE GAP	WHAT OUGHT TO BE
This Is What Exists Now		**This Is What *Ought* to Happen**
"Every Sunday as I sit in church, I notice this group of people who are obviously retarded sitting in the last few rows. They don't bother anyone, and they leave right after the service. But they seem so lonely and out of it."	**G** **A** **P**	"These people are newcomers to our church and ought to be welcomed by the congregation. It would be nice if they could stay for the hospitality hour so members and their children could get to know them. That's what our church is supposed to be all about."
"Every week the hospital in our town releases people who have emotional disturbances to live on their own in the community. A lot of them have lost contact with old friends or relatives. They're just drifting. They live in cheap boarding houses, often on skid row, where they have nothing to do and little to look forward to."	**G** **A** **P**	"There ought to be some place they could go during the day if they are not working or on weekends if they are. They need to be with other people, especially ones who can understand what they've been through and know how hard it is to adjust after years spent in and out of an institution."
"Every year the YMCA has a junior olympics for the kids who attend gym classes. This year, because they've removed a lot of the architectural barriers, my son who is wheelchair-bound attends the sports program. He's going to feel very left out if he's not included in the big event, but everyone seems too worried about problems of safety and insurance to include the kids with handicaps."	**G** **A** **P**	"We ought to offer the kids with physical handicaps a chance to have the same type of activities all the others enjoy."

FIGURE 11.3   Examples of social service GAPs

- She placed ads in newspapers.

- She sponsored a group of high school students, who performed a play about AIDS at schools and churches.

Eventually, many people who worried they might have contracted AIDS found the courage to come to the hospital for testing and care.

In *Designing and Managing Programs: An Effectiveness Based Approach*, Kettner et al. (1990) point out that many people who might need services seek them out only when the possibility of actually receiving them exists. Because they have such low expectations, they often do not even perceive that their GAP is a legitimate one or that they deserve to have it filled.

This can often confuse the public. After a rape crisis center opens in a town, instead of seeing a reduction in the rape statistics, we are likely to see them increase. It looks as if the situation is getting worse, but what might actually be happening is that victims, especially of date rape, who used to feel that there was no possibility of getting justice and who endured their pain in silence, were finding the courage to come forward and report the crime. Now there was a chance that they might be protected and that the abuser might be punished.

STEP 2: COMMITTING OURSELVES TO FILLING THE GAP

Once it has been stated that a GAP exists, someone has to commit her- or himself to the long, painstaking, often thankless planning tasks that can fill it. Unfortunately, gripe sessions too often end with little to show for them but shared frustration. Often people will say:

> What can I do? I don't know anything about starting up a program.

or

> But it has always been that way!

These statements express widespread feelings of powerlessness, but they do not reflect reality. Many programs have grown out of an informal discussion in someone's living room. Park benches in schoolyards where parents gather to talk about their children, their families, and their hopes for the future are often fertile fields for new program ideas. For example, the widely translated, best-selling book *Our Bodies, Ourselves for the New Century* (Boston Women's Health Book Collective, 1998) grew out of a small all-women **consciousness-raising** group that met in the 1970s. The women began asking each other questions about their special issues of health and sexuality. Discovering how little any of them knew, they started doing research. Finding the books limited and written mostly from a male perspective, the women decided to write their own book. That first book (revised over twenty years) was followed by *Ourselves and Our Children* and *Ourselves, Growing Older*.

Programs such as the one above, designed to fill GAPs, do not necessarily need vast sums of money and expertise. They grow out of someone's capacity to keep plugging away, aided by a fertile imagination, self-confidence, and a good **support network**.

Example: Members of a Church Commit Themselves to Filling a GAP

A few years ago, one of the authors of this text was visiting a friend who had just returned from delivering a paper on "supervised visitation" at a professional conference (Speigel, 1992). Surprised because she thought she "knew everything about social programs," the author admitted that she did not have any idea what supervised visitation was. Her friend explained that the supervised visitation program she directed was the brainchild of a member of a local church. Her minister had told the congregation of the problems that families face when an incident of abuse or neglect made

Consciousness raising The process in which people are provoked into giving an issue serious thought, perhaps through suggestion of new points of view to be considered.

Support network The people and places in our lives that offer ongoing practical as well as emotional help.

it impossible for one of the parents to be left alone with his or her child. But, hoping that the abuser would have the incentive to change his or her behavior, so the family unit could eventually be preserved, the court did not want to sever their relationships. So judges mandate that the abusing parent can only visit with the child if a neutral trained observer is present to guarantee safety during the visit. However, this arrangement is almost impossible to manage for most noncustodial parents. State social workers are overburdened and private therapists charge high fees.

So this woman had the idea of using the church as a place for supervised family visits. By having families come at one time in groups, more people could be served for a low cost. Also, families would realize that there were others with similar problems.

The following is the program she designed:

- Each Saturday eighteen families gather at the church, nine in the morning and nine in the afternoon.

- The custodial parent brings the child(ren) to the church where he or she is met by a volunteer facilitator and goes off for a snack.

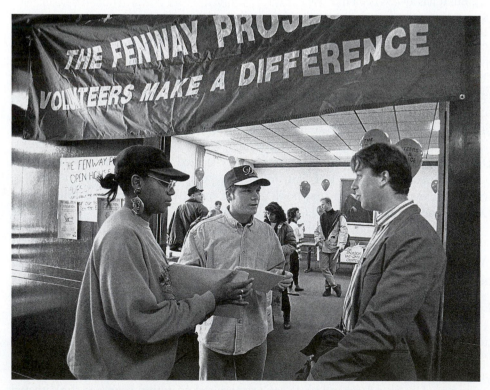

No event, no matter how often it is repeated, is ever taken for granted. Getting a message out to the public takes great imagination and attention to detail. These students are sponsoring a recruitment drive for volunteers.

- The custodial parents gather for a support-group session.

- The noncustodial parent then arrives and the facilitator and child join him or her at a table in the social hall. The table is set with age-appropriate games and craft materials.

- Parent and child interact for an hour while the facilitator sits a few feet away, unobtrusively monitoring the contact. The observer intervenes only if the child is in immediate danger or an inappropriate question is being asked or comment is made.

- Then the child and his or her custodial parent leave.

- The noncustodial parents go into a mandatory support-group meeting.

- The facilitators get together to review how things went and make suggestions.

- In the afternoon the whole program repeats with the second group of parents and facilitators.

The role of the professional social worker, the only paid staff member, is to keep all the balls in the air: training and recruiting the volunteers, most of whom are students, church members, and interested citizens. The worker keeps in contact with the courts and the Department of Social Services.

The program is overseen and the funds are raised by church members as a tangible expression of their convictions about the importance of family values. Because the space is free and all the facilitators are volunteers, the yearly cost of the program is primarily the professional's half-time salary. So far, they have been able to raise this amount through a variety of fund-raising campaigns. Often it is easier to raise money for a very specific program such as this one than for a more amorphous general appeal.

Some people accurately define a problem and immediately propose solutions. But if they start to act too quickly they run the risk of becoming a general without an army. Along with her commitment to act, this woman at the church did careful research before she proposed her idea. She understood that without solid data about the problem, she would never have been able to solicit the support of the congregation, the courts, the Department of Social Services, and the thirty-two volunteers who give up their Saturdays to help their neighbors.

STEP 3: COLLECTING EVIDENCE ABOUT A GAP

Remember the difficulties encountered by Lowell, the Fenway Project volunteer, as he tried to find services for his elderly aunt? Although Raquel, the program coordinator at Fenway, agreed with Lowell that there appeared to be an information GAP about services for the elderly in his hometown, she knew that they had to be *sure* it existed. Maybe it was just Lowell who couldn't find the information he needed. She decided to help him collect evidence to support (or perhaps refute) his assertion that information about geriatric services is not readily available.

They begin their research by collecting data in the public library. They look through directories (both hard copy and on-line) to find social services for the elderly, especially those that help maintain elderly persons in their own homes during a recovery period. They plan to interview people at some of these agencies to get information straight from the source. Before they interview anyone, though, they write up a list of questions to ask, examples of which are shown in Figure 11.4. This way they can make sure that they get the same type of information from each interview. Of course, every GAP one is researching will need specially tailored questions. But these are samples of questions that might be asked.

It is important that the people Raquel and Lowell interview represent a cross section of elderly service workers and consumers. They need to know in whose eyes the GAP exists. The people (and their programs) they interviewed are listed in Figure 11.5. Notice that their hunt for evidence about the GAP also included census data and other library resources.

From their interviews and reading, Raquel and Lowell decided that their initial hunch was correct: Information about available services was not getting to everyone who needed it, especially when they were in crisis. Both the consumers and the

---

COLLECTING EVIDENCE ABOUT THE EXTENT OF A GAP
Services to the Elderly in Aurora

I. Questions to ask organization staff workers:

1. How many senior citizens do you have contact with, either in person or through newsletters?

2. What strategies do you use to get information out about available services to the elderly population and to social agencies?

3. What written guides do you have on elderly programs? Which of them seem most useful? What obstacles stand in the way of reaching some of the elderly?

4. Which groups of elderly citizens and their families do you feel are not being reached?

5. How great a need do you think there is for some type of information service for geriatric programs? What are your suggestions?

II. Questions to ask individual senior citizens or their families:

1. How did you hear about this particular organization (housing project, nursing home, recreational center, or whatever) you attend?

2. If you needed home care, a senior shuttle bus, meals on wheels, day care, or a nursing home, to whom would you turn for that information?

3. How easy is it to get information when you need some kind of services? If it is difficult, why do you think that is so? What are your suggestions to increase knowledge of resources?

FIGURE 11.4   Sample interview questions on services for the elderly

---

COLLECTING EVIDENCE ABOUT THE EXTENT OF A GAP
Services for the Elderly

I. *People we will need to talk to:*

1. Citywide council on elderly affairs in the mayor's office

2. Local chapter of AARP (American Association of Retired Persons), National Council of Older Americans, or OWL (Older Women's League)

3. Nursing Home Director's Group and some residents of local nursing homes

4. The Homecare Corporation

5. The Gray Panthers (a self-help elderly social action group)

6. Project manager and residents at the Susan B. Anthony Elderly Housing Project

7. The Methodist church's friendly visitors program

II. *Publications we will need to read:*

1. Citywide and community newspapers (large-print version if there is one)

2. Newsletters of any senior citizen clubs or groups

3. Directory of services for the elderly

4. Census data for the area

FIGURE 11.5   Sources of information about services for the elderly

professionals agreed that some central source of updated information was sorely needed. Their review of the census data revealed that the elderly population in this area had risen by 20 percent in the last ten years. The articles they read predicted that it will continue to grow.

Now they have evidence to show that outreach to the elderly and to the general public about the full range of elderly home care services is a legitimate GAP. Some agencies call this data-gathering process *conducting a **needs assessment**.* Once they are sure they have a legitimate GAP that needs to be filled, they must find out for what reasons it exists. To do this, they move on to the next step.*

STEP 4: FIGURING OUT CAUSALITY—THE REASONS FOR THE GAP

As Raquel and Lowell were collecting evidence about the size and shape of the GAP in referral services, they were constantly asking their informants "why" questions such as:

> **Needs assessment**
> Methods used to find out precisely what one particular person, group, or community needs to solve its problems and expand opportunities.

*A useful resource Lowell could have used to generate ideas about agencies to look for is a book entitled *Making Aging in Place Work* (Pastalan, 1999).

- WHY do you think the public has so little knowledge about your program?

- WHY do the booklets you publish seem to reach one group of professionals or elderly citizens more than another?

- WHY haven't you tried using other media to inform them?

The answers to these questions begin the difficult process of estimating the reasons for the GAP. *Reasons will suggest remedies.* Although we can never be absolutely certain about the reasons for a problem, the process of identifying possible causes and then ranking them in importance is a vital one. It creates the foundation upon which the whole planning process is built.

Figure 11.6 shows the list of reasons Raquel and Lowell created after studying the interviews and reading journal articles on the subject. See how program ideas seem to flow logically from each of them! There is no way, of course, that they can design one program that deals with all the reasons. So they rank the listed items, giving some a higher priority than others. Finally, they will have to decide which reasons to deal with first.

Now the two young planners are ready to go public, looking to find others who will join them in filling this unmet need.

POSSIBLE REASONS FOR A GAP
Referral Services for the Elderly

Information about elderly services is not reaching enough people because:

1. The directories of services that do exist are all in the English language and the print is often small and hard to read.

2. Directories of services for the elderly are not distributed widely enough. They are available only at social agencies or hospitals.

3. Directories of services for the elderly seem to be very specialized, concentrating on only one type of service. Often they don't mention alternative services available at other agencies.

4. The elderly are often homebound and use television and radio more frequently than books and newspapers for their information.

5. Often the elderly and their families don't prepare for emergencies and must do their planning when a crisis occurs, when they are least able to seek out resources rationally.

6. Many people assume that all service programs for the elderly are charity and resist exploring resources that might have a social stigma.

7. Programs change so often that staff are unaware of new ones or those which have been discontinued.

8. The best referrals are made by knowledgeable people, not directories; however, agencies are short of experienced staff.

FIGURE 11.6   Possible reasons for a GAP in referral services

STEP 5: RAISING CONSCIOUSNESS ABOUT A GAP

Even after a GAP has been identified, evidence about its size, shape, and causes has been marshaled and some possible reasons for it have been outlined, the demand that it be filled can fall on deaf ears. Lots of other people must agree that it is a problem before it can move up to the top of the agenda for the client, the agency, the bureaucrats, and the legislators.

Raquel and Lowell, enlisting the assistance of the students in a class on aging at their university, conducted the following consciousness-raising activities to spread concern about their GAP.

1. They wrote up a brief report, presenting their evidence that there is a lack of information about available resources and giving examples of the havoc it wreaks on the elderly homebound.

2. They met with the president of a senior citizen center to solicit his group's support.

3. They met with the chairperson of the Council on Aging and got her enthusiastic support.

4. They got themselves invited to speak about the problem at two local churches.

5. They convinced the editor of the local newspaper to write a feature story about the plight of elderly homebound people who cannot find support services.

6. They spoke on the local cable TV station about the GAP.

Phase 2: Magnifying

Having gathered evidence and marshaled enthusiastic support, Raquel and Lowell are now ready to begin **magnifying**. During this phase they will collect, sort out, and then choose concrete program ideas—vital components of the program design process. Figure 11.7 shows the steps they followed.

Magnifying
Looking at a program or problem within the larger context of the community, laws, professional field, and so forth.

Now, their imaginations can work overtime. Although looking for innovative ideas, they will not simply dismiss as old hat those program ideas that already exist. Actually, few really new ideas are ever born. Most program concepts are variations on a few central themes. They will borrow a technique from here, an approach from there. They will recombine basic program interventions, giving them a new twist, one that is especially suited to this population, problem, and town.

Before they design their plan, Raquel and Lowell need to be reassured that although we strive for a perfect solution, in the real world one will rarely be found. Program designs have to be flexible and responsive to constant feedback. As soon as they have planned the program, they will want to start redoing the design. Programs are organic, living creatures with unpredictable demands and personalities.

STEP 1: CONDUCTING AN INVENTORY OF OTHER PROGRAMS

Throughout this book we have stressed the critical importance of obtaining first-hand knowledge of program resources in the local community. But when designing

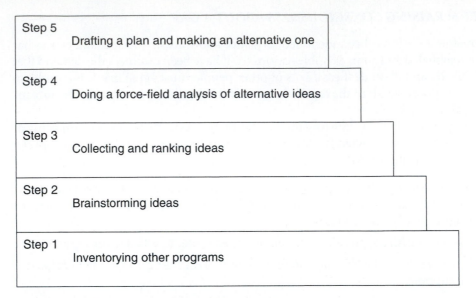

FIGURE 11.7   The process of magnifying a problem

an action plan, we look within and far beyond the boundaries of our own town, because *program ideas cross-fertilize from one region or country to another.* For example, the concept of the ombudsperson—a red-tape cutter—now found in many U.S. city halls, universities, and hospitals, was borrowed from Scandinavia. The program design for the Samaritans, a volunteer suicide hot line, was imported from England. Crèches—overnight shelters for young children whose parents have to leave them in emergencies—originated in France.

After visiting a poor, developing country in Latin America, a social planning student observed:

> On this trip I was impressed by the way in which ideas flow in all directions. When I visited the country's only residential school for the blind, staff members told me how much they wanted to study in the United States. They wanted to learn about the newest Braille machines and mobility training techniques. Their country is very far behind us in special needs programming. I noted with regret that all their new public buildings are being constructed with complete disregard of the architectural barriers that exclude people who are physically disabled. In the future, when they become more conscious of integrating people with special needs, they'll have to have to spend thousands of dollars replacing steps with ramps and modifying bathrooms.
>
> Yet, surprisingly, they had some very innovative approaches that far outdistanced ours. For example, to meet the needs of urban, two-worker couples with elderly disabled relatives, they have constructed nursing and old-age homes. Yet, wanting to keep the traditional, extended family as intact as possible, they arrange to transport the elderly residents back to the homes of their relatives for weekends and holidays. I've not heard of many homes for the elderly doing that in the United States. Because we are concerned about the increasing isolation of the elderly, I suspect that idea will eventually catch on here.

This was a good lesson for me. Although we are advanced in some areas, we still have plenty to learn from a developing country.

Sometimes program approaches are transplanted whole from one place to another. At other times, however, new program ideas leapfrog off each other. Watch how this idea played out in real life:

In the travel section of our newspaper several years ago there was an article about a travel agency that arranges for tourists to stay in elegant castles and manor houses when visiting foreign countries. A few years later, other tourist companies began arranging accommodations in more humble kinds of homes in both Europe and Latin America. Eventually this commercial travel idea reached the human services. It changed from a profit-making enterprise into a nonprofit support network for a special population. A senior citizen council in a Midwestern city set up a vacation home-exchange program for elderly citizens on limited incomes. In this plan, older people living in modest homes can arrange a low-cost holiday trip. For only the cost of transportation, they can explore the countryside or a big city by exchanging their apartment for that of another elderly person. Because improving the quality of life for our elderly is an increasingly important concern, this innovative idea is likely to spread. Perhaps as a logical extension there might be a home-exchange program for physically challenged people, and so on.

Elderhostel, a nonprofit program for people over 55 years of age, sponsors educational travel programs on college campuses all over the world. It has filled the GAP in the cash flow problem of many colleges caused by the decrease in college enrollment, especially in summer sessions. At the same time, it provides low-cost educational vacations for seniors on fixed incomes. With more people retiring in good health, Elderhostel has grown by leaps and bounds. An agency that started as a summer program on a few campuses now runs all year-round in hundreds of locations all over the world.

Program ideas also leapfrog from one problem area to another. The GAP in referral services for the elderly that Raquel analyzed has been filled in one local community by a program called the Geriatric Resource Center. Two years before it was begun, a Divorce Resource and Mediation Center was started in a nearby town. Several years before that, a Child Care Resource Center was begun. We cannot be sure that each was the ancestor of the next, but the program format of specialized resource centers that help a specific population has certainly spread.

Once you see yourself as a planner, you are likely to get new program ideas almost every time you read a newspaper, watch a television show, or attend a lecture or seminar. You will not be able to act on all of them, but you can store program designs away for future use.

STEP 2: BRAINSTORMING IDEAS

Brainstorming is a very simple yet elegant planning technique that quickly produces a great many ideas, some mundane and impractical, a few marvelously creative (Osborn, 1963). It energizes the staff of the Fenway Project, freeing them of their usual reserve by sweeping them into the contagion of shared problem solving.

Brainstorming
A technique in which people generate ideas under time pressure and without judgment so that their most innovative thoughts can flow.

They do it at staff meetings in groups of threes. Everyone can easily be heard and encouraged to participate. A brainstorming assignment must be very clear. It begins with a question, for instance:

> If we had $100 in our treasury, what trips would we take?
>
> If you were made dean of this college, what are the ten most important changes you'd make?
>
> If we open up this program to persons who are blind, what parts of it would have to be changed? In what ways?

A time limit of five or ten minutes is set for each session. Pressure encourages members to keep throwing out ideas. The group leader begins the creative juices flowing by suggesting a few ideas of his own—the more innovative the better. Participants are told that there is a premium placed on far-ranging thinking. There are a few simple rules for brainstorming (Coover, Deacon, Esser, & Moore, 1978; Dale & Mitiguy, 1978; Siegel, 1996).

- Do not censor your ideas, let them flow. Even if they sound silly, impractical, or naive, they can be sorted out and discarded later.

- Do not censor anyone else's ideas by judging them or by communicating distaste, scorn, or ridicule.

- Give encouragement and support and expect it from others.

- Build on each other's ideas, use them, and change them.

- Move quickly and try to get as many ideas out as possible.

- List ideas on paper so that they are not lost in the flow of talk.

STEP 3: COLLECTING AND RANKING IDEAS

At the Fenway Project quarterly retreat, Raquel and the other staff members were asked to brainstorm ways to spend the $1,000 grant they were awarded by the Office of Student Affairs. The ideas they came up with were listed on a chalkboard and then divided into categories:

1. Senior citizen programs
2. Youth after-school programs
3. Programs for developmentally delayed adults
4. Teenager programs
5. Special one-time projects
6. Recruitment of volunteers

Then they divided the categories according to the following criteria:

Programs we can do ourselves

Programs we can try to get other groups to sponsor

and still another dimension:

Programs that do not cost money

Programs that do cost money

Then they edited the lists, discarding ideas that seemed impractical or that evoked little interest. They put check marks next to those that excited almost everyone. These lists will be carried over from one quarter to the next. As new ideas come up, they will be added. If a human service major wants to do an internship at the Fenway Project, he or she can look at this list to see what program ideas are waiting to be developed.

The Fenway Project also keeps a wish list. Staff members suggest equipment or funding they would like to obtain if there is any money left at the end of the fiscal year. Three weeks before the budget closes, they review the auditor's printouts. They see how much money they were allocated and how much they have spent and then pick and choose what they can still afford to buy. If any individuals or organizations offer to make monetary donations, they refer to their wish list and suggest an item. The current wish list of the Fenway Project looks like this:

- A laser printer, a scanner, and a digital camera
- A paint job for the office
- Slides to use for class presentations
- A catcher's mitt and a left-handed fielder's mitt
- A new coffee urn

STEP 4: DOING A FORCE-FIELD ANALYSIS

After a program idea has survived the sorting and ranking process it is time to analyze its chances of success. To do this, Raquel uses a simple but effective technique called **force-field analysis.** She first looks at the forces that might help the program get started and those barriers that are likely to stand in its way. She gains confidence by reviewing the positive factors, but she is also alerted to the barriers posed by the negatives. She looks at how they balance out.

Some Fenway Project youth staff are working with the Hi-Teens, a club of adolescents who live in the local public housing project. The staff has decided that the group needs a really good activity to pull the members together into a cohesive unit. They brainstormed with the teenagers, analyzed their list of ideas, and everyone agreed they wanted a weekend camping trip. Now they must think through how likely it is that they will be able to plan and successfully carry out the idea. Systematically, they list the positive and negative forces, as in Figure 11.8.

Force-field analysis
A systematic way of looking at the negatives and positives of an idea or event in order to understand it fully, anticipate problems, and estimate chances of success.

FORCE-FIELD ANALYSIS
Topic: Hi-Teens' Weekend Camping Trip

The Positives +
(What we have going for us)

1. We have been on several one-day trips, and they've worked out well.

2. It's January now, so we have lots of time to make a reservation at a camp site for the spring.

3. We all get along very well.

4. Our group leader has a lot of camping experience.

5. Because most of the members voted for this idea, we should get good cooperation from them.

The Negatives –
(What might get in our way)

1. We have no money in our treasury.

2. Some parents may refuse to give permission, especially if it's boys and girls together.

3. The camping sites are pretty far away, and we don't have any transportation.

4. Carlos, our group leader, has finals at college in the spring and may not have the time to take us.

FIGURE 11.8   A sample force-field analysis

If the negative forces are too overwhelming, they will move on to the next idea. Many of these inner-city teenagers have already experienced too much frustration and failure in their lives. They need a program that is grounded in reality and success. Their force-field list looks reasonably balanced. It will take a lot of work to turn those negatives into positives, but they think they can do it. If ignored, the negatives might sabotage their best planning efforts.

After completing the force-field analysis, they brainstorm strategies that might overcome or neutralize those negative forces. Figure 11.9 lists the strategies to overcome one negative force listed in Figure 11.8, "parents' resistance to a coed trip." Now, they need to construct an action plan, making sure that potential obstacles to their plans are dealt with and that everything they have decided to do is clear to all the members.

STEP 5: CREATING A PROGRAM PROPOSAL AND MAKING A WORK PLAN

No matter how informal the group, it is imperative that the program plan they hope to implement be written down so that everyone can review it fully and those who become involved later on can be accurately oriented to it. The program proposal will be the road map. It keeps folks on course and invites others (especially funders) to come on board. Figure 11.10 lists what the proposal should include. As a first step in

---

FORCE-FIELD ANALYSIS STRATEGY PLANNING

The negative force

Strategies to overcome the negative force

Some parents may refuse to give permission, especially if it's boys and girls together.

1. Ask one or two parents to chaperone the trip.

2. Go in two separate groups of boys and girls; combine for some activities.

3. Have the overnight at the house of one of the members.

4. Have the parents who are likely to give permission talk to the ones who are against it.

5. Have the group leader meet with all the parents to discuss the trip.

FIGURE 11.9   A sample of force-field analysis strategy planning

drafting the plan, we need to look back at our negative forces. How can we overcome the negative forces? In the minutes of the teenagers' meeting (prepared by the college student volunteer) you can see how they began that process.

> We voted eight to one that we would have a two-day camping trip in the country in the late spring. We want the trip to include both boys and girls. We will schedule it for a weekend after Carlos's finals. We will have a meeting with all the parents this month to try to convince them to let us go and see what help they can give us. Some of the boys worried that the parents would resist. So then we spent more time figuring out what to do to get the parents to say okay.

In Figure 11.9 you can see some of the strategies they came up with.

They ended their meeting by deciding that they would raise the money through a car wash. It would be held on Saturday from 11:00 A.M. to 4:00 P.M. in front of the local housing project. Tiger and Arnie agreed to be in charge of it.

That plan may sound pretty clear, but it needs to be spelled out in greater detail and it needs an alternative. "The best-laid plans of mice and men (and women) often go astray." Every planner knows Murphy's Law:

If anything can go wrong, it will!

So the young people had better plan the camping trip and car wash with some fallback arrangements. There must always be a plan A, B, C, and D. Perhaps they cannot get a majority of the parents to approve the coed overnight trip, which is

Whether you are asking for extra funding or have the funds but need permission from the director or staff group to embark on a new program, it is critically important that all the details of the proposed plan be set down on paper. In the process of doing this, the planners themselves will become much clearer and ultimately more persuasive. The proposal shows that you have done your homework and that you have a feasible plan and credible planners.

The proposal should include:*

1. Title page—with name of program, who it is being presented to and by whom.

2. Abstract—a brief overview of the agency, problem (GAP) program activities, funding request, and planners. No more than one scant page, the abstract should be very tight and clear. It may be all that is ever looked at if many proposals are in a pile in a funder's in-box.

3. Table of contents—each part of the proposal should be numbered for each reference when the program is being discussed.

4. Problem statement—What (GAP) is this program trying to fill? How did the problem get identified, how long has it been going on, what are its consequences? This part would include backup data, surveys, professional articles, anecdotal evidence.

5. Background to the problem—brief information about the agency or persons making the proposal, who does it serve, how, when did it begin, staff, funding, facility, and geographic area.

6. Goals of the program—this includes hopeful outcomes spelled out very operationally and in very specific terms.

7. Proposed activities—Exactly what are you planning to do, when, and how? What staff will be needed, what facility, what equipment? This should also include a work plan or time line in this section or a separate one.

8. Budget—How much money will be needed for exactly what, and how much will need to be raised for the new program, and what in-kind donations are expected?

9. Evaluation—What methods will you use to assess how successfully your program activities have met your goals or hoped-for outcomes, over what period of time?

10. Additional supporting documents—this section would include bibliography if applicable, charts, and letters of support or concern.**

* Many funding agencies will have their own special format to follow.

**For a sample program proposal, see Schram (1997, pp. 220–226).

FIGURE 11.10   Writing the Program Proposal

plan A, and, therefore, plan B might be that they will try to get the parents to agree to a one-day coed trip. Plan C could be separate overnight trips, one for the girls and one for the boys.

Because it might rain on the weekend they choose, they will book an alternate date for the next weekend. If Carlos cannot go because of his schoolwork, they will ask Mr. Devon, the gym coach, if he would be willing to go.

Of course, we can never anticipate all the twists of fate, but good planners try to cover as many bases as they can. Clients do not need workers to protect them from all possible failures. Rather, they need workers who encourage them to plan realistically.

Creating a sensible contingency plan is a problem-solving skill that is valuable in every phase of work, school, and social life. Parades are often rained on, but good planners bring umbrellas!

A vital part of the process of drafting a plan is estimating how much money it will take and how much money the group has or can raise. Although all of us resist making a budget, it is surprising how much clearer every part of a plan becomes when we have finished the budget-making process. Finances always are the bottom line. That does not mean that everything must cost a lot of money. As we get more skillful, we find many ways to get donations and make do with very little.

Phase 3: Microscoping

For the **microscoping** phase of the planning process we take off our creative, think-big hat and put on the green visor of the accountant. Now we must focus all our attention on the minute details of our specific plan. We must make sure that it will work as smoothly as possible. The steps we follow are listed in Figure 11.11.

In this phase we must nail down vague ideas. Using pad and paper, computers, datebooks, clocks, and directories of resources, the teenagers make checklists (and double-checklists). The mindset of the microscoper is neat and orderly, leaving little to chance.

Many experienced workers have adopted the anxious stance of the microscoper after failing several classes in the "school of hard knocks." A student intern at the Fenway Project wrote the following about his fieldwork:

> I still carry with me the vivid memory of facing sixty disappointed, angry adults and children on a hot street corner. Although I had booked the buses for their annual family picnic at Riverside Amusement Park, I had neglected to double-check the bus company's arrangements. The buses never showed! Many of these folks had planned their vacations around this yearly outing. Few have the cars or money to take their own

Microscoping Looking at a program or problem and seeing within it all the component parts and steps of action needed.

FIGURE 11.11   The process of microscoping a problem

Step 4
    Evaluating and following up

Step 3
    Establishing time schedules

Step 2
    Specifying and assigning tasks to be done

Step 1
    Building a resource bank

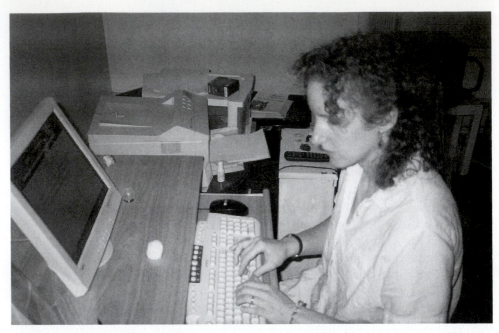

Sitting at a computer is much less glamorous than other parts of the planning process, but when a file or report is missing, the cost in human energy and pain can be great.

trips to the country. They counted on my planning ability, and I hadn't come through for them. Now I've learned to double- (or even triple-) check every time I lease a bus.

Every human service worker can recount a story of a catastrophe that destroyed a program. Perhaps the DVD for the cartoon show for little kids did not work, or the CD player for a dance was broken, or the staff member in charge of food bought only half the number of frankfurters needed for the barbecue.

Mistakes creep into our work in subtle and not so subtle ways. Chances are you will find in your own mail at least one advertisement for a conference, meeting, or open house that has the wrong date on it or fails to note that baby-sitting is provided or that there are special rates for students and senior citizens. Perhaps you have encountered the frustration of receiving an invitation mailed so late that the event has already passed.

With charts, graphs, checklists, and yellow stick-on papers on the refrigerator door, the microscoper tries to minimize small errors that can destroy months of hard work. Although there are no guarantees against errors, if we share the work of planning with others, we tap a large reservoir of energy and skills. This offers some protection.

The following anonymous poem hangs on the wall of the Fenway Project as a reminder of Murphy's Law:

I have a spelling checker
It came with my PC.
It plainly marks four my revue
Miss stakes I cannot sea
I've run this poem threw it,
I'm sure your please to no.
It's letter perfect in its weigh,
My checker toll me sew.

Now we will look at each of the steps in microscoping that can turn proposed programs into solid realities.

STEP 1: BUILDING A RESOURCE BANK

Every action plan must draw on its own **resource bank.** Planners need to figure out what is needed and what resources are readily available. Each of us is an integral part of a network of friends, family, peers, and work associates. They share many of their resources with us, and we in turn reciprocate. We turn first to them when looking for resources. No person or group, no matter how poor or troubled, is totally devoid of resources. By asking questions, we stimulate people to think about their own and others' resources.

Resource bank
People, places, services, or written materials that help people meet needs and reach goals.

After exploring all their contacts, the members did a resource analysis so that they could see what they were still missing and how they might fill any GAPs (see Figure 11.12 for a chart of some of the resources they needed). All the ideas about where to find resources had to be carefully checked out—some materialized and some fell through. The creative hustling continued. The teens were surprised to

---

RESOURCE ANALYSIS
Hi-Teens' Camping Trip

Resources we need	Resources we have	Status	Possible sources
lantern (3)	John has 2 Carol has 1	ok	
stove (1)	Veronica's dad has 1	ok	
tents (to sleep 14)	Flora has tent for six; Don can borrow one for six	need tent space for 2 more	• check out YMCA • Althea will ask her camp director • check Boy Scout troop

FIGURE 11.12   A sample resource analysis

find that most of the people they asked to help them said "yes." Generally people are very willing to lend a hand if asked to donate a specific resource or service that suits their capacity and time schedule. They are more likely to continue helping if their contribution is acknowledged (Ries & Leakfield, 1998; Shore, 1995). We never can say "thank you" too often.

STEP 2: SPECIFYING AND ASSIGNING TASKS

Most of us feel totally overwhelmed at the beginning of any new action plan—perhaps we are anticipating putting on a carnival, forming a tenant committee, or returning to school after twenty years of homemaking. New staff members or volunteers inevitably experience that initial panicky question:

> Who me...
> > *speak in front of a room full of faculty members?*
> > *take fifty screaming kids to the circus?*
> > *walk through that neighborhood?*

Most workers quickly learn, however, that the most important part of creating an action plan is the ability to break down the big tasks into a series of smaller tasks. Thus they will not be overwhelmed or immobilized by the enormity of what they have been assigned. When the goal is broken down into many small tasks, rank ordered by immediacy, and then delegated to different people, the end seems reachable. Logically, each task depends on the successful completion of the one that came before. In Figure 11.13, you can see the task list that was constructed by the Hi-Teens. It demonstrated to their parents that they had done their homework and understood how much work the trip would involve.

The meeting with the parents of the Hi-Teens convinced most of them to let their children go on the overnight coed camping trip. Once that barrier was overcome, the teenagers could concentrate on the specifics of planning the weekend. With the help of a Fenway Project youth worker who was an experienced backpacker, they delegated each item on their task list. Figure 11.14 shows a sample of the way they did it.

Although all this list making can seem needlessly bureaucratic, especially for a group of teens, it is an absolute rule of planning that *if definite assignments are not made or are made but not put in writing, the morale of the group can deteriorate as a result of needless bickering or wasted effort:*

> But I thought you were responsible for the paper goods!
> Well, whose job was it to bring the matches?
> They say they never received our reservation form for the campsite!

Every committee needs task specifications and a coordinator. See *Management of Human Service Programs* by J. A. Lewis, M. D. Lewis, T. Packard, and F. Souflec (2001). Even though a committee of four teens agreed to do the food shopping, one person had to be the "coordinator," "key person," or "honcho." *Accountability is the*

TASKS THAT NEED TO BE DONE
Hi-Teens' Camping Trip

1. Get a campsite

2. Round up camping equipment

3. Get signed permission slips

4. Organize transportation

5. Plan food

6. Shop for food

7. Practice camping skills

8. Get first-aid supplies

9. Practice first-aid skills

10. Make a budget*

11. Raise money

12. Plan schedule and activities for weekend

13. Decide on rules of trip

FIGURE 11.13 A sample task analysis

*Budgeting is a major human service task. A book such as *Financial and Strategic Management for Non-Profit Organizations* (Bryce, 2000) can provide needed guidance.

JOB ASSIGNMENTS
Hi-Teens' Camping Trip, Major Tasks

Tasks:	Coordinated by:	Assisted by:
1. Get the campsite	Carlos	Ron, Flora, & Jefferson
2. Round up camping equipment	Anita	all members
3. Get signed permission slips	Jefferson	all members

FIGURE 11.14 A sample job-assignment list

key to moving an action plan along to completion. Each of the coordinators had to make a list of the smaller tasks that are the components of each job. Then these had to be assigned, as in Figure 11.14. In Figure 11.15 you can see the small tasks within each job and the assignments.

Every task must be thought about and followed up. At this stage, the accountant's compulsion to keep track of every penny and make the books balance comes

SMALL TASKS WITHIN A JOB
Getting a Campsite for the Hi-Teens' Trip

	Who will do it
1. Call Girl Scouts, Boy Scouts, 4-H headquarters, state park. Get names of camp sites between here and Nesoba County.	Ron & Flora
2. Call (or look up) each one of them and find out the following: • Location—Where they are located and are they on a public transportation line? • Costs—What do they charge for one night? Any extra costs? What do they require for deposit? Is it refundable? • Facilities—Do they have an indoor shelter, swimming area, grills, picnic tables, hot showers, parking lot, tent bases, others?	Ron & Flora
3. Choose one site and one alternative.	All
4. Try to arrange a visit or find someone who has been there and has firsthand information.	Jefferson
5. Send deposit and reservation form; make rain date.	Carlos
6. Make sure to get back a confirmation in writing.	Carlos
7. Call two days beforehand to double-check arrangements.	Carlos

FIGURE 11.15   A sample list of subtasks

into play. As we figure out and execute the tasks of each job, nothing can be left to chance. At the risk of being a nag, we must, hopefully with charm and humor, keep after everyone and everything. It is never enough simply to mail a letter or wait patiently for people to return our phone calls.

When the Hi-Teens wanted to make sure that their parents' meeting would be well attended, they did more than simply send a notice to each family. This is what they did: They sent reminder cards a few days before (or e-mail when possible); the club leader phoned or visited each family; if the parents were hesitant about coming, the group leader asked what he could do to make it possible for them; if the time was inconvenient, for many of them, he rescheduled the meeting or he asked parents if they needed a baby-sitter and he tried to get a volunteer to help out; if parents were worried about not speaking or understanding English, he tried to locate a translator.

STEP 3: ESTABLISHING A TIME FLOW CHART

Time flow chart
A diagram of the tasks that need to be done in a certain period of time by specific individuals.

Once tasks are broken into component parts and delegated, they must be put into a time framework called a **time flow chart**. Some tasks need to be done before others; some need more time than others. For example, if the teenagers use up most of their meetings planning their menu or arguing about curfew before they get around to booking the campsite, there may be no place available for the trip. First things come first! Drawing a picture of a logical sequence of events helps to visualize what lies ahead. It also gives some benchmarks along the way. If someone asks, "How's it coming along?" they can say, "Fine, everything seems to be moving on schedule," or "We seem to be getting bogged down by X, Y, or Z."

Nothing dooms a planning process as much as unrealistic time expectations. As we look over the chart, we notice possible stumbling blocks. We readjust our time line to avoid them. If the public schools' spring vacation falls in April and all the fund-raising is planned for then, we may be set up for defeat. If we are counting on outdoor sales and fairs to raise money, we have to remember they do best in warm weather. Few of us, clients or workers, are superpeople. We cannot manage to complete a task in too small a time period. Anxiety and immobility can be the prices we pay for pushing too hard. In Figure 11.16 you can see the time flow chart the group constructed.

For the days of the overnight the group will need several more flow charts, resource lists, and agendas. If they are going to have a campfire, someone needs to build it and put it out. A talent show needs a time frame and, if prizes will be given, someone has to obtain them. And so it goes. A time flow chart can use units of hours and even minutes during the actual events.

	TIME FLOW CHART **Hi-Teens' Camping Trip**						
	TIMES						
TASKS	December	January	February	March	April	May 9	May 12–30
	Hold parents' meeting	Look for campsite Give out permission slips Make budget	Reserve campsite Slips due back Plan fund-raising	Hold fund-raising events Practice camping skills Practice first aid	Reconfirm campsite Funds all collected Plan menu Plan activities and daily schedule Decide on rules Gather equipment	Shop Leave at noon	Return equipment Send out thank-you notes Write up report on trip

FIGURE 11.16   A sample time flow chart

Try making a time flow chart the next time you have a term paper due. See how close you can come to avoiding the night-before-the-deadline stampede to the library or the problem of a last-minute discovery that your printer is broken. But be honest with yourself. If you are a habitual late starter, do not try to begin three months before it is due; you will only feel guilty and unsuccessful. But perhaps you can start one or two weeks before you normally would. Pat yourself on the back for utilizing a planning technique that improves your chances of success and can aid clients in the same way.

Of course, there are very few action plans that actually proceed as written, but a flow chart helps people organize their efforts in the best possible way. In fact, it is a general rule of thumb that everything is likely to take twice as long as you think it should.

STEP 4: EVALUATING THE PLAN AND FOLLOWING UP

Evaluation is always the final act that closes the information loop on the old plan and sets the stage for a new one. In order for the teenagers and the youth workers to learn and grow, they need a feedback system. Are they on schedule and are things progressing well?

Because the Fenway Project staff and volunteers turn over frequently, program continuity and growth are hard to achieve. Before leaving, the program coordinators must store their knowledge in accessible form to orient the next year's workers.

Record keeping and report writing are especially critical when a group has just finished a large-scale planning effort such as an annual neighborhood fair or conference. Lists of prices, the names of the bands and supply houses, and copies of receipts and permits are invaluable documents. That information, plus comments on the quality of the goods and services that were used, will help next year's staff hit the ground running. Each worker should be able to learn from his or her predecessor. Financial management of a program can be a vital part of its success or failure (Fei, 1998).

Process and Product Evaluations

In addition to factual records, we must also evaluate two dimensions of the activity we have planned, both the *process*—how we planned it—and the *product*—how it turned out. Sometimes the two can be different (Clifton & Dahms, 1993; Martin & Kettner, 1996).

The Hi-Teens had a wonderful time on their trip. The experience helped build group cohesion, the members learned new skills, and they gained a greater appreciation of the outdoors. They rate the *outcome* very highly. But in the planning process, many of the young people did not keep their commitments. Carlos, the group leader, is annoyed at them. He ended up getting most of the equipment for them, checking up on the reservation, and filling in for absent members at their fundraising car wash. The group needs to improve its *process*. They must meet together in a debriefing session and discuss what went wrong with the way they delegated and double-checked their assigned tasks. Of course, they should also be reminded to take credit for all the things they did do well.

To systematically review the process they used, members will ask each other:

- How accurate was their original list of tasks?
- Did they think of everything that was needed?
- Did they set realistic time limits?
- What would they repeat and what would they do differently next time?

The techniques used to evaluate an intervention depend on the nature of the program: how complicated it was, how many people were involved, and what the evaluation will be used for. For a camping trip with a group of teens, a good discussion and brief report including comments of supervisors and parents is plenty. But if we are evaluating a large conference or the first few months of operation of a community residence for teenagers, staff must conduct in-depth interviews with clients and collect statistics, questionnaires, and the opinions of outsiders (Alter & Evans, 1990; Mark, 1996; Marlow, 1993; Smith, 1990). Almost any technique used with an open mind and a genuine desire to learn from experience will offer us some insights.

We must be especially careful not to turn our attention away from an event before all the closure work is completed. Thank-you notes have to be written, bills have to be paid, and lost or damaged equipment must be replaced or fixed. Groups

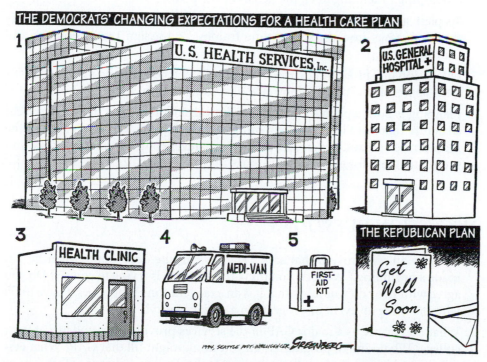

Few plans ever end up exactly as first envisioned. Often they are compromised beyond recognition. Compare the grand scheme for universal health care at the start of the process with the current situation.

also need to spend some time saying good-bye, sharing their photos, or writing an article for a newsletter. There are always next steps to be taken.

SUMMARY

1. The planning process used in organizing events in our personal lives is similar to, but less formal than, the one used by human service workers.

2. The basic tools of the planning process include a pen and pencil, computer (or word processor), e-mail and faxes, calendar/memo book, clock, resource directories, and many thoughtful questions.

3. When planning within a group, large paper sheets or a chalkboard ensure widespread understanding. Minutes keep members informed about decisions and commitments that have been made.

4. Question generation forms an information loop that leads to action, reflection, and new action.

5. The techniques of the planner include troubleshooting (defining the problem), magnifying (seeing it with its background context and complexity), and microscoping (attending to all the details of the plan).

6. To plan successfully, we separate events into their component parts, identify the small tasks in each, set up time frames, and assign responsibilities and coordinators.

7. Evaluation of a program focuses on the product (the outcome of the intervention) as well as the process (how it was conducted from inception on).

8. Planning is both a people skill and a technical skill. Functioning within a clear structure that has a logical system brings out the best in everyone, enabling the most limited or troubled people to make whatever contribution is possible and preparing them for an event.

DISCUSSION QUESTIONS

1. There is an old proverb that says, "He has half the deed done, when he has made a beginning." What do you think this proverb is trying to convey? Do you agree with it, or do you think that it is an exaggeration? What does it have to do with planning an event or program in a social agency?

2. What do you see as a major GAP in the services provided for students at your college? What kind of program(s) do you think might fill that GAP? What evidence would you have to gather to convince the person in charge of that area or division that it is a GAP that must be filled with a new program or strategy?

3. What do you think is meant by the saying, "Life is lived forward, but understood backward"? What do you think that saying has to do with the process of program evaluation?

WEB RESOURCES FOR FURTHER STUDY

Strategic Planning
www.mapnp.org/library/plan_dec/str_plan/str_plan.htm

Additional information on the strategic planning process.

Nonprofits
www.nonprofits.org
www.sc.edu/swan/

Information on nonprofit organizations and the kind of work they do that might help in creating models for new programs.

Proposals and Funding
http://fdncenter.org
www.cfda.gov/public/faprs.htm

Information on available sources of funding and proposal writing.

CHAPTER 12

Organizing and Changing Systems

We have read in the previous chapters about the ways in which human service workers strive to improve and protect the mental health of people. In this chapter, we explain why they must be equally concerned about the mental health of social systems—the environments in which their clients live and work. Often the rules, regulations, and mode of operation of a system can create or increase an individual's problems. To alleviate his or her distress, we must go to the sources of the problem, perhaps changing those elements that are damaging the clients.

We point out, however, that even when human service workers are convinced that the pressures exerted on their clients come from unhealthy systems, they often resist becoming change agents. We suggest reasons for these defeatist or fearful attitudes and ways they can be overcome.

Then we look at the methods of changing both the structure of an unhealthy social system and the hearts and minds of the people who work or live within it. When workers are trying to pass

a law or change the behavior of bureaucrats they begin by *educating*. By systematically documenting the inadequacies of current practices, they hope to change behavior. But if that effort does not create the desired changes, they try *persuasion* techniques. They offer incentives for positive changes and threaten to punish continued inadequacies through the courts or legislature. If there is still resistance to change, they might resort to *pressure*, using the tactics pioneered by labor unions: organizing a protest demonstration or going on strike to illustrate their frustration and stop the process of business as usual.

To organize a change campaign, workers must know a great deal about their communities. They must figure out the sources of power within them and involve the local citizens in genuine decision making. The risks of social change strategies are great, but so too are the potential rewards. Improved conditions may result in fewer people coming to us to solve their individual problems. We stress that even very small changes can have dramatic impact on the lives of ordinary people.

GETTING TO THE SOURCE OF THE PROBLEM

We can think of no better way to start this chapter on organizing and changing systems than by retelling a parable attributed to the late Saul Alinsky, who was one of this country's most imaginative and dedicated community change agents (Alinsky, 1969, 1971).

A Parable

A woman is taking a stroll along a riverbank. Suddenly she hears a cry for help and jumps into the water to rescue a drowning man. After saving the first man, she is forced to jump back into the river to save another and then still another. After she has dragged four men from the river, she looks around in disgust and starts to leave. An onlooker says, "Hey, I see another guy in the water, where are you going?" She replies, "I can't hang around here all day long rescuing drowning victims. I'm going upstream to stop the son of a bitch who's pushing them all in."

Stopping Problems at Their Source

The point Alinsky is making is that it is never enough to just rescue victims from their troubles, important as that is. We have to try to change the situations that are creating their problems. Then, hopefully, we can cut off the problem at its source so that new victims are not constantly being produced.

For those of you who are mechanically inclined, visualize a machine that makes Ping-Pong balls. Every once in a while it goofs and produces one that is not round enough. A worker tosses the defective balls into a bin. Later on, another worker takes the odd-shaped balls out of the reject pile and tries to round them off. But it would save time and money in the long run if they fixed the machine so that it did not make so many mistakes.

To translate this analogy into human service work, we will describe the case of Marty, a young adult of Mexican American background. He was raised on a run-down farm on the wrong side of the tracks in a rural community. He attended a sub-standard elementary school that did not stimulate him. When his mother needed surgery and his family lost their farm because they could not pay the mortgage, Marty was forced to drop out of high school and seek work. He soon discovered that the few jobs available in his town were given to people who had more skills or education than he did. He found that luck and chance and connections played a part also.

He had always tinkered with old cars and was a natural mechanic. But the garage owner held stereotypes about people from the Mexican American community—he was convinced that all Chicanos were lazy and dishonest. As a result, when a job at the garage became available, Marty was rejected.

Marty became depressed about his bleak future and found momentary relief in drugs. Once he became so frustrated that he lashed out, vandalizing the garage. He got caught and enmeshed in the criminal justice system. He spent two months in jail, where he was brutalized by both his cellmate and a guard. By the time the probation worker encountered Marty, he needed a whole series of direct-care and counseling strategies to overcome his addiction and rehabilitate his shattered self-esteem. Now he also had a prison record holding him back.

This young man's problems might have been prevented if there had been:

- Decent housing in an integrated area
- Adequate education, both academic and vocational
- Affordable health insurance
- Mortgage assistance to save family farms

- Drug and alcohol education
- Job-training and placement programs
- Protection from discriminatory employment practices
- A criminal justice system with the resources to protect and rehabilitate offenders

The lack of these basic services helped create and maintain Marty's situation. Like a snowball rolling down a hill, his problems kept getting bigger. In their book, *Social Welfare: A History of the American Response to Need,* Axinn and Stern (2001) conclude that poor people too often come off as second best—scapegoats for circumstances beyond their control.

Human service workers cannot change all of the dysfunctional systems that impinge on the Martys of our country. Nor is it likely that they can change one system in a massive way. But all of us can, in our daily work, create small yet significant improvements in the social systems that surround our clients.

What Can One Worker Do?

When working with Marty, for example, we might find that helping him file a complaint against a discriminatory employer has two major outcomes. First, it gives him the feeling that he can take some control over his destiny. And second, if he succeeds in winning the case, not only will he get a badly needed job, but other Mexican Americans who follow him may also find it possible to work there. If this young man joins a group of citizens who succeed in bringing bilingual and multicultural programs to the local elementary school, that might improve the life chances of his neighbor's children also.

Filing a grievance when you believe a law or regulation is not working properly or drafting a proposal and lobbying for funds to start a program to fill an unmet social need are examples of systems organizing and changing strategies. They support our efforts to deliver direct services to people.

These strategies rely on the same activities and skills as do direct-service strategies. They start with careful collecting of data, contracting, and building a trusting relationship. Worker acts flow out of well-designed and monitored action plans and are refined through reflection and evaluation. Although there are many similarities between direct-care and systems-change interventions, there are, of course, some significant differences in emphasis.

CHECKING ON THE MENTAL HEALTH QUOTIENT (MHQ) OF A SYSTEM

A counselor trying to help a child who is experiencing difficulty in school begins by seeking information about the child's health, family situation, and scores on achievement and IQ (intelligence quotient) tests. Many stop at that point, only seeking out the causal factors within the child and the family. But we believe that the hunt for relevant insights cannot stop there. The competent worker must go on further, to look at the *system* in which the child is functioning. The worker must gather data about the MHQ (mental health quotient) of that student's classroom and school. We must always look at both the *internal* as well as the *external* sources of stress. Ultimately we will need to intervene in both sets of forces.

Traditionally, workers in this field have often neglected the second step, looking at the system. It was the community mental health movement, with its focus on integrating institutionalized people back into the community, that alerted us to the need to seek causality beyond the client. The civil rights struggles of the 1960s also convinced us that the problems individuals face can be made better or worse by forces exerted by their environments.

You can grasp this concept of the "system-as-problem-producer" if you think back to a time when you watched people rudely shoving each other in order to grab a cab at the airport—tempers flared and anxiety levels rose as each person struggled to outmaneuver the others. Clearly, the environment with its chaotic method of allocating benefits exerts a negative impact on otherwise reasonably polite people. If a sensible airport manager inaugurated a system in which numbers are assigned to passengers in some equitable way, everyone could relax. It might take time to get a cab, but each person would be sure that his or her turn was coming. A passenger could risk leaving the line for a moment to carry the luggage of an elderly man or to help a harried mother with a toddler in a stroller and a heavy suitcase.

The airport analogy holds true for the bakery, the baseball game, the classroom, and any other environment in which people seek services or goods. All of us have the potential to act in a variety of negative and positive ways. What is it in an environment that brings out the best and worst in you?

Human service delivery systems—their rules, routines, and personality conflicts—all need to be examined. We must develop our personal method of measuring the MHQ of a system. For example, before we begin to plan counseling interventions for the little girl who runs around her classroom fighting with her classmates, we should check the organizational climate of her classroom and school. Some places are so disorganized or mindlessly rigid that they encourage disruptive behavior in a child who has some tendency in that direction. In a more sensibly organized environment she might behave quite appropriately.

After we observe a client in a classroom or in a hospital ward, we might conclude that certain characteristics of the environment seem to be producing problems rather than solving them. *Thus the system, rather than the client, should be the major focus of our change efforts.* Yet despite recognition of this fact, research indicates that workers often continue to try to change the client by counseling, rather than change the environment by using organizing interventions (Brager, Specht, & Torczyner, 1987; Kahn, 1995; Perlman, 1975).

Ryan, in his classic book *Blaming the Victim* (1976), asserts that focusing change efforts on the client rather than on the system that is malfunctioning, leads us to design social programs that are at best irrelevant and at worst deceptively cruel. Why are so many human service workers unable to confront honestly the primary causes of a client's problem? We think one reason is that workers tend to accept society's negative attitudes toward social activism, even though social activism is required if systems are ever to change for the better.

ATTITUDES TOWARD
SYSTEMS-CHANGE INTERVENTIONS

As we grew up, many of us might have heard adults in our families declare:

You can't fight city hall!

It's not *what* you know but *who* you know!

Good guys finish last!

Well-brought-up people (especially females) don't make waves or rock the boat!

These homespun bromides encourage us to believe that working for change in a rational way is virtually impossible. Stereotypes of **change agents** encourage us to shy away from that role. One prominent stereotype depicts change agents as cartoon-character 1960s activists and bomb-throwing anarchists, bearded, grubby, and deranged. Or they are depicted as naive Don Quixotes, futilely tilting at windmills. On the other side lie the stereotypes that depict change agents as saintly crusaders—Joan of Arc or Mother Teresa. Perhaps you have assumed that change agents must be charismatic leaders like the Rev. Martin Luther King Jr. or President John F. Kennedy. That too is a stereotype.

When people see human service workers walking a picket line or speaking out at a school board meeting, they are often shocked by such aggressiveness. Activists are often accused by their own colleagues of behaving unprofessionally (Reeser & Epstein, 1990).

The social critic George Bernard Shaw has given us a fitting answer to that accusation. He often declared that reasonable people adapted themselves to the world as it was. Only the unreasonable ones persisted in trying to get the world to change. Thus, all progress depends on unreasonable people! We agree with Shaw and hope that there will be times when you decide you must take a strong stand on behalf of a client despite an accusation that you too are being "unreasonable."

Bertha Reynolds, one of the outstanding leaders in the history of the profession of social work, argued that it is the obligation of social workers to take partisan political stands and work for structured change in the socioeconomic system (Reynolds, 1963).

To paint an accurate picture of change agents, we must discard all our preconceptions of who they are and what they do. We need to explore our ambivalent attitudes toward social change. Then we will need to replace the unrealistic attitudes with the conviction that each of us should use our skills to bring about change in a system, just as we do in a counseling intervention.

Change agents
Workers who use their skills to bring about change in an unhealthy agency or situation, either alone or in concert with others.

The Price of Silence

First they came for the immigrants
And I did not speak up
Because I was not an immigrant

Then they came for the teenaged mothers
And I did not speak up
Because I was not one of them

Then they came for the Gays & Lesbians
And I did not speak up
Because I was not Lesbian or Gay

Then they came for the people of color
But as they left me alone
I did not speak up

Then they came for the Jews,
The elderly, the radicals, the farmers,
The "disabled", the trade unionists,
The poor, the artists...
But i believed they were doing it for me
And I did not speak up

Then they came for me
And by then
There was no one left to speak up

This statement is adapted from one written by a pastor who was killed in a Nazi concentration camp. It eloquently warns us that if we do not try to stop injustice when it starts, it will spread and eventually engulf each of us.

Working to change an unhealthy system does raise unique value dilemmas for the human service worker, especially for one who is accustomed to delivering direct services to clients. The following is a look at what can happen to some of our basic attitudes and values when a worker takes on an adversarial or confrontational role. As you read about the day-to-day tasks of a human service worker who uses all the techniques we will be discussing in this chapter, see if you can spot the moments of potential conflicts.

INTERVIEW

Sara Wong, Staff Worker, Riverside Tenants Organizing Council

The Riverside Tenants Organizing Council (RTOC) is made up of over 700 members who live in the Riverside area. We have never taken any government funds, but we have gotten a few small grants from private foundations. The council is run by a group of dedicated volunteers. We stay financially afloat through begging and borrowing from churches, community centers, and businesses in the area. The RTOC is a citizens' group concerned about the housing conditions in the neighborhood. We have a vision of the kind of affordable housing we'd like to see, but because the legislative issues change so often, we stay pretty fluid. The members respond to what's being proposed by the landlords, the big developers, and the city officials who deal with urban renewal, development, public housing, and safety. So, although the members of the social action committees vary from one year to the next, there is always an issue that needs to be worked on.

Ongoing tenant services are at the base of the RTOC. The housing clinic is held Wednesday evening in the community room of All Souls Church. At least eight volunteers are available to assist any tenants who come in with a problem. There is always one lawyer on duty at the clinic and three or four law students. There is a retired man who is 87 and hasn't missed a housing clinic night since we opened. We also depend on some of the community college students. We interview from ten to as many as fifty people each night. Some tenants believe that their landlords are demanding too large a rent increase while not making necessary repairs. Some tenants never have enough heat or hot water, and others have rodent infestations or no locks on doors and mailboxes.

When tenants don't know where to turn, they come to see us. We steer them to the appropriate city official. We explain their legal rights so they can take the necessary steps. Sometimes they just need someone to translate the jargon of leases and court orders into simple language so that the words make sense. Occasionally someone brings in an eviction notice. We go all the way with them, even attending the hearings or going as their representative if they are too elderly or ill to attend. A lot of the houses in our area are being converted into condominiums, so tenants either have to buy their apartments or move. The tenants are being pushed out so the area can be upgraded. These are really tough cases.

My job is to make the clinics run smoothly. I make sure the office is set up, the volunteers arrive, the phone bills are paid, and the advertisements get out. You name it, the buck stops with me!

I also coordinate the housing hot line. We answer questions and refer callers if they have other issues. I'm also in charge of publications. We put out booklets about tenants' rights in three languages: English, Greek, and Mandarin Chinese. We're putting out a Braille booklet that will be used citywide. Once a month we publish a newsletter, we write a column for the local newspaper, and we produce a monthly call-in show on cable TV.

I conduct workshops, orienting volunteers to housing laws and interviewing techniques. I speak at different church or civic groups. I am also the contact person with the legal services agency, the Council of Elders, the housing authority, and the landlords' association. Finally, I'm responsible for organizing our monthly open meetings. The officers and committee heads do the speech making but I am the chief cook and bottle washer. As the only paid staff member, I facilitate everyone's work. When a lawyer who works all day is donating time he or she could be spending at home, I make sure it isn't wasted.

It can be frustrating, but the satisfaction when we turn around a bad situation is incredible. Housing is—along with food—the main support in a person's life. What good is it to counsel someone when they don't have a decent place to live or the heat is turned off and they are sick all the time? You feel powerless when your shelter is being threatened. We work to reverse that. The landlords say it is a business and they have a right to get more money. Of course they deserve a fair profit, but I can't be sympathetic to them when I see elderly people and single parents with their children shoved out of housing into shelters.

I started volunteering here when I was a college freshman. I found this agency when I couldn't get my landlord to fix the locks on my door after we had a robbery. The volunteers helped me, and I've been here ever since.

There is no such thing as a typical day. When I am organizing a membership meeting or a clinic or if I'm speaking at a church, I'll be working at night. I take time off during the day to attend classes. I'm trying to finish my bachelor's degree so I can become a lawyer or paralegal. The legal system is a good route to help people who have personal problems. Even with a law degree, I'd still be doing human service work.

The detail work in this job is very tedious. I would much rather go to a meeting with a developer at his swanky office and be part of a negotiation than balance the checkbook or fix up some lawyer's bad spelling. I have stuffed so many envelopes in the last two years I could qualify as a speed stuffer. Sometimes I wonder if anyone reads what I write, photo-copy, stuff, stamp, and mail. But that comes along with the job and must be done.

There are frustrations in this work. When you think you are close to winning, the person who has filed the complaint gives up and moves. You can't blame the person, but you feel annoyed at everyone—the tenant as well as the landlord. Even when the laws are fair, they aren't being enforced and the people at the bottom of the heap get dumped on. I know families who have been "urban renewed" three or four times in a year. Their kids go to a different school every few months. They are like refugees. Their kids get in trouble, and everyone calls them an unstable family. It's an unstable world and they are doing the best they can.

But sometimes there are tremendous victories. One family moves into a nice place, and you know they couldn't have managed it without the help of RTOC. Perhaps one young lawyer who is going to practice corporate law sees the world from the other side of the fence. I know that will matter when he's working for a real estate firm. More low- and moderate-income housing is being built now for the physically disabled. The lobbying we did to pass that bill made a difference. I make a difference!

DILEMMAS OF THE CHANGE AGENT

Workers Must Choose Sides

When we believe that the needs of one group are being neglected and the needs of another are given an unfair advantage or that one of our clients is being punished by an unjust rule, we are making a judgment of right and wrong. When Sara helps a group of tenants who have been living with inhuman conditions organize a rent strike, she is taking sides in the struggle between landlords and tenants. Although she realizes that the landlord may have a temporary cash-flow problem when rent money is withheld, if she is convinced that the tenants are being exploited she cannot expend much of her energy worrying about the landlord's problems. But she has been trained to be empathetic and caring to everyone!

Such adversarial situations also occurred when Sara did counseling and when she was a recreation worker. But in this job they occur with alarming regularity. The pull between competing needs and outlooks is painful. It is often impossible to find a compromise. In this job she often feels more like a lawyer than a human service worker. Having chosen to represent the interests of the tenants, she advocates for them with tenacity. She becomes adversarial even though that is not her usual inclination. It is a difficult balancing act.

Workers Must Choose among Competing Values

In addition to choosing sides between adversaries in a dispute, Sara is often forced to make almost impossible choices between competing values. This is frequently the case for social change agents.

For example, in writing about their experiences as welfare rights organizers in the rural South in the 1960s, several idealistic young human service workers described how they found the maintenance needs of their organization conflicting with the service needs of individual clients (Kurzman, 1971). In order to recruit new members to the Welfare Rights Organization, they would offer to accompany clients into their eligibility interviews, coaching them right in front of the welfare investigators. They were especially interested in recruiting articulate, energetic clients—most often, young single parents—who would be the most likely to give their time and energy to expanding the welfare rights group. Yet, it was frequently the elderly, infirm clients who begged them for help with their welfare and disability applications or appeals. Though desperately needy, they were also bound by the old traditions and fears engendered by experiencing a lifetime of segregation. They were sometimes the least likely to sign a petition, attend a rally, or become leaders in the welfare reform movement. Striking a comfortable balance between giving service to the most needy and building up the social change group gave many a worker a sleepless night.

Workers Must Overcome Resistance to Change with No Guarantee of Reward

All interventions encounter resistance. But social change efforts exert a special kind of drain on our time and energy. They follow unpredictable courses down twisting, perilous roads leading to many dead ends. There are dubious rewards at the end of the path, and both client and worker can burn out from their seemingly futile investment of time and energy. Bringing a complaint of housing discrimination, for example, can involve endless postponements, which result in several years of waiting for a trial date. By the time the trial rolls around, the apartment in dispute is probably occupied; and even if your client wins the case, the current tenant in the disputed apartment cannot be displaced. The law that prohibits housing discrimination has no teeth in it. The RTOC has been trying to pass a law that would prohibit the landlord from renting the apartment while it is under contention. But given the power of the Real Estate Association, they do not have much of a chance of getting that enacted.

Many times clients have backed off from pursuing their complaints even when it looked as if they might win because they feared that their landlords would retaliate. The threat of eviction or shutting off their heat in the winter and other forms of harassment often abruptly terminate protests. Sara cannot in good conscience promise people that the RTOC can protect them. Direct-service interventions carry risks also, but they are rarely as consistently perilous as these.

Given the slim chances of winning most of the protests her agency is involved with, one wonders why she continues. Sara feels, at least for the present, that though the risks of failure may be much greater in her kind of job, so too are the rewards. When they win one reform in the housing policies of the town or of a major real estate firm, hundreds of low-income people have their lives substantially improved.

Historically that has proved to be a correct assumption. With the stroke of a pen, President Franklin Delano Roosevelt signed the Social Security Act in 1935 and, since then, millions of elderly people have been able to look forward to some measure of security in their retirement years. An army of counselors working with each of those older people, one person at a time, could not possibly have achieved such positive results.

Yet, surprisingly, there is a great deal of inertia after a new policy has been enacted. Often nothing changes until informed consumers rattle the cages of the bureaucracy. Implementation should be a rational process, but barriers of community indifference, lack of information, and bureaucratic rigidity slow down real progress (Bobo, Kendall, & Max, 1996).

Workers Lack Models

Systems-change skills are made more difficult to learn because we lack role models in our personal and professional lives. There is also a woeful lack of written materials about successful social change efforts. Not surprisingly, workers who thrive on the unstructured, rough-and-tumble nature of social change often resist sitting down and putting their thoughts on paper. Many excellent change efforts go undocumented and unrewarded (Rivera & Erlich, 1995).

However, there are some written materials, and we urge students to seek out those books that give firsthand accounts of workers engaged in systems-change efforts (Bobo et al., 1996; Boyte, 1980; Delgado, 1986; Greenberg, 1969; Kahn, 1970; Kurzman, 1971; Russell, 1989). See also the Web resources listed at the end of the chapter.

Dr. Martin Luther King Jr. understood and brilliantly employed the three escalating steps of the organizing process. He educated, persuaded, and pressured, mobilizing thousands of people to question and eventually overturn the laws and practices of racial segregation.

CHANGES ARE GENERATED FROM THE TOP DOWN AND FROM THE BOTTOM UP

Change flows in two directions. Like a giant waterfall, it flows from the top down, dragging the stones and sand along in its wake. Just as often, like a volcano, it simmers beneath the surface and then bubbles up from the bottom, engulfing everything in its path.

When it starts from the top of the system, it usually comes in the form of an administrative or legislative fiat. A board of directors, a supervisor, or an administrator announces a new policy or reduces or expands a budget item. It occurs when new legislation is passed. It can happen when the courts rule on a significant landmark case. Change can be propelled by the writing of a memo banning discrimination against one or another class of tenants or the passage or repeal of a rent-control ordinance. Sometimes seemingly benign words inserted in or deleted from an official policy dramatically change the course of life for many human beings.

Clients, workers, and students usually lack the formal authority to change destructive policies. But they can force change from the bottom up through the weight of their numbers and the power that weight can mobilize. Sometimes bottom-up change comes through the ballot box. Often it comes from citizen initiative or agitation. When homeless squatters break into a building that is boarded up and demand that city officials rehabilitate it, they are attempting to create change. The movement to accelerate the testing of new AIDS medications was spurred on by public demonstrations by citizen activists. Although these AIDS protests seemed to be unruly and filled with anger, they were a catalyst in forcing the Food and Drug Administration to speed up their medication approval process.

Case histories of change efforts reveal that most of the time, struggles to create change and resistance against change are going on simultaneously, at both the top and bottom of the system. In the history of public welfare, for example, positive changes in benefits emanating from the top of the bureaucracy have often been initiated only after it looked as if the bubbling up from the bottom, from the grass roots, would spill over into uncontrolled disruptions (Piven & Cloward, 1971).

The recent congressional actions that dramatically scaled back the social welfare system were spearheaded by many angry conservative legislators. Whether there will be effective grass roots opposition to these cutbacks as the U.S. economy slows down will depend on how accurately the elected officials have read the mood of their constituents. In any event, we can expect there to be much ferment at the top and bottom of the society as the shifting away from postdepression ideology accelerates.

Change efforts must be directed at all points of a system—the top, the bottom, and in between. But rarely can any one group or person spread thin enough to cover all the bases. Even if they could, however, different styles of organizing are needed to confront different parts of a system, for different issues, and to keep up with the changing public mood and world events.

Change agents come in two basic models: the in-fighter and the outside agitator. *In-fighters* are legitimate members of the established authority who work for or administer a particular system. They might be directors of hospitals, supervisors of social service agencies, judges, or politicians. *Outside agitators* are neither employed by nor beholden to any of the established systems.

Sara is an example of an outside agitator. She stands outside the bureaucracy of both the public and private housing sectors. She dresses, talks, and acts differently than she would if she were working for the Housing and Urban Development agency (HUD). But sometimes Sara and a worker at HUD may share a similar change goal. Their techniques are different because they work on different rungs of the change ladder. If they build a coalition around a common goal using different change strategies, they can create powerful momentum for change (Seaver, 1971).

In the civil rights era, it was often said that the agitation of militant grass roots groups, such as those led by Malcolm X and Stokely Carmichael, provoked the established authorities into dealing with the more moderate groups such as the National Association for the Advancement of Colored People (NAACP) and the Urban League. Malcolm X stirred the pot of protest in the streets of Harlem and Martin Luther King Jr. organized nonviolent marches, while the NAACP filed one lawsuit after another.

It is important to realize that if they work alone, neither enlightened leaders at the top of a system nor masses of angry people at the bottom of it are likely to create major, permanent changes.

Guarding Change

Change must be guarded after it has been won. Once instituted, it must be constantly monitored. If left unattended, a new law or policy can turn out to be totally ineffective. It can be "business as usual" unless an organized constituency monitors the process of implementation. The Supreme Court desegregation decision of 1954 is a good example of this. Although the decision made in *Brown v. The Board of Education* outlawed racial segregation in every public school in the land, it has taken hundreds of individual lawsuits and the constant watchfulness of citizens' groups to achieve even the modest amount of school desegregation we now have, five decades later. If a school is segregated and no one complains about it, it is likely just to stay that way! (See Ehrlander, M. F., 2002; Patterson, J., 2001.)

The Targets of Change

Changes such as the Supreme Court school desegregation decision must have two thrusts. First, change agents must create new *structures* composed of rules and regulations that translate the vision of change into a new reality. But that is never enough. For change to take root in a system, it must also become an integral part of the *consciousness* of the people involved.

Once people are committed to overturning segregation in a particular school system, they must marshal the evidence that it is segregated and bring it to court. They must persuade a judge to order the school board to draw up an integration plan. If the parents, school administrators, or some other organization do not like the plan or the way it is working, they must return to court to negotiate adjustments. If the school board continues to refuse to draw up an acceptable plan, the schools may be taken over by the courts as they once were in Boston, Massachusetts.

However, no matter how good the plan is on paper, on the day a desegregated school opens, the attitudes of the school and town officials, parents, and teachers determine whether the elaborate plans have any chance of succeeding. Ultimately, a new law is only as effective as the feelings that swirl around it.

If women, former mental patients, immigrants, or people with disabilities do not use the protection of the laws that guarantee their rights, those laws are worth nothing. On the reverse side, if a law is routinely circumvented by large numbers of people, it cannot be enforced. This was the case with the prohibition of alcohol in the 1920s. This law was consistently violated by the usually law-abiding general public. Alcohol was legally banned, which was a major structural change, but the desire (consciousness) of the population to use liquor as a means of pleasure or escape never changed. Today we face a similar situation with marijuana. Though it is illegal, both a Supreme Court judge and a two-term president admit to having smoked it.

Learning a lesson from the failure of Prohibition, antismoking advocates proceed on both fronts—structure and consciousness. They have changed the structure of smoking by prohibiting cigarettes from being advertised on television and passing smoking bans in government buildings and in many public spaces, such as movie theaters and restaurants. In addition, they have succeeded in placing warning labels on cigarette packages and have lobbied for bans on smoking in airplanes and work-places. Currently, the antismoking change efforts have moved into the courtroom. In high-profile lawsuits, the attorneys-general of several states have sued the major tobacco companies to recover the money the state health care systems have expended caring for citizens who have become disabled or have died from smoking-related illnesses.

And they continue to change the hearts and minds of smokers through smoke-awareness seminars and "I quit" days. Although many Americans still smoke, by targeting structure as well as consciousness, antismoking advocates have begun to tip the balance. Now it is often the smoker who is on the defensive.

The women's movement pioneered the use of consciousness-raising techniques. Out of this movement have come step-by-step procedures for conducting consciousness-raising groups in which members examine their current situation by thinking about the impact of current structures and by suggesting necessary structural changes (Culbert, 1976).

Feminist organizers have long understood that laws redressing gender inequality were a *necessary* first step but would not be *sufficient* to bring about major changes. Many women had to be convinced, for example, that they had a legitimate right to demand equal pay for their labor. They also needed to build up courage and group solidarity in order to press for remedies when equality was withheld from them.

The struggle of American women for liberation, social justice, and self-development has been waxing and waning for 150 years. In an article on women and organizing, Marie Weil (1986) says:

> The entire history and development of feminism can be seen as a process of community organization—from development of critical consciousness regarding the status of women and the oppression of minorities, to demystifying and reclaiming history, through the development of social and political action movements, including the creation of specialized organizations and programs to serve the needs of women. (p. 188)

Weil points out that many of the pioneers of social work and community organizing were women. They included Jane Addams, Dorothea Dix, Julia Lathrop, and Florence Kelley. Despite this rich heritage, men came to dominate the field of community organizing as they did other fields (Weil, 1986).

In general, feminist organizing tends to be more concerned with the quality of interaction between the members of a group and with the individual concerns of members rather than the kind of macho organizing that focuses only on results. With a single-minded focus on results, leaders might be tempted to view members as faceless creatures who can be manipulated to achieve outcomes. Trying to avoid this trap, Ella Baker, who organized the Student Nonviolent Coordinating Committee (SNCC) during the civil rights movement, always started each meeting by asking if members had any personal concerns that needed to be dealt with before they settled down to planning organizing strategies. Only after they dealt with their own pressing issues would their minds be free enough to turn to the needs of the movement.

Now, on college campuses, both administrators and student activists work to change the definitions of appropriate sexual conduct. Policies defining date rape and sexual harassment, with stiff penalties for transgressions, have been drawn up. And seminars and workshops are conducted to sensitize students and staff to the new definitions and the structured process of grievance.

METHODS OF ORGANIZING AND CHANGING SYSTEMS

Change methods fall into roughly three categories of escalating intensity: *educating, persuading,* and *pressuring.* We always start out by trying to educate the public and the powers that be about the need for change. If that is not sufficient to bring about change, we try to persuade them. Finally, if change still is resisted, we resort to pressure.

Educating to Create Change

When a change effort begins, we point out the problems (the GAPs), systematically document them, and suggest solutions. Sara spends a large amount of her time compiling statistics about the number of homeless or underhoused people in her town. She reads housing journals from all over the country and goes to conferences to find out what other groups are doing to solve the problem of the lack of affordable housing. She digests the material and helps produce a monthly newsletter that is sent to members, politicians, and businesspeople.

Whenever new subsidized or tax-abated housing is proposed, a committee from the RTOC reviews the plan to make sure it protects the interests of low-income people. Then they testify before the Riverside Planning Board to give their opinions and suggest changes.

Sara has learned the importance of having facts ready when she visits a legislator to **lobby** for change. Often she is competing with real estate developers who have assembled their own set of data printed in a fancy booklet. Although she complained about having to study statistics and research methods in college, she has come to appreciate their power and is grateful that she can read and interpret budgets, census data, and other weighty documents. The volunteer lawyers do much of the actual negotiating, but she needs to understand enough to explain the RTOC position and answer questions about it.

Lobby An attempt to convince decision makers to support one's ideas or proposed actions.

Sometimes as a result of an educational campaign, people realize how destructive a certain rule, policy, or action is and agree to change it. If that happens, then the change effort is successful and it terminates. But many times, exposing an unhealthy situation and suggesting ways of dealing with it are not enough.

So the change agents turn to the second, more powerful change method.

Persuading to Create Change

Persuasion strategies use both the carrot and the stick. They reward constructive changes and threaten sanctions for continued negative practices. For example, if employers lack the resources but are willing to hire workers who have disabilities (as they are legally bound to do), they might be granted the "carrot" of tax reductions or be given loans to build the ramps or install the special phone equipment they will need. Or, if developers are willing to build affordable housing in low-income communities, they might be given grants-in-aid, tax abatements, and special technical-assistance programs. But even with incentives, we recognize that change does not come about easily. Systems need money and technical know-how, but they also need goodwill to forge new ways of thinking.

If, despite all the incentives, discrimination is still practiced, then the "stick" might be threatened or used. Sanctions on this second level usually involve withholding money, denying permits, or causing public humiliation. For example, some towns list in the local newspaper the names of landlords who have been cited for health and safety violations. Or they list on the post office bulletin board the names and pictures of "deadbeat dads" (noncustodial parents who have not paid court-ordered child support for long periods of time).

The RTOC has used persuasion in other ways. It has organized public rallies supporting or opposing a proposed housing plan, it has collected signatures on petitions, and it has organized letter-writing campaigns.

Pressuring to Create Change

When education and persuasion fail to bring about change, the RTOC resorts to pressure tactics. They go into court to punish, restrain, or force compliance. If these formal channels of appeal are too weak or slow, the pressure tactics of **direct action** are used. They picket or boycott an office, or conduct a sit-in and refuse to move, or find some other way to disrupt business as usual.

Direct action
Interfering with the orderly conduct of a system that is the target of change.

Believing they answer to a higher code of ethics, the agents of change sometimes take the law into their own hands. The Reverend Martin Luther King Jr. encouraged people to do this when Rosa Parks was arrested for refusing to yield her seat on a bus to a white passenger. In accordance with the laws of Montgomery, Alabama, she was wrong. But she and the other members of the black community believed that they had the right to disobey an unjust and morally repugnant law. In order to force change, they boycotted the buses for almost one year. Faced with the possibility of a bankrupt bus company as well as many bankrupt stores, the town officials capitulated and the law was changed.

Forty years later, those who believe that abortion, although legal, violates religious or ethical principles, formed Operation Rescue. They chained themselves to the doors of family planning clinics, blocking the entrances. They have intercepted people walking into the clinics and attempted to disrupt the functioning of these agencies to rescue the "unborn children." As the Supreme Court and state legislatures debated

A little fish swimming alone can easily be gobbled up. But when lots of little fishes get organized, it's amazing what they can accomplish.

the pros and cons of abortion, these activists have taken direct action on their convictions. The issue of stem cell research using human embryos has now taken center stage in public debate. The sides are shaping up on this issue. In the next few years we will see many groups—pro and con—using all of these change methods.

Choosing Which Method to Use and Who Should Lead the Struggle

We make no value judgments about which set of change strategies is better, more appropriate, or more professional. Obviously Sara, like other change agents, always hopes that exposing the facts about a problem will lead to solutions. But she knows that change comes slowly and often encounters a great deal of resistance. An elderly woman soon to be evicted from her apartment or a baby eating lead paint chips cannot keep waiting for help as the wheels of a bureaucractic grievance procedure grind on.

Thus, each strategy plays a role at a particular time with a particular problem in a change campaign. The important point to remember is that in order to maintain credibility, change agents must climb each step of the ladder before escalating to the final, most aggressive one. Each set of strategies must be carefully mapped out and executed, using the kind of planning models we have already described.

Frequently, visionaries or charismatic people take a prominent role in a change effort. They become identified with it. Mr. Pulashnik, an RTOC activist, is a recent immigrant from the Ukraine. He has the ability to rivet an audience with his eloquence and his rage. When a group of homeless families broke into a boarded-up apartment house, vowing to stay until the city made the apartments habitable, he was their spokesperson. It might have seemed to the public that he was the person who galvanized the city council into action. But that was not so. A phalanx of law students and their professor, a priest, a candy store owner, three housewives, Sara, and the members of eight homeless families all played significant roles. Before the news of the takeover made a front page splash, many people had spent months collecting information, negotiating, and forging **coalitions.** If there had not been widespread participation and support for "Operation Move-in," it could have been swept aside with one quick police action or simply ignored until the squatters gave up and left. *All change efforts must be group endeavors.*

When she first began her job, Sara was brimming over with energy and enthusiasm. Occasionally those wonderful qualities got in the way of careful planning. Tenants who seemed very motivated to file a complaint about poor housing conditions often would not follow through. She organized a rally to protest the closing of the local supermarket and, to her great embarrassment, reporters outnumbered neighborhood residents. Sara did not realize then that she first had to prepare the ground before the seeds could grow. She learned that preparation consists of:

- Learning about the history of the problem and the systems involved in it
- Locating the sources of **power** and estimating their potential for change
- Getting to know the local community through both formal and informal channels of information

Coalition   A loose amalgam of people or groups who support a similar idea or goal.

Power
The capacity to influence others to achieve certain desired ends.

Learning about the History of the Problem and the System

Whatever the nature of the change we hope to bring about—more responsive routines in a day care classroom, more humane treatment for victims of domestic violence, changes in the governance of a recreation center—our first task is to learn about the full dimension of the problem. We accumulate the hard facts of the situation by asking questions such as:

- How widespread is the problem?
- How long has it been like this?
- How did this problem come about?
- Is it getting better or worse?

- What evidence backs up our estimate?
- Who benefits and who loses from this situation?
- What will happen in the future if the situation does not change?
- What solutions have others suggested? Which ones have been tried?

Sara located an investigative reporter who was also interested in the problem of corruption in the housing authority. He uncovered valuable information and brought it to the attention of the public. On another occasion she recruited assistance from a business professor. He and his students studied the feasibility of turning abandoned buildings into low-cost condominiums. Facts and allies are powerful weapons.

Locating the Sources of Power and Potential for Change

Before the RTOC begins a change effort, the members need to know just where the power lies to make the proposed changes. Sara has discovered that this is more complex than it at first appears. When dealing with city government, several agencies, bureaus, and commissions have overlapping jurisdiction. Sara worked with a committee trying to clean up a vacant lot and turn it into a playground. She soon found out how Alice felt when she went down the rabbit hole into Wonderland. Everyone who answered the phone was eager to pass her along to another person. After many calls, she was right back with the first person again.

In trying to get that vacant lot cleaned up, she discovered that the health department was concerned about it only if she could prove it was rat infested (rat bites are health hazards). She discovered that the sanitation department could not clean it up because it was private property. They said they would be happy to clean it after it became a park. And she discovered that the lot was condemned for nonpayment of taxes many years earlier. In addition, no one at city hall could find a record of who held the title to the land.

With patience, time, persistence, and lots of help from friends, the RTOC finally unraveled the threads that led to the desk of the person who could cut through the red tape and say, "Okay!" A bit of green grass now exists where only rubbish grew before. Sara often eats her lunch in that park and grins with pride (and scowls at children who try to pick the flowers).

THE FORMAL AND INFORMAL SOURCES OF POWER

Finding the genuine movers and shakers is made more complicated by the existence of two types of power hierarchies: (1) the *formal power structure*, which is composed of those people who have the official authority to make decisions, and (2) the *informal power structure*, which is composed of those people who *actually* make the decisions.

If you think about how decisions get made in your family system, in your college, or in a social agency you have worked in, you can grasp the complex reality of power. Locating the real decision makers in any system is a skill gained from many years of going down blind alleys and returning to try again. It develops out of having the courage to ask everyone involved with the system a lot of concrete questions, thinking about the answers, and then relying on your own intuition.

Sara has learned how to ask questions that might unveil the realities of power. Compare the following two questions. Which one is likely to give her the clearest picture?

Mr. Knight, who makes the policy decisions about hiring staff in your agency?

or

Mr. Knight, would you please describe exactly how the hiring of the project manager was done?

Of course, good questions do not guarantee accurate answers. But if you have ever watched a skilled television interviewer, you can appreciate the art of phrasing questions that elicit rich information.

POWER AND CHANGE

Another reality that Sara has discovered is that power is in a state of perpetual flux, and change is always possible. If she gets turned down on a request one day, she tries again later as the situation or the cast of characters changes. An election, a turnover in staff, or a downturn in the economy can change a "yes" into a "no" and vice versa.

No system is ever totally closed. Every system, no matter how rigid it appears, is vulnerable to change. When Sara gets frustrated and begins to believe the housing situation will never improve, she reminds herself of the dramatic international changes of the recent past. Sara's mother describes signing petitions and demonstrating for nuclear disarmament. At that time the world tottered on the brink of nuclear destruction, as the United States and the former Soviet Union faced each other from opposite corners. But almost overnight, the Soviet Empire came apart at the seams and "Ban the Bomb" buttons became collectors' items. After seventy years of power, the "evil empire" became a supplicant, coming to the West for advice and loans.

Getting to Know the Resources of the Community

Just as each client is rooted within a variety of systems—home, school, workplace, and peer groups—so too are systems rooted within communities. Before we attempt to change one part of a system, we must learn about its context. Communities are the sum total of their history, ethnicity, economics, geography, and relationships with the larger city or town.

The word *community* is often used in two ways. First, it is used to describe a physical entity. The Riverside community, for example, has homes, shops, streets, and boundary lines. However, we also might use the term to describe a community of interest, a group with which we identify. It need not have a geographic boundary. Perhaps we see ourselves as belonging to the gay community, the Christian community, the university community, or the macrobiotic community. In this section we will be dealing primarily with understanding the geographic community.

Understanding the physical layout of a community as well as its spirit helps us design strategies to cope with its problems. When Sara was a student she helped to conduct an attitude survey in Riverside. Crime and vandalism had been escalating, and one summer evening a near-riot occurred when the police tried to disperse a group of teenagers congregating on a corner. When the surveys were tabulated, the researchers found that a major complaint of community members was the lack of decent public transportation. Because they could not get to the stores and factories of the nearby city, many residents had given up hope of ever obtaining steady, decent-paying employment. Hopelessness led to frustration, which then led to aggressiveness and destructiveness. When the Riverside Citizens Committee was formed, obtaining transportation was its major priority. Each community has its own agenda. Human service workers have to learn to read it.

When Sara takes a job in a new community, she will have to start learning about it from scratch. She will not be able to communicate with the people she works with if she does not have, at her fingertips, the details of their daily lives. (See Kahn, S., 1995; Vollbracht, J., 2002). She will begin her education by creating a community profile. She does this by searching out answers to the following kinds of questions:

- Where does this neighborhood begin and end?
- What are the differences between what the map defines as the neighborhood and how the community describes its boundary lines?
- Which is considered a central location?
- Where do different age groups and interest groups congregate?
- Where is the "other side of the tracks"?
- Where are the significant dividing lines between the rich and poor and between one racial or religious group and another?

Before scheduling any meetings, Sara will need to know how the neighbors feel about coming out at night or entering certain areas. She will need to know if in this community parents are likely to bring their children to meetings. If so, she will need to arrange child care. She will need to know what significant events her meetings might conflict with (like the local church Bingo game or ethnic holidays).

She will have to find out what languages people speak so she can arrange for translators if needed. In Riverside, many of the elderly speak English but cannot read and write it, having emigrated from Greece as adults. The newest residents are Chinese whose primary dialect is Mandarin. Sara speaks a bit of Cantonese, but most words are almost totally different. She has had to find community activists or other professionals to translate her meeting notices. The RTOC has a phone message about the housing clinic in three different languages.

Even the refreshments she serves at meetings mirror the preferences or dietary restrictions of her Greek and Chinese members. And their festivals and holidays are celebrated and acknowledged as well.

FORMAL CHANNELS OF INFORMATION

Even though Sara had volunteered in the Riverside community and helped to conduct its community survey, when she started her job she still had much to learn. She found many valuable sources of information at the library and on the Internet (Kjosness, J., & Bar, L., 2004). She looked up the census data, read reports written by different city agencies, and read the town budget. She even looked back over old copies of the *Riverside News.*

Then she made a list of the people in town she needed to meet. Her list included politicians, school board members, clergy, directors of social agencies, and especially the local heroes and town characters. Although she did not formally interview each one, she did have a series of questions she tried to work into her conversations whenever she got a chance to meet a person on her list.

INFORMAL CHANNELS OF INFORMATION

The formal channels of information were valuable, but Sara found that walking and driving slowly in and out of the community's streets was just as important. Often the official version of the economic or recreational life of the community contradicted what she saw with her own eyes.

The boarded-up stores she observed and the neighborhood park strewn with beer bottles and sleeping men and women told her more about its spirit and daily life than did the statistics on parks and unemployment. Through the use of the senses—looking, listening, feeling, smelling—human service workers can round out their profile and identify glaring GAPs in services.

Whenever possible, Sara drops into a service at a local church, attends a parents' association meeting, and stops by the American Legion fair or the police versus firefighters challenge baseball game. She makes a point of doing her laundry near her office because the laundromat is a great place to chat with folks, and it has a bulletin board full of notices about events she might never hear of otherwise.

The one neighborhood landmark that Sara never goes to is Niarchos, the local bar. She thinks that it would be a great place to learn about the hopes, fears, and creative ideas of many of the older Greek Ameri7can residents. But she also knows that in Riverside it is not considered an appropriate place for a single woman, especially a young one of Chinese ancestry. She tries hard not to offend local customs while still maintaining her own personality and purpose.

MAKING SENSE OF WHAT WE HAVE FOUND

After observing an institution or a slice of community life, we try to make sense out of what we have seen and heard. This process involves three steps:

1. *Observation*—What exactly did I see?
2. *Speculation*—What might it mean?
3. *Reaction*—How do I feel about it?

Observation   We describe exactly what we have seen with no interpretation or evaluation. This guards us from jumping to premature conclusions. As a famous television detective used to say, "Just give me the facts, Ma'am!" After a visit to a local public school, for example, Sara describes what she has seen:

> *At the school I saw a lot of students milling in the hallways. There was a lot of noise, and some small fights broke out while I was there.*

instead of

> *I visited the public school, and it was a zoo.*

Speculation   We propose alternative interpretations of what we have seen and heard. By observing a place or person for only a few moments, Sara cannot possibly know what might have led to whatever behavior she has observed. Later on, after learning more about that school, she may find out which one of these interpretations is more accurate. These are her speculations on her observations.

Observation	Speculation
At the school I saw a lot of students milling in the hallways. There was a lot of noise, and some small fights broke out while I was there.	1. The school usually has very poor discipline. 2. There was some kind of recess or break in classes. 3. Something had just happened that was upsetting the pupils.

Reaction   Only at the end of an observation can we give our personal reactions. Now we express how what we have seen or heard strikes us emotionally—in the stomach (or gut) rather than in the head. Sara might conclude her discussion of the visit to the school this way:

Observation	Reaction
At the school I saw a lot of students milling in the hallways. There was a lot of noise, and some small fights broke out while I was there.	I felt a little scared; the atmosphere was so tense. I got the impression of neglect and unhappiness.

PLANNING AND IMPLEMENTING A CHANGE EFFORT

Reaching Out to the Public*

No matter how brilliant our ideas, they are destined to fail if we do not have active broad-based support. We always seek coalitions with groups of clients and their families, influential community members, other human service workers, and the ordinary, not-to-be-ignored taxpayers.

Imagine that you have been assigned the job of establishing a new family residential center in the Riverside community for mothers who have AIDS. First, you found the latest information on AIDS treatment and committed yourself to keeping current. (The *POZ* and *A+U* magazines are excellent ongoing resources.) For two years you have been working with a citywide coalition to get funds. You gathered thousands of signatures on petitions. You went to the state capitol and spent days meeting with your legislators. You helped organize a sit-in demonstration on the steps of the capitol with PWAs (People with AIDS). Finally, a bill was passed and funds were appropriated. Your group has written a program proposal. They want to manage one of the three facilities that will be funded. Now you should be able to start the program. Well, not quite yet!

Assuming you are lucky enough to find an affordable building in an accessible location, you still must negotiate a complex maze of obstacles. You will need to use all your understanding of the formal and informal power systems of the community to obtain the permits and licenses needed to transform a private house into a non-profit group home. You will have to get permits from the building department to make renovations. You will have to meet the fire and health department regulations. The police department will probably be concerned about neighborhood safety and the extra cars the center will bring into a narrow street with limited parking.

You and your group (and your lawyer) will have to appear before the town zoning board to convince them to grant a variance to its usual rule that prohibits anything but a private home in a residential neighborhood.

---

*For further step-by-step organizing techniques see Brager, Specht and Torczyner, 1987; Dale, 1978; Kahn, 1970; Mitiguy, 1978; Mizrahi and Morrison, 1993; Morse, S., 2004; Rivera and Erlich, 1995; Russell, 1989; Shaw, 1996; Speeter, 1978a, 1978b; Weissberg, 1999; and Wharf and Clague, 1997. For organizing manuals, contact the Center for Third World Organizing, 3861 Martin Luther King Jr. Way, Oakland, CA 94609.

Then you will have to face the members of the Park Street Block Association. They are planning to protest that the proposed center will lower the value of their houses. They are also terrified that their children might get AIDS from the children who will live at the house. At an emotional meeting they pour out their fear and rage. Renting or buying a house for a community-based human service program is almost always a politically sensitive issue. Inevitably you will run up against the NIMBY syndrome—"I agree that those people need a place to live, but

Not In My Back Yard."

Anticipating all these obstacles, you and your board have carefully laid the groundwork to defuse the protests. For six months you have been actively reaching out to everyone who might be an ally. You have been presenting accurate data about AIDS, hoping to show that the risk of contagion from the mothers and children who will live in the house is minimal. You also have been reassuring the community that the house will be so well maintained that it will add to the value of the neighborhood, not detract from it. These are just a few of the outreach activities your group might do:

- Speak at every church, mosque, and synagogue in the community

- Appear on a panel discussion about the proposed residence on local cable television

- Run public-service announcements on the radio

- Recruit an advisory committee of local influential people

- Set up an interview with the local newspaper

- Run a series of workshops at the local high school

- Speak at a Parent–Teachers Association meeting

- Convince a famous sports figure who is HIV positive (and heterosexual) to speak at a neighborhood rally

- Organize a walkathon to raise money for AIDS research

- Speak to the Chamber of Commerce to assure them that the center will patronize local businesses

- Publish a monthly newsletter of your activities and progress

- Organize and keep current a web site about the house

Even after successfully working your way through red tape and most of the resistance, you will need to continue to stay in close touch with the community. Some of the typical ways social programs do that are:

- Have an open house

- Become members of the Block Association and other civic groups in town

- Offer free, anonymous AIDS tests or another benefit to the neighborhood

- Encourage the Boy Scouts, Girl Scouts, and other groups to use your back yard for their fund-raising events, or your living room for meetings

By keeping the channels of communication open in both directions, you will be able to accomplish several of your goals. Your staff will:

- Receive constant, current feedback so that complaints can be dealt with before they explode into conflicts

- Recruit volunteers and obtain donations of materials and services to supplement the scanty budget of the program

- Obtain referrals of clients

- Mobilize supporters for your grant renewal or to protect the program when budget cuts are threatened

INVOLVING THE PUBLIC IN THE DECISION-MAKING PROCESS

The most potent vehicle for creating significant change in any sector of the community is the ongoing, genuine participation—the give and take of ideas—of those who will be affected. Psychologists and sociologists have found that when workers are asked to help design changes in their work routine, they tend to be receptive to innovation. When they feel excluded from decisions they tend to resist even positive change, subtly sabotaging and undermining it (Klein, 1953; Mondros & Wilson, 1994).

As change agents, we encourage people to articulate their complaints and visualize solutions. Yet some human service workers fear putting too much power in the hands of clients or citizens. This is especially so when the clients are emotionally troubled, physically handicapped, or burdened with the daily problems of getting food, clothing, and shelter. Although the professional's hesitations are understandable, there are at least three excellent arguments in favor of giving clients and citizens key roles in maintaining and changing systems (Fisher, 1994).

1. *Client and citizen involvement is efficient and effective.* Time and again, clients complain that social researchers spend needless time and money arriving at conclusions about social causation that the clients themselves could have supplied gratis. Although this is a pretty cynical view, it carries a kernel of truth. No matter how troubled or disorganized they may be, clients do have enormous insights into their problems, aspirations, culture, and lifestyle. No matter how skillful we are at understanding systems, clients undoubtedly know their world better than we ever can.

   Rather than sitting in her office wondering why so few tenants attended a workshop on applying for fuel subsidies or consulting recognized community leaders about the problem, Sara went to the laundromat, school playground, and local park and asked. She has found that one-shot research projects or twice-a-year open meetings do not sufficiently mobilize the ideas or energy of the neighbors. She constantly works at sharpening the RTOC's ability to solicit ongoing client and community feedback. That feedback has to be a regular part of the planning of every workshop and the evaluating of it after it is completed.

2. *Client and citizen involvement has therapeutic and protective value.* Many of the people who arrive at the doors of human service agencies already have been overwhelmed by bureaucracies, unresponsive cumbersome institutions, urban ghettos, and suburban isolation. Feeling alienated and vulnerable—one small ant on a very big hill—they desperately yearn to play a significant role in the systems that affect their lives. When we counsel clients, we carefully guard their right to choose their own path. We must also do that as we pursue change.

    Viable decision making about the administration of prisons, mental hospitals, counseling agencies, community residences, day care centers, nursing homes, and the like helps release positive forces for change. These forces might have lain dormant, but they have not atrophied. Participation in change efforts as equals rather than as passive recipients guards clients against the further development of their sense of powerlessness. It also protects change efforts from the self-interest of entrenched leaders and workers who might perpetuate their own powerful roles. One of the few truths we know that has no exceptions is *"Power tends to corrupt and absolute power corrupts absolutely."*

    We always have to be careful of our capacity to manipulate. Brager et al. (1987) point out that client trust in us is shaken when the worker engages in manipulative acts.

3. *Client and citizen involvement in decision making is both a moral right and a legal obligation.* Juggling the rights of individuals and neighborhoods with the rights of the larger society requires the wisdom of Solomon. Sara tries to find answers for questions that probably have no definitive answers:

    > Why should landlords be forced to abide by rent controls rather than charging whatever the traffic can bear like other nonregulated industries?

    > Why should people who work hard and save money have it taxed by the government to support housing for mothers who have children and no ability to support them?

All sides of these controversial issues have strong proponents. Although social policy issues are perplexing, they must be decided in an open marketplace of ideas. In some towns, rent-control legislation constricts the amount of money a landlord can charge, and in other towns each time a house is sold a portion of the proceeds goes into a fund to purchase affordable housing or open space for parks. Some towns spend tax money on building subsidized units, and other towns do nothing and hope that low-income people will move away. Whatever the arrangement, it is always open to change. The public can vote to change policies and they can vote for candidates who espouse their positions. Thus, participation is built into our system at every level, either directly or indirectly.

In education, the federal government leaves to local jurisdictions a great deal of freedom to teach the curriculum as they choose. But, with the passage of Public Law 94-142 in 1974, the federal government has assumed a central role in deciding what kind of services must be offered to students with disabilities. The Education for All Children Act also mandates citizen participation. Every educational plan created for a child with special needs requires parental consent. If the parents withhold their consent, they can mediate with public officials, then arbitrate, and then finally go to court. If the lower court disagrees with them, they can go up to a higher court. Currently there is a growing push for mandated academic testing and an effort to require passing a standardized test in order to graduate. Parent groups have begun to mobilize on both sides of this hotly contested issue.

Many health and environmental laws require the approval of community planning groups. Social welfare and housing laws require advisory or review panels of citizens and consumers. These panels periodically review the work of public agencies and have some say in whether their funding is expanded or downsized.

Thus, whether or not human service workers are convinced that their clients can handle the responsibility or that participation has intrinsic value, they have no choice but to include it in most publicly funded programs. The challenge is to learn how to implement the mandate for participation so that it works well.

Decision Making and Participation

Citizen decision making is essential in a democracy, but both skeptics and supporters of participation agree that many barriers stand in its way. Citizens often lack time, self-confidence, specialized knowledge of resources and alternatives, articulateness, and objectivity. No less an authority than Thomas Jefferson, however, offered an answer to the public's unreadiness to assume power. In a letter to William Charles Jarvis, dated September 28, 1820, he wrote:

> . . . I know of no safe repository of the ultimate powers of this society but the people themselves; and if we think them not enlightened enough to exercise their control with a wholesome discretion, the remedy is not to take it from them, but to inform their discretion.

An in-depth examination of several day care programs that had strong parental and citizen participation identified five crucial building blocks that help inform the discretion of citizens (Schram, 1975). Let's look at each of them (Figure 12.1). You can use them in the future when you are given the task of building a strong advisory committee, house council, or board of directors.

A. *Commitment.* After the third meeting in a row when a vote cannot be taken on a grant proposal to rehabilitate a derelict house in the neighborhood because there is no quorum, Sara might be tempted to throw up her hands and yell,

FIGURE 12.1   The building blocks of participation

"Damn it, I'll decide myself!" But even if shared decision making is not working very well, she still cannot abandon it.

She must grit her teeth and try a new approach to solicit the opinions of the members. She could call each one and take a telephone poll, or she could write a letter (and enclose a stamped, self-addressed postcard) and ask for written feedback. She must continue to believe that six hesitant, low-income tenants will eventually make a sounder decision about the rehabilitation proposal than she could make alone. She understands that there are low points in every group's participation history.

Because of her deep commitment to the process of citizen input, she usually finds a way to make it work. When it does not work (for example, by not acting soon enough they lose an election or a grant), she does not resort to blaming the members of the board. Their lives are complex, and she believes that they do the best they can. During the next funding cycle she will give them more advance notice, tack one meeting onto another, or take a telephone survey to obtain a vote. And there usually is a next time.

B. *Clear mandate.* Participation has the best chance of working when the contract governing the process is clear. Discussing each of the details of by-laws or personnel practices seems to most of us like tedious nitpicking. However, carefully written rules of the road are the backdrop against which rational participation can take place. Vague generalities doom shared decision making. Compare the following statements in the by-laws of two different community residences for adults who are in recovery from drug addition. The clarity of the second statement offers residents more of a chance of gaining significant participation than the generality of the first.

> Residents will play an active role in running the house.

Compare that vague mandate with this very clearly specified process of decision making.

> Once a week there will be a two-hour meeting during which activities for the next seven days will be planned. Each member will have one vote. All activities must get the majority of votes and must fall within the recreation funds allocated for that week.

C. *Appropriate structure.* Every participation effort needs a tailor-made participation structure. The format must be the right one for the mix of purpose, participants, and set of tasks. Unfortunately, most of us know of few alternative models of structure. We drift into the familiar, having elections for president, vice president, secretary, and treasurer. Then we establish a weekly or monthly meeting.

But not all groups need the same kind of officers, nor do they need to meet on a regular, arbitrary schedule. Some decisions need the face-to-face interaction of a meeting; many just need a polling of opinions in a variety of ways. Some tasks need not be done by everyone but can be delegated to committees. Some jobs on a board like RTOC's might pay a small salary for a limited amount of time. A neighborhood resident who recently returned to school was given the job of rewriting the Tenants' Rights Handbook. She sold ads to some local merchants and churches. The proceeds from the ads and the small purchase price for the book covered her two-week salary. Once a year the RTOC sponsors a citywide affordable housing and homelessness conference. The fees the professionals pay to attend it cover the small stipend of the member who does the secretarial work involved.

Some committees can be ad hoc, taking on one task and then disbanding when it is completed. Sara has found that it is much easier to ask a resident to take on a task if it has a beginning and ending time attached to it. Although she turned down the job of chair of the fund-raising committee, for example, Ms. Kazantakis was willing to run two bake sales a year. That was a role that did not overwhelm her.

Carving out a structure is like sculpting a face. No two are identical. Experimentation and imagination are the keys to success. But if the structure is not designed, an informal one will evolve anyway, with all its attendant fuzziness and potential for conflict.

D. *Knowledge and skills.* Few of the tenants in Riverside have ever made the kinds of decisions that organizing a social change movement entails. Sara has often passed on to the members the knowledge and skills she has learned in college courses as well as the skills she has acquired from volunteering in local political campaigns.

When the board of RTOC was hiring an architectural consultant to advise them on the building rehabilitation project, Sara showed them how to use the role-playing she had learned in counseling classes to prepare for the interviews. Before they met with the city commissioner of housing, they also role-played stating their demands and anticipating his objections under the experienced eye of one of their volunteer lawyers.

Sara has brought in sample budgets from other groups to show them what is usually included. When they wrote their by-laws, she invited a guest from an older established neighborhood association who had already gone through the process. And now that they have been meeting for several years, they can reach out and help other fledgling groups.

E. *Supports that enable participation.* No matter what the issue—a tenant council is lobbying for legislation to control the spread of condominiums in a low-income area or a recreation center's board is deciding whether to hold an open house—some people will inevitably invest more time, energy, and enthusiasm than will others. Those who do the work need to be warmly thanked, whether it be with a letter of appreciation, a dinner, or a certificate of appreciation.

Less active people also need encouragement. Resources can support the growth of democracy. Perhaps if child care were provided during meetings, more people might come. Sara has found that if she rotates the locations and schedules of meetings, it becomes easier for some folks to attend. Sometimes she suggests to one member that he or she carpool with someone she knows is coming. She always makes it a point to offer rides to members because very few of them can afford to maintain a car and walking long distances at night can be frightening.

She also tries to remember that as important as RTOC is, each member and coworker has a personal life outside of the organization, and that life also needs to be nurtured. So she builds time into meetings so members can swap news of job openings or available apartments. The group often has potluck birthday or wedding celebrations. She takes the time to visit a sick colleague or member. It is these touches of warmth that provide tangible rewards for the members' investment of energy.

Because RTOC is often on one side of a confrontation, it is especially important that the human service worker and participants form a supportive group. They will need to shore each other up when they become discouraged or fearful. The sense of exhilaration that comes from being part of a united and valuable effort is the bright side of the frustration and hard work of an organizing campaign.

Changing the Rules, Regulations, and Power Arrangements of a System

Just as every worker has a boss, so every public or private organization has some type of governing body. Decisions are generally made in a board room, courtroom, or legislative chamber. It is to these groups that the members of RTOC turn when they become frustrated trying to cope with a housing problem that is not getting solved at the local level. After they determine where the next level of power lies, they try to educate those officials.

For many years the tenants in Riverside had been complaining about garbage collection that was very sporadic. When garbage was collected, the empty cans were often thrown in the street where buses would reduce them to junk metal. The smell of garbage, especially in the summer, hung over their neighborhood. Letters written to the manager of the sanitation department got polite answers but no improvement. A petition demanding regularly scheduled and more careful sanitation service was circulated. Two hundred people signed their names, but nothing changed. So, for three weeks an elderly homebound RTOC volunteer sat by her window marking down the times the trucks arrived on her corner and what the sanitation workers actually did.

To remove the "Whites Only" signs in public accommodations in the southern states, advocates went all the way to the U.S. Supreme Court. Our society still must deal with the legacy of humiliation and resentment such segregation engendered.

Armed with all these data, Sara helped several tenants arrange a meeting with the regional director of sanitation. He listened courteously and promised to discipline his staff. For two months the situation improved, but it drifted back to its original state. Summer came and the stench of garbage increased. The fear of rat infestation increased along with it.

APPEALING TO ELECTED OFFICIALS

Sara realized they had to go over the head of the regional sanitation director. One of the experienced members of RTOC suggested that the tenants appeal to their local town council. Sara panicked. Since her public school social studies lessons, the legislative process had always seemed very overwhelming to her. But, as she soon discovered, in day-to-day practice social change agents must inevitably deal with local, state, and federal elected officials. And when taxpayers have complaints that are not being taken seriously, they have a right to expect that those who are paid by their tax money will respond to their legitimate requests.

Sara made the appointment with Councillor Irene Haupt, who represented the Riverside neighborhood. The tenants practiced stating their demands in a tense late-night session. They went in with a written agenda, with evidence collected by the homebound volunteer, and with their petitions. Ms. Haupt, anticipating an upcoming hotly contested reelection campaign, seemed very impressed with the 200 signatures. Each of those signatures represented a potential vote she might capture.

Ms. Haupt investigated the sanitation department's operations. Eventually the regional administrator was censured by the board. Sara was surprised to find that Ms. Haupt genuinely appreciated the feedback she got from the residents. She encouraged them to return to discuss their suggestions to improve the derelict park in their area. She listened to their complaints about the lack of police foot patrols and promised to begin working on that GAP. Sara has found that legislators often depend on citizen groups. They cannot know everything that is going on in their districts, and the voters are their eyes and ears.

RTOC is often consulted by a town councillor or by a state representative who wants to hear their ideas or solicit support when legislation about housing is proposed. The members have established credibility as people who do their homework. They also have built a reputation of having good memories, especially on election day!

Although they might think of themselves as apolitical, human service workers cannot be. They visit their statehouse when budgets are being discussed by legislators. If they do not lobby for the funding of social welfare programs, perhaps no one else will! The opponents of affordable housing, humane correctional programs, or shelters for battered women are likely to be there, telling their side of the story. They are demanding that money be diverted from social programs to fund their priorities. They too will have research documents and signatures on petitions. Thus, as Sara has learned, understanding how to present a case to a legislator is not a skill reserved just for community organizers. This is a skill she will take with her into every human service job she does. She will also use it in her personal life as a citizen of her own community.

TURNING TO THE COURTS FOR REDRESS OF GRIEVANCES

Although the sanitation complaint was resolved on the legislative level, at other times Sara has needed to follow the path to the courthouse. If she is convinced that an inequity in the wording or practice of a law stands in the way of a client getting fair treatment, the RTOC either tries to get the law repealed or asks a judge to change the way it has been interpreted or implemented.

Lawyers from legal services programs (initially funded by the federal poverty program), private attorneys doing pro bono work, and nonprofit groups such as the American Civil Liberties Union (ACLU) and the Southern Poverty Law Center carry these cases into court. They work on behalf of limited-income people, especially when they are convinced that their civil rights are being violated. When homeless residents of Riverside were being routinely gathered up by the police and forced to go to shelters against their will, these lawyers filed a suit on their behalf.

Although the volunteer lawyers do the actual juggling of the incomprehensible legal words and motions, Sara plays a role too. Because she knew many of the homeless residents, she was the one who talked to them about participating in the lawsuit. She provided them with information at every step. And she also gave them the emotional support that helped them hang on through the endless delays before their case was finally heard.

Rewards of Social Change Interventions

Most human service jobs do not require as much time, energy, and skill at social change as Sara's role at RTOC. But all workers will, at some point, encounter an unyielding barrier that stands between their client and the service he or she needs. Then, even on a very small scale, the worker acts as a change agent. As the federal government continues to shift away from publicly funded programs and the slack is picked up by the private sector, human service workers will have to continually monitor the output of social programs. Would you stand by quietly if:

> . . . a disoriented elderly woman you counsel was being evicted from her home because the landlord wanted to sell her apartment as a condominium?

> . . . a young man just released from prison wanted to find work as an electrician and the union representative told him they would not take anyone with a prison record?

> . . . the mother of a Cambodian youngster was told that she would have to wait six months for an educational assessment because the school psychologist was too busy?

> . . . a person was running for office in your town on a platform of cutting out all the frills and was targeting the only teenage recreation center, a meals-on-wheels program for elderly shut-ins, and a van to transport adults who were physically disabled to their sheltered workshop?

We hope your answer is a resounding, "Of course not!" Walking a picket line and knocking on a stranger's door to explain a community problem can at first be intimidating. Licking stamps, stuffing envelopes, handing out leaflets, and making endless phone calls is tedious. And losing a struggle after months of hard work can be devastating. Sara does all of these tasks, and she has faced many disappointments.

Yet she has also had incredible highs when desperately needed services were begun or reinstated after being cut back. The day the first tenants move into the housing development she has worked on for so long will be filled with indescribable joy.

Every organizer can tell stories about coworkers or citizens who, after experiencing a new sense of their own power, went back to school to finish their degree, took a more responsible job, conquered an addiction, or returned home feeling more hopeful about their children's futures.

Deborah Rosenfelt sums up the legacies of a social change campaign in her study of the aftereffects of a dramatic labor dispute in the mines of New Mexico in the 1950s. A group of poor Chicana women defied years of their community's machismo tradition and the prospect of spending several days in jail and continued to walk a picket line for months in the place of their coal miner husbands. The men had been forbidden to strike by a court order.

Thirty years later she interviewed those women. That strike had been the most significant event of their lives. For most, the relationships with their husbands had changed dramatically as their roles reversed during the strike. But, afterward, their roles in the family gradually regressed to the old inequality. The women's feelings of self-confidence had also gradually faded, they said . . . but not completely! (Wilson & Rosenfelt, 1978).

Although it often appears as if the field of human services has, like the field of social work, moved away from social change and become enmeshed solely in clinical and direct-service practice, that might not be the full picture. Terry Mizrahi (2000), a professor of social work and a long-time activist, asserts in her book that organizing for change both within and outside professional groups is, in fact, on the upswing. With a shaky economy, questionable welfare reform, and a world community reeling from the impact of globalization and terrorism, we agree with her assessment. Community efforts to come together and work for positive change have never been more necessary. And they need not be gigantic efforts. In *Stopping at Every Lemonade Stand*, Vollbracht (2002) describes all the small acts all of us can make that build up a safer and more satisfying community, one that nurtures children—and everyone else.

SUMMARY

1. Individual problems are often caused by factors rooted in the social environment.

2. Changes in the social environment can help one troubled individual, but more importantly, they can prevent the development of similar problems in others.

3. Systems-organizing and systems-change strategies rely on the same basic activities and skills as the direct-service strategies. They begin with data collection and terminate with evaluation.

4. Before forming an action plan to counsel a client, the human service worker must check out the mental health of the systems within which the client lives and works.

5. Human service workers need to explore their ambivalent or unrealistic attitudes toward change agents.

6. Momentum for change generates from the top down through legislative or administrative fiat. It also generates from the bottom up through the actions of organized citizens and clients. Often it is generating from the top and bottom of the system simultaneously.

7. Human service workers attempt to change both the structure of an unhealthy system as well as the consciousness of the people in it.

8. The three escalating methods of organizing for change are education, persuasion, and pressure.

9. Before a change effort begins, organizers research the background of the problem and locate where the power to make change really resides. They need to prepare a community profile to assess resources and understand the lifestyles of the people involved in the organizing.

10. Organizers use outreach techniques to solicit public support and participation in generating ideas and making decisions and to overcome resistance to change.

11. Citizen participation depends on obtaining strong commitment, clear mandates, appropriate structure, knowledge, skills, and participation supports.

12. To change the rules, regulations, and power arrangements of a system, organizers disseminate information, rally support, lobby decision makers, and take direct action when other techniques have not worked.

13. Working to change systems is time- and energy-consuming, frustrating, and often fruitless. Even very small changes can result in dramatic improvements. The potential rewards of all our change efforts can have widespread ramifications that change many people's life situations.

DISCUSSION QUESTIONS

1. George Bernard Shaw, a social critic of his times, is reported to have said that only unreasonable people will not accept the world as it is—therefore all change depends on "unreasonable people." How do you feel about that statement; does it make sense to you? Would you feel comfortable in the role of "an unreasonable person"? Can you think of some famous people who might fit that description?

2. What kind of change efforts have you been involved in within your own hometown or on your college campus? Who started them, what techniques did they use, how did the effort work out? Remember these change efforts need not be major campaigns. If you can't think of any change efforts in your own experiences, what kind of change efforts have you heard of or seen in your community or on the college campus? Have you seen or read about any groups that asserted their position for or against a woman's right to an abortion, or for or against gun control? What kind of tactics did they use to influence the public or legislators?

3. Is there any form of student governance on your campus? Where would you go to find the sources of power that might be able to change a rule or regulation that you feel is unfair or not fairly implemented?

WEB RESOURCES FOR FURTHER STUDY

Organizing Projects

www.lemonade-stand.com (see bibliography for book citation)

http://neighborhoodsonline.net

Immediately usable ideas on small community organizing projects that enhance cohesion.

Organizing Strategies

www.nfg.org/cotb/

www.netaction.org/training/reader.htm

www.nonviolence.org/support

Concrete organizing strategies and an organizer's toolbox

Government Agencies

www.house.gov/

www.os.dhhs.gov/

The House of Representatives and the Department of Health and Human Services.

CHAPTER 13

Understanding Legal Issues

Although human service workers are not expected to act as lawyers for a client, they must be able to interpret much of the legal language and conditions found in government rules and regulations, as well as in the personnel practices and guidelines of their agency. Workers also need to know when and where to seek advice when they cannot fathom the meaning of court rulings or legislative mandates that affect their clients' lives.

Human service workers practice the skills of giving accurate testimony in a court case or legislative hearing, to which they might be called as an expert witness. Sometimes they are asked to make recommendations to a judge about the fitness of a parent in a custody dispute or give their opinion on whether to commit someone for involuntary treatment. They should know where to refer an undocumented immigrant or a client who has been denied a benefit and wants to appeal that decision.

Our country has an especially complex set of overlapping laws and regulations. If a social service mandate is created on the federal level, then all fifty states must implement it in a similar way. But often each state is permitted to compose its own rules. So the worker must learn to hit the ground running when moving from one geographic area to another or from a job with one client population to another.

Laws about the rights to privacy and confidentiality, as well as the right to receive or reject treatment, are particularly controversial in our field. Workers may have to make ethical judgments about what information they can share with their clients or supervisors. Like doctors, human service workers can be accused of malpractice. Although these are not common occurrences, workers can protect themselves and their agencies by understanding the ins and outs of the legal system and by being scrupulously careful with their notes of interviews and with their accountings for program income and expenditures. Good practice is ultimately the best defense.

CLEVELAND, OH: On October 5, 1994, the American Civil Liberties Union of Ohio filed a lawsuit against the City of Cleveland on behalf of four homeless plaintiffs and the Northeast Ohio Coalition for the Homeless. The plaintiffs allege that Cleveland police officers, under the direction of their superiors, engaged in "dumping" homeless people—a charge that the defendants flatly deny. The complaint seeks injunctive relief to halt an unconstitutional practice under which police officers physically remove homeless and/or destitute individuals from certain sectors of the city, transport them against their will to various distant locations, and abandon them.

ACLU's Kevin O'Neill interviewed nearly forty homeless people and discovered that Cleveland police officers have at least three devices they use to keep homeless people away from the downtown business district. These devices included commanding people to leave, citations for disorderly conduct, and dumping. There have been no complaints of dumping since the filing of this lawsuit. However, Levin speculates that problems with dumping could begin again this year when Jacob's Field opens for baseball and the Rock and Roll Hall of Fame opens for business (*Spare Change,* 1995).

LEGAL ISSUES THAT CAN CONFRONT A WORKER

The above case is one example of the many kinds of legal issues that a human service worker might deal with. It is impossible in one chapter to cover all the legal issues that affect human service workers. Not only can they can seem overwhelming, but no human service worker knows the ins and outs of every issue. However, it is vital that we be sensitive to legal rights and dilemmas and that we seek further help when on shaky ground. Knowing where to turn and being willing to ask for help are the strengths of the conscientious worker.

To begin your thinking about legal issues, take the following quiz. We would be surprised if you knew all the answers. Legal issues in the human services can be complicated.

Question 1: An 18-year-old high school student began to wonder just what her teachers had been writing in her record since she started school. She asked her homeroom teacher if she could look at her cumulative school record. The teacher said no, because it would violate the confidence of all those teachers who had counted on some measure of confidentiality. Did the teacher break the law?

Question 2: In 1974 the State of Georgia set up a central computer bank to store mental health information about its citizens. State officials requested all clinics and community mental health centers to send in the following information for each new patient: background data, Social Security number, the nature of the patient's primary disability, previous mental health services, and diagnosis.

A human service worker at a community mental health clinic asked all of her clients to sign this medical release authorization, which read:

> The state wants to keep a record of name, Social Security number, and the type of problem of every person who comes for mental health services. The reason why the state wants this information is so that it can keep track of mental health services and clients throughout the state. If you sign this paper it means that you give us permission to send your name, Social Security number, and diagnosis to the state offices in the capital, where it will be placed in the mental health computer file. (Rosen, 1976, p. 285)

What is wrong with what the worker did?

Question 3: Felicia, a 23-year-old woman who had been adopted, wrote to the state registrar of vital statistics in Minnesota to request a copy of her original birth certificate. After receiving it, she went to the agency that had placed her with her adoptive parents to ask their help in finding her biological parents, who were named on the birth certificate. The adoption worker agreed to help her with this search (Weidell, 1980). At the same time, Felicia's 21-year-old brother Paul, who had been placed for adoption in Massachusetts where his biological mother had moved from Minnesota, wrote to the registrar of vital statistics for his original birth certificate, and they refused to send it to him. He went to the adoption agency, and they refused to help him.

Why did the adoption agency in Minnesota help Felicia, whereas the agency in Massachusetts refused to help Paul?

If you knew the answers to these questions, you are better informed about legal issues than a good many experienced human service workers. One study found that a significant proportion of mental health professionals are either ignorant of or they ignore their legal obligations (Swoboda, Elwork, Sales, & Levine, 1978, p. 448). Until recently, legal issues either have not been taught at all in human service training programs or have been dealt with superficially.

Here are the answers to the questions:

Answer 1: Yes, the teacher broke the law. According to the Family Educational Rights and Privacy Act, often called the Buckley Amendment, educational institutions that receive federal aid must make students' records available to them if they are 18 or older and to their parents when they are minors. This law probably also applies to the records of school guidance counselors, although there is some continuing debate about that (Bershoff, 1975, p. 367).

Answer 2: The State of Georgia, which requested this very personal information for its computer records, *did not* show sufficient concern for its citizens' right to privacy. Some states have adopted progressive privacy laws, and some states have constitutional provisions protecting the right of privacy. However, clients did not have to sign that Medical Release Authorization in order to receive service from the clinic. The mistake the worker made was not telling clients this. A study showed that when clients were told the following in addition to the first part of the statement, the majority of them chose not to sign the statement:

> If you do not sign this paper, this identifying information will not be sent to the state offices in the capital and will only be kept locally. The services you get will not depend on your choice. In other words, if you don't sign you will get the same services from us as if you did sign. (Rosen, 1976, p. 285)

The principle of consent assumes that people are informed about what they are giving consent to and that it is freely given, without any real or implied threats. If people think they will be refused services if they don't sign the consent form, most will sign.

Answer 3: The Minnesota agency helped Felicia in the search for her biological parents, whereas the Massachusetts agency refused Paul, because Minnesota passed a law that allowed adoptees who are at least 21 years old to obtain their original birth certificate if the biological parents have consented to the search. Massachusetts law does not allow birth records to be revealed for such a search.

Variations in the Law

Notice as you read those questions and answers that some laws apply *equally* to everyone in the United States (for example, letting students see their records), while other laws (opening adoption records) *vary* from state to state. As you read this chapter, some of the laws we discuss are probably already in the process of being changed by state or federal legislatures or by a court decision. Even lawyers must do constant research to keep abreast of current law in a particular field. Although most human service workers cannot know the law in the same way, they should strive to keep abreast of the particular body of law that applies to the major problems of their agency population.

THE LAW AS RESOURCE

Laws can give people rights and resources, and therefore, workers need to know them. Suppose that a human service worker is helping a blind child and the child's family to find an appropriate school. If the worker did not know that the Education for All Handicapped Children Act requires that handicapped children be placed in the most nearly normal setting, the worker might try to find a placement in a residential school for the blind rather than in the local school system. And when the worker arranged an interdisciplinary team evaluation, which is also required by law, he or she might neglect to include the parents, not knowing that the law requires their participation.

This process of finding information, evaluating it as it applies to a particular problem, assessing the needs of the person or group you are working with, and finding the correct fit between person and resource is the same problem-solving process that human service workers use in all the interventions discussed in this book.

Street-Level Bureaucracy

Street-level bureaucracy
The way laws and regulations are implemented by human service workers at the level of direct contact with clients.

Although laws are passed at various government levels—federal, state, and local—most beginning human service workers will encounter those laws that affect their practice at the level of the agency in which they work. Michael Lipsky (1980a) calls this **street-level bureaucracy.** Laws and policies are implemented on the streets where people live. A law sets the broad outlines of a program, but the face of the law that clients see is the face of the agency worker who delivers the service. Moving up the bureaucratic ladder, the worker sees the face of the law in the face of her or his supervisor and the agency director, who interpret how regulations shall be put in practice in that particular agency. In a large government agency, those regulations have been written by the state officials of that bureaucracy according to the way they interpret the law.

Regulations: Bureaucratic Interpretations of Law

After laws are passed, they cannot affect anyone's life until the money is appropriated and the regulations spelling out how to implement the laws are written. *Agencies don't make laws, but their regulations define how the law will be put into practice.* They end up having the same force as a law. For example, the Rehabilitation Act for the Physically and Mentally Disabled was passed by Congress in 1973. The regulations making key portions of it effective were not signed by the Secretary of Health, Education, and Welfare (HEW) until 1977, when several disabled people protested the four-year hiatus by sitting in at the HEW office. The 1973 law stated, among other things, that barriers that prevent the handicapped from gaining access to various facilities should be removed. Yet the ramps replacing curbs at crosswalks to accommodate wheelchairs, the audiocassettes opening museum tours to the blind, or the captioned news for hearing-impaired television viewers did not appear until the Secretary of HEW signed those regulations and set the procedures in motion.

Regulations are generally more specific than laws. For example, a law about licensing day care centers may say that the center shall be operated with "due regard for health and sanitation." But it is the regulations that specify a minimum number of toilets and the water temperature for dishwashing (Brieland & Goldfarb, 1987, p. 29).

Sometimes, in order to save money, officials make regulations that do not conform to the law, or they break their own regulations. This happened in 1981 when the Reagan administration ordered accelerated reviews of Social Security disability cases using what a Minnesota federal district court called "arbitrary," "capricious," and "irrational" standards to evaluate applicants' eligibility for the benefits (National Association of Social Workers, 1983). Thousands of eligible people were terminated until Congress reviewed the process, slowed the rate of review, and provided for continuation of benefits during the appeals process. An attorney for the Mental Health Law Project, which brought suit in Minnesota on behalf of the disproportionate numbers of mentally ill people who were terminated, said,

> "the court confirmed that SSA, in its eagerness to reduce the disability rolls, has been systematically violating both the law as spelled out by Congress and its own regulations." (p. 9)

In Massachusetts doctors were reviewing these Social Security disability cases without giving physical exams, and 80 percent of their decisions were ultimately overturned by administrative law judges. A legislative commission that investigated this said that "the doctors are following Social Security Administration *regulations,* while the administrative law judges are relying on federal *law* when they overturn the doctors' decisions" ("Law on Disabilities," 1983).

"CATCH-22" REGULATIONS

Regulations can put clients in a "Catch-22,"* a situation in which they are "damned if they do and damned if they don't."

Suppose that a toddler has outgrown his or her crib and needs a child-size bed. In the state where the child lives, the welfare officials who drew up the regulations decided that public money should not be spent on beds. Therefore, the 3-year-old will stay crammed in the crib or sleep on the floor.

Or suppose that a woman has been told by her landlord that she must leave her apartment. She agrees and then asks welfare for money to pay a security deposit on another apartment. The officials who wrote the regulations, however, specify that she must *show* the worker a court eviction order or already be evicted before the welfare department can help her pay the security deposit.

CONFLICTING JURISDICTIONS AND REGULATIONS

The picture may be further complicated by the different levels of government involved in the same program. This catches the client in a web of conflicting jurisdictions and regulations. Fuel assistance for poor people is one such example. A federal program provides money that some states supplement. If a state requires a client to apply first to a federal antipoverty agency for fuel assistance before applying to the state welfare department, the client can get a bureaucratic runaround and perhaps live in a freezing home until the confusing tangle is unraveled.

States and localities often implement programs that are not federally mandated. Sometimes they even challenge federal regulations. For example, at one time a federal drug abuse program had a regulation that required all states receiving money from the program to put personal data on patients into a centralized computer. Massachusetts refused to do so on the grounds that it would violate patients' confidentiality. Some states have stronger privacy laws than does the federal government.**

If the foregoing discussion has been confusing, imagine what it feels like to be a client. You might have only a dim understanding of who gives the money and makes the regulations. When you complain, you are told, "*We* don't make the regulations. The 'feds' (state, county, city) make them." Local, state, and federal bureaucrats sometimes fight each other about policies and regulations, passing the

---

*"Catch-22" refers to a novel of the same name by Joseph Heller (1961) and describes dilemmas that are impossible to solve because of contradictory requirements.

**The federal law regarding disclosure of drug information was later changed to prohibit it in all states.

Deciding exactly what are the limits of protests is a challenge for constitutional scholars and community residents. These members of the white supremacist KKK can march in Washington, D.C., but may no longer hide their faces behind their sheets.

buck from one to the other when clients complain. Advocating for clients in these situations requires patience, tenacity, and the concerted efforts of many people and organizations.

AMBIGUOUS WORDING

Regulations are sometimes worded so ambiguously that citizen groups or individual clients challenge them, claiming they give a false interpretation of the original intent of the law. Sometimes the laws themselves are ambiguous and loosely written. When a confusing regulation is stacked on top of a confusing law, conscientious workers are also caught in a bind. How can one interpret them? Many bureaucrats are becoming increasingly aware of the immobility caused by ambiguous intent or language, and now and then agency workers are pleasantly surprised to find on their desks a revision of agency regulations written in *plain, easy-to-understand English*. Sometimes these regulations give examples, which can make complex rulings easier to comprehend.

Some people argue that the ambiguity of regulations is intentional. When clients don't understand what they are entitled to, they are less likely to ask for those rights.

Learning the Regulations

Few things are more frustrating to a consumer than being served by a poorly informed worker. Think of how you feel when you ask for information about housing, financial aid, or degree requirements from a college employee and are given the runaround! A worker who is confused by the full meaning of a regulation should discuss it with a supervisor or a colleague. If the confusion persists, it is best to turn to a lawyer who specializes in this area. Most large agencies, such as a Department of Social Services or a Department of Vocational Rehabilitation, have legal divisions. In addition, there are many public-service law groups that specialize in children's rights, welfare reform, the needs of the physically disabled or developmentally delayed, and so forth. When a new law is passed or a regulation promulgated, memos and newsletters are distributed and conferences are organized to help workers and consumers understand and use its provisions.

Without these forms of public information, none of us—human service worker, client, or lawyer—would be able to keep clear about the endless changes and refinements in social service law.

Unfortunately, the federal government has been cutting back on legal services for the poor since the Nixon administration. President Reagan tried unsuccessfully to eliminate them altogether. In 1995 the Republican-controlled Congress made cutbacks of over 25 percent in an already weakened legal services. The struggle continues today. Bureaucrats and public officials resist protests against their rules and try to weaken organizations that challenge them. Because there are not nearly enough legal services for all the people who need them, human service workers will need to learn more than ever about the law in order to be able to help their clients.

THE LAW AS RESTRICTION

Laws provide resources and rights; they also limit them. City councils and state and federal legislatures create programs; they also cut them. Delinquency and correctional programs and agencies that investigate child abuse and neglect are examples of the government policing people's behavior. Human service workers in these programs need to be sensitive to the *stigmatizing* effects that such programs have on the clientele. They work to combat the **stigma** through social action and sensitive individual and group counseling. People may need to be stopped when their behavior is endangering themselves or others, but social stigma cripples rather than rehabilitates.

Stigma Something that detracts from the character or reputation of a person or group; mark of disgrace or reproach.

Human service workers work with many stigmatized clients:

1. When parents have been accused of child abuse and a child-protection worker goes to their home to investigate, the parents inevitably feel stigmatized, regardless of whether or not they actually did abuse their child.

2. When a child has been labeled a "delinquent," that label becomes a stigma that can create a self-fulfilling prophecy.

3. When patients in a drug or alcohol abuse program have their names put in a centralized computer, they have legitimate fears about how this information will be used.

4. When ex-convicts mention their prison record, they usually have a hard time getting a job because of employers' fears.

5. When people test positive for HIV, they have legitimate fears that they will be discriminated against.

LAWS EVERY WORKER NEEDS TO KNOW

These are some areas of law that all human service workers need to understand:

- Confidentiality
- Privileged communication
- Privacy
- Due process

Some laws affect one specific field of practice. For example, only those involved with the courts need a thorough understanding of the probation and parole regulations of that particular county or state.

Confidentiality, privileged communication, and privacy, however, affect all fields of service delivery. What do they mean as legal concepts to human service workers? To summarize, a human service worker promises confidentiality to a client in order to protect the client's privacy and develop trust between them. In a few human service relationships, the law treats those confidences as privileged communication, protected from being divulged in court. The only way that information should be shared with others outside the worker–client relationship is for the client to give informed consent. We shall discuss these concepts further in the sections that follow.

Confidentiality

Confidentiality is important in order to build trust. People are not likely to reveal anything embarrassing or intimate if they cannot rely on the helping person to keep secrets. Confidentiality means protecting a person's privacy and respecting that person's autonomy. Some people have such strong feelings against exposing their lives to public view that they will ask for help or reveal themselves only in dire circumstances.

Most people want the right to control information about themselves. People don't like having secret files about them that they can't look at or having credit records given out that might damage their ability to get a loan or buy a car. People get angry when they talk to someone in confidence and that person spreads their secrets to others without permission. We feel betrayed if a person violates our trust.

The psychotherapeutic relationship depends the most on confidentiality. People need to feel free to express their most private thoughts, feelings, and impulses. Some psychotherapists have gone to jail rather than testify in court about their patients. Some therapists have stopped including highly personal material in their notes to protect clients' confidences in case the notes are subpoenaed by a court.

Social agencies usually have a specific policy on confidentiality, but these statements are often vaguely worded, containing many "ifs," "ands," and "buts," which create many loopholes. In practice many agencies freely give out information about clients to other agencies, human services data banks, police or court officials, schools, employers, landlords, and researchers from both public and private groups. One experienced worker laments:

> It is not unusual for intake workers to have their new clients routinely sign a handful of blank consent forms "to make it easier for everyone." These forms authorize the agency to seek or release information about the client to almost everybody at any time under any circumstances. With the client's signature already obtained, the worker can fill in the blanks later when a need arises to disclose data. This system doesn't allow the client to maintain any meaningful control over the content of his case record. Thus, many settings (and federal regulations) are requiring that the client's consent be "informed." (Wilson, 1980, pp. 189–190)

This violation of confidentiality is not ethical, but it is legal. Two lawyers who studied the daily practices of public agencies concluded that clients of welfare or other social service agencies have no legal right to privacy and no legal way to fight a breach of confidentiality except where the federal Privacy Act or a state privacy act covers the agency's operations (Hayden & Novik, 1980, p. 68).

Privileged Communication

Privileged communication
Legal protection of confidences revealed in certain specified relationships.

Privileged communication gives *legal protection* to some human service workers against having to reveal a client's confidences in court, unless the client consents. It has historical roots in the privileged communication of the lawyer–client relationship, which held that confidences told to the lawyer must be kept secret not only to protect the client but, more importantly, to protect the right of all clients to be represented by counsel. Privileged communication is essential to ensure that clients will confide in their lawyers.

Recently, however, some states have freed lawyers to violate a client's confidentiality if they believe doing so could prevent injury or death to another person. California passed such a law in 2003, which states that the attorney–client privilege can be broken when a lawyer "reasonably believes" that disclosure is necessary to prevent a criminal act by any person, including a client, that could result in death or substantial injury. While disclosure is discretionary, not mandatory, the law was opposed by many lawyers and by the San Diego County Bar Association, which feared that it would "discourage clients from being forthright and complete" (*The Recorder,* 2004). Those supporting the law included the Gray Panthers and the California District Attorney's Association.

Privileged communication has been extended to other relationships in which trust is of the utmost importance—husband and wife, priest and penitent, psychiatrist and patient, journalist and source, and sometimes psychologist and client and social worker and client. Although it protects certain professionals from having to reveal confidences in court, it is not an absolute privilege. In fact, there is considerable disagreement and debate about this concept, even among lawyers. Some argue that privileged communication should be restricted when there is a threat to society, as when a client tells about a crime he or she has committed or is contemplating.

Human service workers are sometimes caught in an agonizing bind when they are subpoenaed by a court to testify. The worker may have promised clients that the information given them was confidential, honestly believing that she could guarantee confidentiality, but the state she works in does not provide the legal protection of privileged communication. The following are three examples of cases that have been contested in court.

1. *Director of a rape crisis center threatened with jail for refusing to give the court a rape crisis file.* Nassrine Farhoody, director of a rape crisis center in Worcester, Massachusetts, refused to release records of a client's rape counseling, which put her in contempt of court. She faced a jail sentence, but fought the case all the way up to the state's Supreme Judicial Court, which decided in her favor in July 1996 and tightened access to rape counseling records. The confidentiality of rape counseling sessions in Massachusetts is now as protected as the confessional with a priest. The woman whose records Farhoody refused to release during the rape trial came close to saying, "Turn over the records. I can't deal with this" (Coleman, 1997). But each time, Farhoody assured her she was willing to carry the burden. "She keeps saying she's only doing her job.... I love that woman," said Darlene, who doesn't want her last name used (Coleman, 1997).

2. *Rape victims' center defends confidentiality.* Erin Marie Ellis, the executive director of Washington County's Sexual Assault Resource Center in Oregon, was in court with her 9-year-old child, ready to be sent to jail for challenging a defense lawyer's subpoena seeking records on a rape victim whom the center counseled. A judge quashed the subpoena on a technicality on the eve of trial, but the case highlighted the ongoing effort by advocates statewide working for nonprofit, sexual assault crisis centers to protect their clients and maintain confidentiality.

    "Once we start losing control of our records, it greatly diminishes our ability to do our work and do it well," Ellis said (Bernstein, M., 2004).

Oregon state law does not grant rape crisis counselors special "privilege" from disclosure of their case records. About thirty other states afford rape victims protections for their counseling records, with several states providing absolute confidentiality, similar to attorney–client privileges, said Gina McClard, associate director of the National Crime Victim Law Institute at Lewis & Clark Law School in Portland.

"This is a privacy issue for rape victims, but it's also a crime-prevention and a crime-fighting tool," McClard said. "Rape is the least-reported crime. There's no reason we should put up another barrier" (Bernstein, M., 2004).

3. *Eighteen agencies refuse to turn over records to Department of Social Services.* In another successful court suit in 1982, eighteen agencies in New York City that had contracts with the New York City Department of Social Services were threatened with having their funds cut off if they did not turn over their clients' case records to that agency. A U.S. district court judge ruled in the agencies' favor, saying the information in the records "may well be constitutionally protected in that it touches upon intimate personal and family matters and was disclosed in confidence with some reasonable expectation of privacy" (National Association of Social Workers, 1982, p. 3).

Women's crisis intervention agencies in Maine scored a victory for confidentiality in 2004 when the state enacted a law to protect victims of domestic violence attempting to elude their assailants. The law established a program that provides a designated address to individuals who have relocated or plan to move to a location unknown to their abuser. It also provides participants with a first-class mail forwarding service and a designated address that has no relationship to the participant's actual address. As a result of the program, victims of domestic violence, sexual assault, and stalking are able to interact with businesses, government agencies, and other organizations without disclosing their actual address (Higgins, 2004).

Some research projects have been charged with violating confidentiality. For example, a research project that involved drug testing of high school athletes in Oregon did not protect the students' confidentiality because students who refused to participate in the research or who tested positive for drugs came to the attention of coaches and principals, were prohibited from engaging in school sports, and could be suspended from school. "Considering the profound social and psychological importance of peer relationships among adolescents, the loss of confidentiality results in humiliation as well as the public airing of drug-using status, assuming that the test result is a true positive. Confidentiality requires that the consequences of trial participation not be subject to publicity of any form in which individuals are reasonably at risk of identification" (Shamoo, 2004).

Agencies sometimes invoke confidentiality as a way of avoiding public scrutiny of their failings. Child welfare agencies have legitimate reasons for assuring their clients that information will be kept confidential. Many people would not report child abuse if their identity were known; people who have been charged with abus-

This cartoon points up the differences in the way the government treats a birth control pill for women and a sexual enhancement pill for men.

ing children do not want publicity. Yet when an agency is failing to protect the children who are in its care from abuse, it may not be possible to correct the agency's failings unless the public is informed and presses for change through the legislature. In 1999, two children age 11 and 9, who had been in the custody and care of the New Jersey Division of Youth and Family Services (DYFS) for more than five years, brought a class action suit which alleged a systemic failure of the agency to protect them and twenty other children from harm "and to provide their families with support and services to maintain adequate health and safety" (*New Jersey Law Journal*, 2003).

Since then, the tragic death of a foster child, Faheem Williams, and the abuse of his siblings, who were known to DYFS, encouraged the plaintiffs and interveners to request a modification of the existing confidentiality order in the class action suit. They asked for public disclosure of materials pertaining to child fatality and near-fatality cases. The *New York Times* and the The *Newark Star Ledger* joined the suit, requesting permission to publish the information. The U.S. District Court of New Jersey ruled that since DYFS is a public agency, the public has a right to know some relevant information regarding the health and safety of the children. The court gave the newspapers the right to review about 10 percent of the agency's files related to child death reports and other substantiated reports, but not identifying information about children currently in the custody of DYFS. The court attempted to "strike that balance between protecting the privacy interests with the public's right to know" (*New Jersey Law Journal*, 2003).

PROFESSIONS AND PRIVILEGED COMMUNICATION

Although privileged communication protects both the client and the professional, the confidence belongs only to the client, and only the client can waive it. Some states grant the privilege to clinical psychologists and to social workers. Human service professionals try to get broader legal coverage and stricter laws.

The confidentiality of a patient's communications with a psychotherapist was guaranteed on a federal level in a 1996 Supreme Court decision, *Jaffee v. Redmond*. The Health Insurance Portability and Accountability Act of 1996 required rules to be drawn up governing the privacy of health and mental health information. The rules were four years in the making, and in 2001 the Department of Health and Human Services announced them. The rules now:

- Require clients' consent in order to disclose health information for the purpose of treatment, payment, and health care operations.

- Preserve state laws' stronger privacy protections, where they exist.

- Recognize that psychotherapy notes require a greater level of protection than other types of health records (Moss, 2001).

- Prohibit employers from receiving personal health data, except for the administration of health plans.

- Make people who misuse private medical records, such as selling them, subject to fines or imprisonment (O'Harrow, 2001).

However, the rules allowed doctors, hospitals, other health services, and some of their business associates to use personal health records for marketing and fund-raising. In response to customer concerns that the marketing provision in the law did not protect privacy, the Department of Health and Human Services modified the law in August 2002 to prohibit selling lists of patients or enrollees to third parties without an individual's prior authorization. However, marketing to doctors is still permitted.

The new rules also say that sick patients will not be required to visit a pharmacy themselves to pick up a prescription, but can send a family member of a friend instead (U.S. Privacy, 2002).

You have probably seen the effects of this law when your doctor or hospital handed you a "Notice of Privacy Practices" brochure and asked you to sign a form saying that you had read it. You may notice greater privacy in the reception room and changes in sign-in sheets so that patients can't see each other's names.

Despite this law, a national survey showed that an overwhelming number of Americans fear their psychological health records are not kept confidential, particularly from their employers. And most people are not aware that many insurance plans require a diagnosis of mental illness to cover ongoing counseling. Many people are reluctant to seek psychological health care for fear their psychological health records may be shared with their employers or others. Two-thirds of Americans would not be likely to tell their employer they were seeing a mental health professional, and 70 percent would not tell their work associates. Half of Americans said they would hesitate to see a counselor if a mental illness diagnosis were required. To address these concerns and ease the strong stigma that is still prevalent in America, some health care professionals created a counseling service called OnMind Psychological Services, based in Kansas City, Mo., which does not participate in insurance plans and does not require a diagnosis of mental illness for treatment. They charge fees directly, but their fees are at least 50 percent lower than national averages (*PR Newswire*, 2004, May 17).

If human service workers do not have the protection of privileged communication, they must decide, with the help of their agencies, what to do if they are subpoenaed to appear in court with certain information. Even though a subpoena looks impressive, even frightening, you need not automatically comply with it. You can challenge its validity or relevance or the information it requests. You can contest it, with the help of a lawyer, by claiming privileged communication or other legal regulations. Most agencies have legal consultation.

LIMITS ON PRIVILEGED COMMUNICATION

There are certain legal limits on privileged communication. Privileged communication laws do not grant protection from reporting child abuse. All fifty states have passed some form of mandatory child abuse and neglect reporting law.

Some highly publicized cases of priests and church youth workers sexually abusing children have helped to create public demand for applying these laws to priests. In Massachusetts, a youth worker at a church pleaded guilty to dozens of child sex abuse and pornography charges, and a former priest was accused of repeatedly molesting children during a twenty-seven-year career in the church. Two dozen of the priest's seventy-seven alleged victims sued Cardinal Bernard F. Law for transferring the priest from parish to parish.

Some states have extended the reporting requirement to include reporting the abuse or neglect of people who are disabled or incompetent, particularly the dependent elderly (Gothard, 1995, p. 1580).

Most states have passed laws mandating that police arrest a person who batters another person and have also passed laws that mandate treatment programs for those convicted of domestic violence. Work with batterers poses dilemmas regarding confidentiality because counselors are required to report on the progress of the treatment to the court. Most treatment programs for batterers have a written contract explaining that because both the court and the agency want the victim to be safe, they will contact both the court and the victim to inform them of the batterer's progress in treatment. Participants are required to sign this contract before beginning treatment (Buttell, 1998).

Probation and parole officers and counselors who work with prisoners cannot assure their clients of confidentiality because they are required to report violations of probation, parole, or prison rules to the authorities. Clients should be informed immediately of the many limitations of confidentiality.

Workers in agencies receiving federal funds are prohibited by federal regulations from disclosing information about a client's substance abuse without the client's consent. But even the federal code of regulations allows disclosure of confidential information in cases involving such offenses as child abuse, homicide, rape, or aggravated assault (Landers, 1998).

PRIVILEGED COMMUNICATION AND INDIVIDUAL AND COMMUNITY RIGHTS

Laws often require the professional to break confidentiality if there is a possibility of a crime being committed. A landmark case, *Tarasoff v. California Board of Regents*, occurred at the University of California in 1974. An 18-year-old high school senior told the school psychologist in a therapy session that he planned to kill a girl when she returned from a midsemester vacation with her parents. The psychologist agonized over the ethical dilemma she was in. Should she break the confidence of the therapy relationship? Was the murder threat genuine? Convinced that it was, she called the campus police and asked them to take the student into custody for possible commitment. The police took him in, but, convinced that he was rational, released him on his promise to stay away from the girl. The psychologist wondered if she should warn the young woman but, following her interpretation of the American Psychological Association Code of Ethics,* did not do so. The student carried out his threat eight weeks after he had confided in the psychologist. The parents of the dead girl sued the psychologist, the school, the psychologist's supervisor, and the campus police. They charged them with negligence in failing to warn the girl of the student's threat. The court ruled that the psychologist *was* negligent in failing to warn the young woman.

There are no easy answers. If you know that in an interview you will not be able to keep everything confidential, tell the clients in advance. Discuss with them what you must reveal. If you are a probation officer working with juvenile delinquents, you are legally required to tell the court if a juvenile has violated parole. If you are an assistance payments worker in the Department of Welfare, you are required to act if your clients have broken welfare regulations. If your clients know these rules, they can make their own decisions about what to tell you.

Privacy

Privacy The right to be left alone.

Privacy can be defined as the "right to be left alone." In many state constitutions, it is defined as an individual's right to decide how much to share private thoughts, feel-

---

*APA's Principle 6(a): "Information received in confidence is revealed only after most careful deliberation and when there is clear and imminent danger to an individual or to society, and then only to appropriate professional workers or public authorities" (American Psychological Association, 1963, p. 57).

ings, and facts of one's personal life. In other words, no one has a right to make public anything about a person that the person wants to be kept secret. Before a human service worker gives information about a client to someone outside the relationship, the client must give **informed consent.** This means that the client understands *exactly what the consequences of the consent will be* before giving it and that *consent is given willingly,* without any coercion or fear of reprisal.

Most human service professional societies have codes of ethics that are intended to provide their members with guidance on how to protect clients' privacy. However, these codes are rarely revised often enough to keep up with changing circumstances. They are not always helpful guides to the legality of any one particular action. Here are two examples:

1. "Research project on drug use violates privacy." In a junior high school in Pennsylvania, a consulting firm wanted to administer questionnaires for a study designed to identify potential drug users. The school psychologist, seeking guidance from the codes of ethics of the American Psychological Association and the National Association of School Psychologists, followed what she interpreted as their guidelines in requesting the consent of the research subjects. Some parents, however, sued the school to prohibit the research study, and the federal district court (*Merriken v. Cressman*) agreed with them. The court concluded that even if the subject signed a release, it did not constitute *informed consent,* because the students and parents were not given enough facts about the reasons for the test or the ways in which the test was going to be used to identify and counsel potential drug users. In balancing the right of the individual to privacy and the right of the government to invade that privacy for the sake of the public interest, the court struck the balance on the side of individual privacy, believing that "There is too much of a chance that the wrong people for the wrong reasons will be singled out and counseled in the wrong manner" (Bershoff, 1975, p. 367).

2. "Court says that state agencies giving records to each other violates privacy." The question of whether state records in one bureaucracy should be made available to another without client consent was tested in Massachusetts in 1979, and the client won. Jose Torres, represented by the Juvenile Law Reform Project, was the plaintiff in a class-action suit against the state's Department of Mental Health and Department of Education.

   The suit was brought in an attempt to obtain services for Torres and other emotionally disturbed adolescents. In preparing the state's defense, the attorney general obtained information about Torres that was in the state's Department of Social Services files. When this action was contested by Torres and his lawyer, the Supreme Court of Massachusetts ruled that this disclosure of information about Torres amounted to "an unwarranted invasion of his privacy" ("Privacy and State Records," 1984). The attorney general was wrong to assume that you give up your rights when you sue the state ("Privacy and State Records," 1984).

Informed consent
Agreement given with the understanding of the full implications of what one is agreeing to.

COMPUTER DATA AND PRIVACY

The federal Privacy Act of 1974 says that people have a right to control information about themselves and to prevent its use without their consent "for purposes wholly unrelated to those for which it was collected" (Massachusetts Civil Liberties Union, 1983). Yet, in their eagerness to find fraud, some welfare departments are routinely doing computer matches with bank records and records of other benefit programs such as Social Security, unemployment compensation, and so forth, *without the consent* of the recipients.

In Massachusetts, for example, the Department of Welfare in 1982 gave the Social Security numbers of all welfare recipients to 117 Massachusetts banks. When the department received the list of people whose assets were over the allowable limit, it immediately sent out benefit termination notices to all the people on the list, without first discussing it with the recipients. John Shattuck, the national legislative director of the American Civil Liberties Union, pointed out that this was a violation of the Fourth Amendment to the Constitution, which prohibits unreasonable searches and seizures. Computer matches of unrelated files have generally been "fishing expeditions" directed against large numbers of people on the chance that something will turn up (Massachusetts Civil Liberties Union, 1983). Further, Shattuck says, they violate the legal principle on which law is based in the United States, that *a person is innocent until proven guilty.* Many of the people on the list were in fact innocent of fraud.

CRIMINAL RECORDS AND PRIVACY

A seven-year study of FBI criminal-history files gives us cause to worry about the use of records to invade our privacy. According to professor Kenneth Laudon, an expert in information systems at New York University who conducted the study, the persistently high error rate of these records makes them "a bigger blacklist than existed during the McCarthy period"* (Gelbspan, 1986). Laudon warns us that "today, there is a gargantuan, runaway system of records on individuals which is unregulated and unaccountable" (Gelbspan, 1986, p. 15).

Records are increasingly used by private and government employers to screen job applicants. Because they are often inaccurate, every year several million Americans are being unjustly denied jobs. The most common flaw involves records that list arrests but fail to distinguish between people convicted of crimes and those who were never brought to trial or who were acquitted. The impact of this falls hardest on black and Latino men and the poor because they experience a disproportionate number of arrests that are later dismissed. Representative Don Edwards (D-Calif.), chairman of the House subcommittee on civil and constitutional rights, said, "We are only perpetuating their disadvantages when we use those arrests to deny them jobs" (Gelbspan, 1986, p. 15).

*The "McCarthy period" refers to the years during the 1950s when Senator Joseph McCarthy conducted what some describe as a "witch hunt" against people whom he alleged to be Communists or Communist sympathizers.

Criminal records are used for screening even menial jobs. According to Diane Gordon, a political science professor at the City University of New York, "You can't even be a...janitor in a day care center if you have a criminal record of any kind" (Gelbspan, 1986, p. 15). How can ex-offenders stay out of jail if they can't find work?

CLIENT ACCESS TO RECORDS

In order to protect privacy, people need to know what has been said about them and have the opportunity to correct misinformation. Clients of human service agencies sometimes ask to read their records. Some states have privacy laws regulating this. The Privacy Act of 1974 and the Family Educational Rights and Privacy Act (Buckley Amendment) are the two main federal privacy laws.

The Privacy Act of 1974 gives certain rights of privacy to clients of federal programs, particularly the right to read and copy one's own record and to insist that it be corrected or updated if its accuracy is questionable. The client must give consent for the record to be used for any purpose other than that for which it was specifically compiled. The heaviest public demands for information have been made of the CIA, FBI, and Treasury Department. Federal social service agencies, such as the Veterans' Administration (VA), are also subject to the Privacy Act.

A study of several agencies' policies regarding client access to records showed that, of all the agencies studied, the VA had the highest percentage (84 percent) of workers who reported that their agency had written policies on client access to records. All VA policies provided clients with access to their records. However, only about one-fourth of the VA agencies routinely *told* clients about these rights; the remaining three-fourths would make the record available *if* it was requested. Obviously, if most clients don't know they have a right, they are not likely to seek it out and use it (Abel & Johnson, 1978).

When a program is partially or totally federally funded, as with Medicaid and the Title XX social services programs, clients who have appealed an agency action and have a scheduled hearing have a right to examine their case files before the hearing. Any federally administered social service program, such as the Supplemental Security Income program, is covered by the Privacy Act provisions for client access and correction.

OPEN ACCESS TO RECORD KEEPING

Some professional organizations, including the National Association of Social Workers, favor open access to records, but there is debate about this within all the human service fields. Our own position is that an open-record policy encourages honesty between worker and client. That makes for a trusting relationship. We like this guideline that one author offers:

> Pretend that your client is sitting beside you reading everything as you write in his record. Consider consciously what should and should not be documented, and figure out the most effective way of wording what has to be said. Be aware of things that might

upset the consumer, but that must be recorded, and be prepared to deal with your client's reaction. (Wilson, 1980, p. 197)

PRIVACY FOR WELFARE RECIPIENTS

When people have been stigmatized and treated in a demeaning manner, they are also likely to have their privacy invaded; all of these things erode peoples' pride. Welfare applications, for example, ask detailed personal questions to decide if the applicant is eligible. The federal–state Parent Locator Service (PLS) of the Child Support Enforcement Program has been especially prone to use "police state" tactics in its zeal to track down fathers who don't pay child support.

> In some states PLS paternity investigations have required women to complete questionnaires revealing all of their sexual relationships, including dates and places and the names of witnesses, and to take polygraph (lie detector) tests. (Hayden & Novik, 1980, pp. 68–69)

In Massachusetts welfare recipients and their advocates raised such a vehement protest about a "sex questionnaire" that it was quickly dropped.

When people are examined for their suitability for workfare in New York City, interviews with recipients with psychological problems are conducted in public spaces and not by doctors. Recipients are not given the results of their exams unless they specifically request them. Inside the waiting room, "waits are long, tempers short. People are moved in bunches by security guards through the crowds, off to have their blood drawn. One morning, the receptionist was observed openly mocking Spanish speakers" (Sexton, 1997a, p. 17).

The privacy of welfare recipients in Michigan is invaded by mandatory drug testing of all state welfare benefit applicants. Michigan is the only state in the nation to institute a policy of mandatory drug testing of welfare recipients, although the 1996 Welfare Reform Act authorized (but did not require) states to impose mandatory drug testing as a prerequisite to receiving welfare assistance. This policy was opposed by physicians, social workers, public health workers, and substance abuse treatment professionals, who filed an *amicus curiae* brief with the U.S. Court of Appeals in January 2001. The brief argued that mandatory drug testing is a marked deterrent on the willingness of individuals, particularly pregnant and parenting women, to access essential medical and social services (Vallianatos, 2001a).

The brief stated that this invasion of privacy was not justified by any special need to protect public safety. It identified other shortcomings of the policy:

- The use of drug testing is narrow in scope and fails to detect obstacles to employment and problematic family relationships.

- Drug testing does not detect child abuse or neglect.

- Suspicionless drug testing erodes the trust between welfare recipients and benefit workers—such as by promoting the fear that drug testing will result in removal of children from the home (Vallianatos, 2001b).

A federal appeals court upheld the Michigan program in 2002, but in 2003 the ACLU reached a settlement with the Family Independence Agency of Michigan which states that the FIA can now require drug testing of welfare recipients only where there is a reasonable suspicion that the recipient is using drugs (*ACLU Online Newsletter*, 2003).

PRIVACY IN A TIME OF WAR

As we write, there are both domestic wars and a foreign war in progress. Both are affecting our right to privacy. Domestically, there is a war over the legal right to have an abortion. The Bush administration has claimed in legal proceedings that it does not believe that there is any legal protection for the confidentiality of the doctor–patient relationship.

In 2004, the Justice Department demanded to subpoena the records of patients who had received abortion care at a Chicago hospital.

> In his ruling on the decision, Charles P. Kocoros, the Chief Judge for the U.S. District Court, Northern District of Illinois, noted: "The government counters that federal law governs this case and because federal common law does not recognize a physician–patient privilege, the medical records of Dr. Hammond's patients must be disclosed subject to the subpoena."

The judge denied the Justice Department's demand to subpoena the records. Kate Michelman, president of NARAL Pro-Choice America, said: "Americans will be shocked to find out that the Bush Administration has taken the position that there is no right to medical privacy. To assert that the government has an unfettered right to root around in our private medical records is beyond appalling, and brings to mind the basic question in the debate over a woman's right to choose—who decides?"

Shortly after September 11, the Justice Department submitted to Congress a law that they dubbed the "USA Patriot Act," an acronym for "Uniting and Strengthening America by Providing Appropriate Tools Required to Intercept and Obstruct Terrorism." It was rushed through Congress in several days, no hearings were held, and it went largely unread. Within two years of its passage by Congress, 238 cities and towns had passed resolutions against it, as had three state legislatures, and many more were planning to do so. "Local and state governments reanimate the practice of self-rule by opposing the Patriot Act's assault on the personal privacy, free flow of information, and freedom of association that lie at the heart of democracy" (Scarry, 2004).

The Patriot Act contains provisions that increase the ability of federal officers of the executive branch to enter and search a person's house, to survey private medical records, business records, library records, and educational records, and to monitor telephone, e-mail, and Internet use. It strikes most heavily against non-citizens. In the words of the Boulder, Colorado, resolution, it enables the federal government "to detain and investigate citizens and non-citizens," and to carry out "surveillance of citizens and non-citizens." It permits the incarceration of noncitizens for seven days without charge, and for six-month periods indefinitely without access to counsel if the attorney general "determines release would endanger either the country or individual persons" (Scarry, 2004).

Elaine Scarry sums up the dangers of the Patriot Act to democracy:

> The Patriot Act inverts the constitutional requirement that people's lives be private and the work of government officials be public; it instead crafts a set of conditions in which our inner lives become transparent and the workings of the government become opaque. Either one of these outcomes would imperil democracy; together they not only injure the country but also cut off the avenues of repair.
>
> When we say that democracy requires that the people's privacy be ensured, we do not mean that our lives remain secret; we mean instead that we ourselves individually control the degree to which, and the people to whom, our inner lives are revealed. From *Griswold v. Connecticut* (1965) to the recent *Lawrence v. Texas* (2003), the Supreme Court has affirmed that privacy is a fundamental constitutional value and located its roots in the First, Third, Fourth, and Fifth Amendments.... The constitutional scholar Kenneth Karst has argued that privacy...means first of all "informational privacy"—control over personal information and judgments. Such privacy is in turn the basis of a person's capacity for friendship and intimacy. It is also the foundation of moral autonomy and liberty, since freedom is premised on making important decisions based on independent judgment. Inhabitants of a country who lose the guarantee of privacy also eventually lose the capacity for making friends and the capacity for political freedom. (Scarry, 2004)

Due Process

Due process
Procedural
mechanisms that
secure or protect
one's legal rights.

Due process means that, under the Fifth and Fourteenth Amendments to the U.S. Constitution, individuals are entitled to "due process of law"—including notice of the charge, an open trial, and right to counsel—before they can be deprived by the government of life, liberty, or property. In recent years, due-process protection has been extended to include some social agency practices. This was done to curb "the broad discretion available to officials and employees of public agencies and institutions and the arbitrary or illegal acts that have sometimes resulted" (Dickson, 1976, p. 274).

If someone does something to you that you think is unfair, you naturally want to find out why, give your side, and rectify the wrong. You may want others to support you—perhaps a lawyer. Clients of human service agencies want the same. They often disagree with agency policy and workers' actions. They need some protection against arbitrary decisions.

FULL AND PARTIAL DUE PROCESS

There can be either full or partial due-process procedures. In situations in which a person might be seriously damaged by a decision, full due-process proceedings are usually allowed. These include representation by a lawyer, the right to present evidence and witnesses, the right to cross-examine witnesses, the right to a written statement of findings, and the right to a trial by judge and/or jury.

When there is less potential harm to an individual, or when a full-blown judicial hearing would be costly, laws provide partial due process. Generally they grant an administrative hearing and notice of charges and perhaps assistance in preparing and presenting the case (Dickson, 1976, p. 275).

Most human service organizations give partial due process in a dispute with a client. Clients generally have a right to appeal an agency decision, and the agency holds an administrative hearing before an impartial examiner. Agencies sometimes allow legal assistance or an advocate from another human service organization, an advocacy support group, or even a well-informed friend.

DUE PROCESS IN HUMAN SERVICE ORGANIZATIONS

Clients of most human service organizations had few legal rights to appeal an agency decision before 1970. In that year, the U.S. Supreme Court decided, in *Goldberg v. Kelly,* that the due-process amendments of the Constitution applied to welfare hearings. Eventually the same principles were applied to schools, prisons, parole proceedings, Title XX (federally financed) social services, mental hospitals and institutions for the mentally retarded, the physically disabled, juvenile delinquents, and other service consumers.

Soon after the Goldberg ruling, there was a sharp rise in administrative hearings. Many people who did not agree with this expansion of entitlements began to attack those procedures, saying they were going too far. There were demands for change, and certain due-process procedures were made less stringent. Welfare hearings were made more informal, and in the 1976 *Mathews v. Eldridge* case, the Supreme Court allowed disability benefits to be cut off *before* a hearing, although the *Goldberg v. Kelly* decision had stipulated that a hearing be held before adverse action was taken.

Despite the increase in the numbers of welfare appeals, few recipients even know that a fair hearing is possible. Nationwide, the appeal rate for denials and terminations of welfare grants is only 6 percent, and three-fourths of those came from four states: New York, California, Massachusetts, and Texas (Handler, 1979, p. 60).

Yet, *when recipients do appeal, they frequently are granted benefits that the agency had just denied. Workers should encourage clients to appeal an adverse decision of a hearing examiner or of a judge.* Many lower-court or administrative-agency decisions are overturned on appeal. Help your client to be persistent and aggressive. A study in New York City showed that close to half of the welfare clients who appeal had a victory (Handler, 1979, p. 60).

In the Supplemental Security Income and Social Security Disability Insurance programs, the Social Security Administration often denies that a person is disabled. In a large number of such cases, an administrative law judge grants disability benefits to clients who appeal (Heller, 1981).

Toward hope and healing for America.

Dave, Ruth and Margie Waterbury

We're living proof that families with lesbian and gay kids can be whole, happy and worthy of all that this great country promises.

Laws often reflect public opinion. This family is helping create a favorable climate for gays and lesbians so that laws will not oppress their lesbian daughter.

It is easier to appeal a decision in some agencies than in others. One person standing alone is always at a disadvantage when confronting an institution, but there are even more obstacles when that person lives in the institution and depends on it for food, clothing, shelter, and care (Handler, 1979, p. 69).

Although children gained some due-process rights in the Gault case, they do not have the right to refuse institutionalization against their parents' wishes. The Supreme Court decided in the 1979 *Parham v. J. L. and J. R.* case that parents have the right to institutionalize their children without the children's consent. Justice Brennan, one of three dissenters, argued, "It is a blind assumption that parents act in their child's best interests when making commitment decisions" (Frank, 1980, p. 379). Should parents be given full control over their children? Until what age? Under what circumstances?

HELPING CLIENTS GET THEIR LEGAL RIGHTS

During the 1960s and early 1970s, clients' rights were greatly expanded through the organizing of grass roots groups, including:

- The Welfare Rights Organization
- The Mental Patients' Liberation Front
- Feminist health collectives
- Children's rights advocates

Although the rights they gained still don't necessarily fulfill all their needs, clients are slightly less powerless. In recent years, however, the government has been whittling down those gains. Federal legislation has cut out or weakened client-participation provisions that gave social service consumers a way to monitor and change programs that affected them.

Title I of the Elementary and Secondary Education Act, which provides enriched resources for educationally disadvantaged children, used to give parents a share in the schools' decision making. But recent legislation has weakened their role and only gives them a watered-down advisory role. Title XX of the Social Security Act, which provides for social services, has also weakened its consumer-participation provisions. Class-action suits, which represent an entire class of clients rather than just one individual, have been severely curtailed.

Due-process rights were significantly eroded in 1996 by both the Immigration Act and the Personal Responsibility Act. Immigrants who are deported or imprisoned have no right of appeal, and recipients of Temporary Assistance to Needy Families (TANF, formerly AFDC) are not guaranteed a right of appeal against unfavorable decisions by the federal law, although states may still allow it.

Strategies

Human service workers, on the front lines with clients, must devise ever more ingenious strategies to help them secure their rights. Following is a description of some of these strategies:

1. *Human service workers need to be fully informed about their clients' legal rights, and they need to clearly inform their clients.* Reciting clients' rights at the beginning of your working relationship is rarely enough. Clients are under stress when applying for benefits or services. They might not hear or understand your full meaning. They frequently need to be told about their rights again, in other contexts and with fresh emphasis.

   Some advocacy groups publish booklets that spell out the rights of their constituents in clear, easy-to-understand language. If none exists in your area, consider helping your clients to write one.

Legal services groups sometimes publish manuals, and welfare rights activists in several states are publishing newspapers to inform people of their rights. There are also nationwide advocacy groups that publish useful information about legislation and people's rights.*

2. Even if you are convinced that you are correct in denying a particular benefit, you must remember that *the client always has the right to appeal a worker's decision.* The conscientious worker reminds the client of that right. Perhaps new evidence will come to light. Perhaps you made a mistake. An appeal is a chance to make sure a decision has been fair. If another agency has denied benefits to the client, the primary worker might investigate that denial, urging the client to appeal if there is a shadow of a doubt about the decision. The client may need help from a lawyer or an advocate to prepare or pursue the appeal. An updated resource file of legal services, advocates, and consumer groups is invaluable.

3. *The worker should encourage clients to learn as much as they can about their rights.* There are never enough low-cost legal services, so people will often need to defend themselves. Find out if there is a relevant self-help group that your clients can join. Welfare recipients, mental patients, adoptees, birth parents, adoptive families, divorced fathers, battered wives, people who are disabled, nursing-home residents, prisoners, families and friends of prisoners, and many others have advocacy groups that go to bat for clients.

4. Human service workers can help in due-process hearings by interviewing participants, collecting evidence, and helping in the preparation of cases. They also serve as **expert witnesses,** testifying in court on the basis of their specialized knowledge or experience in the field. If, for example, there is a question about whether a specific patient can manage his or her life outside the hospital, a worker in a community residence for the mentally ill could compare that patient with the residents he or she works with, establishing the likelihood of success or failure.

Expert witness
A person who is especially knowledgeable in a particular field and who is asked to give testimony based on that knowledge in a court trial.

*In the area of children's services, the Children's Defense Fund (1520 New Hampshire Ave., NW, Washington, D.C. 20036) publishes *CDF Reports.* In the area of aging, the Gray Panthers publish the *Gray Panther Network* at 3635 Chestnut St., Philadelphia, PA 19104. (This is actually an intergenerational organization.) Food Research and Action Center publishes information on food programs, including food stamps and school breakfast and lunch programs. The American Civil Liberties Union has published a series of books on various groups' rights. The National Association of Social Workers has published a booklet on confidentiality and privileged communication entitled *General Counsel Law Notes on Client Confidentiality and Privileged Communications;* it is available from NASW, Information Center/640, 750 First St., NE, Suite 700, Washington, D.C. 20002-4241 (send $1.10 and a self-addressed 6 × 9 envelope with your request). *Survival News* is a welfare rights newspaper that tells people about their rights and benefits. Subscription is free to low-income people. Write to Survivors, Inc., 95 Standard St., Mattapan, MA 02126.

This cartoon refers to a government program to encourage marriage of women on welfare. It humorously points out that there is no government interference in the marriage habits of middle-income women, even if they want help in finding a mate.

5. Welfare rights advocates often advise welfare recipients to take someone with them to *all* of their interviews at the welfare office to give them support and to ensure fair treatment by the welfare worker.

6. Workers who believe that an agency practice is harmful to a client must decide whether to challenge the agency or "go along to get along." Often a professional organization will support the worker in challenging the agency. For example, the National Association of Social Workers gave a Whistleblowers Award and some legal assistance to a social worker who sued the U.S. Public Health Service (PHS). The worker, Donald Soeken, was forced to retire from PHS due to what he described as substantial animosity from his supervisors after he testified on behalf of a patient's family that the patient at St. Elizabeth Hospital was not treated in a timely fashion after the diagnosis of cancer ("Two Cases Given Legal Aid Grants," 2001).

SOME CURRENT LEGAL ISSUES

There are some hotly contested issues in the human services that, although they do not apply equally to all workers, have wide-ranging implications and should be thought about. These include the **right to treatment,** the right to treatment or education in the **least restrictive setting,** and the **right to refuse treatment.**

To help you visualize how a human service worker might be called on to deal with some of these issues, we present an interview with Donald Boucher, who worked in a mental hospital for adolescents while completing his undergraduate degree in social work.

Right to treatment Legal assurance that a person who is placed in an institution that purports to give treatment does, in fact, receive treatment.

Least restrictive setting The type of treatment and location that provide the greatest amount of freedom to a client (who often has a specific disability).

Right to refuse treatment Legal protection granted to a person who does not want the treatment that is prescribed by professionals.

INTERVIEW

Donald Boucher, Mental Health Worker

Donald Boucher has worked as a mental health counselor at a private psychiatric hospital that has a seventeen-bed coed treatment program for youths from 12 to 19 years old. They stay from fourteen days to five or six months. The policies of the program are strict, based on firm limit and goal setting to modify behavior.

Donald's job was to help with the scheduled daily activities, to maintain the safety of the clients, and to enforce the rules. He believes that those rules are sometimes too strict and actually prevent genuine treatment. On two occasions, parents protested hospital practices because they believed that the treatment was harmful to their children. Donald describes these two situations:

1. A 14-year-old girl had a severe eating disorder called bulimia. She would vomit in front of staff and patients, sometimes at the dinner table. Because of her behavior, the other patients didn't want to be around her, and the staff was also repulsed by her actions.

   She was placed in isolation in her room with no contact with other patients and limited staff contact. She was not allowed to participate in group counseling sessions with her peers. She wasn't allowed to leave her room and had no individual counseling sessions while in isolation. She was punished in the hope that her negative behavior would be extinguished. Instead, she became more and more detached. She was kept isolated for about four months.

   Her mother was outraged when she learned what was going on. She told the hospital that her daughter desperately needed to learn socialization skills, but instead she was isolated and ignored. She wasn't getting treatment she needed to overcome her illness.

   The mother sent a letter to her hometown newspaper, and it was published. She also sent copies of the letter to politicians and others who she thought would be shocked to find out how the hospital is run. The newspaper called the hospital a "snake pit." This prompted an investigation, which resulted in some improvement.

2. The second case concerned a teenage girl who would behave violently even when no one provoked her. Once, for example, she began kicking a staff person in the head for no apparent reason. He just happened to be near her when she had this outburst. At other times, she was calm, rational, and very pleasant.

   At this hospital, when clients behave positively, they earn more privileges. They climb a ladder of steps of increased privileges and freedoms, such as being able to go for a walk outside along the grounds. This particular client had climbed to a very high level. She was doing very well with her positive behavior. However, one act changed all this for her.

   When the clients aren't actively involved in counseling sessions, they have to go to their rooms. They are not allowed to socialize with other clients outside of supervised group sessions. One day this client, out of boredom, sat in the doorway of her room and was carrying on a conversation across the hall with another client. A staff person caught her doing this, reminded her of the rules, and told her to go inside her room and stop talking. Angry, she refused to move. She was then physically carried into her room. She kicked and screamed. She was then put in restraints and stripped of all the privileges it had taken her so long to earn.

Her family, who were very involved in her recovery, were upset by the punishment she received for such a small infraction of the rules. They wrote letters and made complaints, which resulted in an investigation.

One of the positive changes that came about as a result of both families' complaints was the creation of a common room where the clients can socialize and participate in recreational activities instead of staying isolated in their rooms. Also, the entire program became more humane, with less harsh punishment for minor infractions. Donald feels that the changes were a step in the right direction.

Right to Adequate Treatment

The patients' rights movement of the 1960s and 1970s asserted that mental hospitals and institutions for the retarded were more like prisons than hospitals. Patients, ex-patients, and their advocates turned to the courts for relief. The first "right to treatment" case, *Wyatt v. Stickney*, came in Alabama in 1971. The court ordered the state social service officials to provide a specified quality of treatment for institutionalized mentally retarded people. The court argued that when a person is involuntarily committed without the same type of due process given even to criminals, that person has a *constitutional right to receive adequate treatment.*

A 1974 Florida decision, *Donaldson v. O'Connor*, asserted that if a person was dangerous, he or she could be committed involuntarily. But the state had a responsibility to give that person adequate treatment. Some other states followed suit, prohibiting involuntary commitment to a mental institution *unless* the person is a clear danger to self or others.

On June 18, 1982, the U.S. Supreme Court made a decision in *Youngberg v. Romeo*, which established, for the first time, constitutional rights for people committed to institutions for the mentally retarded. It guaranteed a minimum level of training and development (Barbash, 1982).

The parents who protested the treatment their daughters received in the hospital where Donald Boucher worked probably knew they had a right to demand *adequate* treatment for their children. Their protest techniques succeeded in making the hospital more responsive, so they didn't have to go to court. The hospital knew that the parents had a legal basis for a suit if they chose that route. *Legal suits that establish precedents make it easier for people to bring about change without having to resort to costly and time-consuming suits.*

Right to Treatment in the Least Restrictive Setting

The right to be treated in the "least restrictive setting" means that the conditions should allow the most possible freedom. Implicit in the right to treatment is the constitutional issue, does the state have the right to *force* treatment on people? The

Fifth and Fourteenth Amendments to the Constitution specify that a citizen's liberty shall not be deprived except in accord with due process of law. When the state decides to provide a service for a particular group of disturbed or disturbing citizens, it must do so in a manner that restricts their basic liberties as little as possible.

In deciding what treatment to use, an agency and its workers must consider which treatment will do the least to restrict the client's full growth. This concept has been applied by courts to residential mental health and mental retardation facilities, juvenile institutions, and educational facilities in the Education for All Handicapped Children Act. Perhaps you sat next to a pupil with a learning disability or physical impairment. It is this act that gave the student the right to occupy that seat.

Mainstreaming
Putting people who have emotional or physical disabilities into the mainstream of society as much as possible. The Education for All Handicapped Children Act (94.142) requires that all children be taught in regular schools and classrooms whenever possible.

The Education for All Handicapped Children Act requires that all children be "mainstreamed" into regular classrooms *whenever that is possible.* **Mainstreaming** means that schools must make every effort to put special-needs students in as normal a classroom setting as possible. Many hard-fought battles have raged between parents and their advocates and school systems, arguing about the definition of "the best setting" for a particular child. Teachers who aren't used to teaching children with disabilities have had to develop new skills. States and school systems have spent a great deal of money developing the facilities and expertise to incorporate children with special needs into public schools.

The Supreme Court ruled in 1999, in what is called the "Olmstead decision," that states may be violating the Americans with Disabilities Act if they provide care to people with disabilities in an institutional setting when they could be appropriately served in a home or community-based setting. This decision was made in regard to two women with developmental disabilities and mental illness who were residents of a psychiatric hospital, but it has been interpreted to extend to people with physical as well as mental disabilities, to those in nursing homes and other institutional settings in addition to psychiatric hospitals, and to those who live in the community and are at risk for institutionalization (GAO Testimony, 2001).

Right to Refuse Treatment

Efforts to force treatment onto clients are problematic. Can the state insist on counseling as a condition for obtaining a divorce or retaining custody of a child, even though counseling requires trust and a readiness to change? There will be many court cases before this issue is resolved—if in fact it ever is.

Mental patients have challenged the states' right to commit them to an institution and employ psychosurgery, shock therapy, aversion therapy, seclusion, restraints, drug therapy, or behavioral modifications that withhold food and privileges. Courts consider whether the patient was legally competent to be involved in a treatment decision, and if so, whether the institution obtained the patient's informed consent. Courts also consider whether the treatment is experimental or traditional and how intrusive and potentially dangerous it is. Psychosurgery, aversion therapy, and shock therapy, for example, are considered much riskier than other behavioral strategies.

The Importance of Written Plans

Written documentation of a treatment plan is often required. The Education for All Handicapped Children Act is very specific about these plans. Also, the Developmental Disabilities and Rights Act requires program plans for institutions and for individuals in community programs that receive federal funds. Whether or not a written plan is required by law, it is helpful to have one. It ensures continuity of service (Burgdorf & Burgdorf, 1977, p. 127).

SUMMARY

1. Many human service workers are unaware of their legal obligations. Human service training programs have often omitted such issues or have treated them superficially.

2. Federal laws apply equally to all states. Other laws vary from one state to another. Because laws change frequently, a human service worker needs to keep up-to-date on changes.

3. Laws are a resource; many human service programs were created by laws. In order to help clients obtain their entitlements, workers need to understand these laws.

4. After laws have been passed, a government agency draws up the regulations, which are the bureaucratic procedures that put the law into practice.

5. Some regulations are so restrictive that they make life very difficult for clients.

6. Some programs are governed by several government jurisdictions, and clients often get a bureaucratic runaround.

7. Some regulations are worded ambiguously, either intentionally or because bureaucrats are unable to write clear English. If clients do not understand their rights, they are not likely to claim them.

8. People enmeshed in the legal system are often stigmatized. Human service workers need to combat this stigma.

9. There are some laws that every worker needs to know. These include laws concerning confidentiality, privileged communication, privacy, and due process.

10. In order to protect privacy, clients need to know what is said about them in records so they can correct them if they want to.

11. Agencies comply with privacy laws to varying degrees. Those that are covered by federal privacy laws are more likely to allow open access to records, but they do not always comply with the law or inform clients of their right to read their records.

12. Open access to records causes workers to be more careful in their recording. There are pros and cons to an open-access policy. The authors favor open access.

13. Welfare recipients have few legal guarantees of privacy. The Parent Locator Service is particularly intrusive.

14. Privileged communication protects the confidences of the client–worker relationship in some cases, but it is not complete protection, nor is it extended to all professions in all states. The privilege belongs to the client, not to the worker.

15. Due process assures a client the right to disagree with a worker's decision. Most clients of human service agencies are granted only partial due-process procedures.

16. Human service workers should help clients appeal adverse decisions, which might be reversed on appeal.

17. Federal legislation is weakening or eliminating provisions that allow clients decision-making power in federal programs; therefore, self-help advocacy groups are increasingly important.

18. Workers should learn about clients' legal rights and inform clients about them.

19. Current legal issues that human service workers should be aware of include the right to obtain treatment, the right to treatment or education in the least restrictive setting, and the right to refuse treatment.

20. Written plans are often required by law, as is client involvement in writing them.

DISCUSSION QUESTIONS

1. Should parents be given full control over their children? If so, until what age? Under what circumstances?

2. What are the pros and cons of allowing clients to read their own records?

3. The state makes many intrusions into the privacy of welfare recipients but very few in the lives of children and their parents who receive Social Security. Why do you think this is? Do you think the state has the right to investigate the personal behavior of welfare recipients?

4. People with criminal records can be kept out of public housing and many kinds of jobs. They can also be prevented from voting. What do you think of this?

WEB RESOURCES FOR FURTHER STUDY

The Center for Law and Social Policy (CLASP)
www.clasp.org/

The Center for Law and Social Policy (CLASP), is a national, nonprofit organization which conducts research, policy analysis, technical assistance, and advocacy on issues related to economic security for low-income families with children. In addition, CLASP is a leader in the national effort to establish equal justice for all. Family policy projects include welfare reform, workforce development, child care, child support enforcement, child welfare, couples and marriage policy, and reproductive health and teen parents.

Welfare Law Center
www.welfarelaw.org/

The Welfare Law Center works with and on behalf of low-income people to ensure that adequate income support—public funding provided on the basis of need—is available whenever and to the extent necessary to meet basic needs and foster healthy human and family development. Their LINC project promotes low-income groups' use of technology. Their web page for low-income groups is www.lincproject.org. The constantly expanding web page includes their *Directory of Low-Income Organizations Working on Welfare* with information on 157 groups in forty states.

FindLaw for the Public
http://consumer.pub.findlaw.com

FindLaw for the Public offers extensive plain-English legal information, such as user-friendly articles, guides, forms, and FAQ pages to help people and businesses understand and deal with legal issues. Their resources include West Legal Directory, the Internet's largest directory of lawyers and legal professionals, as well as many resources for lawyers.

CHAPTER 14

Staying Current and Avoiding Burnout

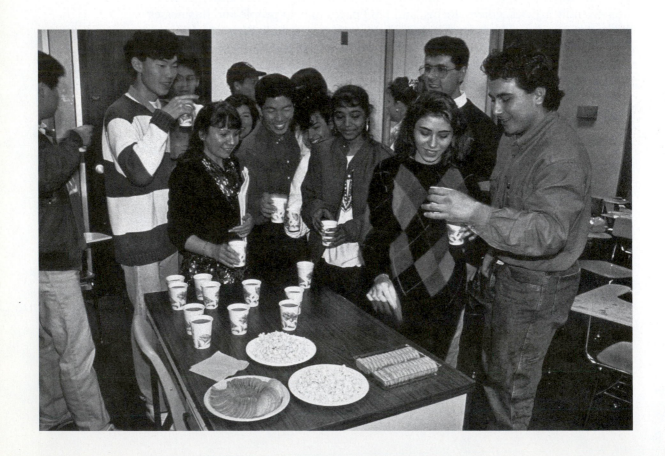

Throughout this book, we have underscored the complex nature of our work. There is no doubt that people and their problems are uniquely fascinating and endlessly frustrating. We also have described the intense sense of self-worth and satisfaction a worker can gain when a child is reunited with a healthy family or a previously homeless person moves into a rehabilitated apartment. You can hear these ups and downs, in each of the worker interviews.

How do we accentuate the positive moments of the small successes and how do we insulate ourselves from all the pain around us without becoming callous? These are questions you will continue to ask.

In this chapter, we have a frank discussion of the emotional and physical symptoms of burnout. If it does engulf you at some point, you will be able to identify the beginnings of it and start designing your process of renewal. We also discuss the many reasons why periods of burnout might happen to even the strongest of us. Increased bureaucratization of the field, low salaries, time pressures, and a shrinking pool of available resources and public support are the chief culprits.

After sounding the alarm, we describe many of the ways workers have found to deal with those inevitable times when the troubles of the world and the assaults of the budget cutters make us feel hopeless. Total capitulation to the forces of bureaucracy, angry rejection of all rules, blaming the clients for their problems, and withdrawing into the "nine to five" niche are all nonproductive coping mechanisms. Seeking out the support of one's peers, supervisors, and family and fighting the bureaucratization by creating new, humane ways of delivering services are productive approaches. So too are carefully choosing your battles, using the channels of your professional organization or union, and setting limits on yourself and others. Job rotation and taking time off to pursue another set of interests for a while can also refresh us. Pursuing a hobby, exercising, and using your sense of humor are all healing.

The word *crispy* may not refer to crackers when it is used by human service workers; it may describe a burned-out worker. One of the authors first heard it at a college human service career day.

I had invited two of my former students to talk about their human service jobs. The first, Kathie, was all fired up and spoke energetically about her work in child protection and foster care. Sure, she said, her job had its hard moments, but that did not stop her from doing a good job or figuring out ways to solve the problems.

The second speaker, Brian, whom the teacher remembered as a bright and enthusiastic student, talked in a depressed monotone about the problems of his job that he felt were insurmountable. He droned on about his work as a probation officer in a juvenile court, complaining about large caseloads, ungrateful and manipulative clients, inadequate resources, coworkers who goofed off, other agencies that refused referrals, insensitive judges, and mountains of paperwork.

After the speeches were over, I commented to Kathie about Brian's lack of enthusiasm. Kathie replied, "He's not just burnt out, he's crispy—*for sure!*"

Human service work draws on our deepest impulses to form important relationships and on our curiosity about what makes us think, feel, and act the way we do. It gives us a chance to laugh and play with people, to solve problems with them, to cry and grieve with them, to share the joy of their successes, to share their anger at injustice, and to work with them to change unjust systems. What job can be more important than that?

In fact there is evidence that by helping others, people improve their mental health, their physical well-being, and even their longevity. A University of Michigan study of 423 elderly couples followed for five years found that the people who reported helping others—even if was just giving emotional support to a spouse—were only about half as likely to die within those five years as those who did not. Another study of 2000 Presbyterians found that improved mental health seemed to be more closely linked to giving help than to receiving it. However, when helping involves constant or exhausting demands, the toll it takes clearly outweighs any good it does (Goldberg, 2003).

Any work is exciting only as long as we are growing in it—expanding our self-awareness, learning more about the job, feeling good about our ability to do it, gaining more power over the conditions of work, and getting some measure of success from it. In order to grow, we need the following supports from our environment:

- Working conditions that make it possible to do our best
- Support and respect from our peers and supervisors
- Freedom from unconstructive criticism and control
- Ability to share in decision making
- Some stability

It is the same with flowers: They grow luxuriously only when they have the right conditions of sun, soil, and water; if those are lacking, they wilt and die. Continual change in the human service field brings excitement and adventure as well as tension. When the change is too rapid or when it brings a political climate that is unsympathetic, it is hard for workers to do their best work.

BURNOUT

The term *burnout* and the slang terms for its varying degrees of intensity have been coined to describe the mood that human service workers sink into when they have lost their spark. The concept has—to coin a pun—caught fire. Newspapers print articles about it, workshops and conferences are held on it, teachers' unions devote entire issues of their professional journals to it, books are written about it, and there are now "burnout experts." Reed (1979) says that burnout "disproportionately strikes those in the helping professions—teachers, counselors, social workers. It's related to stress and can last for years. It's harmful physically to the individual and psychologically to all those around him" (p. 12).

Symptoms of Burnout

Grey (1979) says these five symptoms of stress are easily identified:

- Difficulty in sleeping

- Irritability

- Upset stomach

- Headaches

- Shortness of breath

Burnout may lead human service workers to stop caring about the people they work with, perhaps to sneer at them, laugh at them, label them, or treat them in derogatory ways. It causes workers to exaggerate differences between clients and themselves, seeing clients as "less good, less capable, and more blameworthy than themselves" (Maslach, 1978, p. 113).

Some workers escape their job by drinking or taking drugs or staying away from work—calling in sick or pretending to be at work when they are not. In place of enthusiasm, a sense of futility sets in. Some workers develop a callousness and cynicism to protect themselves from feeling anything. Behind this callousness may be an idealist who became overwhelmed by the job and stopped caring. Starting out with empathy for victims, he or she ends up being a victim blamer.

One woman who worked for the Save the Children agency in Vietnam during the war watched this process happen in herself. She said that when she went to Vietnam, she was fired up with enthusiasm about saving the victims of the war. But there was never enough medical staff, supplies, or equipment, and the destruction of war was too devastating for the staff to handle. In order to get even a few hours of sleep so they could start again the next day, they had to push the doors shut against the bodies of people screaming and pressing to get in for emergency medical treatment. She began to resent the people for their insatiable demands and for making her act like that. She never in her life dreamed that she would be slamming a door on people in such desperate straits. She had to go home to rebuild her sense of self.

CAUSES OF BURNOUT

There are at least two ways to analyze the phenomenon of burnout. One, based on individual psychology, emphasizes the emotional stress of working with problems that can reactivate the worker's unconscious childhood conflicts (Littner, 1957). The other approach, based on sociological theory, examines the social system in which human services are embedded and claims that the system itself creates the stresses. Karger (1981) argues that the very term *burnout* is misleading because it focuses on the subjective state of the individual. He would substitute the term **alienation,** a sociological term used to describe the way that the structure of a job distances people from their work, from each other, and from themselves. This would put the focus *on the organization and the larger society.* Both the psychological and the sociological points of view are correct, but they often ignore each other's insights.

Alienation
A sociological term used to describe the way the structure of a job or organization distances people from their work, from each other, and from themselves.

Psychological Conflicts

The powerful emotional stress and thorny problems that human service workers deal with daily often touch deep responsive chords in them: A worker who was neglected as a child may impute neglect when parents are merely casual in their parenting style; one whose parents were extremely strict may seethe with fury at seemingly overdemanding parents. Many beginning workers are still dealing with their own issues of dependence and independence from family, mate, religion, and cultural group. Often it is difficult for them to sort out when their own struggles and those of their clients begin and end. For young workers, identification with the problems of teenagers or young adults can easily cross the line into **overidentification.**

Overidentification
The process of relating so completely to another person's feelings and/or experiences that one cannot separate oneself from the other person.

Sometimes the goals of the work itself cause ambivalence and anxiety, even when the worker basically agrees with the agency's mission. You can feel strongly about the importance of protecting children from abuse, but accusing parents of perpetrating that abuse, and even removing children from their homes, can cause intense anxiety.

Workers in abortion clinics are also under emotional stress because of the nature of the work. Carol Joffe (1983) studied workers in one clinic and found that, even though the workers supported a woman's right to choose an abortion, they did not believe that abortion should be done as a method of contraception. They loved babies, were happy when a client decided to go through with her pregnancy, and were joyous when one of their own staff had a baby. They were more pro-choice than pro-abortion. Yet, in the embattled political atmosphere that surrounds abortion, they were forced to "cling, at least publicly, to a rhetorical pro-abortion position" (Joffe, 1983, p. 318). The politics of abortion rights forced them into a rigidity they did not really feel, and this created stress.

Conflicting Social Values

Combined with these very personal stresses are the even more serious strains induced by the ambivalent values of our social system, which gives only grudging support to universal social services. Welfare workers are in the front line of this conflict. To illustrate how one worker deals with these conflicts, following is an interview with Rick Colbath Hess.

INTERVIEW

Rick Colbath Hess, Director of MassSERVE

Rick Colbath Hess is the founder of MassSERVE, an organization dedicated to improving the working conditions of human service workers. We present here an interview with him, conducted by a staff member of the Mass Human Services Coalition in October 2001 (Mass Human Services Coalition, 2001).

SHW: We'd like to talk to you about the whole direct care worker crisis that's rampant throughout human services and in particular, what MassSERVE has been doing about it. So perhaps we could start by you giving a little background on the founding of MassSERVE.

RC: "Well, there were essentially a bunch of human service workers who came together who didn't feel like they had a voice in any other place. Their organizations were not unionized and they felt like they should have a voice in the political process and they came together and people were very upset about the working conditions and what was going on in the field and out of that came MassSERVE. That's the short version."

SHW: Could you tell us a little bit about your own experience as a direct care worker? Or how you became involved in this cause and effort?

RC: "Sure. I've been in human services now for seventeen or eighteen years, I've worked with homeless people, I've worked with people with drug addictions, I've worked with people in food pantries, I've worked with program creation, and my last job was at Catholic Charities, and when I went around interviewing for that job, I went to many many different agencies and they were all dropping their personnel policies and going to worker at will provisions and I realized at the time that there was really a powershift in the dynamics of what was happening in the field and that people really didn't have much say at work because providers were also losing their say and it was trickling down to the workers. After working at Catholic Charities for three years I had children and—let me see how to say this—I was essentially demoted for trying to negotiate a child-friendly work schedule and there was really nowhere for me to turn for help, and out of that experience really came my organization. I ended up being laid off from that job and I started organizing (MassSERVE) and putting together a lot of people that had been talking around these issues.

"Also in my internships at social work school, I saw how depressed everybody was. People were essentially responding the way they would respond to crisis, fight or flight. Half the staff was depressed in my internships and the other half was angry as hell and the energy was very misdirected. People did not seem to be able to respond to the political crisis at the time: the crisis of privatization, the degradation of human services, both at the service level and at the employee level."

SHW: Well now MassSERVE has put forward a possible solution to the direct care worker crisis; the Human Services Worker Living Wage Bill. Could you tell us a little bit more about the genesis of the bill and what coalition has emerged in support of it?

RC: "Well, the bill came out of looking at the whole field, who was suffering the most, looking at research and seeing that when you push the bottom up, everybody else goes up too. And also following the Living Wage movement nationally and seeing what a success it's had and we had a number of goals at MassSERVE but we decided that wages were the most pressing at the time and we started working on developing a strategy around the living wage bill. And from that we were able to try to pull together—one of the advantages of the organizing that we're doing is that being a worker organization, we don't go directly after providers, we essentially view the state as the provider. Without moving the state you can't change much of the conditions in the work field. We were able to pull providers, unions and recipient groups together which has been a very hard thing and phenomenal kind of thing that came together."

SHW: Well now there is a very large dollar amount attached to the Living Wage Bill, in the range of $100 million, what's it going to take to get the state to be willing to make that kind of investment. What do YOU think it's going to take to get that bill passed?

RC: "Well clearly…all salaries need to be upgraded, not just people at the bottom, there needs to be more training and possibly some kind of career ladder, [where] salary is tied to education and experience, that world view—I think there are many places in other parts of the world where it's a very professional field where you actually get trained and people get paid much higher. I think if it was looked at more professionally, then salaries would go up and that quality of care would go up. And I think that another one of the long-term strategies is essentially for the union providers and recipient groups to work together and to find their common ground to push for legislation to improve all their lots."

The Bind of the Double Message

Humanitarian ethos
A dedication to promoting the welfare of humanity, especially through the elimination of pain and suffering.

Careerism
A single-minded preoccupation with getting ahead in a career to the exclusion of other interests or values.

As we discussed in Chapter 2, powerful forces are trying to dismantle most, if not all, government support for social welfare. As a result, "social workers are caught between the privatization of profits and the socialization of the costs from that profit making" (O'Connor, 1973, cited by Arches, 1991).

The human service profession is built on a **humanitarian ethos,** but everyone in our society does not fully subscribe to it. And therein lies the conflict. Communities rarely provide the full resources of money, time, and caring to allow the human service worker to do the kind of job that needs to be done. One writer says that the modern welfare state has converted the ideal of service into cynicism or self-serving **careerism** (building your career at the expense of other values). This has made some committed and idealistic workers so disillusioned that they leave public service. This in turn makes it less likely that agencies will change, because the most idealistic workers often leave.

Workers face many double messages in this country. They are continually in conflict about whether to help clients summon their energies for change or to make the client more obedient in order to fit better into the agency's way of "helping." They may want to advocate for their clients to get more services, but the agency, with an eye on the budget, probably wants to limit services. Workers may want to work with clients as allies in shaping the policies and practices of the agency, but the agency does not encourage input from clients or alliances between workers and clients. Although the agency proclaims its desire to "help," that help may merely mean manipulation. All of these contradictions mirror the ambivalence society has about its poor.

> It is the front-line worker who is called upon to broker these contradictions and rationalize them to the client and to her or himself.... Public defenders committed to the ideal of providing the indigent with legal representation find themselves in court without time even to interview the client, let alone prepare adequately. Teachers find that the more pressing the need for creative classroom instruction, the more likely is the school to be overcrowded, and the more inundated the teacher is with disciplinary and housekeeping chores. When welfare workers in Massachusetts are assigned the statutory maximum of 180 cases (and others stack up, uncovered), or when judges have dozens of cases to dispose of daily, the possibility of personalized assessment becomes submerged in the need to process the work.
>
> Although public agencies empowered under various legislative acts are required to serve everyone who is eligible, they often cannot do so with their limited resources. Some react to this imbalance by devising ways to keep people from applying for service and by delivering an inaccessible or inferior product. Public programs often cannot charge fees, but they can set "prices" by inflicting indignities such as requiring long waits or limiting information.
>
> Obviously, these techniques contradict the ostensible program goals. Yet a worker who provides superior service will be rewarded only with additional clients. Greater availability or quality of services like health care, or greater accessibility of effective counseling to families in crisis, simply attracts more customers and harder cases. Adding capacity fails to solve the worker's perennial problem of inadequate resources (although it may in fact extend mediocre service to more people).
>
> The worker in public welfare programs confronts the dilemma of the fabled highway planner of the congested Long Island Expressway. The engineers kept adding additional lanes on the theory that this would alleviate traffic jams. However, the increased capacity only attracted more drivers, so that congestion was perpetuated, albeit at higher traffic levels. (Lipsky, 1980a, pp. 33–34)

Agencies respond to this pressure by following the Peter Principle (which suggests that services expand until they reach the point of mediocrity). More people may be served, but they are not served well. Agencies often sacrifice their original service goals in order to meet their bureaucratic needs. For example, when the job market shrinks, vocational placement agencies change their objectives from finding people jobs to "job counseling."

Increased Bureaucratization

Bureaucracy has become pervasive within the past few decades, and social agencies too have followed that trend. Increased bureaucratization means more centralization, more hierarchical control, larger workplaces, and decreased autonomy for workers. "Authority and discipline imposed by sponsors undermine autonomous input. Rigidly enforced and scheduled work hours and quotas are common" (Arches, 1991, p. 202).

Butler studied 404 members of the Virginia National Association of Social Workers in 1986 to assess job satisfaction. Not surprisingly, she found that workers who had high levels of daily frustration and emotional intensity, excessive bureaucratic demand, and too much paperwork were less likely to be satisfied (Butler, 1990, pp. 115–116). Those who worked in large agencies were also less satisfied. Thirteen percent of the workers studied had a full-time private practice, and 17 percent had a part-time private practice.

Butler (1990) says that the level of dissatisfaction with large agencies

> sends a clear message to management. Social work managers in large bureaucratic organizations need to find ways to organize their work units into smaller groups. The advantages of working in a small group include better support from co-workers, more effective communication between management and staff, greater flexibility in work hours, and less bureaucratic red tape. Large businesses have found ways to break up their organizations into small work groups, and so can large human service agencies. (p. 115)

Low Salaries and Decreased Satisfaction

Another factor that caused discontent among some workers in Butler's study was low salaries, which apparently was one reason that some workers left agency work to go into private practice. Other studies show that in social work, men are more satisfied with their jobs than women. Men's salaries are consistently higher than those of women in both service and administration positions. One author speculated that women's lower job satisfaction might be partly due to feelings of discrimination because men hold a disproportionate number of administrative positions in the profession (Glicken, 1977).

Insurance and Government Reimbursement

When insurance companies dictate the kind of treatment to be given and the way of giving it, workers no longer decide how the work gets done. This affects social workers in private practice as well as in agencies. Private insurance companies only reimburse for psychotherapy, diagnosis, and evaluation. They do not reimburse for marital counseling unless the client is given a diagnosis from what has become the "bible" of diagnosis, the DSM-IV—the *Diagnostic and Statistical Manual of Mental Disorders, Fourth Edition* (American Psychiatric Association, 1995). Every request for reimbursement in *any* field of practice must be accompanied by a diagnosis from DSM-IV. This means that much of our work is not reimbursable, including nursing-home placements, foster care, client-related meetings, and advocacy.

Even when a practice is reimbursable, the insurance company sets the time limits. Workers make cynical jokes about "sixty-day miracle cures" for psychiatric patients. They are discharged as "cured" from the hospital when the insurance runs out, whether or not they act or *feel* cured.

Workers may not be able to choose the treatment of choice because of insurance requirements. "For example, if only 12 visits are reimbursable, then planned short-term therapy is likely to be used whether or not it is deemed clinically the best treatment by the social worker" (Ortiz & Bassoff, 1988, p. 116). Medicare establishes time limits for treatment of each diagnosis under its system of Diagnostic Related Groups (DRGs). Ethical dilemmas abound.

> In some agencies, social workers are encouraged to double-book clients so that the outside coverage will still pay for the worker's time if one of the clients does not show up. If both show up, someone is forced to cool their heels in the waiting room. In other settings, social workers are pressured to drop clients who do not show up for two consecutive appointments. (Arches, 1991, p. 203)

Arches (1991) studied 275 registered social workers in Massachusetts in 1988 to assess the level of job satisfaction and burnout and found that one source of stress was that agencies have several financial sponsors and each sponsor has different demands. The workers in her study "reported working in agencies with an average of five external sponsors" (p. 203). For example, a family agency might receive money from several insurance companies, Medicaid, Medicare, state contracts, and the federal government. The agency is responsible to each of these sources of money, and the worker must comply with their demands as well as the agency's demands.

Time Pressures

When there is not enough time, the helping impulse may become extinguished. Careful listening takes time and patience. In fact, according to a Princeton University study, time is one of the most important reinforcers of the helping impulse (Shenker, 1971).

Three groups of theological seminary students were given a speech to read at a nearby building. On the way to the building, they encountered a man lying on the ground acting as if he were suffering (this was arranged by the researchers). One group of seminarians was told they had plenty of time; another, just enough time; and another, that they were already late. The ones who stopped to help most often were the ones with the most time (63 percent of "low hurry," 45 percent of "intermediate hurry," and 10 percent of "high hurry" men stopped). The researchers speculated that in the biblical parable of the Good Samaritan, the Samaritan, being a man of low public status, had little important business to attend to, so that he had the time to help. One could imagine the priest and Levite, "prominent public figures, hurrying along with little black books full of meetings and appointments, glancing furtively at their sun dials as they go" (Shenker, 1971, p. 25).

Lack of Resources Outside the Agency

Even if workers are lucky enough to be at an agency with enough money to hire competent staff, keep caseloads to a manageable size, and provide good supervision and a supportive environment, they are not home free. As long as other agencies are not as lucky, the impact is still felt by the clients and workers of all agencies. In the following narrative, Priscilla Shade (1981) tells of how state cutbacks in medical benefits to General Relief recipients affected her work in the welfare department:

> What this left workers like me to cope with were cases like the man who'd had surgery of the colon, who, with medical benefits cut, couldn't afford colostomy bags—life-sustaining medical supplies—because he got so little money on General Relief. He'd come in the office and get sick right there. Of course I was hysterically dumping him and clients like him back on City Hospital. At the hospital they went crazy from the patient overload. It also put the doctors there in the position of seeing a patient who may not have been disabled for the minimum of thirty days that was required for eligibility, but the doctor knew the patient would have nothing to eat if he didn't say he or she was disabled for thirty days. So all of a sudden, doctors were put in a position of having to lie for the client: they were caught right in the middle. (p. 28)

Shade goes on to describe how her work was affected when the state eliminated General Relief for the unemployed:

> Those clients who were merely unemployed and now cut off from General Relief began to reappear with a variety of illnesses related to their mental state. This meant an additional burden for caseworkers. In the end, clients got no "stopgap" assistance for unemployment, caseworkers were saddled with heavier "crisis" caseloads, the state footed a higher bill—and no one was helped. (p. 30)

Shade also describes how the housing shortage forced workers to do "shelter shuffling," sending deinstitutionalized mentally ill homeless people from one shelter to another because of the differing eligibility criteria of shelters, and how workers are caught in the middle of contradictory agency policies. She tells how at one point, the state provided professional services to clients while ignoring their basic needs for food and shelter.

> When I worked in the services division I learned to beg, borrow, and steal. I got to know a lot of people and I got to know where I could beg this, where I could borrow that, and where I could get $5 for groceries. I depended on the private agencies. I went outside the system. It strained every resource I could ever think of—even my own pocketbook. I was broke every week. (p. 30)

Lack of Support from the Agency

A worker's frustrations in the face of inadequate resources can be eased when the agency goes to bat for its workers, helping them do the job despite problems. But if the agency *blames* the workers for its own inadequacies (as sometimes happens), workers are likely to feel angry, guilty, and depressed. Some government funding sources and agency bureaucracies have tried to deal with their workload problems by introducing management methods that stress accountability and speeded-up work.

Agencies are increasingly under the gun for **accountability** and effectiveness. This can cause anxiety that sometimes interferes with doing quality work because of the new concern with quantity and numbers. Although workers should always be concerned about their effectiveness, attempts to *prove* effectiveness in narrowly conceived mechanical ways can be useless at best and intimidating at worst. Workers may have to write down the way they spend every minute of the day in an efficiency study. New managers and management techniques come and go. The concern with numbers and quantification can lead people to adopt techniques they are not comfortable with and use them in absurd ways.

> **Accountability**
> A requirement, usually imposed by a funding source, that an agency performs according to a certain set of standards.

Buckholdt and Gubrium (1979) studied a children's residential treatment institution that had recently adopted behavior modification as its treatment method because its funding sources insisted on some numerical proof of effectiveness. Behavioral modification offered more precision than the psychodynamic strategies the institution had previously used. The actual treatment seemed to continue more or less as it had before—loving and caring and time-consuming, the days filled with activities. It was probably one of the best run institutions in the area, perhaps the nation. Yet the workers, anxious to prove their effectiveness, became preoccupied with quantifying the children's behavior—how many temper tantrums, how many refusals to do homework, how many small thefts—in an effort to prove that they had solved these problems.

We return to Priscilla Shade's (1981) account of her work in the welfare department to illustrate how an agency can subvert a worker's desire to help people:

> The worst thing was that the worker was caught in the middle—caught in the contradictions of programs that provided, for instance, job counseling to clients when there was little hope of employment. Then, too, workers were faced daily with programs that provided preventive health screening for children; while other policies cut down on the amount and quality of food that could be purchased by the family. In effect, well-intentioned programs were being established while other policies undermined them. Those of us whose job was to help people found ourselves working in a system that did not allow it. (p. 30)

Pressures Exerted by Clients

Workers are not the only ones who become angry and frustrated when resources are inadequate or rules are restrictive. Clients feel the same but often express their negative reactions to the worker because that is the person who face-to-face denies them the resources they need. The legislators who voted the inadequate funding are shadowy figures. Today, the worker not only has to face clients' anger but also has to face continual value dilemmas. In an effort to help their clients find the resources they need for survival, workers often devise their own methods of playing the system, or they look the other way as their clients do so. One British author describes the kinds of dilemmas that workers face daily:

> How many social workers, for example, ignore the illegal fiddling of some of their clients against the Department of Health and Social Security, an organization which social workers surely see as being unkind to themselves as well as to their clients? How many probation officers turn a blind eye to the breaches of the probation order by offenses of their clients? How many social workers simply do not care about the fact that a client earns a pound or so more than social security regulations permit by working behind a pub bar at night? These are questions to which we do not know the answers, and perhaps nothing more than discretion will prevent us from ever knowing. But our commonsense knowledge tells us, as insiders to the codes and signals of the profession, that the social worker sometimes serves the function of a…Robin Hood who, if he is not actually robbing the rich to feed the poor, is aiding and abetting the offense. (Pearson, 1975, p. 65)

A few welfare workers, on the other hand, regard bureaucratic rules with almost religious reverence and are on the lookout even during their leisure time for clients who are working part time without reporting their wages.

INVOLUNTARY CLIENTS

Involuntary clients
Clients who are forced to use a social service, usually by a court.

Some clients are angry because they never asked to be clients, and they fight their client status every step of the way. Such **involuntary clients** include parents accused of child abuse and neglect, juvenile or adult offenders who are imprisoned or on probation, involuntarily committed mental patients, some old people in rest homes or nursing homes, children in treatment programs, and people caught driving under the influence of alcohol. Through patient and empathetic work, many of these people can be encouraged to participate, and some end up being genuinely grateful for the worker's intervention. Some continue to resist even the most patient and caring of workers.

T. S. Szasz (1965), a psychiatrist who thought and wrote a great deal about the involuntary status of clients, argued that when the power differential inherent in the relationship is made clear and explicit, both you and the client can deal more honestly with each other (p. 56). Some human service work is used for social control, so it is important to distinguish between social control and social service, both for theoretical clarity and to help us understand our relationships with clients. Clients of probation or parole officers may regard their workers as police officers who are not to be trusted. Child-protection workers investigating an abuse complaint should not be surprised if they are also regarded as police officers, because they are symbolically entering a client's home with the long arm of the law.

Stigma, Discrimination, and Status Ranking

The poor, the physically disabled, the retarded, the mentally ill, and the prisoner are often stigmatized by the larger society. People who work with them find that some of that stigma rubs off on them. Workers may often discover this when telling their friends or relatives about the nature of their jobs. Perhaps they have just gone on a home visit in a very poor section of town, or they have just gone to court with a youthful offender accused of a violent crime. People may say, "Aren't they dirty?" "Why do you want to help him?" Some people can brush off these remarks, which only reinforce their commitment. Yet such constant reminders of the low social esteem in which their daily tasks are held can be demoralizing.

The public often makes distinctions between and within groups of people, continuing the age-old stereotypes of "deserving" and "undeserving" clients. Among the least stigmatized are the more affluent clients who take their interpersonal problems to the offices of private psychiatrists or mental health clinics. Among the most stigmatized are the drug addicts and alcoholics who live and socialize on the local skid row. Because human service workers are part of the same society that creates these stigmas, they also sometimes measure their clientele by the same yardstick. In child-welfare agencies, adoption workers may have dinner with prospective adoptive parents, but they almost never dine with the unmarried mothers who produce the babies for the adoptive parents.

A stigma is only effective if you believe it. A worker like Rick Colbath Hess refuses to accept the stigma that society puts on clients and the people who work with them. Rick sees all people as equally valuable and does not divide his clients into "deserving" and "undeserving." Nor does he consider his social status diminished because he works with stigmatized clients.

Added to the stigma problem is the status problem. There are often sharp and painful status differences between professionals within an agency. A worker with an associate's degree from a community college may be doing exactly the same work and doing it just as competently as a worker with a BSW degree from a four-year college; yet the pay for the associate's degree worker will probably be less, the possibility of being promoted without further credentials may be nil, and—to rub even more salt into the wound—the BSW worker might even be insensitive enough to remind the worker with the associate's degree of the supposed superiority of the BSW degree.

DEALING WITH DANGER

Human service workers usually work with poor people and some of them live in neighborhoods that contain some violence. Naturally a worker wants to avoid violence, yet needs to work in those neighborhoods. When a worker shows excessive anxiety about it, disproportionate to the reality, clients can interpret that as contempt or hostility toward all the people who live in the neighborhood. Yet some caution is realistic, and clients know that better than anyone. They can give you good advice about taking precautionary steps. It is important to establish collegial relationships with neighborhood people so they trust you and show concern for your safety, just as you are concerned for their safety.

Human service workers have sometimes been assaulted by their clients, and even murdered. Bureau of Labor Statistics data for 1993 showed health care and social services workers having a higher incidence of assault injuries than any other field (OSHA, 1998). Definitions of violence vary, depending on the person doing the defining. Some people consider a verbal threat to be violence, while others do not. The most prevalent form of violence is verbal threat (Kadushin, 1992). Physical assaults are not as prevalent. Research shows that younger and less-experienced staff are at greatest risk of client assault in community residential mental health programs (Flannery, Fisher, & Walker, 2000; Flannery, Lizotte, Laudani, Staffieri, & Walker, 2001).

Workers often deny that they can become victims at the hands of their clients, thereby overlooking the potential for danger (Maier, 1996). This leaves them more vulnerable because they do not take realistic steps to protect themselves, and it also denies the agency information that they could use to help protect workers. Your agency has a responsibility to keep you safe and you should expect, even demand, practices that protect you from possible danger and that give you support when you encounter a threatening situation. You should expect support from your supervisor and from your colleagues. Sometimes colleagues are not as supportive as they should be because they want to deny that the same thing could happen to them. None of us is invulnerable, and we all need support.

Hazards of the Work

Most human service workers go into the field because they have ideals and a vision about helping people and optimism about the possibilities of change. This is an absolute requirement for the work; when ideals die and turn to cynicism, that is burnout. Yet an occupational hazard for human service workers is that the desire to be of help can turn into a rescue fantasy—a belief that they *have to do it all,* and if clients don't change in a desired way, the worker has failed.

> No matter how much you care, show concern, or even love, students will quit, inmates will mess up, patients will die, depressives will commit suicide, and parolees will violate the conditions of their paroles. It's natural to feel that a portion of the failure is your responsibility. Maybe you really did the best you could. If you had to do it over again, perhaps you would do some things differently. Perhaps that will help you with the next challenge. Failure is especially hard on the new staff member who is fired up with humanitarian zeal to help, to give, and to serve. Your own well-being and sanity may be at stake if you accept more than your portion of any failures. (Russo, 1980, pp. 157–158)

Even those workers who do not succumb to rescue fantasies or the need to be omnipotent in the clients' lives can be dragged under by the sheer weight of people's problems, many of which may be essentially unsolvable. Sometimes the feelings of helplessness and of being overwhelmed come from the simple fact that life is often painful and that some pain cannot be removed, some problems cannot be solved, and the best you can do is simply reach out and show that you care. Here is an account of one student's feelings about the pain of the human drama in her fieldwork:

> Sometimes when I go into the home and I haven't been there for a while, I'm almost afraid to ask, "Well, how are things with you, Mrs. J.?" I know that she'll begin to catalogue all the things that are wrong with her. Her health is really in a terrible state, and it's hard for her to get used to all the tubes and bags and the feelings that she can't do anything by herself. And then she'll tell me that her son didn't show up after he swore he would. And, damn him, why can't he visit once in a while? She seems like she's such a decent person and she really cares about him. A visit would make such a difference in her morale, but I can't drag him in, and what can I say to her to make it okay—that he is just too busy with his own life to visit a sick old lady, the person who raised him and looked after him when he needed it?

For all of us, there is often a wide gap between what we wish we could do and what we can do. As human service workers, this gap can be particularly painful when we feel we are behaving differently with our clients than we were taught to behave in our college classes. Human service workers can lament, along with doctors, that no one comes to see them when they are feeling good. In some ways that is true. We often encounter people at their worst, when they are the most abusive, discouraged, depressed, overwhelmed, angry. Frequently they have already had their problems for many years. Inadequate housing, poor schools, bad marriages, and destructive parenting patterns did not appear overnight and will not disappear overnight; so several things happen. Our clients often slip back into destructive patterns of behavior even after they see other possibilities. The alcoholic adult makes a hundred vows that will probably be broken and covers each with a hundred excuses—the same ones we ourselves use when we explain why we have abandoned our exercise program again or have broken our diets:

- I'm not really hooked.
- I'll just do it one more time to get me through this hard stretch.
- When things calm down, I'll stop drinking (overeating, taking dope, being beaten or beating).
- Just one more binge and then I'll quit!

The parent council that quite justifiably complained that no one ever listened to their opinions before still has barely a quorum even though you are committed to not submitting the next budget without their approval. You *really, really* mean to share the power with them yet they still don't show up in any significant numbers. So here you sit, making the decisions for them!

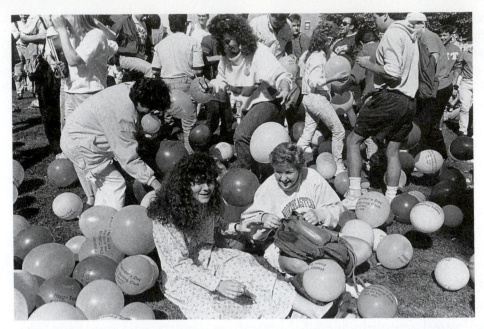

For all its frustrations, working with people, interacting with them at their best (as well as their worst), is perhaps the greatest natural high in the world.

Often when our clients are feeling better about their lives and possibilities, they take off, and we never know just how well they are doing and how well we did with them. Sometimes they even need to deny that we were of any help to them at all. Sometimes we encourage them to feel their own sense of power by minimizing the contributions we may have made. But being human and having our own needs for stroking, we can at times get angry at them when they fall back into old behaviors or seem to be rejecting us or putting down the help we have given them.

Some days being a human service worker can be a thankless task. You have to look in the mirror and say, "Hey, I just did a damn good piece of work!" You'll probably have a supervisor, coworker, or good friend who gives you strokes for your good work just in case you don't get them from anyone else. We shouldn't need to be constantly thanked and fussed over, but we are all human and need a small pat on the back from time to time.

SOME REACTIONS TO STRESSFUL CONDITIONS

Some ways of reacting perpetuate feelings of powerlessness, and others help workers to gain power and autonomy for themselves and their clients. The following five common reactions illustrate *the least creative ways* of coping with job stress; they do not involve an *active struggle* to take charge and master one's work environment (Wenocur & Sherman, 1980).

Total Capitulation

A patient in the hospital where she worked asked Ginny, the social service aide, if he could look at his medical records. Ginny said she'd ask her supervisor, who promptly said, "No, patients have never been allowed to look at their records. That's our policy. We've always done it this way." That made sense to Ginny. If things had always been done that way, that's the way she wanted to do them too. All her life she had tried hard to do things the way other people did them. She had only to pick up a slight cue from her parents, her teachers, her minister to set her on the straight and narrow path; she never rocked the boat. Needless to say, Ginny never went out on a limb to fight for patients' rights to read their records or for anything else. She simply closed off whatever empathy she had brought to the job and spent a lot of time shuffling papers. She lasted a long time.

Total Noncapitulation

In the course of his twenty-two years, Rafael had variously been described as a "maverick," "agitator," "radical," "unrealistic," and "immature." In his job at the Department of Welfare, he was constantly furious at the bureaucracy, "the stupid regs," "the dumb supervisor," "the crummy welfare grants," "the stupid, greedy, and corrupt legislators" (and he used other, less printable terms). He always agreed with his clients when they railed against the system; yet he never controlled his anger long enough to analyze the system or to help his clients understand it or work to change staff attitudes or regulations. His radical friends described him as a "rebel without a cause," not the kind of radical who got to the roots of problems. Rafael was fired after six months on the job; he had achieved little positive change but was well on the way to his first heart attack.

Niche Finding

After Bisi finished college, she got a job at the county Department of Child Welfare, where she was given a caseload of eighty foster children, plus their foster and birth parents. The workload overwhelmed her; she could never get on top of it. In the morning, she reached in her box to take out the telephone messages written on pink memo slips that had piled up when she was out in the field the day before. She held her breath as she read them, hoping she wouldn't find the dreaded message from a foster parent—"Take Johnny out today. I can't stand him a minute longer!" or "Susie's run away. Call the police!" As she reached the point of being unable to stand it anymore, the agency offered her a special intake job, with a lower caseload. One can certainly understand Bisi's finding a safe niche for herself—any one of us might do the same. Workers like Bisi find an area of expertise or a special position in the organization.

If workers concentrate only on their particular niche, they gain real but limited power in one small segment of an agency, but they have opted out of trying to change the entire agency. However, it is also possible that, having found a job that uses her full talents, Bisi will have *more* energy to devote to changing the agency.

Becoming a Victim Martyr

Following is a narrative by one worker who tried to do too much.

> We were so terribly understaffed when I first went to work at the recreation center that I found myself doing everything from running the dance to cleaning up afterwards. It killed me to have to keep saying "no" to the kids every time they'd come up with something they wanted to do. So, little by little, I'd give in—one weekend it would be a camping trip, another a disco party, and soon I realized I'd worked seven Saturday nights in a row. Well, my boyfriend was getting really annoyed. He's a computer programmer who works very hard but doesn't take his work home with him, so on the weekends he's ready to play. I dragged him with me when I took the kids places, and he was terrific with them, but he began resenting the fact that we were never alone.
>
> After a while I also began to miss the closeness we used to have. I got flak from other friends, too—they'd want to talk with me and I'd be falling asleep from sheer physical exhaustion. Suddenly I realized that at 23 I didn't have the stamina of my 14-year-old group members. I also realized that I still had to clean my apartment and do the laundry, and my world was getting messier and messier. Somehow I got through that summer, but in the fall I told the director that this center absolutely had to have more staff if it was really going to respond to the neighborhood kids. I knew I was falling apart and couldn't keep up the one-handed tennis match much longer.

This worker quickly fell into the trap of being a "victim martyr," believing that she *had* to fulfill totally all the tasks the agency *claimed* it was doing. The job was impossible to do by herself, but she believed the implicit message of the agency that she had to do it. This is sometimes called a *double bind*—a person is given two contradictory messages. She obeyed the part of the message that said, "You must do it because we say that's what we do," but was continually facing the other message: "But you can't do it—no one can alone." Until she faced that issue with the agency, she was unable to lead a well-balanced life of her own.

Some victim martyrs have the additional burden of working in agencies where the clients are angry and powerless. The victimized workers identify with the clients' anger and powerlessness, feeling the same themselves, but then get stuck in a powerless position and feel unable to change the system (Wenocur & Sherman, 1980, pp. 14–15).

It is easy to be sucked into the role of victim martyr, because most workers genuinely want to help and place high demands on themselves. Knowing our limits helps both us and the agency to face reality in a constructive way.

**"I'd like to schedule a time management seminar on
my calendar...as soon as I find time to buy a calendar. "**

Withdrawal

Many workers withdraw from the overwhelming pressures of the job by quitting.
This may sometimes be a move essential for one's mental health, yet, needless to
say, it doesn't change anything for the agency or the workers (Wenocur & Sherman,
1980, pp. 14–16).

Although we have described these five reactions as "pure types," people are
more complex than that and generally react in various ways to their jobs. Priscilla
Shade, for example, fought valiantly for her clients for a time, but finally felt that it
was hopeless and quit the job to be a full-time mother. Here is her description of
that process:

> I dealt with the welfare department's Wonderland-like working conditions by venting
> my anger. I raved a lot. I screamed. I called Legal Aid. I exerted political pressure. I went
> and testified in district and federal courts against rulings that affected clients. In the in-
> stance where medical benefits were cut from General Relief, I and a group of co-workers
> went to our state legislator. His assistant, who also had contacts in the human services
> department, had been told that people were dying for lack of medical benefits. So in
> six weeks the legislature—without going through the usual public hearings—restored
> medical benefits to people who were on General Relief.... In the end, though, the
> workers and clients were driven apart. This is what happened to me. Slowly I was go-
> ing down. And no matter what I did, the policy makers were going to come up with
> some beaut tomorrow that would put me three feet behind where I was the day before.
> So when the baby sitter who was taking care of my child suddenly got sick, I decided
> I'd be a full-time mother again.... Even with the best of intentions, programs don't

work when they're erratic, underfunded, and understaffed. And starting new programs while crippling others will not help. Ultimately, client advocacy is not an option for the line worker: it is a requirement. For only advocacy will enable workers to obtain the means to do their job, hopefully in a decent and humane way. (Shade, 1981, p. 31)

STAYING ALIVE—POSITIVE ADJUSTMENTS

"The major responsibility for avoiding staff burnout rests with the administration: this is what administrators are paid to deal with" (Weissman, Epstein, & Savage, 1983, p. 301). Just as workers are held accountable for their work, agencies too should be held accountable. Weissman (1973) believes that agencies avoid examining their own efficiency and effectiveness by focusing on the efficiency and effectiveness of their employees, and he recommends "bottom up" evaluations, that is, having workers evaluate their supervisors and directors as well as the other way around. We would add to this that clients should also be routinely asked to evaluate both their workers and the agency.

Combating Stress

The welfare department is particularly vulnerable to shifts and contradictions in social policy, and those of course are reflected in the workplace. However, even within the constraints imposed on them by the legislature, courts, and governor's office, managers of welfare offices have some options. They do not have to operate according to the "dixie cup—use them up and throw them away—school of management" (Bramhall & Ezell, 1991, p. 33). There are many things they can do:

1. They can take principled stands with the legislature and governor against policies that limit their ability to help people.

2. They can enlist workers in advocacy for clients and encourage alliances between workers and clients.

3. They can go to bat for higher pay and better working conditions for workers.

Support groups
Groups in which members help each other to clarify or act on certain issues.

4. They can set up **support groups** in which workers can share their feelings and frustrations with each other and brainstorm to solve problems in the agency.

5. They can recognize the pressure that workers are under and give them encouragement and support.

6. They can involve the frontline staff as partners in decision making and create smaller and more intimate work groups.

7. They can pay attention to workers' stress levels and do whatever is necessary to keep them from burning out, including:

Varying a worker's tasks

Instituting flex time

Limiting a person's work hours

Keeping a roster of on-call workers to maintain client-staff ratios during periods of absenteeism

Providing carefully graduated levels of responsibility for new staff

Streamlining paperwork

8. They can make the workplace surroundings as pleasant and clean as possible (Bramhall & Ezell, 1991, p. 35).

9. They can set up child care space in the waiting room and enlist volunteers to care for children of waiting clients.

10. They can involve clients in decision-making bodies.

Problem Solving

The reality is that administrators are under the gun to save money and are responding to pressure. They often lose sight of both workers' and clients' needs. Everyone in an agency needs to be involved in solving its problems.

Many of the skills involved in solving work problems in an agency are the same analytical and change skills that workers have learned in dealing with clients. Workers who do certain kinds of work, such as in rape crisis or battered women's centers, no longer see these problems as just individual troubles. They involve their clients in a social and political analysis of their problems. It is a relief to clients to realize they are not alone. Using the same skills, workers can involve their colleagues in analyzing agency problems. This gets workers beyond incessant criticism of the agency that goes nowhere, and it helps them gain mastery of agency problems (Bramhall & Ezell, 1991, p. 329).

If workers feel powerless and helpless, how can they help clients feel less so? Workers cannot provide models for growth for clients or help them gain mastery over their lives unless they are taking some control over their own work lives. How is that done? We have pointed out that when people analyze the reasons for their burnout, they tend to overemphasize either the personal or the organizational reasons, rarely balancing the two. The same dichotomy happens when people prescribe remedies. Although some can look at both personal and political issues as all of a piece, many prescribe only individual remedies (biofeedback, meditation, relaxation techniques, job rotation). Others insist that the only solution to worker stress is to change the whole agency and even the whole social system. Both sets of remedies have utility but they need to be combined. Certainly, a rigid and authoritarian agency working with a stigmatized clientele on a shoestring budget can literally produce a pain in the neck, stomach, head, or gut of the worker, but even in the "good" agency, with a low caseload and lots of support, we will still find ourselves under occasional stress simply because we are dealing with people's emotions and unmet needs.

Gaining Power through Knowledge

In order to get power in an agency, you need to understand the social and political economy of the agency and how it fits into society. As one sociologist put it, you need to break out of "occupationally trained incapacity to rise above a series of cases" (Mills, 1943, p. 171) in order to figure out what society *really* wants you to do with these clients, what society *really* expects of you, what is *really* known about the kinds of problems your clients have.

Your study of your own agency should begin with close observation, perhaps using your journal to document your observations and thoughts. Notice who does what and why, who is especially rewarded and why, what kinds of behavior in both workers and clients is valued. Supplement your own observations by studying what others have said about these issues in books or at workshops, conferences, visits to other agencies, formal courses, and your own informal support group. Remember that *knowledge is power,* and if you do not understand "what is coming down," you will be buffeted about by mysterious forces.

Getting an award for good work is a morale-booster. These members of Survivors, Inc., a welfare rights group, are receiving an award from one of their founders, Boston Women's Fund.

In order to understand our own position in an agency and intervene helpfully in people's lives, we need to see them and their environments as clearly as possible. For example, some of the "whys" that might occur to you in a foster care agency are:

1. Why are so many children being moved so often from one home to another?
2. Why do children stay so long in foster care?
3. Why is it so hard to find foster homes for adolescents?
4. Why don't some social workers and foster parents want the biological parents to see more of their children?
5. Why is my caseload so high and my pay so low?

In child-protection work, an area with a high rate of burnout, a study of the job should include an analysis of the structure of the worker's job. One expert on the child-welfare system maintains that high burnout is at least partly caused by the fact that the worker is asked to perform the two incompatible roles of policing and providing supportive help to families (Pelton, 1989). Pelton argues that, in order to develop the trust necessary to provide the supportive help that families need, families must voluntarily choose the help. Because workers often meet families with a real or implied threat to invoke the state's power to remove their children, it is impossible for families to trust the workers. Pelton believes that the two roles should be separated, creating special police units to handle the coercive functions and freeing social workers to give help that families genuinely need and want.

Along with your independent study, you will need to join with others, both coworkers and clients, in seeking answers. One person working alone can conceivably change an organization, but that is rare, and it is a lonely road. We stress, again, that change comes about through people working together.

Getting Support

SUPERVISION

Social agencies have traditionally relied on supervision to train workers and to give them support in their work. The profession of social work has probably relied more than any other profession or trade on long-term, one-to-one supervision. Although it can have its benefits, not all human service workers are happy with the kind of supervision they interpret as enforced dependence for their entire career.

There are good and bad aspects to traditional supervision. The best part is that a supportive supervisor can help human service workers function at their full potential, often helping them discover creativity and strength they never knew they had. Such a supervisor can help prevent burnout and poor-quality service.

One research project (Berkeley Planning Associates, 1978) that evaluated child abuse and neglect programs concluded that the most important factor in keeping workers actively engaged was supportive program leadership. This was especially important to younger and more inexperienced workers. Workers functioned best when they:

- Were active participants in supervision
- Were encouraged to be innovative
- Were given clear communication and expectations from supervisors
- Were not required to follow formalized rules rigidly when it was more helpful to the clients to bend the rules

Good supervisors:

- Took the work seriously
- Emphasized its importance
- Encouraged workers to get the job done
- Were neither passive nor authoritarian
- Provided support and structure
- Conveyed a sense of trust in staff
- Gave direct feedback to workers on their performance
- Helped workers find resources in the community
- Provided strong advocacy on behalf of the clients and workers within the agency

The same research report showed that workers who had poor supervision burned out at a much greater rate than did workers with good leadership.

IDEAL SUPERVISION

One of the most important qualities of a good supervisor is the ability to allow workers the freedom and responsibility for their own work. An overcontrolling supervisor encourages dependence and childish subservience. Workers under the tutelage of such a person never develop their own creativity. The study on child abuse and neglect demonstrated that workers became seriously demoralized when they were not given autonomy.

Most of us would agree that we can, and need to, learn from more experienced and knowledgeable people both in our professional and our personal lives. In any job, a worker should expect good supervision at a regularly scheduled time—perhaps an hour or two a week set aside to talk about work-related problems and plan for future activities. Supervision need not be done only on a one-to-one basis. Informal peer supervision and formal group sessions, which are regularly scheduled discussion groups of agency workers and selected consultants, can replace or supplement it. In many human service agencies, most of the staff supervision is done through groups. Some people think this is better than one-to-one supervision because "the group has a way of maintaining honesty; the supervisor shares power with the group members, and they add their power to his. One result can be a lessening of the threat of the conference held behind closed doors" (Abels, 1979, p. 141).

OTHER FORMS OF SUPERVISION

Other forms of group supervision are **case conferences,** core evaluations, or staffings, in which the workers concentrate on one particular client's problem or on one key issue affecting groups of clients. The child neglect and abuse study mentioned previously concluded that work was more likely to be successful when the workers used multidisciplinary teams to review more serious or complex cases at intake and at some other point in the treatment process (at least once every six months). Using such teams, which might include teachers, homemakers, lay therapists, social workers, psychologists, nurses, and doctors, helped workers learn how to handle a particular case and similar cases in the future. Workers also did better in these projects when they had case conferences in which two or more workers reviewed their progress on a case once every three months and when they used outside consultants from different disciplines on more complex cases.

> **Case conferences** Conferences about a particular client in which staff members pool their information and share resources.

Sometimes lawyers are members of the problem-solving team. A group of lawyers called Volunteers of Legal Service give pro bono legal advice to the doctors and social workers at some New York City hospitals. The lawyers, from the firm of Cravath, Swaine & Moore, take cases in areas such as housing, public benefits, special education, employment, and immigration. One of the lawyers works with the Lead Poison Prevention Program at Montefiore Hospital.

> The program holds a weekly clinic for children with lead poisoning, seeing about 400 children each year. Most of the children get lead poisoning from old paint in their homes. Cynthia Martinez, a social worker in the program, considers the availability of lawyers to be a "fantastic resource." "Landlords," she says, "pay attention when lawyers step into the picture." (Dean, W., 2003)

SUPERVISION AS A PROBLEM-SOLVING PROCESS

A supervisor's broadly ranging knowledge is not enough, however, if he or she does not know how to pass the knowledge along. Supervision is a problem-solving relationship. A worker must feel safe in supervisory relationships before he or she will risk honestly admitting insecurities, mistakes, and ignorance. A supervisor who acts like a "snoopervisor," always checking up and looking over the worker's shoulder for mistakes, ready to mark them down on an evaluation sheet, is not someone with whom subordinates will willingly discuss problems. In fact, many will respond to this assault by playing games, telling the supervisor what he or she wants to hear while shoving their real problems under the rug.

If supervisors are secure, they can invite workers to tell them what helps or hinders them about the supervisor's way of working. Open discussion is the best way to work out problems in supervision. If the supervisor feels too threatened by this, or if it is impossible to change supervisors, one must look around for support elsewhere.

SUPERVISORS AND WORKERS' SELF-ESTEEM

Because human service workers "as a rule, are easily convinced that they are doing a poor job" (Feldman, 1979, p. 365), one of the supervisor's most important jobs is to help workers gain confidence in the effective work they are actually doing, often without being aware of it. For example, there are times in a working relationship with a client when the client needs to express anger and be critical of a worker. Such an expression may be a sign that the worker has helped a client feel free enough to express anger. Yet anger is hard to take, and a worker may feel that he or she has failed. A supervisor, understanding the relationship more objectively, can help the worker understand the anger as a sign of progress and can also show the worker points at which the worker "felt empathy and was able to perceive her client's need and respond constructively—without herself being aware of it.… (Analyzing with workers their intuitively correct responses is the best way of teaching.)" (Feldman, 1979, p. 263).

Formal and Informal Groups

Another study of worker effectiveness and morale showed that workers needed informal peer support (Maslach, 1966, p. 16). In high-morale agencies, workers were encouraged to choose a consultant on their own, either a fellow worker whom they respected and trusted or someone outside of the agency. Human service students or trainees in fieldwork placements often turn to a field supervisor from their college in addition to the one appointed at their field agency. This doubling up of supervisors can be an asset or a liability, of course, according to the skill and commitment of all involved.

INFORMAL NETWORKS

The informal conversations we have with our friends and fellow workers are the most common way of sharing experiences. These take place during coffee breaks, over lunch, after work on the telephone, at each other's homes, and during shared entertainment. These conversations give us the emotional support to keep at our demanding jobs. They are one way to check out, add to, and revise our store of knowledge about our work. Sometimes they can improve our practice. We may share innovative ideas; but we may also share ignorance, prejudice, and stereotypes. If the conversation stays on the level of griping, it can increase anxiety and keep people mired in helplessness. One needs to gripe, but if one never moves on to analysis and action, complaining can be counterproductive.

Informal networks are essential for survival on the job. Sociologist Howard Polsky (1962) studied a residential treatment center for delinquent youths and found that the live-in cottage parents felt, and in fact were, the most isolated and vulnerable of all the staff members because they did not have a reference group—friends they could go home to and share ideas and feelings with. The social workers, on the other hand, commuting together back to New York City and spending evenings with family and friends, returned to work the next day emotionally replenished for their bouts with the rage, wisecracks, con games, and sadness of these youngsters who had been taken from their homes by the state. The cottage parents' lack of an alternative status reference group had a negative impact on the treatment they gave to the teenagers in their care:

> Lacking an alternative status reference group, the cottage parent becomes dependent upon, and conforming to, the boys' delinquent orientation and eventually adjusts to it by taking over and utilizing modified delinquent techniques. The extreme concern with cottage loyalty and the violent condemnation of "ratting" cement the cottage parent to the boys' subculture and perpetuate a vicious circle which insulates the cottage from the rest of the therapeutic milieu. (Polsky, 1962, p. 135)

FORMALLY ORGANIZED SUPPORT GROUPS

A more formally organized support group may or may not include one's friends. It may consist only of colleagues on the job, or it may be an explicitly political group that is open to people from other agencies who want to clarify their thinking about their work. They may be a study group that meets regularly, chooses readings to discuss, and perhaps invites specialists to discuss certain issues. A study group is most effective when people give it a high priority in their lives, meet regularly, and use the group to analyze the workplace: how it is affecting each member and how members can individually and collectively deal with their work-related frustrations. It can become quite an effective tool for collectively tackling problems in the workplace, and it can give enormous psychological support to its members. Wenocur and Sherman (1980, p. 21) suggest a few important items to discuss:

How the organization heightens the guilt of the workers

The role of dependency in keeping workers in patterns of victimization

How workers identify with the powerlessness of their clients

The forms of accommodation the members have adopted in order to survive in the agency

Most of the literature on burnout emphasizes the crucial importance of support groups. One child-welfare agency held a support group for child abuse workers to deal with the severe stresses of the job (Copans, Kress, Gundy, Rogan, & Field, 1979). The group met for one and one-half hours once a week for six months to "examine the feelings aroused in workers by their work and to discuss how these feelings aided or interfered with effective delivery of care" (p. 302). During these meetings, eleven major sets of feelings that often interfere with effective delivery of care were identified:

- Anxiety about the effects of a decision
- Need for emotional gratification from clients

- Lack of professional support
- Denial and inhibition of anger
- Feelings of incompetence
- Denial and projection of responsibility
- Difficulty in separating personal from professional responsibility
- Feelings of being victimized
- Ambivalent feelings toward clients and about one's professional role
- The need to be in control

In all of these areas, workers got emotional support and helpful suggestions for dealing with the problem. Every single group member suffered from feelings of incompetence.

> One very competent worker said that she felt professionally inadequate most of the time. Since she rarely received comments on her work, she assumed it was not good. It was a great relief to her to discover that others shared these feelings of failure. As a result of recognizing this problem in the group, many workers returned to their agencies and asked for critical feedback on their work. Most of them also felt much less incompetent, as they could see from case discussions that there is generally no "best way" or "right answer" in such work. (Copans et al., 1979, p. 305)

One of the reasons for this widespread feeling of incompetence among human service workers is that they are not sure whether their work is effective. Most researchers on burnout assume that when workers' morale is high, their work is effective and productive. Weissman and his colleagues, however, believe that this is the wrong way to look at it. They assert that worker morale will improve when the *agency* is effective. They would shift the focus from the individual worker to the agency.

> There is nothing more satisfying to professionals than spending their work lives in an organization that they feel is effective.... The competence of the agency should be as high a priority to the profession as the competence of individual practitioners. If agencies are not effective, clients suffer, and workers suffer. (Copans et al., 1979, p. 331)

Researchers at the Wellesley Center for Research on Women studied stress in the service sector of the economy and found that "regardless of how demanding their jobs were, workers who felt they weren't making a contribution to the lives of others were more distressed." Their advice to employers in the service sector was to design jobs that permit individuals to be effective service providers, to make a difference to others. "This won't make the stress of a demanding service job any easier to bear, but it may prevent job-related distress from worsening" (Center for Research on Women, 2000, p. 7).

PROFESSIONAL ORGANIZATIONS

A professional organization forges links between people in the same field. Collectively, these people share their values and their knowledge and support each other in job searching and other concrete ways. Most organizations have at least one professional journal that provides a platform for workers to carry on their professional debates and to share their research and practice experiences. Most human service organizations have a code of ethical practice. Workers often derive support by holding on to their professional values, even though these may at times be in conflict with those practiced in the agency. The profession often uses the clout afforded by its numbers to improve agency practice and to lobby for better social services.

UNIONS

There is often no sharp distinction between a professional organization and a union; some professional organizations such as the National Education Association (NEA) and the American Association of University Professors (AAUP) started as professional associations but have gradually taken on the traditional functions of a trade union. Generally, professional organizations do not engage in contract negotiations or in job actions such as slowdowns or strikes.

As the country's workforce has increasingly moved into service occupations, professionals such as teachers and human service workers are unionizing much more now than in the past. The greatest increase in unionization recently has been among professionals in education, government service, and nonprofit organizations.

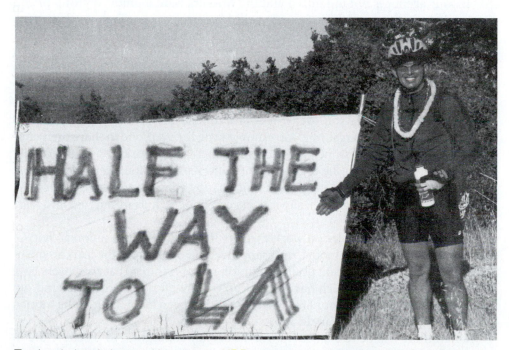

Turning their pain into positive energy, AIDS activists organize fund-raising long-distance bike rides all around the country. They provide money for medical research while increasing their own fitness.

One of the most important reasons workers give for leaving human service agencies is their lack of control over their working conditions. Unions are often perceived as the most powerful tool to wrest some of that control from management. Some social service unions have a limited vision of their task, bargaining mainly for wages, hours, and fringe benefits, while others struggle for a greater worker role in decision making and for changes in systems. A spokesperson for the American Federation of State, County, and Municipal Employees (AFSCME), which has organized many human service workers, tells of his union's concern for those broader issues.

> In addition to the general concern about wages, hours, and working conditions, two other factors become important in white collar campaigns: promotional opportunities and professional standards.... An added factor, often important in professional campaigns, is a desire for representation at the planning or policy level. Social caseworkers, for example, express a concern about the heavy case load which hinders their effectiveness in giving clients their full attention. Caseworkers seek a voice in dealing with this problem. (Curtin, 1970, pp. 12, 15)

The organization that Rick Colbath Hess founded is one model for human service workers to improve their working conditions. This is especially important for direct care workers, who often have lower salaries and worse working conditions than others in the field.

If your agency is not unionized and the workers want a union, a group of you can work on it. Study all the unions that could represent you. Find out their track record on organizing and bargaining; check out what salaries their staff earn. (There's no reason why union bureaucrats should be living in luxury while human service workers scrimp.) See what issues they are willing to take a stand on; ask how elitist or hierarchical they are in their own decision making. Do they believe the membership or the union staff should call the shots? How much are the dues? Do they have a fund to tide you over if it comes to a strike? Can they give you legal assistance and help in bargaining? Give ample time for everyone to share their concerns about what might happen to the clients if there was a work stoppage and what they are prepared to do if the organizing or contract negotiation gets sticky. Don't be surprised if the agency management is not happy about the prospect of workers organizing. Even human service supervisors can have serious misgivings and fears of turmoil and conflict.

Some organizations play on workers' fears in order to reduce union activity— fear of being fired, not promoted, or disapproved of. Sometimes the fears are justified. One reason for the recent decline in union membership is that employers have fired union organizers, which has made people more afraid to organize. Find out from the union leaders in your area whether this has been happening in the human service field and what you can do about it.

Often there will be resistance from some agency colleagues, who believe that it is unprofessional to organize. As the economic crunch hits more middle-class people, however, they tend to look for a union's protection. Finally, if workers are in a small private agency that contracts out work from the state, they may find they need to form coalitions with fellow workers in similar small agencies before unionizing in order to grow large enough to influence management.

Some of the workers who have been successfully organized by Service Employees International Union (SEIU) recently include:

- Thousands of health care workers at Catholic Healthcare West, the largest hospital chain in California (Stern, 2001)

- Thousands of janitors from New Jersey to Maryland, who have won raises from $5.50 an hour to more than $9 an hour (Stern, 2001)

- 80,000 home care workers in Southern California (Mancillas, 2001)

- 604 people in Milwaukee, Wisconsin, who care for their parents, employed by the nonprofit agency New Health Services (NHS). This was the first large-scale organizing in Milwaukee at the low end of the wage scale since the 1997 launch of "W-2," Wisconsin's welfare reform system initiated by then-governor Tommy Thompson. Many former welfare recipients are employed by NHS. These workers were paid at the rate of $7.10 an hour, with no benefits of any kind. After their union was certified, they went on to negotiate a contract for higher wages, improved training, health insurance, and pension benefits (Glenn, 2001b). Many feminists have long argued for paying wages to caretakers. This campaign is the first to organize people who care for their own parents.

Choosing Your Fights

After analyzing your situation and setting up your support groups, you will then need to set priorities on what you want to change in your work situation. You can't change everything at once, so decide what it is that you simply can't live with any more. Say that your gripes include having to punch a time clock at 8:30 and carrying a caseload of 180 people—all with inadequate secretarial staff to prepare court documents, write letters, and do publicity. Which of these is most important? You will probably decide that the clock punching is least important, so you won't take on that fight just yet. There is no point in risking a major confrontation on a minor issue, especially one that doesn't compromise any basic principles, when there are other things much more crucial to your effectiveness or job satisfaction.

Make a cost–benefit analysis of your issue. How much might it cost you in terms of job risk, disapproval from the boss, and so on, and what are the possible benefits? Which side of the scale tips—risks or benefits? Don't overestimate the risks, especially if you have substantial group support. People tend to err on the side of caution when some risk might actually reap large benefits. The more people you have with you, the more you reduce your risks. It is harder to reprimand or even fire ten people than one. Watch out for divide-and-conquer tactics. Agency management may lay off the people with the least formal training first, and the others may assume they have escaped. Later, management may pick off the trained workers or lower their salaries. The more people you include in your struggle, the better your chance of success.

Creative Ways of Working

One way of keeping the spark alive on the job is to experiment with new ideas. It may be hard to think of new ways to do your work when so many people are telling you, "But we've always done it this way." Yet well-thought-out experimentation is often worth the risks it might entail. Clearly, it keeps one enthusiastic.

Working with people in groups rather than as individuals can sometimes save time. You might make an overly large caseload more manageable by such devices as conducting group intakes for adoption applicants. Foster parents can be trained in groups to care for children; they can also help the worker to recruit other foster parents. Group counseling for unemployed people and support groups for parents, teens, families of alcoholics, and others can all be both time-saving and sometimes more effective than individual work. One study found that treatment of abusive and neglectful parents was most effective when parents were involved in mutual support groups such as Parents Anonymous and when parent aides were used (Berkeley Planning Associates, 1978). Encouraging and supporting clients to help themselves and each other cuts down on your caseload and pressures while strengthening your clients' abilities.

If you can get enough support from your colleagues, clients, and community, you might persuade your agency to change the way it does the work. One staff member of a sheltered workshop for retarded people said this in her letter of protest to the agency board:

> While I was told that teaching clients would be at least a part of my job, this has not been the case so far. In the weeks I've been at [the workshop], I've spent a total of half an hour working on money skills with a client, and that was only because I put other things aside and took initiative to do so. In reality, my job consists of fixing and counting chess pieces and mascara brushes, inspecting bathrooms, opening boxes of calculators. How about if I spend two hours a day teaching clients to do these tasks? I understand they must be done but think it is a ridiculous use of my skills. From 10:00–12:00 I could work on routine sorting tasks and from 1:00–3:00 hold a money management workshop. I'd like six weeks to stick with this schedule and then I'll report back on how it's working.

Programs that allow scope for creativity make space for workers and clients to grow. The ultimate goal of any human service work is the mutual empowerment of clients, workers, and the community. Workers can reach out to clients and the community to explore and discuss alternative modes of service.

Varying the Work

Another way to survive on the job is to vary the work by rotating duties with other workers, alternating between intense involvement with clients and less emotionally draining administrative work, or taking time out from regular tasks to do a special project or attend a course or conference. Workers often break a cycle of defeat by figuring out which clients are the most draining on them and making trade-offs with other workers who have different kinds of tolerances and bring a new insight to a stalled group or individual case process.

Sharing Ideas

One of the most important ways of enjoying your work is to know you are doing a good job. That is a good reason to continue to sharpen your skills throughout your career. It is stimulating to share ideas with others, both verbally and in writing. You can be part of the "community of scholars" at work, in the community, and in your profession by writing letters to the editor of your local newspaper, composing practice notes and accounts for your professional journal, and, if you have a bent for more formal research and theoretical speculation, producing articles that present your thinking and research.

CLARITY OF THOUGHT AND WRITING

Most human service concepts can be expressed in clear language. The beginning student should be wary of articles or lectures that are overly abstract or filled with labels, jargon, categories, and excessive complexity.

English writer George Orwell (famous for his political novel *1984*) warned us about pretentious diction in his classic essay, "Politics and the English Language" (1950). He illustrates his point by translating a passage from the Bible into "modern English of the worst sort." Here is the original passage from *Ecclesiastes*:

> I returned and saw under the sun, that the race is not to the swift nor the battle to the strong, neither yet bread to the wise, nor yet riches to men of understanding, nor yet favour to men of skill; but time and chance happeneth to them all.

Here it is in modern "jargonese" English:

> Objective consideration of contemporary phenomena compels the conclusion that success or failure in competitive activities exhibits no tendency to be commensurate with innate capacity, but that a considerable element of the unpredictable must invariably be taken into account. (Orwell, 1950, p. 92)

Clear thinking demands honesty, not pretentiousness, and in studying the field of human services, students should demand clarity of teachers and supervisors and should strive for honest expression in their own writing. Orwell's guidelines for writing can be helpful to all of us:

   i. Never use a metaphor, simile or other figure of speech which you are used to seeing in print.
  ii. Never use a long word where a short one will do.
 iii. If it is possible to cut a word out, always cut it out.

iv. Never use the passive where you can use the active.

v. Never use a foreign phrase, a scientific word, or a jargon word if you can think of an everyday English equivalent.

vi. Break any of these rules sooner than say anything outright barbarous. (Orwell, 1950, p. 100)

Orwell tells us that our writing style will be clearer and more forceful if we speak in the active rather than passive voice. An active style forces us to take responsibility for our thoughts. When I say, "I think…," I announce that I am the author of that thought and am willing to take both the praise and the blame for it. If, on the other hand, I want to duck responsibility for the thought, I might say, "It has been thought…." A person who thinks and writes in the active voice is more likely to be actively engaged in dialogue that shapes practice.

AVOIDING ABBREVIATIONS

In addition to avoiding pretentiousness in our speaking and writing, we also need to avoid the casual drift into speaking in human service abbreviations—the secret code of our field. It is very easy to say to a parent, "After your child has been cored, we'll apply to OCD for CHINS or Title XX money, and we'll find a less restrictive setting for your child," when what you want them to know is, "After the study and evaluation of your child's special needs are completed, we can apply to the Office of Child Development for money from the Children in Need of Service fund or the Supplementary Security Act. We'll also find a school that will provide him with the best, most normal education."

If you are sure that the parent knows the jargon, then speaking in abbreviations or professional terms is, of course, acceptable. But we must always check to make sure we aren't speaking in a "foreign language." Barbara Schram recalls an example of this in the 1960s, the time of the War on Poverty:

> When I was on the board of a poverty program funded by the Office of Economic Opportunity (fondly known as O.E.O.), we were always having one or another crisis with our funding and must have mentioned O.E.O.—cursing or praising it—at least twenty times in the course of one board meeting. At the close of one particularly dramatic meeting, I realized that one of the new board members, known for her militancy in neighborhood politics, was remarkably quiet, and in fact she had abstained from voting on several important issues. When I took her aside after the meeting and asked her why she was acting in this untypically laid-back manner, she explained that much of the meeting had been a jumble to her. "What," she asked me, "did oleo (the local word for oleomargarine, the butter substitute) have to do with the poverty program?" My heart sank when I realized that we unwittingly excluded through our use of "insider's" abbreviations the very person we most wanted to involve. It taught me a lesson I will not soon forget.

Of course, no matter how conscious we are, code words and initials will creep into our writing and speaking. If you as a new worker are plunged into a bowl of alphabet soup, the only way to keep from drowning is to interrupt the action politely and ask for an explanation.

Setting Limits on Self and Others

Finally, you need to know how to protect yourself from the unrealistic demands that people make on you. You need to learn to recognize your limits and let others know when you have reached them. Learn to say "no" without feeling guilty. Take time out when you're feeling drained. If you've just had a nerve-wracking experience with a client and your knees are shaking, let your supervisor know that you need to take a walk or talk it out. If you're exhausted after a few years on the job, try to take a leave of absence, if you can afford it. You may come back refreshed, with new ideas.

You need to learn how not to take your work home with you, and you need to take good care of yourself outside the job. There are lots of ways to do this. Our list would include good nutrition, regular exercise, rest, recreation, reading, and friendships. Some people find meditation, relaxation techniques, or biofeedback helpful. One psychologist in a teachers' stress counseling program talks of how some people neglect their health: "Many teachers subsist on coffee and nicotine. They don't eat breakfast, but they might drink coffee with sugar, or a Coke, with a doughnut. They get sugared up. It makes them sleepy, cranky, and inefficient" (Grey, 1979, p. 6).

However we manage to do it, we must keep our spontaneity and spirit of play alive. If we lose our joy, how can we bring joy and hope to our clients?

SUMMARY

1. Human service work can be one of the most exciting careers in the world, but only as long as one can grow in the job and feel successful in it.

2. Growth requires support from peers, supervisors, and the society that sponsors your agency.

3. If support is not forthcoming, a human service job can create stress, which leads to burnout.

4. Symptoms of burnout can include sleep problems, irritability, upset stomach, headaches, and shortness of breath. Workers may become cynical and hard-hearted, stop caring about the clients, and treat them with contempt.

5. Burnout can be caused by both psychological and environmental stress.

6. Agencies that serve the poor seldom have enough resources.

7. Pressure for accountability can cause agencies to take refuge in sorting and counting behavior, which may not reflect the true quality of their work.

8. Clients exert pressures on the worker when resources are restricted.

9. Work stress is increased when the client has not chosen to come to the agency, as in child-protection work.

10. Clients of agencies are often stigmatized by society. Those who work with them are sometimes included in this stigmatization.

11. Hazards of human service work include workers' rescue fantasies, the fact that some problems cannot be solved, and the enormity of the problems.

12. Some of the less creative reactions to the pressures of work include capitulation, total noncapitulation, niche finding, withdrawal, and becoming a victim martyr.

13. Taking control of one's work situation involves understanding the social and political structure of the agency and its relationship to the larger society.

14. Support groups, professional organizations, and unions are important sources of support.

15. Individual methods of change include finding more creative ways of doing the work, varying the work, improving one's competence, and joining the "community of scholars" by contributing to the dialogue of the profession.

16. Clarity of thought and writing help one to maintain a forceful presence in the human service profession.

17. Workers need to protect themselves from impossible demands and learn how to say "no" without feeling guilty.

18. Taking care of oneself includes good nutrition, regular exercise, rest, recreation, reading, and enjoying friendships.

DISCUSSION QUESTIONS

1. If you were in charge of a social agency, how would you structure it to avoid worker burnout?

2. Imagine that you are a worker who wants to form a union to improve wages and working conditions. The administrator of your agency calls a meeting to warn workers about the dangers of unions and makes a veiled threat that workers might be fired if they try to form a union. How would you respond to this?

3. What are some examples of federal and state laws that might contribute to worker burnout?

4. What are some examples of agency regulations that might contribute to worker burnout?

5. Describe what you would consider to be the ideal supervisor, and the ideal method of supervision.

WEB RESOURCES FOR FURTHER STUDY

American Federation of State, County, and Municipal Employees (AFSCME)
www.afsme.org

AFSCME is the largest and fastest growing public service employee's union, with 1.4 million members. It organizes workers in all areas of government, health, education, and other services, both public and private.

Employment Relations Advice
www.employmentrelationsadvice.com/sitemap.htm

This site gives advice and assistance on the subjects of personnel management, employment relations, and employment law.

Employer–Employee
www.employer-employee.com

This site has information on various aspects of the employer–employee relationship.

Service Employees International Union (SEIU)
www.seiu.org

SEIU has 1.7 million working people and 120,000 retirees unified to improve their jobs and their communities. Members include nurses, doctors, health technicians, workers in local government, state employees, security officers, janitors, nursing home workers, home care workers, public school workers, social workers, and people in many other jobs.

Glossary

Accent responses. Repeating, as a question or with some emphasis, a word or short phrase that the client has just said.

Accountability. A requirement, usually imposed by a funding source, that an agency performs according to a certain set of standards.

Adult Children of Alcoholics (ACOA). A self-help support group run on the model of Alcoholics Anonymous for adults whose parent(s) were alcoholics.

Advising. Telling a client what to do. Used with caution, if at all, in interviews, because it incorrectly assumes that one person knows what is best for another.

Ageism. The practice of discriminating against people because they are old; attitudes associated with the practice.

Aid to Families with Dependent Children (AFDC). The title of the Social Security Act that authorized public financial assistance for parents of dependent children. It is now called Temporary Assistance to Needy Families (TANF).

Al-Anon. The self-help group for the families of alcoholics.

Alateen. The self-help group for teenage children of alcoholics.

Alcoholics Anonymous (AA). A self-help organization that uses a specific twelve-step program for recovery from the addiction to alcohol.

Alienation. A sociological term used to describe the way the structure of a job or organization distances people from their work, from each other, and from themselves.

Americans with Disabilities Act (ADA). A congressional mandate that guarantees many rights to people with physical and mental disabilities, especially in the fields of employment and architectural access.

Anxiety disorder. A biological condition in which feelings of extreme fear, tension, and dread often overwhelm the person, even when there is no apparent threat to their well-being.

Artificial insemination. The practice of implanting semen into a woman's uterus by a method other than sexual intercourse.

Assessment summary. A summary recording that analyzes the observations and information that the worker has obtained through interviews.

Attention deficit hyperactivity disorder (AD/HD). A biological condition with early onset and often long duration that interferes with a person's capacity to focus and sustain interest, especially when the agenda is set by an outside authority, as in the school or work setting.

Aversive behavioral treatment. A form of behavior modification based primarily on punishment rather than reward.

Battered women. Women who have been physically abused.

Behaviorist. A theorist who believes that behavior can be shaped or changed by the systematic application of rewards for behavioral compliance with the demands of the caregiver or therapist.

Bicultural theory. A theory asserting that although people are socialized into their minority culture through family and ethnic community, they are also influenced by the dominant culture through social institutions and the mass media.

Brainstorming.　A technique in which people generate ideas under pressure and without judgment so that their most innovative thoughts can flow.

Building the contract.　Making an agreement, whether verbal or written, about the purpose and goal of the work that the helpee and helper do together.

Bureaucratization.　Increased organizational centralization, hierarchical control, larger workplaces, and decreased autonomy for workers.

Careerism.　A single-minded preoccupation with getting ahead in a career to the exclusion of other interests or values.

Career ladder.　A specific path of jobs that relates accomplishment and tenure to upward mobility.

Case conferences.　Conferences about a particular client in which staff members pool their information and share resources.

Change agents.　Workers who use their skills to bring about change in an unhealthy agency or situation, either alone or in concert with others.

Charismatic leader.　A person who profoundly influences others through the dynamism of personality.

Charity Organization Societies (COSs).　The earliest professional social work agencies, organized first in England and later in the United States; they claimed to deliver "scientific charity" through case-by-case work of "friendly visitors."

Child-saving movement.　A term used to describe the efforts of reformers in the late nineteenth and early twentieth centuries to rescue children from "unwholesome influences." The movement led to the development of children's institutions, foster care, and the juvenile court.

Clarifying.　Seeking further understanding of what has been said in an interview.

Coalition.　A loose amalgam of people or groups who support a similar idea or goal.

Co-dependency.　A mutually destructive relationship between a person who is addicted and his or her significant other that helps to continue, rather than break, the addiction.

Community residences.　Small living units, houses, or apartments located in communities that serve people who have disabilities or other special situations that render them unable to live on their own. (Also known as halfway houses; group homes.)

Comparable worth.　Describing and paying wages for jobs according to their inherent difficulty and worth in order to help equalize women's wages with men's.

Computerized recording.　Recording in a computer contacts with, and information about, clients.

Confidentiality.　Keeping information that the client reveals to the worker secret.

Conflict resolution.　The way in which a group handles sharp differences in opinion or digressions from accepted standards.

Confronting.　A tactic used by the interviewer to point out to the interviewee discrepancies or inconsistencies in an interviewee's words or behavior.

Consciousness raising.　The process in which people are provoked into giving an issue serious thought, perhaps through suggestion of new points of view to be considered.

Contracting out.　A system whereby a government agency contracts with a private agency to do some specified work for pay.

Corporate restructuring.　A process of shifting resources within corporations, resulting in lower pay for workers and higher pay for executives and in the laying off of workers. This is brought on partially by technological developments and investment decisions and partially by a decision to cut labor costs in order to maximize profits.

Cover terms.　Terms that describe some aspect of culturally significant meaning and experience.

Deindustrialization.　Changes in the U.S. economy in recent decades that have reduced the number of jobs in the manufacturing industry and increased the number of jobs in the service sector.

Deinstitutionalization.　A large-scale reform movement that took people out of institutions and hospitals and returned them to their community with special services to aid their reintegration.

Descriptors.   Blocks of descriptive information, systematically collected, used to build a composite portrait of selected cultural characteristics more or less shared by a set of clients.

Deserving versus undeserving.   The discriminatory classification of people into higher and lower categories, considering some people to be more worthy of receiving benefits and services than others.

Dialectical.   Refers to the principle that an idea or event (thesis) generates its opposite (antithesis), leading to a reconciliation of opposites (synthesis) and a continuation of the dialectical process.

Direct action.   Interfering with the orderly conduct of a system that is the target of change.

Direct-service strategies (intervention, roles).   Worker actions that deliver services directly to clients.

Disabilities Resource Center (DRC).   An office that coordinates the academic support services that enable students with physical, mental, or educational disabilities to pursue their class work.

Door openers.   An invitation to say more about something that the interviewee has brought up, preferably in the form of an open-ended request for information.

Due process.   Procedural mechanisms that secure or protect one's legal rights.

Early intervention program.   Program that attempts to deal with a person's (often a child's) problem at the first sign of difficulty.

Employee assistance programs (EAPs).   Supportive services dealing with mental health or financial or legal issues that are offered directly to employees by their company or agency. Their goal is to reduce worker turnover and raise productivity.

Empathy.   An attempt to put oneself in the shoes of another person, to feel or think of a problem from another perspective.

Encouraging and reassuring.   Providing a message of hopefulness in an attempt to inspire confidence, often without regard to what a person is actually feeling.

Entitlements.   Benefits and services that people are legally entitled to, as compared to those that are given at the discretion of officials.

Ethics of helping.   An ethical commitment to helping others rather than engaging in dog-eat-dog competition.

Euthanasia.   Active intervention in hastening death, usually made by a doctor with the permission of the dying person or the family.

Expert witness.   A person who is especially knowledgeable in a particular field and who is asked to give testimony based on that knowledge in a court trial.

External barriers.   Barriers in the environment that make it difficult for a person to receive help.

Facilitators.   People involved in helping to move group members in the direction of their goal.

Family preservation.   A commitment to provide the resources and supports that can hold together or reunite a family unit, especially to provide stability to the children.

Feedback.   Both positive and negative critical comments on particular actions, statements, or other factors.

Fee-for-service.   A prearranged amount of money that will be paid to a health care provider each time he or she delivers a specific service to a plan member in accordance with the plan's criteria for that service.

Feminization of poverty.   The phenomenon of increasing poverty among women, particularly among female heads of families.

Force-field analysis.   A systematic way of looking at the negatives and positives of an idea or event in order to understand it fully, anticipate problems, and estimate chances of success.

Furthering responses.   Responses that encourage clients to continue talking.

GAP.   A necessary service or resource that is lacking in a program or in services that might help solve a problem.

Gatekeeper.   A person in the health plan organization who decides whether a prescribed medical service will be paid for based on its set of criteria for care.

Generalist. A worker who is knowledgeable about a wide range of resources and subgroups and who can use a variety of helping interventions.

Global questions. General, open-ended questions about some aspect of the interviewee's life.

Goal-oriented recording. A specialized form of summary recording that focuses on the goals in a case and the proposed methods of reaching those goals.

Grass roots programs. Programs started by those persons who do not hold the official decision-making positions within a system but have a stake in the outcome of its services or policies.

Group bond or cohesion. A complex set of forces that welds each member to the group and to each other.

Group structure. The sum total of rules and regulations that govern how a group organizes itself to do its work.

Head Start. A federally funded preschool program that aims to increase the readiness for public school of children from low-income families. It was begun by the War on Poverty in the 1960s.

Health Maintenance Organization (HMO). A health care institution or association of doctors that contracts with its members to collect a fixed sum of money monthly or yearly in exchange for doctor visits, tests, medications, hospital care, and preventive services as needed.

Hobbes, Thomas. A seventeenth-century philosopher who believed that people need a strong authority in order to regulate their desires.

Homophobia. An unreasoning fear or loathing of any person who has an intimate sexual relationship with a person of the same sex.

Hot line. Telephone service that gives information or short-term counseling on a variety of human-service issues.

Humanitarian ethos. A dedication to promoting the welfare of humanity, especially through the elimination of pain and suffering.

Human service networks (or delivery systems). The programs and entitlements that offer help in dealing with different but complementary parts of an overall problem.

Image of an agency. The reputation that a social agency has established in the community.

Indirect question. A question or statement that encourages the fullest possible expression of the interviewee's thoughts and feelings.

Information loop. A circular method of constantly refining one's interventions on the basis of careful questioning and absorbing of evaluative feedback.

Informed choice. A choice that is made after being given all the relevant information about the issue.

Informed consent. Agreement given with the understanding of the full implications of what one is agreeing to.

Institutional philosophy of social welfare. A philosophy that looks at people as being embedded in a social system and as having predictable developmental needs.

Institutional racism (sexism). Discrimination against a racial group (or gender) practiced by an organization or an institution, usually perpetuated by an interconnected system of policies and practices.

Intake interview. An interview (form) soliciting relevant information before the delivery of a service begins.

Internal barriers. Emotions or attitudes within a person that make it difficult for him or her to seek help.

Interpreting. A form of response that speculates on the meaning of an interviewee's statement or behavior.

Intervention plan. Specific acts or words aimed at moving persons or programs toward their goal.

In vitro fertilization. Fertilization of a woman's egg outside her body in a petri dish.

Involuntary clients. Clients who are forced to use a social service, usually by a court.

Laissez-faire style. A leadership style in which the worker allows the process of the group to flow with a minimum amount of leader direction.

Leadership acts and roles. Influential behavior (feelings, acts, or words) that move a group toward its primary purposes and/or maintain the group.

Least restrictive setting. The type of treatment and location that provide the greatest amount of freedom to a client (who often has a specific disability).

Legal services.   Organizations, generally supported by state or federal governments, that provide legal services to low-income people.

Linkage technology.   The acts involved in referring a client to another agency, worker, or resource.

Lobby.   An attempt to convince decision makers to support one's ideas or proposed actions.

Locke, John.   A seventeenth-century English philosopher and scientist who believed that if people followed their own self-interest, a rational, just society would result.

Magnifying.   Looking at a program or problem within the larger context of the community, laws, professional field, and so forth.

Mainstreaming.   Putting people who have emotional or physical disabilities into the mainstream of society as much as possible. The Education for All Handicapped Children Act (94.142) requires that all children be taught in regular schools and classrooms whenever possible.

Managed health care.   A prepaid system in which an individual must choose among the doctors included in a particular plan, such as a Health Maintenance Organization. It generally stresses preventive health care but is often used as a cost-cutting measure.

Mandated treatment.   Treatment that is legally required by the courts or by government officials.

Manipulation.   Trying to influence someone's behavior or thoughts by covert, unstated methods rather than open, explicit methods.

Means-tested programs.   Programs that are only available to the poor, whose assets fall below a certain set eligibility level.

Medicaid.   A program that pays for the medical treatment of poor people, administered by states and paid for by federal and state funds.

Mental Patients' Liberation Front (MPLF).   An organization of people who are or have been patients in psychiatric hospitals and who oppose many established psychiatric practices. They have established support groups and alternative institutions.

Microscoping.   Looking at a program or problem and seeing within it all the component parts and steps of action needed.

Minimal verbal or nonverbal response.   A small response to the interviewee, such as a nod or a look of interest, to encourage the interviewee to continue.

Multicausality.   The view that personal or social problems are caused by many interacting factors, often too complex to allow a precise assessment of causality.

Needs assessment.   Methods used to find out precisely what one particular person, group, or community needs to solve its problems and expand opportunities.

Negotiate a contract.   An attempt on the part of the helper and the helpee to forge an agreement about what will be included in their work together.

New Careers for the Poor movement.   A movement that began in the 1960s to train workers who do not have extensive formal credentials for human service jobs.

Nonjudgmental.   Refers to an attitude that withholds moral judgments on another person's behavior, attitude, or values.

Norming.   A process of arriving at mutually acceptable rules, regulations, and standards of behavior.

Norms.   Mutually acceptable rules, regulations, and standards of behavior.

Objective data.   Data based on unbiased facts, not affected by personal feelings or prejudice.

Open-ended questions.   Questions asked in such a way that they allow for a variety of responses.

Opening the interview.   The first stage of an interview, when worker and client begin to play out their expectations of each other and develop a way of working together.

Opportunity theory.   The theory that people are prevented from getting out of poverty because of the lack of social opportunities rather than because of individual defects.

Overidentification.   The process of relating so completely to another person's feelings and/or experiences that one cannot separate oneself from the other person.

Paraphrasing or restating.   Putting the interviewee's words in another form without changing the content in order to encourage the interviewee to go on.

Permanency planning.   An attempt to create, in a timely fashion, a plan for a child that will return him or her safely to the family of origin or legally frees the child to be adopted.

Personal Responsibility Act.   This bill was passed by Congress in 1996 and signed by former President Clinton and ended federal entitlements to needy families. It replaced AFDC with the Temporary Aid to Needy Families (TANF) Act, which gave grants to the states to administer work-related and time-limited programs of aid.

Physical attending.   Making oneself physically receptive to the interviewee.

Power.   The capacity to influence others to achieve certain desired ends.

Preparatory empathy.   An attempt to put oneself in the shoes of another person, to feel or think of a problem from another perspective, even before encountering a client, to sensitize the worker.

Primary purpose.   The main goal of an agency that determines the work it does.

Primary reference groups.   Groups in which a person is intimately involved, including family and friends who influence one's attitudes and values.

Principle of less eligibility.   The principle that the amount of welfare given to people should be less than the lowest wage so that people will not be tempted to take welfare rather than get a wage-earning job.

Principle of reciprocity.   The principle that social relationships are based to some extent on an analysis of trade-offs that determines what each person must give to the relationship in order to get back certain benefits.

Privacy.   The right to be left alone.

Privatization.   Changing the funding and administration of social welfare programs from the public to the private sector.

Privileged communication.   Legal protection of confidences revealed in certain specified relationships.

Problem-solving skills.   Systematic techniques that aid in achieving a goal in the most efficient and effective manner.

Professional helping relationship.   A relationship between a worker and client(s) that follows a pattern determined by the goals and ethics of the human service field.

Program design or Program proposal.   The thoughtful mapping out of a program so that it includes an analysis of tasks, strategies, resources, responsibilities, schedules, a budget, and an evaluation plan.

Progressives.   Members of the Progressive party in the early twentieth century who favored social reforms such as abolition of child labor, juvenile courts, and more individualized treatment of the mentally ill.

Progressive taxes.   Taxes that tax rich people at a higher rate than those who are less affluent.

Psychosocial model of disability.   A model that looks at the entire environment of the person, including social attitudes, attitudes of other individuals, and the society that the able-bodied have created.

Public-health approach.   A preventive approach to social problems as opposed to a remedial approach. It implements large-scale programs to meet people's basic health and nutritional needs in order to prevent illness.

Racism.   Hatred or intolerance of another race or other races. Belief that one's own race is superior.

Reassuring.   Making statements that seek to restore someone's confidence.

Referral file.   An updated list of all available resources in a human service area with notations about the special characteristics or qualifications of each.

Referral statement.   An initial verbal or written statement that explains the reasons a client is being sent to or has chosen a specific resource, person, or agency.

Reflecting.   An interviewer response that puts into words what the interviewer thinks the interviewee might be feeling.

Rescue fantasy.   A fantasy that envisions saving someone from his or her fate.

Residual philosophy of social welfare.   A philosophy that believes the problem that requires help is not a "normal" social need, but arises because of special circumstances brought about by individual deficiency.

Residential treatment center.   A facility providing mental and physical services for a specific problem population which requires that the person being treated stay within its walls for a specified period of time.

Resource bank.   People, places, services, or written materials that help people meet needs and reach goals.

Respite care.   Provision of a paid worker to relieve a person who is a primary caretaker so that the caretaker can pursue outside tasks or have some free time.

Restraining order.   A document issued by a judge that prohibits a specific person from approaching another person who feels that he or she is being threatened.

Right to refuse treatment.   Legal protection granted to a person who does not want the treatment that is prescribed by professionals.

Right to treatment.   Legal assurance that a person who is placed in an institution that purports to give treatment does, in fact, receive treatment.

Root causes.   The critical causes of a particular problem that seem to have contributed most significantly to its emergence.

Rousseau, Jean-Jacques.   An eighteenth-century Swiss-French philosopher who believed that people were good by nature but corrupted by civilization.

Self-determination.   People's right to determine their own life plan without interference.

Settlement house movement.   The movement of the late nineteenth and early twentieth centuries that established agencies in city slums of England and the United States, where professionals gave group services and engaged in social action on behalf of the slum dwellers.

Shelter industry.   The system of using private hotels as shelters for the homeless. It has become a profitable industry in the last several decades.

Shift from industrial to service jobs.   Changes in the United States economy in recent decades that have reduced the number of jobs in the manufacturing industry and increased the number of jobs in the service sector.

Social Darwinism.   The application of Charles Darwin's theories of evolution to the human sphere by sociologist Herbert Spencer. The concept "the survival of the fittest" was used to justify accumulation of wealth and disregard of the needs of the poor.

Stereotype.   To make generalizations based on little or no information about people or a subject. The generalizations are invested with special meaning and shared by a group of people.

Stigma.   Something that detracts from the character or reputation of a person or group; mark of disgrace or reproach.

Street-level bureaucracy.   The way laws and regulations are implemented by human service workers at the level of direct contact with clients.

Subjective data.   Personal opinions about the client's attitude, situation, and behavior that may or may not be objectively true.

Substance abuse.   The misuse of substances such as alcohol and drugs.

Suggesting.   Giving a mild form of advice, generally made tentatively.

Support groups.   Groups in which members help each other to clarify or act on certain issues.

Support network.   The people and places in our lives that offer ongoing practical as well as emotional help.

Surrogate parenting.   The procedure in which a fertile woman conceives and bears a child for an infertile woman by being impregnated with the husband's sperm.

Systems-change strategies (interventions). Acts aimed at helping clients by creating or improving the organizations that are supposed to deliver services to them.

Task-focused casework.   A method of helping a person with a problem by focusing on the immediate priorities of the client and the small steps involved in realizing, or seeking to realize, the ultimate goal.

Therapeutic or rehabilitative. Types of groups whose members usually have in common a mental or physical problem of some magnitude. Usually led by a professionally trained leader.

Third-party payment. Payments made by insurance companies or government programs for medical expenses incurred by individuals.

Time flow chart. A diagram of the tasks that need to be done in a certain period of time by specific individuals.

Trade-offs. Those things that must be sacrificed to obtain another hoped-for benefit.

Troubleshooter. The person who is alert for signs or symptoms that indicate the existence of an actual or potential problem.

Twelve-step program. A program of healing activities designed by the founders of Alcoholics Anonymous.

Unintended consequences of reform. Events that occur as a result of reform measures that were not planned or anticipated by the reformers.

Universal programs. Programs that provide income supports and social services to both the affluent and the poor.

Value conflicts. Disagreement brought about by differences in values between people.

Value dilemmas. A situation in which competing values make it difficult, if not impossible, to determine the correct choice.

Verbal following responses. Any of a number of responses that let clients know they have been heard and understood.

Victim blaming. Blaming a person for his or her own misfortune rather than considering the social forces that contributed to the problem.

References

Abel, C. M., & Johnson, H. W. (1978, January). Clients' access to records: Policy and attitudes. *Social Work 23* (1), 42–46.

Abels, P. A. (1979). On the nature of supervision: The medium is the group. In C. E. Munson (Ed.), *Social work supervision* (pp. 174–179). New York: Free Press.

Aber, J. L., Bennett, N. G., Conley, D. C., & Li, J. (1997). The effects of poverty on child health and development. *Annual Review of Public Health 18,* 463–483.

Abramovitz, M. (1986). The privatization of the welfare state: A review. *Social Work 31,* 257–264.

Abramovitz, M. (1988). *Regulating the lives of women: Social welfare policy from colonial times to the present.* Boston: South End Press.

Abramovitz, M. (1992, Summer). Poor women in a bind: Social reproduction without social supports. *Affilia,* 23–43.

Abrams, J. (2000, December 2). *The Atlanta Journal and Constitution,* p. A9. *ACLU Online Newsletter* (2003, December 18). Drug policy. www.aclu.org.

Adams, M. (2002, November). "Showing good faith towards Muslims. *HR Magazine.*

Addams, J. (1902). *Democracy and social ethics.* New York: Macmillan.

AFSC (2001). *Everyone is deserving.* Philadelphia: American Friends Service Committee.

Albelda, R., & Tilly, C. (1994). *Glass ceilings and bottomless pits: Women, income, and poverty in Massachusetts.* Boston: Women's Statewide Legislative Network.

Albelda, R., & Tilly, C. (1997). *Glass ceilings and bottomless pits.* Boston: South End Press.

Albelda, R., Withorn, A., & Navin, C. (1998, July). Poor timing: An analysis of welfare time limits. *Sojourner.*

Albert, E. (1989). AIDS and the press: The creation and transformation of a social problem. In Joel Best (Ed.), *Images of Issues* (pp. 39–54). New York: Aldine de Gruyter.

Alexander, B. (2003). The state of the nation's housing: 2003. Joint Center for Housing Studies for Harvard University. Cambridge, MA.

Alinksy, S. (1969). *Reveille for radicals.* New York: Vintage Books.

Alinksy, S. (1971). *Rules for radicals: A practical primer for realistic radicals.* New York: Random House.

Allard, M. A., Albelda, R., Cotten, M. E., & Cosenza, C. (1997). *In harm's way? Domestic violence, AFDC receipt, and welfare reform in Massachusetts.* Boston: University of Massachusetts Press.

Allport, G. (1954). *The nature of prejudice.* Reading, MA: Addison-Wesley.

All Things Considered. (1992, May 20). National Public Radio.

All Things Considered. (1995, November 21). National Public Radio.

All Things Considered. (1998a, January 5). National Public Radio.

All Things Considered. (1998b, April 7). National Public Radio.

Alonzo-Zaldivar. (2004, May 2). Democrats urge immigration changes. *Boston Globe,* p. A19.

Alter, C., & Evans, W. (1990). *Evaluating your practice: A guide to self-assessment.* New York: Springer.

Alter, J. (1994, February 12). The name of the game is shame. *Newsweek,* p. 41.

Alvarez, L. (1997, August 25). For Hispanic lawmakers, time to take the offensive. *New York Times.*

America's families better off today than in 1997, but not all share equally in economic gains. (2000, October 24). The Urban Institute. www.urban.org.

American Association of University Women. (1978). *Community action tool catalog: Techniques and strategies for successful action programs.* Washington, DC: Author.

American Psychiatric Association. (1995). *Diagnostic and statistical manual of mental disorders* (4th ed.). Washington, DC: Author.

American Psychological Association. (1963). Ethical standards of psychologists. *American Psychologist 18,* 56–60.

Anderson, R. (2004). A single-payer response to the health care crisis. Physicians for a National Health Program. www.pnhjp.org/news/2004/June/a_singlepayer_respon.php.

Andrews, H. B. (1995). *Group design and leadership.* Boston: Allyn & Bacon.

Appleby, G. A., & Anastas, J. W. (1992). Social work practice with lesbians and gays. In A. T. Morales & B. W. Sheafor (Eds.), *Social work: A profession of many faces* (pp. 347–381). Boston: Allyn & Bacon.

Arches, J. (1991). Social structure, burnout, and job satisfaction. *Social Work 36*(3), 202–206.

Ariel, S. (1999). *Culturally competent family therapy: A general model.* Westport, CT: Greenwood Press.

Aronowitz, S., & DiFazio, W. (1994). *The jobless future: Sci-tech and the dogma of work.* Minneapolis, MN: University of Minnesota Press.

Atkinson, L., & Kunkel, O. D. (1992). Should social workers participate in treatment only if the client consents to such treatment freely and without coercion? In E. Gambrill & R. Pruger (Eds.), *Controversial issues in social work.* pp. 157–172. Boston: Allyn & Bacon.

Axinn, J., & Stern, M. (2001). *Social welfare: A history of the American response to need* (5th ed.). Boston: Allyn & Bacon.

Ayres, B. D., Jr. (1997, November 21). California immigration law is ruled to be partly illegal. *The New York Times,* p. 11.

Baker, C. S. (2001). Charitable Choice. The Employment Project. www.nomorejobs.org/charitable.htm.

Bales, R. (1950). *Interaction process analysis.* Cambridge, MA: Addison-Wesley.

Bales, R., & Borgatta, E. F. (1995). Size of group as a factor in the interaction profile. In A. D. Hare, E. F. Borgatta, & R. F. Bales (Eds.), *Small Groups* (pp. 396–413). New York: Alfred Knopf.

Banfield, E. (1974). *The unheavenly city.* Boston: Little, Brown.

Barbash, F. (1982, June 19). Justices rule for mentally retarded. *Boston Globe,* p. 13.

Barkley, R. (1981). *Hyperactive children.* New York: Guilford Press.

Barkley, R. (1997). *Attention deficit disorder: A clinical workbook.* New York: Guilford Press.

Barker, R. L. (1995). Private Practice. In *Encyclopedia of Social Work,* 19th ed. (Vol. 3, pp. 1905–1906). Washington, DC: National Association of Social Workers.

Barlett, D. L., & Steele, J. B. (1992). *America: What went wrong?* Kansas City, MO: Andrews & McMeel.

Barry, E. (2000, February 20). Stranded. *Boston Globe,* pp. A1, A26.

Barry, E. (2002, March 3). Group stirs debate over schizophrenia. *Boston Globe,* p. B1.

Bass, A. (1992, February 3). Illness coupled with stigma. *Boston Globe,* p. 16.

Bass, B. M., & Stogdill, R. M. (1990). *Handbook of leadership.* New York: Free Press.

Bassuk, E. (1995, July). Dilemmas in counting the homeless: Introduction. *American Journal of Orthopsychiatry* 65(3), 318–319.

Bassuk, E., Browne, A., & Buckner, J. C. (1996, October). Single mothers and welfare. *Scientific American.*

Battle, M. (1990). National Association of Social Workers. In *Encyclopedia of Social Work: 1990 Supplement* (18th ed.) (pp. 232–233). Silver Spring, MD: National Association of Social Workers.

Becker, H. J. (1978). Curricula of associate degree mental health/Human service training programs. *Community Mental Health 14,* 133–145.

Becvar, D. S., & Pontious, S. L. (2000). Complementary alternative medicine in health and mental health: Implications for social work practice. *Social Work in Health Care, 31* (3) 39–57.

Bell, W. (1965). *Aid to dependent children.* New York: Columbia University Press.

Benjamin, A. (1981). *The helping interview* (3rd ed.). Boston: Houghton Mifflin.

Berenson, B. G., & Mitchell, K. M. (1974). *Confrontation: For better or worse!* Amherst, MA: Human Resource Development Press.

Bergstein, B. (2002, January 31). Now she'll meet mother's sperm donor. *Boston Globe,* p. A2.

Berkeley Planning Associates. (1978, August). *Evaluation of child abuse and neglect demonstration projects, 1974–1977* (Vols. 1 & 2, DHEW Publication No. (PHS) 79-3217-1). Hyattsville, Md: National Center for Health Services Research, U.S. Department of Health, Education and Welfare.

Berney, L. (1984, January 15). Social, moral issues in case of 96-year-old. *Boston Globe,* p. B4.

Bernstein, J. (1995, January-February). Welfare-bashing redux: The return of Charles Murray. *The Humanist,* 22–25.

Bernstein, M. (2004, March 16). Rape victims' center defends confidentiality. *The Oregonian.*

Bernstein, N. (1996a, August 20). Criminal and welfare rules raise new issues of fairness. *New York Times,* p. A16.

Bernstein. N. (1996b, September 15). Giant companies entering race to run state welfare programs. *New York Times,* pp. 1, 26.

Berrick, J. O. (1995). *Faces of poverty: Portraits of women and children on welfare.* New York: Oxford University Press.

Bershoff, D. N. (1975). Professional ethics and legal responsibilities: On the horns of a dilemma. *Journal of School Psychology 13*(4), 359–376.

Bertcher, H. J. (1994). *Group participation: Techniques for leaders and members* (2nd ed.). Thousand Oaks, CA: Sage.

Besharov, D. (2004, March 6). There's more welfare to reform. www.nytimes.com/2004/03/06/opinion/06BESH.htm.

Best, J. (Ed.). (1989). *Images of issues.* New York: Aldine de Gruyter.

Bettelheim, B. (1950). *Love is not enough: The treatment of emotionally disturbed children.* Glencoe, IL: Free Press.

Bettelheim, B. (1960). *The informed heart: Autonomy in a mass age.* Glencoe, IL: Free Press.

Billies, M., Boushey, H., Dorow, H., Lane, M., Pollack, A., & Yau, K. K. (1997). *Welfare, workfare, and jobs.* New York: Urban Justice Center Organizing Project.

Bill of Wrath. (1998, May 11). *The Nation 266*(17), 3.

Blau, J. (1992). *The visible poor: Homelessness in the United States.* New York: Oxford University Press.

Bluestone, B., & Harrison, B. (1992, May 26). Poverty wages vs. the 'high road' to economic recovery. *Boston Globe,* p. 11.

Bobo, K., Kendall, J., & Max, S. (1996). *Organizing for social change* (2nd ed.). Washington, DC: Seven Locks Press.

Boston Globe (1998, September), p. A3.

Boston Phoenix (2004, May 7). Bad times for the middle class, p. 8.

Boston Women's Health Book Collective. (1978). *Ourselves and our children.* New York: Random House.

Boston Women's Health Book Collective. (1987). P. B. Doress & D. L. Siegal (Eds.). *Ourselves, growing older.* New York: Simon and Schuster.

Boston Women's Health Book Collective. (1992). *The new our bodies, ourselves.* New York: Simon & Schuster.

Boston Women's Health Book Collective. (1998). *Our bodies, ourselves for a new century.* New York: Simon & Schuster.

Boyd, Julia A. (1990). Ethnic and cultural diversity: Keys to power. In L. S. Brown & M. P. Root (Eds.). *Diversity and complexity in feminist therapy* (pp. 151–167). New York: Harrington Park Press.

Boyte, H. C. (1980). *The backyard revolution: Understanding the new citizen movement.* Philadelphia: Temple University Press.

Brager, G., Specht, H., & Torczyner, J. L. (1987). *Community organization* (2nd ed.). New York: Columbia University Press.

Bragg, R. (1995, April 14). Georgia, passing child support, discovers its potential limits. *New York Times,* p. A1.

Bramhall, M., & Ezell, S. (1991, Summer). How agencies can prevent burnout. *Public Welfare,* 33–37.

Brawley, E. A. (1980, March). *Emerging human service education programs: Characteristics and implications for social work education and practice.* [unpublished report prepared for the Joint Board Committee of the National Association of Social Workers and the Council on Social Work Education].

Breggin, P. (1991). *Toxic psychiatry.* New York: St. Martin's Press.

Breitbart, V., & Schram, B. (1978, September). Rocking the cradle without rocking the boat: An analysis of twenty-four child-raising manuals. *Bulletin of the Council on Interracial Books for Children 9*(6 & 7), 4.

Brieland, D., & Goldfarb, S. Z. (1987). Legal issues and legal services. In *Encyclopedia of Social Work* (pp. 29–33). Silver Spring, MD: National Association of Social Workers.

Brimelow, P. (1995). *Alien nation: Common sense about America's immigration disaster.* New York: Random House.

Brock, S. E., Sandoval, J., & Lewis, S. (2001). *Preparing for crisis in the schools: A manual for building school crisis response teams.* New York: Wiley.

Brown, C. (1965). *Manchild in the promised land.* New York: Macmillan.

Bryce, H. J. (2000). *Financial and strategic management for non-profit organizations* (3rd ed.). San Francisco: Jossey-Bass.

Buckholdt, D. R., & Gubrium, J. F. (1979). *Caretakers.* Beverly Hills, CA: Sage.

Bureau of Labor Statistics (2003). Age 16–19: Percent jobless and percent employed in June 1948–2003. Washington, DC, Bureau of the Census.

Burgdorf, M. P., & Burgdorf, R. L., Jr. (1977). Law. In P. J. Valletutti & F. Christoplos, Eds., *Interdisciplinary approaches to human services* (pp. 111–134). Baltimore, MD: University Park Press.

Burt, M., & Laudan, L. (2000, February). America's homeless II: Populations and services. Oral presentation at the Urban Institute First Tuesday's Forum. Washington, DC.

Butler, B. B. (1990). Job satisfaction: Management's continuing challenge. *Social Work 35*(2), 25–29.

Butler, R. N. (1975). *Why survive? Being old in America.* New York: Harper & Row.

Buttell, F. (1998, Spring). Issues and ethics in social work with batterers. *The New Social Worker.*

Butterfield, F. (2000, April 26). Racial disparities seen as pervasive in juvenile justice. *New York Times,* pp. 1, 18.

Butterfield, F. (2001, September 2). States ease laws on time in prison. *New York Times,* p. A1.

Butterworth, I. A. (2001). The components and impact of stigma associated with EAP counseling. *Employee Assistance Quarterly 16*(3), 1–8.

Cahill, S. (2000). Tip of the iceberg or bump in the road? The initial impact of welfare reform in Dorchester. Boston: Massachusetts Human Services Coalition.

Callicutt, J. W. (1987). Mental health services. In A. Menahan (Ed.), *Encyclopedia of Social Work* (18th ed., p. 126). Silver Spring, MD: National Association of Social Workers.

Canada, G. (1998). *Reaching up for manhood: Transforming the lives of boys in America.* Boston: Beacon Press.

Carden, A. (1994). Wife abuse and the wife abuser: Review and recommendations. *The Counseling Psychologist 22,* 539–582.

Carkhuff, R. R. (1969). *Helping and human relations: Practice and research.* New York: Holt, Rinehart & Winston.

Carkhuff, R. R. (1972). Differential functioning of lay and professional helpers. *Journal of Counseling Psychology* 15, 117–126.

Carkhuff, R. R., & Berenson, B. J. (1968). *Beyond counseling and therapy.* New York: Holt, Rinehart & Winston.

Carter, B. (1995, July). Looking at families through the gay lens: An interview with Betty Carter. *In the Family,* 12–15.

Cassidy, J. (1997, July 14). The melting pot myth. *The New Yorker,* 40–43.

Cass, C. (2004, May 28). 1 in 75 men were in prison or jail in 2003. *Boston Globe.*

Center for Research on Women, Wellesley College (1999/2000, Fall/Winter). *Research Report* (20), 1.

CensusScope (2000). Population by race. www.censusscope.org.

Chamberlin, J. (1998). *On our own.* London: RAP.

Chambers, C. A. (1980). *Seedtime of reform: American social service and social action 1918–1933.* Westport, CT: Greenwood Press.

Chandler, D. L. (1997, May 11). In shift, many anthropologists see race as social construct. *Boston Globe,* p. A30.

Chappell, D. (2004, May 8). If affirmative action fails…what then? *New York Times.*

Chasnoff, I. J. (1989). Drug use in women: Establishing a standard of care. *Annals of the New York Academy of Science 562,* 208–210.

Chesler, P. (1972). *Women and madness.* New York: Avon Books.

Child Welfare League of America (2004a). Quick facts about foster care. www.cwla.org/programs/fostercare/factsheet.htm.

Child Welfare League of America (2004b). Kinship care: About the program. www.cwla.org/programs/kinship/kinshipaboutpage.htm.

Child Welfare League of America (2004c). Adoption fact sheet. www.cwla.org/programs/adoption/adoptionfactsheet.htm.

Children's Defense Fund (2000). *Families struggling to make it in the workforce: A post-welfare report.* Washington, DC.

Children's Defense Fund (2004a). *Testimony of the Children's Defense Fund on the impact on children of proposed federal marriage initiative.* Washington DC: Author.

Children's Defense Fund (2004b). Child health. www.childrensdefense.org/childhealth/chip/default.asp.

Children's Defense Fund (2004c). The Child Tax Credit. *The Access Handbook.* Washington, DC.

Children's Defense Fund (2004d). Tax and benefits outreach. www.childrensdefense.org/benefits/default.asp.

Church leaders protest cutbacks. (1992, February 5). *Boston Globe,* p. B1.

Cities not able to provide jobs for those on aid. (1997a, November 22). *Boston Globe,* p. 7.

Claiborne, W. (2001, August 3). *Boston Globe,* p. A2.

Clarke, K. (1998, June). America behind bars. *U.S. Catholic 63*(6), 10–17.

Clifton, R., & Dahms, A. M. (1993). *Grassroots organizations: A resource book* (2nd ed.). Prospect Heights, IL: Waveland Press.

Cloward, R. A., & Ohlin, L. E. (1964). *Delinquency and opportunity: A theory of delinquent gangs.* New York: Free Press.

Clymer, A. (1996, August 5). In Congress, they learn to live with Clinton. *International Herald Tribune,* p. 4.

CMS/OACT (2003). Medicare enrollees. www.cms.hhs.gov/researchers/pubs/datacompendium/2002/02pg30.pdf.

CNN.com.U.S. News (2000, August 8). www.cnn.com/2000/US/08/08/teen.births.ap/.

Coalition of Battered Women's Advocates. (1988, November 1). *Position Paper on Child Welfare.* Unpublished manuscript.

Cockburn, A. (1995, November 27). The white man's answer. *The Nation,* 656–657.

Coleman, S. (1997, January 28). The woman who said no. *Boston Globe,* pp. D1, D6.

Coles, R. (1977). *Privileged ones: The well-off and the rich in America.* Boston: Little, Brown.

Collins, C. (1995, May/June). Aid to dependent corporations. *Dollars & Sense,* pp. 6–10.

Collins, P. H. (1990). *Black feminist thought: Knowledge, consciousness, and the politics of empowerment.* London: Harper Collins.

Conklin, M. (1997, March 26). Out in the cold: Washington shows drug addicts the door. *The Progressive,* pp. 25–27.

Conniff, R. (1997, March 22). Girding for disaster. *The Progressive.*

Cooper, M. (1997, June 2). When push comes to shove: Who is welfare reform really helping? *The Nation,* pp. 11–15.

Coover, V., Deacon, C., Esser, R., & Moore, P. (1978). *Resource manual for a living revolution.* Philadelphia: New Society Press.

Copans, S., Kress, H., Gundy, J. H., Rogan, J., & Field, F. (1979, January–February). The stresses of treating child abuse. Excerpted from *Children Today 8,* 22–35. In H. Weissman, I. Epstein, & A. Savage (Eds.), *Agency-based social work: Neglected aspects of clinical practice.* Philadelphia: Temple University Press 1983.

Corcoran, K. J., & Vandiver, V. (1996). *Maneuvering the maze of managed care: Skills for the mental health practitioners.* New York: Free Press.

Cottle, T. J. (1974). *A family album.* New York: Harper & Row.

Court rejects curb on immigrant care. (1998, August 14). *International Herald Tribune,* p. 8.

Crary, D. (2003, January 2). Imprisoned mothers fight to keep children. *Boston Globe.*

Culbert, S. A. (1976). Consciousness raising: A five stage model for social and organizational change. In W. Bennis, K. Benne, & R. Chin (Eds.), *The planning of change* (3rd ed., pp. 231–245). New York: Holt, Rinehart & Winston.

Curtin, E. R. (1970). *White-collar unionization.* New York: National Industrial Conference Board.

Cyrus-Lutz, C., & Gaitz, C. M. (1972, Summer). Psychiatrists' attitudes toward the aged and aging. *Gerontologist 12,* Pt. I, 163–167.

The Daily Review. (2004, April 6). Welfare reform requires funds for day care.

Dale, D. (1978). *How to make citizen involvement work: Strategies for developing clout.* Amherst, MA: Citizen's Involvement Training Project, University of Massachusetts.

Dale, D., Magnani, D., & Miller, R. (1979). *Beyond experts: A guide for citizen group training.* Amherst, MA: Citizen's Involvement Training Project, University of Massachusetts.

Dale, D., & Mitiguy, N. (1978). *Planning for a change: A citizen's guide to creative planning and program development.* Amherst, MA: Citizen's Involvement Training Project, University of Massachusetts.

D'Augelli, A. R., D'Augelli, J. F., & Danish, S. J. (1981). *Helping others.* Monterey, CA: Brooks/Cole.

Davis, M. H. (1994). *Empathy: A social psychological approach.* Madison, WI: Brown & Benchmark.

Davis, M. (1998, July). The illegitimacy game. *Sojourner,* 10.

A deadly silence on AIDS. (1991, September 27). *Boston Globe,* p. B2.

Dean, W. (2003, July 7). In the service of children. "Pro Bono Digest," *New York Law Journal.*

de Cunha, P. (1983, Spring). The feel of culture shock. *Bilingual Journal 7*(3), 15–17.

Deen, T. (2003). Rights Discrimination against Muslim increases in US. IPS Homepage, World News. www.oneworld.org.

Delgado, G. (1986). *Organizing the movement, the roots and growth of ACORN.* Philadelphia: Temple University Press.

Delgado, G. (2000, fall). Racing the welfare debate. *Color Lines,* p. 14.

Dembner, A. (2001, September 21). Medicare waste raises cost of drugs by $1b. *Boston Globe,* p. A2.

Democratic Policy Committee. (1999, February 11). DPC Fact Sheet. Washington, D.C.

Denniston, L. (2001, March 22). Drug test ruling backs pregnant women's privacy. *Boston Globe,* p. A3.

Dentzer, S. (1998, January–February). A guide to managed care, Part 2. *Modern Maturity,* pp. 35–41.

DeParle, J. (1997, September 11). As rules on welfare tighten, its recipients gain in stature. *New York Times,* pp. A1, A28.

Department of Human Services. (1981). *Human service education program extracts.* Evanston, IL: National College of Education.

Department of Justice, Americans with Disabilities Act (2001). www.usdoj.gov.80/cit/ada/pubs/10hrpt.htmlanchor 30598.

Depass, T. (2003, April). Bay state votes to kill bilingual ed. *Resist,* p. 3.

DeWitt, K. (1995, October 15). Black men say the march in Washington is about them, not Farrakhan. *New York Times,* p. 22.

Diamant, J. (2004, February 10). Christians and Jews split over Gibson's film. *Newhouse News Service.*

Di Giovanni, M. (1996, April 17). Speech at the New England Organization of Human Service Educators.

Dickson, D. T. (1976, July). Law in social work: Impact on due process. *Social Work* 21(4), 274–278.

Dore, M. M., Doris, J. M., & Wright, P. (1995). Identifying substance abuse in maltreating families: A child welfare challenge. *Child Abuse and Neglect 19,* 531–543.

Doten, P. (1991, April 20). Falsely accused, a mother fights back. *Boston Globe,* p. 31.

Douglas, C., Kalman, C., & Kalman, T. (1985). Homophobia among physicians and nurses: An empirical study. *Hospital-Community Psychiatry 36,* 1309–1311.

Dougherty, R. (2001, July 22). Overworked, underpaid, undercover. *Boston Globe,* p. D4.

Dow, M. (2004, June). "Whatever we want to do with you." http://www.nthposition.com/whateverwewantto.php.

Dowdy, Z. B. (1998, June 21). Who pulled the trigger? *Boston Globe,* p. E1.

Drug defense tactic charges U.S. targets blacks unfairly. (1995, August 27). *Boston Globe.*

Drug Policy Alliance (2003). Race and the drug war. http://www.drugpolicy.org/race/.

Dugger, C. W. (1998, March 14). Immigration study finds many below new income limit. *New York Times.*

Dugger, R. (1995, August 14–21). Real populists please stand up. *The Nation,* 159–164.

Dwyer, O., & Tully, E. (1989). *Housing for battered women.* New York: State Office for the Prevention of Domestic Violence.

Edelman, P. (1997, March). The worst thing Bill Clinton has done. *The Atlantic Monthly,* pp. 43–58.

Edelman, P. (2001, April 23). A fairness agenda for the Bush era. *The Nation 272*(16).

Edin, K. J., & Lein, L. (1996). *Making ends meet: How single mothers survive welfare and low-wage work.* New York: Russell Sage Foundation.

Editorial. (1997, November). *Harper's,* pp. 24–29.

Edwards, Richard L. (Ed.). (1995). *Encyclopedia of Social Work,* 19th ed. Washington, DC: NASW Press.

Ehrenreich, B. (2001). *Nickel and dimed: On (not) getting by in America.* New York: Metropolitan Books (Henry Holt & Co.).

Ehrlander, M. F. (2002). *Equal educational opportunity. Brown's elusive mandate.* New York: Oxford University Press.

The Employment Project. (1997, May). No more jobs. Available from the Employment Project, 237 Thompson Street, New York, NY 10012. Vol. 3(5).

Ennis, B. J., & Emery, R. D. (1978). *The rights of mental patients: An American Civil Liberties Union handbook.* New York: Avon Books.

Epstein, L. (1980). *Helping people: The task-centered approach.* St. Louis, MO: C. V. Mosby Co.

Epstein, L. (1992). *Brief treatment and a new look at the task centered approach* (3rd ed.). New York: Macmillan.

Equal choice for the disabled and seniors. (2001, August 3). *The Malden Advocate,* p. 12.

Esber, G. Jr. (1989). Anthropological contributions for social work education. *Practicing Anthropology 11*(3), 4–11.

Evans, D. R., Hearn, M. T., Uhlemann, M. R., & Ivey, A. E. (1979). *Essential interviewing.* Monterey, CA: Brooks/Cole.

Evans, W. P., Fitzgerald, C., & Frantz, C. E. (Eds.). (2000). *Shocking violence: Youth perpetrators and victims: A multi-disciplinary perspective.* Springfield, IL: Charles C. Thomas.

Eysenck, H. (1971). *The IQ argument.* Freeport, NY: Library Press.

Ezorsky, G. (1991). *Racism and justice: The case for affirmative action.* Ithaca, NY: Cornell University Press.

Faatz, A. (1953). *The nature of choice in casework process.* Chapel Hill, NC: University of North Carolina Press.

Families USA. (2004, June). *One in three: Non-elderly Americans without health insurance 2002–2003.* Washington DC.

Fatout, M., & Rose, S. (1995). *Task groups in the human services.* Thousand Oaks, CA: Sage.

Feagin, J. & Sikes, M. (1997). *Living with racism: The Black middle class experience.* Boston: Beacon Press.

Fei, M., & Peter, L. (1998). *Financial management in human services.* New York: Haworth Press.

Feldman, Y. (1979). The supervisory process: An experience in teaching and learning. In C. E. Munson (Ed.), *Social work supervision* (pp. 118–124). New York: Free Press.

Feltham, C., & Horton, I. (2000). *Handbook of counseling and psychotherapy.* Thousand Oaks, CA: Sage.

Feminist Majority (2004). RU486. www.feministmajority.org/rights/ru486btwo.html.

Fetterman, D. M., Kafterian, S. J., & Wandersman, A., (Eds.) (1996). *Empowerment evaluation: Knowledge for self-assessment and accountability.* Thousand Oaks, CA: Sage.

Field, M. A. (1988). *Surrogate motherhood.* Cambridge, MA: Harvard University Press.

Finder, A. (1998, April 12). Evidence is scant that workfare leads to full-time jobs. *New York Times,* pp. 1, 26.

Fineman, H. (1998, July 27). HMOs under the knife. *Newsweek,* 21.

Fisher, R. (1994). *Let the people decide: Neighborhood organizing in America* (updated ed.). New York: Twayne.

Fitzgerald, B. (1998, June 9). Welfare cap in N.J. raised abortion rate, study finds. *Boston Globe,* p. 7.

Flanders, L., Jackson, J., & Shadoan, D. (1997). Media lies. In D. Dujon & A. Withorn (Eds.), *For crying out loud* (pp. 29–39). Boston: South End Press.

Flannery, R. B., Jr., Fisher, H., & Walker, A. P. (2000). Characteristics of patient and staff victims of assaults in community residences by previously nonviolent psychiatric inpatients. *Psychiatric Quarterly 71*, 195–203.

Flannery, R. B. Jr., Lizotte, D., Laudani, L., Staffieri, A., & Walker, A. P. (2001). Violence against women and the assaulted staff action program. *Administration and Policy in Mental Health 28*, 491–498.

Flaubert, G. (1959). *Madame Bovary.* New York: Bantam Books (original work published 1856).

Flaws in immigration law. (1997, September 29). *New York Times,* p. A1.

Fleck-Henderson, A. (1991, June). Moral reasoning in social work practice. *Social Service Review,* pp. 32–36.

Fletcher, M. A. (2000, June 8). Drug war targets blacks unfairly, rights group says. *Boston Globe,* p. A3.

Foot, P. (1979). Active euthanasia with parental consent [Commentary]. *Hastings Center Report,* pp. 20–21. New York: Hastings-on-Hudson.

Foreman, J. (1997, December 19). CDC assesses fertility clinics. *Boston Globe,* p. 24.

Foreman, J. (2003, July 29). A little empathy, please! *Boston Globe Online.* www.boston.com/dailyglobe2/210/science/A_little_empathy_please_ tishtm/3.8.2003.

Forman, J. Jr. (1992, Summer). Fighting against the tide: Defending racial preferences. *New Politics 4*(1), [New series], 171–175.

Foster, S., & Walter, G. G. (1992). *Deaf students in post secondary education.* New York: Routledge.

Foucault, M. (1987). *Mental illness and psychology.* Berkeley: University of California Press.

Foxman, A. (2003, December 7). *Chattanooga Times Free Press.* FRAC (Food Research Action Council). Current News Analysis. Low-income student participation Breakfast Programs doubles since 1990, but stalls in 2002–2003 on key measure. www.frac.org/html/news/1/0403Breakfast.htm.

FRAC (Food Research Action Council). (2004, June 4). One in four workers live at federal poverty level. www.frac.org/htm/newsdigest/06.04.04.htm/#4.

FRAC (Food Research Action Council). (2004a). Food Stamp participation increases in March 2004 to 23.8 million persons. www.frac.org/htm/news/sp/Latest_FSP.html.

FRAC (Food Research Action Council). (2004b). Hunger in the U.S. www.frac.org/html/hunger_in_the_us/hunger_index.html.

FRAC (Food Research Action Council). (2004c). *Child Nutrition Fact Sheet.* National School Lunch Program, Washington, DC, p. 1.

FRAC (Food Research Action Council). (2004d). USDA study finds that income verification in the National School Lunch Program does harm, without doing good. http://www.frac.org/html/federal food programs/cnreauthor/OANEstudies.htm

FRAC News Digest. (2004, June 6). One in four workers live at federal poverty level. http://www.frac.org/html/news/newsdigest/06.04.04.html.#4.

Frame, D. J. (1995). *Managing projects in organizations.* San Francisco: Jossey-Bass.

France, K., & Kish, M. (1995). *Supportive interviewing in human service organizations: Fundamental skills for gathering and encouraging productive change.* Springfield, IL: Charles C. Thomas.

France, K. (1996). *Crisis intervention: A handbook of immediate person-to-person help* (3rd ed.). Springfield, IL: Charles C. Thomas.

Frank, C. C. (1980, June). Children's rights after the Supreme Court's decision on Parham, J. L. and J. R. *Child Welfare 59*(6), 375–380.

Freedberg, S. (1989). Self-determination: Historical perspectives and effects on current practice. *Social Work 34,* 33–38.

Freeman, J. (1972). The tyranny of structurelessness. In A. Koedt, E. Levine, & A. Rapone (Eds.), *Radical feminism* (pp. 285–299). New York: Quadrangle.

Freire, P. (1970). *The pedagogy of the oppressed* (M. B. Ramos, Trans.). New York: Continuum.

Friedlander, D., & Burtless, G. (1995). *Five years after: The long-term effects of welfare-to-work programs.* New York: Russell Sage Foundation.

Friedlander, W. A., & Apte, R. A. (1980). *Introduction to social welfare.* Englewood Cliffs, NJ: Prentice-Hall.

Friedman, D. H., Douglas, E., Hayes, M., & Allard, M. A. (1998). *A policy brief: Massachusetts (T)AFDC case closings October 1993–August 1997.* Boston: University of Massachusetts.

Frisch, N. C., & Kelley, J. (1996). *Healing life's crises: A guide for nurses.* Albany, NY: Delmar.

Gaines, J. (2000, May 1). Racial abuse is alleged at Boston school. *Boston Globe,* pp. A1, A12.

Gallagher, C. (2003). Color-blind privilege: The social and political functions of erasing the color line in post race America. *Race, Gender & Class 10*(4).

The Gallup Organization (2004, May 25). Tuesday briefing.

Gans, H. J. (1992, Fall). The war against the poor. *Dissent,* 461–465.

GAO report reviews state sanction policies and limited data on effects on families. (2000, July). *Welfare News,* p. 2.

GAO Testimony (2001). Long-term care: Implications of Supreme Court's *Olmstead* decision are still unfolding. Statement of Kathryn G. Allen at hearing before the Special Committee on Aging, U.S. Senate, Washington DC, September 24, 2001. Serial No. 107-15. U.S. Government Printing Office, Washington DC.

Gardner, H. (1962). *A thousand clowns.* New York: Penguin Press.

Garfinkel, H. (1965, March). Conditions of successful degradation ceremonies. *American Journal of Sociology 61,* 420–424.

Garland, J. A., Jones, H., & Kolodny, R. (1965). A model for stages of development in social work groups. In S. Bernstein (Ed.), *Explorations in group work.* Boston: Milford House.

Garrett, L. (2004, July 17–18). The politics and profit of AIDS. *International Herald Tribune,* p. 4.

Gartner, A., & Riessman, F. (1977). *Self-help in the human services.* San Francisco: Jossey-Bass.

Gary, L. T. (1991). Feminist practice and family violence, in M. Bricker-Jenkins, N. R. Hooyman, & N. Gottlieb (Eds.), *Feminist social work practice in clinical settings.* Newbury Park CA: Sage.

Gavin, R. (2004, June 7). Temps become permanent fixtures. *Boston Globe,* p. A1.

Gelbspan, R. (1986, October 19). FBI's arrest files often do injustice. *Boston Globe,* p. 15.

Gellman, B. (2000, July 6). West refused to heed early warnings of pandemic. *International Herald Tribune,* pp. 1–2.

Geography IQ (2004). Infant mortality rate. www. geographyiq.com/ranking_Infant_Mortality _Rate_aall.htm.

Gerth, R. H., & Mills, C. W. (Eds.). (1958). *From Max Weber: Essays in sociology.* New York: Oxford, Galaxy.

Gilder, G. (1981). *Wealth and poverty.* New York: Bantam Books.

Gilligan, C. (1982*). In a different voice: Psychological theory of women's development.* Cambridge, MA: Harvard University Press.

Ginsberg, L. (1998). *Careers in social work.* Boston: Allyn & Bacon.

Gitterman, A., & Shulman, L. (Eds.). (1994). *Mutual aid groups, vulnerable populations, and the life cycle* (2nd ed.). New York: Columbia University Press.

Glasser, I. (1992, Spring). Talking liberties. *Civil Liberties 2,* 376.

Glasser, I. (1989). Techniques for teaching anthropology to social work students. *Practicing Anthropology 11*(3), 5–10.

Glenn, D. (2001a, September 3–10). Labor of love. *The Nation 273* (7), pp. 30–34.

Glenn, D. (2001b, Summer). I thought you said she worked full time. *Dissent,* pp. 101–105.

Glicken, M. D. (1977). *A regional study of the job satisfaction of social workers.* Unpublished doctoral dissertation, University of Utah, Salt Lake City.

Golan, N. (1978). *Treatment in crisis situations.* New York: Free Press.

Goldberg, C. (2003, November 28). For good health, it is better to give, science suggests. *Boston Globe,* p. B5.

Goldberg, G. S., & Rosenthal, M. (2002). *Diminishing welfare: A cross-national study of social provision.* Westport, Ct.: Auburn House.

Golden, D. (1990, November 11). Halfway to where? *The Boston Globe Magazine,* pp. 49–50.

Golding, W. (1959). *Lord of the flies.* New York: Capricorn Books.

Goldstein, B. (2004, May/June). Letter to the editor. *Dollars & Sense,* p. 5.

Gonnerman, J. (1997, March 10). Welfare's domestic violence. *The Nation,* 21–23.

Goodman, E. (1996, May 23). Wisconsin welfare plan looks good—until you read the fine print. *Boston Globe,* p. 25.

Goodman, E. (1996, August 8). A modest proposal to rescind childhood. *International Herald Tribune,* p. 6.

Goodman, E. (2001a, March 25). Privacy and pregnancy. *Boston Globe.*

Goodman, E. (2001c, July 8). Here's a new question for pro-lifers: What is life? *Boston Globe,* p. D7.

Gordon, L. (1988). *Heroes of their own lives.* New York: Viking.

Gordon, L. (1994). *Pitied but not entitled: Single mothers and the history of welfare.* New York: Free Press.

Gordon, T. (1970). *Parent effectiveness training.* New York: Peter H. Wyden.

Gornick, J. C. (2001, Summer). Cancel the funeral. *Dissent,* pp. 13–18.

Gorov, L. (1997, December 23). Affirmative-action ban alters terrain in California. *Boston Globe,* p. A1.

Gorov, L. (1999, January 22). Oakland council mulls spanking ban. *Boston Globe.*

Gorz, A. (1987, Spring). S(He) who doesn't work shall eat all the same. *Dissent,* 179–187.

Gothard, S. (1995). Legal issues: Confidentiality and privileged communication. In *Encyclopedia of Social Work* (19th ed.). Washington, DC: NASW.

Gottlieb, N. (Ed.). (1980a). *Alternative social services for women.* New York: Columbia University.

Gottlieb, N. (Ed.). (1980b). Women and mental health. In *Alternative social services for women* (pp. 3–22). New York: Columbia University.

Gowans, P. (2000, October 13). Privatization out of control. workfare-wlc@igc.topica.com.

Green, J. (1982). *Cultural awareness in the human services.* Englewood Cliffs, NJ: Prentice-Hall.

Green, J., & Leigh, J. W. (1989). Teaching ethnographic methods to social service workers. *Practicing Anthropology 11*(3), 8–10.

Greenberg, J. (1965). *The Monday voices.* New York: Avon Books.

Greenberg, M. (1993). *Beyond stereotypes: What state AFDC studies on length of stay tell us about welfare as a way of life.* Washington, DC: Center for Law and Social Policy.

Greenberg, P. (1969). *The devil has slippery shoes.* New York: Macmillan.

Greenberger, S. S. (2001, May 15). Bill would overhaul bilingual education. *Boston Globe,* pp. B1, B5.

Greenhouse, L. (2004, May 18). States can be liable for not making courthouses accessible. *New York Times.*

Greenhouse, S. (1997, July 24). Nonprofit and religious groups to fight workfare in New York. *New York Times,* p. A1.

Greenhouse, S. (1998, April 13). Many participants in workfare take the place of city workers. *New York Times,* pp. A1, B6.

Greenhouse, S. (2001, July 15). U.S. sues New York City over harassment complaints. *New York Times,* p. 25.

Greenstein, R., & Horney, J. (2000, July 7). How much of the enlarged surplus is available for tax and program initiatives? Washington, DC: Center on Budget and Policy Priorities.

Greenstone, J. L., & Leviton, S. C. (2002). *Elements of crisis intervention: Crises and how to respond to them* (2nd ed). Monterey, CA: Wadsworth.

Grey, N. (1979, October). Tucson teachers initiate stress counseling program. *NEA Reporter 18*(6).

Grillo, T. (1997, December 25). Managed care legislation seeks swifter patient appeals. *Boston Globe,* p. B11.

Grossman, H. (1984). *Manual on terminology and classification in mental retardation.* Washington, DC: American Association on Mental Deficiency.

Guetzloe, E. (Ed.). (1999). Violence in children and adults—A threat to public health and safety: A paradigm of prevention. *Preventing School Failure 44*(1), 21–24.

Gutierrez, L. M. (1990, March). Working with women of color: An empowerment perspective. *Social Work 35*(2), 149–153.

Haas, W. (1959, July). Reaching out: A dynamic concept in casework. *Social Work 4,* 41–45.

Hacker, A. (1992, April). Speech at the Socialist Scholars Conference.

Hackney, H., & Cormier, S. (1996). *The professional counselor: A process guide to helping* (3rd ed.). Boston, MA: Allyn & Bacon.

Hall, J. C., Smith, K., & Bradley, A. K. (1970, April). Delivering mental health services to the urban poor. *Social Work 15,* 35–39.

Halmos, P. *The faith of the counsellors.* New York: Schocken Books.

Hammond, C., Hepworth, D. H., & Smith, V. G. (1977). *Improving therapeutic communication.* San Francisco: Jossey-Bass.

Hampton, R. L., Senatore, V., & Guillotta, T. P. (Eds.) (1998). *Substance abuse, family violence and child welfare.* Thousand Oaks, CA: Sage.

Handler, J. F. (1979). *Protecting the social service client.* New York: Academic Press.

Handler, J. F., & White, L. (1999). *Hard labor: Women and work in the post-welfare era.* New York: M. E. Sharpe, Inc.

Hard times for immigrants. (1997, April 4). *New York Times,* p. A34.

Hare, A. P. (1976). *Handbook of small group research* (2nd ed.). New York: Free Press.

Hare, A. P., Borgatta, E. F., & Bales, R. F. (1955). *Small groups.* New York: Alfred Knopf.

Hastings Center. (1979). *Hastings Center report.* New York: Hastings-on-Hudson.

Hayden, T., & Novik, J. (1980). *Your rights to privacy.* New York: Avon Books.

Heller, J. (1961). *Catch-22.* Dell.

Heller, N. (1981). Unpublished manuscript.

Hendricks, J. E. (1995). *Crisis intervention: Contemporary issues for on-site interveners.* Springfield, IL: Charles C. Thomas.

Hepworth, D. H., & Larsen, J. A. (1987). Interviewing. In *Encyclopedia of social work.* Silver Spring, MD: National Association of Social Workers.

Herbert, B. (1996, July 23). Welfare 'reform': Officially sanctioned brutality. *International Herald Tribune,* p. 2.

Herbert, B. (1998, June 14). Hidden agendas. *New York Times,* p. 17.

Herbert, B. (2004, June 11). Punishing the poor. *New York Times.*

Hernandez, R. (1998, June 14). Trimming of the welfare rolls causes crisis for some shelters. *New York Times.*

Herrnstein, R. (1971, September). I.Q. *Atlantic Monthly,* pp. 43–64.

Herrnstein, R., & Murray, C. (1994). *The bell curve: Intelligence and class structure in American life.* New York: Free Press.

Higgins, A. (2004, May 14). Program bolsters violence victims' confidentiality. *Bangor Daily News.*

HIV-related knowledge and stigma. (2001, March 14). *Morbidity and mortality weekly report. Journal of American Medical Association 285,* (10).

Hoff, L. A. (1995). *People in crisis: Understanding and helping* (4th ed.). San Francisco, CA: Jossey-Bass.

Hoff, L. A., & Kazimiera, A. (1998). *Creating excellence in crisis care: A guide to effective training and program design.* San Francisco: Jossey-Bass.

Hoge, W. (1998, August 11). Swedes yearn for the good old days as election nears. *International Herald Tribune,* p. 7.

Holbrook, S. M. (1990, July). Adoption, infertility, and the new reproductive technologies: Problems and prospects for social work and welfare policy. *Social Work 35*(4), 333–337.

Holland, S. (2004). Childhood family assessment in social work practice. Thousand Oaks, CA: Sage.

Holmes, S. A. (1997, December 21). Thinking about race with one-track mind. *New York Times,* pp. 1, 12.

Home stretch support and action group: Voices of homelessness. (2000). Massachusetts Coalition for the Homeless.

hooks, b. (1997). Representing whiteness in the black imagination. In R. Frankenber (Ed.), *Displacing whiteness.* Durham, NC: Duke University Press.

House Committee on Ways and Means, U.S. House of Representatives. (2000). *Green Book 2000.* Washington, DC: U.S. Government Printing Office.

Houston, L. P., & Cohen, A. C. (1972, Fall). The college for human services: A model for alternative professional education. *New Generation 54*(4), pp. 22–23.

Hoyt, M. F. (1995). *Brief therapy and managed care: Readings for contemporary practice.* San Francisco: Jossey-Bass.

Hsu, F. L. K. (1971). *The challenge of the American dream: The Chinese in the United States.* Belmont, CA: Wadsworth.

Human Services Referral Directory of Massachusetts. (2002). Kennebunkport, ME: George D. Hall Co.

Hurley, R. (1969). *Poverty and mental retardation: A causal relationship.* New York: Vintage Books.

Ingram, R. (1992, April). When therapy is oppression. *Transactional Analysis Journal 22*(2), 95–100.

Issues and controversies: Immigration update. (1997, October 10). *Facts on File News Services.*

Jackson, B. (2003, November 24). Poll of teens back Affirmative Action for college admission. *Rocky Mountain News.*

Jackson, D. Z. (2004, June 25). Bush's compassion is all talk. *Boston Globe,* p. A23.

Jackson, D. Z. (2001, August 31). Who's better off this Labor Day? Numbers tell. *Boston Globe,* p. A3.

Jacobs, E. E., Mass, R. L., & Harvill, R. L. (2001) *Group Counseling.* Monterey, CA: Wadsworth.

Janofsky, M. (2001, July 15). States pressed as 3 boys die at boot camps. *New York Times,* pp. A1, A13.

Jarmon, R. L., McFall, J., Kolar, P., & Strom, G. (1997). The changing context of social work practice: Implications and recommendations for social work educators. *Journal of Social Work Education 33,* 29–46.

Jay, J. & Jay, D. (2000). *Love first: A new approach to intervention for alcoholism and drug addiction.* Center City, MN: Hazelden Publishing.

Jenkins, S. (1981). *The ethnic dilemma in social services.* New York: Free Press.

Jenson, J. M., & Howard, M. O. (Eds.) (1999). Youth violence: Current research and recent practice innovations. Washington, DC: NASW Press.

Joffe, C. (1983). Abortion work: Strains, coping strategies, policy implications. In H. Weissman, I. Epstein, & A. Savage (Eds.), *Agency-based social work: Neglected aspects of clinical practice* (pp. 62–67). Philadelphia: Temple University Press.

Johnson, A. (2001). *Privilege, power, and difference.* Mountain View, CA: McGraw Hill.

Johnson, D. (1996, May 19). Wisconsin welfare effort on schools is a failure, study says. *New York Times,* p. 6.

Jordan, B. (1998, March 18–25). The long arm of immigration reform. *Christian Century 115*(9), 15.

Jordan, C. & Franklin, C. (1995). *Clinical assessment for social workers: Quantitative and qualitative methods.* Chicago, Ill: Lyceum Books.

Kadushin, A. (1980). *Child welfare services* (3rd ed.). New York: Macmillan.

Kadushin, A. (1992). *Supervision in social work* (3rd ed.). New York: Columbia University Press.

Kagan, J. (1989). *Unstable ideas: Temperament, cogniton & self.* Cambridge, MA: Harvard University Press.

Kahn, S. (1970). *How people get power.* New York: McGraw-Hill.

Kahn, S. (1995). *Organizing: A guide for grassroots leaders.* Washington, DC: NASW Press.

Kamerman, S. B., & Kahn, A. J. (1976). *Social services in the United States.* Philadelphia: Temple University Press.

Kaminer, W. (1997, November/December). Unholy alliance. *American Prospect 35,* 54–55.

Karger, H. (1981). Burnout as alienation. *Social Service Review 55,* 271–283.

Kates, E. (1998, May). Access to education and training for single parents receiving TAFDC benefits in Massachusetts: Concerns and recommendations for action. Unpublished article.

Katz, M. B. (1989). *The undeserving poor: From the war on poverty to the war on welfare.* New York: Pantheon.

Kaufman, L. (2003, October 20). Are those leaving welfare better off now? Yes and no. *New York Times.*

Keefe, T., & Maypole, D. E. (1983). *Relationships in social service practice: Context and skills.* Monterey, CA: Wadsworth.

Keith-Lucas, A. (1972). *Giving and taking help.* Chapel Hill, NC: University of North Carolina Press.

Kelly, S., & Blythe, B. J. (2000). Family preservation: A potential not yet realized. *Journal of Child Welfare LXXIX* (1), 29–41.

Kernberg, P. F., Chazen, S. E., Frankel, A. K., Hariton, J. R., Kruger, R. S., Scholl, H. H., & Sanders, P. S. (1991). *Children with conduct disorders: A psychotherapy manual.* New York: Basic Books.

Kettner, P. M., Moroney, R. M., & Martin, L. L. (1990). *Designing and managing programs: An effectiveness based approach.* Newbury Park, CA: Sage.

Kiernan, L. A. (1992, May 24). In N. H., a battle over how to protect children. *Boston Globe,* p. B3.

Kilborn, P. (1997, December 10). Mentally ill called victims of cost-cutting. *New York Times,* p. A20.

Kindlon, D., & Thompson, M. (2000). *Raising Cain: Protecting the emotional life of boys.* New York: Ballantine.

Kingston, M. H. (1977). *The woman warrior: Memoirs of a girlhood among ghosts.* New York: Alfred Knopf.

Kinney, J., Haapala, D., Booth, C., & Leavitt, S. (1988). The homebuilder's model. In J. K. Whittaker, J. Kinney, J. Tracy, E. M. Tracy, & C. Booth (Eds.), *Improving practice technology for work with high risk families: Lessons from the homebuilders.* Seattle, WA: Center for Sociological Welfare Research, University of Washington School of Social Work.

Kinsey, A. C., Pomeroy, W. B., & Martin, C. E. (1948). *Sexual behavior in the human male.* Philadelphia: W. B. Saunders.

Kirk, S. A., & Greenley, J. R. (1974). Denying or delivering services? *Social Work 19*(4), 439–447.

Kirkpatrick, M., & Hitchens, D. (1985). Lesbian mothers/Gay fathers. In D. H. Schetky & E. P. Benedek (Eds.), *Emerging issues in child psychiatry and the law.* New York: Brunner/Mazel.

Kirchhoff, S. (2001, August 5). Bush says states may shift Medicaid to add flexibility. *Boston Globe,* p. A3.

Kjosness, J., Barr, L. R., & Rettman, S. (2004). *Research navigator guide: The helping professions.* Boston, MA: Allyn & Bacon.

Klein, A. (2004, April 9). Affirmative-action opponents suffer setbacks in Colorado and Michigan. *Chronicle of Higher Education.*

Klein, A. F. (1953). *Society, democracy and the group.* New York: Morrow.

Kleinfield, N. R. (1983, May 29). Operating for profit at hospital corp. *New York Times,* pp. F1, 22.

Knowles, M., & Knowles, H. (1959). *Introduction to group dynamics.* New York: Association Press.

Knowlton, B. (2004, August 27). Poverty in the U.S. climbs for third year. *International Herald Tribune,* p. 1.

Koedt, A. (1971). The myth of the vaginal orgasm. In *Liberation now: Writings from the womens' liberation movement* (pp. 311–320). New York: Dell.

Kowalczyn, L. (2001, August 6). Despite U.S. law, seniors click on Canada for drugs. *Boston Globe,* p. A1.

Kravetz, D. F., & Rose, S. D. (1973). *Contracts in groups: A workbook.* Dubuque, IA: Kendall-Hunt.

Kruger, R. S., School, H. H., & Sanders, P. S. (1991). *Children with conduct disorders: A psychotherapy manual.* New York: Basic Books

Kurzman, P. A. (1971). *The Mississippi experience: Strategies for welfare rights action.* New York: Association Press.

Kuttner, R. (1998, June 14). In a libertarian era, shades of a police state. *Boston Globe,* p. F7.

Kuttner, R. (2004, April 21). The problem with outsourcing. *Boston Globe,* p. A19.

Lacombe, A. (1997, June 2). Welfare reform and access to jobs in Boston. Prepared for the Bureau of Transportation Statistics.

Lahr, J. (2001, April 16). Been here and gone. *The New Yorker.*

Lakien, A. (1974). *How to get control of your time and your life.* New York: The New American Library.

Landers, S. (1998, May). Balancing confidences, laws, and ethics. *NASW News,* 3.

Latour, F. (2002, June 16). Marching orders: After 10 years, state closes boot camp. *Boston Globe,* p. B1.

Lauffer, A. (1997). *Grants etc.* Thousand Oaks, CA: Sage.

"The law on disabilities." (1983, February 23). *Boston Globe,* p. 18.

Lawrence, S. (2002). *Domestic violence and welfare policy: Research findings that can inform policies on marriage and child well-being.* New York, NY: National Center for Children in Poverty.

Lazarin, M. (2003, November/December). Children of immigrants dare to dream. *Network Connection,* pp. 8–9.

Lefferts, S. (1982). *People's guide to health care* (1st ed.). Stony Brook, NY: Social Services Interdisciplinary Program, State University of New York.

Leichter, H. J., & Mitchell, W. E. (1967). *Kinship and casework.* New York: Russell Sage Foundation.

Lester, B. M., & Tronick, E. Z. (1994). The effects of prenatal cocaine exposure on child outcome. *Infant Mental Health Journal 15,* 107–120.

Levi-Strauss, C. (1974). *Reciprocity, the essence of social life.* In R. L. Coser (Ed.), The family: Its structures and functions (pp. 3–12). New York: St. Martin's Press.

Lewin, K., Lippett, R., & White, R. K. (1939). Patterns of aggressive behavior in experimentally created social climates. *Journal of Social Psychology 10,* 271–299.

Lewis, J. A., Lewis, M.D., Packard, T., & Souflee, F. (2001). *Management of human service programs,* 2nd ed. Pacific Grove, CA: Brooks Cole.

Lewis, N. A. (1997, April 2). With immigration law in effect, battles go on. *New York Times,* p. 1.

Lewis, O. (1961). *The children of Sanchez.* New York: Random House.

Lewis, O. (1966). La vida: *A Puerto Rican family in the culture of poverty—San Juan and New York.* New York: Random House.

Lieberman, M. A., Yalom, I. D., & Miles, M. B. (1973). *Encounter groups: First facts.* New York: Basic Books.

Lima, H. (1998, July). A grass-roots fight to save Section 8. *Street Spirit,* 3.

Lind, M. (1995, April 24). American by invitation. *New Yorker,* pp. 107–113.

Lindblom, C. E., & Cohen, D. K. (1979). *Usable knowledge: Social science and social problem solving.* New York: Simon and Schuster.

Link, B., Phelan, J., Bresnahan, M., Stueve, A., Moore, R., & Susser, E. (1995, July). Lifetime and five-year prevalence of homelessness in the United States: New evidence on an old debate. *American Journal of Orthopsychiatry 65*(3), 42–46.

Lipsky, M. (1980a). *Street-level bureaucracy: Dilemmas of the individual in public services.* New York: Basic Books.

Lipsky, M. (1980b, May/June). The welfare state as workplace. *Working Papers 7*(3), 33–38.

Littner, N. (1957). *The strains and stresses on the child welfare worker.* New York: Child Welfare League of America.

Lloyd, J. C., & Bryce, M. E. (1984). *Placement prevention and family reunification: A handbook for the family centered practitioner* (rev. ed.). Iowa City, IA: National Resource Center on Family Based Services, University of Iowa School of Social Work.

LRP Publications. (2004, April 12). Agencies seek to improve measurement of disability population.

Loughary, J. W., & Ripley, T. (1979). *Helping others help themselves: A guide to counseling skills.* New York: McGraw-Hill.

Lowman, R. L., & Resnick, R. J. (Eds.). (1994). *The mental health professional's guide to managed care.* Washington, DC: The American Psychological Association.

Lukes, C. A., & Land, H. (1990, March). Biculturality and homosexuality. *Social Work 35*(2), 155–161.

Lupo, A. (2001, August 12). In quest of a common language for the bilingual education debate. *Boston Globe,* p. 2, City Weekly.

Lyons, P., & Rittner, B. (1998, April). The construction of the crack babies phenomenon as a social problem. *American Journal of Orthopsychiatry 68*(2), 42–49.

Maas, H. S., & Engler, R. E., Jr. (1959). *Children's need of parents.* New York: Columbia University Press.

MacKenzie, K. R. (Ed.). (1995). *Effective use of group therapy in managed care.* Washington, DC: American Psychiatric Press.

Madara, E. J., & Meese, A. (1998). *The self-help sourcebook: Finding and forming mutual aid self-help groups.* Denville, NJ: The Self-Help Clearing House, Saint Clares-Riverside Medical Center.

Maier, G. J. (1996). Managing threatening behavior: The role of talk down and talk up. *Journal of Psychosocial Nursing, 34*(6), 25–30.

Makela, Klaus, et al. (1996). *Alcoholics anonymous as a mutual help movement: A study in eight societies.* Madison, WI: University of Wisconsin Press.

Malcolm X, & Haley, A. (1966). *The autobiography of Malcolm X.* New York: Grove Press.

Mancillas, J. (2001, September 3/10). Jorge Mancillas replies to "Changing to Organize." *The Nation 273*(7), p. 24.

Mandell, B. (1973). *Where are the children? A class analysis of foster care and adoption.* Lexington, MA: D. C. Heath.

Mandell, B. (Ed.). (1975a). Controlling the 'dangerous classes.' In *Welfare in America* (pp. 104–118). Englewood Cliffs, NJ: Prentice-Hall.

Mandell, B. (Ed.). (1975b). Who rules the social services? In *Welfare in America* (pp. 65–88). Englewood Cliffs, NJ: Prentice-Hall.

Mandell, B. (1995, Spring). Shredding the safety net. *New Politics,* 9–22.

Mandell, B. (1997, Winter). Downsizing the welfare state. *New Politics,* 33–46.

Mandell, B. (2004). Review of Piven, F., Acker, J. Hallock, & Morgan, S. (Eds.). *Work, Welfare and Politics: Confronting Poverty in the Wake of Welfare Reform.* In *Journal of Progressive Human Services 15*(1), pp. 89–104.

Mandell, B. (2004, Summer). Diminishing welfare: A review essay. *New Politics 9*(4), pp. 158–175.

Mandell, B., & Mandell, M. (1992, Winter/Spring). Who are the real thieves? *Survival News 6*(1), 1.

Mandell, M. (1997, Summer). In defense of social security. *New Politics 6*(3), 21–29.

Many reportedly forced off welfare. (1998, March 23). *Boston Globe.*

Mark, R. (1996). *Research made simple: A handbook for social workers.* Thousand Oaks, CA: Sage.

Marlow, C. (1993). *Research methods for generalist social work.* Pacific Grove, CA: Brooks/Cole.

Martice, G., & Clark, R. (1982). *Anti-Semitism in the United States.* New York: Praeger.

Martin, L. L., & Kettner, P. M. (1996). *Measuring the performance of human service programs.* Thousand Oaks, CA: Sage.

Martin, R. (2001). *Listening up: Reinventing ourselves as teachers and students.* Portsmouth, NH: Heinemann.

Maslach, C. (1978). The client role in staff burnout. *Journal of Social Issues 34*(4), 111–124.

Maslach, C. (1966, September). Burned Out. *Human Behavior,* 16–22.

Mason, H. (2003, July 8). Does bilingual education translate to success? The Gallup Organization.

Mass-Care. (1998). The tide is turning in health care reform. Boston, MA.

Mass Human Services Coalition (2001). *State House Watch.* Boston, MA.

Massachusetts Civil Liberties Union. (1983, August). Computer matching serious threat to privacy. *The Docket 13*(2).

Massachusetts Civil Liberties Union. (1984, November). *The Docket 14*(4), 4.

Massachusetts English Plus Coalition (2003, April). *Resist,* p. 5.

Massaro, T. (1998). *Catholic social teaching and United States welfare reform.* Collegeville, MN: The Liturgical Press.

Matchan, L. (1992, January 8). Once homeless, now in tug of war. *Boston Globe,* pp. 1, 9.

Maxwell, M. L. (1998, Fall). Empower. *Social Policy,* 11–16.

Mayer, J., & Timms, N. (1970). *The client speaks: Working class impressions of casework.* Chicago: Aldine Publishing.

McGowan, J. F., & Porter, T. L. (1967). *An introduction to the vocational rehabilitation process.* Washington, DC: U.S. Department of Health, Education, and Welfare, Vocational Rehabilitation Administration.

McGrory, M. (1996, May 25). Me-too tactics on welfare. *Boston Globe,* p. A11.

McKnight, J. (1992, April 22). Speech at Foundations Affecting the Future of Massachusetts' Communities Forum on Community Organizing.

McNamara, E. (1991, December 26). 'Last one over the wall': Battling youth crime with compassion. *Boston Globe,* p. 24.

McNamara, E. (1995, October 20). Where will your mother go now? *Boston Globe,* p. 28.

McRoy, R. G. (1990). A historical overview of black families. In S. Logan, E. M. Freeman, & R. McRoy (Eds.), *Social work practice with black families* (pp. 3–17). White Plains, NY: Longman.

Mead, L. (1986). *Beyond entitlement: The social obligations of citizenship.* New York: Free Press.

Metro. (2004, May 5). State to probe racial profiling, p. 7.

Milgram, S. (1974). *Obedience to authority: An experimental view.* New York: Harper & Row.

Miller, J. (2004, March/April). High and dry: The economic recovery fails to deliver. *Dollars & Sense,* p. 23.

Miller, J. B. (1976). *Toward a new psychology of women.* Boston: Beacon Press.

Miller, J. G. (1991). *Last one over the wall: The Massachusetts experiment in closing reform schools.* Athens, OH: Ohio University Press.

Miller, P. (1992). *The worst of times.* New York: Harper Collins.

Mills, C. W. (1943, September). The professional ideology of social pathologists. *American Journal of Sociology 49*(2), 165–180.

Mills, C. W. (1959). *The sociological imagination.* New York: Oxford University.

Mink, G. (1998). *Welfare's end.* Ithaca, NY: Cornell University Press.

Miranne, K. B., & Young, A. H. (1998, June). Women reading the world: Challenging welfare reform in Wisconsin. *Journal of Sociology and Social Welfare 25*(2), 155–176.

Mishel, L., Bernstein, J., & Schmitt, J. (1995, October). Cutting wages by cutting welfare: The impact of reform on the low-wage labor market. [Briefing paper], Washington, DC: Economic Policy Institute.

Mishra, R. (2002, February 11). Shorter lifespan found in study of cloned mice. *Boston Globe,* p. A1.

Mitiguy, N. (1978). *The rich get richer and the poor write proposals.* Amherst, MA: Citizen's Involvement Training Project, University of Massachusetts.

Mizrahi, T., & Morrison, J. (Eds.). (1993). *Community organization & social administration.* New York: Haworth Press.

Mizrahi, T. (2001). The status of community organizing in 2001: Community practice, context, complexities, contradictions and contributions. *Research on Social Work Practice 11*(2), 176–189.

Mondros, J. B., & Wilson, S. M. (1994). *Organizing for power and empowerment.* New York: Columbia University Press.

U.S. Department of Labor, *Monthly Labor Review.* (1998, July). Washington, DC: Bureau of Labor Statistics.

Morales, A. (1978, July). Institutional racism in mental health and criminal justice. *Social Casework 59*(7), 387–395.

Moran, Tyler. (2000, September). Immigrants still hurting from welfare reform. Boston: Massachusetts Immigration and Refugee Advocacy Coalition.

Morse, S. (2004). How citizens and local leaders can use strategic thinking to build a brighter future. San Francisco, CA.: Jossey-Bass.

Mosher, L., & Berti, L. (1989). *Community mental health: Principles and practice.* New York: Norton.

Moss, M. S. (2001, May). HHS gets additional comments on privacy rules. *NASW News* (46)5, p. 4.

Moynihan, D. P. (1965). *The Negro family: The case for national action.* Washington, DC: U.S. Department of Labor, Office of Policy Planning and Research.

Murphy, S. (1995, December 9). SSI recipients will lose $2.50 a month to the state. *Boston Globe,* p. 18.

Murray, C. A. (1984). *Losing ground: American social policy 1950–1980.* New York: Basic Books.

Murray, C. (1994, October 29). The coming white underclass. *Wall Street Journal.*

Murray, C., & Herrnstein, R. (1994). *The bell curve: Intelligence and class structure in American life.* NY: Free Press.

Musto, D. F. (1988). Evolution of American attitudes toward substance abuse. *Annals of the New York Academy of Science 562,* 3–7.

Nather, D. (2001). Bush plan to promote faith based charities creates dilemma for both. *CQ Weekly 59*(5), 283, 285.

National Academy of Sciences. (1997). Economic, demographic, and fiscal effects of immigration. Washington, DC: National Academy Press.

National Alliance to End Homelessness. (2004, February 2). President's budget undercuts progress in ending homelessness: ¼ million to lose housing assistance. Washington, DC.

National Association of Social Workers. (1982, September). Suit settlement favors confidentiality of records. *NASW News 27*(7), 7.

National Association of Social Workers. (1983, February). Congress, district court chop rate of disability cutoffs. *NASW News 28*(2), 9.

National Center on Child Abuse and Neglect. (1979, September). *Resource Materials,* OHDS, Children's Bureau, DHEW, Publication No. 79–30221. Washington, DC: Department of Health, Education, and Welfare.

National Coalition for the Homeless. (2001, August 9). Why are people homeless? http://nch.ari.net/causes.html.

National Conference of Catholic Bishops. (1986). *Economic justice for all: Pastoral letter on Catholic social teaching and the U.S. economy.* Washington, DC: United States Catholic Conference.

National Commission for Human Service Workers. *Registration and certification of human service workers.* Paper Prepared and Distributed by the National Commission for Human Service Workers (NCHSW). Atlanta, Georgia, July 1982.

National Low Income Housing Coalition. (2000, July 21). Washington, DC: Author.

National Organization for Women (2004, April 9). Pay equity: A long overdue step in the road to equality. www.now.org/press/04–03/04–09.html.

Nelson, T. S., & Tripper, T. S. (Eds.) (1998). *101 more interventions in family therapy.* NY: Haworth Press.

Neukrug, E. (1994). *Theory, practice, and trends in human services: An overview of an emerging profession.* Brooks/Cole: Pacific Grove, CA.

New Jersey Law Journal. (2003, April 28). Charlie and Nadine H. et al. v. Whitman et al.

A new picture of poverty. (1997, November 25). *Boston Globe,* p. 11.

Newman, B. (2001, August 29). Lost in America: Quirk in law creates health-care minefield for legal immigrants. *The Wall Street Journal,* pp. A1, A16.

New York Times. (2001, December 23), pp. 1 and 4wk.

New York Times. (2003, December 31). The budget politics of being poor.

New York Times. (2004, April 17). The perils of cutting Medicaid.

New York Times. (2004, May 22). Affordable housing in crisis.

New York Times. (2004, June 23). A blow to health plan patients.

Nichols, K., & Jenkinson, J. (1991). *Leading a support group.* New York: Chapman & Hall.

Nichols, M., & Porter, K. (1995, March 14). *General assistance programs: Gaps in the safety net.* Washington, DC: Center on Budget and Policy Priorities.

Nickerson, C. (1985, March 10). Reformers' dream that went astray. *Boston Globe,* p. 21.

Norsigian, J., & Newman, S. (2001, August 3). Ban human cloning right now. *Boston Globe,* p. A23.

Northeast Action. (2004, Spring). Worldview and immigrant rights.

NOW (National Organization for Women). (2004, March 26). NOW fights right-wing assault on abortion rights, urges supporters to march on April 25th. www.now.org/press/03–04/03–26.html.

NOW (National Organization for Women). (2004, June 1). Federal judge declares "partial-birth" abortion ban unconstitutional: Exposes right-wing policy as infringement on a woman's right to choose. www.now.org/press/06-04-01.html.

NOW (National Organization for Women). (2004, July 14). Senate majority votes against writing discrimination into Constitution: NOW salutes defeat of Federal Marriage Amendment. www.now.org/press/07-04-07-14.html.

O'Connor, J. (1973). *The fiscal crisis of the state.* New York: St. Martin's Press.

O'Hare, W., Greenstein, R., Mann, T., & Porter, K. (1990, July). *Real life poverty in America: Where the American public would set the poverty line.* Washington, DC: Center on Budget and Policy Priorities and Families USA Foundation Report.

Ojito, M. (1998a, April 20). A record backlog to get citizenship stymies 2 million. *New York Times,* p. B6.

Ojito, M. (1998b, September 4). Immigrant fights off his deportation. *New York Times,* p. B8.

Okun, B. (1991). *Effective helping: Interviewing and counseling techniques* (4th ed.). Pacific Grove, CA: Brooks/Cole.

Okun, B. (1996). *Understanding diverse families: What practitioners need to know.* New York: Guilford Press.

Okun, B., Fried, J., & Okun, M. (1999). *Understanding diversity: A learning-as-practice primer.* Pacific Oaks, CA: Grove/Brooks Cole Publishing Co.

Okun, B., & Rappaport, L. (1980). *Working with families: An introduction to family therapy.* North Scituate, MA: Duxbury Press.

Olasky, M. (1995). *The tragedy of American compassion.* Washington, DC: Regnery Gateway Press.

O'Neill, J. V. (2001a). MCOs hear practitioners' grievances. *NASW News* (46)2, 1–4.

Orentstein, M. (1999). *What every therapist needs to know about learning disabilities.* Binghamton, NY: Haworth Press.

Ortiz, E. T., & Bassoff, B. Z. (1988). Proprietary hospital social work. *Health and Social Work 13,* 114–121.

Orwell, G. (1950). Politics and the English language. In *Shooting an elephant and other essays* (pp. 84–101). London: Secker and Warburg.

Osborn, A. F. (1963). *Applied imagination* (3rd ed.). New York: Scribner's.

Overholser, G. (2001, June 10). The pay gap between CEOs and us. *Boston Globe,* p. C7.

Owen, D. (1964). *English philanthropy 1660–1960.* Cambridge, MA: Harvard University Press.

Pack-Brown, S. P., & Whittington-Clark, L. E. (1998). *Images of me: A guide to group work with African-American women.* Boston: Allyn & Bacon.

Panaro, F. (2004). September 11 doesn't justify discrimination against Muslims, Arabs, and others. Bankers.online.com.

Pantoja, A., & Perry, W. (1992). Community development & restoration: A perspective. In F. G. Rivera & J. L. Erlich (Eds.), *Community organizing in a diverse society* (p. 71). Boston: Allyn & Bacon.

Papadoupoulos, L., Bor. R., Cross, M. C., & Cohn-Shertok, D. C. (2003). *Reporting in counseling and psycotherapy: A trainee's guide to preparing case studies & reports.* New York: Routledge.

Parker, L., & Eisler, P. (2001, April 6–8). *U.S.A. Today,* p. A1.

Parloff, M. B. (1970). Sheltered workshops for the alienated. *International Journal of Psychiatry 9,* 197–204.

Parrott, S., & Greenstein, R. (1995, January). *Welfare, out-of-wedlock childbearing, and poverty: What is the connection?* Washington, DC: Center on Budget and Policy Priorities.

Patterson, J. (2001). *Brown v. Board of Education: A civil rights milestone & its troubled legacy.* New York: Oxford University Press.

Pastalan, L. A. (Ed.). (1999). *Making aging in place work.* Binghamton, NY: Haworth Press.

Patchner, M., & Wattenberg, S. H. (1985). Impact of diagnosis related groups on hospital social service departments. *Social Work 30,* 259–261.

Pear, R. (1998a, May 18). Academy's report says immigration benefits the U.S. *New York Times,* p. A1.

Pear, R. (1998b, August 11). Plagued health care system. *International Herald Tribune,* p. 9.

Pear, R. (2000, September 24). 40 states forfeit health care funds for poor children. *New York Times,* p. 1.

Pear, R. (2003, December 7). Medicare plan for drug costs bars insurance. *New York Times,* p. 1.

Pear, R. (2004, April 26). U.S. finds fault in all 50 states' child welfare. *New York Times.*

Pear, R. (2004, June 23). Electronic cards replace coupons for food stamps. *New York Times.*

Pearce, D. & Brooks. J. (2003). The Self-Sufficiency standard for Massachusetts. Washington, DC: Wider Opportunities for Women.

Pearl, A., & Riessman, F. (1965). *New careers for the poor.* New York: Free Press.

Pearson, G. (1975). The politics of uncertainty: A study in the socialization of the social worker. In H. Jones (Ed.), *Towards a new social work* (pp. 21–23). London: Routledge and Kegan Paul.

Pearson, G. (1977, October). The triad model of cross-cultural counselor training. *Personnel and Guidance Journal 56*(2), 94–100.

Pederson, P. B. (1978, April). Four dimensions of cross-cultural skill in counselor training. *Personnel and Guidance Journal 56*(8), 480–484.

Peek, T. (2000). Families and the nursing home environment: Adaptation in a group context. *Journal of Gerontological Social Work 33*(1), 51–66.

Pelton, L. (1989). *For reasons of poverty.* New York: Praeger.

Perlman, R. (1975). *Consumers and social services.* New York: John Wiley and Sons.

Pertman, A. (2001, May 20). Still illegal, but... *Boston Globe,* p. D1.

Pincus, A. H., & Minahan, A. (1973). *Social work practice: Model and method.* Itasca, IL: F. S. Peacock.

Pipher, M. (1998). *Reviving Ophelia: Saving the lives of adolescent girls.* New York: Ballentine Books.

Piven, F. F., & Cloward, R. A. (1966, May 2). A strategy to end poverty. *The Nation 202*(18), 510–517.

Piven, F. F., & Cloward, R. A. (1971). *Regulating the poor: The functions of public welfare.* New York: Random House.

Piven, F. F., & Cloward, R. A. (1977). *Poor people's movements: Why they succeed, how they fail.* New York: Pantheon.

Platt, A. M. (1977). *The child savers: The invention of delinquency.* Chicago: University of Chicago Press.

Polsky, H. W. (1962). *Cottage six—The social system of delinquent boys in residential treatment.* New York: Russell Sage Foundation.

Polsky, H. W. (1968). *The dynamics of residential treatment.* Chapel Hill, NC: University of North Carolina Press.

Popple, P. R., & Leighninger, L. H. (1990). *Social work, social welfare, and American society.* Boston: Allyn & Bacon.

Portes, A., & Rumbaut, R. (1990). *Immigrant America.* Berkeley, CA: University of California Press.

PR Newswire. (2004, April 19). No cause for celebrating Equal Pay Day, says Michigan Pay Equity Network.

PR Newswire. (2004, May 17). National survey finds confidentiality and forced mental health diagnoses are major barriers to seeking psychological care.

Press, E. (2001, April 9). Lead us not into temptation. *The American Prospect 12*(6), pp. 20–27.

Primislo, E. (1979, January). Confidentiality and privileged communication. *Social Work 24*(1), 10–13.

The Progressive. (1991, July). *56*(7), p. 9.

The Progressive. (1997, November 8).

Project Bread/The Walk for Hunger. (1991). *Children are hungry in Massachusetts: A report of the Massachusetts community childhood hunger identification project.* Boston: Author.

Prothrow-Smith, D. (1987). *Violence protection for adolescents.* Newton, MA: Educational Development Center, Inc.

Psychotherapy Finances. (1998, May). P.O. Box 8979, Jupiter, FL 33468. Vol. 24(5), Issue 289.

Public Health Service. (1980). *Towards a national plan for the chronic mentally ill.* Washington, DC: U.S. Department of Health and Human Services.

Rachels, J. (1979). Active euthanasia with parental consent [Commentary]. *Hastings Center Report.* New York: Hastings-on-Hudson.

Racism, fear of foreigners called on rise worldwide. (1995, October 10). *Boston Globe,* p. A11.

Raphael, J., & Tolman, R. (1997). Trapped by poverty, trapped by abuse: New evidence documenting the relationship between domestic violence and welfare. Ann Arbor, MI: University of Michigan Research Center on Poverty, Risk, and Mental Health.

Reamer, F. (2001, October 15). Social work values resonate, inspire in wake of recent tragedies. *Social Work Today,* pp. 22–23.

The Recorder. (2004, May 14). State Bar to allow lawyers to break confidentiality.

Reed, S. (1979, January 7). Teacher burnout a growing hazard. *New York Times,* p. L12.

Rees, S. (1979). *Social work face to face.* NY: Columbia University Press.

Reeser, L. C., & Epstein, I. (1990). *Professionalism and activism in social work.* New York: Columbia University Press.

Reforming welfare reform. (2000, January 1–16). *The American Prospect.* www.prospect.org.

Reich, R. (2001, May 21). No tax cut. Period. *The American Prospect 12*(9), p. 48.

Reinarman, C., & Levine, H. G. (1989). The crack attack: Politics and media in America's latest drug scare. In J. Best (Ed.), *Images of issues* (pp. 115–137). New York: Aldine de Gruyter.

Reynolds, B. (1963). *An uncharted journey.* New York: Citadel.

Rezendes, M. (1992, November 18). Health plans for poor stress preventive care. *Boston Globe,* pp. 1, 15.

Rhodes, M. L. (1989). *Ethical dilemmas in social work practice.* Milwaukee, WI: Family Service America.

Rhodes, M. (1988, April). Human service dilemmas. Workshop. *Teaching Social Work Ethics.* Regis College, Weston, MA.

Richan, W. C., & Mendelsohn, A. R. (1973). *Social work: The unloved profession.* New York: Franklin Watts.

Richmond, M. (1917). *Social diagnosis.* New York: Russell Sage.

Ridley, C. R. (1995). *Overcoming unintentional racism in counseling and therapy.* Thousand Oaks, CA: Sage.

Ries, J. B., & Leakfield, C. G. (1998). *The research funding guidebook: Getting it, managing it, and renewing it.* Thousand Oaks, CA: Sage.

Riessman, F., & Gartner, A. (1977). *Self-help groups in the human services.* San Francisco, CA: Jossey-Bass.

Riessman, F., & Gartner, A. (1980). *A working guide to self-help groups.* New York: Franklin Watts.

Rifkin, J. (1995). *The end of work: The decline of the global labor force and the dawn of the post-market era.* New York: G. P. Putnam.

Rimer, S. (1998, March 15). Blacks carry load of care for their elderly. *New York Times,* pp. 1, 22.

Rivera, F. G., & Erlich, J. L. (Eds.). (1995). *Community organizing in a diverse society* (2nd ed.). Boston: Allyn & Bacon.

Robinson, W. V. (2000, April 4). Surge in immigrant voters favors Gore. *Boston Globe*, pp. A1, A11.

Rodriguez, C. (2001, June 7). Latino prison count called inaccurate. *Boston Globe*, p. A3.

Rogers, C. (1951). *Client-centered therapy.* Boston: Houghton Mifflin.

Rose, N. (1985). *The labor market and the constraints on work relief in the United States during the 1930s.* Unpublished doctoral dissertation, University of Michigan, Ann Arbor.

Rose, N. (1997). Workfare vs. fair work: Public job creation. In M. Billies, H. Boushey, H. Dorow, M. Lane, A. Pollack, & K. Yau (Eds.), *Welfare, workfare, and jobs* (pp. 62–65). New York: Urban Justice Organizing Project.

Rose, S., & Edelson, J. L. (1990). *Working with children and adolescents in groups.* Santa Fe, NM: Jossey-Bass.

Rosen, C. E. (1976, July). Sign-away pressures. *Social Work 21*(4), 284–287.

Rosen, F. (2001, July 8). The promise of stem cell research. *Boston Globe*, p. D7.

Rosenhan, D. L. (1973, January 19). On being sane in insane places. *Science 179*, 250–258.

Rossen, S. (1987). Hospital social work. In A. Menahan (Ed.), *Encyclopedia of Social Work* (18th ed.) (pp. 816–820). Silver Spring, MD: National Association of Social Workers.

Roth, W. (1987). Disabilities: Physical. In A. Menahan (Ed.), *Encyclopedia of social work* (18th ed.) (p. 67). Silver Spring, MD: National Association of Social Workers.

Rothman, D. (1971). *The discovery of the asylum.* Boston: Little, Brown.

Ruben, D. H. (2001). *Treating adult children of alcoholics: A behavioral approach.* San Diego, CA: Academic Press.

Russell, D. M. (1989). *Political organizing in grassroots politics.* Lanham, MD: University Press of America.

Russo, J. R. (1980). *Serving and surviving as a human service worker.* Monterey, CA: Brooks/Cole.

Ryan, D., & McCarthy, M. (Eds.). (1994). *A student affairs guide to the ADA and disability issues.* Washington, DC: National Association of Student Personnel Administrators.

Ryan, W. (1976). *Blaming the victim.* New York: Random House.

Sacks, O. (1989). *Seeing voices: A journey into the land of the deaf.* Berkeley, CA: University of California.

Sainsbury, E. (1974). *Social work with families: Perceptions of social casework among clients of a family service unit.* London: Routledge.

Salinger, J. D. (1965). *Raise high the roof beam, carpenters and Seymour: An introduction.* New York: Bantam Books.

Salinger, J. D. (1951). *The catcher in the rye.* Boston: Little, Brown.

Saltus, R. (2001, March 29). Congress questions 2 human clone groups. *Boston Globe*, p. A3.

SAMHSA, Office of Applied Studies. (1999). 1999 national household survey on drug abuse. http://www.samhsa.gov/oas/NHSDA/1999/table.

Sanders, B. (1998, Spring). The economy is great, but for whom? *Sanders Scoop.*

Sard, B., & Lubell, J. (2000, February 17). The increasing use of TANF and state matching funds to provide housing assistance to families moving from welfare to work. Center on Budget and Policy Priorities. Washington, DC, p. 3.

Schaefer, R. T. (1989). *Racial and ethnic groups.* Glenview, IL: Scott, Foresman/Little, Brown Higher Education.

Schamess, G., & Lightburn, A., (Eds.) (1998). Humane managed care? Washington, DC: NASW Press.

Schein, V. E. (1995). *Working from the margins: Voices of mothers in poverty.* Ithaca, NY: Cornell University Press.

Schiller, L. Y. (1995). Stages of development in women's groups: A relational model. In R. Kurland & R. Salmon (Eds.). *Group work practice in a troubled society.* NY: Haworth.

Schiller, L. Y. (1997). Rethinking stages of development in women's groups. *Social Work with Groups 20*(3), Handbook of Leadership. NY: Haworth.

Schmitt, E. (1997, November 13). Lawmakers ease immigration curbs approved in 1996. *New York Times*, p. 10.

Schmitt, E. (2001a, May 15). For first time, nuclear families drop below 25% of households. *New York Times*, p. 1.

Schmitt, E. (2001b, July 29). You can come in, you stay out. *New York Times*, p. 5 wk.

Schneider, P. (1991). *Teamwork in the hierarchy: Sustained in the thick of organizational culture.* Unpublished doctoral dissertation, Northeastern University, Boston.

Schoech, D. (1999). *Human services technology: Understanding, designing and implementing computer and Internet applications.* Binghamton, NY: Haworth.

Schram, B. (1975, June). The building blocks of parent decision making. *Day Care and Early Education 2*(5), 8–12.

Schram, B. (1971). The conscious use of color. In P. Kurzman (Ed.), *The Mississippi experience: Strategies for welfare rights organization* (pp. 66–83). New York: Association Press.

Schram, B. (1997). *Creating the small scale social program: Planning, implementation and evaluation.* Thousand Oaks, CA: Sage.

Schram, S. F. (1995). *Words of welfare: The poverty of social science and the social science of poverty.* Minneapolis, MN: University of Minnesota Press.

Schreiber, L. A. (1993, January 17). What kind of abortions do we want? *New York Times Book Review,* pp. 13–14.

Schreter, R. K., Sharfstein, S. S., & Schreter, C. A. (Eds.). (1994). *Allies and adversaries: The impact of managed care on mental health services.* Washington, DC: American Psychiatric Press.

Schulman, L. (1993). *Developing and testing a practice theory: An interactional perspective.* New York: NASW.

Schuman, H., Steeh, C., Bobo, L., & Krysan, M. (1997). *Racial attitudes in America: Trends and interpretations.* Cambridge: Harvard University Press.

Schwartz, W. (1971). On the use of groups in social work practice. In W. Schwartz & S. Zalba (Eds.), *The practice of group work* (pp. 3–24). New York: Columbia University Press.

Sciegas, M., Garnick, D. W., Hogan, C. M., Merrick, E., Goldin, D., Urato, M., & Hodgkin, D. (2001). Employee assistance programs among Fortune 500 firms. *Employee Assistance Quarterly 16*(3), 25–35.

Scripps Howard News Service (2004, June 4). California budget crunch withers welfare reform.

Seaver, T. (1971). The care and feeding of southern welfare departments. In P. A. Kurzman (Ed.), *The Mississippi experience: Strategies for welfare rights organizing* (pp. 53–65). New York: Association Press.

Seever, F. S. (1987). (Review of the book *Professionalism and social change: From settlement house movement to neighborhood centers, 1886 to the present*). *Social Service Review 64*(1), 163.

Sege, I. (1992, May 14). Role of crack babies' environment studied. *Boston Globe,* p. 20.

Seigel, B. (1991, August 7). In the name of the children. *Los Angeles Times Magazine,* p. 1.

Seligman, L. (1996). *Diagnosis and treatment planning in counseling* (2nd ed.). New York: Plenum Press.

Service Employees International Union. (1997, November). *Contracting human services: Recurring scandals and bad performance.* Boston: Author.

Sexton, J. (1997a, October 12). Privacy and pride are submerged at busy workfare evaluation site. *New York Times,* p. 17.

Sexton, J. (1997b, December 22). Only children with severe disabilities need apply. *New York Times,* p. 9.

Shade, P. (1981, Summer). Running to stay in place. *Public Welfare,* 28–31.

Shamoo, A. (2004, Winter). Ethics of research involving mandatory drug testing of high school athletes in Oregon. *American Journal of Bioethics.*

Shaw, R. (1996). *The activists' handbook: A primer for the 1990s and beyond.* Berkeley: University of California Press.

Sheehan, S. (1981, June 8). A reporter at large (Creedmoor-Part III). *New Yorker.*

Sheldrick, C. (1999). The management of risk in adolescence. *Journal of Child Psychology, Psychiatry, and Allied Disorders 40*(4), 507–518.

Shenker, I. (1971, April 10). Test of Samaritan parable: Just who aids the helpless? *New York Times,* p. 25.

Sherman, A. (1994). *Wasting America's future: The Children's Defense Fund report on the costs of child poverty.* Boston: Beacon Press.

Shertzer, B., & Stone, S. (1980). *Fundamentals of counseling* (3rd. ed.). Boston: Houghton Mifflin.

Shore, W. H. (1995). *Revolution of the heart: A new strategy for creating wealth & meaningful change.* New York: Riverside Books.

Shulman, L. (1979). *The skills of helping individuals and groups.* Itasca, IL: F. E. Peacock.

Shuyter, G. V. (1999). *Improving organizational performance: A practical guide book for the human service field.* Thousand Oaks, CA: Sage.

Siegel, G. B. (1996). *Mass interviewing and the marshaling of ideas to improve performance.* Lanham, MD: University Press of America.

Silk, L. (1981, November–December). A walk on the supply side. *Harvard Business Review.*

Silverman, E. J. (1998, May 17). State ripped on welfare reform. *Boston Herald,* p. 1.

Simanis, J. G. (1990, January). National expenditures on social security and health in selected countries. *Social Security Bulletin 53*(1), 12.

Simmel, G. (1955). The significance of numbers for social life. In A. D. Hare, E. F. Borgatta, & R. F. Bales (Eds.), *Small groups* (pp. 9–15). New York: Alfred Knopf.

Simon, M. (2001, September). Children's health insurance: Available, but unused. *NEA Today,* p. 31.

Skinner, B. F. (1974). *About behaviorism.* New York: Alfred A. Knopf.

Slaughter, J. (1998). Endorsing the lean machine. *New Politics 7*(4), pp. 71–76.

Sloan, L. M., & Gustavsson, N. S. (Eds.). (1998). *Violence against lesbian, gay & bisexual people.* Binghamton, NY: Haworth.

Smith, A. C. (1999, September 28). Care of mentally ill prisoners questioned. *St. Petersburg Times.* www.sptimes.com/news/92899/state/care_of_mentally_ill_shtml.

Smith, M. J. (1990). *Program evaluation in the human services.* New York: Springer.

Smith, P. (1993, February 16). 'Queen' star McKee takes on role of bolstering black clout. *Boston Globe,* pp. 25, 30.

Social Security Administration. (1997). *Social Security Bulletin,* Vol. 60, No. 4. Washington, DC: Author.

Social Security Administration. (2001). *Social Security On Line.* www.ssa.gov/policy.

Social Security Administration (2004a). Table 1, All OASDI benefits by program and type of benefit, May 2003–May 2004. www.ssa.gov/policy/docs/statcomps/oasdi_monthly/2004–05/table1.html.

Social Security Administration (2004b). SSI statistics, May 2004, Table 1. Recipients (by type of payment, total payments, and average monthly payment, May 2003–May 2004). www.ssa.gov/policy/docs/statcomps/ssi_monthly/2004–5/table1.html.

Social Security Administration (2004c). Table 10. DI benefits, by type of beneficiary, Mary 2003–May 2004. www.ssa.gov/policy/docs/statcomps/oasdi_monthly/2004-05/table10/html.

Sojourner. (2001, July/August). *26*(11/12).

Solomon, A. (2001, May 6). A cure for poverty. *New York Times Magazine,* pp. 112–117.

Somers, S. (1988). *Keeping secrets.* New York: Warner Books.

Sourander, A., Helstela, L., Helenrus, H., & Pina, J. (2000). Persistance of bullying from childhood to adolescence: A longitudinal 8 year follow-up study. *Child Abuse and Neglect (The International Journal) 24*(7), 873–881.

Southern Regional Education Board. (1969, December). Roles and functions for mental health workers: A report of a symposium. Atlanta, GA: Community Mental Health Worker Project.

Spalter-Roth, R., Blurr, B., Hartmann, H., & Shaw, L. (1995). *Welfare that works: The working lives of AFDC recipients.* Washington, DC: Institute for Women's Policy Research.

Spare Change. (1995, November 15). 4(8).

Specht, H. (1990, September). Social work and the popular psychotherapies. *Social Service Review,* 19–24.

Speeter, G. (1978a). *Playing their game our way, using the political process to meet community needs.* Amherst, MA: Citizen's Involvement Training Project, University of Massachusetts.

Speeter, G. (1978b). *Power: A repossession manual, organizing strategies for citizens.* Amherst, MA: Citizen's Involvement Training Project, University of Massachusetts.

Speigel, B. (1992). The supervised visitation program at the New York Society for Ethical Culture. Paper presented at the Vermont Child Study Association's Conference on Supervised Visitation Programs, 1992.

Spock, B. (1976). *Baby and child care* (4th ed.). New York: Hawthorn Books.

Spock, B. (1946). *Common sense book of baby and childcare.* New York: Meredith Press.

Spock, B., & Morgan, M. (1989). *Spock on Spock. A memoir of growing up with the century.* New York: Pantheon Books.

Spradley, J. (1979). *The ethnographic interview.* New York: Holt, Rinehart & Winston.

Srole, L., Lengner, T., Michael, S., Kirkpatrick, P., Opler, M., & Rennie, T. (1975). *Mental health in the metropolis.* New York: Harper Torchbooks.

Stack, C. (1974). *All our kin: Strategies for survival in a black community.* New York: Harper & Row.

Staples, R. (1988). The black American family. In C. H. Mindel (Ed.), *Ethnic families in America* (pp. 303–324). New York: Elsevier.

Steadman, H. J., McCarty, D. W., & Morrissey, J. P. (1989). *The mentally ill in jail: Planning for essential services.* New York: Guilford Press.

Steele, C. M., & Aronson, J. (1995, August). Stereotype vulnerability and the intellectual test performance of African-Americans. Paper presented at the American Psychological Association.

Stein, C. (2004, May 5). Wages don't figure in rebound. *Boston Globe*, p. A1.

Stern, A. L. (2001, September 3). Andrew L. Stern replies to "Changing to Organize." *The Nation 273*(7), p. 23.

Sterngold, J. (2001, October 7). Legal residency hopes of millions dashed. *New York Times*, p. A20.

Stevenson, R. W. (2001a, August 12). A new threat to the president's agenda: The tax cut. *New York Times*, p. 1wk.

Stewart, B. (1998, August 7). From sleeping in a train station to writing about it. *International Herald Tribune*, p. 10.

Stoesz, D., & Karger, H. (1991, April). The corporatisation of the United States welfare state. *Journal of Social Policy 20*(2), 157–171.

Stogdill, R. M. (1948). Personal factors associated with leadership: A survey of the literature. *Journal of Psychology 25*, 37–71.

Stogdill, R. M., & Coons, A. E. (1957). Leader behavior: Its description and measurement. Columbus, OH: Bureau of Business Research, Ohio State University.

Stolberg, S. G. (2001, May 13). Shouldn't a pill be colorblind? *New York Times*, pp. 1 & 3 wk.

Stone, D., Patton, B., Heen, S., & Fisher, P. (2000). *Difficult conversations: How to discuss what matters most*. New York: Penguin Books.

Sue, D. W., Ivey, A. E., & Pederson, P. (1996). *A theory of multicultural counseling and therapy*. Pacific Grove, CA: Brooks/Cole.

Survival News. (1996, Spring).

Survival tips. (1998, Fall). *Survival News*, p. 23.

Swarns, R. L. (1998, April 14). Mothers poised for workfare face acute lack of day care. *New York Times*, pp. A1, A21.

Sweeney, E. P. (2000, February 29). Recent studies indicate that many parents who are current or former welfare recipients have disabilities or other medical conditions. Center on Budget and Policy Priorities.

Swoboda, J. S., Elwork, A., Sales, B. D., & Levine, D. (1978, August). Knowledge of and compliance with privileged communication and child abuse reporting laws. *Professional Psychology 9*(3), 448–457.

Szasz, T. S. (1965). *Psychiatric justice*. New York: Macmillan.

Szasz, T. S. (1961). *The myth of mental illness*. New York: Harper & Row.

Szyndrowski, D. (1999). Impact of domestic violence on adolescent aggression in the schools. *Preventing School Failure 44*(1), 9–11.

Talk of the Nation. (2004, January 15). National Public Radio.

Talk of the Nation. (2004, April 15). National Public Radio.

Tarasoff v. Regents of University of California, 13, C. 3d, 177, 529, P. 2d. 533, 118, Cal. Rptr. 129, 1974.

Tilly, C. (1998, Winter). Part-time work: A mobilizing issue. *New Politics VI*(4), pp. 19–26.

Time.com. (2001). www.time.com/time/nation/article/0,8599,131350,00.html.

A tome keeps track of social policy. (1998, August 12). *International Herald Tribune*, p. 5.

Townsend, P. Speech at the Socialist Scholars Conference, New York City, April 25, 1992.

Toy, V. (1998, April 15). Tough workfare rules used as way to cut welfare rolls. *New York Times*, pp. A1, A27.

Trillin, C. (2001, September 3). New grub streets. *The New Yorker*, pp. 42–48.

Trimmer, S. (1964). *The economy of charity* (1801). Cited in *English Philanthropy 1660–1960*, by David Owen. Cambridge, MA: Harvard University Press, 1964.

Truax, C. B., & Carkhuff, R. R. (1967). *Toward effective counseling and psychotherapy*. Chicago: Aldine.

Truax, C. B., & Mitchell, K. M. (1971). Research on certain therapists' interpersonal skills in relation to process and outcomes. In A. E. Bergin & S. L. Garfield (Eds.), *Handbook of psychotherapy and behavior change*. New York: Wiley.

Tuckman, B. (1965). Developmental sequence in small groups. *Psychological Bulletin 63*(6), 384–399.

Turnbull, Lornet (2004, March 16). Single parents, unmarried couples give new definitions to 'family.' *Seattle Times*.

Two cases given legal aid grants. (2001, February). *NASW News 46*(2), p. 12.

Unemployed Workers (2004). Laid off and left out: America's workers deserve better. www.unemployedworkers.org/helpful_statistics/nationalstatistics/index.cfm.

United for a Fair Economy. (1997, September). Milking the health care money machine. *Too Much*.

United for a Fair Economy. (1998, June 16). Flyer. *Think Again*.

United for a Fair Economy. (2001, Spring). *Too Much.* Boston: Author.

United Press International. (2004, April 26). Welfare kids staying longer in foster care.

Urban Institute. (1996). *Potential effects of congressional welfare reform legislation.* Washington, DC: Author.

Urdang, E. (1999). The influence of managed care on the MSW social work student development of the professional self. *Smith College Studies in Social Work 70*(1), pp. 3–25.

U.S. Bureau of the Census. (1993). *Asset ownership of households.* Washington, DC: Government Printing Office.

U.S. Bureau of the Census. (1999). *Housing vacancies and home ownership annual statistics.* Washington, DC: Government Printing Office.

U.S. Bureau of the Census. (2000, May 26). Annual population estimates by sex, race, and Hispanic origin. Current Population Report P25–1095. Washington, DC: Government Printing Office.

U.S. Bureau of the Census. (2002). Poverty: 2002 highlights. www.census.gov/hhes/poverty02/povo2hi.html.

U.S. Bureau of the Census. (2003a). Poverty status of families by type of family. www.census.gov/prod/2003pubs/p60–222.pdf.

U.S. Bureau of the Census. (2003b). Annual Demographic Survey. http://ferret.bls.census.gov/macro/032003/pov/new01_100_01htm.

U.S. Conference of Mayors. (2003). *Hunger and Homelessness 2003.* Washington, DC.

U.S. Congress, House Ways and Means Committee. (2000). *The Green Book-2000.* Washington, DC: U.S. Government Printing Office.

U.S. Department of Agriculture. (2004). Special Supplemental Nutrition Program for Women, Infants and Children (WIC). www.fns.usda.gov/pd/WIC_monthly.htm.

U.S. Department of Commerce. (2001). *Statistical Abstract of the United States, 2001.* Washington, DC: Bureau of the Census. Poverty rates, p. 40.

U.S. Department of Commerce. (2003, September 30). Numbers of Americans with and without health insurance rise, Census Bureau reports. Press release. Bureau of the Census.

U.S. Department of Health and Human Services. (1998). *National Center for Chronic Disease Prevention and Health Promotion.* Washington, DC: U.S. Government Printing Office.

U.S. Department of Health and Human Services. (2004). www.acf.hhs.gov/programs/ofa.

U.S. Department of Health and Human Services. (2004, February 13). *Federal Register: Volume 69*(30), pp. 7336–7338.

U.S. Department of Housing and Urban Development, Division of Policy Studies. (1989). *Report on the 1988 national survey of shelters for the homeless 14.* Washington, DC: Author.

U.S. Department of Labor. (1998, August). Glossary of Compensation Terms. Bureau of Labor Statistics, Report No. 923.

U.S. high court denies appeal in fetus abuse case. (1998, May 26). *Reuters,* http://classic.elibrary.com/getdoc.cgi.

U.S. Newswire. (2003, November 20). GAO report finds continued, unexplained gender wage gap; Women's progress of 1980s unmatched in subsequent years, reports IWPR.

U.S. Newswire. (2004, February 12). Bush Administration violates doctor-patient confidentiality, says NARAL Pro-Choice America.

U.S. Newswire. (2004, March 11). National Council on Disability opinion editorial on Temporary Assistance for Needy Families and people with disabilities.

U.S. Newswire. (2004, March 30). Welfare rolls drop again, says HHS.

U.S. Privacy: Health Insurance and Accountability Act 1996: Synopsis. (2002). www.gpit.ie/presentations/Gregg%Palmer.pdf.

Upshur, C. (1982*). How to set up & operate a non-profit organization.* Englewood Cliffs, NJ: Prentice-Hall.

Valentine, P. (1997, February 5). Maryland suspends licenses over child support: Thousands of parents lose the right to drive. *Washington Post.*

Vallianatos, C. (2001a). Association backing given in two cases. *NASW News* (46)14, p. 11.

Vallianatos, C. (2001b). Managed care is faulted. *NASW News* (46)17.

Van Ornum, W. (1990). *Crisis counseling with children & adolescents: A guide for nonprofessional counselors.* New York: Continuum.

Vicini, J. (1999, March 9). Justice Department attempt to speed deportations is set back. *Boston Globe,* p. A5.

Vogel, R. (1979, November 11). Teachers' colleges shift their focus to 'related fields.' *New York Times,* p. 32.

Vollbracht, J. (2002). *Stopping at every lemonade stand: How to create a culture that cares for kids.* New York: Penguin Books.

Vonnegut, K. (1991). *Fates worse than death.* New York: G. P. Putnam.

Vonnegut, K. (1990). *Hocus pocus.* New York: G. P. Putnam.

Walker, R. (1995, January–February). California rages against the dying of the light. *New Left Review 209,* 42–74.

Warner, R. (1989). Deinstitutionalization: How did we get where we are? *Journal of Social Issues 45*(3), 17–30.

Warner, R. (1983). The effect of the labor market on mental hospital and prison use: An international comparison. *Administration in Mental Health 10,* 239–258.

Warren, J. (2000, April 30). Crusader for the poor: "Good news" in welfare is a sham. *Chicago Tribune.*

Washington, W. (2001, March 5). HUD eyes cuts in rental funding. *Boston Globe,* p. A1.

Washington, W. (2004, May 31). Bush takes spotlight off Medicare drug benefit. *Boston Globe,* p. A1.

Watkins, T. R., & Gonzales, R. (1982). Outreach to Mexican Americans. *Social Work 27,* 68–73.

Weaker safety net. (2000, July 4). *International Herald Tribune,* p. 4.

Webster-Stratton, C., & Martin, H. (1994). *Troubled families, problem children.* New York: John Wiley.

Weidell, R. C. (1980, February). Unsealing birth certificates in Minnesota. *Child Welfare 59*(2), 113–119.

Weil, M. (1986). Women, community and organizing. In N. Van Den Bugh & L. Cooper (Eds.), *Feminist vision for social work* (pp. 126–134). Silver Spring, MD: National Association of Social Workers.

Weinbach, R. (2002). *The social worker as manager: A practical guide to success* (4th ed.). Boston: Allyn & Bacon.

Weinstein, M. M. (1998, July 19). Getting litigious with HMO's. *New York Times,* p. 5.

Weissberg, R. (1999). *The politics of empowerment.* Westport, CT: Praeger.

Weissman, A. (1976). Industrial social services: Linkage technology. *Social Casework 57,* 50–54.

Weissman, H. H. (1973). *Overcoming mismanagement in the human service professions* (pp. 47–59). San Francisco: Jossey-Bass.

Weissman, H., Epstein, I., & Savage, A. (1983). *Agency-based social work: Neglected aspects of clinical practice.* Philadelphia: Temple University Press.

Welfare reform: An overview of effects to date. (2001, January). The Brookings Institution. www.brookings.org/wrb/publications/Pb/Pb01.htm.

Welfare reform's uncounted failures. (1998, April 2). *Boston Globe,* p. A22.

Wellstone, P. (1998, July 27/August 3). The people's trust fund. *The Nation,* 5.

Wender, P. (1987). *The hyperactive child, adolescent and adult.* New York: Oxford University Press.

Wenocur, S., & Sherman, W. (1980, March). *Empowering the social worker.* Baltimore, MD: University of Maryland School of Social Work and Community Planning.

Wharf, B., & Clague, M. (Eds.). (1997). *Community organizing: Canadian experiences.* Toronto, Canada: Oxford University Press.

White, B. J., & Madera, E., compiled and edited, web version updated by Kerrin, M. E., & Rothblatt, A. (2004). American self-help clearing house, 1993–2004. Mental Help Net. www.mentalhelpnet/selfhelp/.

Wideman, J. E. (1995, October 30). The politics of prisons: Doing time, marking race. *The Nation 261*(14), 503–505.

Williams, L. (1997). Decades of distortion: *The right's 30-year assault on welfare.* Somerville, MA: Political Research Associates.

Williams, R., Jr. (1966). Prejudice and society. In J. P. Davis (Ed.), *The American Negro reference book* (pp. 727–730). Englewood Cliffs, NJ: Prentice-Hall.

Wilson, M., & Rosenfelt, D. S. (1978). *Salt of the earth: Screenplay and commentary.* Old Westbury, NY: Feminist Press.

Wilson, S. (1980). *Recording: Guidelines for social workers.* New York: Free Press.

Wolfe, B., & Hill, S. (1993). The health, earnings capacity, and poverty of single-mother families. In D. Papadimitriou & E. N. Wolff (Eds.), *Poverty and prosperity in USA in the later twentieth century* (pp. 6–10). New York: Macmillan.

Wolvin, A., & Coakley, C. G. (1992). *Listening* (4th ed.). Dubuque, IA: William C. Brown.

Wong, D. S. (1997, November 29). Food pantries see sharp increase in demand. *Boston Globe,* pp. B1, B4.

Workfare's missing link. (1996, October 21). *New York Times,* p. A31.

Wuthnow, R. (1994). *Sharing the journey: Support groups and America's new quest for community.* New York: Free Press.

Yaffe, J., & Gotthuffer, D. (1999). *Quick guide to the Internet for social work.* Boston: Allyn & Bacon.

Yegidis, B. L., Weinbach, R. W., & Morrison, R. B. (1999). *Research methods for social workers* (3rd ed.). Boston: Allyn & Bacon.

Yenkin, J. (1992, September 10). 30 million Americans go hungry, report says. *Boston Globe,* p 3.

Yoon, Y., Spalter-Roth, R., & Baldwin, M. (1995). *Unemployment insurance: Barriers to access for women and part-time workers.* Washington, DC: National Commission for Employment policy.

Young, L. (2002, February 6). Women and Aging: Bearing the burden of long-term care. Testimony at Joint Hearing before the Special Committee on aging of the committee on Health, Education, Labor, and Pensions of the U.S. Senate. U.S. Government Printing Office: Washington, DC, p. 37.

Zastrow, C. (1993). *Social work with groups* (3rd ed.). Chicago: Nelson-Hall.

Zayas, L., & Katch, M. (1989, January). Contracting with adolescents: An ego-psychological approach. *Social Casework 70*(1), 3–9.

Zeilberger, J., Sampen, S. E., & Sloan, H. N., Jr. (1973). Modification of a child's behavior in the home with the mother as therapist. In J. Fischer (Ed.), *Interpersonal helping* (pp. 224–236). Springfield, IL: Charles C. Thomas.

Zimbardo, P. G., Haney, C., Banks, W. C., & Jaffe, D. (1982). The psychology of imprisonment. In J. C. Brigham & L. Wrightsman (Eds.), *Contemporary issues in social psychology* (4th ed.) (pp. 230–245). Monterey, CA: Brooks/Cole.

Zimbardo, P. (1994, November). *Transforming California's Prisons Into Expensive Old Age Homes for Felons.* San Francisco: Center on Juvenile and Criminal Justice.

Zorza, J. (1991). Woman battering: A major cause of homelessness. *Clearinghouse review: Poverty comes home: Women and children in the 90s, 24*(4). [Special issue]. Chicago: National Clearinghouse for Legal Services.

Index